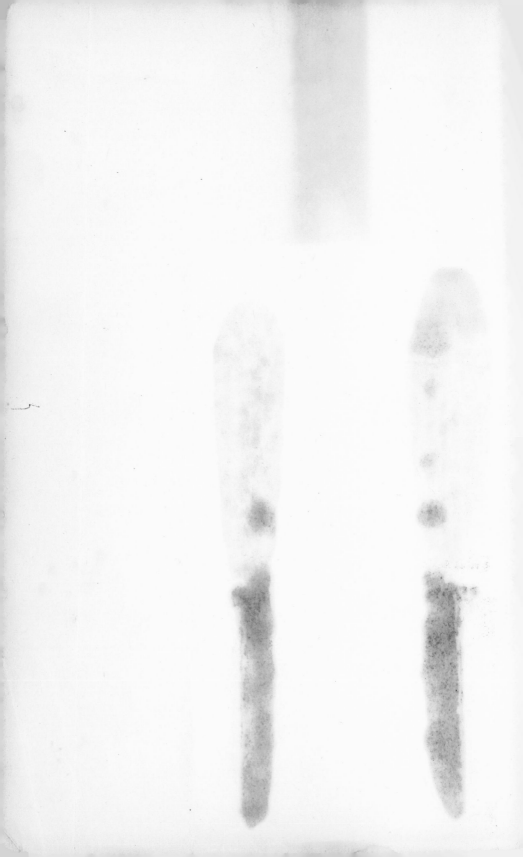

Television
and
Human
Behavior

Television and Human Behavior

By George Comstock, Steven Chaffee,
Natan Katzman, Maxwell McCombs
and Donald Roberts

With the assistance of Thomas Bowers,
Marilyn Fisher, Georg Lindsey and Albert Tims

Columbia University Press
New York

Columbia University Press

New York   Guildford, Surrey

Copyright © 1978 by The Rand Corporation
All Rights Reserved
Printed in the United States of America
10 9 8 7 6 5 4 3 2

Library of Congress Cataloging in Publication Data
Main entry under title:

Television and human behavior.

Bibliography: p.
Includes index.
1. Television—Psychological aspects.
2. Television broadcasting—Social aspects—United
States.   3. Television and children.   I. Comstock,
George A. [DNLM: 1. Child behavior.   2. Social
behavior.   3. Violence.   4. Television.
WS105.5.E9 C739t]
HE8700.8.T34   384.55'01'9   78–5915
ISBN 0–231–04420–8 cloth
ISBN 0–231–04421–6 pbk.

For Merrell Clark

Acknowledgments

AN UNDERTAKING OF this kind inevitably owes a debt to several hundred persons and institutions. We could not possibly list all those who generously replied to our queries, submitted to interviews, supplied us with drafts of material "in press" and papers not publicly available, and offered helpful advice and counsel. There is also the inestimable intellectual debt that we owe to the authors of the research, essays, and various writings on which we have drawn. A full accounting would be impossible, but there are a number of parties who have played such a large and significant part that to omit individual recognition would be unjust. We shall certainly fail even in confining ourselves to such parties by ignoring some who deserve our explicit thanks, but we shall attempt such a partial account on the ground that the greater injustice would be to leave those we shall cite unmentioned.

The largest portion of the financial support for the writing of this volume was provided by the Edna McConnell Clark Foundation. Without this support, it would not have come into existence.

Financial support was also provided by a grant from the John and Mary R. Markle Foundation to The Rand Corporation and by The Rand Corporation itself. This support was instrumental and essential to the completion of this volume.

Our foremost individual obligation is to Merrell Clark, currently senior vice president, The Academy for Educational Development, and formerly vice president, the Edna McConnell Clark Foundation. It is not solely that his interest in television's influence on the way people behave led to the financial support of this undertaking by the Foundation. It is because that support carried no impositions or qualifications, because his reception to the plans and intentions of the authors was informed and sophisticated, and because his confidence was unflagging.

Another person to whom a debt of similar magnitude is owed—but in this instance primarily by the first author, George Comstock—is Dr. Eli A. Rubinstein of the State University of New York, Stony Brook. Comstock served under him as science advisor and senior research coordinator to the Surgeon General's Scientific Advisory Committee on Television and Social Behavior, which issued the report *Television and Growing Up: The Impact of Televised Violence* (1972). Dr. Rubinstein in turn has served the first author in the present undertaking by encouragement, sound counsel, and unguarded criticism.

We are also particularly indebted to Dr. Leland Johnson, then of The Rand Corporation, who provided an environment of freedom that allowed the authors to pursue their vision. Others at Rand to whom a debt is owed are John Hogan and Gustave Shubert.

We certainly must applaud the staff of the Rand library. Neither cheer nor service were defeated by our elephantine bibliographic demands.

Many persons in the television industry were generous with their time and thoughts. These include Dr. Thomas Coffin and Dr. Ronald Milavsky of the National Broadcasting Company, Dr. Joseph Klapper of the Columbia Broadcasting System, and Seymour Amlen and Herman Keld of the American Broadcasting Company.

Kristin Anderson and Nancy Dennis of New York had a central role by recruiting the first author on behalf of the Ford Foundation to help organize a major conference on television research. The richness of the experience they made possible has left its mark on him in many ways, all positive. Others without whom the conference would not have come into being are David Davis, Fred Friendly, and Edward Meade, Jr., of Ford; Dr. Lloyd Morrisett, president of the John and Mary R. Markle Foundation; and Drs. Charles Brownstein and Allen Shinn of the National Science Foundation. Co-sponsored by Ford, Markle, and NSF, the event, summarized in *Television and Children* (Ford Foundation, 1976), contributed significantly to this volume.

We also wish to acknowledge the cooperation of the A. C. Nielsen Company, and particularly Lawrence Frerk, in providing extensive audience data. Much of chapter 3 was possible only because of this assistance.

Among the most difficult of obligations to acknowledge accurately are those where the intellectual component is preeminent, because they often go back far in time, and sometimes do not even bear clearly on the topic at hand. Among those not yet cited to whom the intellectual debt is very large are Dr. Richard Carter of the University of Washington, and Dr. Roger Levien, director of the International Institute for Applied Systems Analysis, Vienna. The former as a professor at Stanford introduced Comstock, Chaffee, and McCombs, his students, to the art of beauty of conceptual schema and scientific theory. The latter, as a department head at The Rand Corporation, quite unknowingly taught George Comstock how to design an undertaking of which this volume represents the concluding step. Two others to whom a similarly large debt is owed are Dr. Nathan Maccoby, director of the Institute for Communication Research at Stanford, and Dr. Wilbur Schramm, professor emeritus at the East-West Center, Honolulu, Hawaii. Their values, thinking, and scientific careers have influenced all the principal authors, to whom each has variously been mentor, teacher, critic, and friend.

Twelve persons whose pointed and ascerbic discussions of the evidence of television's effects are indelible in the mind of George Comstock are those who served as members of the Surgeon General's committee: Drs. Klapper and Coffin, already mentioned, Dr. Ira Cisin of George Washington University, Dr. Irving Janis of Yale University, Dr. Harold Mendelsohn of the University of Denver, Professor Eveline Omwake of Connecticut College, Dr. Charles Pinderhughes of Boston University, Dr. Ithiel de Sola Pool of the Massachusetts Institute of Technology, Dr. Alberta Siegel of Stanford University, Dr. Anthony Wallace of the University of Pennsylvania, Dr. Andrew Watson of the University of Michigan, and Dr. Gerhart Wiebe, now retired from Boston University.

Others whose work and thought influenced this volume, and who have been personally helpful to the authors, are Dr. Charles Atkin of Michigan State University, Dr. Albert Bandura of Stanford University, Dr. Leonard Berkowitz of the University of Wisconsin, Dr. Leo Bogart of the American Newspaper Publishers Association, Douglass Cater of the Aspen Institute, Dr. Paul Ekman of the University of California at San Francisco, Dr. Seymour Feshbach of the University of California at Los Angeles, Dr. George Gerbner of the University of Pennsylvania, Dr. Bradley Greenberg of Michigan State University, Dr. Roderic Gorney of the University of California at Los Angeles, Dr. Randall Harrison of the University of California at San Francisco, Dr. Hilde Himmelweit of the London School of Economics, Dr. Aimee Leifer of Harvard University, Dr. Gerald Lesser of Harvard University, Dr. Robert Liebert of the State University of New York at Stony Brook, Dr. David Loye of the University of California at Los Angeles, Dr. Jack Lyle of the East-West Communication Institute (Hawaii), Dr. William McGuire of Yale University, Dr. Jack McLeod of the University of Wisconsin, Dr. Keith Mielke of Indiana University, Dr. Paul Mussen of the University of California at Berkeley, Dr. Percy Tannenbaum of the University of California at Berkeley, and Dr. Scott Ward of Harvard University.

There are also always those persons with whom friendship has been so entangled with professional exchange that whatever is written shows their influence. Four to whom this applies for George Comstock are Dr. Thomas Cook of Northwestern University, Dr. Stephen Barro and Dr. John Wirt, both of Washington, D.C., and Dr. W. Lee Ruggels of Stanford Research Institute.

Robin E. Cobbey read every word of the final manuscript for errors and gaucheries. Her elegant mind has protected the reader from being imposed upon, and has saved the authors from many embarrassments. Fancy footwork; it deserves to be the talk of the town.

As the reader will have surmised, these acknowledgments bear both the responsibility for the particular debts of George Comstock and the more general obligations of his co-authors. It is hoped that it is not so imbalanced toward the former as to exclude any of the latter. The debt of George Comstock to his co-authors, of course, is boundless. He gladly assigns the pages that follow to the express train of history.

George Comstock
June 1978

Contents

Introduction

TELEVISION AND HUMAN behavior will never be a topic where the questions will have long ago been answered and the issues will become dead. The procedures of social science are too imperfect, the issues too important, the questions too many and too difficult, and both the medium and society too subject to change. Nevertheless, in the 25 years since television began its conquest of our environment a sizable scientific literature about the relationships between it and us has accumulated.

It is a myth that little is known—if we are willing to accept the scientific definition of "known" as a circumstance in which there is verifiable evidence that disposes an observer toward one or another of a set of possible facts or explanations without establishing that such is the case with absolute precision or certainty. Out of vanity, and perhaps a touch of arrogance, we have attempted to cover the entire relevant scientific literature in English. We looked at more than 2500 books, articles, reports, and other documents, including some that fall beyond the usual boundaries of science. We found enough to fill this book with conclusions, although many are tentative and they are interspersed with more than a few speculations.

This is not only a report on what is now known about television and behavior. Because we depart from the norm for reviewing scientific evidence, it is also the evidence in behalf of a promising model for the retrieval and synthesis of scientific information.

Background

There are a number of reasons for a stocktaking at this time. The first would be justification enough. The list makes a reconnaissance seem mandatory.

There is currently a high degree of interest in empirically verifying television's impact on individuals and society. This is reflected in the reassessment of older studies and methodological tenets as well as in a large amount of new research involving a wide variety of disciplines and fields of study. There is activity in social psychology, child development, communications and journalism, political science, business and marketing, sociology, psychiatry, and gerontology. The National Science Foundation, the National Institute of Mental Health, the Office of Child Development, and the John and Mary R. Markle Foundation are particularly visible patrons. Those turning to research for guidance in evaluating television's performance include the Federal Communications Commission and the Federal Trade Commission, several committees of the Congress, various public interest groups, and the advertising and broadcasting industries.

More than 15 years ago, Berelson (1959) began a symposium with the declaration that social scientists could turn away from mass communications because the major questions had been answered. Whatever the plausibility of that view at the time, the feeling today is closer to Schramm's rejoinder: Let's get on with the work.

Second, sufficient time has elapsed since its conclusion in 1972 for the Surgeon General's study of television violence to be placed in perspective. It left a broad legacy—the report of the specially assembled scientific advisory committee, *Television and Growing Up: The Impact of Television Violence,* and five volumes totaling more than 1000 pages of new empirical research bearing on many questions other than violence, and a new cadre of young social scientists interested in television and its impact.

Third, there are the very many changes occurring within the broadcasting industry. There is what could be called "the new responsibility"—the industry's increasing acknowledgment that what it broadcasts sometimes may have unintended and undesired effects. It is exemplified not only by more frequent declarations of responsibility but also by the "family viewing" experiment to make early-evening programming more suitable for children, reductions in the amount of advertising accompanying Saturday morning children's programming, increased efforts to improve entertainment directed at children, and the involvement of all three networks in research on the social impact of television. There also are the many technological, legal, and economic forces reshaping broadcasting. The eventual configuration of network and independent broadcasting, cable, pay television, and in-home recording and playback cannot be predicted, but there is little doubt that the trend is toward greater diversity of choice for the individual viewer. The corollary is that the three networks' ability to shape or reform the medium will be greatly restricted. The multiset household is a step toward making the video experience private; the new technology will be a large stride in the same direction. These events raise many questions for the focus and course of future research that make a summing up of the past necessary.

Fourth, there is the current interest by the social and behavioral sciences in translating research into practical action. The scientist inhabits a different world and speaks a different tongue than do those he wishes to influence. Success will depend in part on fully taking into account the legacy of the findings that sharpen the focus of new research and such experiences as the Surgeon General's study in applying research to policy issues.

Finally, there are the recent shifts within social and behavioral science in regard to the study of television and human behavior. They include the reexamination of certain assumptions about methods, the emergence of new topics, and the revising of the models used to describe television's influence. These shifts are the foundation for a new generation of research, and to understand what they imply we need to see them in the context of what has gone before.

Procedure

Behind this volume lies a somewhat unusual way of evaluating a scientific literature. In the typical case, the author works in what in effect is a state of information deprivation. Resources are limited to personal bookshelves, the nearby library, immediate colleagues, and the personal and organizational ties peculiar to the author. Although occasionally producing masterful efforts (for two examples, see Weiss, 1969, and McGuire, 1969), this procedure runs a number of risks. Coverage is likely to be incomplete, with recent and current research in particular ignored. There may be an unplanned provincialism because the narrow intellectual walls within which any individual works may block unfamiliar or uncongenial concepts, theories, and issues.

This traditional approach does little to speed the entry of new research into the scientific and public discourse, a need that becomes increasingly urgent as a literature grows, new directions are taken at the frontier of activity, and new and more sophisticated techniques are developed. It also fails to provide the comprehensive coverage on which further advances, particularly in the development of sound theory, depend. That the traditional method has been accepted without question until recent years gives one pause over the rationality science extends to its own affairs.

The procedure designed by the first author for this volume attempts to solve such problems. They are particularly severe in the present case because the literature is large and widely scattered; the quantity of very recent work is considerable; and the flow of communication across disciplines is limited.

The procedure has three features: First, a group was assembled to review the literature in a cooperative, interactive, coordinated fashion; second, an information service was established at The Rand Corporation to search through the literature, disseminate materials, critically abstract major documents, and survey the scientific community about current work, important issues, and priorities for the future; third, the first author as principal investigator assumed a very directive role in giving form and substance to the separate parts of this volume, acting similarly to the news editor who assigns, guides, and takes ultimate responsibility for a story while at the same time expecting final treatment to fully reflect the reporter.

The Information Service

The work of the information service resulted in three more specialized volumes. They are:

Television and Human Behavior: A Guide to the Pertinent Scientific Literature. By George Comstock and Marilyn Fisher. Santa Monica, Calif.: The Rand Corporation, 1975. An inclusive bibliography of more than 2300 items, each briefly described, and specialized bibliographies for 11 topics. 344 pages.

Television and Human Behavior: The Key Studies. By George Comstock, with the assistance of F. G. Christen, M. L. Fisher, R. C. Quarles, and W. D. Richards. Santa Monica, Calif.: The Rand Corporation, 1975. Summaries in depth of 450 studies and other documents judged to be particularly important, arranged so that the literature can be readily examined from a variety of perspectives, with each graded by *Michelin*-like stars for current interest. The summaries are introduced by an analysis of methodological issues and trends. 251 pages.

Television and Human Behavior: The Research Horizon, Future and Present. By George Comstock and Georg Lindsey. Santa Monica, Calif.: The Rand Corporation, 1975. A survey of the factors likely to influence future research including the priorities held by the scientific community, the 15 major theoretical and methodological perspectives likely to influence future research, problems raised by the desire to make research relevant to policymaking, and the research underway at the time of writing. 120 pages.

At Work

In addition to the bibliographic and interpretive material in the three Rand volumes, each author was supplied with an individual reference library. The information service particularly ferreted new, unpublished, "in press," and other relatively fugitive items. Each author received complete copies of whatever *he* wanted *and* whatever the first author thought he should have.

What the reader will find in this volume is the result of a reiterative, cooperative process. On the basis of his judgment and comments collected from his co-authors and others, the first author reshaped and expanded the initial drafts of chapters. The coauthors then further revised the portions for which they had been initially responsible. The altered, and in some cases now quite different, drafts were then again subjected to review and revision by the first author, who by the nature of this final responsibility must accept blame for errors and omissions. It is because of this process that chapters are not individually labeled by authorship, although certainly their central thrust and perspective are attributable to those responsible for the initial drafts.* This is not an anthology, but an attempt at orchestration.

* Persons responsible for the initial draft of each chapter: Katzman, Chapters 2, 3, and 4; Roberts, Chapter 5; McCombs (with the assistance of Bowers), Chapter 7;

The project began in the fall of 1973, and was initially intended to take one year. It eventually took more than three. The decision to make generally available in the Rand series the work of the information service interrupted progress on this summative volume, necessitating a certain amount of updating. The major factor, however, was simply that everything took longer to do well than expected.

Implications

The method by which this book was put together has left its mark. It is in the pervading tone, the individual phrase, the organization, the topics and issues emphasized, and the range of coverage. We offer this volume, then, not only as our treatise on television and human behavior, but also as an advertisement in behalf of the method behind it.

In this particular case, there was an exceptional fit between method and subject, hardly surprising with the former designed specifically for the latter. Nevertheless, the problems the method was intended to alleviate are very general ones and new research often suffers from the loss or delay of information. We turn now to television and human behavior, but we ask the reader to be open also for what the ensuing pages have to say about the retrieval and synthesis of scientific information.

and Chaffee (with the assistance of Tims), Chapter 8. Others were the primary responsibility of the first author. Fisher managed the information service; Lindsey conducted its survey of current research.

Television
and
Human
Behavior

Chapter

1

Overview

TELEVISION HAS INTRODUCED a fifth and artificial season to the four natural ones around which people have always organized their lives. This new influence, like the natural seasons, has a specific place in the calendar. Each fall and winter, new programs are introduced, accompanied by increased viewing and attention. It even has its own holiday, Super Bowl Sunday. It differs from the natural seasons by remaining with us in some guise throughout the year. By 1976, almost every American home had television, and that fall the average television household had a set on almost seven hours a day. It is difficult to conceive that in December of 1945, Gallup was asking the country:

"Do you know what television is?"
"Have you ever seen a television set in operation?"

Now, 25 years after television began to become common in the American home, the resulting scientific literature consists of about 2500 items—experiments, surveys, case studies, content analyses, and various interpretive reviews and commentaries. What does it tell us?

The study of the role of the mass media in American life has been filled with controversy, principally over the capability of social and behavioral science to say anything with much authority about such a complex issue. The controversy has been particularly noisome because there are few persons who do not think of themselves as experts in regard to the mass media. As a citizen wrote the National Institute of Mental Health after the Surgeon General's study of television violence, "You should have asked me. You could have saved the money."

The themes are as old as the mass media and tools of inves-

1

tigation, as this account about the effects of a different medium illustrates:

ELLINGTON REFUTES CRY THAT
SWING STARTED SEX CRIMES!

In refutation of the hue and cry against swing music by Arthur Cremin, of the New York Schools for Music, in which the instructor attributed the recent wave of sex crimes to the current "hot" jazz vogue, Duke Ellington, prominent composer-pianist-bandsman, denounced Cremin's psychological experiments as being totally unfair and completely lacking in authoritative material.

Cremin, in his recent attack, said he would prove through tests he conducted that swing music produced debased emotions in human beings. He is reported to have placed a young man and woman in a room alone, first playing a series of symphonic recordings followed by a set of swing recordings. According to the teacher, the young couple remained formal throughout the first renditions, but as the music turned to jazz, they became familiar and more personal towards one another.

"If this experiment is earnestly offered as proof for the ill effects derived from swing music," said Duke Ellington, in discussing the matter before the Musician's Circle of New York, "then the facts must be totally discounted as not being a true psychology test, for there was no 'proper constant'—a prerequisite of an accurate experiment of this nature."

Ellington, who studied psychology during his collegiate courses at Howard University, further commented . . . "Music invigorates emotions to certain degrees, but on the other hand, so do baseball and football games. If music can be proved a neurotic influence, then I'm certain you will find Stravinsky's 'Le Sacre Du Printemps' a great deal more exciting, emotionally, than a slow 'ride' arrangement of 'Body and Soul' or even a fast rendition of 'Tiger Rag.' "

—down beat, December 1937*

An aside by Thomas Pynchon in *Gravity's Rainbow* is relevant here:

Proverbs for Paranoids, 3: If they can get you asking the wrong questions, they don't have to worry about answers.

This is the key to making good use of evidence from social and behavioral science on the role of television in our lives. Ask science a question its methods can answer. For example, science

* Reprinted by permission of *down beat* magazine.

cannot tell us conclusively whether television violence contributes to serious crime because its methods are too imperfect. It can empirically test hypotheses whose confirmation or disconfirmation alters the probability that such a proposition is true and verify the consistency of observed fact with such a proposition. Conclusions of a grander sort depend on judgments about the acceptability of various assumptions and the risk of error that is tolerable. Consequently, the argument that there is no conclusive scientific evidence on this and other broad causal relationships is not impressive. The wrong question is being asked.

From the beginning, television has been principally entertainment. Only a small proportion of total broadcast time has been devoted to news and public affairs, although the coverage of certain specific events—election campaigns, assassinations, congressional investigations, and space flights—has absorbed the nation's attention. The shape of that entertainment has been remarkably constant despite oscillations in violence, the decline of westerns, the fall and rise of game shows, and the rise and fall from popularity of featured performers. Fiction in some guise has been the principal component. In the daytime, it appears as soap operas and situation comedies. In prime time, it has appeared as general drama, feature films, situation comedy, westerns, and mystery, suspense, and detective-and-police tales. Action and adventure have always been central in evening entertainment. Variety has been peripheral because of its dependence on extraordinary personalities, a sparse commodity. In the mid-1970s, situation comedy became increasingly common, partly as the result of the search by the networks for programming in which the infliction of injurious or lethal violence is unlikely. Sports draw huge audiences, but account for a relatively small portion of total viewing time.

The dominant figure in television drama has been the youthful adult white male. For 25 years, he has occupied a large majority of major roles. Women have far less often been seen in central roles. The elderly, children, and blacks and other minorities have been seen relatively infrequently, although appearances of blacks increased sharply in the late 1960s as the result of network policy.

Occupationally, television drama is a world of law enforcement or crime, professionals, males, and persons with atypical or no visible means of support. The departure from reality into the fantasy of violence, upper status, and freedom from economic restraint is marked.

The quantity of violent programs in a season has oscillated

over the years. The oscillations apparently are caused by the rush of the industry toward a violent genre as soon as ratings demonstrate its popularity, followed by a retreat as the newly formed mob of violent programs dilute the audience for violence and ratings for many fall below acceptability. Interpersonal physical and verbal abuse, however, has been demonstrated to be unrelated either to the size of audience for the episodes of network series or to the liking for episodes expressed by viewers.

Violence is often the means to an end in television drama. The use of illegal or socially disapproved means to achieve socially approved ends is a staple. Otherwise, television appears to be noncontroversial in its treatment of topics, with some tendency to favor the interests of advertisers. For example, in the portrayal of behavior related to the environment, the totality of messages has been in accord with public dispositions regarding pollution, nature, and conservation, evasive where there is high controversy (as in the case of population control), and in accord with the interests of advertisers favoring private over public transportation.

The quantity of violence in television prime-time drama and on Saturday mornings, like the number of programs of a violent type, has oscillated over the years. The principal result so far of efforts to reduce violence has been a decline in killing. Downward trends in other measures have generally been followed by upward shifts. Increased pressures—from the government and the public, but particularly from advertisers—conceivably may foretell a different story. One of the most striking aspects of television violence so far has been the high degree to which characters fall victim to crime or violence, for a rate of victimization far in excess of that risked by the average viewer. Women have seldom been seen as professionals. Typically, they have been sex objects and providers of affection and support to the achieving male.

Male dominance has also been typical in commericals. Women have usually been portrayed in a few limited roles, principally leisure activities. When the sexes are fairly evenly divided in the audience, male appearances predominate. When women are almost certain to be the major purchasers of a product (as they are particularly of products advertised in the daytime)—and even in the commercials they are usually shown as its users—males are nevertheless most often seen as informed experts about the product's value and use.

The segment of the broadcast schedule the networks devote to news has regularly been the focus of debate. The principal issue has been bias, either in the reporting of controversial events such as the Vietnam war and the subsequent invasion of Cambodia, or in election campaign coverage. It is, of course, impossible to reach conclusions about coverage that has not been studied, or about future coverage. The question is made particularly difficult by two factors: the criteria for judging bias is itself often a matter of debate, and news is inevitably the creature of events which may favor one side or another. Many critics of national television news have been able to offer arguments that merit attention. However, the many analyses of news content do *not* provide much support for the contention of bias, either in regard to major stories or election campaigns. Nor do the various strong criticisms of network coverage during the Nixon years by officials associated with that Administration appear to have affected coverage, except perhaps to introduce a very slightly greater degree of caution in the handling of stories.

Public television—as those who advocate it in the interests of diversity would expect—differs sharply. The principal difference is the presentation of a greater proportion of children's, news, and public affairs programming. However, a major trend discernible over the past decade has been toward a greater emphasis on entertainment, although entertainment different in character from that on commercial television.

One thoroughly studied topic is the public's viewing behavior. Over the past 15 years, the amount each television household uses its set has steadily increased. Use of television has always been greater in the United States among those of lower socioeconomic status. However, when the increasing consumption by those of lower socioeconomic status began to level off—as would be expected because of the ceiling imposed on total possible viewing time by other activities—the viewing by those of higher socioeconomic status began to climb more sharply. By the mid-1970s, viewing was greater by those of higher socioeconomic status than it had been a decade before by those of lower status. This appears to represent a final step in the pervasive adoption of television by our society in which those at first most resistant— possibly because of greater affinity for "print" and "book" culture—began to approach the amount of viewing of those who turned to television more readily.

However, the convergence in amount of viewing by those of lower and higher socioeconomic status conceivably may not end in the greater homogeneity of media experience that these trends imply. The new technologies—such as cable television and in-home playback—require greater income for access, and thus may lead to those of higher socioeconomic status fashioning a television environment of their own.

Average amount of viewing changes throughout the life cycle. Viewing increases from childhood through elementary school, decreases through the high school and college years, then increases again to a level that persists throughout adult life until a further increase in the later years. Those over 65 view more than adults in general. Viewing tends to vary inversely with other demands. Thus, it is decreased by the social and educational demands of adolescence, and by the demands on younger adults of child-rearing, social life, and career development, and increased by the reduced occupational demands of retirement. Certain segments of the audience definitely are heavier-than-average viewers. Among these are women, blacks, the elderly, and children.

Viewing over a typical day arches up sharply, like the back of a beast ready to pounce. The pattern for the fall of 1976 is typical, although average hours of weekly viewing are less in summer and greater in winter. In the morning hours, only about 9 percent of Americans of all ages were watching television. By early evening the figure was 30 percent. Later, the figure approached 45 percent, before declining to about 17 percent around midnight. The peak is an audience of more than 95 million.

It would be a mistake to think that the arch is identical for all segments of the audience. The viewing cycle differs over the day and week by age and sex. Younger adult women (18–49 years of age) reach an early peak in mid-afternoon, decline, then rise to a much higher prime-time peak between 8 and 10 P.M. Adult men view little during the day and begin their rise in early evening to their sole, prime-time peak. Older women and men (50-plus) behave similarly, except that the peaks occur sooner, viewing by both men and women is heavier, and viewing by men is proportionately greater. During the weekend, viewing by men and women, both older and younger, is similar.

The cycle for children and teenagers is different. Young children (2–5 years of age) reach an early peak in mid-morning, decline until mid-afternoon, then rise to a new, markedly higher peak at about 5 P.M., followed by a slight decline (presumably because of some meals without television) then rise to a final similar peak about 8 P.M. Older children (6–11 years of age) reach a slight, presumably preschool, peak at 8 A.M., then decline until mid-afternoon when the rising curve resembles that for young children with two notable exceptions: the final evening peak is much higher, and viewing into the later evening is heavier. Teenagers behave similarly to adult males with viewing slight until early evening when the rise to a prime-time peak begins. Viewing by teenage girls is typically heavier than by boys except for a sharp 5:30–7:30 P.M. dip—an unexplained phenomenon alternatively attributable to kitchen chores, some other activity, a distaste for news, or some combination of these factors.

The data make clear the large place of television viewing in the lives of the young. At their first daily peak in the morning in the fall of 1976, less than a third of all young children were in the audience; during two evening peaks, the figure was about 45 percent. At their first evening peak, about 40 percent of all older children were in the audience, and at the second, the figure was about 55 percent. By 10 P.M., only about 12 percent of younger children remained in the audience, but the figure for older children was almost twice that. Teenagers are generally not heavy viewers, but in their prime-time peak about 40 percent were in the audience. Slightly more than half of all children under 12 were in the audience between 8 and 9 P.M. weekdays. The figure declined to 30 percent for 9–10 P.M. and to 13 percent during the half-hour before 11 P.M. The huge size of the prime-time audience means that children make up a modest proportion, but their rate of viewing means that in absolute numbers the evening audience of younger children is very large—in the fall of 1976, about 18 million at any given moment in the 8–9 P.M. period. On Saturday mornings, when children dominate the much smaller audience, the number of younger children viewing during the peak between 9 and 11 P.M. was only slightly greater—about 19 million.

These varied viewing patterns reflect the effects of available time, alternative demands and opportunities, and the appeal of programming at the various hours. From the perspective of the television industry, which seeks to maximize its audience, these data pose the question of how the height of these curves can be increased. In their various applications in programming decisions, they lead to such industry concepts as "audience flow" (the shifts of viewers away from and toward the medium and from channel to channel during the broadcast day), "lead-in" (usually applied to a program but more properly thought of as the demographic composition of the audience at a given time that may affect the size and character of the audience for subsequent programming), and "least objectionable programming" (that content which will attract the maximum audience as the result of the phenomenon that many choose to view before deciding what to view). From the perspective of the social or behavioral scientist, these data represent the fit of the medium to the varied lives of these disparate segments of the audience. From the perspective of the public-interest advocate concerned about the effects of television, they are the facts of who is viewing what, and therefore the metric of possible impact.

Another measure of the public's response to television is its beliefs about the medium and its evaluation of the medium's performance. There are several main threads. Between 1960 and 1970, the public became somewhat disenchanted with television, although its evaluation of the medium remained on the whole highly favorable. Compared to the other mass media—magazines, newspapers, and radio—television has risen in esteem. It has dramatically replaced the newspaper as the medium first in public favor. The most criticized aspects of television are commercials. A majority believe that there are too many, but an identical majority believe the presence of commercials is a fair price to pay for television. Other aspects drawing considerable criticism, particularly in regard to children, are sex-related and other content judged inappropriate for the young, and violence. Despite the generally favorable evaluation given television compared to other media, it is also more often cited as the medium that is getting worse. It is not waggish to suggest that this is not an anomaly but a reflection of greater sensitivity to the medium that has become predominant among the mass media.

When the public focuses on news, television increasingly has received acclaim. In 1960, television was slightly overshadowed by newspapers in being judged by the public as the principal source of news, the provider of the most complete coverage, and the most credible source. By 1970, television had become the unambiguous leader on all these counts. Despite this generally favorable evaluation, about a fourth of the public believes television news is biased. However, complaints come about equally from conservatives and liberals. This means that to the degree that people believe the news to be biased, it is equally so to partisans, not that there is unanimous perception of nonbias.

The widely declared esteem for television news is qualified by certain facts. The term "television news" to which the public responds in most studies encompasses both network national news and local news. A large proportion of the adult public—in one national sample more than half over a two week period—do not watch network national news. Reading of newspapers appears to be more frequent. The viewing of local news, ignored implicitly or explicitly in many studies, is greater. The esteem for television decreases and that for newspapers increases when the subject is local and not national news. The implication is that to some degree the public's expression of reliance on "television news" represents a response to the medium as symbol or eternal presence at the hearth rather than a measure of its actual importance as a regular news source.

Like television viewing, favorability toward the medium—in beliefs and in the evaluation of its performance—is inversely related to socioeconomic status, as measured by income or education. Favorability also is greater among blacks and older adults. However, when the viewing choices of those higher and lower in socioeconomic status are compared, differences are minor, and even total amount of viewing by the mid-1970s had become more similar. The implication is that television so well performs its function as an entertainer that it largely overcomes scruples based on attitudes.

There are a variety of ways in which television affects the experiences of its audience beyond hours spent viewing. These concomitants of television include the behavior before the set during viewing, the effects on allocation of leisure time, the influence on other activities, the dynamics of program choice, the impact on other media, and the various uses and gratifications of the medium.

Television certainly brought something new to the household by dimming the lights and turning faces toward the screen. Behavior before the set is unique to television because, despite the similarities to the movies, the home is not a theater. The viewing of television is typically discontinuous and accompanied by some other activity. Eating very often accompanies viewing. People leave and enter the room, sew, converse, play games, read, give full attention to something else, turn back to the screen. Any given time estimate of viewing represents continuing attention and withdrawal. This oscillating inattention is not unrelated to content; people give least constant attention to commercials and news, and the most to movies and other drama.

The impact of television on the expenditure of leisure time has been sizable. Television has markedly increased the total amount of time spent with the mass media. Television viewing as a primary activity, excluding very disrupted viewing while doing something else, consumes more of the leisure time of Americans than any other activity. Among almost 40 kinds of primary activities—exclusive categories into which the 24 hours of the day can be divided—television viewing falls behind only sleep and time spent at work. Despite the variations in total viewing attributable to sex, age, ethnicity, and socioeconomic status, it is a rare set of circumstances where television viewing is not the predominant leisure activity.

Television's absorption of leisure naturally occurs at the expense of other activities. One of television's most marked effects appears to have been to reduce time spent sleeping. It also appears to have reduced time spent in social gatherings away from home, in radio listening, in reading books, in miscellaneous leisure, in conversation, in travel related to leisure, in movie-going, in religious activities, and in household tasks. Television appears in some instances to have increased public participation by drawing attention to events that might otherwise be overlooked. Thus, it may boost a previously not-so-popular sport or cultural activity. However, in the case of minor league baseball in the United States, it appears to have severely reduced attendance by bringing major league baseball into the home.

The conflict of taste among family members that is implied by the decision to view one program rather than another is sharply attenuated by the growing number of multiset homes and by the degree to which only one or a few family members are viewing at a particular time of day. By the mid-1970s, more than half of households of three or more persons had more than one set. During the day, an adult female is typically alone to choose programs, or else she is there with her child or children. Disagreement increases with the group's heterogeneity, and is resolved by a democratic majority, or by normative social standing and authority. Children and parents will view separately when there is disagreement in a multiset household. When there is only one set or children and parents are committed to viewing together, children's tastes rule about as often as do the tastes of parents. When parents agree, they typically prevail over children. When a child and either parent agree, they typically prevail over the other parent. When husbands and wives disagree, which is about half the time, husbands more often prevail. When children disagree, the older is likely to prevail. Parents report considerable lack of mutual agreement, but children report little conflict, which suggests that children do not believe the existing lack of agreement as a very serious matter.

The greater amount of time spent with television increases the incursion of common experience bearing on an extraordinary range of topics, from political and social crises to relations between the sexes. This increase, of course, is attributable to the attention given television and involves some decrease in the time given to other media. The basic rule is that a new mass medium will displace older media when it performs their functions either with greater convenience, reduced financial expenditure, or in a more satisfying way. However, a mass medium may also alter the character and the functions served by other media as these older media attempt to compete. The popularity of a new medium implies a redistribution of media use because consumer expenditures for media are roughly a constant proportion of income, so that expenditures for a new medium imply a reduction in expenditures for old. Television has reshaped the other media, and it is likely that the television we know will itself be reshaped by new technology offering different opportunities and options in regard to information, news, and entertainment.

Any medium and any content may serve for a given individual almost any purpose and may provide almost any conceivable gratification. For a few, a crime caper movie may serve as a lesson about the unlawful acquisition of wealth; for the majority, it will serve simply as entertainment. Television news may be viewed by many for information and some will use such information as the weather report to plan the following day's activities, while for others it will serve simply as diversion, like the presentations preceding or following. However, every medium and every type of content has its normative or central character. In American society, the central use and gratification of television is entertainment. Entertainment is not only predominant in content, but the seeking of entertainment is the predominant rationale offered by the public for viewing television. Television also appears to be largely viewed for itself, rather than for the specific programs; the decision to view is typically more influential than the decision what to view at any particular part of the day.

A major focus has been television's role in the lives of the young. Children as a group are heavy viewers, with viewing increasing through elementary school. Viewing decreases during the high school and college years, but adolescents nevertheless view substantial amounts of television. The major concern has been over possible negative effects. In this respect, television has inherited the villainous posture attributed by critics to whatever mode of storytelling at the time—comic book, movie, radio drama, or ancient tale-spinning and epic poetry—seemed to attract the young. Nevertheless, there are certain traits peculiar to television which justify concern—it occupies extraordinary amounts of time, it is omnipresent, access is difficult to regulate, and most of its programming is designed for adults with no regard for the responses of children.

What research depicts is quite complex, not without apparent inconsistencies, and leaves many questions unanswered. Regular viewing begins long before the first grade, and preferences and tastes begin almost as soon as viewing. Sex differences in taste and preference appear early and continue. Age differences are noticeable, and with them come differences between blacks and whites. There are marked individual differences in amount of viewing and in tastes and preferences. The most plausible way to examine television is as a factor whose place and influence varies with the characteristics and particular age or developmental stage of the young person.

Four topics in particular have drawn attention—television advertising, political socialization, antisocial effects, and "prosocial" effects.

Research on the influence of commercials during growing up is just beginning. Attention to commercials appears to decrease with age, which means exposure is inversely related to the knowledge and experience necessary for critically evaluating them. Very young children do not comprehend the self-interested persuasive nature of commercials. With such understanding comes skepticism and distrust. Even among adolescents, who display the most distrust, there is some attention to and acquisition of information from commercials. Commercials appear to inspire appeals to parents to purchase products. One study found that by the end of the five weeks of the campaign, Christmas toy advertising overcame the defenses of early resisters and those who previously did not prefer television-advertised items began to choose them. The major questions, such as influences on health-related practices, such as dietary preferences, and on basic values, such as materialism or acquisitiveness, remain to be addressed.

Television is *probably* an important factor in the image and expectations young persons hold in regard to politics and government. This is probably so despite the modest degree of attention young persons give to news and public affairs programming. The very nature of public events makes the mass media a major source of information. Children and adolescents frequently cite television as their main source of public-affairs knowledge. Television appears to be more important than teachers or parents for information on continuing events, such as the Vietnam war. However, parents appear to have a strong influence on the direction of opinion. There are many questions not yet studied. To some degree, the wrong question may have been asked in studies which dismissed television as unimportant because it did not change attitudes. The wrong question may also be asked when the focus is solely on news and public-affairs programming, because political socialization involves many issues, such as what constitutes power, the appropriate means for problem solving, and the character of law enforcement, on which there is a large quantity of relevant portrayals in television entertainment. The varied studies so far suggest that television's influence is usually indirect, principally by providing information whose evaluation and eventual influence depends heavily on interpersonal relationships, but nevertheless important because information is a major ingredient in political socialization.

The most studied topic has been the influence of television on antisocial behavior. Television viewing itself appears to be unrelated to either aggression or antisocial behavior. The viewing of television violence appears to increase the likelihood of subsequent aggressiveness. This conclusion derives from the pattern of results of dozens of laboratory experiments, field experiments, and surveys. It also hides many complexities. The relationship of television violence to aggression and antisocial behavior is a topic that reveals the strengths and weaknesses of social and behavioral science, and illustrates many of the problems in drawing generalizations applicable to future events from the limited circumstances of specific studies.

The evidence is that television may increase aggression by teaching viewers previously unfamiliar hostile acts, by generally encouraging in various ways the use of aggression, and by triggering aggressive behavior both imitative and different in kind from what has been viewed. Effects are never certain because real-life aggression is strongly influenced by situational factors, and this strong role for situational factors means that the absence of an immediate effect does not rule out a delayed impact when the behavior in question may be more propitious. The likelihood of subsequent aggressiveness is increased by portrayals in which the aggressor is justified in his act, is rewarded, escapes punishment, or is engaged in the intent to inflict harm. Such likelihood is also increased by portrayals which are realistic and by similarities between cues in the portrayal and in the environment.

Television violence under certain circumstances is capable of reducing subsequent aggressiveness, but the cause appears to be inhibition following upon anxiety over aggression rather than catharsis. The quantity of studies with consistent results provide considerable confidence about the relationship between television violence and subsequent aggression, but the studies do not provide direct evidence on whether television contributes widely or generally to serious antisocial behavior.

In recent years, increasing attention has been given to television's contribution to socially desirable, or "prosocial," behavior. The few studies done to date indicate that television portrayals can increase the likelihood of certain kinds of behavior other than aggression, although there are many differences between raising the likelihood of negatively sanctioned behavior, such as aggression, and doing so for positively sanctioned behavior.

Learning appears to underlie all other influences. Children and adolescents learn from television in a variety of ways. Both knowledge and behavior are subject to influence by television. Television probably should be considered a major agent of socialization, although its influence is often indirect and contingent on interpersonal relations and other factors.

Four other segments of the audience—women, blacks, the poor, and the elderly—are also of high interest. Each has an atypical relationship to television. They are all, as groups, heavy viewers. They are usually portrayed on the screen either in trite fashion, in lesser roles, or relatively infrequently. Increasingly, they have become the subject of concern over whether they are served well by the mass media. Women and the elderly are heavy viewers because they are less frequently in the labor force, and instead remain at home, where television is adjacent. The social roles assigned women apparently fate them to be heavy viewers, for both younger and older women view more on the average than their male peers. Blacks are extraordinarily favorably disposed toward television. The reasons are highly speculative, but one possibility is a fortuitous conjunction of the histories of the medium and the group. The poor typically rely heavily on television among the media, probably because of a lack of the education that would orient them more toward print media. Blacks, the poor, and the elderly are all more likely to look upon television as a source of knowledge and information. The larger effects of television on these portions of the audience are unknown, but there are intriguing bits of data and much speculation.

There are two bodies of findings which can best be examined together in order to interpret the evidence most easily, because in both cases there are calculated attempts to persuade—these are the data on television and politics, and on television and advertising. When they are examined together, political and campaign news coverage, political advertising, and product advertising, display certain similarities and differences.

In both areas, there are instances in which paid-for campaigns appear to have had a significant impact. However, the very many factors which influence decisions make the clear-cut demonstration of effects on behavior uncommon. In politics, television appears to affect knowledge and information and to define the context in which voting decisions are made. Along with the other mass media, it helps to establish the agenda of personalities and issues to which the public responds. Television has an important role because it is the ultimate mass medium in focusing the nation's attention on the same topics, persons, and messages. During elections, it is now a principal means of increasing the salience of politics, stimulating the expression of partisanship, and orienting the public toward the eventual act of voting. However, television's influence on the outcome of elections is limited by voters' party allegiances prior to a specific campaign and their tendency typically to reach a decision by the time of the nominating conventions, the carrying by television of roughly balanced news coverage and political advertising for the various candidates (this becomes to some degree self-cancelling with respect to the emphasis given one side or another), and the preoccupation of television news with events and personalities amenable to visual coverage rather than issues.

The trend toward reduced party allegiance over the past 15 years and the presence of unusual numbers of undecided or wavering voters (such as in the 1976 presidential election), increase the opportunity for television to have an effect. The evidence from the many studies of the 1960 Nixon-Kennedy debates does not lead to any conclusion about their effect on the outcome, although it appears that individual voters were affected in various ways in their beliefs and prceptions. Evidence from 1976 suggests that in this close election, where voter indecision was high and the Ford–Carter debates were an electoral media event, television played a particularly significant role in facilitating the reaching of a decision by individual voters about which of the major candidates to vote for.

Television has probably altered the way political campaigns are fought, and thereby reshaped politics, but this is precisely the important kind of "effect" that is not readily measurable by social and behavioral science. Politics and advertising most overlap in the case of political advertising, which despite certain sharp differences shares many similarities with product advertising. Advertising obviously can affect knowledge, information, attitudes, and behavior, but the various conditions on which such effects are contingent are numerous and complex.

There is a very large scientific literature on the effects on subsequent behavior of exposure to a television portrayal. This literature derives from a number of disparate theories of human behavior, and although much of it deals with effects on aggressive or antisocial behavior, the implications apply to a far wider, highly varied range of behavior. Among the concepts or conditions on which a behavioral effect appears to be contingent are the state of physiological arousal, the perceived consequences of the behavior in question, the perceived reality or "authenticity" of the television portrayal, the alternatives for behaving in the situation at hand, the salience of the behavior in question at the particular time and in the particular circumstances, and the opportunity to perform it.

Obviously, there is no facile answer to the question of whether the viewing of a portrayal will influence behavior. However, by synthesizing the large and varied body of evidence, it is possible to develop a single explanatory model. Our approach is to present the model, then test it against the evidence; this, of course, is a heuristic device and the sequence of events was actually the laborious construction of the model by reviewing the findings one by one. The result is an integrated picture of the psychological dynamics behind any kind of behavioral effect.

It is likely that social and behavioral science will assume an increasing role in television policy-making. Its impact is likely to be particularly great in the regulation of television advertising, where new issues have emerged in regard to effects on children, and in the highly varied self-regulatory actions undertaken by the television industry in response to pressure from the government and public. However, it also has a role in the evaluation of the effectiveness of policies adopted primarily on legal, economic, or ideological grounds. There is a lengthy agenda of topics which future research should address, many with significance for future policy. Progress in the practical application of research to the problems of mass communications depends on the solution of three problems. (1) The difficulty of generalizing from research to real life can be alleviated (a) by the use of multiple methods of investigation, dissimilar in their deficiencies, to focus on the same question, and (b) by the further development of theory, which implies the wide use—despite the objections raised against its artificiality in the case of television—of the laboratory-type experiment. (2) The polyglot and fragmented nature of the scientific study of television can be partially overcome (a) by the use of focused, coordinated research programs directed by persons expert and sophisticated in communications studies in which research is organized around a theme or topic, with particular attention to encouraging cooperation among investigators, insuring coverage of important issues, and the avoiding of redundancy, with a publications program to bring about speedy, effective dissemination of results to social and behavioral scientists, the television industry, and the public, and (by) the the inauguration of a specialized information service specifically designed to address the needs of the field. (3) The usefulness of social and behavioral science in policymaking of all kinds, in the government, in the industry, and on the part of citizen and advocacy groups, can be increased (a) by altering the intellectual milieu in which social and behavioral scientists function to give them greater knowledge of the way broadcasting operates so that they can devise research that is more pertinent, and (b) by altering the organizational milieu in which policymakers function to give them greater and more effective access to social and behavioral science's expertise.

Chapter

What's On

IN A TYPICAL year, the approximately 720 commercial television stations in the United States broadcast 4.7 *million* hours of programming.* Because television is so pervasive, even those who do not watch very often know the twin "truths" about this programming—it is extremely varied, ranging from what might be called audiovisual babble to news coverage of momentous and occasionally tragic events; and it is all the same, varying little from day-to-day, station-to-station, or year-to-year. Besides these two patently self-evident, if paradoxical, "facts," there is also a great deal more which can be said with some precision because of the attention social scientists have devoted to analyzing television content.

We begin with an examination of the nature of content analysis. This is necessary because content analyses are often mistaken for something they are not, such as the study of the effects *of* television on viewers, and also often unjustifiably derided for not doing what they are not designed or intended to do.

We then evaluate the state of scientific knowledge about television content in regard to:

Types of programs broadcast, including data on differences among networks and between commercial and noncommercial broadcasters, and on the time consumed by commercials.

Themes that are typical in television drama, with special attention to the implicit and "hidden" messages of the soap opera.

Portrayals as they relate to social class, race, and occupation, with

---

* Estimated on the assumption that the average broadcast day for commercial stations is 18 hours. The figure would rise to over 6.0 million on the assumption of a 24-hour broadcast day. Data from *Addenda to Television Factbook,* No. 47, April 3, 1978. Television Digest: Washington, D.C.

particular attention to any tendency of television to distort social reality.

News coverage, with particular attention to the evidence on bias in television news.

Violence, including data on trends and the debate which has occurred over the measurement of television violence.

The Technique Examined

Holsti (1969) defines content analysis as "any technique for making inferences by objectively and systematically identifying specific characteristics of messages." This concise statement has a number of implications.

Inferences

The first implication concerns the making of inferences. To do so, some sort of comparison is necessary. The standard for the comparison may be objective, such as content of another kind, or at another time, place, or medium; or the frequency of real-life occurrence. It may also be implicit or intuitive, and thus value-based, such as establishing a standard of zero in order to assess news bias. An inference depends upon the introduction of a standard against which the measure in question may be judged.

Inferences cannot be drawn solely from content analyses of television—either about effects on viewers or about motives of communicators. Knowledge of content must be supplemented by evidence that such content has particular effects or betrays particular motives. Nor does a content analysis "evaluate" the performance of a broadcaster until some standard of judgment invoking a set of values is applied to the data.

Reliability

The second implication is that, because what is to be counted must be objectively and systematically specified, the results must be "reliable"—that is, unaffected by differences in the recorders or the circumstances under which the recording takes place. Whatever specified characteristics are to be identified, they must be equally identifiable by all who use the mode of categorization.

The rules and definitions are intended to permit any recorder to bring back the same results from the same initial content. Of course, the most interesting concepts are sometimes the most difficult to define clearly for objective and systematic specification.

Validity

The third implication is that the characteristics to be identified must be proper indicators of the concept to be measured. To phrase it in the language of the philosophy of science, operations must validly reflect conceptual definitions. An example of the problem is found in the debate over the relationship between the number of television stations and the diversity of programs in a community. One group defines diversity as the number of different *programs.* Another uses the number of different *kinds* of programs. Both definitions allow for objective and systematic measurement, but tabulations in each case lead to quite different inferences.

Often, resolving the validity problem in the case of television requires adjudicating among equally objective measures. When they are inconsistent in trend, inferences are difficult to make and must be carefully qualified.

Another aspect involves the selection of the sample of television content. Our knowledge of "television" in the United States is inevitably distorted because analyses have been largely limited to what are currently broadcasting the three networks, although non-network stations and non-network programs on stations affiliated with networks contribute sizable portions of the total fare consumed by viewers. Two examples stand out: (1) Locally produced news typically accounts for as much or more audience-viewing time than network news, but analyses of TV news have been limited almost exclusively to that of the three networks. (2) Children spend a great deal of time watching locally scheduled situation comedy and violent adventure reruns between school and prime time, yet measures of the content of children's viewing usually ignore such programming. The problem is simply that because of the variation across communities, locally scheduled programming is less amenable to study than network programming.

With these qualifications in mind, we can turn to the findings about the messages conveyed by television.

Basic Dimensions

Most television viewing occurs in the evening, in what commercial television labels prime time; and during this 8 to 11 P.M. period nine out of ten viewers watch network programs. The regular network schedule during these hours is exclusively entertainment (table 2.1). When the total broadcast day over a week for a typical year is examined, there is only a slight shift in the predominance of entertainment with about 12 percent devoted to news and information.

The networks in the mid-1970s differed somewhat in types of entertainment programs offered in the evening, principally in the disinclination of one network to schedule situation comedy. The most frequent types of programs were situation comedies (in number of programs) and mystery and suspense drama (in hours of programming). Over time, the networks tend to vary similarly in content, as exemplified by the relative decline over the past decades on all three networks of evening western, quiz and game, and variety programs.

Network programming dominates American television. About 90 percent of the 717 privately owned commercial television stations in the United States are affiliated with one of the three networks and the networks provide about two-thirds of their programming. The few nonaffiliated stations subsist on syndicated programs broadcast in previous seasons on the networks, movies, and purchases of original programming either produced for sale outside of or rejected by the networks. There has been a trend in recent years toward independent distribution of new, original programming comparable in quality to that disseminated through the networks. The availability of such programming for purchase by both affiliates and nonaffiliates will increase competitiveness and sensitivity to signals of shifts in public taste, but is unlikely to alter in any way the basic makeup of the programming available to the public. The principal difference brought about by the presence of an independent station in a market appears to be an increase in the quantity of violent programming broadcast in a community (Milavsky, 1977), a result of such stations' reliance on old material of fairly certain appeal.

Shifts in network programming are a function of popularity as defined by size of audience. The fate of individual programs and whole genres of programs is determined by their success in at-

Table 2.1 Patterns in Television Programming

Part A: One Week of Network Prime Time, Fall 1976

Program Type	Hours
Situation comedy	12.5
Suspense and mystery drama	16.5
General drama (includes adventure, science fiction, general and western drama)	13.0
Variety	7.0
Feature film	11.5

Part B: Three Networks for One Week of Prime Time, Fall 1976

Program Type	Number of Programs (in half hours)		
	ABC	CBS	NBC
Situation comedy	8	13	2
Suspense and mystery drama			
Official police	8	6	6
Private detective	0	4	5
General drama	8	6	10
Variety	2	6	2
Feature film	8	4	11

SOURCE: TV Guide, October 2–8, 1976.

SOURCE: A. C. Nielsen Co.

Part C: One Week of Network and Public Television, 1972

Network (N = 253 hours)		Public (N = 29 hours)	
Program Type	Percent	Program Type	Percent
News/public affairs	12	News/public affairs	30
Children's	8	Children's	40
Other	80	Other	30
Sports (9)		Cultural (9)	
Quiz, audience participation (14)		Musical performance (7)	
Daytime serials (16)		Nonmusical performance (14)	
Feature films (11)			
Comedy/variety (18)			
Drama/adventure (12)			

Part D: A Week of Evening Programs on New York Public Television (WNET), 1966 and 1975

Program Type	Hours Per Week (in percent)	
	1966 (N = 19)	1975 (N = 21)
Academic instruction	4	—
Nonacademic instruction	8	19
Light entertainment	7	31
Cultural information	12	—
Cultural entertainment	37	24
News/public affairs	28	27
Other	3	—

SOURCE: Adapted from N. I. Katzman. 1973. *One Week of Public Television: April 1972.* Washington, D.C.: Corporation for Public Broadcasting.

SOURCE: Adapted from National Broadcasting Company, Social Research Department, 1976. *Public television.* New York: National Broadcasting Co.

tracting viewers. The rise and fall of the ratings for a type of program very roughly parallels its frequency in the television schedule. When such trends since 1955 are analyzed, the shift up or down in average ratings for a type of program over a two-year period successfully predicts the rise or fall in the frequency of the programs in the subsequent two-year period—a delay that allows for rescheduling and the production of new programs—in about two-thirds of the instances in which there was some change in both (table 2.2). As we shall see later in this chapter, this very evident tendency for ratings—which reflect the proportion of the total audience watching a program—to determine future program selection is made even more clear in the case of violent programs.

Public television, intended to offer programming not available on commercial channels, naturally differs considerably from commercial television even in gross dimensions (table 2.1). The principal differences at such a level are in the greater emphasis of public television on news and public affairs programming and on children's programs. Commercial and public television differ so much that different classification schemes are typically employed in the analysis of their content (Katzman, 1973, 1975). Nevertheless, a rough grouping by news and public affairs programming, children's programs, and other content leaves no doubt that com-

Table 2.2 Ratings and Subsequent Schedule Changes for Evening Programs for the Three Networks (1955–1976)

Type of Program	Trends in Ratings and Broadcast Schedule, by Two-Year Delay [a]		
	Consistent	Inconsistent	Unclassifiable [b]
Western	7	1	1
Quiz	4	2	—
Suspense and mystery drama	5	2	2
Situation comedy	6	2	1
Variety	3	5	1
Total	25	12	5

SOURCE: Data compiled from A. C. Nielsen Co., National Audience Demographics Report.

[a] Upward or downward shift in average ratings over two-year period for a type of program compared to changes in number of such programs scheduled in subsequent two-year period—i.e., ratings trend in 1955–57 compared to scheduling trend in 1957–59.

[b] No shift either in ratings or program frequency.

mercial television is far more oriented toward general audience entertainment, and that a very substantial amount of non-news and non-public-affairs programming on public television is devoted to children's programs (table 2.1).

As we shall see, the bond that has developed between the audience and commercial television in the United States defines the medium as principally a provider of entertainment (chapters 4 and 6), although the public rates its performance as a news medium very highly (chapter 3). This observation implies no valuation of this role; it is simply a fact.

Television is not primarily a medium of entertainment in all societies, but it is typically so, and the assumption of this role appears to be related to the attempt to attract and please a large, heterogeneous audience. Public television in the United States would appear not to be immune to the dynamics involved. We shall see that its audience has been increasing (chapter 3). At the same time, there has also been a trend toward more light entertainment (*Jennie; Upstairs, Downstairs; Monty Python*), as exemplified by a comparison of the evening programming in 1975 with that of a decade earlier of the New York station, public television's major urban outlet (table 2.1). Again, no valuation is implied in the recognition of this trend; it is an observation of fact.

Public television programs are viewed by such relatively small audiences that their content has little weight in what the American public sees on television. This is not so for commercials. Bechtel, Achelpohl, and Akers (1972) installed cameras in the living rooms of 20 midwestern homes to record what was going on while the television set was on. When we examine what people actually viewed, one item stands out—15 percent of all viewing time was spent looking at commercials (table 2.3), a figure roughly equivalent to the proportion of time alloted to commercials during prime time. Commercials were the least attentively viewed of any other program category (see chapter 4), but this does not alter the conclusion that paid advertising constitutes a substantial portion of the viewing experience of Americans, and one that has far greater weight in the television experience of the public as a whole than does public television.

Table 2.3 Program Types by Percentage of Total Actual Watching Time by All Individuals [N = 20 families (93 persons)]

Program Type	Percent of Total Watching Time
Family programs and variety	20.8
Films (movies)	18.5
Commercials	15.0
Children's shows and cartoons	11.8
Suspense	10.6
Sports	8.6
News, weather, informative programs	5.6
Melodrama	3.1
Talk show	2.5
Game show	2.4
Religious	0.2

SOURCE: Adapted from R. B. Bechtel, C. Achelpohl and R. Akers. 1972. Correlates between observed behavior and questionnaire responses on television viewing. In E. A. Rubinstein, G. A. Comstock and J. P. Murray (eds.). *Television and Social Behavior*. Vol. 4, *Television in Day-to-Day Life: Patterns of Use*. Washington, D.C.: Government Printing Office, pp. 274–344.

Television Themes

There has been extensive journalistic, interpretative, and (often) caustic comment on the themes of television entertainment, but not a great deal of empirical research. The research which does exist bears on several rather specific topics—the western, the soap opera, means and ends, and the environment.

The Western

Topping (1965) analyzed 16 prime-time westerns broadcast in a single week in the early 1960s. He coded the behavior of heroes, protagonists (those helped by the heroes), and villains to determine their views of the world, and found all three types of characters to be "individualistic"; but that was the limit of similarities. Villains viewed human nature as immutably evil, while heroes and protagonists tended to feel that people were basically good and might be open to change. Protagonists generally felt that man can master nature, whereas villains were less likely to think so; heroes fell between the two. Ten of sixteen villains focus on the present, while heroes and protagonists are far more likely to focus on the future. It would appear that western villains are less "modern" in outlook than heroes or protagonists; thus the drama centers on the triumph of what we understand as social progress.

Analysis of 100 western films from the late 1950s—a genre that has been a staple of television—similarly suggests that such dramas are embroidered, however tackily, around basic human conflicts. In this instance, the films were found to feature either conflicts between good and evil personified in two males or a version of the Oedipus conflict requiring a central role for a woman as well as for two men (Emery, 1959a, 1959b).

We do not have comparable data on the urban law enforcement dramas so popular in the 1970s, but we would suspect that there would be many thematic similarities. Both westerns and urban crime dramas are concerned with the punishment of criminal deviance and both feature unofficial as well as official agents of law enforcement. Furthermore, the crime drama has replaced the western in viewer esteem, which encourages us to expect similarities at their heart that would permit such substitution.

The Soap Opera

More recently, several researchers have examined the content of the daytime television soap opera. Katzman (1972a) analyzes "problems and events" during one week in April 1970. Four main strands were identified in the 14 soap operas broadcast, covering 85 independent problems and events:

Criminal and undesirable activity:
  blackmail
  bigamy
  3 threats or instances of violence
  2 murders
  2 other deaths
  poison
  illegal drug traffic
  a man in prison
Social problems:
  3 cases of business difficulties
  3 professional men on probation or fired
  2 cases of drunkenness
  4 youths involved with drugs
  4 offspring of parents not married to each other
  adoption of a child
  5 cases of family estrangement

Medical developments:
  2 mental illnesses
  4 psychosomatic illnesses
  5 cases of physical disability
  4 pregnancies
  3 successful medical treatments
  2 instances of important medical research
Romantic and marital affairs:
  3 romances in trouble
  3 new romances
  4 marriages in trouble
  8 clear cases of marital infidelity
  2 cases of potential marital infidelity
  3 divorces or annulments
  a reconciliation of a married couple
  7 impending marriages

The author summarizes:

> On the whole, the world of the soap opera was full of troubles. Problems seem to keep the shows moving along. They are not major problems like war, forest fires, outlaw bands or national security. Rather, they are "realistic" problems of shady business deals, illness, young people and drugs, marital infidelity, and so forth.

Ramsdell (1973) spent more than 600 hours watching eight soap operas offered by a single network in 1971–72, a total which is not out of line with the average annual viewing of the typical soap opera fan. Among the findings:

Illegitimacy is common among soap families.
Abortion is not accepted.
Divorce is common.
Death is presented openly and realistically.
Some couples live together before marriage.
Senior citizens are part of family structure.
Juvenile delinquency, frequently drug-related, is common.
Social drinking is an essential ingredient of action.
World and national problems are not considered.

These two studies and a third conducted by Downing (1974) are consistent in their reports of the age, sex, and occupational status of characters in soap operas. Males are primarily "profes-sionals" (Ramsdell reports "better than 50 percent," Downing reports 58 percent, and Katzman reports 60 percent) while females are either housewives ("a majority"; 30 percent; "a third") or have lower-status positions.

There is a solid core of female professionals (Ramsdell says 14 percent; Downing reports 19 percent; Katzman reports 5 percent "doctors, lawyers and businessmen," but excludes nurses or other lower level professionals). However, there is some disagreement about how they are presented. Ramsdell insists that "the career woman is not dealt with gently in the soaps, most frequently being depicted as villainous or emotionally unstable." Downing, on the other hand, is not surprised to find that "professional women are portrayed sympathetically on daytime serial drama." One notes without surprise that in quantifiable areas there is general agreement, but when conclusions are drawn from examples or personal impressions there is conflict.

A summary consistent with most data is that:
. . . the world of the soap opera is populated by male and female adults—mainly male professionals, their wives and lovers and their female assistants and secretaries. These people almost always appear indoors (most often in a living room), where they spend most of their time talking. During their conversations males tend to pair off with females. The males tend to be the same age as the women or older, and they are less likely to have been married. Over 90 percent of the conversations are about people, typically people who are not present at the time. When the topic is not business or small talk, conversations turn to family matters (where negative comments equal positive comments), the more favorable aspects of romantic relationships, and ever-present health problems. (Katzman, 1972a; p. 211)

Means and Ends

An often cited analysis of television content is the report of Larsen, Gray, and Fortis (1963) on goals and goal achievement in drama (table 2.4). They chose 18 network programs divided into three categories—programs aimed at adults, programs for a mixed audience ("kidult"), and children's programs.

The most frequently sought goal was "sentiment," defined as a desire for justice or fairness unaccompanied by personal or tangible reward. Next was "affection," reflecting a desire for devotion, friendship, passion, or the gratification of strong emotional needs such as hate, followed by "self-preservation." These three accounted for about 70 percent of goals sought.

Table 2.4 Goals and Their Means of Achievement in Television Drama

Part A: Goals by Program Type (in percent)

Goals	Adult[a] (N = 172)	Kidult (N = 133)	Child (N = 106)	Combined (N = 411)
Property	6.4	20.3	25.4	15.8
Self-preservation	29.1	10.5	12.3	18.8
Affection	28.5	13.5	20.8	21.7
Sentiment	18.0	39.8	19.8	25.6
Power and prestige	5.2	9.8	18.9	10.2
Psychological	7.6	4.5	2.8	5.4
Other	5.2	1.6	0.0	2.5
Total	100.0	100.0	100.0	100.0

Part B: Means of Achievement by Program Type (in percent)

Means of Achievement	Adult (N = 236)	Kidult (N = 198)	Child (N = 181)	Combined (N = 615)
Socially Disapproved				
Nonlegal	7.2	5.1	9.4	7.2
Violent	31.8	20.2	47.0	32.6
Escape	17.4	3.5	6.1	9.6
Total disapproved	56.4	28.8	62.5	49.4
Socially Approved				
Legal	8.1	14.6	6.6	9.7
Total approved	8.1	14.6	6.6	9.7
Other				
Economic	4.7	11.1	6.1	7.2
Organizational	8.5	19.7	8.3	12.0
Chance	7.2	10.1	8.8	8.7
Miscellaneous	15.1	15.7	7.7	13.0
Total other	35.5	56.6	30.9	40.9
Total	100.0	100.0	100.0	100.0

SOURCE: Adapted from O. N. Larsen, L. N. Gray, and J. G. Fortis. 1963. Goals and goal-achievement methods in television content: Models for anomie? *Sociological Inquiry*, 33, 180–98.

[a] N = Number of instances coded.
Adult = all dramas after 9 P.M.
Kidult = 4 situation comedies and two cowboy programs.
Child = 5 early evening animated series and *Walt Disney Presents*.

Goal achievement was marked by the prevalence of socially disapproved means, of which violence was the most frequent. Children's programs used violent means more frequently than adult and "kidult" programs. Half of all goals for all program types studied were achieved through socially disapproved means. We would expect sizable use of socially disapproved means from the typical presence of villains in dramas of conflict. What is significant is that success so often followed from transgression, and that the ends so achieved would not by themselves lead a viewer to reject what had been depicted about their pursuit.

The data, of course, are now relatively old. By the mid-1970s, 17 of the 18 series had vanished from first-run network presentation. Nevertheless, the results are interesting as a benchmark and naturally raise questions about current goals and means in television drama. What goals are presently pursued? What means are used? We possess very little data about the themes, plots, and general value systems of current television programs.

The Environment

Heffner and Kramer (1972) describe the content of a week of 1971 network programs in terms of environmental statements (table 2.5). This, like the analyses of television violence we cover later, is an example of research focused on a prominent "issue" in regard to television content. They found 570 statements concerning environmental phenomena fairly evenly divided among five major categories, although rather definite advocacy is detectable (or, in one case, skirting of an issue) within each category. Television's message was against pollution, for conservation, very favorable toward nature, and in favor of private rather than public transportation. Television tended to obscure any position on population growth by placing such statements within larger statements about other issues, in sharp contrast to its handling of pollution statements, where about 85 percent of the antipollution statements (which include two-thirds of all statements) were direct and straightforward.

These results are in accord with the view of television as an essentially conservative agency reflecting public values but protective of its own interest. The direction of its advocacy is in accord with views to which the public at least verbally subscribes— *against* pollution, *for* conservation of resources, and *favorable* toward nature. It is noncommittal where there is explosive con-

What's On

Table 2.5 Treatment of the Environment by Network Television Programs: Distribution of Statements About the Environment

Topic	Percent of All Environment Statements (N = 570)[a]	Percent of Total Statement Time (N = 1090 min.)	Analysis of Statements
Pollution	23	28	67 percent of the statements are against pollution; about 85 percent of these are *direct*, straightforward statements against pollution
Transportation	20	16	59 percent of the statements support private transportation; 22 percent support mass transportation
Attitudes toward nature	19	18	87 percent of the statements express a positive attitude; less than 10 percent are negative
Resource conservation	16	18	61 percent of the statements support attitudes or actions conducive to conservation; 26 percent support resource-depleting attitudes or actions
Population growth	15	14	81 percent of population-growth statements are overshadowed by other issues in the statement and can be said to be indirect rather than direct
General and miscellaneous	7	6	————

SOURCE: Adapted from R. D. Heffner, and E. H. Kramer. 1972. Network television's environmental content. Unpublished manuscript, Rutgers University.

[a] Statements were coded from a composite, weighted network television week drawn from a seven-week period with a total of 372 programs or 262 hours and 43 minutes of television time.

troversy—neither for nor against population control. And in the case of a conflict with its derivation of income from advertisers of automobiles, gasoline, and other private-transportation products, it acts in its own interest—*for* private transportation. What is remarkable is that a picture so like what we should expect if television were a self-interested individual emerges as the sum of the thousands of individual decisions that lie behind television programs and commercials.

Social Differentiation on Television

There have been a number of studies of television's portrayal of various social strata, minorities, and occupations. Two issues inescapably arise in their review:

> The meaning of a deviation from real-life in the portrayals. The criteria by which portrayals can be said to exemplify a stereotype, and particularly an uncomplimentary one.

Portrayals often are evaluated by comparing them to a statistic representing real life, such as a census datum. We have already seen that by such a criterion soap operas overrepresent male professionals. The research we shall now examine finds similar distortions. The introduction of such a criterion is not a judgment of the merit of the portrayals. Television, like Elizabethan drama, Broadway plays, the modern (or any) novel, movies, and any medium of fiction, presents a created world that cannot be expected to contain a probability sample of real life. The issues in each instance are the distortions of the created world in question. The standard of reality is convenient, and in the case of television particularly appealing, because it is a mass medium whose portrayals enter—as have none other—into the homes of the public whose individual lives provide that standard.

Portrayals also are often evaluated by their conformity to the mental image called a stereotype. The standard here is no more than the observer's perception of what he believes to be a trite, conventional, or unrealistically narrow image. Portrayals are said to be stereotypic both because of their sameness to each other and their consistency with the image held by the public. The perception of a stereotype depends on a value judgment, for there is no objective, empirical basis for their presence or absence. Many would argue that stereotypic portrayals are inherently bad because they slight human diversity, but assigning merit or its lack to a stereotype is otherwise not so easy.

The difficulty for those determined to pass judgment on the merits of portrayals is that the standard to be imposed is often not clear. Deviation from the real world may conflict or support a publicly held stereotype; a stereotypic portrayal may or may not be in the interests of a particular group. Those who would sit in judgment need their full baggage of values.

Social Class and Occupations

When television was still in its infancy, Head (1954) published an analysis of 209 network-distributed drama programs that were on the air during the spring of 1952. Among other things, he reports that "in most real communities, the lowest [social class] is the largest and the upper class is the smallest; whereas precisely the opposite is true of the fictional community of television drama." Gentile and Miller (1961) report an analysis of 21 hours of prime-time television during December 1956 covering 18 dramatic and eight quiz programs. The overwhelming majority (62 percent of all characters and 81 percent of nonhistorical characters) of occupational roles was judged to be "middle class" and there were relatively few (6 percent to 7 percent) identifiable working-class characters.

Several years later, DeFleur (1964) examined the occupational roles in 250 half-hour time periods. His programs were chosen from all those shown on four local channels during hours when many children were watching and where recognizable, modern work was being carried out. Cartoons, commercials, new programs, quiz shows and westerns were excluded. The television labor force was compared to the actual composition of the labor force:

> Professional workers were substantially overrepresented. Nearly a third of the labor force on television was engaged in professional occupations of relatively high social prestige. A similar concentration was noted in the category of managers, officials, and proprietors.

Seggar and Wheeler (1973) drew a similar sample—250 half hour segments chosen randomly from 3:30 to 11 P.M. weekdays and 10 A.M. to 11 P.M. weekends. Like DeFleur, they included only programs which portrayed "people interacting in modern settings in which activities revealed occupational status." When the two studies are compared, we find a 34 percent increase in the number of identifiable occupational roles consuming three or more minutes—from 436 to 586. This suggests an increase in occupational depictions over the decade.* On other counts, Seggar and Wheeler are consistent with DeFleur and other earlier stud-

*Seggar and Wheeler coded portrayals of 15 seconds or more, of which there were 1830; however, their data allowed the calculation of three-minute portrayals for comparison with DeFleur, who confined himself to this larger unit.

ies. When compared with labor-force statistics, "There was an overrepresentation of all groups in the professional and managerial fields . . . [and] there was an underrepresentation of all groups in occupations with little prestige, except in the service area."†

Ethnic Portrayal

Seggar and Wheeler also analyze the portrayal of ethnic groups. White Americans were slightly overrepresented (television, 75 percent; census, 70 percent), British characters appeared even more frequently (6.6 percent) than black Americans (6.3 percent)—and blacks appeared less frequently than their distribution in the population (11 percent). The distribution of occupation by ethnicity showed that white Americans and black Americans were given the highest status positions—with no statistically significant differences between the two groups—and that non-American and Chicano characters were assigned job roles relatively lower in status than other television characters. Table 2.6 presents our summary of these data.

Table 2.6 Television Portrayals by Occupational Category and Ethnicity (In Percent)

	Ethnic Group [a]				
Occupational Category	White (N = 1362)	Black (N = 115)	British (N = 121)	Chicano (N = 97)	European (N = 62)
Professional and technical	38.6	35.7	23.9	24.2	23.7
Managers, officials, proprietors	10.2	18.3	14.0	8.1	18.6
Craftsmen and foremen	6.9	1.7	1.6	1.6	1.0
Service workers	23.8	33.0	36.4	43.5	46.4
Clerical, sales, operatives, household, laborers	20.5	11.3	24.1	22.6	10.3

SOURCE: Adapted from J. F. Seggar and P. Wheeler. 1973. World of work on TV: Ethnic and sex representation in TV drama. *Journal of Broadcasting*, 17, 201–14.
[a] N = Number of portrayals of 15 or more seconds duration.

†The overrepresentation of "service" workers is a rather complex matter that seems to have been complicated by the difference between counting 15-second appearances and three-minute appearances. DeFleur identified less than 12 percent of his characters as service workers, but Seggar and Wheeler put 26 percent of their characters in the category. Has television changed in nine years? Do many service workers have brief walk-on roles? Or are both things true? The data now provide no answer.

When the distribution of television occupations is compared to labor-force data, several different patterns emerge. All ethnic groups are overrepresented in the professional and technical group, and blacks are overrepresented in managerial positions. Similarly, all ethnic groups are underrepresented in the lower-status positions, and blacks most strongly so.

When Seggar and Wheeler examined ethnic portrayal by sorting appearances into those which occupied more versus less than three minutes, they found that whites were most likely to have major parts in programs. Of 1362 white Americans, 35.9 percent appeared for at least three minutes; of Europeans, 35.1 percent; of the black Americans, 27.8 percent; of the British, 22.3 percent; and of the Chicanos, only 16.1 percent.

In Head's (1954) early study, characters other than white Americans represented 11 percent of 1578 characters identified in 209 programs—a proportion less than half of that found 20 years later by Seggar and Wheeler. Head found that ethnic minorities were "markedly more engaged in domestic and other service work and in small proprietorship . . . [and they were] markedly less often engaged in police and protective work and white-collar jobs." Head also reports that in terms of affective and ethical status, ethnic minorities were presented favorably. Only two of 56 blacks were depicted as "bad" and only four others were "unsympathetic" characters. In fact, ethnic minorities were less likely than white Americans to be depicted as unsympathetic.

Dominick and Greenberg (1970) analyzed three seasons beginning in 1967–68, at which time the networks adopted a policy of increasing the presentation of blacks on television. Unsurprisingly, the networks were quite effective in changing the makeup of television. Dominick and Greenberg found that the number of commercials featuring blacks more than doubled over the three years, although 88 percent of daytime and 90 percent of prime-time advertisements still contained no blacks in the fall of 1969.

Commercials in which blacks appeared generally contained several times as many characters as those in which they did not. Implicitly, therefore, blacks usually gained admittance as part of a group. But this trend was also diminishing—the median number of people included in commercials containing blacks fell from ten to six over the three years. Blacks had already been present in about a quarter of "public service" ads, and this proportion did not change. Product ad appearances jumped from 3 percent (day) and 4 percent (prime time) to 8 percent (day) and 10 percent (prime time). The sharpest increase in the use of blacks in advertising was among "promotional" ads to acquaint viewers with coming television programs. By 1969, blacks appeared in 25 percent (day) and 20 percent (prime time), a large increase over the 10 percent and 6 percent figures for 1967. Additional data indicate that within commercials where they appear, blacks were increasingly receiving major roles and decreasingly receiving background positions.

Dominick and Greenberg also analyzed the appearance of blacks in television drama. During the daytime, there was little change in frequency of portrayals over the three years; roughly a quarter of the soap operas included at least one black character. What did change was quality of portrayal—the proportion of black characters given major roles. In 1967, 8 percent of the 25 blacks in soap operas had a major role; by 1969 the proportion had jumped to 47 percent of 34 characters. The change in policy also had a striking effect on frequency of blacks in prime-time television. There, the proportion of dramas containing blacks rose sharply from 34 percent to 52 percent in 1968, but did not increase in 1969. However, the portrayal of blacks in major prime-time roles declined negligibly over the three years.

The analysis of annual samples of prime-time and Saturday morning programming suggest that nonwhite representation in drama has increased since the 1969–70 season (United States Commission on Civil Rights, 1977). In this instance, the data consist of the proportions over six seasons ending in 1974–75 of about 5600 major and minor characters who were nonwhite. In 1969–70, the figure was 7 percent; in 1974–75, 13 percent. However, there is no justification for inferring a continuing trend, for the peak of 14 percent occurred in 1972–73. These data do not disabuse us of three impressions about television: the upper spheres of work appear more frequently than they are enjoyed in real life, nonwhites also enjoy such fictionally ascribed status, but there is somewhat more favorable ascription for whites.

Dominick (1973) analyzed television crime and law enforcement during a week of prime-time network drama and comedy programming in February 1972. Nonwhites constituted 14 percent of the law enforcers, 7 percent of the criminals, and 27 percent of the victims of television crime. When comparisons were made with real-life statistics it was found that nonwhites were greatly underrepresented both as criminals and as victims of crime.

Mendelson and Young (1972), in a study of the content of Saturday morning children's programs, examined 440 identifiable characters representing one morning of content for three networks in November 1971: 30 percent were nonhuman; of the humans, 87 percent were white, and 13 percent were black or other nonwhite minorities; over 60 percent of the programs with human characters presented no black or minority characters; less than a third of all human characters had identifiable occupations. There were not enough nonwhites to analyze occupational status, but an important finding was that blacks were portrayed as almost universally good. There were a few black heroes, and no black villains. The few black leaders always had white co-leaders, but white leaders usually did not have black co-leaders. Race and racial issues were never discussed.

Mendelson and Young also provided interesting data on the portrayal of white foreigners. Good characters *rarely* spoke with an accent on Saturday children's programs. Over half the villains had accents—most commonly German or Russian. In addition, gypsies, Swiss, French, and Italian characters were portrayed with derogatory stereotypes.

These findings are consistent with some of those already cited. Black Americans appear relatively infrequently, but are given relatively positive stereotypes when they do. It is "foreigners" (and sometimes Asians and Latinos) who are given negative characteristics and relatively menial occupations.

Minority group members appear more often in commercials on children's programs. Winick et al. (1973) found minority persons in about a quarter of a sample of children's commercials, and in all cases there was at least one closeup of the minority person.

C. C. Clark (1969) proposes that mass-media depiction of minorities is evolving through three stages: nonrecognition, ridicule, and regulation. He finds that television treatment of blacks has passed through nonrecognition and ridicule (in the context of comedy such as *Amos and Andy* and *Beulah*) and is now in the "regulation" stage. In this stage, black Americans are portrayed as upholders of the institutions of society. Clark lists all black characters in starring dramatic roles in 1968, and convincingly shows that, with the exception of one program, they all have some connection to the maintenance of law and order. The addition of such programs as *Sanford and Son, Good Times,* and *That's My Mama* to the situation comedies may have changed the distribution of black roles on television. (Of course, in 1974–75 law enforcement was the most frequent program type, regardless of race.)

Males and Females

We have already noted that male and female roles in soap operas are quite different. Although there are roughly equal numbers of men and women in the programs, the men have a higher occupational status while the women include a high proportion of housewives. Both Downing (1974) and Katzman (1972a) report that female soap opera characters tend to be younger than male characters; and the latter found that about 60 percent of all conversations involved a man and a woman conversing—and two-thirds of these involved young-adult or mature men conversing with women who were the same age or younger.

The problems of reporting on portrayals of males and females are similar to those for social strata, minorities, and occupations. The notions of conformity to real-life demography and stereotyping are heuristic for analyzing the data, but the presence or absence of such qualities are not synonymous with merit, nor should one presume an invariant association between fidelity to life and the absence of a stereotype; belief and convention, even among the public and in popular culture, do not always lie.

In his early research, Head (1954) found that there were twice as many men as women among characters in network dramatic programs. DeFleur (1964) reports that women composed 16 percent of the television labor force compared to 31 percent of the actual labor force. Of course, women not identifiable as employed would increase the proportion of female characters in DeFleur's sample, but the point is not underrepresentation of females but underrepresentation of female job-holding. DeFleur's data also indicate that women were far more likely than men to appear as clerical or private household workers and far less likely then men to appear as managers or service workers.

More recently, Seggar and Wheeler (1973) report that 18 percent of the television labor force was female. This is also an underrepresentation when compared to the actual labor force. Other comparisons with the labor force indicate that television:

Overrepresents females in professional and technical roles.

Overrepresents males in professional and technical roles, but overrepresents females to a greater degree.

Underrepresents females in clerical and operative roles.

Overrepresents males as service workers but underrepresents them as craftsmen, foremen, and operatives.

Five occupations—nurse, secretary, entertainer, maid, and model—account for half of all the employed women. Men are employed in a far wider range of occupations. The top five male occupations—policeman, physician, musician, diplomat, and serviceman—account for only 29 percent of the employed men. The authors conclude that "both males and females were shown in stereotypic roles, but female imagery was more limited than that of the male."

In the television world of crime and law enforcement, Dominick (1973) found that 95 percent of the upholders of justice were male; television criminals were 84 percent male and 16 percent female; television murder victims were 80 percent male and 20 percent female. The sex distribution of criminals and victims is almost an exact match of the distribution found in *FBI Uniform Crime Reports,* so neither sex is over or underrepresented.

Tedesco (1974) reports on the sex roles for "major characters" in a four-year sample of prime-time network dramatic characters. She found that only 28 percent of these characters were women. Of the female characters, 60 percent were not employed, while only 36 percent of the males had no occupation. An examination of all employed television females reveals that 53 percent were entertainers, clerical workers, or employed in health or education; 25 percent of the males were in these occupations. By contrast, 57 percent of the male characters were managers, law enforcers, military or government professionals; 28 percent of the females were in these occupations.

Tedesco also studied personality characteristics and nonoccupational roles (table 2,7). Men were more likely to be bad persons, unsuccessful, unhappy, serious instead of comic, unmarried, and violent. Women were more likely to be happy, comic instead of serious, married, and nonviolent. In addition, Tedesco reports that the sexes differed on six personality scales. Women were more attractive, sociable, warm, and peaceful. Men were more powerful, smart, rational, and stable.

McNeil (1975) similarly found in the analysis of 43 programs representing 1973 prime-time series that women differed from men in personal characteristics. Women were more frequently concerned with family, marital, and romantic problems, more fre-

Table 2.7 Personality Characteristics and Nonoccupational Roles by Sex [a]

Characteristics More Likely to Be Found in Males		
Personality Characteristic or Role	Percent Males (N = 556)	Percent Females (N = 219)
Bad person	15.5	4.6
Unsuccessful	19.0	13.2
Unhappy	15.3	8.2
Serious role	62.9	44.3
Nonwhite	9.9	4.6
Unmarried	61.5	45.2
Violent	44.8	20.2
Characteristics More Likely to Be Found in Females		
Personality Characteristic or Role	Percent Males (N = 556)	Percent Females (N = 219)
Happy	27.3	37.0
Comic role	16.4	25.6
White	89.6	94.0
Married	32.4	51.1
Nonviolent	55.2	79.9

SOURCE: Adapted from Nancy Signorielli Tedesco. 1974. Patterns in prime time. *Journal of Communication*, 24, 119–24.

[a] Based on prime-time network dramatic (noncartoon) television programming, 1969–1972.

quently had their problems solved by the intervention of another party, when employed were more often supervised by another person, and far more often were clearly identified as to marital status.

Children's Television

Levinson (1973) limited consideration to sex roles in Saturday children's cartoons on the three networks and found patterns quite similar to those reported for prime-time programs. Men outnumbered women by three to one. This ratio was found among *all* characters; among the 58 "stars" of the programs and among teenage characters the ratio was two to one. Even three-quarters of the animal characters with determinable sexes were males. Occupational roles for males covered a wider range, while females were most frequently pretty teenagers or, if adults, housewives.

Two studies have examined sex roles in the commercials that are on the air during Saturday children's programs. Chulay and Francis (1974) found that 81 percent of the commercials with people contained males, while 65 percent contained females (35 percent included only males, 19 percent only females, and the rest both sexes). Winick et al. (1973) found that 58 percent of children's commercials contained boys, while only 36 percent contained girls. The agreement over male dominance in portrayals is striking, since toy commercials account for about two-thirds of the former sample and were excluded in the latter.

Chulay and Francis also found that girls in children's commercials were most likely to be shown in ads for food, games, and dolls; boys were associated with games and "male" toys such as cars and planes. Girls were most likely to be shown playing in a bedroom. Boys were most likely to be outdoors. Sometimes children in commercials were given imaginary occupations: 53 percent of the girls were shown as housewife or mother, 29 percent were models and 9 percent were stewardesses; 39 percent of the boys were shown as race drivers, 29 percent were in the military, and another 22 percent were pilots. The authors conclude that children's advertising "does not show the idea of women being independent and successful in the business world," and that women are "merely" presented in the traditional stereotyped roles.

The Adult Sales Pitch

Bardwick and Schumann (1967) offer a subjective and nonquantified analysis of the themes of commercials directed to adults. They argue that the principal themes are seduction, omnipotent status, unlimited money, acceptance, and admiration. They believe sex roles are contradictory: women are either sex objects or nurturant mother figures; men are dominating, sexy, aggressive and knowledgeable when out of the home, but passive, infantile and emasculated within it.

Some empirical evidence is consistent with this interpretation. Courtney and Whipple (1974) divide presence in commercials into "voice-overs" (off screen announcing) and "product representative" (on screen). Men accounted for almost 90 percent of voice-overs, even for products directed entirely toward a female audience. On the other hand, women seemed to be as likely as men to appear as product representatives in current commercials, during prime-time hours, although men are still more frequent (two to one) salespeople. Dominick and Rauch (1972) found that three-quarters of all ads using females were for kitchen or bathroom products.

The general findings among the various studies are that:

Women are overrepresented in family and home roles and settings and are seldom seen in nontraditional roles.

Men are shown in a wide range of roles and leisure activities, as beneficiaries of women's work, and as dominant decision-makers regarding products such as cars and insurance.

It is interesting to note one difference between the empirical findings and Bardwick and Schumann's discussion. Reviewing four post-1971 studies, Courtney and Whipple conclude that there is considerable agreement that women are sex-typed as housewives or in subordinate roles but there is no indication that women appear in any significant numbers as sex objects, a clear objection voiced by Bardwick and Schumann. Perhaps the demise of cigarette advertising and the absence of ads for liquor on television can help explain the difference.

McArthur and Resko (1975) examine sex roles in a sample of 199 commercials aired in 1971 on the three networks. Again, males were found to be overrepresented (70 percent) in evening commercials. Women were less likely to be employed, less likely to be given the "expert" or authority role, more likely to be defined in relation to others (wife, girlfriend), and more likely to be

Table 2.8 Men and Women as Users and Authorities in Television Commercials for Three Product Types[a]

	Percent Users		Percent Authorities	
Product	Male	Female	Male	Female
Home products	16	84	86	14
Body products	33	67	78	22
Food products	40	60	95	5

SOURCE: Adapted from L. Z. McArthur and B. G. Resko. 1975. The portrayal of men and women in American television commercials. *Journal of Social Psychology,* 97, 209–20.

[a] Based on sample of 199 commercials drawn from network weekday broadcasts in 1971.

identified with a "home" product. Table 2.8 illustrates the different roles for the sexes as users and authorities in commercials for three types of product.

All the evidence concerning sex roles on television is consistent. Whether characters are in commercials, soap operas, dramas, or children's programs, women are shown either as home-oriented or in lower-status jobs. Their proportion in the television labor force is far below the proportion of working women in the United States, and the range of things that television women do is much narrower than that of men. It is unfortunate that there are no comparable data (using similar samples and definitions) over long periods of time. Although one would *expect* depictions of sex roles to be changing, the data are insufficient to clearly document rate or type of change.

A Government Report

The U.S. Civil rights Commission's report, *Window Dressing on the Set: Women and Minorities in Television* (1977), is consistent in its findings with the sociology of television entertainment and commercials that we have depicted. Its analysis of more than 5600 characters in prime-time and Saturday morning programming for six seasons beginning in 1969–70 simply confirms the impressions conveyed by the numerous analyses of the past years. Minority representation has increased somewhat; women comprise a minor proportion of the television population; higher status occupations appear more frequently than in the labor force, and women as well as men, non-whites as well as whites, appear to benefit from this anomaly; and differences in status ascribed tend to favor whites and males.

However, the report does document a phenomenon that could easily be overlooked. Television is the great recycler among the media. From almost the beginning, it has relied on old movies to fill in late and other off-hours, and as soon as it had its own stock of programming, it began to use reruns of various series to fill in the less-frequented portions of its programming schedule. The motive is much the same as that which justifies libraries; it is cheaper to borrow than to buy fresh. What is not at once apparent is that such reliance on second-hand content often will give currency to the social properties of a distant era. What has happened in this instance is that television has conveyed to several generations a view of the world in which "No tickee, no laundry!" would be accepted as anthropological observation.

As *Window Dressing on the Set* argues, the television screen has preserved for new audiences the perspectives that many film and television program producers today undoubtedly would avoid. There are the westerns that paint the American Indian as a bloodthirsty savage, a coward, or a drunk. His proclivity to ride in circles around white prey until their uncanny riflemanship decimate his numbers almost to the point of defeat is known to millions of children. There are the undeniably endearing *I Love Lucy* reruns that nevertheless exploit the competent woman as zany broad. There are the movies of the *Fu Manchu* genre depicting the Chinese as occupants of sinister environments where the black market, nefarious transactions, and opium smoking are the norms. Musically talented, humorous, self-deprecating blacks ("Feets, get movin'!") found happiness and joy in their own society or served white masters with no complaint of working conditions. Western towns presumably often had a Chinese laundryman, but many western movies portray him in servile indifference in contrast to the courage and recklessness of Caucasians. In more modern settings, the Oriental emerged as Charlie Chan the detective-sage who advocated such policies as, "Confucious say, 'Man should never hurry except to catch a flea.' " These are all depictions that largely exist on the television screen not for any reasons of particular attunement to the beliefs and values of viewers, although they undeniably have proved entertaining, but because they are embedded in films and videotapes whose reuse is dictated by economics.

The report also covers the treatment of women and minorities on television news. The conclusions here are succinct: By the criterion of appearance as news reporters or commentators, women and minorities are underrepresented—although we would add that no viewer could escape the conclusion that their representation has increased markedly in recent years. By the criterion of news coverage, women and minorities are similarly underrepresented. As we discuss later in this chapter, it is not easy to find a standard by which to assess the adequacy of news coverage, and such a finding leaves us uncertain whether responsibility lies with imbalance in coverage or with the lesser prominence of women and minorities in the actual events of the day.

Television News

No type of television content has been the focus of more controversy than network news. We shall see later that its command
on public attention (chapter 3) and its likely influence (chapter 7)
are probably more limited than this attention would lead one to
expect.

The Administration

Critics of television news have not been prone to find balanced
presentations. The most prominent attack is probably that of
former Vice-President Spiro Agnew in a speech on November 13,
1969, charging that network news emphasized the negative,
represented the views of a monolithic Eastern clique, gave a false,
unfair picture of the Nixon Administration, and was liberal to a
degree far distant from the views of the majority of the audience.
The critique drew widespread attention because it reflected the
Nixon Administration's perception of television news.

Data collected by Lowry (1971b) bear on the verisimilitude of
this attack. The three networks were monitored over 45 newscasts
in the summer of 1970. This procedure yielded 820 news items for
analysis.

Among Agnew's criticisms was the contention that "bad"
news—dissent, confrontation, the irrational, violence—was over-
emphasized. Lowry found that a third of all the news items fell
into one of his five "bad" news categories. There were 282 such
items: 30 percent about armed conflict and war; 28 percent about
crime; 21 percent about international tension; 14 percent about
social conflict, strikes, and riots; and 6 percent about accidents
and disasters.

One hesitates to generalize from such a breakdown. All of the
armed conflict and war items were about the Indochina war and
the fighting in the Middle East, and a quarter of all the crime coverage dealt with the sensational Sharon Tate murder trial. We suspect that the distribution of types of "bad" news would vary
widely over time. The two months studied in this instance were
certainly not similar to a two-month period four years later, when
the problems of the Nixon Administration and the world economy
dominated the news.

Two-thirds of the network news items did not fall into the "bad" news categories (unfortunately, Lowry fails to describe in detail his "other news" items). "Bad" news received relative better "position emphasis" by being placed toward the beginning of a newscast and including visual aids in addition to a newsman reading a story. The greater position emphasis was accounted for by the prominent treatment given items about armed conflict and war and international tension; other types of "bad" news were no better positioned than other items. "Bad" news items were neither longer nor shorter than other news items. One network, ABC, presented significantly more "bad" news and gave it significantly more position emphasis than the other two networks. This is somewhat ironic, since the ABC network had been least criticized by the Administration for its news coverage, and was generally supposed at the time to present the least controversial news coverage. Whether these data, which certainly would substantiate a claim that there is considerable "bad" news on television, justify a conclusion that television news overemphasizes the negative requires the introduction of a value judgment about what constitutes overemphasis.

Pride and Clarke (1973) and Pride and Richards (1974) also contribute evidence on "bad" news. The focus is the treatment of symbols—the President, the police, blacks, students—in the verbal coverage by the three networks of race relations and student protests during 20 months beginning late in 1968. More negative than positive statements were broadcast about such symbols, but in the case of the student movement the degree of negative treatment was very slight. In neither case did the treatment of the various symbols, which often represented parties in opposition, differ substantially. The data do not fit either the view that the Nixon administration received disproportionately harsher treatment, or that the competence and wisdom of figures representing the established order were consistently impugned.

A second Lowry study (1971a) is an analysis of the effects of Agnew's charges on the types of statements made by network newscasts when they refer to the administration—the President, Vice-President, Cabinet, or White House. Agnew's remarks, and a subsequent endorsement of them by President Nixon, were delivered in November and December 1969. Lowry took 45 newscasts from the summer preceding these comments and compared them to 45 newscasts from the summer following the comments. He transcribed all sentences referring to the administration and had them coded into nine categories. Table 2.9 summarizes his results.

The major finding was that all three networks increased the proportion of attributed sentences:—verifiable information associated with a source. Unattributed sentences—verifiable information not associated with a specific source—declined in frequency. One of the most interesting findings was the almost complete lack of judgment sentences at either time period. Inference sentences—"statements about the unknown made on the basis of the known"—included more than half of all sentences about the administration at both time periods and did not change in any noteworthy way. More than nine out of ten inferences were made *without* verbal labels ("tip-offs") such as "it appears that,"

Table 2.9 Sentences About the Administration on Three Network Newscasts, Before and After Agnew's Criticisms (Percent Sentences)

Nature of Sentence	1969 (before)			
	ABC (N = 306)[a]	CBS (N = 261)	NBC (N = 176)	Total (N = 743)
Report/attributed	14	20	22	18
Report/unattributed	27	25	26	26
Inference/labeled	6	4	3	5
Inference/unlabeled	50	48	47	49
Judgment[b]	—	—	—	—
Other	3	3	2	3

Nature of Sentence	1970 (after)			
	ABC (N = 169)	CBS (N = 250)	NBC (N = 141)	Total (N = 560)
Report/attributed	21	26	34	27
Report/unattributed	22	23	21	22
Inference/labeled	1	2	1	2
Inference/unlabeled	54	48	43	49
Judgment[b]	1	—	1	1
Other	1	—	—	—

SOURCE: Adapted from D. T. Lowry. 1971a. Agnew and the network TV news: A before/after content analysis. *Journalism Quarterly*, 48, 205–10.

[a] N = number of sentences referring to Administration.

[b] Represents combination of four categories used by Lowry: (1) judgment sentences/attributed/favorable; (2) judgment sentences/attributed/unfavorable; (3) judgment sentences/unattributed/favorable; and (4) judgment sentences/unattributed/unfavorable.

which clearly identify an inference for the viewer. It seems reasonably clear that the types of sentences used in 1970 differed minimally, if at all, from those used in 1969. Variation among the three networks was greater in each year than variation across time; NBC received 8 and then 13 more percentage points than ABC in the "report/attributed" category.

The clearest difference between the two years seems to be the sharp drop in total coverage given to the administration by the networks. The number of minutes of administration-related material in the 45 sample newscasts fell 32 percent (from 153 to 104), while the number of sentences fell 25 percent (from 743 to 560). Three-quarters of the drop in coverage can be attributed to a sharp decline for ABC. All three networks provided 183 fewer sentences in 1970; ABC accounted for 137 of these, falling from a clear first place in amount of administration coverage to a distant second place. In conclusion, it is difficult to attribute many of the differences between the two years to effects of political pressures. Newsmen perhaps became more likely to identify their sources of information, but variations in the events of the day are probably a more likely source for the differences in quantity of coverage. In the summer of 1969 the Nixon/Agnew Administration was newly installed in office. It may have been creating more news items than it did a year later.

The charge of excessive liberalism implies unjustified emphasis on the desirability of social change. Cutler and Tedesco (1974) indeed found that in the coverage of social conflict national television news gives balanced attention to figures representing social control (those in power) and social change (those not in power) while network drama portraying such conflict gives overwhelming emphasis to the forces of social control. This confirms that television news adheres to the journalistic canon of balanced treatment for those involved in conflict, but whether such a practice constitutes excessive liberalism is obviously a matter of opinion.

War in Southeast Asia

News coverage of U.S. involvement in the Indochina war provoked several controversies in the late sixties and early seventies. Were the networks presenting a "fair" picture? Russo (1971) evaluated transcripts of CBS and NBC newscasts sampled to represent the period from January 1969 to December 1970. He first established a reliable ten-point scale of statements on a "pro-" vs. "anti"-administration "spectrum." Statements in newscasts were then scored in relation to this scale, and each newscast was given a score. The mean value (within a possible range from $+5.0$ to -5.0) over two years was -0.3 for CBS and -0.6 for NBC. These values were not significantly different from each other. The NBC value was significantly lower than zero, indicating that there was a very slight, but definite, anti-administration tone to NBC newscasts. Russo asserts that "there was no 'bias' against the Nixon Administration's policies in Vietnam. . . ." His data do not support such a strong statement—we can be 99 percent certain that the NBC score was on the negative side of the scale. On the other hand, Russo's amplification is more to the point: "The fact that the average bias did not exceed the -1 point on the scale means that, on average, the networks did not exceed the rather weakly anti-administration statement, 'Many people go hungry in South Vietnam.' "

Content analysis of newscasts over the two-year period revealed a slight, nonsignificant, shift in the negative direction. The best interpretation is that there was no notable change over the two years, and that the networks did not "cave in" to the Agnew–Nixon criticism—which came right in the middle of the period studied. Russo also scored bias in regard to nine other topics and found that the two networks did not differ. (It is a pity that ABC was not included in this study, since other research has shown that it is somewhat different from the other two networks.) A relatively pro-Administration tone was found for statements regarding "Vietnamization," and the POW issue; a relatively neutral tone characterized statements about the allies' chances of winning and diplomatic ventures such as the Paris peace talks, and a relatively anti-administration tone characterized statements about civilian casualties, popular support for the war in Vietnam, the Vietnam government, U.S. domestic support for the war, and the President's credibility. Finally, an interesting point is made about the nature of this type of analysis. "Balanced" coverage would include an equal weight of pro- and anti-administration content; but this might not be "fair"—a concept that would vary with views of the war. Some people might believe that "fair" coverage of what actually happened in Vietnam should produce a scale value to one side or the other of zero. Russo's data only indicate relatively *balanced* presentation of pro- and anti-administration material.

The U.S. incursion into Laos in February and March 1971 produced an attack on media coverage of the event by several pro-Administration Senators. Pride and Wamsley (1972) obtained videotapes of CBS and ABC coverage for the period from February 5 to March 5, 1971. Their unit of analysis was every "cut-to-cut segment" of a report about activity relating to the action in Laos. The authors identified two dimensions—"strength" and "morality"—of material related to three objects—the U.S., North Vietnam, and South Vietnam. The strength dimension was applied to segments that discussed strength, activity or potency of any of the three nations. The morality dimension was applied to the morality, principle, credibility, or goodness of each nation. Segments were coded on each dimension as either positive or negative; in cases where the emphasis was balanced, or where the dimensions were not relevant, a "neutral" category was applied. A somewhat modified version of the findings is presented in table 2.10.

Several things are apparent from these data. The overall patterns for both networks are quite similar, although ABC more frequently presented segments that were neutral, and CBS was relatively negative toward U.S. strength while ABC had roughly equal numbers of segments reflecting positive and negative evaluations. Both networks presented relatively balanced coverage of U.S. morality and almost no discussion of the morality of either

Table 2.10 CBS and ABC Coverage of Laos Incursion Related to Strength and Morality of Three Nations

| | Percent of Segments[a] | | | | | |
| | United States | | South Vietnam | | North Vietnam | |
Content	CBS	ABC	CBS	ABC	CBS	ABC
Strength						
positive	13	16	14	12	21	18
negative	23	17	14	13	5	4
Morality						
positive	10	10	0	0	0	0
negative	11	6	1	1	1	1
Neutral	43	51	71	73	72	78

SOURCE: Adapted from R. A. Pride and G. L. Wamsley. 1972. Symbol analysis of network coverage of Laos incursion. *Journalism Quarterly*, 49, 635–40.

[a] Percentages are based on "cut-to-cut segments" as unit of analysis (N = 219 for CBS; 194 for ABC).

South or North Vietnam in regard to the Laotian action. Segments on both networks describing the strength of South Vietnam were about equal with those describing its weakness, but both networks were far more likely to portray North Vietnam as strong. Since intervention in Laos went poorly for the allies, it is not surprising that North Vietnam was given a strong image.

The findings raise difficult aspects of the relationship between analysis and criticism of content. Senator Robert Dole of Kansas, then Republican National Chairman, claimed that CBS coverage was biased because only a small proportion of the statements made were favorable to the U.S. and South Vietnam. One implication was that the remainder of such statements were unfavorable. The data clearly refute such a claim. A majority of statements are nonevaluative. However a deeper problem is the question of what is a "favorable" statement and whether there *should* be a balance. If available facts indicated more strength than weakness for the North Vietnamese, it is hard to cite these data as an indication of bias. The fact that two networks differed significantly (including the statistical sense) in their reports of U.S. strength may indicate a leaning in *either* direction. Perhaps CBS was prone to underestimate the U.S. while ABC was "objective." But maybe ABC was prone to overestimate the U.S. while CBS was correctly presenting events. The morality dimension may provide more of a clue to bias. But on this dimension we find a balanced CBS presentation and a slight pro-U.S. tilt by ABC along with an almost total absence of the dimension in relation to either Vietnamese government.

Election Campaigns

Media coverage of national elections has been a subject of debate among politicians, journalists, and historians for many decades. The major issues has been the balance and fairness of the coverage of the principal contenders. The arrival of network television with its nightly command of a national audience for news exacerbated the contention. The best available evidence on the medium's performance in national elections comes from the 1968 and 1972 presidential elections.

Like wars, elections tend to be special cases that make generalization difficult. Television coverage depends on the campaign strategies adopted by candidates and their particular roles and newsworthiness. The *compared to what?* question repeatedly appears to threaten the inferences that can be drawn from data. In 1971, a number of issues of scientific and political interest were raised by the publication of Edith Efron's *The News Twisters*. The author presented a content analysis of network news between September 16 and November 4, 1968, that led her to conclude there was considerable bias. She found decidedly more favorable treatment of liberal positions and the Democratic candidate, Hubert Humphrey, than of conservative positions and the Republican candidate, Richard Nixon. Stevenson et al. (1973) then analyzed CBS newscasts for the same period using different methods and found no such bias.

Efron focused exclusively on the favorability or unfavorability of reports and opinions in regard to the issues she posited as important and the candidates. Two major units of analysis were the frequency of statements judged as expressing an opinion and the number of words of coverage in reports said to be favorable or unfavorable to a candidate. Efron is quite explicit in stating her view that network coverage inevitably will be biased in favor of liberal positions because, in her opinion, almost all network newsmen are of liberal persuasion. The result, she believes, is to limit and distort coverage not only of conservative but also of radical viewpoints.

She explains her procedures clearly. She did not examine the quantity of material that could be said to be neutral. Her thesis is that bias can be observed only in content that can be said to be evaluative. By implication, because there is no formal statistical check on reliability among coders, she argues that the definitions of favorable and unfavorable opinion and coverage offered are without ambiguity and could be applied by anyone without any risk of markedly different results.

Her technique involves multiple tallying, with every issue and candidate mentioned in a statement receiving credit as the target of unfavorable opinion or words of coverage. Thus, a single paragraph containing an attack unfavorable to positions A and B and a comment judged as favorable to candidate X would be tallied in three separate places. Statements of this kind that refer to a large number of issues and candidates are common in politics. The consequence is that the procedure tends to produce a quantitatively impressive set of tallies from even a few instances of alleged bias.

Stevenson et al. call their study a replication of Efron, but it cannot fairly be called that because they used different techniques. They confined themselves to the CBS newscasts for the same period, because the other two networks did not provide transcripts—a problem Efron evaded by transcribing coverage directly from the screen. They counted lines of coverage which four coders classified as favorable, unfavorable, or neutral. Reliability of coding is statistically supported by an adequate level of intercoder agreement. This procedure leads to quite a different picture than that portrayed by Efron.

The data in table 2.11 indicate that all candidates received more favorable than unfavorable coverage on CBS in 1968. There were no marked differences between the treatment of Humphrey and Nixon, but coverage of George Wallace was less favorable than for these two. Efron, on the other hand, found Humphrey treated far better than Nixon in terms of words of coverage, with Humphrey coverage divided 53 percent favorable to 47 percent unfavorable compared to a startling 6 percent favorable vs. 94 percent unfavorable for Nixon, with Wallace somewhat less favorably treated than Humphrey, 46 percent favorable vs. 54 percent unfavorable. Regarding statements of opinion, the results were similar: 52 percent favorable vs. 48 percent unfavorable for Humphrey and only 17 percent favorable vs. 83 percent unfavorable for Nixon, with Wallace faring by this measure as well as Humphrey, 51 percent favorable vs. 49 percent unfavorable (data from Appendices D and E, *The News Twisters*).

One problem dramatically raised by the Stevenson et al. analysis is the effect of ignoring neutral content. Their study found that nearly *two-thirds* of all CBS candidate coverage was neither

Table 2.11 CBS Coverage of Presidential Candidates (September 16,– November 4, 1968)

		Humphrey	Nixon	Wallace
All *lines* of candidate coverage	Percent favorable lines	23.5	24.5	17.8
	Percent unfavorable lines	11.0	11.7	15.1
	Percent all other lines	65.5	63.8	67.1
	Number of lines	1,459	1,113	962
All *lines* either favorable or unfavorable	Percent favorable	68.1	67.7	54.1
	Percent unfavorable	31.9	32.3	45.9
	Ratio—favorable:unfavorable	2.1:1	2.1:1	1.2:1

SOURCE: Adapted from R. L. Stevenson et al. 1973. Untwisting *The news twisters*. A replication of Efron's study. *Journalism Quarterly, 50,* 211–19.

favorable nor unfavorable (table 2.11). Direct film of candidates (about 40 percent of all lines of transcript), neutral commentary (17 percent) and mixed reports (9 percent) were found to take up twice as much coverage as anything classified as pro- or anti-candidate reports. Surprisingly, the proportions are almost identical for all three major presidential candidates—Humphrey, Nixon, and Wallace.

On the other hand, Stevenson and his colleagues identified one type of imbalance that Efron did not find. Humphrey averaged about three minutes more coverage per week than Nixon and about four minutes more per week than Wallace.

The major issue raised by the Efron study is a general one—the appropriateness and justifiability of procedures employed to detect bias. We would recommend that the concerned reader examine the Efron and Stevenson et al. analyses with some care before deciding whether Efron's approach identified bias in network campaign coverage. However, the Stevenson et al. do make it clear that not everyone would agree with Efron's designation of certain reports as biased. They offer, for example, an item that she described as "report elaborates poetically on public response to Humphrey."

Reporter Morton Dean covered a Wall Street rally. He interviewed a young woman who explained that advance workers for Humphrey had brought sacks of confetti to her office so that it could be thrown as the procession approached. Dean:

> On signal, paper snow, all chopped into little bits, begins to fly from the skyscrapers. From many floors below it takes on the look of a spontaneous demonstration of affection as it drifts lazily into the rain and into the eyes of the thousands who have given up their lunch hours to take a peek at Hubert Humphrey. A short excerpt of Humphrey's speech is interpolated.] By coming to Wall Street, Mr. Humphrey may be more than just hinting at one big problem his campaign has been having—the raising of money, especially in New York State, where some Humphrey-for-President workers say they're having great difficulty meeting the weekly payroll.

The reporter certainly embraces the pathetic fallacy in "paper snow drifting lazily." And statements such as "takes on the look of a spontaneous demonstration" and "may be more than just hinting" are interpretations of events. However, the labeling of this report as pro-Humphrey is dubious. Talk of advance men and false spontaneity has not usually been considered favorable, nor has a discussion of inability to meet a payroll. The fact that thousands gave up their lunch for Humphrey was in his favor; but "to take a peek" is hardly as favorable as "to cheer," "to encourage" or "to support." This passage illustrates the problem of reliability and validity in analysis of television content. The transcript is almost like a projective test for those with strong opinions. Selective attention might make Morton Dean appear to have a bias in either direction.

Paletz and Elson (1976) confine themselves to coverage of the 1972 Democratic convention. In a novel attempt to find an empirical standard by which to evaluate journalistic practice, they query delegates about the conformity of their experience to the impressions conveyed by television coverage of prior conventions. The delegates found their role to be much more businesslike, and activities more orderly, than they believed television had implied. However, a quantitative analysis of NBC coverage did not lead to conclusions of favoritism toward any of the contenders in the selection of persons to be interviewed or of emphasis on the bizarre, atypical, or irrelevant.

Five other studies analyze network coverage of the 1972 presidential campaign. The designs vary. Hence their conclusions refer to somewhat different aspects of network campaign coverage. Some major findings are summarized in table 2.12.

Lowry (1974) analyzed amount, verbal emphasis, and visual treatment of coverage on all three networks for 20 sample days during the 10 weeks between the end of the Republican convention and election day. Newscasts were recorded on audio tape and visual aspects observer-coded. The unit for analysis was a "Nixon story" or a "McGovern story," defined as an account of which one-third or more was directly related to the candidate, his vice-presidential running mate, or others campaigning or speaking for him. This produced 100 Nixon and 68 McGovern stories yielding 788 Nixon and 577 McGovern sentences and totaling, respectively, 8729 and 7476 seconds in length. Thus, Nixon received 47 percent more stories and 33 percent more sentences, but because McGovern stories were longer only 17 percent more airtime.

There were no pronounced differences in the pattern of verbal coverage by anchormen and reporters, except for somewhat more judgmental statements that were anti-Republican than anti-Democratic. However, nonverbal aspects of coverage seemed to favor McGovern. The Democratic candidate received a higher

Table 2.12 Five Analyses of Network Coverage of the 1972 Campaign

Source	Sample	Unit of Analysis	Nixon: McGovern Coverage
Lowry	20 days randomly selected from 53 days prior to election	Number of items[a]	100:68
		Sentences given[a] by newsmen	778:577
		Seconds[a]	8729:7476
Meadow	5 weeks prior to election	Percent time covering[b] "candidate" role	39:61
		Percent time covering[b] any role	52:48
Doll and Bradley	12 days between Labor Day & election	Minutes	86:86
		Items	55:60
Frank	7 selected weeks from conventions to election	Seconds of film coverage of political statement or with voters[c]	3428:6974
		Percentage coverage of Republican and Democratic parties	18:17
Hofstetter	17 weeks prior to election	Number of news stories	475:556
		Minutes	685:902

SOURCE: D. T. Lowry. 1974. Multiple measures of network TV news bias in campaign '72. Paper presented at the meeting of the International Communication Association, New Orleans, April; R. G. Meadow. 1973. Cross-media comparison of coverage of the 1972 presidential campaign. *Journalism Quarterly*, 50, 482–88; H. D. Doll and B. E. Bradley. 1973. A study of the objectivity of television news reporting of the 1972 presidential campaign. Paper presented at the meeting of the Speech Communication Association, New York; R. S. Frank. 1973. *Message Dimensions of Television News*. Lexington, Mass.: Lexington Books, D. C. Heath and Co. Reprinted by permission of the publisher; C. R. Hofstetter. 1976. *Bias in the News*. Columbus: Ohio State University Press.

[a] Includes any coverage of candidate or others campaigning in favor of candidate.

[b] Only includes Nixon and McGovern explicitly.

[c] Totals for Nixon/Agnew and McGovern/Shriver.

proportion of film and tape coverage of the events being reported, and pro-McGovern speakers were given a higher proportion of on-camera time than pro-Nixon speakers. Of course, this "more favorable" treatment occurred *within* a smaller total amount of treatment of the McGovern campaign. It is a matter of opinion whether quantity or quality of coverage is more "favorable" for the individuals involved.

An important distinction regarding network coverage of presidential candidates is made by Meadow (1973). He divided coverage of President Nixon into reports where his role was that of candidate and those where he was functioning as chief executive. He found that during the five weeks prior to election day Nixon received slightly more network coverage than McGovern when Nixon coverage included both roles. When Nixon's coverage was limited to his role as candidate, he received considerably less coverage than McGovern. The apparent discrepancy between the Lowry and Meadow findings is explained by differences in definitions. Meadow only counted items specifically related to the individual candidate. He reports that Agnew received a great deal more coverage than Sargent Shriver (McGovern's running mate); and this probably explains why Lowry discovered more total coverage for the Republican candidates. It should be noted that the major thrust of the Meadow study is a comparison of television and newspaper coverage. He finds that the two media were "remarkably similar" in their treatment of the two candidates.

Doll and Bradley (1973) considered news reports "primarily related to the campaign itself" including reports about the presidential and vice-presidential candidates as well as related campaign items. They report that both campaigns received approximately equal amounts of coverage. This conclusion of balanced treatment is qualified by the data of Frank (1973), who analyzed coverage during seven sample weeks preceding the election. Amount of time devoted to the two parties was almost equally split—with a slight edge for the Republicans. However, amount of film coverage of campaign statements plus candidates mingling with crowds was greater for McGovern and Shriver than it was for Nixon and Agnew.

Frank also reports differences in the "grammar" of network reporting of candidates. He finds that McGovern received more closeup camera shots, more appearances with an audience, and more coverage of direct political statements than Nixon. If these factors are assumed to be favorable to a candidate, then McGovern received somewhat better treatment. However, the composite of all the studies strongly suggests that differential campaign coverage was attributable more to campaign strategies deliberately adopted by the candidates than to biased coverage by the networks.

Richard Nixon campaigned in 1972 from his position as incumbent President. He used "surrogates" to travel across the country and speak in his behalf, taking the position that his duties in office precluded a heavy campaign schedule. Thus, we find that when the two candidates are compared in their "candidate roles" (such data are presented by both Meadow and Frank) there was more network time devoted to McGovern. On the other hand, total network time devoted to Nixon (including both his Presidential and candidate roles) seems to have been a bit greater than that devoted to McGovern. Other measures of campaign coverage seem to indicate equal treatment or slightly more time for the Republican campaign. In this light, it is not an indication of bias to find that McGovern received more film footage making statements and with voters—he did more of that kind of thing. The one indicator that may reveal a bit of biased coverage is Frank's average "tight shot" index.

The difficulty of inferring bias when the events covered are not the same is illustrated by the greater average of closeups of McGovern than of Nixon. Bias would be more readily inferrable if the occurrence of such "tight shots" were averaged over events of the same kind, such as parades or airport rallies. Otherwise, it remains uncertain whether differences are attributable to differential treatment of the candidates or of events. The former might justifiably be considered bias, the latter a convention of video reporting.

The issues we raised in regard to the Efron study led Hofstetter (1976) to construct a novel model for analyzing news bias. For his interpretation of data from 17 weeks of news on all three networks prior to the 1972 presidential election, he introduces the concepts of *structural* and *political* bias. The former is defined as bias introduced by the character of the medium, which like all media packages events into news in accord with the needs peculiar to satisfying its particular audience. The latter is defined as bias introduced by political partisanship or prejudice. Because there is no readily available empirical standard for either outside of the performance of the news media themselves, structural bias is said to occur when treatment is similar across networks, and political bias is said to occur when there is differing treatment among the networks, and coverage by one or more networks is dissimilar for the opposing candidates. From these data, it appears that in 1972 there was structural bias, but very little evidence of political bias (as the author remarks, ". . . network news coverage about politics was amazingly similar in profile"). The data also lead to the same conclusion about political bias when simply examined for consistent favorable treatment for Nixon or McGovern.

This view (as the author acknowledges) does not allow for the possibility that political bias may be similar across networks due to commonly held prejudices and partisanship. However, it does illustrate brilliantly the dilemma of detecting bias when there is no absolute standard as to what constitutes fair, even, and balanced coverage, since the very nature of news as the reflector of uneven events means that such coverage is not necessarily equivalent to equality of treatment.

Network Diversity

We know a surprising amount about diversity among the networks because every study comparing in any way the news of even two networks provides evidence. What is not clear is the significance to be attached to this evidence. When do differences seem to distinct portraits? Should we decry sameness, or hold diversity in suspicion for its proof that news is invention, possibly imperfect invention, as well as event?

Lemert (1974) found that on weekdays in February–March 1971 70 percent of the stories were covered by two or more networks. Nearly 58 percent of all stories were carried by all three networks. Certainly, this indicates considerable duplication; but should we emphasize that 58 percent of the stories were covered the same day by all three networks, or should we emphasize that 42 percent were *not* carried by all three? Since ABC averaged 16.9 stories per broadcast while CBS averaged 19.3 and NBC averaged 21.3, it would have been possible for all three networks to duplicate a maximum of the lowest figure. This would have produced an 88 percent maximum duplication rate. Lemert further reports that the bulk of overlapping stories are "hard-straight-official" reports, rather than features or reporter-initiated material. Overlapping feature stories could not be expected, and this further emphasizes the degree of similarity in network coverage of "routine" news stories.

B. D. Singer (1970) compares news coverage by CBS with that of CBC, a Canadian network. The main consideration was number of stories and air time devoted to "aggressive" items such as war, violence, and protest. The evidence clearly indicates that CBS presented a great deal more aggressive content—about twice as much. A comparison of CBS with NBC over an eight-day period (the CBS vs. CBC comparison covered 21 days) indicated that the two U.S. networks were different, but much more similar to each other than they were to the Canadian newscasts. This finding was not diminished when stories about the American involvement in the Indochina war were removed from the analysis. Total news time devoted to aggressive content by CBS was 51 percent including Indochina war items and 40 percent excluding such items. The comparable figures for CBC were 27 percent and 19 percent. These data were obtained two months prior to Lowry's study of "bad" news, which showed that CBS carried 31 percent "bad" news items and fell below ABC (44 percent) and close to NBC (30 percent). Although Lowry's definitions do not coincide with Singer's, it seems fair to conclude that the U.S. networks are indeed more similar to each other than any one is to the Canadian network.

Nevertheless, the evidence of measurable differences that in some instances seem to amount to significant diversity is irrefutable. Lowry (1971a, 1971b) found divergence in the emphasis on "bad" news, in the reliance on attributed reports, and one network accounted for most of a decline in coverage of the administration. Pride and Clarke (1973) found one network giving greater attention to race relations. Pride and Richards (1974) found attention to the student movement to vary and that the anchorman on one network assumed a more prominent, interpretative role. Pride and Wamsley (1972), although documenting strikingly similar patterns in ABC and CBS coverage of the Vietnam war, also document a greater emphasis on U.S. weaknesses at one network and a greater use of statements that were neither positive or negative about the participants. Hofstetter (1976) and Frank (1973) find substantial differences in coverage of the 1972 presidential campaign. None of the uncovered diversity, however, encourages a conclusion of bias toward those involved in contention.

The Lyle and Stone (1971) study of local and national newscasts in a moderate-size California city, provides data on the relative degree of overlap for different types of stories. They found that 22 stories were carried by all three stations; this indicates that 66 presentations—about 10 percent of all stories on all stations—were covered by all three stations. On the other hand, 53 percent of all presentations were "exclusives"—not covered by any other station. Local news was most likely to be exclusive; 134 of 194 stories (69 percent) were not carried by another station. Sports and weather coverage was 48 percent exclusive. And exclusives included 163 of 351 nonlocal news items (46 percent).

We believe that evidence of diversity, wherever it has arisen in the past and whenever it arises in the future, should be the basis for self-scrutiny on the part of those responsible for news broadcasts. Certainly there is some absurdity in three such expensive and proud endeavors as network news duplicating one another—although not as much, perhaps, as in the simultaneous scheduling that minimizes audience access to news—but divergence in reporting is not a guarantee of journalistic health. Divergence also can be the signal for high-handedness, narrow vision, or omission. What we must ask is that divergence reflect reasoned judgment, not happenstance or habit. In this way, we can enlist evidence of diversity in behalf of the public's need to be informed.

Evaluating the News

The data from the past do not support the contention that network news coverage has been politically imbalanced. The data do document sufficient differences in coverage for a viewer to prefer one or another of the networks. The data do not lead us to embrace "bias" to describe network news. These, of course, are our evaluations.

The central problem for the inferring of bias is that there is no recognized formula for computing its presence. The conformity of news to actuality is judged on the basis of the observer's conception of that actuality. The mass media encourage the myth that events determine news because this protects them from criticism. This is strategically judicious, but does not enhance their reputation as mirrors of reality.

In fact, in all media, journalists manufacture news by the way they select what to present and how they treat it. This obvious but often ignored truism is reflected in the finding of little daily correlation between amount of violence on newspaper front pages and in television news (D. G. Clark and Blankenburg, 1972). It is documented in the case of public events, in which the impression television conveys may be quite different from that of those actually in attendance (Lang and Lang, 1953). Close examination of television newsroom practices (Altheide, 1976; Bailey and Lichty, 1972; Epstein, 1973a, 1973b; Warner, 1971) also make this quite clear. Television as a medium appears to be biased toward events that make for good visual coverage, toward brief, succinct reports that more nearly approximate a newspaper's front page than its full contents, toward emphasis on personalities; and national television is biased toward events of high interest to viewers in all regions. This is the import of the bias that television brings to news. What the findings confirm is not lack of bias but lack of systematic political bias by newscasters or networks. Whether the particular biases of television or of journalism itself deleteriously distort the portrayal of events is not easily discoverable among empirical data and will largely remain a matter of subjective judgment.

That this is so does not obviate the need for continuing empirical scrutiny of the performance of television news. What has been true in the past may not hold in the future, and judgment will always benefit from the sobriety of fact.

Missing Items

Our portrait of television news is unfortunately incomplete because there are no extensive studies of local television news. Whereas each of the three networks presents 30 minutes of national news each evening, almost every local station presents at least one hour (in some cities, two) a day of local newscasts. Local news typically rivals network news in ratings, and occupies more minutes of broadcast time. The ignoring of local news by analysts is thus a major omission.

Finally, we are surprised that studies of network news have been limited and so sporadic. We applaud the indefatigable Frank (1973) for tabulating 29 different dimensions of broadcast news, but on the whole we find that only a few news topics and dimensions of their treatment have received attention, Dominick's (1977) documentation of the domination of "national" news by Washington, D.C., New York, and California demonstrates that analyses need not be confined to the coverage of contentions. And the Cutler and Tedesco (1974) analysis of the prominence given forces of social control and of social change is a reminder that the analysis of contention does not proscribe innovativeness. We are also disappointed that network news has not received continuous regular examination. The sole continuity is the result of the fascination of the drama of Presidential election. Despite its prominence as a focus of debate, and alleged importance in the life of the nation, network news has not been the subject of such continuous monitoring as has violence, to which we turn next.

Violence

The first documentation of the quantity of violence in television drama and cartoons occurred in the early 1950s when television was still a stranger in many American homes. Smythe (1954) reports on the several studies sponsored in 1952 and 1953 by the National Association of Educational Broadcasters. The data for 1953 tell the story. In one week on seven New York City channels there were 3421 threats and actual acts of violence. There was an average of 6.2 threats or acts per hour. Television directed at children had more than three times this average. The rate here was 22.4 threats or acts per hour, and the highest of all rates was for children's comedy drama, where there were 36.6 per hour.

The two major conclusions have not been altered by the intervening decades:

There is a great deal of violence in television drama.
Violence is very frequent in television directed at children.

The Measurement Debate

However, a great deal of data has been collected since that tells us more about the nature of television violence.* The single richest source is the much-publicized "Violence Profile" of Gerbner and Gross (Gerbner, 1972b; Gerbner and Gross, 1976; Gerbner et al., 1977).

Since the 1967–68 season, one fall week of prime-time and weekend morning television for all three networks has been analyzed each year. Television programs are videotaped for later coding. Analysis is limited to dramatic content that tells a story. News, documentaries, specials, variety programs, and sports are excluded. Typical hours for weekday and Saturday evenings are 7:30–11 P.M.; for Sunday evening, 7–11 P.M.; and for Saturday and Sunday morning, 8 A.M.–2:30 P.M. The definition of violence employed is, "the overt expression of physical force against self or other, compelling action against one's will on pain of being hurt

---

* "Television violence" has been variously defined. Most of the studies have been concerned with violence in television entertainment, and in particular in fictional entertainment, such as drama and cartoons. Sports, news, and public affairs content are usually excluded, although in some studies violence in such content is analyzed.

or killed, or actually hurting or killing." Coding covers frequency, perpetrators and victims, environment, and nature of violent acts.

The resulting data have been the focus of debates that raise significant if possibly unresolvable issues about any measurement of television violence. The controversies center on:

The definition of violence employed and its consequences for identifying violent content.

The meaningfulness of the "violence index" constructed to give a shorthand measure of the level and fluctuation of violence.

The usefulness of a gross measure of television violence.

The generalizability from the sampled content.

In table 2.13, we simulate a debate between an *Admirer* and a *Critic* to emphasize the principal points at issue (Coffin and Tuchman, 1972a, 1972b; Eleey, Gerbner, and Tedesco, 1972a, 1972b; Gerbner, 1972a; Gerbner et al., 1977; Owen, Beebe, and Manning, 1974). We do not fully share either viewpoint.

It has been argued that under Gerbner and Gross's definition, certain programs can wrongfully be identified as violent, if comedy, accidents, and acts of nature are included. We agree that comedy is not superficially thought of as violent, but we cannot reasonably reject Gerbner and Gross's contention that violence should be measured wherever it occurs and not on the basis of format. It has also been argued that the definition leads to an overestimation of the occurrence of criminal acts or malevolent physically hurtful human conflict; we agree that this is so if the measures are mistakenly interpreted to be confined to such behavior.

We are not disturbed that there is disagreement over the programs identified as violent in one year by the Gerbner and Gross data and by the *Christian Science Monitor* and by the National Association for Better Broadcasting (NABB), although the latter two are in close agreement. Such disagreement is expected. We doubt whether the explanation inheres in the "unscientific" nature of the *Monitor* and NABB ratings, although their methods are far below rigorous criteria for content analysis. The disagreement occurs simply because the *Monitor* and the NABB designate programs normally perceived as violent while Gerbner and Gross tabulate violence wherever it occurs, using a normative definition of violence. Thus, we find moderately high, significant, but far from perfect correlations between the ranking of programs as violent

What's On

Table 2.13 Two Perspectives on the Gerbner and Gross Violence
Measurement

Issues	Critic	Admirer
Comparability with other ratings of violent programs	Many programs that would be identified as violent would not be so identified by others	This is to be expected; in each case, the methods are different
Definition of violence	Because the definition focuses on behavior and events and not context, comedy may be scored as violent, and actual events such as accidents and natural disasters are included; yet neither comedy nor news events are equivalent to the interpersonal attacks usually thought of as television violence	Violence is defined normatively and measured wherever it occurs; whether or not comedy programs are "violent" is an empirical issue and accidents and natural disasters that fit such a definition cannot justifiably be ignored
Composition of the violence index	The violence index is entirely arbitrary, with weights assigned and some components counted twice for no reason other than caprice; the result is misleading	The violence index is intended as a heuristic device and has no faults that are not common to indices, since the purpose of an index is to provide a single score for a complex set of components; we use the index as a device to focus attention on the variables comprising it and their contribution to its change or stability
The sample	The sample consists of one fall week of prime-time and weekend morning programming each year and cannot be said to represent "television" because it excludes news and sports, television at other times, television that does not tell a story, and non-network television	The sample is intended to reflect the character of each season's television fiction for the general and child audiences and is appropriate for the purpose
Usefulness	Policy cannot be based on the measures because of their arbitrariness, inclusiveness, and inability to single out harmful violence, and they invite misinterpretation	Measurement of violence as normatively defined has scientific merit and provides the most justifiable reflection of the amount and character of violence in mass entertainment until we can be certain about what kind of violence is harmful

by the Gerbner and Gross data and by the public (.69) and by television critics (.75) (B. S. Greenberg and Gordon, 1972b); these
correlations probably underestimate the correspondence over the
concept of violence because of the unnecessary inaccuracy of the
Gerbner and Gross data. They have limited their study to one episode for each series, but use them to create rankings that presumably reflect seasonal or more general standings. When programs were identified as violent by Gerbner and Gross and by the
coding of synopses from *TV Guide,* there was almost 90 percent
agreement, with most of the disagreement occurring over comedy
programs (D. G. Clark and Blankenburg, 1972). Our conclusion is
not that the Gerbner and Gross data are in any way incorrect but
that the use of a normative definition of violence requires some
qualification in interpretation, and that programs identified as violent by its use conform more perfectly to the normative perception when comedy or other formats normally considered inconsistent with violence are excluded.

The Gerbner and Gross violence index (table 2.14) under-
standably has aroused the ire of many. We agree that it is an arbitrary combination of factors. There is no necessary reason for the
inclusion of any component, the formula for combining them, or
the weights involved. We also agree that shifts in the index are
not readily interpretable unless the index is accepted as synonymous with violence. Even if the definition, the time sample, and
the rules of program inclusion and exclusion are accepted, any
difference over the kind of violence that should be emphasized
would render the index an imperfect indicator. Gerbner and

Table 2.14 Computation of Gerbner and Gross Violence Index

Violence Index $= \%P + 2(R/P) + 2(R/H) + \%V + \%K$

Where

$\%P =$ percentage of programs studied (i.e., network evening plus children's,
nonstoryline excluded) in which there is violence

$R/P =$ number of violent episodes *per program*

$R/H =$ number of violent episodes *per hour*

$\%V =$ percentage of *leading characters* involved in violence—either commit
act or as victim

$\%K =$ percentage of leading characters involved in killing—either as killer or
victim

SOURCE: G. Gerbner. 1972b. Violence in television drama: Trends and symbolic
functions. In G. A. Comstock and E. A. Rubinstein (eds.), *Television and Social
Behavior.* Vol. 1, *Media content and control.* Washington, D.C.: Government
Printing Office, Pp. 28–187.

Gross argue that indices by definition are arbitrary combinations and that their index serves them as a heuristic device leading to the analysis of the shifts in components behind the trend in the index. We concur, but we would emphasize that the index requires acceptance before the figures generated can be taken as representative of the level or change in television violence.

The usefulness of a gross measure of television violence has been questioned on several grounds. We share the fear of those critics who warn that any measure will encourage public and governmental attacks on the medium by many who imperfectly understand the measure, but we do not see this as an argument against measurement. We believe that the examination of the fictional content of the medium that is modern society's most popular purveyor of stories and the most pervasive of all mass media is justifiable on scientific grounds alone. We do not agree with those who argue that any use of a measure of violence must be predicated on evidence that the kind of violence in question has been demonstrated to be harmful. We would argue that a policy expressing concern over violence is sufficient for empirical measurement.

We would emphasize that the Gerbner and Gross data do not give any weight to the variety of aspects of television portrayals demonstrated to increase the likelihood of subsequent aggressiveness that we discuss later (chapters 5 and 8). We doubt whether any empirical measure could encompass such contextual aspects adequately enough to satisfy those accustomed to thinking of the immense subtleties that distinguish one drama from another, and the criticism that some crucial element is overlooked will always remain with content analysis. However, it must be recognized that the Gerbner and Gross data do not reflect any of the specific factors that have been demonstrated to heighten the impact of violent portrayals on behavior.

The reply of Gerbner and Gross that from an evidentiary standpoint it is too soon to assume that aggressiveness is the principal outcome of television violence, and that the evocation of fear and distrust through the depiction of the world as violent and dangerous may be the more important effect, explains this absence. Behind this view is their theory of the social function of the fiction on television. They argue that television violence helps to maintain the existing social order by reinforcing beliefs about who is powerful or dangerous and increasing belief in the likelihood of risk and danger. Thus, television is said to "cultivate" beliefs and perceptions.

This view is consistent with the differences in violent portrayals among ethnic and socioeconomic groups and the sexes, which we shall review. It also gains support from the finding that among both adults and children heavy viewing of television is associated with greater belief in the likelihood of falling victim to a crime or being harmed (Foundation for Child Development, 1977; Gerbner). However, there are many possible explanations for this relationship, and they must be explored before we accept television viewing as the cause of this phenomenon; nevertheless, the belief's existence across the boundaries of age, sex, education, socioeconomic status, and amount of exposure to other mass media is highly suggestive.

The "cultivation" perspective has led Gerbner and Gross to calculate "victimization ratios" for various demographic categories that purportedly indicate the relative degree of risk portrayed. These consist of the ratio of perpetrators to victims of violence in each category, omitting those not all involved in violence. Groups that have quite high ratios are women, the poor, and the elderly. In accord with Gerbner and Gross's theory, television would especially "cultivate" insecurity among such viewers.

The problem with a "victimization ratio" is that it is an entirely arbitrary indicator. Other measures, such as the actual number or percentage of persons who are victims in a given category, would generally reverse the pattern toward greater victimization of groups with less social power because of the predominance of white males in action drama. We cannot accept Gerbner and Gross's "victimization ratio" as clearly conveying to viewers the alleged pattern. We also do not reject it because it is eminently possible that the valid approach is to focus solely on the pattern of dominance among those involved in violence. Such an approach derives its plausibility from its consistency with the social order, but since it was developed with knowledge of this order this is hardly verification. What we would like to see is some empirical demonstration that this measure is more valid than others, but we cannot join critics who would discard it, because it may well represent insight into a means by which television drama affects its audience.

The Gerbner and Gross sample has been criticized for its time span and for what it excludes. We do not agree with those who assert that several weeks scattered over the fall-winter season would produce very different results, but it would certainly increase the accurate reflection of the season. We do believe that the variability within a season makes anything other than very marked differences or shifts among networks difficult to interpret, and this is especially so for the violence index because of its arbitrary character.

We think the sample is adequate to reflect each fall season's network programming of fiction for general and child audiences. It certainly does not reflect television as a whole; it excludes independent stations and non-network broadcasting. Nor does it reflect network television as a whole; it excludes news, sports, specials, and variety programs. In some respects, these omissions may give a falsely high and in others a falsely low impression of the quantity of violence on television. It is ironic that those who advocate measuring violence within a sphere of content (fiction, wherever it occurs) ignore it in content outside this sphere.

In sum, Gerbner and Gross's "violence profile" must be understood in terms of its limitations. It nevertheless is a valuable source for knowledge of television's fiction and its violent content.

Character, Level, and Trends

We now turn to the data. We begin with the *character* of television violence:

> Violence is often portrayed as not leading to physical discomfort—so much so that degree of pain and suffering cannot be coded.
> Most programs over the past decade have been set in the present, in the United States, and in an urban environment, so naturally most violence also has occurred in such circumstances, but the highest rates of violence tend to occur in circumstances set apart from American reality in time, geography, or surroundings.
> Portrayals of falling victim to violence are frequent, the number of characters who are victims outnumber those who inflict violence, and the likelihood of falling victim to violence on television is 50 times greater than the real-life statistical likelihood.
> The committing of violence has been inversely related to socioeconomic status and more frequent among nonwhites and foreigners over the past decade, but this pattern has shifted from season to season, and the relatively infrequent appearance of characters who are at the extremes of socioeconomic status, nonwhite, or foreign, means that the greatest quantity of violence is committed by white middle-class Americans.
> The principal leading characters in noncartoon television drama, most of which involves some violence, tend to be in the

prime of life, male, American, and middle or upper class—and this dominance is probably partly attributable to violence because such characters are especially fit for conflict, danger, and risk.

By the Gerbner and Gross victimization ratio, victims of violence are disproportionately found among groups less powerful in the real society—they tend to be female, old, lower class, foreign, or nonwhite. When we apply the criterion of the proportion falling victim to violence out of the total of such characters, we come to precisely the opposite conclusion about women and the elderly. This anomaly arises because markedly fewer of these two groups are involved in violence either as victims or as perpetrators than white males, but when they are, victims are proportionately more frequent.

We now turn to the *level* and *trend* of violence. Because the Gerbner and Gross index is an arbitrarily weighted composite, we first present specific single measures for different types of programs (figures 2.1 through 2.5). We conclude by comparing Gerbner and Gross's data with CBS data that illustrate the sensitivity of conclusions about trends to the method of measurement (figures 2.6 and 2.7). We find that (Gerbner and Gross, 1976; Gerbner et al., 1977):

Violence is very prevalent in television drama, with about 80 percent of all programs over the past decade containing one or more violent episodes. The highest incidence of violence of course occurs in action-type programs (crime, adventure, and western drama and cartoons), and these have been a substantial component of network programming, with their proportion of all noncartoon, general programs ranging between 40 and 60 percent over the past decade.

Programs directed at children have typically scored high on most measures of violence except for killing. Cartoons have consistently exceeded all other categories of programs, including action-type, in number of violent episodes per hour despite a steady decline for five years beginning in 1969–70. That 100 percent of cartoons contained violence in the 1976–77 season is most fairly considered an anomaly, since live drama has become more common in children's weekend programming and there were only five cartoons during the fall week analyzed, compared to two or three dozen in earlier seasons. However, the figures for all daytime weekend programming, a period whose drama is largely intended for children, indicate a very substantial degree of violence and an upturn in the 1976–77 season to a 100 percent score.

Considerable violence occurs in a comic or humorous con-

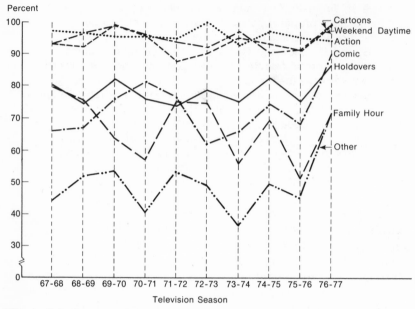

Figure 2.1. Percent of programs containing violence.

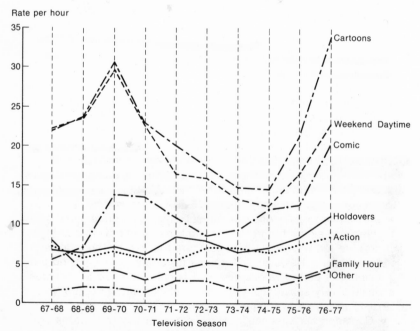

Figure 2.2. Number of violent episodes per hour.

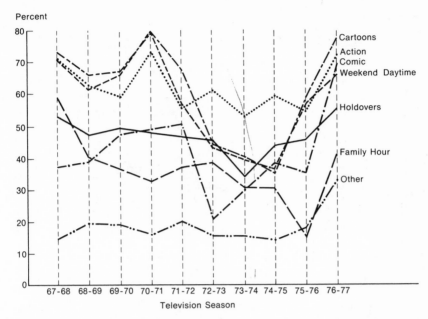

Figure 2.3. Percent of leading characters committing violent acts.

Figure 2.4. Percent leading characters involved in violence as perpetrator or victim or both.

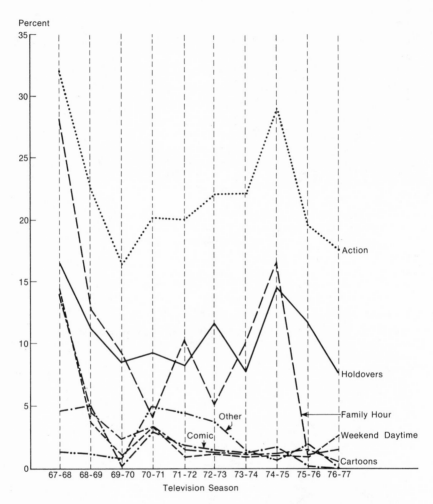

Figure 2.5. Percent leading characters involved in killing as perpetrator or victim or both.

NOTES (figures 2.1–2.5): Cartoons: all animated programs; Action: all western, crime, action-adventure programs (cartoons not included); Other: all programs other than western, crime, and action-adventure (cartoons not included); Comic: all programs mostly humorous in tone, including such cartoons; Holdovers: all programs also broadcast in the previous year, including such cartoons.

SOURCE (figures 2.1–2.5): G. Gerbner, L. Gross, M. F. Eleey, M. Jackson-Beeck, S. Jeffries-Fox, and N. Signorielli. 1977. *Violence Profile No. 8: Trends in Network Television Drama and Viewer Conceptions of Social Reality: 1967–1976*. Philadelphia: Annenberg School of Communications, University of Pennsylvania.

text—comic programs are far from violence-free, and "comic" cartoons are about as violent as adventure and super hero cartoons. ⌐

We single out "comic" programs—cartoons and drama humorous in tone—because of the dispute about whether humorous fare should be included in the measurement of violence. The fact that such programs stand fairly high in quantity of violence and fluctuate in a different way than programs in other categories justify their measurement on the grounds of scientific curiosity; whether they should be pooled with action dramas in a "violence index" is open to debate.

There have been sporadic shifts in the various measures of violence over the past decade, but few that suggest any definite trend. For some types of programming and for some measures, there has been stability. In other instances, there have been oscillations that at various points in time appeared to be trends. These were illusions. The rate of violent incidents per hour—probably the most sensitive and plausible reflector of quantity of violence—declined between 1969–70 and 1974–75 for three overlapping categories —cartoon, weekend daytime, and comic programs—then rose. Among action-type programs, the rate appears to have risen gently over the decade. Meanwhile, the proportion of these four genres of programs with some violence has remained about the same, while the figure for other categories has risen and fallen.

The sole exception to the absence of trends occurs over the involvement of leading characters in violence of any kind and their involvement in killing, either as victims or perpetrators. Even here a sensitive eye and a taste for qualification are required. After 1967–68, there appeared to be a marked decline in the proportion of leading characters involved in violence or in killing. There remains a detectable trend for action-type programs. Killing appears to have been eliminated from weekend daytime and cartoon programs, the two categories that most closely reflect programming aimed at children. However, once we leave children's programming we become more conscious of shifts and peaks that interrupt trends than of any trends.

Although the adoption of "family viewing" in early 1975 reduced violence in the 1975–76 season during the pre-9 P.M. period affected, other trends give this the appearance of an aberration. Since 1973–74, total violence as measured by the Gerbner and Gross violence index increased in the hours after the 9 P.M. "family viewing" cutoff. Moreover, the termination of "family viewing" by a federal court (see Chapter 9) was followed by an increase to levels greater than before the initiation of this programming innovation,

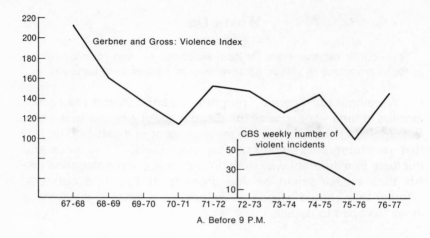

A. Before 9 P.M.

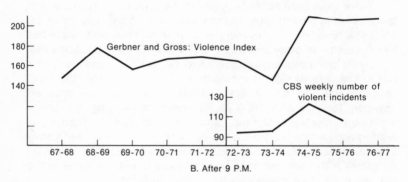

B. After 9 P.M.

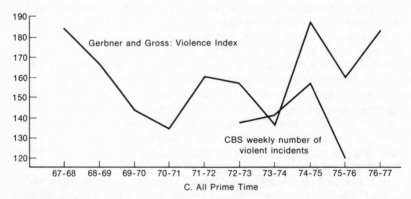

C. All Prime Time

Figure 2.6. Alternative measures of broad trends in violence.

SOURCES: G. Gerbner, L. Gross, M. F. Eleey, M. Jackson-Beeck, S. Jeffries-Fox, and N. Signorielli. 1977. *Violence Profile No. 8: Trends in Network Television Drama and Viewer Conceptions of Social Reality, 1967–1976.* Philadelphia: Annenberg School of Communications, University of Pennsylvania. Columbia Broadcasting System, Office of Social Research. 1976. Network prime-time violence tabulations for 1975–76 season. Unpublished manuscript.

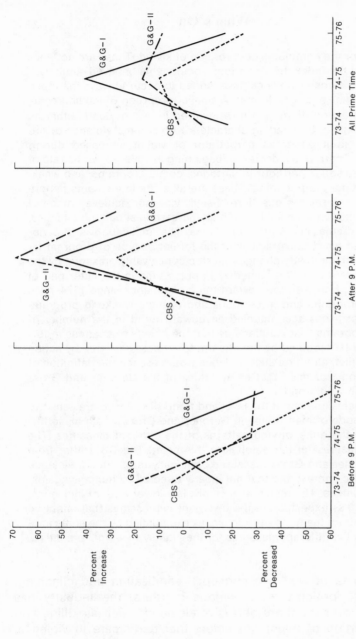

Figure 2.7. Percent loss or gain in measures of violence from season to season.

NOTE: G&G-I = Gerbner and Gross Violence Index (table 2.14). G&G-II = Number of violent incidents in one week of fall programming for all three networks. CBS = Average number of violent incidents for all three networks (13-week average, 1975–76; 2-week average, for previous seasons).

except for the continuing suppression of killing. These are not anomalies of the index, for its various components behaved similarly.

Reductions in violence have tended to occur in ways that have
only a minor effect on format. A smaller proprtion of leading characters in action drama are now involved in violent death either as
killer or killed, but leading characters who commit violence or are
involved in it either as perpetrator or victim increased during
1976–77. There was a decrease, beginning in 1969–70, in the rate of
violent episodes per hour in cartoons, comic programs, and weekend daytime programming. These are all shifts in elements peripheral to the format in question. "Family viewing" achieved much of
its reduction in violence through an increase in situation comedies,
general drama, and variety programs. The implication is that violence will resist constraint until the format or type of program favored by the industry changes—a step conceivably presaged by the
trend toward situation comedies in prime time in the latter part of
the 1970s. However, the upward trend of violence since 1974–75 in
comic programs and in cartoons and daytime weekend programming which has accompanied an upward trend in the number of
such programs, also cautions us that the effects of changes in format may be modified by the attempt to attract audiences by action
and conflict, although such violence would escape the definition of
"television violence" that many critics of the Gerbner and Gross
approach would prefer.

Conclusions about the level and trend of violence are sensitive
to the mode of measurement. Gerbner and Gross's data make this
clear by the quite varying patterns of the different measures. The
CBS measures further emphasize this point. The CBS differ from
the Gerbner and Gross measures principally in excluding violence
in a comic context and that not clearly directed by humans against
other humans. The result, expectedly, is a lower level of incidence.
What is less expected are the divergent impressions that might be
gained about the trend in violence, as exemplified by the shifts indicated by the different measures for the "family viewing," pre-9 P.M.,
period.

The data fit well two concepts: sanitization and clinching.
Faced with criticism from various quarters, the industry has
smoothed over the more obtrusive elements, such as killing and
the proportion of major characters that participate in violence,
and there have been various shifts, possibly defensive, that could
be mistaken for downward trends. In the end, however, change
appears to have been slight.

The total pattern over the decade is testimony to the resil-
ience of violence as a component of television entertainment.

This pattern gives credence to the view that television violence is intractable because it is the inevitable product of the various forces that shape programming (Comstock, 1972). These forces are varied, and emanate from such diverse sources as the values and motives of those who produce television (Baldwin and Lewis, 1972; Cantor, 1971, 1972) and the competitive nature of network programming. The resurgence of violence after the abandonment of "family viewing" as formal policy is illustrative of the dynamics at work. As this is written, the pressure on the industry to reduce violence—from Congress, advocacy groups, advertisers, and such prestigious bodies as the American Medical Association and the national Parent-Teachers Association—is at a peak. Although past experience does not justify optimism on the part of those who would like to see a gross reduction in television violence, the increased pressure—and particularly that from advertisers—may alter the historical pattern. At the same time, as we discuss later in regard to the formulating of policy in regard to television programming (chapter 9), it is clear that particular aspects of portrayals judged by some criterion to be particularly undesirable can be effectively curtailed or eliminated, although such reform may not be reflected in many of the measurements of television violence employed to date.

The measurement of violence and the accompanying debate are certain to continue. The tabulation so far has had considerable impact by drawing public attention. As we point out later (chapter 9), it has furthered the dissatisfaction of advertisers with violence, because it has led to the identification of those whose commercials appear regularly in conjunction with violence. The Social Science Research Council (1975) especially assembled a committee to address the question of constructing a superior violence profile although its recommendation that such a measure be multi-dimensional was unimaginative. Nevertheless, various government officials have repeatedly promised that an improved mode of measurement will be developed (U.S. Congress, 1974).

"Television Violence" in Context

Television drama is obviously not unique in conveying violence. Comic books, movies, novels, popular magazine fiction, television news, and newspapers all present obtrusive quantities of violence. Because of D. G. Clark and Blankenburg's (1972) comparative analysis of a variety of mass media, often covering trends over several decades, we can place "television violence" in context.

Before 1970, violence in theatrical movies, prime-time television drama, the fiction in mass-circulation magazines, and newspaper front pages oscillated sharply (figure 2.8). Since World War II, the trend in movies and newspaper front pages has been upward. The same cannot be said of prime-time television drama, in which the highest peak of violence occurred in the late 1950s; it more nearly appears to have oscillated around a constant. Violence in the mass-circulation-magazine fiction studied (*Saturday Evening Post*) followed neither of these patterns. The trend was downward after 1950, reversing an upward trend.

A positive correlation between violence in a newspaper's front pages and its city's annual homicide and suicide rate is consistent with the view that news roughly follows the incidence of real-life violence. The lack of a correlation between violence in prime-time television drama and violent crime in the Federal Bureau of Investigation's Uniform Crime Report data suggests no such reflective factor in the level of television violence. The positive correlation between the proportion of violent programs and the ratings for such programs in the preceding year instead suggests that such violence reflects the evidence reaching broadcasters about its likely popularity.

The oscillations of violence in television drama tend to peak every four or five years.

The data, based on synopses in *TV Guide,* represent the pattern of the adoption of violent formats. We concur with Clark and Blankenburg that this cycle reflects the pursuit of popularity and the price of that pursuit. When ratings signal that violent programs are becoming popular, more are put on the air. The increased availability of violence dilutes the audience and ratings fall while criticism of the industry rises. There is then a temporary abandonment of violence. What this pattern makes clear is that the industry behaves toward violence as if it were a popular staple with limited—or as an economist might say, "inelastic"—demand.

The evidence, however, does not support the contention that violence enhances popularity—either in terms of series viewing or attractiveness of episodes to channel-switchers. Diener and De-Four (in press) found no correlation between amount of violence in the episodes of 11 series over a season and their Nielsen ratings, when violence was coded to emphasize interpersonal physical or verbal abuse rather than action elements such as car

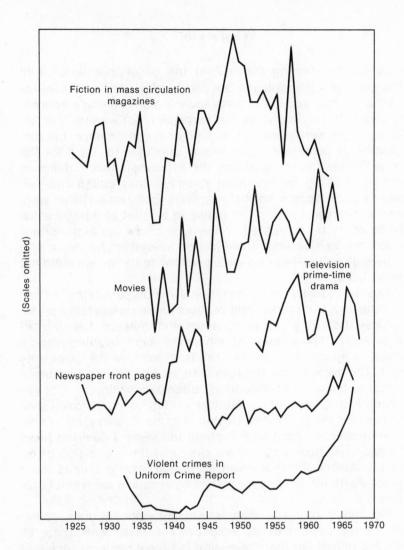

Figure 2.8. Trends in violence: Mass media and real life.

NOTE: Fiction in mass-circulation magazine: percent stories in *Saturday Evening Post* with a violent incident; Movies: percent synopses in *Movies on TV* with violent incident, coded by year of production; Television prime-time drama: percent synopses in *TV Guide* with violent incident; Newspaper front pages: percent stories of violent events for ten days each year on front pages of four urban dailies; Violent crimes in Uniform Crime Report: rate per 100,000 of murder, forcible rape, robbery, and aggravated assault.

SOURCE: Adapted from D. G. Clark and W. B. Blankenburg. 1972. Trends in violent content in selected mass media. In G. A. Comstock and E. A. Rubinstein (eds.), *Television and Social Behavior*. Vol. 1. *Media Content and Control*. Washington, D.C.: Government Printing Office, pp. 188–243.

chases. Such a finding fits neither the belief that series with on-the-average high violence are more attractive to viewers, or that violence may seduce viewers scanning an evening's options. They also found in analyzing the perceptions of viewers that, indeed, episodes were perceived as high or low in violence, but that the degree of perceived violence was unrelated to liking for the episode. To test more rigorously the hypothesis that violence is unrelated to liking for television episodes, they edited two versions of *Police Woman* so that reactions to depictions that were similar in degree of action but unlike in amount of interpersonal violence could be compared. Viewers who saw the high action–low violence version liked this episode as well as did those who saw the high action–high violence version; again, violence did not increase liking.

Thus the industry responds rationally in pursuing signs of format popularity, but market and production factors defeat individual goals—there is a glut of offerings and imitators fall short of creative equity. The solution of enhancing action by interpersonal violence is apparently not the means to achieve the popularity sought. The cycle then continues with action certainly and interpersonal violence as a concomitant often oscillating.

Television drama cannot fairly be said to be more violent than news because the proportion of violent items in newscasts and violent programs in prime time is about the same. Television news and newspaper front pages were similar in the proportion of reports of violence, but television illustrated such accounts more frequently with film or videotape than newspapers did with photographs.

The import of these data is that television is unlike other media in the pattern of its violence. The statements that "all media are violent" or that "television is violent because society is violent" are truisms but hide important distinctions. News, although a concoction from available events, must be somewhat obedient to them. Entertainment need not be, either in principle or, in the case of violence in prime-time drama, in fact. Despite obvious similarities, the various media differ sufficiently in their communicatory properties, their audiences, and their economics for us to believe that it is necessary to explain the frequency and pattern of violence by specific factors operating in each case. Similarities, not differences, may be explained by such slogans as a human need for vicarious violence. What has given "television violence" its prominence as a subject of concern, in addition to the medium's ubiquity, vividness, and daily command of the public's attention is its independence from any necessity other than the character and economics of the industry.

In Conclusion

We have been limited in our depiction of television's messages by what has been studied. Television is certainly what we have said it is, but it is also much more. We look forward to studies that will focus on new questions, such as the possible similarities (and differences) between current types of programs and those they appear to have supplanted, and between such diverse currently popular types of programs as urban law enforcement dramas and situation comedies. The notion of E. Greenberg and Barnett (1971) that similarity of audience composition and not format should be the basis for program classification merits increased attention. By analyzing the content of programs so classified, we presumably would be better able to identify the essential factors responsible for their appeal.

Our conclusions:

Entertainment is the predominant currency of commercial television; network and public television differ primarily in the latter's emphasis on public affairs and children's programming and the former's emphasis on entertainment; no description of television content can ignore the commercial because it consumes more than one of every seven minutes of prime-time viewing.

The themes of television drama revolves around basic human conflicts as exemplified in the confrontation of good guys and bad guys, personal problems, and the role of professionals in solving them; and they often treat socially desirable goals as achievable by socially disapproved means.

Television content, although the product of innumerable independent decisions, resembles what one would expect of a rational individual; the treatment of the environment in drama and commercials is illustrative—consistent with public norms, evasive where there is roiling controversy, and supportive of the economic interests of the industry where they are clear.

Television drama is a created fiction that emphasizes males, professionals, whites, and the middle class, although the portrayal of blacks has increased with a policy of greater ethnic diversity.

As elsewhere, men and women are not equal on television. In

drama, men appear more often, have more dominant roles; women
tend to be more youthful, are typically objects of sexual desire, or
are emotionally supportive of the man's risk-taking. Similar male
dominance occurs in commercials.

Children's television is like prime-time television and its commercials in portraying males as dominant.

The use of the actual makeup of the population and the concept of the stereotype are useful for highlighting the character of
television portrayals, but do not easily lead to a judgment as to the
merit of the portrayals. Such judgment is difficult because neither
conformity to statistical actuality or stereotypic portrayal are necessarily uncomplimentary or inaccurate.

Television news is a selective shaping of stories in accord with
the needs of the medium, and is difficult to evaluate because there
are seldom readily available criteria by which to judge the authenticity of news.

Network television gives considerable attention to bad news,
but because there is no standard for judgment it is impossible to
say whether or not this represents excessive negativism. The networks have differed somewhat in their treatment of news, but by
and large have been very similar. Despite the many controversies,
there is little evidence of partisan bias in coverage of national politics and major public events.

Violence in network television drama emphasizes victimization
and the prowess of the white male; it has changed in some respects
over the past decade, and has been reduced to some extent, but on
the whole it has remained much the same—including a consistently
high level in children's programming; historically the quantity of violent programs has fluctuated cyclically as the result of the competitive economics of the industry, but the evidence suggests that
amount of interpersonal physical and verbal abuse in programs is
unrelated to audience popularity or viewers' expressions of liking
for the program.

Chapter

The Audience

SINCE THE LATE 1950s, almost everyone in the United States has been living in a dwelling with a television set. In the fall of 1976, Nielsen data indicate that the average home had the set turned on for almost seven hours every day.

The universal availability and extensive daily use make television the ubiquitous mass medium. Its saturation is simply the result of the attentiveness of the public—a tribute to the courting skills of broadcasters whose economic success depends on winning and holding a large audience attractive to advertisers. When we look closely at the television audience, we discover that it is actually many audiences, among which there are a number of differences in the amount of viewing as well as in other television-related behavior and attitudes. This quite definite variation within the audience qualifies—but does not significantly alter—the fact that substantial involvement in television viewing in modern America is an experience common across demographic boundaries. Among the topics we shall cover in our depiction of the audience are:

The character of the audience for television, with particular attention to trends over time, the relationships between viewing and age, sex, and time of day; the variation in composition of the audience over the day and evening; and the way the audience differs for different kinds of programs.

The makeup and size of the audience for television news.

The makeup of the audience for violent television drama.

The relationship between nondemographic personal attributes and viewing.

The black audience and how it differs from the white audience.

The attitudes held by the public about television, with particular attention to the public's evaluation of television's performance.

The esteem in which television is held as a news source by the public, with particular attention to the degree of credibility attributed to television in comparison to that attributed to other media.

Trends and Patterns

Because of their freshness and comprehensiveness, we chose to analyze new data from the A. C. Nielsen Company. They are by several years more recent and they permit examination of a wider range of questions than data available in published sources.

Most of the data are from the fall of 1976. The patterns they reflect are typical of television in the United States since the late 1950s, although there is a trend toward the reduction of differences related to socioeconomic status and the level of viewing has reached an historic high.

However, every body of data has its limitations. In the present case, we shall be restricted to using the same descriptive categories as Nielsen, or some estimate based upon them, and the Nielsen sample, although excellent for a broad description of the audience, is not large enough for detailed analysis of certain populations of great interest, such as blacks. For these reasons, the analysis of Nielsen data will be followed by a summary of evidence on certain issues from other studies.

The Nielsen sample consists of 1200 homes with television sets wired directly by telephone line to a computer. The sample is designed to provide a portrait of the television-viewing behavior of the American public. The 1200 homes constitute a continuing panel, but 20 percent are replaced each year—so that no family is a Nielsen family for more than five years. Excellent data on trends are thereby provided. The automatic measurement makes the data highly reliable in regard to whether sets are on, and to which channel they are tuned. Information on household characteristics of viewers is obtained from a second national sample of 2300 homes where diaries are maintained on who views what. Data from the two samples are coordinated to produce the eventual portrait of viewing behavior.

Nielsen sampling and recruitment have been the subject of debate. Are the sample homes a true stratified random sample? Certainly there is some reason to worry about sample bias due to refusals to participate. However, under the realities imposed by finite resources, we believe that Nielsen data are far more trustworthy than those available from other sources. And in many cases they are the only available data pertaining to the entire population. Further, internal comparisons are probably quite valid, unless we assume complex interactions between viewing, refusal to participate, and demographics.

The limitations of the Nielsen data derive from the purpose for which the data are collected. That purpose is the needs of those engaged in the buying and selling of advertising time. Nielsen depicts a program's popularity and the characteristics of its audience—the two features that determine the value of air time. Size of audience is the principal factor, although the most valuable segment of the audience is the "young adult," 18- through 49-year, age group. They achieve this status both by size—they constitue not quite half of the population—and by their expendable income and rate of consumption, which make them predominant in consumer purchases. From the perspective of the network or station, the Nielsen data are used to discard programs that fail to draw adequately, with success defined as equaling or beating other broadcasters in the same time period. From the perspective of the advertiser, the data are used to direct purchases toward time periods where audience size and characteristics are satisfactory. The data take life in the decision-making largely in two guises—the *rating,* which represents *the proportion of the total potential sets* tuned to a program for several minutes or more; and the *share,* which represents the proportion of the total sets *in use at a particular time* that are tuned to a particular program during an average minute. The rating and the share determine whether or not a program will survive through a season or from one season to another.

From the perspective of the social and behavioral scientist, the data reflect the social phenomena of time use and taste. From that of critics and advocacy groups, they are the bases for disdain or alarm. It is in the statistics of who views when that the content of the programming takes on meaning.

The Nielsen data are commensurate with the needs of the parties in the marketplace for the television advertising time, and no more. The automatic measurement is precise and operating but unattended sets are a minor factor; however, the simultaneous diaries are necessary to learn precisely who is viewing when. There should be no illusion that the behavior reflected in the resulting estimates is constant attention to the set, for as we shall see in the next chapter "television viewing" is not synonymous with quietly watching.

Broad Trends

In the fall of 1976 the average home with television had the set turned on for 6.82 hours every day. This was an increase of almost an hour per day from the 1963 level. These fall averages, however, are about 9 percent higher than a 12-month average because of lighter summer viewing.

As figure 3.1 shows, the early steady increase in hours per day is largely attributable to a sharp increase between 1963 and 1970 in viewing in households whose head was relatively less educated. Over this period, television use in lower-education households rose from 5.94 to 6.80 hours, an increase of 15 percent compared to the 2 percent increase in higher-education households. In the next three years, the trend changed. There was no increase for lower education households, but there was a substantial increase for higher-education households of about 10 percent—from 5.60 to 6.15 hours.

What is the explanation for the change in the pattern? It is easy to believe that the sharp increase in viewing by lower-education households contained its own demise, because it absorbed much of the time still available for watching television. The sudden upward shift in the trend for higher-education households is more problematical. Perhaps this rise reflects the first significant appearance in the tabulation of the better educated of the first television generation. For this generation, a set was simply an ordinary but constant presence in the home, and therefore a good education might be less inhibiting to viewing. There is no available evidence either for or against such a proposition. The upward shift is certainly not attributable to any gross swelling of the better educated viewers by persons whose backgrounds in some other way would incline them toward greater viewing. Growth in the size of the category over the period has not been great and the proportion of households meeting the education criterion had previously increased steadily, without a dramatic rise in viewing. With the purchase of a color set viewing temporarily increases, a fact that will annually provide some increase in the nation's total viewing until color ownership (three-fourths of television households in 1975) becomes universal. But this phenomenon appears

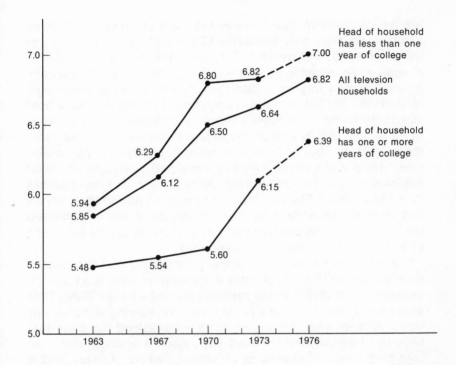

Figure 3.1. Average hours per day television on in the household, 1963–1976.

NOTE: Data for 1976 educational categories (----) estimated on basis of prior trend and relationship to data for all television households.
SOURCE: A. C. Nielsen Company, National Audience Demographics Report.

unrelated to the pattern. In fact, because acquisition of a color set is directly related to socioeconomic status, if color were involved we would expect the shift for higher-education households to precede that for lower-education households.

The progressive rise in television use clearly exceeds anything that could be attributed to changes in demographic patterns. However, population changes undoubtedly have played their role, as they surely will in the future. What is always difficult to predict is the net impact of trends on household television consumption. The very gradual rise in the proportion who are elderly implies increased consumption. The implication of the baby boom of the late 1940s are shifts in television use as two waves run on—those born then, now in their late twenties and thirties, and their children, now about 8 to 12 years of age. The swelling of the adult ranks, and eventually those of the elderly, implies little change or an increase in viewing; the entrance into adolescence of the children implies a decrease. Overshadowing these age-related changes are associated alterations in lifestyles. Household size is declining, with more younger adults and elderly persons living alone. This is one of the explanations for the more rapid increase in number of television households than in population size. Living alone implies greater individual viewing than might otherwise occur, but reduced set use because of the fewer parties in the household. The net impact of these varied trends is uncertain, and becomes even more problematical when it is realized that adjustments in programming may occur to satisfy any signs of a change in the makeup of the public.

We do have some confidence in hazarding that the general steady increase in hours per day of viewing represents an accommodation attributable to the previous level of viewing. Behind the gross trend are individuals whose norm of viewing is constantly rising, as each year there is some viewing beyond the norm that becomes incorporated the next year. Such a shifting norm can take place only for rare kinds of behavior whose primary limit is available time; the same trend would probably have occurred for radio were there no television.

We are not surprised to find that most of the increase in the early 1970s occurred during the day and after 11 P.M. (Lyle, 1975), and not in prime time, where available time for viewing has already been largely consumed.* That the increase comes from blocks of time during which television was previously not viewed rather than from even heavier viewing during prime time supports the notion that the natural limit to the amount of time for viewing is approaching (J. P. Robinson, 1969). However, the trend over the past 15 years suggests that time set aside for other, presumably necessary, activities may be more easily foreshortened or abandoned than one might have supposed.

---

*The term prime time derives from the higher price chargeable for advertising time in the evening when the audience is especially large. It is considered to end at 11 P.M. when the audience dwindles. From the network's perspective, it begins with network dissemination, which in the mid-1970s was 8 P.M. From the local station's perspective, it begins at 7 or 7:30 P.M. when the evening audience begins to swell. The 8 P.M. network figure is the result of Federal Communications Commission regulations intended to encourage local broadcasting that prohibit network evening dissemination before that hour.

Nevertheless, we are very hesitant to make the obvious prediction that viewing will continue to increase, for the prognosticator's graveyard displays too many epitaphs in memory of those who simply extrapolated trend lines into the blue future. The increasing shift of women into the labor force is certain to result in a decline in daytime set use. Thus, the increases that have occurred outside of prime time may quickly be offset by the departure of the foundation for non-prime-time viewing, the housewife.

Other factors endangering the growth curve for commercial broadcasting, besides the finite nature of available time and the possibility—certainly not endorsed by history—that the competitiveness of the networks will entrap them in formulas rejected by some sizable portion of the viewing public, are the various technological innovations that may draw viewers away. As we discuss later (chapter 4), those who can afford them are quickly becoming able to construct their own video environments.

All in all, correcting for seasonal fluctuation, we estimate that in 1976, the most recent year for which we have data, the television was on for 2278 hours in the average household with television.

Amount of television viewing varies by sex and age. Figure 3.2 presents data for fall of 1967 and 1976 for individuals. Several patterns are evident:

Viewing by individuals increased over the last six years. However, the increase was not identical for all groups.

Children watch about the same amount of television per week as adults, although at different times. Children from 2 to 5 years watch somewhat more than those 6 to 11 years old (29 vs. 26.7 hours per week in the fall of 1976).

Teenagers watch the fewest hours of television. The 21.9 hours in the fall of 1976 was almost 7 hours less than average.

Men from 18 to 49 watch less television than the other adult groups although there was an increase of 5.1 hours per week between 1967 and 1976. This remarkable 26 percent increase is the most dramatic for any group.

Men over 50 years old watch more than men under 50. Their total viewing increased over the past six years to 31.9 hours a week, about 7 more than younger men.

Women from 18 to 49 watch more hours than men the same age. 'n the fall of 1976, these younger adult women viewed almost 7 hours ɔer week more than younger adult men. Their total viewing haɔ increased by more than 4 hours in the last three years, and they remain above the overall average for individual viewing, with over 31 hours a week.

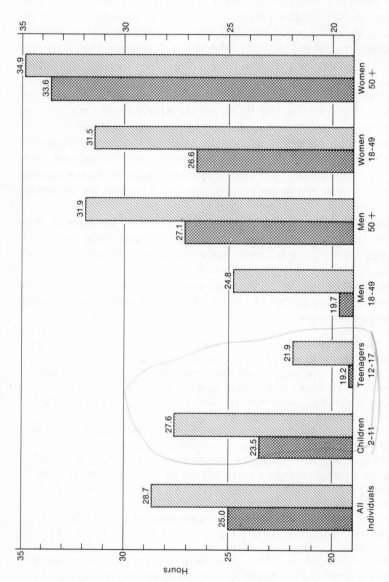

Figure 3.2. Hours per week television viewing for different groups—1967 (dark bars) compared to 1976 (light bars).

SOURCE: A. C. Nielsen Co., National Audience Demographics Report.

Women over 50 watch far more television than any of the other groups. Their fall 1976 total of nearly 35 hours per week is 3.4 hours a week more than younger adult women and 3 hours a week more than men over 50.

Viewing declines between elementary school and high school, rises in adulthood, and rises again quite markedly after age 50, particularly for men. In the fall of 1976, both men and women over 50 watched several hours a week more than younger adults.

Three Other Variables

The relationship of viewing to age and sex has been examined. Other factors are also strongly related to the amount of television viewed by individuals. Three major such variables will be examined in the next seven bar graphs: number of people in household, household income, and education of head of household. The three variables are clearly related, especially education and income, but although available data do not allow for multivariate analysis by household, it seems reasonable to assume some degree of independent effect for each. Figure 3.3 presents average weekly viewing by *individuals* over these variables.

People who live alone or with one other person typically watch much more television than people who live in households containing three or more people. This finding deserves emphasis because our analysis leads to a conclusion quite different from that of the pattern usually described. A well-known and repeatedly documented finding has been that *households* with more people have the set turned on more than those with less people. This is true. In the fall of 1976, homes with five or more people had their sets on for an average of more than nine hours a day, over three and one-half more hours than daily use in one- and two-person households. However, the household use of television is an accumulation of *all* individual use—the *individual* in the larger household on the average actually watches less television. The decline in average viewing by individuals is continuous across the various sizes of household (table 3.1).

The roots of this pattern are found in the household's composition. Small (one- and two-persons) households are composed of about 60 percent persons 50 and older and 1 percent children. Larger households typically constitute families with adults and children. Older persons watch a great deal of television, which contributes strongly to high average viewing in small households.

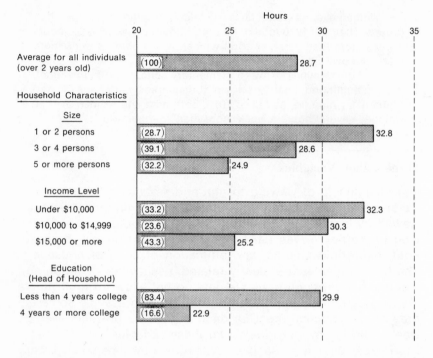

Figure 3.3. Average hours of television viewing per week for all individuals by household characteristics, fall 1976. (Figures in parentheses are percent of all individuals in a given household type. 100% = 201.46 million.)

SOURCE: A. C. Nielsen Co., National Audience Demographics Report.

In larger households there is usually a wide spectrum of ages and the more members there are the longer the set will be on; but the audience before the set will be changing with different persons viewing at different times.

The next variable examined in figure 3.3 is household income. Over 33 percent of the population live in homes with under $10,000 annual income. Persons in lower-income households watch considerably more television—an additional half-hour a day more in the fall of 1976—than the average for all individuals. Higher-income people watch the least television, but individuals in homes earning $15,000 or more in the fall of 1976 nevertheless averaged over three and one-half hours of television a day.

The pattern for individuals by household education level is similar. If the head of household has finished four or more years

Table 3.1 Individual and Household Viewing Compared (In Average Hours Per Day, Fall 1976)

		Average By Household Size		
		1–2	3–4	5+
	Average for All Individuals	Persons	Persons	Persons
Children 2–11	3.9	—ª	3.9	3.8
Teenagers 12–17	3.1	—	3.2	3.0
Men 18–49	3.5	3.9	3.6	3.1
Men 50+	4.6	4.8	4.3	—
Women 18–49	4.5	4.7	4.7	4.0
Women 50+	5.0	5.0	5.0	—
All Individuals	4.1	4.7	4.1	3.6

SOURCE: A. C. Nielsen Company, National Audience Demographics Report.
ª Below sample size needed for estimate.

of college, the household in the fall of 1976 watches an average of seven hours less television per week than households with less than four years of college.

Children and Youth

Children vary very little in viewing as a function of household size (figure 3.4). This is possibly attributable to the set being on longer in larger households, giving children greater opportunity to view television. Teenagers and adults, except for women 50 and over, more markedly view for fewer hours in larger households.

Socioeconomic status is a major factor. Children in households with annual incomes of $15,000 or greater view several hours a day less than those in households with lower income. (The large amount of viewing for children in households with annual income of $10,000 to $14,999 compared to that in households with greater or less income, depicted in figure 3.4 by the unshaded bars, is a departure from data for other time periods and previous years. As a result, the shaded bars representing data from a month earlier than all the other data in this series of graphs are included because they conform to the more usual pattern. Data nowhere else in the series depart in any exceptional way from the typical.) Education of head of household, in most instances a parent, makes a great difference. Viewing was more than six hours greater in the fall of 1976 when parental educational level was less than completion of four years of college. Otherwise (and relying on the greater typicality of the shaded

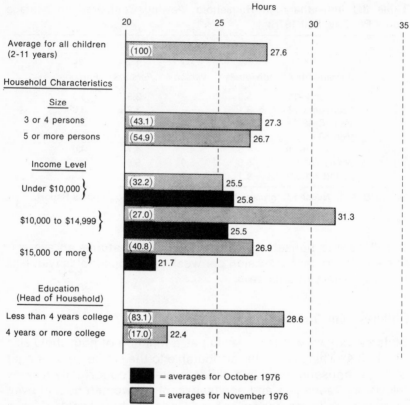

Figure 3.4. Average hours of television viewing per week for children (2–11 years) by household characteristics, fall 1976. (Figures in parentheses are percent of all children 2–11 years in a given household type. 100% = 33.93 million.)
SOURCE: A. C. Nielsen Co., National Audience Demographics Report.

bars), the most striking feature of children's viewing is its lack of variation by household characteristics.

Teenagers are the only group that averaged as few as about three hours of viewing a day in the fall of 1976. As figure 3.5 indicates, teenage viewing roughly follows the pattern for children. Viewing is inversely related to parental education, but less markedly so than for children, and the greater viewing in smaller households is accentuated. This is a trend of interest, because the lower total viewing by teenagers increases the importance of absolute differences. The overall low viewing level reflects the greater demands and attractiveness of activities and friends out-

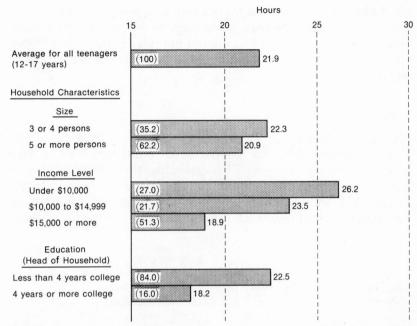

Figure 3.5. Average hours of television viewing per week for teenagers (12–17 years) by household characteristics, fall 1976. (Figures in parentheses are percent of all teenagers 12–17 years in a given household type. 100% = 24.52 million.)
SOURCE: A. C. Nielsen Co., National Audience Demographics Report.

side the home. The sharper inverse relationship between viewing and household size may reflect an adolescent desire to evade family members.

The 27 percent of all teenagers in lower income homes watch far more television than teenagers in higher income homes. The 26.2 hours a week spent watching television in the fall of 1976 is 39 percent higher than viewing in homes with incomes of $15,000 or more per year.

The other side of the teenager viewing pattern is the relatively low viewing level in affluent and educated households. About half the teenagers reside in upper-income households, and in the fall of 1976 they watched only 18.9 hours a week. The 16 percent of teenagers in higher education households watched the least total hours (18.2) of any demographic group in the data. Again, this is an indication of teenage desires and habits. The better educated, more affluent teenager has more alternative leisure-time activities and also probably devotes more time to his or her education. When television programming is not entirely to the taste of teenagers, the more affluent have both the chance and the motive to reject it.

Adults

We have already noted that women watch more than men in all types of households, that people 50 or older watch more than younger adults in all types of households, that individuals living alone or with one other person watch more than those in larger households, and that those with lower incomes and lower education watch more. Figures 3.6 through 3.9 give the details of these

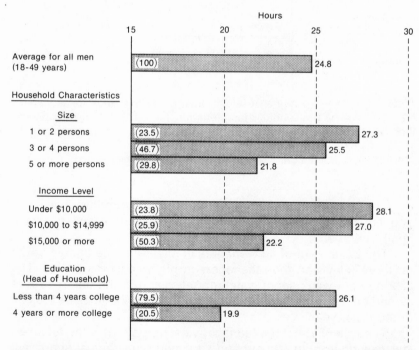

Figure 3.6. Average hours of television viewing per week for men (18–49 years) by household characteristics, fall 1976. (Figures in parentheses are percent of all men 18–49 years in a given household type. 100% = 44.25 million.)

SOURCE: A. C. Nielsen Co., National Audience Demographics Report.

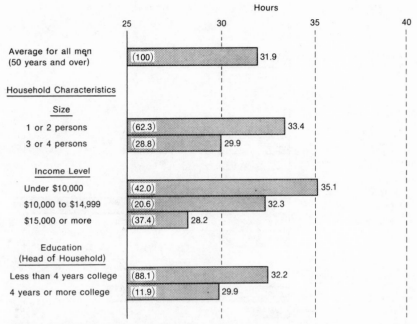

Figure 3.7. Average hours of television viewing per week for men (50 and over) by household characteristics, fall 1976. (Figures in parentheses are percent of all men 50 and over in a given household type. 100% = 23.39 million.)
SOURCE: A. C. Nielsen Co., National Audience Demographics Report.

effects for four types of adult viewers. Some details deserve mention:

The difference in amount of viewing between small and large households is greater for men than for women. For example, men 18 to 49 watched almost two more hours in the fall of 1976 when in one- or two-person households than in three- or four-person households, but women only watched one-half hour more; for persons 50 and over the pattern holds for men but not for women.

For women 18 to 49, lower income means far more than the ordinary amount of viewing. Those in households with income under $10,000 watched almost 13.5 more hours per week in the fall of 1976 than those in households with $15,000 or more in income; men watched only about an hour more.

Although both men and women of lesser education watch more (with the exception of older women), education makes more dif-

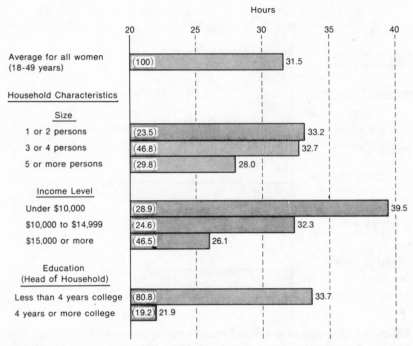

Figure 3.8. Average hours of television viewing per week for women (18–49 years) by household characteristics, fall 1976. (Figures in parentheses are percent of all women 18–49 in a given household type. 100% = 46.63 million.)

SOURCE: A. C. Nielsen Co., National Audience Demographics Report.

ference for women 18 to 49. For men 18 to 49, the difference in the fall of 1976 was about six hours, but for women about twelve hours.

Perhaps these differences reflect the impact of varying kinds of isolation. A man living alone or with one other person more frequently finds himself with little to do than a woman, for whom a certain amount of housework is the norm. Women with lower income and less education are relatively less likely than males to have become involved in activities other than housework, particularly outside the home. In these various circumstances, television may be the solution for nothing to do.

Time of Day

Not only do persons with different characteristics watch different amounts of television, they also watch at different times of the

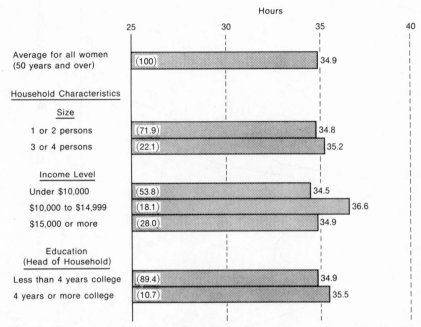

Figure 3.9. Average hours of television viewing per week for women (50 and over) by household characteristics, fall 1976. (Figures in parentheses are percent of all women 50 and over in a given household type. 100% = 28.74 million.)
SOURCE: A. C. Nielsen Co., National Audience Demographics Report.

day and on different days of the week. Figures 3.10 to 3.13 display viewing for the fall of 1976 by age and sex from 7 A.M. to 6 P.M. for weekdays and 6 P.M. to 1 A.M. for all seven days. Figure 3.14 displays Saturday and Sunday viewing prior to 6 P.M. by children versus all others.

The pattern of viewing among children reflects the rhythm of their lives and the programs that are on the air at a given time of day. Preschool children are quite likely to watch television in the morning. Between 8 and 10 A.M., more than 20 percent of all children in this age group were watching television during the average minute of the average weekday in the fall of 1976. There was a peak of nearly 24 percent between 9:30 and 10 A.M. This is a period in which older siblings are off at school, afternoon women's programs have not yet started, and content aimed at young children is on the air. Later, in the early afternoon, viewing falls off as television sets are turned to "housewife" material. Yet,

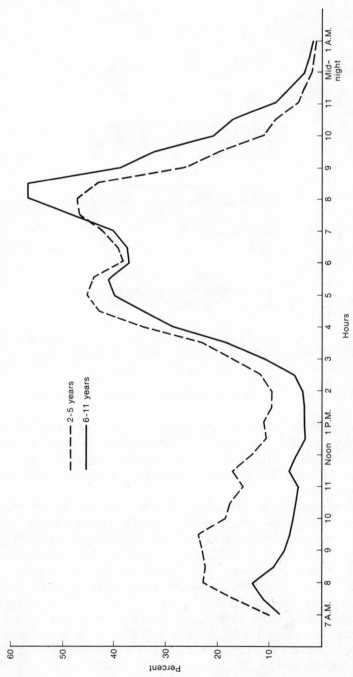

Figure 3.10. Percent children (2–5 and 6–11 years old) viewing television by time of day, fall 1976. (Monday–Friday 7 A.M. to 6 P.M.; Monday–Sunday 6 P.M. to 1 A.M.)

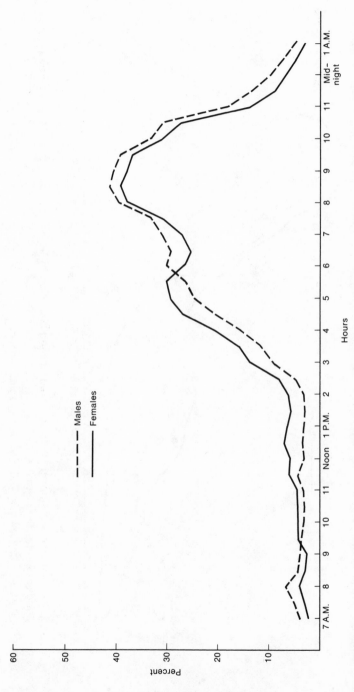

Figure 3.11. Percent male and female teenagers (12–17 years) viewing television by time of day, fall 1976. (Monday–Friday 7 A.M. to 6 P.M.; Monday–Sunday 6 P.M. to 1 A.M.)
SOURCE: A. C. Nielson Co., National Audience Demographics Report.

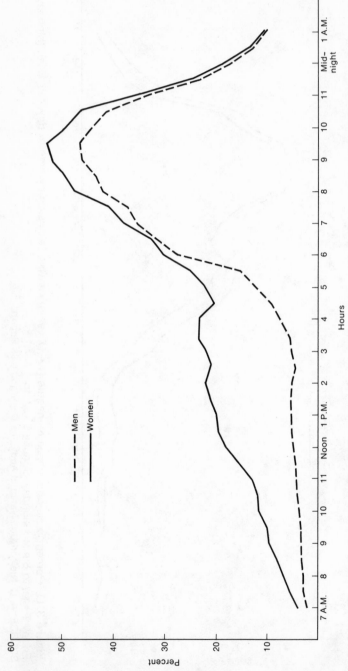

Figure 3.12. Percent men and women 18–49 years old viewing television by time of day, fall 1976. (Monday–Friday 7 A.M. to 6 P.M.; Monday–Sunday 6 P.M. to 1 A.M.)

SOURCE: A. C. Nielsen Co., National Audience Demographics Report.

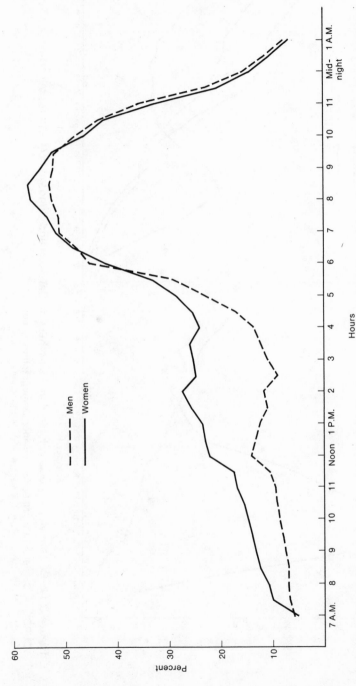

Figure 3.13. Percent men and women 50 years and over viewing television by time of day, fall 1976. (Monday–Friday A.M. to 6 P.M.; Monday–Sunday 6 P.M. to 1 A.M.).

SOURCE: A. C. Nielsen Co., National Audience Demographics Report.

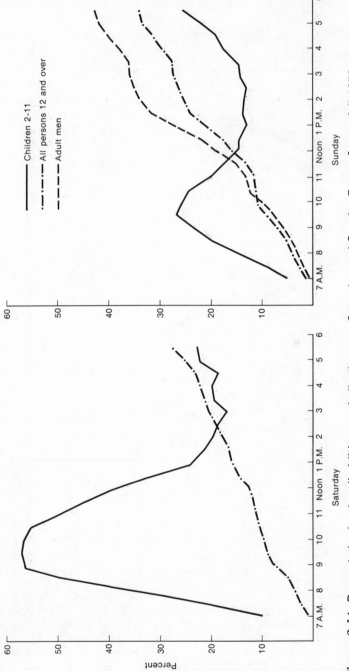

Figure 3.14. Percent viewing by all children and all others on Saturday and Sunday 7 A.M.–6 P.M., fall 1976.

SOURCE: A. C. Nielsen Co., National Audience Demographics Report.

more than 10 percent of all children from 2 to 5 in the fall of 1976 were watching television during the average minute. In the afternoon, older children return from school and broadcasters offer a mix of old cartoons, reruns of situation comedies, and other children's programs. The audience among 2 to 5 year olds climbs to a peak value between 5 and 5:30 P.M., with about 45 percent watching the average minute in the fall of 1976.

Between 6 and 7 P.M. there is a clear dinnertime dip. This does not appear in adult viewing patterns and may be due as much to aversion to early evening news as it is related to requirements of the dinner table. From 7:30 to 8 P.M. viewing climbs again but then falls off very sharply as the young children go to bed. At 8 P.M., 47 percent in the fall of 1976 were watching television; at 9 P.M., 26 percent; at 10 P.M., 11 percent.

Elementary school children are not able to watch television until school is out in the afternoon. There is some early morning viewing among 6 to 11 year olds. This probably reflects varying hours at which school begins; in some places there are split sessions, so it is possible for children to watch television before going to school.

When school is out, there is a sharp and continuous increase in viewing throughout the late afternoon. A plateau is reached from 5 to 6 P.M., when more than a third—about 40 percent in the fall of 1976—of all 6 to 11 year olds typically are watching television. There follows a dinnertime dip parallel to that for 2 to 5 year olds, after which an increasing proportion of these children turn to television. About 56 percent of all 6 to 11 year olds were watching television between 8 and 9 P.M. during the average minute in the fall of 1976, seven days a week. Between 9 and 10 P.M., the average was about 36 percent. The 6 to 11 year old audience fell below 20 percent only after 10:30 P.M.

With two exceptions, viewing habits of adolescent boys and girls (ages 12 to 17) are quite similar. The exceptions, clearly seen in figure 3.11, are the higher viewing rate for teenage girls between the end of school and dinnertime and the clear dip that appears among teenage girls but is much less pronounced among teenage boys at dinnertime. This probably reflects mealtime sex roles; girls are more likely than boys to be called into service when the family eats.

From the early morning through the end of the school day, very few teenagers watch television; we assume that very few are at home. Starting at about 2 P.M., there is an increase in teenage viewers.*

We have seen that adolescents watch fewer total hours of television than any of the other age and sex groups. They are less likely than younger children to watch in the daytime or early evening.† They are also less likely than adults to watch in the evening. The high peak of teenage viewing, from 8 to 10 P.M. typically represents about 40 percent of all teenagers watching the average television minute. Bedtime causes a rapid decline by 11 P.M. During the fall of 1976, only 16 percent were watching, compared to more than 30 percent of all adults.

Age, Sex, and the Viewing Cycle

Earlier, we saw that total viewing for adult men vs. women differed, as did viewing for people under 50 vs. those 50 and over. Figures 3.12 and 3.13 further document age and sex differences by displaying the viewing cycles that occur each day for various segments of the audience.

At any hour, women who are 18 to 49 years of age are more likely to be watching television than their male peers. The proportion watching climbs steadily to a peak between 3 and 4 P.M. Television programming over the morning and afternoon consists of situation comedies, game shows, and soap operas, with soap operas becoming more frequent in the early afternoon. The latter win a high proportion of the potential housewife audience. The degree to which soap operas are attractive to younger adult women—and, for that matter, to younger adult men—is probably much greater than the size of the television audience indicates, because many women and most men of this age are at work and do not have the opportunity to view. Viewing dips to almost 20 percent between 4 and 5 P.M. when the children seem to be controlling the set. It climbs again to a high of over 50 percent from 9 and 10 P.M. and then falls off at the end of the evening, although about one out of every seven women 18 to 49 years of age are still watching television between midnight and 1 A.M.

*The increase is less sharp than that for younger children—over a third of 2 to 11 year olds in the fall of 1976 were watching at 4:30, while about a fifth of the teenagers were watching. It is also less sharp for teenage boys, who averaged 4.5 fewer percentage points of viewership when compared with girls in the period from 2:30 to 6:00 P.M.

† More than 30 percent of the younger children are viewing television after 4:30 P.M. The same figure for teenagers is not reached until 7:30 P.P.

Most men between 18 and 49 are, of course, at work, so it is not surprising that very few of them are watching television before 5 P.M. The proportion viewing increases rapidly through the evening news hour to nearly 37 percent at 7:30 P.M. The increase then becomes less rapid, leading to a peak of about 46 percent. Throughout prime time, there is a greater proportion of female viewers; after 11 P.M., viewing by the two sexes is almost identical.

The pattern for men and women 50 years or older is quite similar to that for younger adults, except that the older people are more likely to watch and begin to watch earlier (see figure 3.13). Increasing numbers of older women turn to television as the morning progresses. By noon, in these 1976 data, more than 20 percent are watching. In fact, from noon to 11 P.M. never are fewer than 20 percent of all older women watching television. There is a slight decline in the late afternoon that probably reflects both program preferences and household activities. But then more and more join the audience until between 7 and 9:30 P.M. over half of all women 50 and older are viewing.

Viewing among both older women and older men peaks sooner and begins to decline sooner than among those younger. This has often been erroneously taken to mean that early prime-time hours are more "elderly" than later prime-time hours. It should be emphasized that until 10 P.M. for older women and 11:30 P.M. for older men, there is a higher proportion of viewers in the older group than in the younger adult group at every hour of the day.

The daily viewing cycle for older men reflects the modification by increased age of the cycle for younger adult males. There is a relatively low level of viewing throughout the working day. The level is higher than that for younger men, and it includes a small peak between noon and 2 P.M. Then, from 5:30 to 7 P.M. there is a rapid increase that parallels the increase among older women. Between 7 and 10 P.M. more than half of all men 50 and older are tuned to television. Later at night the proportion declines. However, until 11:30 P.M. there is always a higher proportion of older men than younger men watching television.

Weekend viewing from morning to early evening is of interest because school and employment are no longer factors. Figure 3.14 shows the very high proportion of children watching the average minute of television on Saturday morning. Sunday morning viewing is also relatively greater among children than among older persons, but the level is not nearly so high.

During these weekend hours there are no major differences between viewing by teenagers, younger adults, and older adults; therefore the data are pooled in figure 3.14 as "all persons 12 and older." The one age and sex difference is that weekend afternoon sports coverage—and especially Sunday football in the autumn period covered by these data—attracts a higher than average proportion of all adult men in the late afternoon.*

Audience Composition

We shall now turn these age and sex data around to construct a portrait of audience composition. So far, we have been looking at the viewing behavior of different components of the audience. Now, we shall see how each group contributes to the total audience.

The data are displayed in table 3.2.

Because there are a different number of persons in each of the age and sex groupings, the proportion of a group viewing at a particular time is not equivalent to their share of the total audience. Adults 18 to 49 years old in 1976 constituted about 45 percent of all persons over two years of age in households with television. The result is that despite the average heavier viewing by older adults, they never outnumber younger adults in the audience. Between 1 and 7:30 P.M. weekdays (two categories combined in table 3.2) there are about equal numbers of older and younger adult males, but far more younger than older adult females, with the difference largely attributable to more frequent viewing by younger adult females in the early part of the afternoon. From 4:30 to 7:30 P.M. weekdays, there are only slightly more younger than older adult females, but earlier in the day, between 10 A.M. and 4:30 P.M. (two categories combined in table 3.2), younger outnumber older adult women by a considerable margin. The most noteworthy difference during the day reflects work. There are far more female than male adults in the audience, but the difference is less for those 50 and over. Almost 45 percent of the total potential audience is viewing daily during the 8 to 11 P.M. prime-time period, almost 13 percent are children 11 years of age and under; another 10 percent are teenagers; and almost half the audience are in the younger adult category of 18 to 49 years of age.

*There is no meaningful difference between the viewing of older and younger adult men. Teenage boys watch more weekend sports coverage than their female peers but less than younger and older adult men.

Table 3.2 Composition of Television Audience by Time of Day, Fall 1976 [a] (For composition at a given time of day, read across)

| | Segments of Audience | | | | | | | | |
| Time of Day | Children | | Teen-agers | Women | | Men | | Total Viewers (in millions) | Viewers in This Time Period as Percent of Total Potential Audience |
	2–5	6–11	12–17	18–49	50 and over	18–49	50 and over		
Mon.–Fri. 7–10 A.M.	17.4	12.6	6.7	23.3	20.6	8.5	11.0	14.6	7.3
Mon.–Fri. 10 A.M.–1 P.M.	9.8	4.9	5.4	33.3	25.3	9.0	12.3	20.6	10.2
Mon.–Fri. 1–4:30 P.M.	8.0	7.5	7.6	34.6	25.0	8.0	9.4	28.8	14.3
Mon.–Fri. 4:30–7:30 P.M.	9.0	13.5	10.7	21.0	18.1	14.5	13.2	61.4	30.5
Mon.–Sun. 8–11 P.M.	3.7	8.8	10.0	25.9	16.6	21.7	13.2	89.2	44.3
Mon.–Sun. 11:30 P.M.–1 A.M.	1.0	2.9	7.4	31.5	15.5	28.0	13.6	28.4	14.1
Sat. 7 A.M.–1 P.M.	19.5	31.3	14.0	13.2	5.7	10.9	5.5	27.6	13.7
Total persons in television households									
N (in millions)	(12.8)	(21.1)	(24.5)	(46.6)	(28.7)	(44.3)	(23.4)	—	(201.5)
% of total	6.4	10.5	12.2	23.2	14.3	22.0	11.6		100.0

SOURCE: A. C. Nielsen Co., National Audience Demographics Report.
[a] Estimates represent audience size during average minute within time period.

We gain from these data a keen sense of the importance of young viewers at certain times. Weekdays between 7 and 10 A.M., about a third of the audience is under 12. The figure in the fall of 1976 was 30 percent. On Saturday mornings, the figure increases dramatically. In the fall of 1976, about half of all children under 12 were viewing. At the same time, we do not escape from the realization that because the evening audience is so huge the relatively small audience share of those under 12, about 13 percent of those viewing, represents a very large number of persons—about 11 million between 8 and 11 P.M. weekdays and Saturday and Sunday.

Programs and Audiences

The popularity of various types of programs and as a result their frequency in network television schedules has varied over the history of American television. Variety programs, evening quiz and game shows, and westerns have declined in importance; evening quiz and game shows and westerns became at least temporarily extinct or near-extinct in the 1970s. Quiz and game shows, of course, continue in the hour immediately before network prime time, because they are among the more popular of syndicated programs available to local stations. General drama was in decline, but revived in the mid-1970s by the dramatization in miniseries of such popular novels as *Rich Man, Poor Man* and *The Captains and the Kings.* This concept of high-quality serialization with a finite end probably reached its apotheosis in the dramatization on ABC early in 1977 of Alex Haley's *Roots,* which drew the largest audience in television history. Evening situation comedies have risen and fallen in number, but by the mid-1970s were more frequent than ever. Soap operas, daytime game shows, evening news, weekend sports, and weekend children's programs have become staples of programming outside of prime time. Evening suspense and mystery programs, like situation comedies, have risen and fallen in number. They have been very frequent in the late 1950s and early 1960s, and again in the 1970s. Feature films first became prominent in prime time in the 1967–1968 season, and since have been a regular component of evening programing.

Figure 3.15 uses Nielsen ratings to describe the average audience for different types of network programs. Audience composition varies widely. Although these ratings have been largely stable over the years, there has obviously been some volatility attributa-

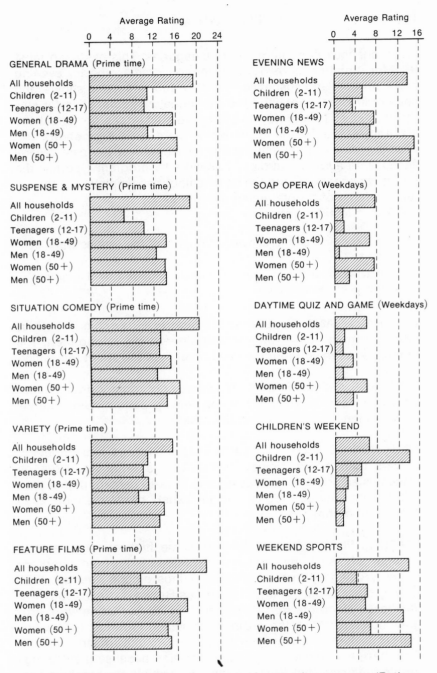

Figure 3.15. Average ratings for types of network programs. (Ratings = Percent total potential audience tuned to a particular program.)

SOURCE: A. C. Nielsen Co., National Audience Demographics Report.

ble to changes in content within categories. This has been most true for situation comedy and general drama; sports, evening news, mystery and suspense, weekday quiz and game shows, and soap operas have retained their essential characteristics for several decades. This minor long-term volatility does not affect the accuracy of the ratings for depicting the audience for an era and probably only slightly distorts the depiction over the past several decades. In addition, audience analysis by program type has the inherent appeal of using the same categories employed in the actual reaching of programming decisions.

Two questions can be posed:

What distinguishes the audience for each of the various types of programs?

What types of programs are particularly preferred by the various segments of the audience?

GENERAL DRAMA. General drama programs have higher ratings among women—both younger and older—than among men. The ratings between younger men and older men are about the same.

SUSPENSE AND MYSTERY. Suspense and mystery dramas conform more closely to the general viewing pattern. Older adults watch slightly more than younger adults.

SITUATION COMEDY AND VARIETY. Females are more frequent viewers than males; however, the average rating for situation comedies among older adults is more than 10 percent higher than it is among younger adults, and for variety programs more than 30 percent higher.

FEATURE FILMS. Feature films have the highest rating among younger adults of any category of prime-time programs and are the only category that has higher ratings among younger than among older adults. The journalist Les Brown, in *Television: The Business Behind the Box* (1971), astutely notes that network programmers are not in the business of selling products to viewers. Their business is the selling of viewers to advertisers. Feature films have become prominent on television because their ratings profile indicates that they are the best vehicle for reaching that principal consumer population—younger adults of both sexes. For this purpose, variety programs are least attractive. General drama, situation comedy, and suspense and mystery all attract substantial portions of the younger adult audience, but in each case the rating is lower than for feature films and markedly so for men.

EVENING NEWS. Commercials for pills, tonics, and denture adhesives dominate the advertising for network evening news. Where are the soft drink and sporty car ads? Figure 3.15 provides the answer. Although network evening news achieves respectable "household" ratings, we find that only about 7 percent of younger adults view the average minute, compared to a figure more than doublt that for older adults. In fact, ratings among older adults are about the same for the average minute of the evening news as they are for the various prime-time program types.

SOAP OPERAS. It is not surprising to find that daytime viewing of soap operas and quiz and game shows is highest among women. Younger and older women have about the same likelihood of watching soap operas while the older women are much more likely to be interested in the daytime quiz and game programs.

These profiles clarify some of the aspects of figures 3.12 and 3.13. Differences between younger and older adults in the early evening period can be better understood in light of the finding that older viewers are far more likely to watch evening news programs. Viewing by more older than younger adults in early prime time and a narrower difference in late prime time is associated with the scheduling of situation comedies and variety programs earlier than suspense and mystery dramas and feature films. Similarly, the greater proportion viewing early in the day and the earlier peak in viewing among older women is associated with the generally earlier scheduling of game shows than soap operas, which draw a much larger proportion of younger women.

PREFERENCES. The various segments obviously have different preferences. Children are most likely to watch the children's weekend schedule. However, the proportions of 2 to 11 year olds watching situation comedies, general drama, and variety programs are also relatively high. Children are less likely to be watching suspense and mystery programs, feature films, news, and sports.

The available data allow analysis of network programs only. Figure 3.10 indicated that children do a considerable amount of viewing between the end of school and the start of the evening news. During this period they are watching locally originated materials primarily—situation comedy and action drama and cartoon reruns.

Among the program types for which we have data, the trend seems to be a leveling of children's ratings across program types. Children's viewing of situation comedy is still the highest rated among prime-time programs, with about 13 percent of the potential audience viewing. General drama and variety programs are second with about 11 percent.

Teenagers have highest prime-time rating figures for situation comedy and feature films and lowest viewing for the average minute for variety programs, with the other three types of programs falling between these. In 1973, general drama was highest rated and variety was lowest rated.

Younger women are more likely to be watching feature films and dramas than variety programs. Older women are most frequently found watching situation comedies and dramas. They are also frequent viewers of feature films, evening news, and suspense and mystery. Variety programs attract the lowest prime-time proportion of women 50 and over.

Feature films, suspense and mystery programs, and sports are seen by a higher proportion of younger men than any other type of program. Since 1973 there has been an increase in younger male audience for feature films. Sports and suspense and mystery viewing have remained about the same. Highest ratings for older men are for feature films; then come situation comedy, suspense and mystery, evening news, weekend sports, and general drama. Lowest ratings are for variety programs.

Public Television

Proportionately, the audience for public television is so small that a description of the viewing behavior of the American people would not be seriously distorted were no mention of it made. In 1975, public television on the VHF channels receivable by all television sets in two major television markets, New York and Chicago, had an average of only 3 percent of the audience viewing during evening hours and 3 and 4 percent, respectively, of the daytime audience (NBC, 1976). These estimates of audience share

are similar to the average of 1.5 percent of television households found to be tuned in during the evening in November of 1974 in five major markets where public television was available on VHF (Katzman and Farr, 1975). In Los Angeles in 1975, public television on the less accessible UHF channel had an average of 2 percent of the audience during the evening and under 1 percent of the daytime audience (NBC, 1976). Nationally, it is estimated that in 1975 public television attracted an average of less than 2 percent of the total audience viewing during the evening (NBC, 1976).

Despite the proportionate smallness of the public television audience, it cannot be said to be small in absolute numbers. Two percent of the typical average fall commercial television audience during the evening in the late 1970s is about 1.8 million persons. Furthermore, when cumulative figures representing viewing one or more times over an extended period are substituted for average viewing during a minute or hour of a particular day, it becomes clear that public television attracts a sizeable proportion of the audience. For example, in a four-week period in 1974 such a cumulative audience totaled 32 million households (Lyle, 1975).

The available audience for public television is restricted by problems of transmission and reception. There are sizable areas of the West and Midwest where no public television signals penetrate. In addition, about 65 percent of the 264 public television stations in 1976 were UHF, including the stations in 10 of the top 25 television markets, which means that many households within their signal areas could not receive them. UHF was not required on U.S. television sets until 1964. It is variously estimated that in the mid-1970s between 80 percent (Lyle, 1975) and 90 percent (NBC, 1976) of U.S. households could receive public television signals. However, any figure based on transmission coverage and UHF capability in the home is in practical terms an overestimate, because UHF reception in some homes within a transmission area will be marginal, particularly in the typical circumstance in which VHF stations are also operating (Rubin, 1974).

Public television also differs in other ways from commercial television outside of its financial support, which comes from subsidies and contributions from the government, private foundations, and the public rather than from the sale of time to advertisers. Its stations vary considerably in their programming, with some largely devoted to educational content that has limited community appeal. In addition, the average hours of broadcasting

The Audience

per week in 1975 was 75 compared to 126 for commercial stations (NBC, 1976). These circumstances further delimit public television's capability to attract a large audience.

The viewing of public television is positively related to household income and the education and occupational status of the head of household (tables 3.3 and 3.4). This relationship between viewing and socioeconomic status is the reverse of that for commercial television. Although the ability to receive public television—a function of residence in or near an urban center and possession of a newer, UHF-equipped set—historically has been positively related to socioeconomic status, the relationship between viewing and status occurs when accessibility of public television is equivalent (table 3.4). The relationship would appear to depend largely on the greater appeal of the content of public television to those of higher socioeconomic status.

As we shall see in the next chapter, this deviation from the pattern for commercial television in the United States parallels that occurring in some societies with television systems that do not attempt to meet the entertainment desires of the mass audience. This suggests that the U.S. pattern might not be sharply al-

Table 3.3 Viewing of Public Television over Four Weeks (Major evening programs distributed by the Public Broadcasting Service,[a] January 28–February 24, 1974)

	Audience Cumulative (%)	Average Number of 77 Programs Watched
Total U.S. television households	31.4	3.3
Occupation of head of household		
Not in labor force	27.1	3.8
Blue collar	26.4	2.7
Professional and white collar	38.9	3.5
Education of head of household		
3 years high school or less	25.1	2.4
4 years high school	26.2	3.1
1 or more years college	42.8	3.9
Working woman	30.4	2.9
Household income		
Under $5000	19.7	3.5
$5000–$9999	27.5	3.4
$10,000–$14,999	37.4	3.2
$15,000 and over	40.5	3.4

SOURCE: J. Lyle. 1975. *The people look at public television 1974.* Washington, D.C.: Corporation for Public Broadcasting.

[a] Not equivalent to all public television.

Table 3.4 Reception and Viewing of Public Television by Education
(Base N = 100%)

	Percent Able to Receive Public Television (in 1970)	Percent of Those Able To Receive Public Television Who Watched Once a Week (in 1970)
Education		
Grade school	27 (345)	24 (94)
High school	51 (1011)	35 (518)
College	63 (480)	49 (304)

SOURCE: Adapted from R. T. Bower. 1973. *Television and the Public.* New York: Holt, Rinehart and Winston, 1973.

tered, although certainly total viewing would grossly increase, if public television were the only television available.

Public television also differs from commercial television in the distribution of its audience across the broadcast schedule. A sizable proportion of public television viewing occurs outside of prime time because of the drawing power of such children's programs as *Sesame Street, The Electric Company,* and *Mister Rogers' Neighborhood.* For example, nationally during a week late in 1973 about half of the 31 percent of all television households who tuned to public television at least once did so during the day (Katzman and Farr, 1975).

Nevertheless, the public television audience during the evening has been increasing. The cumulative figure for a week increased from 13 percent in 1966 to 32 percent in 1975 of the total audience for television (NBC, 1976). A series of special Nielsen studies indicate that between 1970–1971 and 1973–1974, the proportion viewing some evening public television increased by 50 percent (Lyle, 1975). This trend is probably attributable in large part to the increasing emphasis of public television on entertainment, exemplified by such popular evening programs as *Jennie, Monty Python,* and "Masterpiece Theater" productions of *Upstairs, Downstairs* and the Lord Peter Wimsey mystery stories.

The inverse relationship between socioeconomic status and viewing does not mean that public television does not draw a substantial number of viewers from lower socioeconomic and minority groups. In a four-week period in 1975, major evening programs were viewed by one out of five households with an annual income of $5000 or less and one out of four households in which the education of the head of household was three years or less of high school (Lyle, 1975). These represent a considerable degree of attention, although far less than the approximately 40 percent for households with incomes of $10,000 or more and the approximately 37 percent for households where the education of head of household was four years of high school or greater.

A series of studies in 1974 in Boston, Dallas–Fort Worth, Denver, Los Angeles, New York, and Washington, D.C., did not find marked differences in the proportions of blacks, Hispanics, and whites in the viewing of public television (Lyle, 1975). However, this apparent equivalence of attraction is attributable to the viewing of children's programs in minority households. The principal factor has been *Sesame Street*. A series of studies indicate that the proportion of black children viewing *Sesame Street* is about equal to and certainly not markedly less than the proportion of white children (Cook et al., 1975; Lyle, 1975). Data from black households in four major markets—Chicago, Detroit, Philadelphia, and Washington, D.C.—indicate that with some exceptions viewing by black households is entirely accounted for by children's programs. The role of children in altering the socioeconomic pattern of viewing is illustrated by a 1974 study of Nashville, in which education of head of household made little difference when there were children of preschool or elementary age, but made an enormous difference (with greater education associated with greater likelihood of viewing) where there were no children of these ages (Lyle, 1975).

The proportionate smallness of the public television audience at any given moment somewhat beclouds the service provided by public television because the viewers attracted over an extended period of time are ignored. In table 3.3, we see that about a third of all households over a four-week period in early 1974 viewed one or more of the major evening programs, with three the average number. The evening figure the previous fall was about the same and rose to about 50 percent when daytime programming is included (Lyle, 1975). The import of these audience estimates is that for a substantial portion of viewers public television at one time or another offers programming preferred over that available on commercial television.

It is likely that the trend toward a larger audience for public television will continue. The federal Broadcast Financing Act of 1976 appears to assure substantial and increasing funding through 1981. A network study of the prospects for public broadcasting predicts that it will increasingly approximate a fourth network, with a number of high-quality programs with fairly broad appeal, and that its national average prime-time share of the audience conceivably could increase from the 2 percent of 1975 to 4 or 5 percent by 1980 (NBC, 1976). What this will portend for the composition of its audience is something only the future will reveal, but we suspect that increased size will not change the pattern as long as public television does not pursue a mass audience.

We conclude that:

Public television constitutes a quantitatively small but distinctive and growing portion of the American public's television experience.

The size and character of the audience for public television is primarily the function of its content and not of the limits imposed on the available audience. Limiting factors such as nonuniversal transmission or the bias toward households of upper socioeconomic status (resulting from the necessity in some areas of owning a set of UHF capability) play some small part.

Public television as a medium is not inherently less acceptable to the well-educated and thus more print-oriented segments of the public than to those with less education, as the inverse relationship for commercial television between viewing and socioeconomic status is reversed for public television.

News and Violence

Television News

We found that network evening news fails to match the appeal of the five major Nielsen entertainment categories—general drama, suspense and mystery, situation comedy, variety, and feature films. We now take a closer look at the audience for television news.

Israel and Robinson (1972), on the basis of television viewing diaries collected from a national probability sample of about 7000 during the 1969–1970 season, report in regard to heavy or more-frequent-than-ordinary network evening news viewing:

Regular news viewers are disproportionately drawn from the elderly, regardless of education or amount of total viewing.
Regular news viewing is curvilinearly related to education, with those least and most educated viewing most.
Regular news viewing is higher among males than females and is especially high among college-educated blacks.

J. P. Robinson (1971), on the basis of the same data, reports that more than half of the adult population did not watch a single national evening news program in a two-week period. The impression this leaves is in startling contrast to the one given by the often-cited finding that 65 percent of Americans report getting most of their news from "television" (Roper, 1975).

This apparent discrepancy can be explained, first, by the confinement of the Robinson analysis to *network* evening news, whereas Roper's 65 percent figure includes local news as well. The contrast is entirely consistent with findings that local news often outdraws network news; for example, in a Corporation for Public Broadcasting study (Katzman, 1974), four out of five homes over a week had seen a local newscast but only half had seen a network newscast. Second, the degree to which television is said to be a major source depends upon whether the referent is national or local events. Television's standing is highest for national news, which is the referent in the case of the 65 percent.

We conclude:

There is a regular audience for network evening news—drawn disproportionately from the elderly, persons with relatively high and low education, males, and college-educated blacks.

Network evening news reaches far fewer persons than one would suppose from the public's acclaim of television as a news source, which is inflated by not distinguishing between network and local news and by employing a referent—national news—which evokes acclaim for "television."

Television Violence

Israel and Robinson (1972), using such national television diary data for three seasons ending in 1969–1970, also analyze the makeup of the regular audience for violent television drama. Who are the heavy viewers of violence? We find that when total viewing, which would affect exposure to violence because violence is so prevalent, is controlled:

Regular viewing of violence is inversely related to education and income—those poorer and less educated are more likely to be regular viewers of violence.

Regular viewing of violence is high for those over 50, blacks, and those 18 to 24 who are high-school dropouts.

Male and female heavy viewers of violence are alike, except that race—not education and income—is the major predictor of regular viewing of violence by women.

Personal Attributes and Viewing

There is some evidence that various permanent or transient personal attributes of a nondemographic nature are related to both the amount and type of programs viewed. The attributes that have received the principal amount of attention so far are mental ability, alienation, and anxiety.

Several studies at different times and involving quite unlike samples of young persons have found an inverse relationship between amount of viewing and mental ability (Lefkowitz et al., 1972; McLeod, Atkin, and Chaffee, 1972a; Schramm, Lyle, and Parker, 1961). Comparisons between similar samples a decade apart suggest that such a relationship may be disappearing (Lyle and Hoffman, 1972a). If so, this is another example of the increasingly uniform accommodation to television by all individuals. Whether there has been any relationship between viewing and mental ability among adults is moot.

Several studies investigate the possibility of a relationship between feelings of alienation and amount of viewing. The concept, which refers to estrangement from self or others, has been variously measured. J. P. Robinson (1972c) reports that, in a national sample of adults, alienation and low self-conception were positively related to viewing and controlling for 12 other variables, such as education, sex, or race; various indices of media consumption weakened but did not eliminate the relationships. McLeod, Ward and Tancill (1965) found statistically significant correlations between amount of viewing and age (positive), occupational status (inverse), and education (inverse), but not with alienation. Sargent and Stempel (1968) found that persons on poverty relief rolls watched much more television than a sample of the general public, but high alienation was associated with less likelihood of being a heavy viewer and greater television news viewing. These studies give the impression that any relationship that may exist between alienation and television viewing is complex and subtle.

The possibility of relationships between anxiety, stress, and social coping and television viewing have also been explored. Hazard (1967) found high anxiety positively related to choice of fantasy in television viewing. Pearlin (1959) found personal stress positively related to amount of "escapist" programming viewed. D. K. Davis (1974) found that persons with difficulties in personal adjustment were more likely to report using television as a distraction or as a replacement for interaction with others.

A plausible explanation for such relationships is that television provides relief from psychological discomfort. The belief that television is the medium best-suited for escape is consistent with a finding that television programs are perceived as more likely than magazines to provide immediate gratification (Rees, 1967). However, there is no justification for assuming such a process. Mere viewing of fantasy does not ensure that escape is the motive; entertainment and diversion might also be responsible.

We were made particularly cautious by the finding that among children television is not at all their typical recourse when in states of personal discomfort and unhappiness. At these times solitude, games, reading, and particularly listening to music are preferred; but television is very popular, especially among younger children, for entertainment and diversion (Lyle and Hoffman, 1972a). It is also plausible that discomfort may lead to unoccupied time, and television is the most convenient way to fill it. Conversely, it is conceivable that the observed relationships reflect the nurturing by television of such discomfort.

The possible relationships between personal attributes of a nondemographic character and television viewing have remained largely unexplored. Those that have received attention have been examined to only a modest degree. Our conclusions reflect ignorance more than knowledge:

> Personal attributes and the amount and kind of television viewed may be related, but the nature, degree, and cause of such relationships are uncertain.
> The much clearer relationships to television behavior that have been found for demographic variables such as income, education, age, and race probably reflect the truly superior predictive power of these variables; but they also partly reflect the fact that these attri-

butes do not contain those problems of definition and measurement that leave the personality variables weak and sometimes conjectural.

Although for some people television may reduce anxiety, deliver relief from feelings of alienation, and offer distraction from coping with life, there is no very convincing evidence that such effects occur in any consistent way for any sizable segment of the audience.

The Black Audience

The evidence is that the viewing patterns of blacks differ from those of whites, and that the differences are *not* wholly explained by differences in income or education. We find that:

Black households watch more television, especially during the day.
Black viewers prefer different programs.

Three of the strongest patterns of viewing among the total population have been found to be reversed among blacks. Bogart (1972b) reports on a large survey, which included over 1400 nonwhites. Among whites, the older, less educated, and lower income groups were more likely to watch television; among blacks, the younger adults, those with more education, and those in higher income homes watched more television (table 3.5). This departure by blacks from the demographics found among whites in regard to television is consistent with the data reported by Bower (1973) for his national sample of 2000 adults, who also presents convincing evidence that blacks, as we discuss in some detail later (chapter 6), are much more likely to be "superfans" of television in the intensity of their expressions of liking for the medium than are whites.

Blacks as a group also differ from the white majority in their program preferences. The data available for scrutiny make that much clear, but they do not isolate the degree to which this is attributable to socioeconomic rather than ethnic differences. Such ambiguities should be expected when the shifts in programming make it difficult to distinguish between continuity and change in viewer tastes.

There is no doubt that blacks of all ages prefer programs featuring black performers. Beyond this fact, the element at the heart

Table 3.5 Average Hours Per Week of Prime-Time Television Viewing by Race

	Whites (hours)	Estimated Base N	Blacks (hours)	Estimated Base N
Age				
18–34	8.9	4486	10.4	563
35–49	9.3	4216	9.1	420
50 and over	10.2	5160	8.0	477
Income				
$10,000 and over	8.9	7183	10.0	213
$5,000–$9,999	9.7	4336	9.5	523.
Less than $5,000	10.1	2342	8.8	725
Education				
Some college or more	8.1	5336	8.5	188
High school graduate	9.8	4659	11.2	321
Less than high school	10.1	3866	8.7	952

SOURCE: Adapted from L. Bogart. 1972b. Negro and white media exposure: New evidence. *Journalism Quarterly,* 49, 15–21.

NOTE: Data are based on special analysis of data from 1970 W. R. Simmons National Study of Media Audience. Base N's are estimates—original data was weighted for analysis; therefore percentages apply to adjusted figures, not to actual number of interviews.

of the differences that exist between the black and white audiences is not so clear. The substantial correlation between favorite programs for adult whites and blacks sharing in low socioeconomic status (Greenberg and Dervin, 1970) suggests that a sizable portion of the differences are attributable to the larger proportion of low-income persons in the black population, while the absence of a near-perfect correlation, in conjunction with the differences in viewing and attitudes for black and white groups similar in education and income (Bower, 1973; Bogart, 1972b), suggests that ethnicity is also partly responsible. When we examine adolescents and children, we become more convinced of ethnic differences, for here socioeconomic status seems to divide white tastes while leaving black tastes largely unaffected (Greenberg and Dervin, 1970).

Two sets of data collected about a decade apart suggest some consistency in black-white differences. Carey (1966) reports on two national samples of 5000 families, of which 10 percent were black. The results for the fall of 1963 are representative. When programs were ranked by audience size, there were four that were in the top ten among both races (*Perry Mason, The*

Nurses, Red Skelton, and *Ed Sullivan*). The remainder of the top ten among blacks included another variety program, a movie series, and four action/adventure series that did *not* feature family units. The remainder of the top ten among whites includes three situation comedies featuring families, two westerns featuring families, and one western not built around a family. A special A. C. Nielsen report on the black audience during the first quarter of 1974 provides data perhaps made less opaque by the dust of time. Again, there were four programs that were in the top ten for both races (*All in the Family, MASH, Sanford and Son,* and *Streets of San Francisco*). The remainder of the top ten among blacks (eight programs because of ties) included two situation comedies featuring blacks, two variety programs featuring blacks, and four action/adventure programs that did not feature family units. Among whites, the remainder of the top ten included three situation comedies that did not feature blacks, a drama series featuring a family (*The Waltons*), a medical series with a strong family appeal (*Marcus Welby, M.D.*), and a variety program with a white host. These data would lead us to conclude that the black audience, besides preferring black performers, has a greater preference for action/adventure series, and especially those emphasizing singular heroes or avoiding family connotations, and a lower preference for situation comedy and programs featuring family units. However, when we focus more narrowly on younger black viewers we are forced to reshape this conclusion.

We were ready to conclude that blacks are less likely than whites to enjoy programs that center on the activities of a family, such as *The Waltons* or *Bonanza.* However, young blacks actually have a higher preference than their white peers for such programs.

Two samples are involved. B. S. Greenberg and Dervin (1970) and Surlin and Dominick (1970) analyze data from the same sample of about 300 tenth- and eleventh-grade northern teenagers. Fletcher (1969) analyzes the data from a sample of about 460 sixth- to twelfth-grade southern teenagers. Table 3.6 shows the principal findings. When family income is examined, with the influence of race eliminated, poor youngsters have a higher preference for "family"-type programs than higher-income whites. When poor blacks and whites are compared, the blacks have the higher preference. Of course, because the proportion of poor blacks is much higher than whites, black teenagers as a group have much stronger preference for such content.

Table 3.6 Race, Income, and Preference for Family-Type Programs

	Percent Naming One or More Family-Type Programs As a Favorite
White Teen-agers (N)	
Low income family (122)	51
Middle income family (93)	19
Low Income Teen-agers (N)	
Blacks (84)	65
Whites (122)	51

SOURCE: Adapted from S. H. Surlin and J. R. Dominick. 1970. Television's function as a "third parent" for black and white teen-agers. *Journal of Broadcasting,* 15, 55–64.

Why? We are inclined to concur with the interpretation of Surlin and Dominick that the disadvantaged youths are using television to learn about family relationships not present in their own lives. In any case, it is clear that contrary findings on blacks' preference for programs featuring family units are attributable to differences between adult and teenage blacks.

The Public's Evaluation of Television

There have been numerous highly vocal complaints from individuals and organizations about the performance of American television throughout its history. The targets have included the amount and quality of commercials, the portrayal of racial and sexual stereotypes, the exclusion minorities from entertainment programs, the quantity of violence in television drama, the quality of programming for children, and the fairness of network news. Nevertheless, the public as a whole has expressed high esteem for television, although in certain instances and in regard to certain topics there has been considerable dissatisfaction; and television at the beginning of the 1970s was held in less esteem than at the beginning of the 1960s.

Three sources inform us of public attitudes toward the medium. The first is Steiner's 1960 national survey; the second is Bower's similar 1970 survey (Steiner, 1963; Bower, 1973). Steiner and Bower both interviewed a representative sample of about

Table 3.7 Shift in Public Perceptions of Television

	Adult Responses on Six-Point Scale			
	Percent in Three "Favorable" Positions		Percent in "Most Favorable" Position	
"Television is Generally":	*1960*	*1970*	*1960*	*1970*
Lots of variety/all the same	70	69	35	28
On everybody's mind/nobody cares much	79	68	33	21
Getting better/getting worse	68	54	25	16
Keeps changing/stays the same	62	64	23	22
Serious/playful	47	50	8	7
Too "highbrow"/too "simple-minded"	36	35	4	3
Relaxing/upsetting	83	83	43	33
Interesting/uninteresting	82	78	42	31
For me/not for me	76	71	41	27
Important/unimportant	77	73	39	30
Informative/not informative	84	85	39	35
Lots of fun/not much fun	77	73	32	22
Exciting/dull	77	71	30	19
Wonderful/terrible	77	70	28	19
Imaginative/no imagination	75	72	26	19
In good taste/in bad taste	76	70	24	18
Generally excellent/generally bad	73	69	22	15

SOURCE: Adapted from R. T. Bower. 1973. *Television and the Public.* New York: Holt, Rinehart and Winston.

2000 adults, supplemented by diary data on viewing for a smaller sample representing a particular community. Bower repeated about a third of the questions from Steiner's study, producing data on shifts in attitudes. The third is a series of nine surveys over the 15 years between 1959 and 1974 conducted by The Roper Organization, Inc. (1975).

Table 3.7 summarizes the data on perceptions and shifts in perceptions. The first two columns show the overwhelming tendency at both points in time to evaluate television favorably. The two columns at the right indicate that degree of favorability has declined.* An adequate summary is given by Bower:

* In regard to general favorability, the data indicate that wherever a scale measuring perceptions was clearly evaluative, a large majority rated television on the positive side of the scale. In regard to the decreased degree of favorability, the data show that the proportion choosing the most favorable position on these scales has declined.

> Compared to ten years ago, television is now *less* exciting, *less* interesting, *less* wonderful, *less* everything good. . . . People are not leaping in droves from a feeling that television is "wonderful" to a feeling that it is "terrible." They are merely slipping down the scale a bit from a quite high evaluation to a somewhat lower one.

Bower has added the scores of the seven more clearly evaluative scales to create an overall public rating of television's performance.*

In 1960, the mean score was 24.3. By 1970, it had fallen to 22.3. Although Bower presents a complex analysis of differences in attitudes toward television among different demographic groups, the results are fairly straightforward and consistent at both times:

> Blacks have a more favorable response to the medium than whites.
>
> People with a higher level of education have less favorable attitudes toward the medium than people with a lower level of education.
>
> Adults over 50 and under 30 have more favorable attitudes than those between 30 and 50 years old.

The decline in favorability has been general across demographic categories: men and women, grade-school educated and high-school educated, people over 60 and people under 30—all were less likely to give an extremely favorable rating to television in 1970 than in 1960. Despite this shift, television remains in fairly high esteem.

Beliefs about the desirability of television viewing were measured by the question, "Do you think that you spend too much time watching television or would you say that you don't have a chance to see as much as you would really like to see?" In 1960, 26 percent said they missed things, whereas only 18 percent said they spent too much time viewing; in 1970, the figures were 21 percent for each group. People with more education were more likely to say they watched too much in both years. However, the bulk of the shift is attributable to a fall in television's standing among those with a grade-school education. In 1960, 34 percent said they didn't have a chance to see as much as they wanted,

---

*The seven scales were: exciting/dull; important/unimportant; generally excellent/generally bad; in good taste/in bad taste; interesting/uninteresting; wonderful/terrible; for me/not for me.

and only 9 percent said they watched too much. In 1970, the figures were 20 percent and 14 percent.

To investigate motives for viewing, respondents were presented with 15 alternative "reasons" and asked whether they usually, occasionally, rarely, or never viewed for each particular reason. There is remarkably little change over the decade. Table 3.8 summarizes the proportion of "usually" responses for the five most frequently cited reasons.

Table 3.8 Motives for Viewing

Reason	Percent Adults Saying They "Usually" Watch for a Given Reason	
	1960	1970
To see a specific program I enjoy very much	80	81
Because it's a pleasant way to spend an evening	55	41
To see a special program I've heard a lot about	54	50
Because I feel like watching television	50	46
Because I think I can learn something	36	34

SOURCE: Adapted from R. T. Bower. 1973. *Television and the Public.* New York: Holt, Rinehart and Winston.

People are saying that they watch to see particular programs (items 1 and 3), for general enjoyment (items 2 and 4), and, less frequently, to learn something (item 5). Motives have remained stable with the exception of the selection of television as a pleasant way to spend an evening (item 2), where the decline marks the medium's progress from being special to becoming ordinary. The other ten reasons for watching, which include to be sociable, to escape, and for background noise, are mentioned far less frequently.

Between 1960 and 1970, the average of the proportion of programs "you generally watch" said to be "extremely enjoyable" increased from 44 to 50 percent. This contrasts with the decline in favorability toward the medium. It makes sense when we also note that an increasing proportion of programs was found to be "disappointing."

We conclude that:

Motives for viewing have not changed, but people are watching more.

Despite watching more, attitudes toward television have become less favorable.

The anomaly is explained by the public's greater selectivity—people have increased both in their pleasure with what they want to watch and their readiness to dislike a program. The public's rating of television is unarguably favorable.

As we report in some detail later (chapter 7), the public expresses some dissatisfaction over television advertising, but the proportion concurring that there are too many commercials—about three-fourths—is about the same as the proportion agreeing that commercials are a "fair price" for entertainment; there is no evidence of great or deep hostility to television advertising. About half said that television was harmful to children because they "see things they shouldn't," with about a third of the objections concerning exposure to violence and the rest focusing on issues of morality, such as sexual suggestiveness, "bad" language, portrayals of drinking and smoking, treatment of "adult" themes, teaching of "wrong values," and the like. The concern over violence is similar to the 43 percent in another national sample at about the same time (LoSciuto, 1972) who agreed that there was too much violence on television. Public anxiety about television violence has not abated, for in 1977 a Roper poll reported that about 40 percent of American adults believe that seeing "too much fighting and other kinds of violent action" on television is a principal cause of "some children being more aggressive and abusive than they should be" (*Television Digest,* 1977).

Studies conducted in two California cities for the Corporation for Public Broadcasting compare public concern over five aspects of television (Katzman, 1974; Katzman and Lasselle, 1974). The results are summarized in table 3.9.

In one city, people were more concerned with the number of commercials than they were with the amount of violence; in the other, the trend was reversed. In both cases, violence and the number of commercials were most frequently seen as "very serious problems," with news bias, sex and language problems, and children's programming far behind.

When Steiner and Bower asked people whether children are better off with television or better off without television, a great majority replied that children are better off *with* the medium. In fact, the proportion increased from 70 percent in 1960 to 76 percent in 1970 and parents (79 percent) were even more likely than nonparents (72 percent) to say that children were better off with television. The 1970 data indicate that, among nonparents and

Table 3.9 Public Concern over Five Aspects of Television ("Do you think that _____ is a very serious problem, a somewhat serious problem, or not a serious problem?")

Aspect of Television:	Percent Saying "Very serious problem"	
	San Jose (N = 320)	Sacramento (N = 388)
The number of commercials on television	35	34
The amount of violence on television	29	40
The amount of bias in television news coverage	17	21
The amount of sex, suggestiveness, and bad language on television	16	30
The quality of children's programs on television	16	16

SOURCE: Adapted from N. I. Katzman. 1974. *Community Survey, Sacramento, California.* Washington, D.C.: Corporation for Public Broadcasting, and N. I. Katzman and S. Lasselle. 1974. *Community Survey, San Jose, California.* Washington, D.C.: Corporation for Public Broadcasting.

parents, those with more education are somewhat *more* likely to say that when everything is taken into consideration children are better off with television than they would be without it. Given the known complexity of attitudes, it is not hard to reconcile this with the finding, reported earlier, that education is inversely related to holding favorable attitudes toward television. We cautiously interpret it as reflecting the greater ability of the better educated to accept change and their lesser inclination to see a threat in increased access to information.

When people are asked to compare the major mass communication media, television comes out far ahead of the others. The data are summarized in table 3.10. It is said to be most entertaining, to present things most intelligently, to be most educational, to do the most for the public, to create the most interest in new things, and it is the medium that people would most want to keep if they had to choose only one. Such responses have increased since 1960.

The sole negative trend is the frequency with which television is cited as the medium that is getting better or getting worse all the time. Between 1960 and 1970, the proportion citing television as getting worse increased (up 17 percentage points) and the proportion citing it as getting better decreased (down 11 percentage points).

At the same time, the degree to which television is singled out as best performing critical tasks has increased. In regard to

Table 3.10 Television vs. Other Mass Media

"Which one of these would you say. . . .?"	Percent of public in early 1970s saying . . . (bracketed figures are percent change over decade)				
	Television	Magazines	Newspapers	Radio	Don't Know, No Answer
is the most entertaining?	72 [+4]	5 [−4]	9 [−4]	14 [+5]	0 [−1]
presents things most intelligently?	38 [+11]	18 [−9]	28 [−5]	9 [+1]	8 [+3]
is the most educational?	46 [+14]	20 [−11]	26 [−5]	4 [+1]	5 [+2]·
does the most for the public?	48 [+14]	2 [−1]	28 [−16]	13 [+2]	10 [+2]
getting worse all the time?	41 [+17]	18 [+1]	14 [+4]	5 [−9]	22 [−13]
is the least important to you?	13 [−2]	53 [+4]	9 [+2]	20 [+5]	5 [−2]
creates most interest in new things?	61 [+5]	16 [−2]	14 [−4]	5 [+1]	5 [+1]
does the least for the public?	10 [−3]	50 [+3]	7 [+2]	13 [+1]	20 [−3]
getting better all the time?	38 [−11]	8 [−3]	11 [0]	15 [+5]	28 [+9]
you most want to keep?[a]	59 [+17]	4 [0]	19 [−13]	17 [−2]	1 [−2]

SOURCE: Adapted from R. T. Bower. 1973. *Television and the Public.* New York: Holt, Rinehart and Winston; The Roper Organization, Inc. 1975. *Trends in Public Attitudes toward Television and Other Mass Media, 1959–1974.* New York: Television Information Office.

[a] Statistics for this question are based on Roper surveys conducted in November 1974 and December 1959. All others are based on Bower data from 1970 and 1960.

which of the media present things most intelligently and is most educational, the public in 1960 was about equally divided between newspapers, magazines, and television. And a greater number (44 percent) picked newspapers over television (34 percent) as doing most for the public. In 1970, television was much more often cited on each of these criteria than any other medium. When a national sample was asked, in November 1974, which of the media they would keep if they could have only one, 59 percent picked television (Roper, 1975). In December 1959, only 42 percent had picked television, and newspapers were a close second. Television's distancing of its rivals is especially impressive because it has occurred even among the better educated, who are its most frequent critics. In 1959, 47 percent of college-educated persons would have preferred to keep newspapers and only 27 percent would have kept television. In 1961, the two media were neck and neck. By 1974, the college educated show the same trend as the general population in preference for television over newspapers, with 45 percent picking television compared to 26 percent for newspapers.

We conclude that:

Commercials and television violence offend or worry a sizable proportion of the viewing public.

Although commercials annoy a sizable proportion of the viewing public, a very large proportion of that public believes such annoyance is a fair price for the benefits derived from free television.

Although television violence draws the disapproval of a sizable proportion of the viewing public, the size of the audience for mystery and suspense drama suggests that such disapproval deters few from viewing violent fare.

Television is rated by the public as superior to other mass media on most counts, and it has dramatically replaced the newspaper as the number one medium in public esteem.

Television is also increasingly cited as the medium which is getting worse and decreasingly cited as the medium which is getting better, a finding that we cautiously interpret as reflecting the greater attention which one would expect the public to display toward the number one medium.

Television As a News Source

In the period between the Roper poll of late 1959 and the poll of late 1974, television replaced the newspaper as the most frequently mentioned source of information. This finding alone simply reflects evidence of increased reliance on television news, but is not necessarily an evaluation of television's merits as a conveyer of news and information. Television, however, also overtook newspapers as the medium people would be most inclined to believe "if you got conflicting or different reports of the same news story." And television has also caught up with newspapers in the proportion of people who say it gives the most *complete* news coverage, despite the ability of print media to provide a far greater quantity of stories of greater length.

In a question similar to Roper's "most inclined to believe"

item, Steiner and then Bower asked which of four media gives the fairest, most unbiased news. Again, between 1960 and 1970 television replaced newspapers as the most credible medium (see table 3.11).

Table 3.11 Television vs. Other Mass Media News Sources

	Percent of public in early 1970s saying . . . (bracketed figures are percent change over decade)				
"Which one of these would you say. . . . ?"	Television	Magazines	Newspapers	Radio	Don't Know, No Answer
is source of most of your news?[a]	65 [+14]	4 [−4]	47 [−10]	21 [−13]	1 [0]
would you be most inclined to believe?[b]	51 [+22]	8 [−2]	20 [−12]	8 [−4]	13 [−4]
gives the most complete news coverage?	41 [+22]	4 [+1]	39 [−20]	14 [−4]	2 [+1]
brings you the latest news most quickly?	54 [+18]	0 [0]	6 [+1]	39 [−18]	1 [−1]
gives the fairest, most unbiased news?	33 [+4]	9 [0]	23 [−8]	19 [−3]	16 [+7]

SOURCE: See Table 3.10.

[a] Data for these questions are based on Roper surveys conducted in November 1974 and December 1959; the others are based on Bower data from 1970 and 1960.

[b] Multiple responses allowed for this item.

Bower found no evidence of deep political division in regard to television's news credibility. Liberals and conservatives differed only slightly, with only the barest degree of greater criticism coming from the right than the left.

A national survey of over 2,000 adults conducted by Opinion Research Corporation for *TV Guide* in January and February 1972 (Hickey, 1972) produced results similar to those we have reviewed. Television was the majority (55 percent) choice as the medium that provides the "most complete political reporting and coverage—including political news personalities and events." Low education, low income, increased age, and rural or midwestern locale were associated with the tendency to choose television. The college educated, professionals, upper income groups, and urbanites were less likely to choose television.

When asked which medium was the fairest and most objective in its political reporting, 47 percent selected television. Again, those with better education, higher income, and city dwellers were less likely to choose television. Democrats found television the most objective medium somewhat more frequently (52 percent) than Republicans (43 percent).

A direct question about bias in television indicated that "47 per cent of Americans consider TV reporting to be more objective than it is biased . . . [but] 34 per cent of Americans believe that TV news is more biased than it is objective." An interesting finding was that "when TV political bias does exist," equal proportions of people find it biased in different directions. Writes Hickey:

> A quarter of the public at large sees bias in favor of the Administration, and another quarter detects bias against it; 12 per cent think the Republicans are being treated more kindly, and 13 per cent are equally sure that the Democrats are having their views more hospitably reflected; 16 per cent maintain that liberals are getting cozy treatment, but 14 percent are sure the conservatives are.

Of course not everyone finds television to be the most fair or objective medium. Clotfelter and Peters (1974) report that a sample of U.S. Army officers find television news to be the medium that treats the military fairly least frequently. Neverthless, the norm is represented by the Wisconsin sample of 627 adults analyzed by Jacobson (1969) that rated television more favorably than newspapers or radio as a news source on 16 of 20 semantic differential scales.

We have discussed news as if it were homogeneous. It is not. Among the dimensions by which news can be categorized is one which sharply affects television's standing as the number one news carrier. This is the dimension of local vs. national coverage.

The Roper studies differentiate between use of the media for news differing in degree of local interest. The question asked of samples from 1964 through 1972 was:

> During the last election campaign, from what source did you become best acquainted with the candidates for *city* (*town*) and *county* offices—from the newspapers or radio or television or magazines or talking to people or where? What about candidates for *state* offices? And what about candidates for *national* offices—the Presidency, the Senate and the House of Representatives?

Results for the three presidential-year elections covered are summarized in table 3.12.

Table 3.12 Mass Media as Sources for News About Political Campaigns, 1964–1972

| Type of Office | Percent Citing Each Medium As "Best" Source [a] | | |
	November 1964	November 1968	November 1972
Local			
Television	27	26	28
Newspapers	42	40	43
Other	36	34	35
State			
Television	43	42	43
Newspapers	41	37	42
Other	23	20	22
National			
Television	64	65	65
Newspapers	36	24	29
Other	22	15	21

SOURCE: Adapted from The Roper Organization, Inc. 1973. *What people think of television and other mass media, 1959–1972.* New York: Television Information Office.

[a] Columns for Local, State, and National offices add to more than 100 because multiple replies were accepted.

Two significant patterns are clear. One is that television's purported dominance as a news source is highly dependent upon national news as the referent when the comparison is being made. Newspapers consistently outrank television for news of local campaigns, and the two media are close, with television consistently ranked higher, for news of state-level campaigns. It is only for national political coverage that television is unambiguously dominant.

The other significant pattern is the trend over time. Unlike public declarations of increasing reliance on the favorability toward television news, these measures of uses show no such trend. Reliance on television for each level of news, including national news, is remarkably similar across the eight years and three elections.

The reliance of television on national reportage as the referent for its high ranking by the public as a news source is given further emphasis by Roper data from the 1974 election (table 3.13). In this off-year election, the query about national offices was specifically delimited to "candidates for the U.S. House of Representatives." When news about this most local of national of-

Table 3.13 Localism of News and News Sources, 1974

| | Percent Citing Each Medium as "Best" Source | | |
Type of Office	Television	Newspapers	All Other Sources
Local	30	41	28
State	48	33	16
Congressional	40	35	20

SOURCE: Adapted from The Roper Organization, Inc. 1975. (See Table 3.10.)

fices is at issue, newspapers and television again are very close, although television leads, and television only appears to be clearly dominant for news of the campaigns for the comparatively remote state-level offices.

Carter and Greenberg (1965) examined the effects of alternative wordings of the Roper questions on media use and credibility. They concluded that there was antinewspaper bias in the Roper question on media use, but not in the question on credibility. Our qualification of the standing of television as a news source thus extends only to its coverage, not its credibility.

They also explore the reasons for choosing one or another of the media as most credible and find that they differ, depending on the medium chosen. Persons citing newspapers as more credible generally did so because of general confidence in their completeness, accuracy, and the broad attributes of the medium, and because it sometimes was the only medium used for news. Persons citing television generally did so because of very specific attributes of the medium ("pictures," "you can see it happen," recency of accounts, on-the-spot coverage), perceived bias in other media, and better personnel (the commentators and on-camera reporters). These findings suggest that television may be responsible for changes in what people expect from the news. If so, we should expect accelerated change in all the media as they attempt to conform more perfectly to public expectations.

Clarke and Ruggels (1970) also offer data requiring adjustment of any early impression of television's news dominance. When a Seattle sample was asked in 1967 to indicate which of the media gave the "best coverage," newspapers were chosen somewhat more often than television. We cautiously interpret this finding, which might well derive from some peculiarity of the site, as indicating again that television's dominance depends on the referent ("best coverage" connotes comprehensiveness, where newspapers excell) when the media are rated. There is no reason to believe the sample was invalid, because other patterns are consistent with other studies—the ratings for newspapers rise as news becomes more local, and education is inversely related to choice of broadcast media.

We conclude that:

Television is highly evaluated and has risen in public esteem as a news medium, but the data bear on what people say about television and other news media and not on how they behave in following a particular story or when reports conflict—so that actual relative impact of the media remains in doubt.

Much of the news dominance of television apparent in some data is attributable to the reaction to television as the symbol of modern media rather than a reflection of its actual role, for the following reasons:

The esteem in which television is held as a news source is highly dependent on national news being the kind of coverage at issue.

National news is viewed fairly infrequently compared to the more regular exposure to newspapers.

There has been no progressive reliance on television as a news source either for national, state, or local political campaigns that parallels the increase in the frequency with which it is acclaimed the major news source among the public.

Thus, exposure and evaluation by the public as a whole are not closely related. It is likely that some of television's dominance reflects respondents' descriptions of how they *believe* the world is rather than how they themselves get along in it.

There is no evidence of widespread public dissatisfaction with television news and no evidence of strong political polarization in its evaluation, although conservatives are somewhat more inclined to believe it is biased than liberals.

Television news is not homogeneous, and one must be very careful to qualify the kind of news when describing the public's evaluation of television as a news source.

Chapter

Living with Television

WE NOW TURN to evidence on television's role in everyday life beyond the amount of time spent viewing. Among the topics we will cover are:

Behavior that accompanies television viewing.
Television's place among total leisure time.
Television's influence on other activities.
How the family decides what to view, and the effect of the owning of more than one set on its decisions.
Television's effects on consumption of other media.
The uses and gratifications associated with television viewing.

The total body of studies may be thought of as reporting on the concomitants of television's presence.

When the Set Is On

The Nielsen data presented earlier indicate that the number of hours per day that a television set is on in the average American home is high and has been increasing. Although the total set-in-use hours reported by Nielsen are often higher than those obtained by other surveys, the similarities and the differences among various categories of viewers have been consistently confirmed. However, there is a question that has received only minimal attention and yet is of the utmost importance in regard to exposure to television. To what extent are people actually paying attention to television when the set is on?

Although the samples are small and the methodology exploratory, two important studies provide a fairly clear answer: There is a great deal of inattention to television when people are in a room with a set on. In addition, television has been found to be frequently secondary to some other activity, and there is often a secondary activity when viewing is primary.

During the 1961–62 and 1962–63 television seasons, Allen (1965) placed time-lapse movie cameras (Dynascopes) in 95 homes containing 358 individuals in Oklahoma and Kansas. Viewing and nonviewing behavior were recorded on film at a rate of four frames per minute. The cameras were constantly monitoring television sets and the viewing area, and trained coders viewed almost 1 million individual pictures to determine whether the set was in use and what was happening in the viewing room when a set was in use. The results are summarized in table 4.1.

Table 4.1 Television Viewing When Set in Use, by Time of Day[a]

	Total	Morning	Noon to 6 p.m.	Evening
Hours set-in-use per week	31.8	3.5	9.7	18.6
Average number of viewers per set-in-use per minute	1.42	1.14	1.22	1.58
Hours when nobody in room and set in use	6.0	1.0	2.4	2.6
Hours when nobody viewing screen and set in use	6.8	0.8	2.1	3.9
Nonviewing hours per week when set in use	12.8	1.8	4.5	6.5
Nonviewing hours as percent of set-in-use hours	40	52	47	35

SOURCE: Adapted from C. L. Allen. 1965. Photographing the TV audience. *Journal of Advertising Research, 1965,* 5, 2–8.

[a] Figures are based on average, over four sample sites; $N = 95$ homes (358 persons).

Allen reports that his sample households had their sets turned on for a bit less than 32 hours per week, somewhat below the Nielsen national estimate for 1963. His cameras recorded that for 19 percent of that time there was *nobody* present in the room. In another 21 percent of set-in-use time, someone was in the viewing area, but no one was looking at or facing the television screen. In sum, the cameras revealed that 40 percent of the time that a set was on in a home nobody was paying attention to television.

Patterns of nonviewing varied across time of day, with inattention proportionately greater before than after six P.M. Nonviewing was higher for commercials than the overall average—48 percent of commercial time found either nobody present in the room or nobody in the room paying attention.*

A second study, by Bechtel, Achelpohl and Akers (1972), used videotape to record viewing behavior among 85 people in 20 Kansas homes that voluntarily submitted to the intrusion, which included a camera crew in a van in the yard. They define "viewing" as actively responding to the set or to others in connection with the set, passively watching, or watching while engaged in another activity. The findings are quite similar to those reported by Allen. There was a high proportion of nonviewing, ranging from about a quarter of air time when movies were telecast to almost a half when news programs and commercials were being presented (table 4.2). They also report that when diary reports were compared to videotaped behavior, only three out of every four hours of reported viewing were actually spent with television and that declarations of amount of viewing "yesterday" or "in general" were less accurate than the diary. Given the conflict between estimates derived from diaries and other indirect means

Table 4.2 Percentage of Time Television Watched While Set On

Type of Programming	Percent Time Watched[a]
Movies	76.0
Children's	71.4
Suspense	68.1
Religious	66.7
Family	66.4
Game show	65.9
Talk show	63.7
Melodrama	59.3
Sports events	58.7
News	55.2
Commercial	54.8

SOURCE: Adapted from R. B. Bechtel, C. Achelpohl, and R. Akers. 1972. Correlates between observed behavior and questionnaire responses on television viewing. In E. A. Rubinstein, G. A. Comstock and J. P. Murray (eds.), *Television and Social Behavior.* Vol. 4, *Television in Day-to-Day Life: Patterns of Use.* Washington, D.C.: Government Printing, pp. 274–344.

[a]Time "attending to screen" divided by time set is on; whether for individuals or homes not reported.

*We should note, however, that the *messages* in commercials and in television programs may not have been missed. In neither this nor the next study we shall examine was there any attention to receipt of the audio signal from television or of the relationship between degree or quality of attention and receipt of messages.

and visual recordings of behavior, we would speculate that people often feel that they have "seen" a program even when their exposure has been marginal or only auditory.

Other research clearly supports the inference that a great deal of exposure to television occurs while the viewer is involved with something else. The social scientists who conducted an extraordinary 12-nation study in the mid-1960s of the use of time by adults distinguish between primary involvement and secondary involvement (Szalai, 1972). They found that the proportion of total viewing time that was secondary to some other activity varied across the American, European, and Latin American sites from nil to about 40 percent.

The variation reflects vast differences in the amount of television broadcast over the 24-hour day and the degree of emphasis on light entertainment suitable for divided attention, as well as cultural differences affecting the distribution of time. In western Europe and the United States, the proportion of viewing as a secondary activity was usually substantial.

In the United States, more than one-fourth of all viewing by adults was found to be secondary to some other activity (table 4.3). The proportion varied from 18 percent for employed men to 36 percent for employed women to 38 percent for housewives. The differences are caused by such activities as housework and meal preparation, normally associated with women. These figures underestimate the degree of involvement with another activity during exposure to television because time spent with a secondary activity while television is primary are not included; unfortunately, data on this are not reported in the 12-nation study. However, the impression that a great deal of television viewing is not an exclusive activity is made more firm by another national sample of American adults in which almost a third reported engaging in another activity (other than conversation) while viewing (LoSciuto, 1972).

What is going on when the set is on? Allen notes that children "eat, drink, dress and undress, play, fight, and do other things while in front of the set. . . . Adults eat, drink, sleep, play, argue, fight, and occasionally make love in front of the TV set." Bechtel et al., tell us that "the most consistently frequent type of behavior accompanying viewing, next to talking, is eating."*

* Although they found eating to be most frequent, Bechtel et al. comment that a "surprising variety" of behavior was observed, and report that a *partial* list would include looking out the window, picking nose, scratching (someone else and self), doing homework, smoking, rocking, reading, dancing, lying (on floor, couch,

Table 4.3 Television as a Primary and Secondary Activity in the United States (Data from 44 Cities)

	Average Per Day			
	Employed Men (N = 904)		Employed Women (N = 490)	
Viewing As A:	Minutes	Percent	Minutes	Percent
Primary activity	101	82	65	64
Secondary activity	22	18	36	36
Total	123	100	101	100

	Average Per Day			
	Housewives (N = 587)		All Adults (N = 1981)	
Viewing As A:	Minutes	Percent	Minutes	Percent
Primary activity	96	62	91	72
Secondary activity	58	38	36	28
Total	154	100	127	100

SOURCE: Adapted from A. Szalai (ed.). 1972. *The Use of Time: Daily Activities of Urban and Suburban Populations in Twelve Countries.* The Hague: Mouton and Co., p. 691.

These on-the-spot observations are largely in accord with the pattern for adults in the United States found in the 12-nation data (table 4.4). When television was a secondary activity, the most frequent primary activities were housework, conversation and social interaction (the sum of three categories in table 4.4), and eating, followed by other leisure, reading, and child care. The rather sparse data on ranking of activities accompanying viewing from the other national sample of adults convey a similar pattern (LoSciuto, 1972).

We do not have data on the incursion of other activities as a secondary involvement when viewing is primary. The parallel between the United States data from the 12-nation study, where a distinction is made between primary and secondary activities, and that from the other national sample, where no such distinction is made in the ranking of activities, suggests that the pattern would

---

table) untying knots, sorting wash, preparing meals, setting table, ironing, dressing, undressing, posing, doing exercises, singing, pacing, asking questions about the television program, reciting, wrestling, fighting, crying, throwing objects (toys, books, paper airplanes), scolding children, mimicking the television portrayal, conversing with the television set, eating, drinking, sleeping, playing cards, picking up objects (toys, etc.), conversing, playing board games (Monopoly, Scrabble), answering the phone, crawling, fantasy play, teasing, combing hair.

be much the same—with housework, conversation and social interaction, and eating paramount.

Conversation has a special role in the pattern. The data make it quite clear that when we speak of television viewing as an activity of often-divided attention, we mean much more than that people talk while the set is on. More than three-fourths of all secondary activity during viewing in the United States in the 12-nation data was unrelated to social interaction (table 4.4), although the almost one-fourth of secondary activity devoted to conversation and social interaction, which could easily be labeled conversation, also makes it clear that talking is a frequent accompaniment of viewing. The second national sample, which did not distinguish between social interaction and conversation, found that conversing was sufficiently frequent to raise the total proportion reporting some other activity during a particular period of viewing from almost a third to more than two-third (LoSciuto, 1972). About half of these conversations were related to the television being viewed, and about one-fifth of the sample said they talked about programs after viewing, some of which presumably occurred while viewing additional television. Thus, conversation is not invariably distractive; about as often, it augments or complements the television viewed.

In sum, "television viewing" is correctly thought of as a dis-

Table 4.4 Viewing as a Secondary Activity in the United States (Data from 44 Cities)

	24-Hour Day	
Primary Activity	Percent of Total Time Television Viewing Is a Secondary Activity	Actual Minutes
Housework	25	10
Eating	14	5
Social interaction (away from home)	11	4
Other leisure	10	4
Reading	9	4
Child care	8	3
Social interaction (at home)	7	3
Conversation	3	1
All other	13	5
Total	100	39

SOURCE: Adapted from A. Szalai (ed.). 1972. *The use of time: Daily activities of urban and suburban populations in twelve countries.* The Hague: Mouton and Co.

continuous, often interrupted, and frequently nonexclusive activity for which a measure in hours and minutes serves only as the outer boundary of possible attention. For some portion of such a measure no one is attending, and for other portions attention is divided. Other than social interaction and conversation, the most frequent activities that occur in conjunction with television viewing are housework, eating, other leisure, reading, and child care. Social interaction and conversation occur at least as frequently as housework, and a sizable proportion—perhaps half—of the verbal exchange is devoted to television.

Television and Leisure

It is not surprising to find that, among the people in the 12 nations studied, Americans were most likely to watch television and watched the highest average number of minutes per person per week. In table 4.5, the second and third columns show this pattern quite clearly. A comparison of the third and fourth columns reveals the relative amount of "secondary" viewing that occurs. A comparison of the first column with the data indicating percentage and amount of viewing per day indicates a strong correlation between degree of television ownership and average per capita viewing. This reflects the obvious fact that when there is not ready access to the medium most people cannot spend much, if any, time watching. On the other hand, the fifth column reveals the unexpected finding that among people who watch television in their own home there is very little variation in the amount viewed despite the wide differences in cultures and quantity and character of television broadcasting.

These time-budget studies also indicate that Americans spend more than three-quarters of their total mass media time and as much as 40 percent of their total leisure time with television (the seventh and last columns refer only to proportion of *primary* television viewing within these categories). The data indicate that the proportions are similar among people in other societies who have access to the medium. They also indicate that when television becomes fully available within a society it can be expected to dominate time spent with mass media and to be a major component of total free-time activity.

Among the American adults in these time-budget studies,

Table 4.5 Television Usage and Free Time in 12 Nations[a] for an Average Day (in 1965)

Sample Site	Percent Set Ownership	Percent[b] That Watched Any TV	Minutes of TV Viewing[c]			Total Mass Media[d]		Total Free Time[e]	
			Total	As the Primary Activity	Per Home Viewer	Mins	TV Percent	Mins	TV Percent
USA (Jackson)	98	80	134	101	142	135	75	310	33
USA (44 cities)	97	80	129	92	131	131	70	301	31
East Germany	85	72	100	81	124	108	75	233	35
West Germany	76	64	87	74	128	112	66	300	25
Belgium	72	65	94	84	139	137	61	297	28
Czechoslovakia	72	52	73	66	135	116	57	239	28
West Germany (100 dists)	66	56	74	63	123	98	64	264	24
France	65	65	96	58	107	91	64	245	24
Poland	59	60	82	70	130	120	58	262	27
Peru	54	47	63	54	125	87	62	309	17
USSR	52	40	45	42	109	116	36	249	17
Yugoslavia (m)	49	41	47	41	111	81	51	222	18
Hungary	45	36	45	43	124	85	51	200	22
Yugoslavia (k)	35	35	48	37	127	87	43	311	12
Bulgaria	26	17	17	16	95	79	20	231	7

SOURCE: Adapted from J. P. Robinson, and P. E. Converse. 1972. The impact of television on mass media usages: A cross-national comparison. In A. Szalai (ed.), *The Use of Time: Daily Activities of Urban and Suburban Populations in Twelve Countries.* The Hague: Mouton and Co., pp. 197–212.

[a] Single city chosen for each nation; all industrial, with population from 50,000–150,000. Exceptions: France (6 cities); Yugoslavia (two sample sites [m] and [k]); West Germany (one site plus 100-district national sample); USA (one site plus 44-city national sample).

[b] Percent of people aged 18–65 in homes with someone employed.

[c] *Total* represents the per capita average for the sample, including non-set owners. Viewing both as a primary and secondary activity is included. Viewing *as the primary activity* also represents the per capita average for the sample and permits the calculation of viewing as a secondary activity (Secondary viewing = Total – Primary Viewing). *Per home viewer* is the average for owners of television sets.

[d] *Total mass media* time as a primary activity. *TV percent* defined as primary television minutes divided *by primary mass media minutes.*

[e] *TV percent* defined as primary television minutes divided by total free-time minutes.

television viewing was the single greatest component of leisure-time activity. Even the sum of all time spent in social activity and conversation was 10 to 15 percent less than the time attributed to television viewing as a primary activity. In fact, among 37 "primary" activities—mutually exclusive categories that divide the average day—television viewing ranked third behind sleep and time spent at work among American adults. Table 4.6 is a summary of the proportion of time spent in various free-time activities by the two U.S. samples. It clearly reveals the prominence of television viewing. Yet, even this image is an understatement, since all the "secondary" viewing has been omitted.

The degree of immersion in television in the United States is surely even stronger than the data in table 4.6 suggest. Certain groups who are heavy viewers, such as children, the retired, and the unemployed, are excluded, and the estimated total viewing time of the sample is below that found in other studies of the same period. In addition, per capita viewing has increased considerably since the data were collected. It is clear that television viewing takes up more time than any activity other than work and sleep, and that it dominates mass-media use and leisure time in America.

We have presented data showing that in the United States those with greater education and higher income tend to watch less television. The data from the time-budget studies confirm

Table 4.6 Primary Activities as Percent of Total Free Time in United States

Activity	Percent of Total Free Time	
	In 44 Cities	In Jackson, Michigan
Television viewing	31	33
Newspaper reading	8	8
All other mass media use	6	4
Study	4	3
Religion and organizations	5	5
Socializing and conversation (home and away)	27	26
Leisure travel	6	7
Outdoors, sports, cultural, entertainment	5	4
Resting	3	4
Other leisure activity	6	6

SOURCE: Adapted from A. Szalai (ed.). 1972. *The use of time: Daily activities of urban and suburban populations in twelve countries.* The Hague: Mouton and Co., p. 580.

this, and also show that total "percent of free time devoted to mass media" by Americans declines as education increases, largely because of the domination of mass-media exposure by television. The pattern is not the same in all nations, but this seems to be due to differences in patterns of media availability rather than any other differences in the societies. When television is universally available, groups of lower socioeconomic status use it more and thereby increase their total media usage.

Data presented by Meyersohn (1968) more finely depict the role of television in the pattern of leisure at different income levels in the United States. At lower income levels, there is a *positive* correlation between level of other leisure activity and television viewing—those who mention several indoor activities, those who have more pieces of "leisure equipment," those who belong to more organizations, those who read more newspapers and books, and those who are more frequent moviegoers watch more television than others at lower income levels. At upper income levels, there is a *negative* correlation—people more active in other leisure activity are less likely to watch television. The exception is newspaper reading; upper and lower income people are alike here, with newspaper reading correlated positively with television viewing for both groups.

The relationship between education and media use had earlier been examined by Samuelson, Carter and Ruggels (1963). They reported a negative correlation between education and television viewing, and positive correlations between education and time spent with radio, magazines, and books. Among their conclusions:

> Apparently, demands on time of the more educated man are such that he must choose between watching television or attending to some other medium, whereas the less educated man seems better able to satisfy his wants for both television and other media.

The various sets of available data clearly suggest different patterns of television viewing within different socioeconomic groups. However, these differences become minor when the high level of television viewing for every group is taken into account. The clear differences are not great in magnitude. It is a rare American home in which television is not the dominant leisure activity. In addition, as we reported earlier (chapter 3), the differences appear to be disappearing, with higher status groups having increased amount of viewing at a faster pace in recent years.

Television dominates the free time of children as well as

adults, although such a strong term may not be appropriate for adolescents. Most children watch some television every day and most watch at least two hours per day, although there is great individual variation; amount of viewing increases during the elementary school years, but the trend is in the opposite direction during high school and college (Lyle, 1972). Adolescents as a group also certainly watch considerable television, but the data do not suggest the same dominance over other leisure pursuits. In a sample of Minneapolis high school students, 60 percent said they had not watched any television the previous night (Murray, Cole, and Fedler, 1970), and in a large national probability sample of recent high school graduates, average daily viewing (1.7 hours) was about half the national average (3.0 hours) (J. P. Robinson and Bachman, 1972). There are no similar doubts about younger persons. For example, Long and Henderson (1973) studied suburban, middle-class, fifth-grade children who could read at or above grade level. The partial time-budget for two weeks (table 4.7) indicates that television viewing consumed half the total leisure time and exceeds the closest competitor ("free play") by three-to-two. In addition, television occupied more than ten times as many hours as reading, even though the sample excluded children with reading difficulties.

Like all of the data on leisure where primary activity is not distinguished from secondary activity, the degree of television exposure is underestimated here, because some viewing would also occur when another activity such as homework is the principal

Table 4.7 Time-Budget of Fifth-Grade Children Over Two Weeks

	Average Number of Hours
Nonleisure Activities	
Chores	2.4
Homework	7.7
Total	10.1
Leisure Activities	
Reading	3.1
Organized activity	8.3
Free play	20.0
Television viewing	30.3
Total	61.7

SOURCE: Adapted from B. H. Long and E. H. Henderson. 1973. Children's use of time: Some personal and social correlates. *Elementary School Journal,* 73 (4), 193–199.

focus.* However, the fact that television absorbs so much time when the methodology discounts total time spent with a set turned on makes clear its dominance of leisure.

Television's Influence on Other Activities

After we acknowledge that television sets are on several hours each day in most homes, and that most people report engaging in the rather varied behavior known as "television viewing" for several hours each day, can we say much more about how television has altered behavior? The answer is yes, but the data are limited. The question is not an easy one to answer because of television's ubiquity in the United States and high level of diffusion in many other countries. When television is everywhere, one can only observe the way people behave when it is present in a society; but that does not permit inferences about how that behavior differs from what it was before television—except in the obvious sense that "television viewing" and such behavior as conversing about television represent changes. What is needed, but hard or impossible to obtain now, are data reflecting behavior before television or without television.

Belson, recognizing the vanishing opportunity to obtain data, conducted a series of studies in the 1950s in England, when many homes did not yet have television. The basic technique was to compare the behavior of persons with and without television in their dwellings, with other differences held constant. In a 1959 study in which he followed trends in behavior over time, Belson focused on television's impact on other activities engaged in by adults. The principal measures were reported feelings of *interest* in engaging in an activity and reports of actually engaging in it. Data were collected on 20 kinds of activities, including gardening, movie attendance, and reading, from samples of 450 persons with television and 350 persons without it; time trends could be examined because of variations in length of set ownership.† The results are summarized in figure 4.1. They are:

* For example, Lyle and Hoffman (1972a) found that 81 percent of the first-grade children they studied reported engaging in other activities while watching television, and that more than two-thirds of the sixth- and tenth-grade children reported that they study with a television set on.

† The full list of activities consists of cinema-going; theatre-going; ballet; looking at paintings; politics in Great Britain; membership in associations/clubs; book

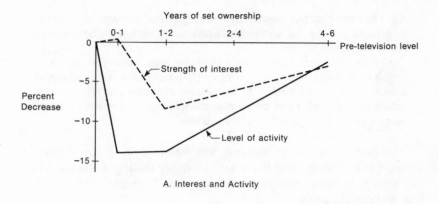

A. Interest and Activity

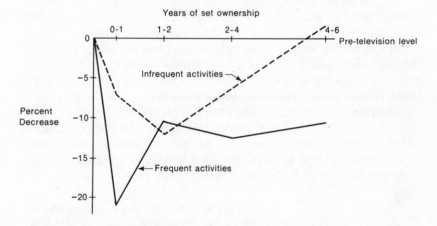

B. Frequent vs. Infrequent Activities

Figure 4.1. Television's effect on other activities over six years.

SOURCE: Adapted from W. A. Belson. 1959. Effects of television on the interests and initiative of adult viewers in Greater London. *British Journal of Psychology*, 50, 145–58.

   Both degree of interest and level of activity were reduced noticeably during the first two years of set ownership.
   Interest was less affected than level of activity.

---

reading; gardening (indoors or outdoors); card playing; playing gramophone records; events in different parts of the world; modern developments in science; international and world affairs; places of historic importance; information about people in other countries; going to see sporting events—major soccer matches, horse racing, or horse jumping; home oriented activities; sociable activities. When the opportunity for direct activity was limited, such as in the case of modern developments in science, activity was defined as reading about the topic.

After the first two years, there was gradual recovery of both interest and activity, but by the end of six years both were below their
initial pre-television level.

When level of activity is examined separately for activities
engaged in frequently and infrequently before television, recovery
after six years is complete for infrequent activities but for frequent
activities the level is not only more sharply reduced in the first two
years but recovery is not at all complete.

In sum, television reduces involvement in other activities
when it is a novelty, and there is a possibly lasting decrease in involvement in more frequently engaged-in activities. Television is
not without its price.

In the same study, Belson also collected data on "initiative,"
defined as "the ability for independent action or original conception." During the first two years of set ownership, there was a lowering apparently attributable to television but not during the third
through sixth years. This is an extremely interesting finding because it suggests an experiential basis for some of the fears that
many voiced when television was a novelty.

Additional findings on the effects of television on other activities come from the multination UNESCO time-budget studies,
which permit comparisons between set owners and nonowners
within sites as well as between sites varying in degree of television diffusion. J. P. Robinson (1972b) finds that:

Television *increases* time spent with the mass media by about
an hour, principally because of the great deal of time devoted to
television.

Television *reduces* amount of total sleep by about 13 minutes.

Television *reduces* the amounts of time devoted to social gatherings away from home, listening to the radio, reading books, in
other leisure, in conversation, on travel related to leisure, the movies, religion, and household tasks.

Few would dispute that television reduces the amount of time
that would be spent in proximity of an operating radio, but a
decline in total time spent with radio since the appearance of television would appear to counter the evidence offered the eye and
the ear by the transistor. Nevertheless, a comparison of the
average hours per day spent listening to the radio in the United
States before television (Bogart, 1972a) with radio listening in
1965–1966 as a primary and secondary activity (Szalai, 1972),

makes it clear that less time is now spent with radio than before the appearance of television.

The most extensive longitudinal study of television's impact in the United States traces the pattern of viewing and other activities in New Brunswick, New Jersey, over a decade during which set ownership increased from one percent to almost 100 percent of all households (Cunningham and Walsh, 1958; Coffin, 1955). The data are consistent with the findings covered so far. Television initially decreased radio listening, movie attendance, magazine reading, and participation in social activities outside the home, but as it ceased to be a novelty there was some resumption in these activities with no decrease in amount of time spent viewing television.

When television was introduced, there was extensive speculation about what the influence would be on spectator sports, concerts, and such competing kinds of entertainment as the movies. The evidence is widely scattered, although much of it has been collected by Bogart (1972a). The story seems to be that television can increase attendance at various kinds of events. For example, Belson (1959) concluded that television led to a 47 percent increase in horse racing and horse jumping attendance and an 18 percent increase in attendance at major soccer matches.

Television apparently can also decrease attendance at various kinds of events. For example, minor league baseball attendance fell from 42 to 10 million between 1949 and 1969 and motion picture attendance declined from 41 to 19 million between 1960 and 1970 and from 82 to 34 million between 1946 and 1956—although population was increasing over these various periods (Bogart, 1972a). These changes are probably attributable to television, although there is no way to know what the trends would have been in its absence.

There are several factors that are difficult to untangle. By televising them, television can increase public interest in—and therefore attendance at—sports or other activities. This is probably what occurred in England. But television can also decrease attendance if it provides access to similar events of higher quality. American minor league baseball, for example, faced the competition of televised major league baseball. Television coverage will bolster a sport or activity through the fees paid for broadcasting privileges, and will most certainly increase public attention to it. This produces a very delicate balance in which the benefits of television coverage continually threaten the events given exposure; television coverage has certainly made football the principal national spectator sport, yet colleges and owners of professional football teams are in constant fright that coverage will decrease net revenues by adversely affecting paid attendance.

Television can also decrease attendance by more conveniently or economically fulfilling the psychological or social functions served by a particular type of event. This probably is what happened in the case of American movies, which faced the competition of an in-home purveyor of adventure, comedy, and diversion. In addition, television also offers competition for other activities simply because viewing reduces the amount of time available for expenditure in other ways. The increase in total time spent with the mass media brought about by television thus inevitably means some diminution elsewhere.

Television imposes its own holidays. In the United States, Super Bowl Sunday has become a tradition that is less sport or program than event. This annual confrontation between the champions of the National and American Conferences of the National Football League attracts what is usually the year's largest audience for televised sports. Parties are planned around the game, other obligations are postponed or forgotten, work is rescheduled or abandoned, traffic becomes light, and the mood of the nation is covered in-depth on the front page of the next morning's *New York Times*.

Viewing Decisions

The description of the behavior of people when they are at home with television must take into account the growing number of multi-set households in the United States. Patterns of family interaction regarding television can be quite different in single-set and multi-set homes.

Nielsen reported in 1965 that approximately 22 percent of all television households had more than one set. The estimate rose sharply over the next decade—to a third by 1970, and 46 percent by 1977.

These data somewhat obscure the increasing importance of multi-set homes because they do not take into account household size. In 1975, only 33 percent of one- and two-person households

were multiset, while the figure for three- and four-person households was 48 percent and for larger households, 63 percent.
Thus, family viewing now occurs more often in a multi- than
single-set environment, and research when the single set was
strongly predominant may no longer be fully relevant.

In addition, there is some evidence that the Nielsen data may
underestimate the actual quantity of multi-set households. In two
instances, the Nielsen 1974 estimate of 41 percent is matched, although the data were collected four years earlier. One is a 1970
national probability sample of 2000 adults (Bower, 1973); the
other, a 1970 national sample of 250 families (LoSciuto, 1972).
Because we know the trend is upward, these data rather force-
fully imply a Nielsen underestimate.

Where do we find the television sets in American homes?
Two national studies report a consistent pattern (Bower, 1973;
LoSciuto, 1972): A very large majority—Bower reports 90 percent—have the set or a set in the house's major evening social
room, the living room or "family" room. When there is more than
one set in the house, an equally large majority—again, Bower
reports 90 percent—have a set in a bedroom. The majority of bedroom sets—LoSciuto reports two-thirds—are in adults' bedrooms.

We have emphasized the growth of multi-set households because in households with the same number of members viewing
behavior differs between multi- and single-set households. With
the availability of a second or third set, joint viewing declines, and
the combinations which do view jointly change.

Tables 4.8 and 4.9 summarize what occurs in families with father, mother, and at least one child. When there is only a single

Table 4.8 Single vs. Joint Viewing by Multi- and Single-Set Families on
Average Day

Family Television Status (N)[a]	Percent Reporting Joint Viewing "Likely"	Percent Reporting Single Viewing "Likely"
Single-set (1036)	94	6
Two-set (543)	80	20
Three-set (160)	66	34
Four-set (35)	65	35

SOURCE: Adapted from R. T. Bower. 1973. *Television and the Public.* New York:
Holt, Rinehart and Winston.

[a] N = number of families (father, mother and at least one child).

Table 4.9 Joint Viewing Combinations in Multi- and Single-Set Families

	"Likely" Joint Viewing Instances (In Percent)	
Viewing Combinations	Multi-Set Family (N = 613)[a]	Single-Set Family (N = 443)
Husband-wife	26	17
Children only	26	13
Entire family	34	55
Mother-children	5	9
Father-children	7	4
Others	3	3

SOURCE: See Table 4.8.

[a] N = Instances for joint viewing.

set, 94 percent said some sort of joint viewing during a day was "likely." With a second set, the figure drops to 80 percent, and where there is a third or fourth set, to about 65 percent. And when there is more than one set, husband-wife viewing and viewing by children become markedly more "likely" and viewing by the entire family becomes markedly less likely. In short, multiple sets disrupt the established pattern of family interaction, so that children and adults tend to view independently.

Thus, the question of who determines which programs will be watched when there is conflict becomes less important when there are multiple sets. At the same time, the increasing trend toward multiple sets raises the question of differences that may result in what is viewed by some of the family and of the consequences of the minimization of adult comment and interpretation when children view.

It should not be assumed that access by children to a separate set necessarily means a great difference in what is viewed. There is little evidence on this issue, but the finding reported in one study of a similar correlation between the categories of programs watched by parents and adolescents in single- and multi-set homes (Chaffee, McLeod, and Atkin, 1970) hints that in broad terms the difference may be small. Yet, even if this finding holds generally, there may be important shifts because of the variation of programs within a category. The implied decrease of parental involvement in young persons' viewing is probably more significant than any changes in what is viewed, for as we see later (chapters 5 and 8), any effect of television portrayals on the behavior and attitudes of young viewers appears to be partly dependent on the implied or direct interpretation given these portrayals by parents or other adults.

Nevertheless, the findings on conflict resolution in regard to television watching remain of interest because considerable joint viewing continues, and provides insight into the roles of family members in regard to television. The findings are largely consistent and cover three issues—who prevails in the various possible combinations when there is conflict, how control of the set varies by time of day, and the frequency of mutual agreement vs. conflict.

In regard to who prevails:*

When there is conflict between a single parent and a child or children, the child's choice is viewed as often or only slightly less often as the adult's (Bower, 1973; Wand, 1968).

When a parent and a child disagree with the other parent, the parent-child combination much more often prevails (Wand, 1968).

When both parents disagree with children, the parents much more often prevail (Wand, 1968).

When an older sibling disagrees with a young sibling, the older much more often prevails (Wand, 1968).

When husbands and wives disagree, the huband much more often prevails (Bower, 1973; Lyle and Hoffman, 1972a).†

In regard to variation during the day:

From morning to early afternoon, the wife, typically home alone or with one or more young children, is most likely to choose programs; from late afternoon to early evening, a child or children; and in the evening, a "family" group of two or more (Niven, 1960).

In regard to the frequency of mutual agreement vs. conflict:

---

* Because the Wand (1968) data were collected in Canada in 1965, we purposely emphasize trends, which are likely to be much more reliable than specific results. However, the reader may like to know what those results were: When the conflict was between a single parent and a child or children, the parent prevailed 51 percent of the time; between a parent-child pair and the other parent, the pair prevailed almost two out of three times; between both parents and a child or children, the parents prevailed three out of four times; and between an older and younger sibling, the older prevailed three out of four times.

† Wand (1968) found that women triumphed in three-to-two instances. We place much higher credence in the studies by Bower and by Lyle and Hoffman because of their greater recency, better sample quality, and consistency with each other.

Mutual decisions occurred least often when viewers were mother and children, were more frequent when both parents viewed with children, and were most frequent when two parents viewed alone. Bower (1973), using data from a national proabability sample of about 2000 adults interviewed in 1970, analyzes decision-making for three viewing combinations—mother and children, husband and wife, and the entire family. He found that when mother and children were vewing, 27 percent of the decisions were mutual; but when they were not, the mother held a slight edge (37 percent vs. 33 percent). When two parents plus children were viewing, 42 percent of the decisions were mutual; but in disputes the father (27 percent) held a strong edge over the children (17 percent) and the mother (10 percent). Similarly, husbands were more likely to win viewing disputes with wives (28 vs. 18 percent), although mutual decisions were common (53 percent).

The data suggest that conflict is fairly frequent; adults report that it occurs about three-fourths of the time when viewers were mothers and children, about 60 percent of the time when viewers were children and both parents, and almost half the time for adult couples (Bower, 1973).

However, a majority of children reported that conflict with parents is infrequent. Conflict was said by children to be more frequent with siblings than with parents. Sibling conflict rises between the first and sixth grades, then levels off and possibly declines (Lyle and Hoffman, 1972a).*

A fairly consistent picture emerges. Considerable joint viewing is by mutual consent. Disagreement is partly a function of the heterogeneity of the group. When there is disagreement in a multi-set household, parents and children are likely to view separately. When there is disagreement in a single-set household or where children are committed to view with one or more parents, children prevail about as often as parents. When parents agree, they prevail over children. When child and parent agree, they prevail over the other parent. Husbands and wives disagree about half the time, and husbands more often prevail. When children

---

* Lyle and Hoffman (1972a) studied first, sixth, and tenth graders in a small city near Los Angeles. All three age groups reported more conflict with siblings than with parents. First graders reported relatively little conflict with parents; 60 percent said there never was any. Sixth and tenth graders reported more conflict, but frequency remained quite low; about a third said there never was any, another third said "not very often," and the final third were divided between "now and then" and "pretty often." Conflict among siblings was least frequently reported by first graders; 22 percent said it occurred "pretty often." The figure for sixth graders was 41 percent and for tenth graders, 35 percent.

are in conflict, the older is likely to prevail. Although the frequency of parent-child conflict is high when measured by the absence of mutual agreement reported by parents, children themselves report little conflict—suggesting that either parents are more sensitive to or falsely perceive incompatible desires on the part of children, or that children do not perceive disagreements over television as amounting to much.

A striking phenomenon is the degree to which what is viewed jointly coincides with the choice of children, either because they win in conflicts with another parent or provide the swing vote when the family views together. This pattern, together with the freedom implied by their frequent viewing outside the presence of an adult, particularly in multi-set homes, gives some justice to calling television in America the children's medium, both in terms of their influence on family viewing and in degree of access to content of their choice.

John J. O'Connor wrote in the *New York Times* (October 19, 1977) that ABC won its first place in the ratings in the mid-1970s by calculatedly emphasizing programs that juveniles would prefer. We are ignorant of network guru-ism, but such a strategy certainly accords with what is known about family television behavior.

Television and Other Media

We have seen that television typically increases the total amount of time devoted to the mass media. We have seen that television typically decreases the amount of time devoted to certain other mass media—specifically, radio, books, and movies (J. P. Robinson, 1972b). We have seen that television markedly shrinks the position of its predecessor as the major audiovisual mass medium, the movies (Bogart, 1972a). We have also seen that it can alter the character of other media by forcing them to appeal to their potential audience on new grounds. We concluded that one factor in the escalating violence of movies is their attempt to compete with television (D. G. Clark and Blankenburg, 1972).

The increasingly explicit treatment of sex in movies is also in part probably attributable to competition with television. With violence, the advantage of visual impact that movies enjoy may be offset by the convenience of television, but in the case of sex the competitive advantage of movies is great, because television dares not offend any significant portion of its heterogeneous mass audience. Radio was converted by television from a national to a local medium. Before television, major radio stations carried the news, variety, and drama of three networks to a mass audience. That is now television's role. Radio has become a largely unlinked body of stations each of which caters to a homogeneous audience with a narrow format, of which the playing and promotion of recorded music with each station devoted to one type of music is paramount.*

After televison, the magazines appealing to broad ranges of taste and offering diversion for a mass audience (the *Saturday Evening Post, Collier's, Life, Look*) died, while specialist magazines (*Gourmet, Road and Track, Playboy*) thrived. Comic book sales fell from about 600 million to 300 million between the early 1950s and 1970. In book publishing, the prospects for promotion on television talk shows became a major factor in selecting what would be published, and with the reduction in total time devoted to reading, publishers' interest in works of marginal popularity, especially those in fiction, declined and the emphasis on achieving a pop success—such as produced by Arthur Hailey and Joyce Haber—grew. Fiction, poetry, and drama declined from 22 to 13 percent of all trade titles between 1950 and 1970, although the absolute number of such titles increased.† Obviously, many changes in addition to television have occurred since its advent and have played their part in these trends, but it is difficult not to believe that television has been a major factor.

The redistribution of media use by a newly popular medium is made largely inevitable by the fact that the proportion of consumer income devoted to the media resembles that for a staple. McCombs (1972) convincingly demonstrates that consumer expenditures for the media tend to be a constant proportion of such expenditures, and a slightly declining function of Gross National

* For example, in the Los Angeles basin in the late 1970s there are radio stations with schedules devoted exclusively to Top 40, progressive rock, '50s rock, jazz, classical, big band swing, current rock, country and western, soul, news and talk in English, music and news in Spanish, and religion. This is very diffrent from the days of Jack Benny. FM made more diversity possible, but the growth of FM benefited from and only augmented the trend initiated by television's replacement of radio as the national home entertainment medium.

† "Trade titles" are those intended for sale to the general public through the normal retail outlets. Texts, technical works, and religious books are excluded.

Product. The analysis is particularly convincing because it covers 40 years of American consumer activity and includes not only such obvious items as television sets, radios, newspapers, magazines and books, but also sheet music, musical instruments, maps, and records. The theoretical implication is that media as a class, regardless of the specific mix, have become alloted an essential role in modern life. The practical implication is that the popularity of any new medium can come only at the expense of other media—unless technological advances permit a reduction in the relative amount of expenditure required for access to the media in question. New media thus will almost certainly take from old; what is largely uncertain before the fact is the basis of the exchange and the pattern of media use that will ensue.

A large number of studies since the advent of television (e.g., Bogart, 1972a; J. P. Robinson, 1972b) show that total daily newspaper circulation for many years has steadily increased in proportion to the increase in the adult population, total amount of *time* devoted to newspaper reading is unaffected by television ownership, television in the home decreases the likelihood of persons subscribing to more than one newspaper, and television affects the degree of attention given to certain kinds of newspaper content. For example, television in the home seems to decrease the reading of Sunday comics by adults.

These changes occurred in a time of numerous mergers and a decline in the number of newspapers in major cities, events which may have been influenced by television but in which several other factors undoubtedly played the major roles. In the years immediately after television was introduced, newspaper circulation per 100 households dropped, but it appears that the decline is attributable to factors other than television, such as problems in delivering to new suburbs (Bogart, 1972a). However, the long-term trend may be unfavorable for major city dailies as people continue to move to more distant suburbs where local newspapers will provide community and consumer information and television may suffice for major and national news.

The issue we shall now focus upon is the reason why television—or any other mass medium—affects some other media strongly, some weakly, and some perhaps hardly at all. The hypothesis for which there is the greatest support is that one medium displaces another when it performs the function of the displaced medium in a superior manner—either more efficiently or at lower cost.

In the case of television, we notice immediately that its widespread adoption in the United States was followed by alterations in the popularity of its audiovisual competitor, theater movies; in two major competitors providing in-home diversion for a heterogeneous audience, the mass circulation magazine and national radio; in a major provider of fantasy to young persons, the comic book; and in the longest living mass medium providing fantasy to both young and old, books containing novels, poetry, or drama.

All of this fits the hypothesis. After television, there was decreased use of media which, variously, are audiovisual, provide the mass audience with in-home diversion, and specialize in fantasy—that is, media performing functions which television could be said to perform better. The impression gained from the sequence of these historical events is strengthened by several explicit tests of the hypothesis. In various instances in the early days of television, when a variety of populations alike except for television ownership were compared, the introduction of television was found to decrease use of mass media providing fantasy, such as comic books and library fiction, but to have less or no effect on mass media providing information, such as newspapers and nonfiction books (Himmelweit, Oppenheim, and Vince, 1958; Parker, 1960, 1963; Schramm, Lyle, and Parker, 1961).

We have also seen that a similar set of changes has occurred after the introduction of television in other societies (J. P. Robinson, 1972b; J. P. Robinson and Converse, 1972). Given the consistency of the evidence, one might expect unqualified acceptance of the hypothesis at this point. Instead, we would like to offer some qualifications. The hypothesis of displacement on the basis of functional similarity was originally developed by Himmelweit, Oppenheim, and Vince (1958) and Schramm, Lyle, and Parker (1961). It was devised to explain reductions following the introduction of television in England and the United States in children's use of fantasy-oriented print media that were not accompanied by commensurate reductions in use of information-oriented print media. The most convincing demonstration was Parker's (1963) analysis of library circulation in the 1950s in 14 closely matched pairs of Illinois communities that varied by several years in the introduction of television. Parker found that television reduced library circulation, and that 80 percent of the reduction involved fiction. We agree that the hypothesis is valid for the context in which it was developed, but we believe that there is more to be said, because effects may be more varied than a mere supplanting of other fantasy media by television because it can more efficiently supply such content.

When we examine the data on television viewing in various societies, we find that the inverse relationship between amount of viewing and education which has been observed in the United States since the introduction of television—and which we perceive as "normal" for the medium—does not hold for all societies. In certain of the societies where diffusion of television sets is far from ubiquity, as much or more time is spent viewing by those of higher as by those of lower socioeconomic status (J. P. Robinson and Converse, 1972).

Principally responsible are differences in broadcast schedule and content. What this divergence emphasizes is that beyond its inherent properties television may vary in character, including its emphasis on fantasy; consequently, the media that it may challenge, and the grounds on which the challenge will occur, also will vary.

As J. P. Robinson and Converse (1972) suggest, it will be interesting to see if increased diffusion of television among those of lower socioeconomic status in these societies will result in shifts in programming to meet their interests that in turn will lead to the inverse relationship found in the United States. The fact that a diffusion rate of over 50 percent tends, if imperfectly, to divide societies with an inverse relationship from those where it is positive or null suggests that this may indeed be what the future holds. If so, what we shall have observed is the evolution of a medium so determined by its inherent properties and their great appeal that great differences among the societies have been overcome.

The increasing penetration of society by television suggests an increasing homogeneity of media experience. This is clearly the implication of the convergence in the United States in amount of viewing of those of higher and lower socioeconomic status (figure 3.1). Nevertheless, there is justification for caution in assuming that such a trend foretells a future of such homogeneity. We argue later that changes in the basic structure of American broadcasting are only likely to come from technological developments that force change (chapter 9). The technological developments so far visible all have in common two characteristics—they increase viewer selectivity and options, and they require greater than average income for access. Thus, such innovations as pay- and cable television, increased channel capacity, satellites that enhance the availability of signals, and in-home recording and playback, make it possible for those of higher socioeconomic status to construct for themselves a more perfectly congenial television environment distinct from that available at no cost other than the price of a set, while the purveyors of broadcast television would presumably direct themselves increasingly to those unable or unmotivated to take advantage of the new opportunities. This would accentuate the historic trends in American broadcasting, for maximizing audience size has always implied a lower denominator approach. The outcome would be two "television cultures" rather than the one we now behold. In terms of set *use*, rather than consumption of broadcast television for which set use is now a surrogate, it could mean the dissolution of the inverse relationship with socioeconomic status.

At the same time, media so far have tended to be similar in characteristics across societies. This has led Katz, Gurevitch, and Haas (1973) to posit a model of most likely media interchangeability (figure 4-2). It is based on data from surveys of the Israeli public—adjacent media were named as serving more similar functions than those more distant. The model leads to the hypothesis that adjacent media would be more likely to displace one another than nonadjacent media. What it also makes clear is that position in such a model depends on the public's *perception* of the media, and that this is a function of the combination of factors that give each medium its character, of which fantasy and provision of information are only two dimensions.

We elaborate upon the original formulation of the hypothesis because it assigns to each medium a principal function and does not take into account the obvious multiplicity of functions which a single medium will perform. As J. R. Brown, Cramond, and Wilde (1974) argue, it is probable that a new medium will cause a redistribution of functions among the media. Thus, a new medium could almost totally assume some of the functions of an older me-

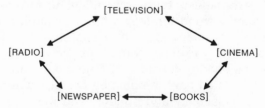

Figure 4.2. Model of media interchangeability.

SOURCE: Adapted from E. Katz, M. Gurevitch, and H. Haas. 1973. On the use of the mass media for important things. *American Sociological Review*, 38, 164–81.

dium without affecting the size of its audience if other important functions served of the old medium were not at all performed by the new medium. Furthermore, the response of the old media to the new may so change one or more of them that new, different functions are provided, and other of the media somehow newly displaced.

We would also point out that sometimes the displacement that occurs may be attributable to mechanisms other than the public's turning away from the older medium. In the case of general circulation magazines, falling circulation alone was not invariably the principal factor. In some instances, circulation was as high or higher than at any time in the past. What occurred was the attraction of advertising revenue to television because it appeared to be a more effective means of reaching the public, which in turn made the magazines economically unviable. In this case, displacement did not so much depend on the superior provision of similar content by television but on the unsurprising inability of magazines to perform in a manner superior to the past so that circulation would increase to offset the advantage television promised to advertisers.

We conclude that:

Television displaces other media when television performs their functions better.

Displacement of one medium by another is caused by the interplay of several fctors—such as content, inherent properties, and the audiences to which they appeal—and the consequence is that the eventual impact of a new medium is hard to predict. The tendency for consumer expenditure for media to be a constant proportion of income means, however, that a new medium's popularity can only occur at the expense of old media, unless old media can proportionately reduce their costs to consumers.

Television may be responsible for a redistribution of functions of the various mass media not apparent from simple before-after differences in the size of their audiences.

The tendency for television to displace fantasy-oriented media does not exclude the possibility of displacement on other dimensions, and the mechanism by which displacement occurs may not be reduced popularity of the displaced medium but its economic viability in the competition for both audience and advertisers when faced with coexistence with television.

Sociological and economic dynamics inhering in broadcast television may mean that widespread social diffusion is synonymous with an inverse relationship between time spent with television and socioeconomic status because diffusion nurtures among broadcasters—regardless of the relationship between the media and the state—a motive to satisfy a mass audience. However, this pattern of set use may be disrupted even in societies where television is ubiquitous by technological innovations that permit those with greater income to construct their own video environments.

What has occurred in the case of television's impact on other media can be expected to occur in regard to new media of the future—*new media alter old.*

Uses and Gratifications of Television

In any society, a given medium has a certain normative character defined by what people expect from it. There are, of course, many qualifications, but each medium's uses and the gratifications derived from that use are different. This occurs although it is obvious that in individual circumstances any medium and any kind of content may serve almost any use or gratification—as any voyeur of sexual transactions would attest.

We have a variety of data on the uses and gratifications served by television. To cover this ground briefly:*

> Different media typically serve different needs, although all may be turned to for entertainment and relaxation, and any one may serve all needs to some degree. For example, children and adolescents are very likely to turn to television for entertainment and relaxation, but are less likely to do so when their feelings have been hurt or they are angry (Lyle and Hoffman, 1972a).
>
> Television may serve some needs better than other media, but there is no reason to think that it is superior in quantity or range of needs especially well served. This point is made quite clear by data from Israel (Katz and Gurevitch, 1976). Among five major media— television, newspapers, books, radio, and movies—television was

---

* "Uses and gratifications" is a label under which almost the entire body of research covered in this book could be organized. We have chosen a different perspective for organizing our evaluation of the scientific literature, and obviously make no attempt to restate this literature in terms of uses and gratifications within a few pages. What we cover here are those studies dealing with uses and gratifications which do not fit well elsewhere, while very briefly summarizing the major findings about the uses and gratifications of television covered in greater detail elsewhere. The most convenient source for recent theory and findings bearing on uses and gratifications of mass media is J. G. Blumler and E. Katz, eds., *The Uses of Mass Communications.* (Beverly Hills: Sage, 1974).

ranked first as satisfying 35 different needs by the public only three times, compared to 19 first rankings for newspapers. Two of these, spending time with the family and being in a festive mood, were said to be "very important" needs by a large majority; one, killing time, was given this status by only about one-sixth of the sample. The precise pattern may be peculiar to Israel, but the larger implication is that television's satisfying of needs is more limited than would seem to be suggested by its popularity, which probably should be interpreted as reflecting the extraordinarily able satisfying of a very few needs.

The uses and gratifications served by specific media change over an individual's lifespan. For example, between the elementary and high school years the degree to which television is turned to for entertainment, for relaxation, and when angry or lonely, decreases, while the degree to which music is turned to for similar gratifications or purposes increases dramatically (Lyle and Hoffman, 1972a).

The public's perception of a medium is not always consistent with its behavior. For example, the public conceives of television as more of a national than local news source, but viewing of local news is at least as frequent as viewing of network evening national news (Roper, 1975; J. P. Robinson, 1971).

The uses of a new medium may be such that established interests and activities are affected. For example, when television was introduced in England the degree of interest and the frequency of engagement in various activities were reduced, and while activities less frequently engaged in prior to television returned to their pre-television levels within six years, those activities more frequently engaged in did not, and may have been permanently affected (Belson, 1959).

Television is very frequently the recourse when there is no involvement in other activities. For example, amount of television viewing by adults is positively correlated with their reporting that they have "time on their hands" (J. P. Robinson, 1972c). Television viewing thus is different from the many activities, including numerous leisure pursuits, which people think of as having their own justification apart from having time on one's hands.

Although "television" as a whole may be thought of as serving various uses and gratifications, different types of programs serve somewhat different sets of these. We infer this from the fact that the audience differs somewhat for different types of programs even when access to the television set would seem to be similar for all persons (see figure 3.15).

The uses and gratifications of television differs for different population groups. For example, blacks view more and like different programs than whites, suggesting that television either serves different purposes for them or that a different pattern of exposure is required for the same purposes to be served (Fletcher, 1969; B. S. Greenberg and Dervin, 1970; Surlin and Dominick, 1970).

But what of television's central character in our society? What do Americans expect from it? The medium is fundamentally perceived as the *entertainer*. Television is highly rated as a news source, and it is used to fill vacant time, yet its principal role from the viewpoint of the public is to provide entertainment and relaxation.

Let us assemble our evidence. Television receives the public's verbal acclaim as a national news source, yet national news does not reach a large proportion of the potential audience (J. P. Robinson, 1971, 1972c). Furthermore, the audience for national news is much smaller than the audience for the various classes of entertainment programs (see figure 3.15). When asked an open-ended question about why television was viewed, about 60 percent of adults in a national sample said they did so for entertainment or relaxation, three times more than offered a motiveless "killing time," and only about 12 percent said they were motivated by a desire to be informed or to learn (LoSciuto, 1972). When a Maryland teenage sample and a large national sample of 19-year-old males were asked, "All things considered, would you say you have learned more about life from television or from school?" school was chosen over television by a ratio of four-to-one. When the public is asked to name favorite programs, there are few choices which do not fall into the entertainment category (J. P. Robinson, 1972c). These findings all suggest that television is principally used for entertainment—although in the course of entertaining it may have all sorts of effects on knowledge and behavior.

We can carry the argument a little further. When we examine the relationship between knowledge of various public figures and media use among a Maryland sample of teenagers and a national sample of adults, we find that with a minor exception neither total amount of television viewing nor amount of viewing of local or national news was related to such knowledge (J. P. Robinson, 1972c).* However, exposure to print media—magazines and news-

---

*The exception was the extremely small number who said they *never* viewed national news or *never* viewed local news, who were somewhat more ignorant than those viewing varying amounts of such news.

papers—was positively correlated with such knowledge. We interpret these findings to mean that persons who are relatively well-informed about public figures—and presumably about other public symbols and events—are not disproportionately drawn to either television as a whole or to television news.

Now we will enlarge our picture. When reasons for watching television are volunteered, almost no one among the public says he does so to see a specific program (LoSciuto, 1972). On the other hand, when asked if one of the reasons for viewing is to see a specific program that is particularly liked, about four-fifths of the public will agree that is one motive (Bower, 1973). When asked about the motive for having viewed a particular program, about 40 percent of a national sample of adults said they watched simply because the program appeared while the channel was already on or someone else wanted to see the program (LoSciuto, 1972). One-fourth of the time a viewer did not watch a program from beginning to end, about a third engaged in some other activity while viewing, and about a third could not give an accurate account of what they had seen (LoSciuto, 1972; J. P. Robinson, 1972c). Although 80 percent affirmed that they "liked" the program viewed, only 40 percent agreed that it was "really worth watching" (J. P. Robinson, 1972c). These data suggest that to a large degree television viewing in America is a largely passive activity where acceptance rather than enthusiasm is the rule.

We have reported that education is inversely related to the favorability of attitudes toward television and amount of television viewing. There is no doubt that there are marked differences among segments of the audience in their relationship to television (see chapters 3 and 7). Nevertheless, when we look at the actual difference between households whose head has or has not attended college in number of hours of viewing, we find that it is not great and has been declining (figure 4.1). In addition, when Bower (1973) compared the stated attitudes and program preferences of adults with their actual viewing, he found education to make a notable difference for the former but not for the latter. Despite more frequent declarations of a desire for more informational and educational programming, the television diet of the better educated was about as heavily weighted with entertainment as that of the less educated. The implications of these findings are that television as entertainer pervades the society, and that this has become progressively so.

Data from Israel are consistent with this view. Katz and Gurevitch (1976) report that with the passage of time after the introduction of television the proportion of the public expecting cultural fare declined. This would appear to be an effect of the medium's success as light entertainer on the public's demands and expectations for the future.

We conclude that:

Television viewing is typically motivated by and serves the desire to be entertained.

The normative role ascribed to television in our society by the public is that of an entertainer—even though television is highly rated as a news source and a wide range of effects on knowledge and behavior may occur.

Much of television is watched as "television" and not for any particular program.

Even when a viewer says he is drawn to a particular program it is hardly ever the merits of an individual episode and often simply the selection of a pleasing example of a particularly satisfying genre.

Viewers typically do not decide to watch a specific program; they make two decisions. The first is *whether* to view, and the second is *what* to view; of these, the first is by far the most important—which means that in the ordinary situation any program largely draws its audience from those who are committed to viewing *something* at that time.

Television's central role as an entertainer holds for both the more and the less educated, and probably for other segments of the population as well, despite variations in attitudes toward television, amount of viewing, and other factors among segments.

Chapter

One Highly Attracted Public

Then shall we simply allow our children to listen to any story anyone happens to make up, and so receive into their minds ideas often the very opposite of those we shall think they ought to have when they are grown up?

—Plato, *The Republic*

IT IS NOT surprising that young persons should be singled out for special attention in regard to television. First, they are—at least during their early years—very heavy consumers of television. Both young boys and girls view for considerably more hours per week than do adult men and women. Second, there is a long tradition of concern over the nature of symbolic messages available to children. A prominent example is Plato's advocacy of censorship as a condition necessary to the rearing of ideal citizens.

Although various media have been the focus of attention at various times, including fairy tales, library holdings, movies, and comic books, the medium that has become the center of the dispute is television. The public concern has been visibly expressed in the attention given to television by Congress, the Federal Communications Commission (FCC), the Federal Trade Commission (FTC), various advocacy groups, and such prestigious organizations as the American Medical Association (AMA) and national Parent-Teachers Association (PTA) to such questions as the effects on the young of television violence, the quality of children's programming, and the possibly detrimental effects of television advertising viewed by the young.

The most publicized reform resulting from such attention was the adoption of "family viewing" by the television industry early in 1975. This innovation imposed restrictions on "violence" and "sex" during two hours of evening telecasting when the young audience is large. (See chapters 2 and 9).

As would be expected, the concern has found considerable reflection in research. There has been extensive investigation of the issue of television violence, including but not confined to the studies commissioned in connection with the Surgeon General's Scientific Advisory Committee (1972), which was convened to examine the issue, and much new research is emerging on the effects on the young of television advertising. In addition, research on numerous other topics related to television's role in socialization and development has been the product of disquiet over the possible influence of the medium.

Such concern with television is related to the accessibility of the medium. The effects of print depend on the child's ability to read. That ability is tied to age and occurs after certain values are presumed to have been established. Aural and pictorial media face no such obstacle. The moving, speaking figure on the screen, along with the words of the storyteller and the cartoon in the comic book, are accessible to even the very young. And television, in particular, is especially accessible because of the medium's ubiquity. It is present in almost every home, and always on call. The storyteller is at least controlled by time; the comic book must be purchased and demands some reading; the child must leave the home and pay to see the motion picture; and, at least for young children, all of these are under a modicum of parental control. The television set is always there and usually on.

The evidence on parental control of children's television viewing indicates that even the preschooler often operates as a free agent in selecting when and what to watch. The information monopoly once enjoyed by parents has been breeched, if not shattered (E. E. Jones and Gerard, 1967; Roberts, 1973).

It should not be surprising that television, more than any other source of symbolic messages, has aroused the concern of parents, teachers, legislators, and the public at large. Nor that much of the research on television and young persons has focused on possible negative effects.

Our evaluation of the evidence on effects on children will cover:

The range and nature of effects with particular attention to the problem of avoiding false issues or overlooking effects.

The pattern of consumption of television, with attention both to quantity and character of viewing and to the motives for viewing.

Effects in such areas of high and special interest as responses to commercials, political socialization, antisocial behavior, and prosocial behavior.

The role of television as a source of learning regardless of the specific topic, with particular attention to the factors upon which a very wide range of effects are contingent.

The degree to which television should be considered an agent of socialization.

The Nature of Effects

Children watch a good deal of television. What are the consequences? Has it affected participation in other activities? Does it arouse emotions? Frighten? Desensitize? Increase anxiety? Do they learn from the medium? If so, what? Does the image of the "real" world the developing young person constructs reflect the image portrayed by television? Perhaps most important, does a young person's own behavior reflect what has been seen on the screen?

There is no one "effect." We would also warn that the term "effect" itself is somewhat misleading in its implication that the bulk of attention should be concentrated on what television does *to* young persons. What young persons do *with* television plays an equally important role in the relationship. When we talk about effects, then, we are talking about a variety of relationships, including:

A broad range of consequences which may follow from viewing a specific program, or program type, or full season of programs.

Direct outcomes, such as the learning of a new fact or behavior from a program.

Indirect outcomes, such as giving up time formerly spent in other activities to sit in front of the television.

Immediate effects, such as emotional arousal during viewing.

Delayed effects, such as the performance of a viewed behavior some time after viewing.

Short-term consequences, such as a behavior learned on Friday but forgotten by Monday.

Long-term consequences, such as attitudes or expectations which may affect behaviors for weeks or years to come.

Communicator-intended effects, such as when *Sesame Street* aims to teach letter recognition.

Unintended effects, such as when a police show producer inadvertently teaches that policemen are violent persons to be avoided.

We do not bother with the commonly asked question, "Are there effects?" It is not fruitful, and diverts attention from a more useful focus by posing questions already answered. It ignores the obvious as well as several decades of research. At the same time, it should not be carelessly concluded that television's effects can be easily anticipated, that they will directly mirror the manifest content present, or that they will be the same for all young persons at all times.

The amount of time spent by young persons in watching television by itself means that there is an "effect," because that is time unavailable for other activities. Moreover, there is ample evidence of a wide variety of other effects. Hence, the important questions have to do with specifying the conditions under which various effects occur and the contingencies facilitating or impeding these effects. The proper effects question is (Berelson, 1948; Roberts, 1973):

Which content,
Under which conditions,
Leads to which effects,
Among which young persons?

Viewing of Television

How Much They Watch

Although we have already devoted considerable attention to viewing patterns in chapter 3, we believe that the high interest in young person's behavior in regard to television and changes in viewing behavior as they grow older justify closer examination.

Except for the Neilsen sampling, surveys that attempt to represent the population of young persons in the United States have not been carried out; and the Nielsen samples of the young are small and analyses are confined to rather roughly defined age categories.

The scientific literature consists of numerous small-scale studies conducted in various parts of the country, with different age groups, at different times of the year, using different measurement procedures and bases for reporting estimates. Thus, although the studies, taken together, have included children manifesting most of the demographic and personal characteristics conventionally employed to describe patterns of media use, it is not surprising to find a range of estimates of "average" amounts of television viewing. For example, on the basis of a seven-day week children between the fifth and eighth grades have been reported to view an average of a little over three hours per day (Schramm, Lyle, and Parker, 1961), over four hours per day (Lyle and Hoffman, 1972a), and almost six hours per day (B. S. Greenberg and Dervin, 1970).

Despite such variations, we find a high degree of convergence across studies: in patterns of relative viewing time for different age and demographic groups, in variables which predict relative amounts of viewing, in evidence indicating that the "average" young viewer is an elusive creature at best, and in the general conclusion that once past infancy most children watch a great deal of television.

Comparisons between the results of early surveys (Himmelweit, Oppenheim, and Vince, 1958; Schramm, Lyle, and Parker, 1961) and more recent work (Chaffee, McLeod, and Atkin, 1970; B. S. Greenberg and Dervin, 1970; Lyle and Hoffman, 1972a, 1972b) suggest an overall increase in children's viewing. Lyle and Hoffman (1972a) estimate an increment of approximately one hour per day over the past two decades.

However, early descriptions of relative age differences in amount of viewing remain valid. The data of Schramm, Lyle, and Parker (1961) have generally stood the test of time.

A composite picture of trends in young persons' viewing as they grow older, based on a number of individual studies, is displayed in figure 5.1. Some two-year-olds are already viewers, and three-year-olds typically are high viewers. Viewing time reaches a peak just before the beginning of elementary school, drops as the school day cuts into the child's available time, increases steadily to another peak around early adolescence, then declines during the high-school years (Chaffee and McLeod, 1972; Lyle and Hoff-

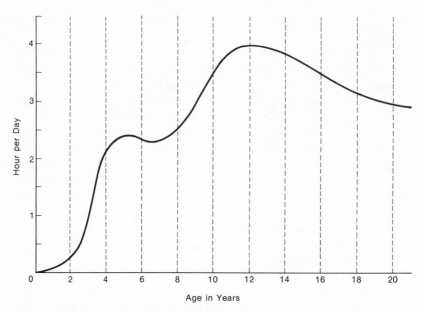

Figure 5.1. Constructed curve of average hours of daily television viewing by age.

NOTE: Hours spent viewing are averages of several studies.

man, 1972a, 1972b; McIntyre and Teevan, 1972; McLeod, Atkin and Chaffee, 1972; Schramm, Lyle and Parker, 1961).

For the most part, these age differences are explained by age-related changes in interests, needs, and opportunities, all of which influence perceptions of available time. For example, the decline in viewing just after early adolescence coincides with increased demands of high school, the onset of activities associated with the teenager's more active social life and greater mobility, availability of competing activities such as sports and clubs, and the emergence of a stronger interest in and more ability to deal with competing media.

Of equal interest is the variation *within* groups. J. P. Murray (1972) found a range of from 5 to 42 hours of viewing per week in a sample of kindergarten and first-grade black boys. Similarly, Lyle and Hoffman (1972a) found that over 25 percent of a sixth-grade sample reported no viewing on a given weekday while another 25 percent viewed more than five and one-half hours. Friedman and Johnson (1972) reported a daily range of two to six hours of viewing among a sample of ninth-grade children and J. P. Robinson and Bachman (1972) gathered estimates of from zero to more than three hours of viewing daily for a sample of 19-year-olds.

Such variations are by no means random. Several of the same variables that predict amount of viewing among adults also predict amount of young persons' exposure. With samples of children, however, the predictive power of many variables tends to be a function of age. The relationship between amount of viewing and such measures of mental ability as IQ scores or grades is an example. While a number of researchers report negative correlations between amount of viewing and mental ability among adolescents (Himmelweit, Oppenheim, and Vince, 1958; Himmelweit and Swift, 1976; Lyle and Hoffman, 1972a; McLeod, Atkin, and Chaffee, 1972a; J. P. Robinson, 1972c; Schramm, Lyle, and Parker, 1961) little or no relationship has been found for younger children. Childers and Ross (1973) examined viewing of 100 fourth- and fifth-graders in relation to IQ scores, grades, and Iowa Tests of Basic Skills scores and found no significant relationships. Several studies (Himmelweit, Oppenheim, and Vince, 1958; Lyle and Hoffman, 1972a; Schramm, Lyle, and Parker 1961) report that many of the brighter sixth-graders tend to be among the heavier viewers of television.

Schramm comments that the probable cause of the lack of any relationship between mental ability and viewing among young children is the brighter young children's tendency to do more of everything—television viewing, radio listening, reading, and so forth. As they grow older, however, brighter children are those more likely to devote more time to and derive more satisfaction from competing media and activities.

It should be noted, though, that Lyle and Hoffman's more recent survey (1972a) found that brighter tenth-graders also tend to view a good deal of television and engage in more competing activities. They suggest that mental ability is no longer related to adolescents' viewing of television to the degree that it was 15 years ago. We agree that one probable result of television's ubiquity has been to reduce such differences, which depend on various norms in regard to the media as well as on young person's characteristics, but we doubt that there is now no longer any relationship at all. Too many other recent studies find some relationship. Moreover, the rationale for why brighter, older children may tend to watch less television is supported by Wade's (1971) study of the relationship between television viewing and creativity. Her results provide strong evidence that the more creative adolescent spends more time and energy on activities that preclude viewing.

Parental socioeconomic status is also inversely related to amount of children's television viewing (Bailyn, 1959; B. S. Greenberg and Dervin, 1970; Himmelweit and Swift, 1976; Lefkowitz, et al., 1972; McIntyre and Teevan, 1972; McLeod, Atkin, and Chaffee, 1972a; Schramm, Lyle, and Parker, 1961), although Lyle and Hoffman (1972a) again suggest that socioeconomic status does not predict as strongly now as it did when Schramm and his colleagues carried out their work. We agree that the relationship has probably become weaker, but, again, we doubt that it no longer exists. Here, too, there are indications that age may modify the predictive power of socioeconomic status measures, although the data are highly tentative, since few studies have made comparisons based on both age and socioeconomic status. Lyle and Hoffman (1972a), for example, report no consistent differences in amount of viewing by sixth-graders from white-collar and blue-collar homes, but do find a consistent, although moderate, tendency for tenth-graders from blue-collar homes to view more. In addition, although the criteria for dividing middle- and lower-class children were slightly different at the two age levels, another study (B. S. Greenberg and Dervin, 1970) indicates that socioeconomic differences in total viewing time are not as large among younger children as among teenagers.

We also find race and ethnic group differences in amount of viewing. B. S. Greenberg and Dervin (1970) and McIntyre and Teevan (1972) found more viewing by black children than by white, and Lyle and Hoffman (1972a) more viewing among Mexican American girls than among their Caucasian counterparts. These data must be interpreted cautiously because uncontrolled social class differences are involved.* We also wonder whether any single index of socioeconomic status is appropriate when try-

---

* At least some of the differences reported by Lyle and Hoffman and by McIntyre and Teevan probably reflect uncontrolled socioeconomic class differences in the samples. Even Greenberg's work, which attempted to control for social class differences using an index of parental occupational prestige, can be questioned on these grounds. For example, among younger children a lack of blacks from high-income families forced adjustment of the classification criteria such that similar cutting points on the occupational prestige index existed only for those children classed as from low-income families. In addition, classification of socioeconomic status was based on the occupation of the "main wage earner" in the family. To the extent that race differences exist in whether that wage-earner was father, or mother, or sibling, even identical cutting points do not ensure comparable socioeconomic groups.

ing to equate blacks and whites in the United States. Fundamentally, measures of socioeconomic status are used as locators of environments and opportunities, but we doubt whether it is reasonable to expect middle-income status or a college education or any other index to predict similar environments, opportunities, or experiences for blacks and whites.

Again there are tentative indications that age may modify race and ethnic group differences in viewing. Although Lyle and Hoffman (1972a) report that ethnic group membership predicted differences only among girls, within that subsample their data also indicate that the differences were roughly twice as large among tenth-graders as among sixth-graders. Similarly, among lower-class children, the only group for which age comparisons are possible in Greenberg's data, race differences in amount of viewing are somewhat larger for teenagers than for elementary-school children.

Girls and boys do not appear to differ greatly in the amount of television they view, although their involvement follows different curves and their preferences diverge as they grow older. In regard to amount of viewing, there are reports of no differences (Schramm, Lyle, and Parker, 1961), of greater viewing by girls (Lyle and Hoffman, 1972a), and of greater viewing by boys (Chaffee and McLeod, 1972; McLeod, Atkin, and Chaffee, 1972a). Very young girls and boys probably do not differ; in elementary school, girls probably view more than boys. By adolescence, boys view more than girls because, as would be expected from earlier female maturation, the downturn in viewing occurs earlier for girls. This temporary female withdrawal from television may be accelerated by their lack of ardor for action-adventure. When adulthood is reached, any ambiguity over sex differences disappears: women view more than men (See chapters 3 and 6).

Several early studies examine the relationship between various psychosocial characteristics and viewing. Young persons classified as insecure in their peer-group relationships, who had difficulties making friends or interacting within a group were found to be heavy television viewers (Himmelweit, Oppenheim and Vince, 1958; Riley and Riley, 1951; Schramm, Lyle, and Parker, 1961). Data gathered in the 1950s from sociometric mapping indicate that teenagers who had few high-school friends and teenagers who aspired to but perceived themselves not to have attained membership in prestige groups were heavier television viewers (Johnstone, 1974).

Parent-child conflict has also been reported to correlate positively with viewing. Maccoby (1954) found that for middle-class elementary-school children, lack of parental warmth, parental restrictiveness, and intrafamily conflict predicted heavier viewing. The relationship did not hold among lower-class children. We believe the interpretation is probably correct that the difference is attributable to the differences in the role of television in the middle- and lower-class families. In the middle-class homes, where parental viewing would be lighter, children could escape from the parents by watching television; in the lower-class homes, television could not serve as an escape from parents because lower-class parents are relatively heavy viewers.

Parent-child conflict has also been measured in terms of the discrepancy between the child's own aspirations and those the child perceived the parents to hold. The greater such "conflict," the more television the child was likely to view, particularly when the child came from a white-collar family (Schramm, Lyle, and Parker, 1961).

More recently, Lyle and Hoffman (1972a) found only a weak positive correlation between high conflict with parents or difficulties with peers and viewing time among sixth- or tenth-graders. They again interpret this as evidence of the dissolution or relationships between viewing and personal characteristics. We again agree that some dissolution would be expected, but doubt whether the relationship has or will vanish. There are simply too many studies which demonstrate that heavy mass-media use is sometimes a symptom of psychosocial malfunctioning.

We also emphasize that the relationships can be very complex. For example, Lyle and Hoffman (1972a) found that first-graders reporting the *lowest* levels of loneliness spent more time with television and less time playing with peers. One possibility is that television is successfully filling a social void. Another is that the first-grader does not define the notion of loneliness the way an adult does. In any case, less time at play—given the consistent finding that children prefer such play to television viewing (Lyle and Hoffman, 1972a; J. P. Murray, 1972; Schramm, Lyle, and Parker, 1961)—makes us suspect that heavy viewing is related to psychosocial malfunctioning.

We would also speculate that the relationship may be age-related. The younger the child, the more he depends on television as an alternative to social interaction.

We must emphasize that a persistent theme throughout this literature is that most children watch television when there is nothing better or more necessary to do. Given a choice between viewing and playing with other children, or between viewing and participating in some organized social activity, the majority of children prefer social interaction. We also find little evidence that television has markedly decreased the amount of time older children spend on homework or other "necessary" activities, and there is good evidence that when the shorter days and inclement weather of the winter months reduce the number of potential alternative activities, viewing increases (Lyle, 1972; Lyle and Hoffman, 1972a; Schramm, Lyle, and Parker, 1961). We thus conclude that one of the important determinants of the amount of television young persons watch appears to be how much time they perceive themselves to have free from other activities, particularly social activities.

What They Watch

What do young persons watch? What characteristics of the developing child and his environment are related to program preferences? Do children attend to programs designed for them, or do they choose "adult" fare?

We find consistent evidence that definite program preferences appear very early and that age continues to be a good predictor of what is viewed throughout the life cycle (Schramm, 1971):

> Almost as soon as children begin to view television, they express definite program preferences (Dominick and Greenberg, 1972; Lyle and Hoffman, 1972a, 1972b; J. P. Murray, 1972; Schramm, Lyle, and Parker, 1961; A. H. Stein and Friedrich, 1972).
>
> The preschool child prefers cartoons, situation comedies, and noncartoon children's programs, generally in that order.
>
> By the first or second grade, situation comedies dominate the list of preferred shows, and their presence as favorites remains substantial well into the beginning of adolescence.
>
> The end of the elementary-school years tends to mark a transition period when, in addition to the situation comedies and even some of the cartoons favored by younger children, action-adventure, music and variety, and various dramatic shows begin to be cited as favorites.
>
> By the middle of the teens, such "adult" entertainment programming tends to dominate the list of preferences (Lyle and Hoffman, 1972a; Schramm, Lyle, and Parker, 1961).

Although Lyle and Hoffman (1972a) comment that the children in their sample almost seem to avoid news programs, a number of investigators report at least some adolescents among the news-viewing audience (Chaffee, McLeod, and Atkin, 1970, 1971; Hawkins, Pingree, and Roberts, 1975; McIntyre and Teevan, 1972; Roberts, Hawkins and Pingree, 1975; J. P. Robinson, 1972c). Roberts and colleagues found that even younger children claim to see news at least once in a while, and Tolley (1973) presents evidence that gradeschoolers do view some news. While it is clear that news and public affairs programming never becomes dominant, it is safe to say that some news viewing begins near the onset of adolescence and gradually increases throughout the high-school years.

We find that the shift toward more adult programming is accompanied by diversification in preferences. It is most clearly seen when the favorite programs of children of different ages are grouped by program categories (table 5.1). Among first-graders, three types of programming account for over 70 percent of all choices, but among sixth- and tenth-graders, six program types are necessary to reach the 70 percent level.

There are many studies that find discrepancies between most

Table 5.1 Favorite Programs of First, Sixth, and Tenth-Grade Children (in percent)

Program Type	First Grade	Sixth Grade	Tenth Grade
Youth-oriented adventure	10	14	20
Situation comedy	22	17	9
Family situation comedy	25	23	9
Police/detective	3	5	6
Cartoon/kiddie	24	5	1
Music/variety/talk	3	5	13
Serial dramas	—	3	9
Dramatic	2	6	13
News	—	1	1
Education/culture	4	3	2
Western	3	8	7
Game	2	4	2
Sports	—	2	2
Movies	2	4	6

SOURCE: Adapted from J. Lyle and H. R. Hoffman. 1972a. Children's use of television and other media. In E. A. Rubinstein, G. A. Comstock, and J. P. Murray (Eds.), *Television and social behavior.* Vol. 4. *Television in day-to-day life: Patterns of use.* Washington, D.C.: Government Printing Office, pp. 129–256.

favored and most viewed shows. Apparently, such discrepancies increase with age. Lyle and Hoffman's (1972a) data, for example, show that two-thirds of the specific programs listed by first-graders as favorites also appear in the list of programs most viewed during a given week. Among sixth-graders, about 40 percent of the favorites appear on the most viewed list. Among tenth-graders, the figure drops to about 30 percent. We suspect the principal factor is opportunity, the general importance of which we discuss in connection with the general psychology of television's behavioral effects (chapter 8). Young persons frequently must share the television set and the likelihood of having to share and negotiate program choices increases with age. The first-grader may have the television to himself on a weekday afternoon when a favorite situation comedy is rerun; the tenth-grader, whose favorite is more likely to appear during prime time, must compete with parents or siblings. This pattern is consistent with the increased number of reports among older children of family conflict over program selection (Lyle and Hoffman, 1972a). In addition, the older the child, the greater the likelihood that he will be engaged in other activities when the program is on.

We were struck by the relative absence of noncartoon children's programs designed both to entertain and to educate from most lists of favorites. Although shows such as *Sesame Street* and *Mister Rogers' Neighborhood* certainly are often cited as favorites by preschool children, such programs are more frequently cited when mothers respond for their children. The proportion of children naming such programs decreases rapidly with age, and by the time children are in the first or second grade almost no mention of these shows occurs (Lyle and Hoffman, 1972a; J. P. Murray, 1972; A. H. Stein and Friedrich, 1972).

We suspect the reason is that while such programs may command large audiences, their appeal is very closely tied to the specific age of the child and they are not favorites. For example, *Sesame Street* is aimed at preschoolers as a group, but Lyle and Hoffman (1972b) found a dramatic drop between ages three and five in the number of children listing it as their favorite show— from almost 30 percent to 12 percent. Roberts and colleagues (1974) report similar findings for a children's program aimed at fourth-, fifth-, and sixth-graders. After viewing four episodes of *Big Blue Marble,* a series designed to increase intercultural understanding, children were asked how frequently they would view it if it were to be broadcast daily. The proportion of children answering "always" or "a lot" dropped from 66 percent among fourth-graders to 28 percent among sixth-graders. Such figures are not valid measures of whether or not children would actually view the program. However, they do indicate that the kind of children's programming that attempts to "educate" as well as to entertain may have to focus on relatively narrow age ranges in order to elicit attention, if only because what is novel and challenging for children at one age might be a bit too difficult for children a year younger and tedious for children a year older.

We thus arrive at a paradox of television. It can assemble a huge young audience for entertainment. Yet, the developmental changes that occur during childhood are so great that when it also tries to educate it is effective for younger children only when it sacrifices that mass audience for a fairly specific age range.

Sex differences in what is viewed occur quite early and continue throughout adolescence. Indications of boys preference for action-type programming can be seen in Lyle and Hoffman's (1972b) data on preschoolers where three times as many boys than girls listed a "violent cartoon" as a favorite, and is quite clear throughout the rest of childhood. Boys constitute the larger proportion of the audience for western, crime, and action-adventure programming. As they grow older, boys are also more likely to view sports and news and public affairs programming. Girls tend to prefer family situation comedies and, to a slight degree, music and variety programming (Chaffee and McLeod, 1972; Lyle and Hoffman, 1972a; McLeod, Atkin, and Chaffee, 1972; J. P. Murray, 1972; Schramm, Lyle, and Parker, 1961).

Ethnic group membership, socioeconomic status, and mental ability are all related to program selection (Fletcher, 1969; B. S. Greenberg and Dervin, 1970; Lyle, 1972; Lyle and Hoffman, 1972a; J. P. Murray, 1972; A. H. Stein and Friedrich, 1972; Surlin and Dominick, 1970). However, it is a brave analyst who would reject the proposition that differences related to these variables are not far clearer than the interpretation that should be applied to such differences. The precise factor that lies behind the differing preferences for specific programs is seldom apparent and typically defies capture.

The use of a program log to find something to view has been found to be more common, and the flipping of the dial for that purpose less common, among children from families of higher socioeconomic status and Caucasian children. Diversity of the programming that wins approval appears to increase with socioeconomic status and with mental ability. These varied findings lead to the conclusion that disadvantage or isolation in any respect may be associated with a narrower television experience.

As we discuss elsewhere (chapters 3 and 6), black youngsters and those from families of lower socioeconomic status have displayed a preference for programs featuring families. Children of ethnic minorities also prefer programs with minority performers. Plausible speculative explanations are the seeking of supplementary familial experience and the identification presumably facilitated by similarity.

We have already reported that viewing of violent programs increases with age (with the qualification that in absolute but not proportional terms there is a decrease in the amount of violence viewed from junior to senior high school, because of the decrease during adolescence in total viewing time) and is higher among boys than girls; and there is consistent evidence that violence viewing is positively related to total viewing time (Chaffee, 1972b; Chaffee and McLeod, 1972; B. S. Greenberg, Ericson, and Vlahos, 1972; McLeod, Atkin, and Chaffee, 1972a). It is therefore not surprising that viewing of violence is related to the same variables as amount of viewing. For example, just as they tend to view less television, brighter children and children from higher socioeconomic backgrounds tend to view less violence (Chaffee and McLeod, 1972; Dominick and Greenberg, 1972; Himmelweit and Swift, 1977; McLeod, Atkin, and Chaffee, 1972a; J. P. Murray, 1972; A. H. Stein and Friedrich, 1972). However, it should be noted that while the negative relationship between measures of mental ability and viewing of violence survive extensive controls for other variables, the same may not be true for the relationship between viewing of violence and socioeconomic status. When Chaffee and McLeod (1972) controlled for other measures of viewing and parent-child interaction, they found no relationship. This finding plus the fact that the relationship between viewing of violence and aggressiveness did not disappear when socioeconomic status was controlled for (McLeod, Atkin, and Chaffee, 1972a) points to the need to consider more psychologically or sociologically meaningful variables. A more productive approach would be to examine variables that might indicate why young persons watch the quantity and kind of television they watch, rather than variables like socioeconomic status which only make possible the description of persons with particular viewing patterns.

Why They Watch

Earlier, we suggested that many of the variables that locate differences in amount of viewing do so because they affect the time each young person perceives to be available to spend with television. That is, older children, brighter children, children from middle-class families may all perceive—and probably have—more alternative activities to which to devote time. Hence, they view less. Similarly, developmental, individual, and social characteristics also locate differential needs, interests, values, and abilities, all of which influence each young person's estimate of whether or not television has a greater claim on time than an alternative.

Given television's accessibility to even the very young, viewing can be conceptualized as a "baseline" activity in which most young children, who by virtue of their age have a limited number of alternatives regardless of various individual or social differences, can and do engage. As they grow older, however, the range of alternatives increases. Children must go to school; they are more geographically mobile; their ability to read develops; their interest in the world beyond the home grows. Time spent viewing then decreases, but it decreases differentially as a result of such factors as mental ability or social class for the simple reason that these variables *also* locate differences in the actual availability of alternatives, in the likelihood of perceiving alternatives, and in factors which locate the attractiveness or necessity of these alternatives. (Some configurations of these variables may also locate increases with maturation in amount of viewing.)

As a result, we are not surprised that some social and individual variables fail to locate significant differences in amount of viewing until the later years of childhood, for it is only then that many variables, such as mental ability, parental income, or residence in a ghetto, will affect alternatives. A child must be old enough to go to summer camp before the economic status of his parents is able to provide this alternative to television.

We believe that the evidence on amount of viewing by young persons indicates that frequently television is watched because it is there when other necessary or attractive alternatives are not. Thus, the various developmental, individual, and social variables that differentiate among children in amount of viewing do so in part because fundamentally they locate the availability of those other alternatives.

But available time is clearly not the only determinant of viewing. Many children who, on the basis of the variables discussed above, should have little available time nevertheless watch a great deal of television. Conversely, some children who would seem to have a great deal of time watch little television. And, finally, available time has little or no impact on program selection once viewing takes place.

The influence of parents is one obvious source of variation in viewing behavior. Such influence may be exercised, for example, by establishing hours during which children can watch, by encouraging or discouraging the viewing of certain programs, or by personal example (Maccoby, 1959). In addition, as has been recently proposed, the kind of family environment that parents develop may guide the child (Chaffee, McLeod, and Atkin, 1971). We shall consider each in turn.

A number of studies have employed various measures of the frequency and nature of parents' attempts to control what their children view (Bower, 1973; Chaffee, McLeod, and Atkin, 1970; B. S. Greenberg and Dervin, 1970; Hess and Goldman, 1962; Lyle and Hoffman, 1972a, 1972b; McLeod, Atkin, and Chaffee, 1972a, 1972b; Niven, 1960; A. H. Stein and Friedrich, 1972). They lead us to conclude that parents are likely to express a good deal of concern over the impact of television on their children, but are much less likely to control the child's viewing directly—particularly the amount of it.

Hess and Goldman (1962) found that most mothers were more concerned with what their children saw than with the amount of time spent viewing; and over 60 percent of the mothers of first-graders interviewed by Lyle and Hoffman (1972a) reported that they placed no restrictions on the amount of time they let their children view. Even when parents do make such restrictions, they are frequently only to set the hour past which children are not allowed to view (B. S. Greenberg and Dervin, 1970). Such a limitation as likely to be an effort to impose a bedtime as it is to control viewing.

Some illustrative data from a national survey are displayed in table 5.2. There is a particularly striking finding. Common sense says that a parent's concern with a child's television viewing will decline as the child matures. In table 5.2, we find this is not far wrong for amount of viewing or the setting of special hours for viewing. Across the various ages, the imposition of controls either declines or holds stable. However, the situation is markedly different for restrictions on specific programs. Here, the percentage

Table 5.2 Parental Response to Child's Viewing by Age of Child

Parental Response	Percent of Parents Reporting Response When Age of Child Is:		
	4–6 Yrs. (N = 197)[a]	7–9 Yrs. (N = 217)	10–12 Yrs. (N = 189)
Control on Viewing Time			
Restrict amount "often"	30	39	34
Set special hours "often"	41	48	46
Control on Specific Content			
Specify programs that can be watched "often"	45	37	46
Switch channel on objectional program "often"	40	27	30
Forbid viewing of certain programs "often"	39	39	52

SOURCE: Adapted from R. T. Bower. 1973. *Television and the Public.* New York: Holt, Rinehart and Winston.
[a] N = Number of parents.

of parents reporting that they often decide what programs the children can watch rises from 37 to 46 percent as the age of the child increases from 7–9 years to 10–12 years. In addition, those who say they often forbid certain programs rises, with the same increase in the age of the child, from 39 to 52 percent.

Why? We interpret these data as a dramatic illustration of parental concern about the role of television in socialization. The ages over which concern rises are precisely the years when adult television drama becomes relevant to the young person's tentative decision-making about his own life and values. It is the specific program content that is at issue. Concerned parents begin to emphasize the models they believe the child should be exposed to, and to deemphasize those they believe the child should be denied. We are particularly confident of our inference because the same data permit us to reject the hypothesis that the parents are concerned over time taken from homework or other activities. If they were, we would expect parents also to restrict total viewing time, or to set special hours. This is not the case.

There is evidence that parents do try to influence program selection (Bower, 1973; Hess and Goldman, 1962; Lyle and Hoffman, 1972a; A. H. Stein and Friedrich, 1972), but such attempts appear to be directed toward forbidding specific programs (usually those with physical violence) rather than toward selecting categories of programs. Moreover, the number of parents who report that they attempt to control content in even a limited way seldom accounts for a majority of those sampled. Indeed, by the time a child reaches mid-adolescence, attempts at parental control of viewing almost vanish. Among one sample of teenagers and parents, only 10 percent of the families reported viewing rules of any kind (Chaffee, McLeod, and Atkin, 1970). Lyle's (1972) summary of these studies, "despite uneasiness and intentions of mothers to guide the viewing of their young children, much of the viewing of even very young children is unsupervised, unmonitored," leads to the conclusion that although direct parental control may exert some influence on some children, such controls are by no means a dominant influence on the viewing behavior of children in general.

The modeling hypothesis holds that much of young persons' viewing behavior—in regard to both quantity and preference—derives from their attempt to behave in an adult manner by following (or "modeling") the example set by parents. On the basis of positive correlations between the patterns of media use among parents and children, the authors of several early studies argued that such observational learning was a primary determinant of how much and what television children viewed (Himmelweit, Oppenheim, and Vince, 1958; Schramm, Lyle, and Parker, 1961). This view prevailed for many years.

Recently, the importance of parental modeling as one of the more potent influences on children's media behavior has been seriously challenged (McLeod, Atkin, and Chaffee, 1972a, 1972b). First, while correlations between indices of media use among parents and children usually reach levels of statistical significance, they account for a relatively small proportion of the variance in viewing behavior—at least among adolescents. Second, many of the obtained parent-child correlations may be due to opportunity rather than modeling—the child may watch a particular program because that is what the parent has switched the channel to and not because he or she is attempting to model parental behavior. Third, parent and child may view similar programs because of some third factor (such as circumstances associated with family socioeconomic status) that influences their viewing independent of social influence between parent and child. Finally, modeling influence may run from child to parent, a process labeled "reverse" modeling (McLeod, Atkin, and Chaffee, 1972a, 1972b). Reverse modeling is supported by several studies that have found substantial numbers of parents stating that they guide their program selection on the basis of children's suggestions (Bottorff, 1970; Chaffee, McLeod, and Atkin, 1971; Clarke, 1963).

We believe the evidence does not indicate that modeling during adolescence typically is an important factor. This conclusion is consistent with the extensive evidence that adolescence is characterized as turning away from parental toward other influences, and the fact that the probability of reacting to stimuli independently rather than in emulation of a model increases with age.

However, we should not abandon the possibility that modeling is important during earlier childhood. Almost all of the data showing its unimportance come from adolescents, for whom we would expect modeling to be less important than for younger persons.

We also suspect that looking for concurrent modeling effects might be looking in the wrong place. Maccoby's (1959) point that the child or adolescent might not display an observed behavior until he reaches the age or circumstances when the behavior becomes appropriate reasonably applies to viewing. A child may observe and internalize the "adult" program selections of parents but fail to manifest them until adulthood. To our knowledge, no studies have examined this hypothesis.

The nature of the parent-child relationship very likely affects the probability that a child will internalize behavior manifested by the parent (Maccoby, 1959). It follows that modeling of parental behavior may be very likely in some types of families and not at all likely in others. Several studies indicate that children are more likely to pattern their behavior after models who are perceived as being warm and nurturant (Bandura and Huston, 1961; Hetherington and Frankie, 1967) or who manifest consistency in exercising contingent rewards and punishments (Bandura, 1969b). Both are dimensions on which parents vary. Such variability would result in only moderate parent-child correlations when various types of families are pooled.

This last finding leads us to the third source of parental influence—the kind of environment for communication that parents provide (Chaffee and McLeod, 1972; Chaffee, McLeod, and Atkin, 1970, 1971; Chaffee, McLeod, and Wackman, 1966; McLeod, Atkin, and Chaffee, 1972a, 1972b; McLeod, Chaffee, and Eswara,

1966; McLeod, Chaffee, and Wackman, 1967). The working hypotheses of research on this topic hold that the pattern of parent–child communication cultivates modes of coping that the child may apply in a wide variety of circumstances, and that the child is primarily affected by the themes or underlying emphases of such communication rather than by the specific content.

Two principal aspects of the underlying structure—the themes and emphases—of child–parent communication have been investigated. One is its social orientation—the parental emphases on maintaining interpersonal harmony by avoiding controversy, repressing emotions, indulging assiduously in "pleasant" conversation. The other is its concept orientation—the emphasis placed by parents on challenging the views of others, on exposure to controversy, and on confonting new and challenging ideas.

These two orientations are not opposite ends of the same continuum. It is easy to imagine parents emphasizing both, neither, or some combination of the two, and empirically, they have been demonstrated to be relatively independent.* As a result, it is possible to construct four different types of family communication (Chaffee and McLeod, 1972; Chaffee, McLeod, and Atkin, 1971):

In *laissez faire* families, neither type of relationship is emphasized—the child is neither prohibited from challenging parental views nor encouraged independently to test the world of contending ideas.

In *protective* families only socio-oriented relationships are stressed—the child is encouraged to maintain interpersonal harmony and is provided little chance to encounter conflicting information.

In *pluralistic* families, concept-oriented relationships, relatively free from social restraints, are emphasized—the child is encouraged to explore new ideas without fear of endangering social relations with parents.

In *consensual* families both orientations are stressed—the child is exposed to controversy and is encouraged to explore, but is simultaneously, and paradoxically, constrained to develop concepts and beliefs consonant with existing socio-oriented relationships.

*The highest correlation between the two dimensions found in several different samples of adolescents by the Wisconsin group is $r = .11$ (Chaffee and McLeod, 1972). Factor analyses also support the interpretation that two orientations form relatively independent dimensions.

Studies of media behavior employing such a family typology as a predictor reveal striking differences in the amount and type of television use across the various family types and in correlations between parents' and young persons' television use (Chaffee and McLeod, 1972; Chaffee, McLeod, and Atkin, 1971). For example:

Parents and young persons from protective families score well above average in total television time, well above the norm in viewing entertainment programming, and well below the norm in viewing news.

Young persons from pluralistic families score lowest in total television time, low in viewing entertainment, and high in viewing news.

Young persons from laissez faire families score lowest in viewing news.

Young persons from consensual families score highest in viewing news (Chaffee and McLeod, 1972; Chaffee, McLeod, and Atkin, 1971).

Illustrative data on adolescent media use are displayed in table 5.3. To emphasize the differences between types of families, the mean in each row has been set to zero and the average score for each type of family is presented in terms of its deviation from that average.

Young persons from homes emphasizing a socio-orientation tend to view much more violence than the norm (Chaffee and McLeod, 1972; McLeod, Atkin, and Chaffee, 1972b). These families also watch more entertainment programs, and we cannot at present say whether the seeking out of entertainment increases exposure to violence or vice versa.

Young persons from socio-oriented families are also more likely to feel that television offers them the opportunity to learn antisocial behavior and, somewhat disturbingly, report *more* parental controls over viewing (Chaffee, McLeod, and Atkin, 1971). One possibility is that these children transgress parental rules more often, and are more frequently punished, of which restriction on television use is one alternative. Another possibility is that these families have higher preference for media restriction when transgressions occur. Still another is that the media, whether or not transgression is greater than normal, are more feared in these families as a cause of transgression. At present, we don't know which interpretation, if any, is more valid. We do

Table 5.3 Adolescent Media Use in Different Types of Families: Deviation From Standard Score[a]

		Type of Family				
Media Use		Laissez faire	Protec- tive	Plural- istic	Consen- sual	Mean Raw Score
Adolescent's television	Jr. High	+02	+35	−38	−01	5.22
time	Sr. High	+08	+22	−18	−07	3.93
Adolescent's television	Jr. High	+02	+08	−15	+03	11.09
entertainment	Sr. High	−07	+16	−04	00	9.81
Adolescent's television	Jr. High	−21	−15	+11	+21	14.83
news	Sr. High	−22	−06	+14	+17	14.47
Adolescent's news reading	Jr. High	−16	−35	+20	+25	9.67
	Sr. High	−19	−09	+15	+14	11.47
(N)	Jr. High	(161)	(145)	(138)	(197)	(641)
(N)	Sr. High	(184)	(131)	(179)	(156)	(650)

SOURCE: Adapted from Table 4 in Parental influences on adolescent media use, by Steven H. Chaffee et al. 1971. *American Behavioral Scientist,* Vol. 14, No. 3 (Jan.–Feb.), 335 and reprinted by permission of the publisher, Sage.

[a] Standard score entries are based on weighted means, setting the overall mean at zero and the standard deviation at unity, within each row. Scores are calculated to two decimal places; decimals are omitted for simplicity. The Mean Raw Scores at the right are index scores that are meaningful only for Junior High versus Senior High comparisons within each category.

believe that the investigation of these possibilities would be worthwhile in regard to clarifying the role of television violence in aggression.

When families are classified along the lines we have been describing, differences in the likelihood that modeling of parental media behavior will occur can be located. Among families that stress socio-relations there are relatively strong correlations between parent-child media use, whereas correlations in families stressing concept-relations are trivial (Chaffee, McLeod, and Atkin, 1971). This suggests that children from homes which stress harmony and adoption of parental values and beliefs are more likely to be modeling parental behavior. This is consistent with what we would expect. Socio-orientation, by emphasizing harmony, should encourage modeling because of the need to acquire harmonious ways of interacting with others and because of the harmony-producing effects of emulating parents.

The type of research we have been describing is new and promising. The evidence so far supports the hypothesis that such communication patterns are associated with different strategies for dealing with persons and information; this in turn suggests that such strategies would influence the role and the effects of television and other media in the lives of young persons.

Special Problems

Research on television's impact on children's social behavior has been problem-oriented. Our knowledge has advanced as science has responded to a number of policy-oriented questions raised by parents, educators, legislators, and special-interest groups. These questions, reflecting fears about specific harmful influences of the medium or concerns that television is not fulfilling its constructive potential, have generally concerned four topics:

Responses to commercials.
Political socialization.
Antisocial behavior.
Prosocial behavior.

Responses to Commercials

Concern over the impact of television advertising on children is nothing new. Parents and critics have long expressed worry over the possible consequences of commercials (Choate, 1975; Jacobs, 1971; Rossiter and Robertson, 1974). They fear that young persons are particularly susceptible to commercial appeals because they lack the necessary skills to defend themselves against highly skillful persuasion; that commercials lead young persons to pressure parents to purchase particular products and thereby create intrafamily conflicts; that the number and nature of television commercials cannot help but socialize children in overmaterialistic ways. Children certainly do see plenty of commercials—more than 20,000 a year, or the equivalent of about three hours of continuous viewing a week (Adler, 1977).

Data gathered by the Council on Children, Media and Merchandising reveal that there has been no lack of effort or money spent by advertisers to investigate children's responses to television commercials. But their sole aim is to build a better commercial, and their findings remain proprietary and secret (Choate, 1973).

Empirical research in the public domain that addresses the question of how children respond to television commercials is in its infancy. Most studies have appeared since 1970, which helps to explain the rather preliminary nature of the data and the enormous number of questions that remain unanswered. Although a few studies that permit causal inferences have begun to be reported, most of our knowledge about children and commercials remains descriptive, based on reports of survey data and focusing on correlates of three types of outcomes: Young persons' attention to commercials; young persons' cognitive and attitudinal responses to commercials; the behavioral impact on young persons of commercials.

ATTENTION. Several studies have examined children's attention to commercials (Ward, 1972b; Ward, Levinson, and Wackman, 1972; Ward, Robertson, and Wackman, 1971; Ward and Wackman, 1973; Wartella and Ettema, 1974). In general, they concur that attention to commercials is negatively related to age. Ward, Levinson, and Wackman (1972), for example, found that children from 5 to 7 paid full attention to commercials about 50 percent of the time while among 11- and 12-year-olds the figure was 33 percent. They found a consistent drop in attention from program to commercial in children ranging from 5 to 12. They also found that older children paid more attention to commercials placed at the beginning of the program and that among younger children there was slightly greater attention to commercials "irrelevant" to them, such as for cleaning products or cosmetics—possibly an indication that commercials are used as a source of knowledge about the unfamiliar. Ward and Wackman (1973) also report that attention is related to cognitive development. They found that the attention of very young children tended to vary little from person to person or commercial to commercial while the attention of somewhat older children was much more differentiated. Other studies report similar findings (Ward, 1972b; Wartella and Ettema, 1974). In sum, then, there is evidence that children do respond to commercials in somewhat different ways than do adults (Steiner, 1966).

COGNITIVE AND ATTITUDINAL RESPONSES. Several studies have examined young persons' understanding of and attitudes toward television commercials. Age is consistently the best predictor, indicating that both cognitive development and the sum of experience influence the way commercials are perceived and processed.

Blatt, Spencer, and Ward (1972) conducted clinical interviews with kindergarten, second-, fourth-, and sixth-grade children and found almost no understanding of the purpose of commercials among the youngest group. Second-graders clearly understood that commercials were meant to sell goods, and fourth-graders were capable of commenting on the techniques used in producing commercials. These researchers also report that kindergarten children do not discriminate between the product and the advertisement and that a great deal of confusion is still present among second-graders; that the youngest children do not discriminate between program and commercial; and, that while young children tend to focus on and recall ads on the basis of a single slogan or concrete element in the commercial, older children manifest a more complex and multidimensional focus and tend to recall ads more on the basis of their own responses to the commercial when it appeared. Ward, Reale and Levinson (1972) substantially replicated these findings with a more structured survey instrument. Howard, Hulbert, and Lehmann (1973) report that an overwhelming proportion of mothers of children between the ages of two and six felt that their children believe commercials to be real and fail to discriminate between commercials and programs, and Rossiter and Robertson (1974), in a study with first-, third-, and fifth-grade boys, found a very strong positive correlation between age and understanding of the nature and intent of television commercials.

Finally, Wackman, Wartella, and Ward (1977; see also Ward, Wackman, and Wartella, 1977) report a large-scale study concerned with the interaction between the level of cognitive development in children and various family influences on the development of their consumer skills as they relate to television advertising. They conducted extensive interviews with over 600 kindergarten, third-, and sixth-grade children and their mothers, obtaining information on a variety of consumer information-processing skills, intrafamily consumer behavior, and level of cognitive development. Results demonstrate not only a strong positive relationship between grade level and understanding of the purpose of television commercials, but also between grade level and such other consumer skills as asking about how well a product will perform when considering its purchase and awareness of an alternate source of information about new products.

The study also delineates several ways that family communication interacts with the child's level of cognitive development to facilitate or impede the child's acquisition of different consumer skills.

There are now at least two studies aimed at exploring whether children understand the disclaimers that frequently appear in commercials. Atkin (1975) found that a combined audio and visual disclaimer was more than twice as effective as a video disclaimer alone. This finding is not too surprising, considering that the children in his study ranged from preschoolers through sixth-graders, a large proportion of whom probably could not read. More to the point, Liebert and her colleagues also report several pilot studies and one more formal examination of children's ability to understand disclaimers (Liebert, et al., 1977). They found that "some assembly required," the standard disclaimer used in many toy commercials (and presented both orally and visually) was understood by fewer than 25 percent of six- and eight-year-olds who saw a test commercial. However, when children viewed the same commercial containing a disclaimer couched in more age-appropriate language—"you have to put it together"—comprehension climbed dramatically, especially among eight-year-olds. Thus, it is clear that a child's comprehension of commercial messages and conventions depends on an interaction between his abilities and the message's characteristics.

Just as children better comprehend the intent and content of television commercials as they grow older, so too do they learn to distrust them. A number of studies have found that distrust in commercials is positively related to age (Blatt, Spencer, and Ward, 1972; Clancy-Hepburn, Hickey, and Nevill, 1974; Rossiter and Robertson, 1974; Ward, Reale, and Levinson, 1972; Ward and Robertson, 1972). Distrust of specific commercials begins to appear by the time children reach the second grade (Blatt, Spencer, and Ward, 1972; Ward, Reale, and Levinson, 1972) and is characterized by Ward (1972b) as "global distrust" by the time children reach the sixth grade.

These studies also indicate that the basis for distrust differs from younger to older children. Among sixth-graders, distrust seems to be a function of the perceived intent of the commercials—which implies a developing ability to defend against such persuasive appeals. Younger children, however, tend to express distrust on the basis of some "mistake" in the commercial's content. An example would be a portrayal that does not fit reality—a man walking through a wall, for example.

Finally, adolescents are very likely to have negative responses to commercials. They characterize them as "stupid," "hypocritical," and "in bad taste." Only one third of the adolescents interviewed by Wackman, Reale, and Ward (1972) and Ward and Robertson (1972) agreed that "TV commercials tell the truth."

Among younger children, Rossiter and Robertson (1974) found a positive relationship between exposure to television and positive attitudes toward commercials. Among junior and senior high school students the same relationship holds, but only for white children—with the relationship more clear among upper- and middle-class white children (Wackman, Reale, and Ward, 1972; Ward and Robertson, 1972). The latter two studies also found that children from families in which consumption of goods and services is frequently discussed are more likely to have positive attitudes toward commercials, and that there is a mild relationship between a measure of materialism and positive attitudes toward commercials, with adolescents who state that material possessions are necessary for happiness more favorable.

In general, then, the available data indicate that as children grow older they become better able to understand commercials and less trusting of them. Nevertheless, even adolescents who express a good deal of dislike for television advertising, continue to pay at least some attention to commercials and acquire some information from them (Ward, 1972b). Not surprisingly, there is a tendency for children from homes where consumption of goods is made salient through conversation, and for children who express materialistic attitudes to be more favorable toward commercials.

BEHAVIORAL IMPACT. A few studies have explored the relationship between television commercials and children's behavior. Young children are seldom in a position to make purchases themselves, so most researchers have relied on parental reports of children's attempts to influence purchases or to express preferences. Recently, however, several laboratory experiments have measured young children's behavior after viewing of commercials. With older children the influence of commercials is measured by their own reports of purchases made in response to television ads.

Howard, Hulbert, and Lehmann (1973) report that almost three-quarters of a sample of mothers of children under six said that television influenced their children to ask that advertised products be bought. Ward and Wackman (1972b) obtained data from over 100 upper- and middle-class mothers of children between the ages of five and twelve that also indicate a high frequency of children's requests for advertised products. According to both studies, the two kinds of items most requested were toys and food, although they disagreed on which ranked first. Ward and Wackman also report that these requests decreased with the age of the child, but that parental yielding increased, and that the time a mother spent watching television was positively related to the child's attempts at influence, to parental yielding, and to parents' perceptions that television commercials caused the attempts at influence.

Frideres (1973) reports findings from interviews with children ages five to eight who were asked what toys they would most like to have and where they first saw or heard about them; 78 percent of the children indicated that they first saw the toy on television. Moreover, the frequency with which television was cited as the source was positively related to the amount of overall television viewing the children reported for the prior week.

Galst and White (1976) conducted one of the more carefully controlled studies of this type. In addition to having parents provide data on preschool children's total television viewing time, they used an experimental televiewing situation to measure the amount of effort the children expended to watch commercials, as opposed to programs, on a television monitor. Subsequently, each child-mother pair participating in the study was accompanied to the supermarket on a shopping trip under conditions where the experimenter appeared to be shopping herself. Here, the number and nature of purchase-influencing attempts made by the children were recorded. Results revealed a strong positive relationship between the child's willingness to watch commercials on the monitor and the number of such attempts. There was also a similar positive correlation between total commercial televiewing time and attempts to influence mothers' purchases.

Rossiter and Robertson (1974) asked 289 first-, third-, and fifth-grade boys in Boston to list what they wanted for Christmas both in early November and in late December, a period spanning the peak toy commercial season. They then developed a measure of the proportion of television-advertised toy and game requests relative to total requests. In addition, they obtained measures of cognitive and attitudinal "defenses" against commercials, the former based on the child's comprehension of the intent and nature of commercials and the latter on perceived believability, liking, and tendency to express desires for products seen in commercials.

One major finding is that children with the strongest defenses to commercials selected fewer television-promoted toys and games early in the Christmas advertising season than did children with weaker defenses, but that after four or five weeks of concentrated advertising, defenses became ineffective predictors of preference. This phenomenon was the result of increased preference for the advertised items among children with initially strong defenses. In short, children's cognitive and attitudinal defenses were operative at the beginning of the peak Christmas toy and game advertising period, but were neutralized by its conclusion.

Another major finding of this study is that before the Christmas advertising period, among first-graders only attitudinal defense was effective in resisting advertised toys. By third grade, cognitive defense assumed some importance, and by fifth grade it was the only effective screen. Thus, there is some evidence for a developmental trend, in which resistance based on attitudes gives way to that based on cognitions as the child grows older.

In a further analysis of the preceding data, Robertson and Rossiter (1977) examined how the child's age, his ability to get along with his peers, and level of parents' education operated to moderate the impact of exposure to television advertising on requests for the advertised product. This analysis revealed a strong relationship between exposure and requests for the product, but requests for the advertised items decreased with age; among high-exposure children requests were reduced among children classified as well-integrated with their peers; and among low exposure children, there was a significant reduction in the number of requests as the educational level of the parents increased. As with the Wackman, Wartella, and Ward (1977) study, this work indicates that background variables have a good deal to do with how children interpret and respond to television commercials.

Several recent experiments have been concerned with the influence of commercials on young children. Goldberg and Gorn (1974) showed boys between eight and eleven years old an episode of *The Flintstones* containing either no commercial, one commercial, or three commercials. The commercials advertised a new toy. After viewing, the boys were given a chance to "win" the advertised toy by working on an essentially insoluble puzzle.

Those who saw the commercials evaluated the advertised toy more favorably than an unadvertised toy and persisted longer in attempting to solve the puzzle than did those who did not see the commercials.

Goldberg and Gorn (1977) also exposed four- and five-year olds either to a ten-minute program with no commercials, to the program with two commercials advertising a new version of a familiar toy, or to the program with the two commerials on successive days (for a total of four exposures to the commercial). Children were then asked whether they would rather play with friends in the sandbox or with the advertised toy. Almost twice as many children who saw the program without the commercials opted for interaction with friends. Similarly, when faced with an option of playing with a "nice boy" without the toy or with a "not so nice boy" who had it, fewer than 35 percent of those who saw the commercials chose the toyless nice boy compared to 70 percent of those who did not see the commercials. A second set of questions addressed to the children concerned the impact of the commercials on parent-child relations. The children were told their mothers had expressed a preference for a tennis ball over the advertised toy. They were then asked which they liked best. Significantly more children from the control group followed their mother's judgment than did those exposed to the commercials. Moreover, when shown photographs of a father and son and told that the father had denied the child's request for the advertised toy, over 60 percent of the children who did not see the commercials felt the boy would still want to "play with his daddy," compared to fewer than 40 percent of those who saw the commercials. Finally, children who did not see the commercials were significantly more likely than children who did to state that a child who did not get the toy would remain happy. The authors interpret their results as indicating that television commercials encourage material as opposed to social orientation in children, that exposure to commercials may lead to parent-child conflict, and exposure can lead to disappointment and unhappiness when products are not obtained.

There is also a paucity of studies with teenagers. Ward and Robertson (1972) report that just over 20 percent of a sample of over 1000 junior and senior high school students reported purchasing two or more items as a result of a television commercial, just under 30 percent reported purchasing one item, and approximately 50 percent reported no influence of commercials on purchases. Wackman, Reale, and Ward (1972) found a slight tendency for black adolescents to be more likely to report purchasing products in response to commercials, but the differences were not large and the sample of black teenagers was so small that the results must be viewed with extreme caution. Milavsky, Pekowsky, and Stipp (1975) conducted a three-year panel study of the impact of television drug advertising on the behavior of teenaged boys. They found a weak positive relationship between exposure to drug commercials and use of proprietary drugs, a weak negative relationship between such exposure and use of illicit drugs, and no relationship between exposure and "an attitude of readiness to take drugs."

As with younger children, several child-centered and environmental variables have been demonstrated that moderate the impact of television commercials on adolescents. Ward and Wackman (1972b), for example, found significant positive relationships between teenagers' reports that they had made purchases as a direct result of television commercials and the amount of intrafamily communication about consumption, the degree to which they perceived commercials to provide socially useful information, and the amount of exposure to magazines. The first two findings indicate that interpersonal communication operates as an important intervening variable between exposure and purchase. In the same vein, Milavsky, Pekowsky, and Stipp's (1975) finding that the relationship between exposure to drug commercials and use of proprietary drugs is stronger among boys from homes where there are many such drugs available implies that commercials are more effective when there are facilitating conditions in the child's environment.

Although the data are sparse, then, we find at least tentative evidence that young persons' behavior is influenced by television commercials. It must be noted, however, that the nature of these data render the results highly tentative. Parental reports of behavior are likely to be biased and young persons' expressions of product preferences are a large step removed from overt behavior.

With the exception of the Goldberg and Gorn study (1977), there is no evidence on the contribution of young persons' exposure to television advertising to the holding of materialistic, consumption-oriented values or to mistrust and cynicism toward other features of the media or nonmedia aspects of life. There is also little research on the influence of such exposure on major and perhaps lifelong consumption practices, such as food preferences, over-the-counter drug use, and other health-related behavior. So far, research has focused on understanding of content, desire for products, and attitudes toward advertising. The entire area of television commercials' impact on children remains largely uncharted.

Political Socialization

Although research on how young persons come to develop their image of politics and government and ultimately become participants in the political process has received mounting attention over the past several decades (Dawson and Prewitt, 1969; Hess and Torney, 1967; Hyman, 1959), until recently little emphasis has been placed on the possible role of the media in that process. Rather, it has been assumed that the important determinants of the political beliefs of young persons operate through interpersonal communication. Thus, the debate has tended to concentrate on the relative influence of family (Chaffee, McLeod, and Wackman, 1973; Jennings and Niemi, 1973), school (Langton and Jennings, 1968, 1969), and, to a lesser extent, peers (Langton, 1967). Chaffee, Ward, and Tipton (1970), however, note that these studies have failed to demonstrate that the primary socialization agents account for much of the variation in political beliefs of young persons. They argue that until we have gathered empirical evidence regarding the role of the mass media in political socialization, media cannot be discounted.

Several factors seem to underlie the lack of attention to the media, and particularly television, as important agents in children's political socialization. First, some studies have indicated that attention to public affairs content—news, election coverage, and the like—is relatively low until mid- or late-adolescence (Lyle and Hoffman, 1972a; Schramm, Lyle, and Parker, 1961), leading to an implicit assumption that since children pay little attention to public affairs programs the media can play only a minor role in political socialization. Second, the most widely employed model for analyzing the media's political impact, that developed by Klapper (1960), confines the media to the role of reinforcing predispositions by selective exposure and attention. The result has been to discourage research on the media and political socialization, although there are many reasons to doubt the operation of selective exposure and attention (Sears and Freedman, 1967), and most of the supporting research only involved adults.

In the past few years, however, attention has been drawn to the possible role of the media in political socialization. A number of studies have found that although public affairs programs seldom rank at the top of young persons' television preferences, substantial numbers of adolescents (Chaffee, Ward, and Tipton, 1970; McIntyre and Teevan, 1972; J. P. Robinson, 1972c) and even grade-school children (Hawkins, Pingree, and Roberts, 1975; Roberts, Hawkins, and Pingree, 1975; Tolley, 1973) watch such programming some of the time. Moreover, when political socialization is broadly conceived of to include, for example, how the young persons come to think about other parts of the world or what constitutes power, several scholars have pointed out that a good deal of information about politics may come from entertainment rather than informational programs (Hirsch, 1971; Torney and Morris, 1972).

In addition, there has been a rethinking about what constitutes a significant effect of exposure to public affairs programs, at least where young persons are concerned. For example, Klapper's (1960) generalizations and a good deal of research into political socialization (Torney, 1972) are cast in terms of attitudes and values. However, such socialization clearly entails more than just the shaping of attitudes. If we define the product of political socialization as an individual's conception or image of government and politics, and of his or her role in relation to that image, then information about politics, interest in government, talking about government, even paying attention to media coverage of politics are all legitimate and significant outcomes of political socialization. Indeed, Chaffee and his colleagues (Chaffee, Ward, and Tipton, 1970) contend that Klapper's position that the media reinforce existing predispositions may not be very relevant to young persons—for the simple reason that they are likely to have few, if any, such predispositions.

Finally, there has been growing sensitivity to the fact that no single socialization agent operates in a vacuum (Leifer, Gordon, and Graves, 1973; Roberts, 1973). Socialization—political or otherwise—is the result of numerous interactions—between the young person and a wide variety of other socialization agents and among socialization agents themselves.

For example, a child may see something on a television news

program that will lead him to discuss it with his parents; or a conversation with his parents might lead him to watch television news. In either case, the child is likely to acquire new or altered information. He may also form a new political attitude or change an old one; and he may choose to watch more public affairs programming as a result—which may alter the quantity and character of his conversations about politics with his parents. And the cycle will begin again. The literature is sparse. However, the few studies which do exist suggest that television and other mass media play an important role.

Data collected by Tolley (1973) are highly consistent with the model we have just proposed. He surveyed 2677 elementary and junior high school pupils ranging in age from seven to fifteen in 14 schools in three eastern states regarding their sources of information about the Vietnam war. He found that among their major sources—including teachers, parents, and friends—television was the most important. Those who watched television news regularly knew more facts about the war. Newspapers also were associated with greater knowledge, but very few read them. Those who opposed the war perceived television news as opposing the war. Those who supported the war perceived television news as supporting it. Parents, and not television, appeared to affect attitudes about the war. In addition, parents were very influential in the acquisition of information, with young persons with parents who were "vocal" pro- or antiwar advocates having greater knowledge. This parental effect occurred not only for the sample as a whole but also among those who were regular evening news viewers.

Although the data do not permit causal inferences, apparently, young people do rely on television for information, but how that information is perceived depends on parental influence. Pro-war parents convert the information to support for the war, antiwar parents to opposition. Therefore, television news had an important role.

A number of other studies indicate that young persons rely on television for political information. Hawkins (1974) asked fourth- and eighth-graders where they obtained their information about the launching of Skylab, the country's first "space station," and the Watergate scandal and found that, overall, children mentioned television and other media more than any other sources. Bailey (1975) found that a large sample of third-, sixth-, and ninth-graders indicated that television is where they learn what the government does. In agreement with Tolley, Alvik (1968) reports that Norwegian grade school children more often cited television than any other source of information about the Vietnam war. The mass media in general and television in particular also led the list when children were asked about important sources of information about other nations (Coldevin, 1971), about foreign peoples (Lambert and Klineberg, 1967), and about war and peace (Haavelsrud, 1971). Hollander (1971) asked a sample of high school seniors a number of open-ended questions about their views on war in general and the Vietnam war in particular, such as causes and consequences. He then asked the students to identify the sources they had used to acquire the information on which the views were based from a list of 18 possible sources ranging from parents to school textbooks. Mass media were the overwhelming choice for most questions, and television was the overwhelming choice among the media. Chaffee, McLeod, and Atkin (1970) asked junior- and senior-high school students to rate the relative importance of parents, friends, teachers, and the mass media as sources of information about politics, and found that media dominated, with television preeminent among the media, at both age levels. More recent data (Chaffee, 1976) indicate that as a source of public affairs information, television is particularly important as the child approaches adolescence, television and newspapers are about equally important in adolescence, and that television declines in importance as the adolescent enters adulthood. In the early twenties a decline for newspapers occurs.

Not only do children say that television is one of the most important sources of information, but in addition several studies have found, like Tolley, positive relationships between knowledge and exposure to public affairs programs. Hawkins (1974) reports that those who often used media for knowledge of public affairs knew more about both Skylab and Watergate. Bailey's (1975) panel study shows positive relationships between attention to television news over time and comprehension of various aspects of government. In addition, two studies provide evidence that exposure is a cause of knowledge. Alper and Leidy (1970) located samples of teenagers, including viewers and nonviewers of the CBS National Citizenship Test, and measured their knowledge of the U.S. Constitution a month before and a week after airing of the program. In order to control for possible differences between samples, the measuring instrument contained items dealing with information not covered in the program in addition to information that was shown on the air. Results indicate no differences in knowledge between the two samples when measured before the broadcast, nor were there difference after the broadcast on the control items. However, on questions dealing with material covered in the program, viewers scored substantially higher.

Chaffee, Ward, and Tipton (1970) collected data at two different times, in May (about one month after the primary election in Wisconsin and again in November within two weeks after the 1968 general election), from a panel of 1291 junior and senior high students. They found media exposure in May to predict later political knowledge. Various analyses indicated that the relationship was attributable to the influence of the media on knowledge, and not the result of greater knowledge leading to greater media exposure. Newspapers were most important, but television also contributed. This is presumptive evidence that exposure to the public affairs information during a campaign increased the political knowledge of young persons. The authors believe the data are inconsistent with the view that the effects of mass communication on political socialization are mostly reinforcement of existing predispositions attributable to "selective exposure," or are largely neutralized by interpersonal influences in a "two-step flow" of communication.

In sum, the various studies do not rule out the very real possibility that children most likely to learn from public affairs programming are also those most likely to view. However, they demonstrate fairly convincingly that those who do view do learn.

There is also a small amount of data hinting that television can influence the political opinions of young persons, particularly when those attitudes or opinions pertain to things not likely to be salient topics of conversation among important interpersonal sources of information. Connell (1971) found that when Australian children were asked to state their opinions on a number of political issues, and were then queried in regard to what the opinions were based on, he found that television was the most frequently cited source on a number of national and international issues. Roberts et al. (1974) also report significant decreases in ethnocentrism and increases in positive attitudes toward foreign lands among fourth-, fifth-, and sixth-grade children after viewing a series of four children's programs with the general theme of the similarity among people around the world. Nevertheless, the evidence certainly does not suggest that television is generally predominant in shaping opinions. Tolley's (1973) finding that parents influence opinions while television supplies information is more plausible, at least for topics where parents voice opinions. A modest role for television is also indicated by Torney's (1972) report that only five percent of a sample of 12,000 young persons cited radio and television as the "best place to look for help in making up your mind about whom to vote for."

We suspect, as do other authors (Alvik, 1968; Connell, 1971; Torney, 1972), that the role of television and other mass media in shaping political attitudes and opinions is usually indirect. The media provide information which young persons submit to others, including parents, for comment and evaluation; and out of this process, in which interpersonal influence is strong, political attitudes and opinions are formed. Where there is little or no explicit interpersonal communication, we would expect the role of the media to be greater.

In accord with this view, several studies also hint that the media have a significant impact on the topics on which young persons develop opinions. Connell (1971) reports that Australian television paid a great deal of attention to the Vietnam war and to the U.S. President, one result of which was that Australian children learned more about the war and the U.S. President than about their own Prime Minister and a variety of domestic issues. He argues that television may be reversing the long-held notion that political concern begins with local issues then turns to the national and international scene. Given the emphasis of much television news, the reverse may be occurring—if local concern ever develops. Further evidence that public-affiars programming sets the agenda of political concern for young persons comes from data reported by Hawkins, Pingree, and Roberts (1975). They asked fourth-, eighth-, and twelfth-graders to list the three most important problems of the U.S. in October 1972 and July 1973, a period during which Watergate became the dominant story in the news media. They found that the problem of "honesty in government" moved from almost total obscurity in October to one of the major issues the following July.

There is also some evidence on the shifting role of the media with age. Roberts, Hawkins, and Pingree (1975), analyzing data from a panel of sixth- and tenth-graders, collected at the beginning and end of the 1972 U.S. Presidential election, found that among tenth-graders, those who reported high attention to public affairs also reported engaging in more intrafamily political discussion, were more likely to know their parents' political affiliation, and were more accepting of interparty conflict; but among sixth-graders, the relationship held only for intrafamily discussion of politics. Chaffee, Ward, and Tipton (1970) found that in junior high, viewing of entertainment appeared to lead to exposure to public affairs programming, but that in senior high, there was no sign of such a sequence.

We find considerable evidence that television has become an important source of information about government, politics, and foreign affairs. Young persons generally name it as a major source, and exposure to television news has been found to be correlated with knowledge, including instances in which the data tend to rule out the possibility that those with greater knowledge made greater use of the medium. There is some evidence that television may be an important contributor to the formation of opinions and attitudes concerning issues that are not likely to receive a great deal of attention from primary socialization agents— and one cannot help but speculate that the array of such issues that are important is rather broad. There is also some indication that television news functions as an agenda setter for children, and that it may motivate them to engage in political discussions with significant others.

We believe that the medium plays a significant role in preparing young persons to become citizens. However, we do not find as much evidence as we would like to have. We find only a few instances in which the role of the mass media in political socialization at various ages is taken into consideration. Yet, it is obvious that the assumption of the role of citizen should occur with a rising curve of involvement which has its particular beginning, shape, and point of leveling off, and that the role of the media and other influences may be quite different at various points on this curve.

Antisocial Behavior

Does viewing televised portrayals of violence increase the likelihood of aggressive behavior on the part of young persons?

Although antisocial behavior conceptually includes far more than aggressive behavior, aggression has received the bulk of attention. Indeed, until recently this question has dominated research concerned with television's influence on children, as evidenced not only by the heavy emphasis placed on the topic in general reviews of the literature on children and television (Liebert, Neale, and Davidson, 1973; Maccoby, 1964; Roberts, 1973; Shirley, 1973) and by numerous books or book chapters (Baker and Ball, 1969; Bandura, 1973; Berkowitz, 1962b; Goranson, 1970; Schramm, 1968b; Surgeon General's Scientific Advisory Committee, 1972), but also by the simple fact that empirical studies addressing at least some aspect of this problem outweigh studies in all other problem areas combined by a ratio of better than four to one.

We will review the evidence in terms of the various methodological genres which have been employed: correlational studies, laboratory experiments, and field experiments.

CORRELATIONAL STUDIES. To establish whether viewing television violence influences aggressive behavior in day-to-day life one must demonstrate a relationship between viewing of violence and aggression that is not accounted for by some third variable (Chaffee, 1972b). Thus, a good deal of research has looked for a correlation between various measures of viewing and various indicators of children's aggressiveness.

At first glance, the results appear to be mixed. Some studies indicate no relationship, some report small positive relationships restricted to particular groups of children, and some consistently demonstrate positive if moderate relationships across a variety of subgroups of children. It is important to note, however, that measures of both exposure to television violence and aggressive behavior have not been put into operation in the same way in the various studies.

Aggressiveness has been measured in terms of the child's responses on antisocial aggression scales, his approval of violence, his perceived utility of violence, his own reports of behaviors ranging from verbal displays of anger to overt physical attacks and delinquent behaviors, his involvement with law enforcement officials, nomination by others, direct observation of behavior, and the like. Measures of violence viewing have ranged from simply coding the presence or absence of a television in the home, through total viewing time and expressed preference for violent television programs, to more direct measures of actual exposure to programming characterized as violent. In this context, when the results of the various surveys are examined in terms of the nature of the measures employed, a good deal of order in the findings appears—order that indicates a positive relationship between viewing of violence and aggressive behavior.

Some of the differences among studies can be attributed to variations in the measures of aggressive behavior. However, the critical difference between studies that do and do not demonstrate a relationship appears to lie in the sensitivity of the measure of violence viewing used by each. The more directly related to actual exposure to violent programming, the more likely positive correlations are to be found. This trend, which amounts to a positive correlation between the accuracy of the measurement of exposure to television violence and aggressiveness, is shown in table 5.4.

For example, several early studies are more relevant to the quite-different question of whether access or exposure to television is related to aggressive behavior. Himmelweit, Oppenheim, and Vince (1958) obtained aggression scores for over 200 ten- and eleven-year-olds in Britain from teacher ratings and personality inventories. When children from homes that had television were compared to children whose homes did not, there was no difference on either of the aggression measures. Similar results are reported by Schramm, Lyle, and Parker (1961) using a sample of Canadian children. The same study also failed to find any differences among sixth- and tenth-grade children classified as heavy versus light television viewers. Scores on a scale of antisocial aggression did not differ as a function of total viewing, although there were moderate positive correlations among tenth-graders who watched a great deal of television and seldom used the print media. Both of these studies concluded that there is little evidence that viewing is related to aggressive behavior.

To the extent that these investigators were concerned with the effects of television violence, they had to assume that exposure to television *per se* was a good proxy for exposure to television violence. More recent research has made it clear that the two correlate only modestly (McLeod, Atkin, and Chaffee, 1972a, 1972b). In short, these studies used a very weak measure of exposure to television violence.

Several studies employing samples of younger children have measured exposure to television violence on the basis of mothers' reports of favorite programs. A. H. Stein and Friedrich (1972) indexed the violence viewing of 97 nursery school children, classifying preferred shows as more or less violent. They then observed the play behavior of these children in a nursery school, and coded the amount of aggressiveness displayed. Results showed little relationship between aggressive behavior and re-

Table 5.4 Summary of Selected Studies Examining Relationships between Various Measures of Viewing and Young Persons' Aggressiveness

Study	Sample	Viewing Measure
A. Studies Using Measures of Total Viewing		
Himmelweit, Oppenheim, and Vince, 1958	1854 10–11- and 13–14-yr.-old British children	Presence or absence of television in the home
Schramm, Lyle, and Parker, 1961	1398 6th- and 10th-graders	Presence or absence of television in the home; self reports of total viewing
B. Studies Using Measures Based on Favorite Programs		
McLeod, Atkin, and Chaffee, 1972a	473 7th- and 10th-graders	Self reports of favorite programs
Eron, 1963	875 3rd-graders	Mothers' report of favorite programs
Friedman and Johnson, 1972	80 junior-high-school boys	Self reports of favorite programs
Lefkowitz et al., 1972	427 19-yr.-olds	Self reports of favorite programs
McIntyre and Teevan, 1972	2270 junior- and senior-high-school students	Self reports of favorite programs
J. P. Robinson and Bachman, 1972	1559 post-high-school males	Self reports of favorite programs
C. Studies Using Measures of Overall Violence Viewing		
Dominick and Greenberg, 1972	838 4th-, 5th- and 6th-graders	Number of programs viewed each week from list of 20 most violent programs
McLeod, Atkin, and Chaffee, 1972a, 1972b	151 junior and senior high school students	Self reports of actual violence viewing per week

ported preference for violent content. Eron (1963) also derived a violence viewing score for 875 third-graders on the basis of mothers' reports of favorite shows. Aggression was measured by a simple count of the number of peers who nominated a child as aggressive. This study found a modest but statistically significant relationship between violence viewing and aggression for boys ($r = +.21$), but no relationship for girls.

Table 5.4 Continued

Aggression Measure	Relation-ship	Qualifications
A. Studies Using Measures of Total Viewing		
Teacher reports of aggressive behavior	0	——
"Anti-social aggression" scale	0	Moderate correlation among 10th-grade boys high in television use and low in print use
B. Studies Using Measures Based on Favorite Programs		
Self report	0	——
Peer ratings	+	For males only
School officials' ratings; self report of aggressive feelings	−	Moderate correlation for measure of aggressive feelings
Peer ratings	0	——
Self report of aggressive behavior	+	For white males only
Self report of aggressive behavior	+	Very weak relationship among males initially high in aggressiveness
C. Studies Using Measures of Overall Violence Viewing		
Self report of attitudes favorable to aggression	+	Relationships withstand controls for sex, socio-economic status, and family attitudes toward violence
Self report of aggressive behavior	+	Relationships withstand extensive partialing

The creation of a violence viewing score based on classification of program preferences is a common procedure in studies that have surveyed adolescents (Chaffee and McLeod, 1972b; Friedman and Johnson, 1972; Lefkowitz, et al., 1972; McIntyre and Teevan, 1972; J. P. Robinson and Bachman, 1972). Children are classified as high or low violence viewers on the basis of a list of three or four "favorite programs," after which scores on a variety of aggression measures are compared. Friedman and Johnson (1972), for example, obtained ratings of aggressiveness from school officials for 80 junior high school boys. They compared the violence viewing scores for the 40 boys nominated as most aggressive to the 40 nominated as least aggressive. The obtained difference was trivial (1.8 vs. 1.6; no significance tests reported). When the boys were reclassified on the basis of their own reports of "aggressive feelings," however, the more aggressive boys listed an average of 2.2 violent favorites while their less agressive counterparts listed only 1.5 violent favorites.

A similar approach was employed by McIntyre and Teevan (1972), who divided a sample of over 2800 junior and senior high school children into low, moderate, or high violence viewers. Their measures of antisocial behavior included students' reports of their own aggressive or violent acts, petty delinquent acts, defiance of parents, "deviant" political behavior, and involvement with law enforcement officials. Results indicated a positive, although weak, relationship between preferences for violent programs and deviant behavior. However, when controls for sex and race were applied, the results held only for white males. They also found a moderate positive relationship, again limited to white males, between violent program preference and expressed approval of violence in others. J. P. Robinson and Bachman (1972) also found a weak, positive relationship between an index of violence viewing and reports of engaging in a variety of aggressive behavior for those initially aggressive in a national sample of post-high-school boys.

Several other studies using such program preference measures, however, have found no support for a relationship between violent favorites and aggression (Chaffee and McLeod, 1972; Lefkowitz et al., 1972). Chaffee (1972b) contends that the only consistent conclusion to be drawn from these studies is that there is evidence for a weak to moderate relationship between preference for television programs featuring violence and adolescent aggressiveness for white males only.

Obviously, a few declared favorites represent only a small proportion of total programs viewed. These investigators assumed that the degree to which favorites were violent would be a valid measure of exposure to television violence, apparently on the grounds that the character of what was singularly liked would be reflected in the rest of viewing. They were wrong. Recent research indicates that the correlation between viewing of violence and expressed preference for specific violent programs is at best modest (Chaffee, 1972b; McLeod, Atkin, and Chaffee, 1972a; 1972b).

Parental reports of what is viewed have generally been found to be undependable (Chaffee, 1972b; Greenberg, Ericson, and Vlahos, 1972; Stipp, 1975), although it is plausible to believe that mothers would be more accurate than fathers, who typically are less often at home, and that mothers of younger children would be most accurate because of the greater maternal attentiveness when children are young. Thus, the Eron (1963) and A. H. Stein and Friedrich (1972) measures have a reasonably strong claim to validity because of the age of the children. With such young children, presumably the mothers' conception of favorites would be strongly influenced by their observation of what the child viewed, a circumstance that would be inversely related to the child's age. Therefore, the Eron finding may reflect a valid relationship for this sample between violence viewing and aggressiveness.

In any case, we are not surprised that there is occasionally found a positive relationship between expressed preference for violent programs and aggressiveness, because there are reasons to expect such a relationship even in the absence of one between violence viewing and aggressiveness. We acknowledge that no such correlation has been found between having a criminal history of violence and such preference (Menzies, 1971).

However, the media may not perform the same function for such persons, who have acted on their impulses and motives, as it would for others. We suspect that aggressive young white males may be guided in their declared or actual affection for particular programs by the degree to which they supply desired role models (Johnson, Friedman, and Gross, 1972). Since most violence in television drama is committed by white males (Gerbner and Gross, 1976), this would lead to their naming violent programs as favorites. In addition, if there is a relationship between actual violence viewing and aggressiveness, we would expect that sometimes a correlation between violent favorites and aggressiveness would occur, because violent favorites cannot help but be a very weak substitute for actual violence viewing.

In sum, "favorite programs" is not a satisfactory substitute for a measure of exposure to television violence. At the same time, there are good reasons why some measures of favorite programs, such as reports of mothers of young children, may serve as a substitute, and good reasons why a preference for violent programs would be modestly correlated with aggressiveness among young males.

Research which measures viewing of violence on the basis of all programs watched in a given period consistently demonstrates a positive relationship between such viewing and aggressiveness. The relationship has persisted when numerous, possibly contaminating, variables have been taken into account and it occurs in samples of typical children. For example, Dominick and Greenberg (1972) tabulated the number of programs watched each week from a list of the 20 most violent programs for over 800 fourth-, fifth-, and sixth-grade boys and girls. Measures of aggressiveness included children's expressed willingness to use violence, perceived effectiveness of violence, suggested use of violence in hypothetical conflict situations, and approval for aggression. The result was a positive correlation between such dispositions, which at the most conservative could be labeled "attitudes favoring aggression," and viewing of violence. The relationship remained when sex, socioeconomic status, and parental approval of aggression were controlled for, although parental approval of aggression was more strongly related to such dispositions than violence viewing. For boys, violence viewing was correlated with willingness to use violence and the perceived effectiveness of violence. For girls, such viewing was correlated with willingness to use violence, perceived effectiveness of violence, and inclination to use violence to resolve conflicts.

McLeod, Atkin, and Chaffee (1972á, 1972b) report even more convincing results. They collected data from 229 seventh-graders and 244 tenth-graders in eight public schools in Maryland, and from 68 seventh-graders and 83 tenth-graders in two Wisconsin schools. The numerous measures cover total amount of television viewing, quantity of violence viewing, aggressiveness, school performance, socioeconomic status, and various individual and family attributes. Viewing of violent television entertainment by adolescents was positively correlated with aggressive behavior. This held for both communities, for boys and girls, and for junior- and senior-high-school samples. It also held when a variety of variables were controlled, including (in addition to sex and age) school performance, socioeconomic class, and total amount of time spent viewing television. Of 38 possible replicates (community × age × sex × aggression subtest) 35 correlation coefficients were positive, 12 significantly.

In short, studies that have employed the most direct measures of violence viewing find correlations between such viewing and various measures of aggressiveness. Moreover, these relationships are not, like those between preference for television violence and aggressiveness, limited only to white males, or even males. They hold for both sexes, for children of different ages and from different communities, and in the face of controls for a wide variety of possible third variables. Therefore, we conclude that the evidence to date indicates that there is a significant correlation between the viewing of violent television programs and aggressive behavior in day-to-day life.

Little more can be said about causality on the basis of these findings alone. That is the kind of question we usually attempt to answer through experimental procedures, whether in the laboratory or the field. There are, however, two sets of survey data which bear more directly on a causal interpretation.

One comes from the McLeod, Atkin, and Chaffee study. In addition to correlating aggression with recent violence viewing, they also correlated it with much earlier violence viewing. The latter was a far less reliable measure than the former, which would depress an obtained correlation, yet the actual correlations were similar. A reasonable inference is that the relationship between earlier viewing and current behavior is in actuality greater than that between current viewing and aggression. This suggests that violence viewing precedes the measured aggression, a relationship consistent with a causal interpretation.

The other comes from a 10-year panel study. Third-grade data were collected in a study of mental health and aggression in childhood behavior. The site was a semirural county in upper state New York. Measures included violence viewing, based on mothers' reports of children's television favorites, and peer ratings of aggressiveness. These are the data reported by Eron (1963). In 1970, ten years later, about half of the original sample was located. Measures again included violence viewing, this time based on self-reports of television favorites, and peer ratings of aggressiveness. The panel results were first reported by Lefkowitz et al. (1972), although they are also available elsewhere (Eron, et al., 1972, 1974; Lefkowitz et al., 1977).

The original sample consisted of 875 boys and girls. In the follow-up, the sample consisted of 211 males and 216 females. The mode of data analysis—cross-lagged correlations, partial correlations and multiple correlations—was chosen to permit inferences regarding the causal influence of watching violent television on aggression in later life.

The principal finding is that for boys only, violence viewing in the third grade is modestly correlated with aggressiveness ten years later (.31), is more weakly correlated with aggressiveness at the same time (.21), and a preference for violent programs ten years later is not at all correlated with earlier aggressiveness (.01). The positive correlation between violence viewing and aggressiveness over the decade was not eliminated when aggressiveness in the third grade was controlled for. Thus, the data suggest that violence viewing precedes later aggressiveness, and operates independently of aggressiveness itself in the earlier period as an influence on later aggressiveness. They also provide no support for the view that early aggressiveness is a cause of a preference for violent programs in later years.

The authors conclude "that there is a probable causative influence of watching violent television programs in early formative years on later aggression. Of course, it is not claimed that television violence is the only cause of aggressive behavior. . . . However, the effect of television violence on aggression is relatively independent of . . . other factors. . . ."* A great deal of discussion and controversy has been stimulated by this study (Chaffee, 1972b; Howitt, 1972; Huesmann et al., 1973; Kaplan, 1972; Kenny, 1972; Neale, 1972; United States Congress, 1972). One reason is its drawing of a causal inference from nonexperimental data; another is the conclusion itself—that exposure to ordinary television violence in the third grade is a "probable" cause of real-life aggressiveness a decade later. A third is simply that it is a ten-year panel study of mass media effects. Longitudinal studies of this duration have frequently been suggested, but this is a "first" in implementation, and thus any problems raise questions about the usefulness of such a design.

We are doubtful that the study should be accepted as demon-

---

* Among the hypotheses "explaining" a correlation between violence viewing and aggressiveness over time with which the overall data were found to be inconsistent were: (a) that third-grade violence viewing stimulates concurrent aggressiveness, and this aggressiveness then stimulates aggressiveness in later life; (b) that third-grade aggressiveness stimulates concurrent violence viewing, and this violence viewing then stimulates aggressiveness in later life; (c) that third-grade aggressiveness stimulates both concurrent violence viewing and aggressiveness in later life; and (d) that third-grade aggressiveness stimulates both aggressiveness and a preference for violent programs in later life. The lack of positive findings for the girls is consistent with the experimental literature, in which girls frequently do not exhibit the same degree of aggressiveness as boys after exposure to televised violence.

strating a causal relationship, because of the various questions that can be raised about the validity and reliability of the measures. At the same time, we cannot dismiss the data entirely on the basis of the objections raised—for example, that the questionnaire items measuring aggressiveness, while all right for the third grade, were no longer appropriate for people ten years older; that the viewing measures involved favorite programs rather than actual viewing; that the third-grade television measure was a mother's report, and not necessarily accurate; that the data are inconsistent because results hold only for boys and not girls; that the second measure of aggression referred only to some past period, but no specific period; and that a necessary statistical assumption that measures of the same variable be identical at both points in time was not met.

Our view is that the data contribute importantly to the evidence on the role of violence viewing in aggressiveness by finding a positive correlation between earlier viewing and later aggressiveness, although such a correlation *by itself* is not open to causal interpretation. Such a view means that we need not be concerned with comparability between measures over time, or otherwise with characteristics of other measures or the pattern of data. As we have said, we accept the mother-based measure of favorites as a fair to good index of violence viewing because of the age of the child, and the aggressiveness measure, although admittedly asking about behavior generally more appropriate for younger persons, should then only produce a diluted index underestimating its relationship to any other variable and not one that would lead to a false conclusion when a positive correlation is found. Thus, the data add an over-time correlation to our collection of same-time (or "synchronous") correlations.

Without any further evidence, this would make causal interpretation somewhat more justifiable. Alone, an over-time correlation is no better than a synchronous correlation for causal inference because any number of third variables may be responsible for the variation in each. However, synchronous and over-time correlations *together* do strengthen the case, because not all explanations that would cover one or the other fit both; thus, the number of possible alternative explanations are reduced. In addition, there are the McLeod, Atkin, and Chaffee (1972a; 1972b) data, which demonstrate that the synchronous correlation withstands numerous tests for the influence of third variables, thereby also eliminating various alternative explanations. Although causal inference from survey data is always problematical, the overall pattern of finding appears to leave only the possibility of some unstudied third variable that would explain both synchronous and over-time correlations. Fortunately, we also have further evidence of a different type, and it is remarkably consistent with the conclusion to which the survey data would seem to lead.

LABORATORY EXPERIMENTS. When the study of the impact of television violence on behavior moves to the laboratory, the researcher is able to make causal inferences. The time order of the variables offers no problem, since the experimenter ensures that exposure to a violent stimulus precedes measurement of subsequent responses. An almost infinite number of third variables that might influence the relationship can be controlled by random assignment of subjects to the various experimental conditions. In addition, the factors possibly affecting the occurrence or magnitude of an effect can be studied by manipulating such variables.

Laboratory study also brings disadvantages with it—the artificiality of the viewing and performance situations, disparities between the experimental and "real" television stimuli, differences between experimental indices and "real" aggression, and the possibility that subjects respond as the experimenter expects because of the unintended communication of experimenter "demand" or expectations. Nevertheless, it is the laboratory experiment that can tell us beyond question what television can do to aggressive behavior when all other things are equal.

The fundamental design is to assign a number of subjects randomly to two or more groups, vary the exposure of the groups to television violence in terms of quantity, degree, or character of the portrayal, and then place the subjects in a situation in which the occurrence or degree of some kind of "aggressive" response may vary. Inferences are based on comparisons among the different groups (or, in some cases of responses of a single group before and after exposure). Possible variations are numerous. Often, a group exposed to no television is included to provide a control; sometimes, the children are frustrated or angered either before viewing or before responding; the measures of aggression may range from direct observation of play to shocking an innocent victim to providing paper and pencil responses; viewing may be individual or in groups; the stimulus may display violence that is justified or unjustified, painful or not painful, rewarded or punished. The nature of the variations depends on the specific question the experimenter asks.

ACQUIRING AGGRESSIVE BEHAVIORS. Several studies demonstrate that young children acquire novel aggressive behaviors from as little as a single viewing of a brief television or film portrayal. In one of the seminal experiments, preschoolers saw a model perform a sequence of highly novel verbal and physical aggression toward an inflated Bobo the Clown doll a large lightweight plastic toy which has sand in the bottom so that it will bounce back when punched (Bandura, Ross, and Ross 1963a). The children were assigned randomly to groups which viewed the aggressive behavior performed by a live human model, a film of the live model, or a film of a costumed model that stimulated a cartoon. There was a fourth, control, group which saw nothing. After viewing the children were mildly frustrated, then allowed to play for 20 minutes in a room containing a Bobo doll, many of the same toys the model had used to attack the doll, and variety of additional toys. Observers coded the children's behavior, recording both imitative and nonimitative aggressive acts. Compared to the control group, all three groups displayed sharply higher levels of aggressive behavior. The children who observed the cartoon simulation showed slightly less aggression than those who had seen the live model or the film, but generally the differences among the three groups were negligible. The largest proportion of aggressive behavior was due to direct imitation. Films of some of the children's post-viewing behavior reveal almost perfect replications of the model's actions, including such unlikely imitative verbal declarations as "Lickit! Stickit!" as the child sat on the doll's head and struck it with the handle of a mallet.

There is also clear evidence that although the child may fail to perform observed behaviors, he may nevertheless have learned them, and will use them later. Display of a behavior depends not only on its acquisition, but on the situation. That this is so is demonstrated by an experiment in which the nursery-school children serving as subjects were exposed to one of three five-minute television portrayals of an adult male. He was either rewarded, punished, or left alone after having attacked a Bobo doll (Bandura, 1965a). Subsequently, the children were observed during play with a Bobo doll for imitation of the observed behavior. They were not rewarded. Then acquisition was measured by asking the children to perform what they could recall in return for a reward of fruit juice and an adhesive-backed picture.

The results are displayed in figure 5.2.

Imitative performance of the aggressive behavior shown on television was greater when the portrayed aggression was re-

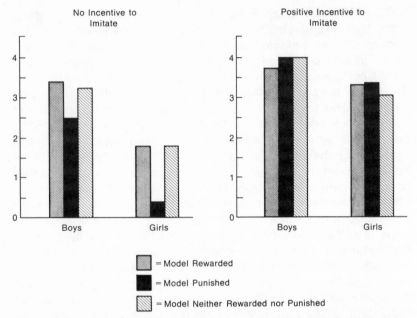

Figure 5.2. Mean number of acts imitating television portrayal under different conditions of reward for model and different conditions of reward for imitation.

SOURCE: Adapted from A. Bandura. 1965a. "Influence of Models' Reinforcement Contingencies on the Acquisition of Imitative Responses." *Journal of Personality and Social Psychology,* 1: 589–95.

warded. Children who saw an aggressive model whose behavior was punished performed significantly fewer imitative aggressive acts than children who saw the model either rewarded or receive neither reward nor punishment. Boys imitated the aggressive models more than girls. However, when a reward was offered to the children for imitating the aggressive model, the differences between the three groups—model rewarded, no consequences, and model punished—disappeared, and the sex difference was greatly reduced. Thus, learning of what was observed occurred regardless of the portrayed consequences.

A number of similar experiments provide evidence of direct imitation of film or videotape displays of novel aggressive behaviors. The novelty serves to ensure that the stimulus is teaching new behavior rather than eliciting already existing ones. The results have been replicated using both realistic and cartoon models with preschool children (Bandura, 1965a; Dubanoski and Parton, 1971; Ellis and Sekyra, 1972; Hanratty et al., 1969), second-graders (Savitsky et al., 1971) and ten-year-olds (Grusec, 1973). Moreover, Hicks (1965, 1968) included both immediate and delayed measures of imitation and found that when preschoolers were provided with an incentive they could recall and perform as much as 40 percent of the model's aggressive actions as long as eight months after viewing.

There is also evidence that aggression may be more likely to be learned than other classes of behavior. Young children are more likely to watch action. A. H. Stein and Friedrich (1972) report that preschoolers recalled little of the "non-action" content portrayed in a short television excerpt. Bandura and Huston (1961), using a live model, found that preschoolers were more likely to imitate behavior performed by a model whom they liked, when liking was manipulated via prior nurturant or nonnurturant interactions with the model. However, they also found that aggressive behaviors were imitated regardless of the relation of the child to the model. As Schramm (1968b) commented: "The implication is that the tendency of children to imitate violence is very strong, and that, while other classes of behavior may not be imitated from a film because the child has no real-life relationship with the model, aggression will be, because it does not require such a relationship."

DISINHIBITION AND FACILITATION OF AGGRESSIVE BEHAVIOR. Any parent knows that most young persons are capable of acting aggressively without acquiring such responses from television. Thus, another issue is whether viewing of violence can induce young persons to perform behavior which, although classed as aggressive, is not necessarily novel or included in the televised portrayal.

Most of the preceding studies coded nonimitative as well as imitative aggression. The results indicate that exposure to violent models also increases the performance of aggressive behaviors that were not displayed in the stimulus. The Bandura, Ross, and Ross (1963a) study found that imitative aggression accounted for the largest proportion of total aggression, but also found that exposure led to significant increases in nonimitative aggression. Exposed children, for example, were subsequently more likely to play with aggressive toys such as guns, although no gun ever appeared in the films.

Many kinds of aggression have been studied. The range is

partially displayed in table 5.5. Although some studies are more convincing than others, there is remarkable consistency in the findings. Under a variety of conditions, exposure to violent portrayals has been found to increase scores on a variety of "aggression" measures. For example, Lovaas (1961) reports that preschoolers who saw an aggressive cartoon were more likely than those who did not to play with a toy that expressed aggression; Mussen and Rutherford (1961) obtained similar results with first graders by measuring their expressed desire to pop a balloon; Stoessel (1972) found that children exposed to aggressive cartoons were more willing to punish a live rat than children in a nonexposed control group. Other studies employing a variety of measures of aggressiveness (some paper and pencil and some not—with subjects ranging from preschool to college age) report greater aggressiveness subsequent to viewing symbolic violence

Table 5.5 Examples of "Measures of Aggression" Used in Various Experimental Studies of the Impact of Television Violence on Young Persons

Type of Measure	Study[a]
Observation of imitative and nonimitative aggressive behavior toward inanimate objects in controlled settings	Bandura, Ross, and Ross, 1963a
Observation of imitative and nonimitative aggressive behavior toward a human in controlled settings	Hanratty et al., 1969
Observation of aggressive behavior in uncontrolled, free-play situations	A. H. Stein and Friedrich, 1972
Shocks ostensibly administered to others	Hartmann, 1965
Noxious noise ostensibly administered to others	Feshbach, 1972
Noxious heat ostensibly administered to others	Liebert and Baron, 1972a
Willingness to punish a live rat	Stoessel, 1972
Preference for "aggressive" vs. "nonaggressive" toys	Lovaas, 1961
Expressed desire to pop a balloon	Mussen and Rutherford, 1961
Paper and pencil responses to hypothetical situations	Leifer and Roberts, 1972
Paper and pencil measures of "hostility"	Berkowitz, Corwin, and Heironimus, 1963
Toleration of aggressive behavior in others	Drabman and Thomas, 1974a

[a] Many of the measures have been employed in a number of studies. The studies listed are illustrative.

(Berkowitz, Corwin and Heironimus, 1963; Collins, 1973b; Collins, Berndt, and Hess, 1974; Emery, 1959a, 1959b; Leifer and Roberts, 1972).

Of course, the practical relevance of these findings can be criticized. Attacks on inanimate objects, choice of aggressive toys, and responses to paper and pencil tests are not identical to actually aggressing against and inflicting pain on humans. The criticism loses much of its force, however, in light of work employing more realistic measures. At least three experiments with young children varied the post-exposure measurement situation. A live adult dressed in a clown suit similar to that worn by the symbolic victim was used, along with the Bobo doll (Hanratty et al., 1969; Hanratty, O'Neal, and Sulzer, 1972; Savitsky et al., 1971). All report more aggression against the Bobo doll than the human. However, all also found that the majority of the children who had seen the non-violent neutral film displayed at least some aggression toward the Bobo, but none engaged in any sort of aggression toward the human clown. Exposure to a violent film, on the other hand, led a number of children in all three studies to physically assault the human clown, sometimes inflicting considerable pain.

Again, the relevance can be questioned. Clowns aren't really human, one may argue, and hence can't really be hurt; and one may object to the close similarity between the symbolic and the live victims. However, there are additional experiments, in which the victims are real persons, the performance is not at all like that portrayed in the film, and the subjects believe that they are inflicting real pain. In these experiments, young persons (usually adolescents) are exposed either to violent or to nonviolent symbolic stimuli, after which they are asked to "assist" the experimenter. For most of the studies, the help consists of administering "shocks" to a "learner" (actually an experimental confederate) whenever he makes an error on an ostensible learning task. Subjects are free to determine the intensity or duration of the shocks, and they believe (incorrectly) that they are administering real pain.

In one of the earlier studies to use this procedure, Walters and Thomas (1963) exposed adolescent males and adult males and females to either a knife-fight scene from the movie *Rebel Without a Cause* or to an educational film. Regardless of the sex or age of the subjects, those who saw the violent film subsequently administered longer shocks. With some variations in the nature of the stimulus and the pre-exposure and exposure conditions, a number of experiments conducted with college students report basically the same results (Berkowitz, 1965; Berkowitz and Geen, 1966, 1967; Geen and Berkowitz, 1966, 1967; Hoyt, 1970).

Hartmann (1965, 1969) used the shock machine with teenage delinquent boys, half of whom were angered before viewing one of three versions of a film showing two boys playing basketball. One film showed an active but nonviolent game. The other two versions culminated in a violent fist fight between the two boys, one focusing on the aggressive acts (hitting, kicking), the other on the punitive consequences of the fight (painful facial expressions). Boys who viewed either of the two fight versions administered more shocks than boys who saw just the game; boys who were angered before the film gave more shocks than those not aroused; aroused boys who saw the painful version gave the most shocks.

Feshbach (1972) modified the procedure so that fourth-, fifth-, and sixth-graders believed they were administering noxious levels of noise rather than shocks to a victim. Children saw either no film or a film of a riot, introduced either as real (a "newsreel") or as fantasy (a "Hollywood movie"). He found that children who viewed the "real" violence were more aggressive than children in the control version. However, data also showed children who viewed the "fantasy" version to be less punitive—a point to which we shall return.

Liebert and Baron (1972a, 1972b) also modified the shock procedure. Children ranging from five to nine years old were offered the opportunity to either help or hurt another child (a confederate) by pushing a button that made a handle the confederate was required to turn either easier to turn (a "Help" button) or that made the handle grow hot (a "Hurt" button). Consistent with most of the preceding findings, children who viewed a violent excerpt from The Untouchables were more willing to hurt than were children who saw an exciting but nonviolent sports sequence. Finally, Collins (1974), in one of the relatively few experimental studies to employ stimuli based on full, although edited, television programs, exposed fourth-, seventh-, and tenth-graders to programs in which the portrayed response to provocation was either aggression or constructive coping. He found that children who viewed the aggressive version gave significantly more and longer hurt responses when compared to children who observed the coping version. When compared to children who viewed a third, control, film, the means for the aggressive condition were higher, but not significantly so.

In sum, we conclude that the influence of violence viewing on aggression is not limited to the acquisition or imitation of portrayed behavior. The studies differ greatly in the degree to which the indicator of aggressiveness employed equals violence that might be performed in day-to-day life, but a good many of them do represent valid indicators of willingness to inflict discomfort or pain on another human being, and across the total array the results are similar. The findings of experiments using different stimuli, different sets of instructions and varied samples of children and young adults are remarkably consistent.

We do not believe that all depictions of violence will make all children more aggressive in all situations. Differences in the nature of the stimuli, the characteristics of the viewers, and the demands and contingencies in the post-viewing situation all mediate differences in the probability and degree of subsequent aggression. It is to these factors that we now turn.

THE ROLE OF TELEVISION CONTENT. Several studies employing stimuli especially prepared for experimental purposes have demonstrated that observation of a model who is explicitly punished for aggressive acts inhibits subsequent aggression among young children (Bandura, 1965a; Bandura, Ross, and Ross, 1963b; Brodbeck, 1955; Leifer and Roberts, 1972). Where aggression is concerned, however, observation of a model rewarded for aggressive acts has been shown to elicit no greater levels of subsequent aggression from children than does seeing a model whose aggressive behavior is associated with no consequences (Bandura, 1965b). Brodbeck (1955) also found that children's levels of aggression rose markedly after viewing a cartoon in which the villain was not punished. It appears that children expect aggressive acts to be punished. When they are not, they behave as if they had seen the model rewarded. Moreover, Bandura, Ross, and Ross (1963b) found that the inhibitory effect of punishment may be highly specific. Nursery school children who saw a model punished for specific aggressive acts subsequently failed to perform those particular acts, but they did engage in other types of aggressive behavior.

Perceived motivations underlying portrayals of violence also mediate aggression. Berkowitz and Rawlings (1963) exposed college students to a violent prizefight scene in which a boxer received a painful beating. In one version, the victim was introduced as deserving of the beating; in the other he was introduced as a sympathetic, unfortunate victim of circumstances. Students who witnessed the justified beating were subsequently more aggressive. Berkowitz (1965) and Berkowitz, Corwin, and Heironimus (1963) found the same result, but only among students who had been angered before viewing, a finding replicated by Berkowitz, Parke, Leyens, and West (1974) with adolescent delinquent boys. Hoyt (1970) included a further variation on the nature of the justification—portraying it as either based on vengeance or on self-defense. Using the shock procedure described above, he found least willingness to inflict pain among college students in the no-justification condition, more willingness in the self-defense condition, and most willingness in the vengeance condition.

Among children, however, the impact of perceived motivation is less clear. Nolan (reported in Leifer and Roberts, 1972) failed to replicate the Berkowitz and Rawlings (1963) study among fourth-, seventh-, and tenth-graders. Collins (1974) and Collins and Zimmermann (1975) report that children who viewed a television program edited to portray explicitly and clearly negative motives for and negative consequences of aggressive behavior subsequently engaged in less aggressiveness and that those who saw such cues ambiguously portrayed engaged in more aggressiveness when compared to a control group. The design of this study, however, makes it difficult to determine whether perceived motivations or perceived consequences played the greater role in inhibiting responses.

These findings point to a problem in generalizing from the results of the studies we have reviewed. For the most part, they employ stimuli especially prepared to test hypotheses about specific variations in content. As a result, they typically present a clear association between the aggressive acts and some other element, such as consequences or motives. Frequently, however, television programs are not so explicit. Crimes at the beginning of a program may not be punished until the end. Aside from the convention that the aggression of heroes is justified (hence "prosocial" in nature), characterization of motives often is unclear. Sometimes, characters express both good and bad motives for their acts. In short, while the evidence from closely controlled laboratory experiments indicates that violent acts may be inhibited to

the degree that they are shown as leading to negative consequences or performed with little or no justification, there is reason to question the effectiveness with which television presents
this message.

For example, Leifer and Roberts (1972) conducted a series of
experiments in which they varied portrayals of both the motives
for and consequences of performing violent acts using full television programs. In addition to demonstrating that comprehension
of motives and consequences was highly dependent on age, they
also found that when full (or slightly edited) television programs
were employed as experimental stimuli, the portrayal of motives
and consequences had little effect on subsequent responses.
Even among older children, who perceived and understood the
cues indicating that punishment was a consequence of violence
or that some of the justifications motivating violence were less
than worthy, there was no evidence that such variations mediated
post-viewing aggression. Only the amount of violence portrayed
in the programs affected subsequent aggressiveness. The more
violence, the more aggressive responses. Similarly, Collins
(1973b) manipulated the temporal association between an aggressive act and negative consequences by inserting commercials between the act and its consequences. Among third-graders he
found that when the consequences were made distant from the
violent act, punishment had no effect on aggressiveness. Younger
children, at least, appeared less capable of associating the consequences with the act in the face of such temporal separation.
Collins (1974), summarizing several studies that used complete or
nearly complete television programs to test the impact of the portrayal of motives and consequences on subsequent aggression,
writes that when a program unambiguously portrays an aggressive actor's motives for aggression as undesirable, and he suffers
the consequences, children's subsequent aggressive responses
are inhibited. However, "if the portrayal is more ambiguous—if
there are scenes in which the actor seems to have more desirable
motives and in which the consequences are less explicitly presented—disinhibition is more likely."

It can be argued that contemporary television frequently
presents aggression in a highly prosocial or justified manner. The
hero often triumphs by administering a sound thrashing to the
criminal. While this is intended to carry the message that crime
does not pay, there is also evidence that it may simultaneously
teach that violence in defense of "right" is both justified and ad-

mirable. Albert (1957), for example, found more aggressiveness among children who saw a film in which the hero won a fight than in those who saw films showing the villain win or no clear-cut winner. Given the evidence that the behaviors of any attractive model are more likely to be emulated than those of less attractive models, perhaps simply the fact that aggression is frequently manifested by the leading figures of many television programs achieves just the opposite of the "crime does not pay" message. Unfortunately, there is no empirical evidence on this topic.

THE ROLE OF INDIVIDUAL DIFFERENCES. A frequent finding is that after viewing, as shown in figure 5.2, boys perform more aggression than girls (Bandura, 1965a; Bandura, Ross, and Ross, 1963a, 1963b; Collins, 1974; Feshbach, 1972; Hicks, 1965; Leifer and Roberts, 1972; Liebert and Baron, 1972a, 1972b). One factor responsible is that social norms permit greater expression of aggression by males. Sex differences also may occur because most televised aggression is performed by males, thus encouraging viewers to label filmed aggression as sex-typed behavior.

A few studies have examined effects of the child's socioeconomic status and race on responses to violent television. Kniveton (1973) found that five- and six-year-old middle-class boys were more influenced by an aggressive adult model, while their working-class counterparts responded more to an aggressive peer model. Thelen and Soltz (1969) found that black, male preschool children enrolled in a Head Start program imitated the aggressive behavior of a white model less when he was rewarded than when he was not, while the reverse was found among white, middle-class children. Thelen (1971) also found that black children recalled more of a model's aggressive behavior when the model was *not* praised than when he was. The paucity of experimental research in which social class and race has served as a control variable makes it difficult to interpret such findings, although it is reasonable to expect that the environmental conditions associated with race and socioeconomic status influence children's perceptions and interpretations of what is viewed on television, including violence.

The relatively few laboratory studies that have looked at the effect of age on aggressive responses to violent television indicate that it is positively related to comprehension of the contingencies surrounding violent portrayals (Leifer and Roberts, 1972).

The relationship of age to aggressive response, however, is less clear. When Leifer and Roberts examined absolute levels of post-exposure aggression, grade was found to be a powerful predictor; older children responded more aggressively. However, data obtained during the construction of their measure of aggression indicate that older children also give more aggressive responses before viewing. In the several experiments in which *change* in aggressiveness from before to after viewing was examined, a curvilinear relationship was found; children in the middle school years responded more aggressively than their younger or older counterparts. This finding was replicated by Collins (1973b).

Collins and Zimmerman (1975) and Liebert and Baron (1972a) also report a relationship between grade and sex in aggressive responses. The former study found that second-grade boys were more willing than second-grade girls or sixth-graders of either sex to press a "hurt" button after viewing a program in which the motives for and consequences of aggression were portrayed ambiguously. The latter study found that younger boys who had seen an excerpt from a violent program played more aggressively than girls or older children. However, these same studies found no such interaction for dependent variables other than these.

Finally, there is evidence that levels of aggression before viewing are among the best predictors of aggressive responses after viewing. Leifer and Roberts (1972), for example, report regression analyses performed on data obtained from several different experiments and consistently find a strong relationship. There is a good deal of evidence that boys and children from families of lower socioeconomic status engage in more aggressive behavior regardless of television, although both sex and status also have been found to be related to greater viewing of violence, and some findings associating television-related aggressiveness with such demographic variables may reflect the contributory influence of a greater inclination toward aggressiveness. However, it also is possible, although there is little evidence on the issue, that more aggressive children are in general more responsive to televised depictions of violence. The Surgeon General's Scientific Advisory Committee on Television and Social Behavior (1972) concluded, on the basis of a variety of evidence, that the impact of television violence on children is most likely to be most significant on children who are already predisposed to behave more aggressively. There is no justification for considering such children as typically deviant; this simply means that those above the median or average score for aggression have often been found to be more affected.

THE ROLE OF THE ENVIRONMENTAL CONTEXT. The more similarity between the setting in which symbolic violence is portrayed and the situation in which the child is given the opportunity to behave aggressively after viewing, the greater the probability that the child will perform aggressive behaviors. For example, in observational learning experiments in which, after viewing, children are placed in a performance situation that repeats the portrayed cues, high levels of aggressiveness are usually obtained. On the other hand, studies which expose children to aggressive cartoons and then place them in situations highly dissimilar from those portrayed tend to obtain lower levels of aggression (Lovaas, 1961).

Berkowitz (1962b) has argued that aggression after viewing violence would be a direct function of the observed cues repeated in the performance situation. One study tested this hypothesis by exposing children to a violent film, then placing them in test situations varying from high to low in similarity to the observed setting (Meyerson, 1966). Imitative aggression was found to increase the more similar the performance situation and the film setting. Berkowitz and his colleagues also report a series of experiments demonstrating that aggressive responding increases to the degree that cues present in the symbolic portrayal are present in the performance situation (Berkowitz, 1965; Berkowitz and Geen, 1967; Geen and Berkowitz, 1966, 1967).

The presence and comments of adult observers also directly influences subsequent aggressive behavior. DeRath (1963) exposed children to television violence in the presence of an adult co-observer who made explicit negative comments about the behavior of the model. After viewing, children who heard those prohibitions inhibited their aggressive behavior in the presence of the co-observer and in the presence of another adult who had not been present when the comments were made. Hicks (1968) conducted an even more elaborate study by having children observe aggression in the presence of an adult who either condemned or praised the actions of the model, or who remained silent. He then placed the children in a performance situation with or without the adult who had made the comments. Compared to the group who heard no comments, when the adult observer was present, children who heard praise for the aggressive model engaged in more imitative aggression, and those who had heard him condemned engaged in less. When the observer was not present, there were no differences between groups and all three engaged in statistically significant degrees of imitative aggression. In other words, at least in the short term the effectiveness of negative sanctions imposed by an adult depends on the presence of the adult.

Thomas and Drabman (1974) replicated the typical imitation experiment with the added condition that children were subsequently placed in a performance situation either alone or in pairs. As usual, observation of an aggressive model produced aggressive imitation. In addition, the amount of aggression displayed was significantly higher when there were *two* children in the performance situation. Thus, by testing children individually we may be grossly underestimating imitative aggression.

THE ROLE OF CATHARSIS. The catharsis hypothesis will be fully discussed in chapter 8. However, since 'much of the current debate over the role of catharsis (Feshbach, 1969, 1972; Feshbach and Singer, 1971; Goranson, 1969a, 1970; Kaplan and Singer, 1977; Liebert, Sobol, and Davidson, 1972) is fueled by concern about the impact of television violence on young persons, we shall briefly cover some of the research here.

The catharsis hypothesis holds, in various formulations, that observing television violence will reduce the likelihood of subsequent aggression. In one version, such an effect is said to occur because vicarious participation in the observed violence will reduce aggressive drive (Feshbach, 1955). In another version, the effect is said to occur primarily for viewers low in the ability to fantasize, and whose capacity to control aggressive impulses by fantasizing about them is therefore augmented by television-supplied fantasies (Feshbach, 1972). Both versions would seem to demand the arousal of aggressive impulses or feelings (accomplished, experimentally, by angering subjects) before viewing in order for catharsis to occur.

Feshbach (1955, 1961) reports two experiments conducted with college-age subjects that appear to support the hypothesis. In the earlier experiment, subjects who had been insulted by the experimenter displayed less punitiveness in rating him when they had been given the opportunity to make up stories that could express hostility, and the amount of hostility expressed in the stories was inversely related to the punitiveness of their ratings. In the later experiment, subjects who had been insulted by the experimenter expressed less hostile imagery on a word association test and displayed less punitiveness in rating the experimenter after seeing a violent film. Feshbach interprets these results as demonstrating that, when angered, vicarious experience with aggression serves to drain off aggressive impulses.

The interpretation of these results also is qualified by a number of studies that provide alternative explanations for at least some of Feshbach's findings or that demonstrate increases in aggressiveness after being angered and exposed to violent television stimuli. Berkowitz and Rawlings (1963) argue that observation of a brutal fight after having been angered may arouse aggression anxiety and guilt, which would inhibit subsequent aggression among those subjects who saw the aggressive film. To test this possibility, college students were angered and exposed to film violence depicted as justified or unjustified. One purpose of the portrayal of justified violence was to create an experimental condition in which inhibitions against aggressiveness would be lowered. If the catharsis explanation holds, then one would expect reduced aggressiveness in this condition because the lowered inhibitions would facilitate vicarious involvement and catharsis. If Berkowitz and Rawlings are correct, the lowered inhibitions should increase aggressiveness. The latter occurred. Their interpretation is further supported by an additional study showing that the level of aggressiveness was lower when subjects were angered and exposed to *unjustified* violence (Berkowitz, 1965),and by Hoyt's (1970) demonstration that angered subjects gave more shocks when the violence they viewed was not only justified but motivated by vengeance—a condition which should legitimize anger and constrain aggression anxiety.

Hartmann's (1965, 1969) study also would seem to fulfill many of the conditions of such an aggression-reduction model. His teenaged, delinquent subjects were not only angered, but one group saw a version of a film focusing on pain cues, the very kind of stimuli that might be expected to arouse aggression anxiety, and thus inhibit aggressive responses. However, the angered teenagers not only were more aggressive overall, but those who were angered and saw the punitive version were the most aggressive.

More recently, in one of the few laboratory studies to report a reduction of aggression based on a behavioral measure, there are the several experiments of Feshbach (1972) already cited. In the clearest of these (experiment 2), nine- through eleven-year-old children were exposed to a film of a riot introduced as either a newsreel or a Hollywood film. On a post-viewing measure of willingness to administer noxious noise to an experimental confederate, children who had seen the "reality" version gave significantly more aggressive responses than children who saw the "fantasy" version. In addition, children who saw the fantasy version administered *less* noise than children, from experiment 1, who had seen no film. Feshbach interprets these data to suggest that when an event is perceived as fictional, subjects can "leave their feelings in the theater," but when perceived as real, tensions are aroused that are expressed in more aggressive responses. In other words, viewing of fantasy aggression as such served to moderate subsequent aggressive behavior.

We question, however, whether this experiment provides a valid test of a catharsis hypothesis since aggressive feelings were not aroused before viewing or the administration of noise. It is possible to view the results as demonstrating that violence perceived to be real is more likely than violence perceived to be fantasy to arouse subsequent aggressive responding, rather than as showing any aggression reducing effect of viewing fantasy violence. And although the fantasy versus no-film comparison would seem to undercut such an arousal hypothesis, it should be noted that the control group data were taken from a prior experiment. Granting that subjects for both experiments came from the same population and were randomly assigned to treatments before any experimental manipulations, comparability of the data still can be legitimately questioned in terms of various threats to validity located by the elapsed time between the first and second experiments (D. T. Campbell and Stanley, 1966).

We believe that, at present, the most that can be said about the ability of televised violence to reduce aggressive behavior is that there is some evidence that under certain conditions such reduction might occur. In those few instances in which such an effect has been found, the dependent measure has not been aggressive behavior but aggressive attitudes or affect. Moreover, the bulk of the research suggests that reduction of aggression is more likely to be a result of anxiety and inhibition about aggression than of any purging to aggressive feelings. And finally, the majority of studies that meet the conditions of a test of catharsis tend to find increases rather than decreases in aggressive behavior after viewing televised violence.

OTHER EFFECTS OF TELEVISION VIOLENCE. One concern has been that exposure to a constant diet of film and television violence might dysfunctionally influence children's emotions. Early work reported that among younger children exposure to violent television led to higher levels of rated anxiety (Himmelweit, Oppenheim, and Vince, 1958; Siegel, 1956). More recently, violent films have been shown to engender physiological arousal among children ranging from preschool through grade school (Cline, Croft, and Courrier, 1972; Osborn and Endsley, 1971) and such arousal has been shown to lead to increase the level of subsequent behavior (Tannenbaum, 1972).

There are also data suggesting that the more violent television a child is exposed to, the less emotionally responsive to portrayals of violence he may be. Cline, Croft, and Courrier (1972), for example, divided a sample of grade-school children into high and low television viewers. A comparison of physiological measures obtained while the children viewed a violent film revealed that the children who came to the study with a history of heavy exposure to television were significantly less responsive. A similar lack of responsiveness to aggressive films among preschoolers who watch a great deal of violent television is reported by A. H. Stein and Friedrich (1972). The typical degree of desensitization does not erase a violent portrayal's capacity to enhance aggressiveness, or the results of the many experiments would be different. However, it may have an undesirable outcome.

Bandura and his colleagues (Bandura, Grusec, and Menlove, 1967; Bandura and Menlove, 1968), for example, have used the principle of exposure leading to desensitization to help children overcome fear of dogs, a decidedly prosocial effect. However, it is also possible that exposure to violence will decrease sensitivity to the possible consequences of violence. In several cleverly designed studies, Drabman and Thomas have created situations in which after viewing a violent or nonviolent film, children ranging from the first through fourth grades are given the responsibility of supervising the behavior of two younger children (Drabman and Thomas, 1974a, 1974b; Thomas and Drabman, 1974). The situation is contrived so that the two children, whose behavior the subjects are asked to follow on a television monitor, misbehave, enter into a fight, and finally destroy property. The dependent variable is the amount of time the subject takes to notify an adult. Those who have seen the violent film take longer. The implication is that observing violent portrayals reduces responsiveness to real-life violence, although the use of video in the measurement situation raises the possibility that the outcome is peculiar to vicarious experience.

LIMITS OF LABORATORY-TYPE EXPERIMENTS. In sum, the evidence produced by a great number of experiments points in one direction—observation of television portrayals of violence can cause subsequent aggressive behavior in children. Nevertheless, there are dangers inherent in generalizing such results to the influence of television in day-to-day life.

In the laboratory, attention is ensured. Stimuli are often brief, focused, and lack the character and plot development characteristic of real programming. Viewing is devoid of both the continuity and distractions of ordinary television experience. Sanctions against aggressive behavior are often removed in order to ensure enough responses so that between-condition comparisons can be made. No matter how overwhelming the experimental findings, a skeptic can always argue that the external validity of the studies is simply not convincing. Some scientists have responded to this criticism by attempting to conduct naturalistic experiments in which the artificialities, but not the prowess for causal inferences, are removed.

NATURALISTIC EXPERIMENTS. We were able to find reports of eight naturalistic experiments. They are described in table 5.6. Seven report an increase in aggressiveness as a function of exposure to television violence, and one reports a decrease. This ratio is rather like that for laboratory experiments. However, there are a number of qualifications to be made in regard to both the individual studies and this genre of method.

Steuer, Applefield, and Smith (1971) rated the free-play behavior of five pairs of matched preschoolers for ten days before any experimental treatment. For the following eleven days the free-play rating period was preceded by viewing of a ten-minute cartoon. One member of each pair saw an aggressive cartoon, the other member a non-aggressive cartoon. The outcomes are displayed in Figure 6.3. The changes in play behavior as a function of the television treatment are striking. In all five pairs, the child who observed the aggressive cartoon engaged in more hitting, throwing of objects at others, kicking, and so forth. Although for one pair the difference between the children who had seen the violent and nonviolent shows was only one point and there was little change from the baseline period, in some pairs the dif-

Table 5.6 Summary of Naturalistic Experiments Examining Young Persons' Responses to Television Violence

Study (Duration)	Subjects (N)	Treatment
	A. Studies with Young Children	
Cameron and Janky, 1971 (7 weeks)	Kindergarten children (N = 254)	Parents controlled television diet for 3 weeks
A. H. Stein and Friedrich, 1972 (9 weeks)	Preschool children (N = 97)	Approx. 10–30 minutes per day of aggressive, neutral or prosocial television for 4 weeks
Steuer, Applefield, and Smith, 1971 (3 weeks)	5 pairs matched pre-schoolers (N = 10)	10 minutes per day of aggres-sive or nonaggressive cartoons for 11 days
	B. Studies with Adolescents	
Feshbach and Singer, 1971 (8 weeks)	8–18 yr. old boys from 7 residential boys' homes and private schools (N = 625)	Minimum 6 hrs. per week vio-lent or non-violent televi-sion for 6 weeks
Parke et al., 1977 (2 studies)		
Study 1 (7 weeks)	14–18 yr. old boys from residential institution for juvenile delinquents (N = 60)	Exposure to either aggressive or neutral feature length films for 5 nights
Study 2 (7 weeks) (Replication of Study 1)	Same institution; differ-ent 14–18 yr. old male subjects (N = 120)	Exposure to either aggressive or neutral feature length film *equal in viewer interest di-mension* for 5 nights (re-peated exposure condition); 2 additional groups for one night (single exposure con-dition)
Leyens et al., 1975 (3 weeks) (Belgian replication of Parke et al.)	13–18 yr. old boys from residential institution for juvenile offenders in Belgium (N = 85)	Exposure to either aggressive or neutral feature length film for 5 nights
Wells, 1973 (12 weeks) (Replica-tion of Feshbach and Singer)	7th–9th grade boys in 10 residential schools (N = 567)	Minimum 6 hours per week violent of nonviolent televi-sion diet for 7 weeks

[a]Results as reported by authors. See text for questions raised about some results.

Table 5.6 Continued

Aggression Measure	Results[a]
A. Studies with Young Children	
Parent ratings of "aggressive" behavior	Slight increase in aggressive behavior among violence viewers
Ratings of free-play behavior before, during and after treatment	Children initially high in aggression who saw violent programs revealed increased aggressive behavior
Ratings of free-play behavior before and during treatment	Increased aggressive behavior among children who saw violent cartoons
B. Studies with Adolescents	
Various self reports, teacher ratings, and observations of behavior before, during and after treatment	Decreases on some measures of aggression for boys from boys' homes who saw violent television
Observation of aggressive behavior in free situations before, during and after treatment	Increased aggressive behavior among violence viewers; greatest for subjects initially high in aggressiveness
Observation of aggressive behavior in free situations before, during, and after treatment (commencing earlier than Study 1); in addition, single exposure subjects verbal aggression measured in laboratory	Increased aggressive behavior among subjects exposed to violent television in both conditions (greatest for initially high-aggressive subjects in *single* violence exposure condition; no difference between initially low- and high-aggressive subjects in *repeated* violence exposure condition
Observation of aggressive behavior in free situations before, during, and after treatment	Increased aggressive behavior among violence viewers; greatest for subjects initially high in aggressiveness
Various self reports, teacher ratings, and observations of behavior before, during, and after treatment	Increased aggressive behavior among subjects exposed to violent television who were initially high in aggressiveness

ference was as great as 28 points and there were dramatic increases in aggressive behavior from the baseline period.

In three naturalistic experiments, two in the United States and one in Europe, adolescent boys who viewed violent films for five successive weeknights engaged in greater subsequent real-life aggressiveness than those who viewed nonviolent films (Leyens, et al., 1975; Parke, et al., 1977).

The stimuli, the circumstances of exposure, and the dependent measures were selected to approximate ordinary television and movie experience and subsequent activity.* In all three, subjects were inmates at schools for delinquent boys.

In the first U.S. experiment (Parke, et al., 1977), the boys were observed and scored in regard to a variety of aggressive and other behaviors three days a week over a three-week period. Then one group saw a different violent movie on each of five consecutive nights, while the other group saw five nights of nonviolent films. No other television or films were viewed. Each of the two groups was made up of the entire population of residential cottages to which individuals originally had been assigned at random by the institution.

The second U.S. experiment (Parke et al., 1977) and the European experiment (Leyens et al., 1975) followed the same basic design. However, the second U.S. experiment involved two additional experimental conditions—a group which saw only one violent movie, and a group which saw only one nonviolent movie.

The strongest findings were for the overall measure of aggression which covered noninterpersonal as well as interpersonal aggression. However, there was also evidence that interpersonal aggression was affected in the same way. In addition, in the second U.S. experiment, a laboratory measure of aggression was similarly affected. This convergence of results provides some validation for such laboratory measures.

The violent films were rated by the subjects as more interesting and enjoyable, and viewing of the violent films was accompanied by greater verbal and physical activity. However, it is important to note that measures of subsequent general activity were *not* affected by the films. This finding leads to the rejection of the hypothesis that increased aggressiveness after viewing a violent film simply reflects an increase in the general level of activity. The

* The violent series included *Death Rides a Horse, The Champion,* and *The Chase,* while the nonviolent series included *Ride the Wild Surf* and *Buena Sera, Mrs. Campbell.*

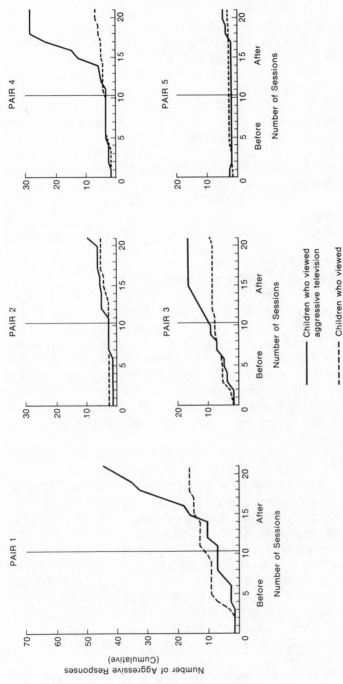

Figure 5.3. Aggressive responses during play in pairs of children exposed and not exposed to television violence.

SOURCE: Adapted from F. B. Steuer, J. M. Applefield, and R. Smith. 1971. Televised aggression and the interpersonal aggression of preschool children. *Journal of Experimental Child Psychology*, 11:442–47.

data for the single film groups in the second U.S. experiment, together with data comparing early and later behavior during the week for those who viewed five movies, provide no evidence on whether the effects of exposure to media violence are increased or decreased by repetition.

The four naturalistic experiments, one involving preschool children, three involving adolescents, are quite convincing. Neither the stimuli, exposure situation, or measurement situation were artificial. For all four, the results are consistent with each other and with the laboratory experiments. In addition, one provides empirical validation of the similarity in responsiveness to television violence of laboratory measures of aggressiveness and real-life measures.

The four remaining naturalistic experiments turn our attention to certain problems inherent to the genre. They are the studies by Cameron and Janky (1971), Feshbach and Singer (1971), A. H. Stein and Friedrich (1972), and Wells (1973).

Cameron and Janky (1971) asked parents of kindergarten children to impose viewing diets varying in violence and to rate changes in behavior during and after the several weeks of the experiment. The findings are questionable because parents knew the treatment in which the child had been placed; controls over viewing were not stringent; the parent ratings are an unknown mixture of fact and expectation; the control over viewing may have interacted with content. In any case, the result was that those assigned to view more violence were rated as becoming more aggressive.

Feshbach and Singer (1971) and Wells (1973) both exposed groups of boys in residential schools either to a diet of violent or nonviolent television over a period of several weeks. In both studies, some schools were private schools, representing high socieoeconomic backgrounds, and some were boys' homes, representing lower socioeconomic backgrounds. In the Wells study, 567 boys in the seventh through ninth grades in 10 residential schools were exposed to the two diets for seven weeks, with half the boys in each school assigned to each diet. In the Feshbach and Singer study, 625 boys 8 to 18 years of age in seven residential schools were similarly exposed for six weeks. In both studies, attrition for various reasons reduced the sample available for analysis by more than 20 percent, although attrition was greatest in Feshbach and Singer.

The Wells study was undertaken as a replication of Feshbach

and Singer, with methodological improvements. It differs from the original field experiment by including more schools, by using a more homogeneous sample in terms of age, by extending the experimental period, by taking pre-experiment measures so that groups could be matched on initial aggressiveness, by obtaining measures of pre-experimental television preferences, by employing professional field staff to train in-school raters, and by including ratings by nonschool visitors unaware of experimental assignments. However, the basic design and the use of behavioral ratings as a principal measure remained the same.

Feshbach and Singer report an association for the boys in boys' homes between exposure to a diet of violent television and lessened aggressiveness toward peers. They interpreted their findings as supporting the hypothesis that violent television stimulates fantasy which can serve as a substitute for aggressive behavior, and thus can aid children in controlling aggression. Wells found, for his analogous lower socioeconomic sample, increased verbal aggression against peers associated with the nonviolent diet, as did Feshbach and Singer, and increased physical aggression against peers associated with the violent diet, contrary to Feshbach and Singer. However, both trends were of low magnitude. Wells interprets his findings as indicating that the "control" nonviolent group was actually more comparable to an "experimental" or "treatment" group because the television diet deviated from the ordinary diet, and that the increased verbal aggression could be attributed to the results of frustration at being denied the customary and normative access to preferred violent entertainment.

A. H. Stein and Friedrich (1972 also, Friedrich and Stein 1973) exposed 97 preschoolers to either violent or neutral or prosocial television programs for 10 to 30 minutes per day over a period of four weeks, and coded free play behavior not only during the exposure period but for three weeks before and two weeks after exposure. The authors conclude that among the half of the children initially rated as highest in aggression in the baseline period, exposure to the aggressive programs resulted in more aggressive behavior in the everyday play situation.

We are not so certain. The inference about effects on aggression depends on a significantly slower decline in aggressiveness over the experimental period for those exposed to the violent diet than for those in the other groups. This would support the plausible hypothesis that television violence maintains aggressive behavior that would disappear in its absence. However, when we examine the pre-treatment scores, we find that the shifts are very much related to initial position, and the greater declines outside the violence condition are plausibly attributed to the failure of the attempted randomization of subjects.

These final four naturalistic experiments illustrate the very large challenge faced by this approach. It is easy to argue that the problem of validity can be solved by moving experimental techniques from the laboratory to the street or playground. It is not so easy to implement them successfully. For example, randomization, which is crucial for causal inference, is often difficult to achieve in real life, although fairly easy in the laboratory. And television viewing, because people have decided preferences and know in most instances what others are able to watch, is difficult to manipulate in real life so that it can serve as an independent variable.

We believe that naturalistic experiments therefore require even more than ordinary scrutiny, because the risks of false inference are greater. We would also suggest that they be undertaken in tandem with laboratory experiments so that inferences can be validated by methods each of which does not suffer from identical risks and weaknesses.

OTHER ANTISOCIAL EFFECTS. In addition to television's impact on aggressive behavior, some research has examined other effects which, like aggression, are undesirable in most circumstances. Most of these studies have been concerned with imitative learning *per se* rather than with any effect of television. Nevertheless, some of the behavior focused on, such as the willingness of a child to violate rules after viewing the rule-breaking or the inconsistencies between the words and deeds of a model, is very relevant to television, which often portrays people who deviate from accepted social norms, explicitly break stated rules, and say one thing while doing another.

Shirley (1973) provides a detailed review. All of the results come from laboratory experiments similar in design to those employed in studies of the imitation of aggression. Typically, children are advised that a certain type of activity is prohibited. They are then exposed to a live, filmed or videotaped model who, in various circumstances, conforms to or deviates from the rule. Subsequently, the children are placed in a situation where they have the opportunity to conform or deviate. The impact of the modeled behavior is then usually assessed in terms of the latency, frequency or amount of deviation displayed by the children.

We can summarize the results of studies employing film or videotaped models briefly. Children who see a model deviate from a stated rule are subsequently more likely to deviate themselves than are children who saw a model conform or children who saw no model at all (G.M. Stein and Bryan, 1972; Walters, Leat, and Mezei, 1963; Walters and Parke, 1964; Wolf, 1972, 1973; Wolf and Cheyne, 1972). G. M. Stein and Bryan (1972) also found that children exposed to a model who both practiced and preached rule breaking deviated more than did children exposed to one who practiced and preached conformity, but that children who witnessed models whose words and deeds were inconsistent (a frequent occurrence in television and films) deviated the most. Children who see models rewarded for deviation or who witness deviation with no consequences have been shown subsequently to deviate more than children who observed a model punished or no model at all (Walters, Leat, and Mezei, 1963; Walters and Parke, 1964; Walters, Parke, and Cane, 1965). In short, laboratory studies find that observation of a deviating model increases the violation of rules among children, that performed behavior is more influential than verbal exhortation, and that the same vicarious contingencies of reward and punishment that affect aggression also affect other types of deviation. No work has been conducted using complete television programs, or even excerpts of regular broadcast television. Given the nature of much television content it seems that this particular area of antisocial behavior is worth a great deal more attention.

OVERALL CONCLUSIONS. The evidence at present favors the hypothesis that exposure to television violence increases the likelihood of subsequent aggressiveness. Two recent studies covering several years in the lives of their young viewers do not alter our conclusion, although one is inconsistent with it. Belson (1977) reports that his CBS-sponsored study of English teenage delinquents isolates violence viewing as contributing to criminal acts and the inflicting of unwelcome physical violence on others. Milavsky (1977) reports that his NBC-sponsored study of American elementary and high school pupils has found no relationship, positive or negative, between violence viewing and classroom aggressiveness among the elementary school boys in the sample. Both, involving different measures and methods and focusing on different populations, are certain to be the subject of intensive scrutiny. What neither does is erase the record of findings; what they are certain to do is further sensitize us to the complexity of conditions and circumstances on which any relationship, in real life or within the confines of the analysis of data, may depend.

Meanwhile, Andison (1978) reported a headcount of the results of all empirical attempts to link aggression with exposure to television violence. When the 67 studies were divided into those reporting negative (exposure to violence related to reduced aggression, a result favoring a catharsis interpretation), null (nonsignificant), or positive results, a very large majority fell into the latter category. This pattern was unaffected by age of the population under study, by method, or by the measure of aggression; whether subjects were of college age or nursery school children, whether aggression was measured by delivery of electric shocks or ratings by peers, or whether the method was laboratory-type experiment, field experiment, or survey, there were more positive than null and negative outcomes.

We are skeptical of the head-count approach because it does not intrinsically provide protection against biases that may permeate a single genre of studies. For example, one could argue that experiments under-report null results because of the norms of scientific publication favoring statistically significant outcomes for experiments, and that those published favor the violence viewing–aggression hypothesis because investigators have been more attracted to this issue, and thus have intuitively favored portrayals likely to have such an effect, with a net effect of strong experimental evidence biased in one direction. Our analysis has emphasized the particular merits of each genre of method, rather than the quantitative direction of the findings. We could have reached a similar conclusion with fewer studies, but our confidence would have been severely shaken had the studies we examined not been complementary by having dissimilar liabilities and assets. The variety of methods encompassed by the Andison tabulation greatly enhances its credibility—much more so than the datum that more than 30,000 persons are represented. We are certainly not at all surprised that the results for surveys were less strong than for other methods, for—in addition to the just-discussed possibility that the experiments skew the results in favor of the hypothesis—as we argue (chapter 8), in real life situational factors often minimized in experiments play a strong part in any media effect.

In sum, we conclude that:

Children watch a great deal of violent television and, although many questions can be raised about individual studies, there consistently has been found a relationship between viewing of violence and various measures of aggressiveness. This remains true even when the findings of studies most open to criticism are ignored. In surveys, violence viewing in every day life has been shown to be correlated with everyday aggressiveness, and this relationship has withstood the test of controlling for the influence of a variety of third variables. In laboratory experiments, it has been demonstrated that televised portrayals of violence frequently will be imitated by young children. In laboratory experiments, it has been demonstrated that televised portrayals of violence increase the likelihood or degree of subsequent nonimitative aggression. In naturalistic experiments, exposure to complete violent films and programs in relatively ordinary viewing circumstances has been shown to increase subsequent aggression in real-life circumstances.

Children as young as preschoolers can learn new aggressive behaviors from as little as a single exposure to a brief symbolic portrayal, and aggressive behavior appears particularly likely to be learned.

Exposure to television portrayals of violence can disinhibit or facilitate the performance of previously acquired classes of aggressive behavior.

Although aggression after violence viewing is governed by sanctions operating in the social situation, the salience and effectiveness of those sanctions can be influenced by the way in which television violence is portrayed. When violence is portrayed as punished, aggressiveness is more likely to be inhibited. When portrayed as rewarded, when portrayed as leading to no consequences, when portrayed as justified, and when performed by an attractive character—all common characteristics of contemporary television programming—the probability of subsequent aggression increases.

Boys, younger children, and more aggressive children are more influenced by television violence, probably because they are less completely socialized against performing aggressive behavior.

Heavy exposure to television violence conceivably may desensitize children to the negative consequences of real-life violence.

The effects of violent television content can be at least somewhat moderated by the comments and interpretations of adults who observe with the children.

We would also draw attention to the nature of the evidence. The great strength of the research on television and aggression is that a full range of possible methods has been employed instead of a single genre and that this variety has yielded interpretable results. The methods include surveys, panel studies, laboratory experiments, and naturalistic experiments. The reason this diversity provides strength is that, as we have observed in our analysis, each genre has characteristics that open it to criticism, but which are not the same for all.

As a result, the protection against erroneous inference, the satisfaction of skeptics, and the confounding of those whose vested interests inspire interpretations uninfluenced by the findings, require that a multiplicity of methods be employed. So far, television and aggression is the sole area of television research where this strength exists.

Prosocial Behavior

As a result of the evidence that has been gathered on the subject of television and aggression, several investigators have hypothesized that television can influence more socially desirable, or "prosocial," behavior in much the same way (Bryan and Walbek, 1970a, 1970b; Leifer, Gordon, and Graves, 1973; Liebert, Neale, and Davidson, 1973; Liebert and Poulos, 1974; Poulos and Liebert, 1972).*

Such research is in its infancy. However, the early findings suggest that under certain circumstances televised portrayals can increase the likelihood of subsequent socially desirable behavior.

We would warn that one cannot assume a perfect analogy between what has been found in regard to the influence of television on aggression and its influence on socially desirable behavior. The encouragement of socially unacceptable behavior, which

---

* Lively debate often occurs about who is to judge what is "prosocial." This is a meaningless dispute, since the term is simply a convenient code word for behavior that is widely deemed to be desirable in situations where aggressiveness and violence are not deemed to be appropriate. "Antisocial" similarly is no more than a convenient code word for behavior that is widely deemed to be inappropriate in many situations. It is understood by all that the actual "prosocial" or "antisocial" quality of a real-life act depends both on the circumstances and on the subjective values of the observers (one man's robbery is another man's revolution, just as one man's ruthless aggression is another's intervention on behalf of peace).

involves the breaking of norms, is not quite the same as encouraging prosocial behavior, which involves the establishment or reinforcing of norms.

For example, several studies have shown that the aggressive behavior of children increases after viewing symbolic models who behave aggressively but are not punished (Bandura, 1965a; Brodbeck, 1955). Presumably children bring expectations of punishment for aggression with them to the viewing situation, and when such expectations are disconfirmed, much the same behavioral outcomes as observing a model rewarded take place. When the behavior is prosocial, however, the contingencies may not function in the same way. If we assume that children probably expect that a prosocial behavior, like sharing, is valued and worthy of reward, then it is reasonable to expect that if they observe a model who shares but is not rewarded, their expectations will be disconfirmed. This should lead to less sharing behavior than that displayed after observing a rewarded model. Elliott and Vasta (1970), however, found no difference in the sharing behavior of children who observed a nonrewarded model as opposed to one who received a toy for sharing (although when the reward was made large and salient, combining a toy with verbal reinforcement, there was more subsequent sharing than in the no-reward condition). This suggests that disconfirmation of children's expectations that reward or punishment will follow a particular kind of behavior may operate somewhat differentially depending on whether that behavior has been previously labeled as acceptable or unacceptable (rewardable or punishable).

RESEARCH WITH PREPARED STIMULI. Several researchers have demonstrated the therapeutic potential of television, particularly as it pertains to teaching children to overcome fears. As we noted earlier, Bandura and Menlove (1968) found that exposing preschool children who were initially fearful of dogs to a series of films that depicted other young children approaching and playing with a dog greatly increased their own willingness to do so. No decrease in fear was found among children exposed to films of Disneyland and Marineland. This study also found that the reduction in fear of dogs was maintained a month after exposure, and that children exposed to multiple models interacting with a variety of dogs were even less fearful when measured a month later. Hill, Liebert, and Mott (1968) obtained substantially the same results with preschool boys after a single viewing of a film that showed an initially fearful child approach a dog being played with by an older, fearless youngster. A similar procedure leading to a similar reduction in fear has been reported by Weisbrod and Bryan (1972) with regard to children who are fearful of snakes.

Poulos and Davidson (1971) showed a film to children between the ages of four and seven years old who had been reported by parents to be afraid of the dentist. In the film an eight-year-old boy climbs fearlessly into a dentist's chair while a fearful four-year-old girl watches. The girl gradually loses her fear and willingly climbs into the chair. After viewing, children were shown pictures of a fireman, policeman, doctor, and dentist and were asked which one they would like to visit. Those who had seen the film said they were more willing to visit the dentist than children who had not seen the film. Finally, O'Connor (1969) found that exposing initially withdrawn nursery school children to a film portraying a peer model engaging in successively more challenging social activities and being rewarded for joining in, dramatically increased subjects' subsequent social interactions in the school.

One study has used a brief television portrayal to influence children's self-control regarding delay of gratification, and several have looked at the impact of symbolic models on individual adherence to rules. Yates (1974) obtained a measure of nine-year-olds' preference for an immediate small reward as opposed to a more valuable reward for which they had to wait a week. Several weeks later, children saw one of four videotapes in which an adult either modeled delay of gratification, explained reasons for delay, modeled and explained, or acted in a neutral manner. Post-viewing measures revealed that children in all three treatment conditions became more willing to wait for the more valuable reward and that the effect was still present four weeks later. Data also indicated that the modeled behavior combined with verbalizations of reasons to delay were the most effective stimuli.

Self-control underlies the research discussed so far, as it does several studies of children's adherence to or deviation from rules. Several of these studies found that young children who viewed a peer model conform to an explicitly stated rule subsequently deviated from that rule less than children who viewed no model (Wolf, 1973; Wolf and Cheyne, 1972). These studies also found that a film model is equally as effective as a live model, and that when a model's behavior and spoken explanations are inconsistent, children are more likely to forget the rule governing the behavior. G. M. Stein and Bryan (1972) found that third- and fourth-grade girls who saw a television portrayal of a girl who was successful playing a game and who explained the rules against cheating subsequently cheated less than those who saw a model who was less successful and verbalized the same rules. Moreover, subjects who saw the successful model more accurately recalled the rules governing the game. Another study conducted with kindergarten boys found that a film of a boy punished for playing with forbidden toys inhibited subsequent deviation relative to a control group who saw no film (Walters, Leat, and Mezei, 1963).

Thus, we find evidence that in the somewhat constrained and artificial environment of the laboratory experiment, film or television stimuli can influence at least three different types of children's self-control behavior—courage, delay of gratification, and adherence to rules. These findings are convincing because they have been replicated in studies that have used live instead of film- or television-mediated models (Poulos, 1975; Shirley, 1973).

Laboratory experiments have also looked at the impact of portrayals on children's friendliness and willingness to share. Three studies coded children's displays of affection or friendliness after they had viewed a model exhibiting such behavior toward a doll. One reports more imitative affection toward such a doll among preschool children who had viewed the model compared to those who had not (Fryear and Thelen, 1969). Results also indicated that the female model had more impact on girls than on boys. A second experiment used mentally retarded subjects among whom there were a number of children, and also found more friendly behavior toward dolls after viewing (Fechter, 1971). There remains a question about whether these results generalize beyond dolls, however, for the same study found no increase in friendly behavior toward other humans, and Tasch (1970) observed no change in the behavior of preschoolers toward other preschoolers after watching an adult model behave in a friendly manner toward a doll. At least in terms of friendliness, the influence of a symbolic model may be highly specific.

Several studies have been concerned with imitation of sharing behavior; usually such behavior is measured in terms of willingness to donate resources to a worthy cause. In the typical study, a child views a model who is shown playing a game and winning prizes (such as money, tokens, or candy). After winning, the model either does or does not give some part of the winnings to a charity. The child is then allowed to play the same game and "win," after which he or she has the option to donate winnings.

Studies employing live models have found that compared to a no-model control group, simply exposing children to an exemplar who shares increases subsequent sharing (Shirley, 1973). Research using videotaped models has obtained similar results with children ranging from five through eleven years old (Bryan and Walbek, 1970a; Elliott and Vasta, 1970; Liebert, Fernandez, and Gill, 1969).

Most work with symbolic models, however, has been more concerned with the effect of different ways of portraying the sharing behavior than with simply examining the effect of observing the deed itself. For example, in the Elliott and Vasta (1970) experiment, preschoolers saw a peer model win and donate candies with varying consequences. In one version, the model was not rewarded; in a second, the model was rewarded with a toy; in a third, the model was rewarded with the toy and the reason for the reward was explicitly stated. Although all three treatments increased donations compared to the no-model condition, the most effective portrayal included both the reward and the verbal statement. Moreover, there was no difference between the no-consequences and the reward-only conditions. This study also found some evidence for generalization of sharing, since subjects who saw the models were more willing to share both candy and pennies, only the first of which had been portrayed in the videotapes.

Morris, Marshall, and Miller (1973) report that relative to a control group, children who viewed a model punished for behaving selfishly in a situation in which sharing was an option subsequently shared more, and that it made little difference whether the punishment was contingent or noncontingent on the model's refusal to share. Bryan (1971), on the other hand, had a model express positive affect ("I'm happy!") either immediately upon donating pennies to the March of Dimes or after a slight delay. His results indicate that, at least for first- and second-grade boys, the more contingent declaration led to more donating behavior.

Bryan and his colleagues (Bryan, 1970; Bryan, Redfield, and Mader, 1971; Bryan and Walbek, 1970a, 1970b) have also examined the different influence on generosity of a model's words as opposed to deeds. In these studies, various combinations of stimuli portray models engaging in either generous, neutral, or selfish behavior and verbally expressing either generous, neutral, or selfish exhortations. Measures include both children's subsequent behavior and their evaluations of the various models. In terms of judgments of the model's attractiveness, the weight of the evidence indicates that a model who practices generosity is evaluated more positively than one who practices greed. Results regarding verbal exhortations are somewhat less consistent, but tend to show that children perceive models who preach generosity to be more attractive than models who make neutral comments. They, in turn, are rated as more attractive than models who preach greed. The subsequent behavior of the children, however, seems primarily governed by the model's behavior (Bryan and Schwartz, 1971). Exhortations make little difference in children's subsequent behavior; the behavior of the model does.

Thus, we find evidence that observing a generous model leads children to behave more generously within the context of an experiment. The effect has been obtained with boys and girls ranging from preschool through the sixth grade. There is little evidence for age differences in imitative sharing, and no consistent pattern of sex differences has been found. Contingencies associated with the portrayed sharing behavior, such as reward or punishment, also influence the likelihood and degree of subsequent imitation.

STIMULI APPROXIMATING TELEVISION CONTENT. Evidence of television's influence on everyday prosocial behavior is just beginning to accumulate. There are few equivalents to the studies discussed in regard to aggression that attempt to reflect everyday long-term influence or short-term influence in ordinary situations.

There is evidence that children do recieve prosocial messages when television contains them. A quota sample survey of over 700 children between the ages of seven and eleven who viewed an episode of *Fat Albert and the Cosby Kids* indicates that 90 percent received at least one prosocial message (Columbia Broadcasting System/Office of Social Research, 1974). Silverman (1977) found that many five-year-olds and almost all seven-year-olds who viewed versions of *Sesame Street* edited to emphasize cooperative behavior understood the message of most "cooperation segments." Poulos (1975) presents evidence that comprehension of prosocial messages can be dramatically increased with careful engineering and cooperation between research and production personnel. She describes an effort to produce "prosocial commercials"—30-second spots exemplifying positive social behavior. Comprehension scores of kindergarten, first- and second-graders ranged from 38 to 67 percent correct for the initial attempts. With careful refinement of the spots, it was possible to raise the score to 93 percent correct.

Not surprisingly, two programs, *Mister Rogers' Neighborhood* and *Sesame Street,* have received a good deal of research attention. A. H. Friedrich and Stein (1975) showed kindergarten children either a series of neutral television programs or a series of four episodes of *Mister Rogers' Neighborhood.* The latter series focused on attempts of various characters to understand, reassure, and help a character fearful of being replaced by a "fancy new visitor." To assess whether additional training would enhance the program's influence, children who viewed the treatment programs were further divided into four groups: no further activity, verbal labeling of the behaviors portrayed, role playing of the behaviors displayed, and verbal labeling and role playing. After viewing and training, children completed a test that included items specific to the portrayals and items involving similar but not identical situations. Compared to children who viewed the neutral films, children in all four treatment groups could "correctly" answer more questions about prosocial behavior. There was also evidence that, among girls, verbal labeling led to slightly more learning.

A. H. Friedrich and Stein (1975) also included two behavioral measures. The first examined helping behavior in a fantasy context by having children interact with a puppet who manifested some of the same jealous behaviors portrayed in the program. The second placed children in a situation where they could help another child by repairing a piece of damaged art work. In both instances, behavior was observed and coded. Both measures revealed an increase in prosocial behavior after viewing *Mister Rogers' Neighborhood.* The enhancing effect of further training was also indicated by the boys who had engaged in the role playing condition, who subsequently engaged in more nonverbal helping behavior. A. H. Stein et al. (1973) also report an experiment in which, after viewing a minimum of four episodes of aggressive, neutral, or prosocial programming, four- and five-year-olds were divided into same-sex pairs and placed in a situation requiring that they build a structure demanding careful balancing of parts—a difficult and frustrating task for children of this age, and one that gave ample opportunity for either cooperation or aggression to occur. A concealed observer coded the children's social interaction for interpersonal aggressive and prosocial behaviors. For boys, a fairly coherent pattern emerged: those shown aggressive programs engaged in high levels of aggression and low levels of prosocial behavior; those shown prosocial programs engaged in low levels of aggression and high levels of prosocial behavior; those shown neutral programs engaged in high levels of both types of behavior.

In the naturalistic experiment discussed earlier, A. H. Stein and Friedrich (1972) found that preschoolers exposed to the prosocial television diet showed an increase in self-control behavior (tolerance of delay, obedience to rules, persistence in tasks) in the day-to-day nursery-school environment. Moreover, children from lower socioeconomic status families who viewed prosocial programs increased prosocial interpersonal behavior (verbalization of feelings, nurturance of others, cooperation).

Coates and his colleagues (Coates, Pusser, and Goodman, 1976) also observed the free-play behavior of preschool children before and after exposing them to a week of either *Sesame Street* or *Mister Rogers' Neighborhood.* They found that for children with a low pre-exposure rate, viewing *Sesame Street* increased the frequency of giving positive reinforcement and punishment to others in the preschool. It also increased the number of social contacts with other children and adults. For viewers of *Mister Rogers' Neighborhood,* pre-exposure rates made no difference; that is, there was an increase in the giving of positive reinforcements and in the number of social contacts made among all children who viewed the program.

Silverman (1977) reports less impact on the cooperative behavior of children exposed to specifically edited versions of *Sesame Street.* She showed three-, five-, and seven-year-olds a 15-minute version of the program that either emphasized the resolution of conflict via cooperation, emphasized cooperation but made no mention of conflict as an antecedent condition, or dealt only with cognitive skills such as letter and number recognition. After viewing, pairs of children participated in a game demanding cooperation in order for any gains to be made, and responded to questions testing their understanding of the concept of cooperation and their comprehension of the film. Although the data show that exposure to the treatment films influenced the cognitions about cooperation of five- and seven-year-olds, there was no increase in cooperative game behavior among children of any age. Moreover, there was a negative impact on the youngest children who viewed the conflict-resolution version; those children tended to be less cooperative than their control group counterparts. Silverman speculates that her behavioral measure was too gross to be sensitive to some effects that might be attributable to the prosocial messages, but she also interprets the data as suggesting that televised examples of prosocial behavior may not influence behavior even when cognitions are affected.

Still another study employing *Sesame Street* materials is reported by Gorn, Goldberg, and Kanungo (1976), who were concerned with the potential impact of the program on racial attitudes. They showed three- to five-year-old, white, Canadian children 12-minute versions of *Sesame Street* that included specially made inserts portraying children of other racial groups playing in either a segregated or integrated setting. Compared to a control group not exposed to the inserts, children who observed the programs with the inserts showed significantly more preference for playing with non-white children as opposed to white children when asked to choose potential playmates from sets of photos. This study also included a condition that exposed some children to an insert with a French Canadian boy. Results indicate a strong preference for him regardless of whether or not his cultural identity was evident.

In sum, with the exception of Silverman's (1977) dissertation, the work of these investigators has consistently demonstrated that viewing "real" prosocial programs can increase prosocial behavior at least among preschool children. Their work also indicates that, depending on the measure employed, the effect tends to be greater among boys and among children from lower socioeconomic families. Moreover, the impact of these programs can be enhanced via training, a finding with significant implications for parents who are concerned enough to view television with their children.

Poulos (1975) also reports increased cooperation after viewing a prosocial commercial portraying cooperation. The spot showed a boy and girl arguing over a swing, then resolving the conflict by deciding to take turns pushing one another. After viewing, pairs of second-, third-, and fourth-grade children played a game designed so that competition would increase one child's reward, but cooperation would facilitate the earning of points (exchangeable for prizes) for both. Among children who viewed the prosocial commercial there was no difference in the average amount of time spent cooperating and competing (151 seconds versus 146 seconds); among children who viewed a typical children's commercial, however, there was a difference that approached significance in the direction of more competition (89 seconds cooperation versus 207 seconds competition). Viewing the prosocial spot increased cooperation and decreased competition.

Collins (1974) gave fourth-, seventh-, and tenth-graders an opportunity to "help" or "hurt" another (fictitious) child by pressing the appropriate button on a machine typically used in aggression studies after viewing a television show edited to portray either an aggressive or a coping response to a threatening situation. We reported earlier that the aggressive version led to a higher level of hurting responses. The results also show that relative to a control group that viewed a neutral program, children who viewed the constructive coping portrayal not only gave fewer and shorter "hurt" responses, but pressed the "help" button more often and for a longer period of time. The data also indicate no differences in arousal attributable to the two treatment programs. Collins speculates that modeled prosocial responses to an arousal-inducing provocation may be even more potent than a modeled aggressive response.

Rubinstein et al. (1974) report an experiment in which first graders viewed one of three unedited television programs—an episode of *Lassie* in which a small boy risked his life to save an endangered puppy, an episode of *Lassie* that featured dogs in a positive light but portrayed no example of a human helping a dog, or an episode of *The Brady Bunch,* a family situation comedy. After viewing, children were first introduced to a situation engineered so that they were faced with a choice between persisting at a button-pushing game, thereby amassing points that could be exchanged for prizes, or beaking off from the game to push another button that would bring assistance to (fictitious) puppies in distress, thereby reducing the number of points they could win. The illusion of a troubled puppy was created by asking the children to monitor a kennel by earphones, and to press the button signaling the attendant that the dogs might be in distress if the child heard barking over the earphones. The dependent measure was the button-pressing in response to barks. The principal findings are displayed in figure 5.4. Children who saw the helping version of the *Lassie* program pressed the help button significantly longer. Here, viewing an example of beneficent intervention led to an increase in helping behavior that also demanded a kind of self-sacrifice. It is also important to note that the conditions involved a television episode with content similar to the later situation in

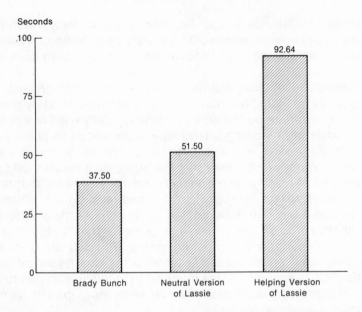

Figure 5.4. Time children spent seeking help for distressed puppy after exposure to varying television programs.

SOURCE: Adapted from E. A. Rubinstein, R. M. Liebert, J. M. Neale, and R. W. Poulos. 1974. *Assessing Television's Influence on Children's Prosocial Behavior.* Stony Brook, N.Y.: Brookdale International Institute, 1974. (Occasional paper 74–11.)

which analogous behavior could be displayed. This contrivance of similarity between the stimulus and test situation reflects the results of an earlier experiment, in which a *Lassie* episode with many instances of helping behavior had increased later helping, but did not affect other kinds of prosocial behavior.

In sum, we find the evidence from laboratory experiments that have used especially prepared films or videotapes to enhance prosocial behavior indicates that children's positive actions can be influenced by such portrayals. Although the stimuli are briefer than actual programs, clearly focus on the relevant behavior, and contain artificial measurement situations, the data clearly suggest that television has the potential for positive impact. This expectation is reinforced by the few studies that have employed stimuli that more nearly approximate the kind of television programming that is actually found, and nonartificial measurement situations. Although some of those who have conducted naturalistic experiments report differences in the impact of prosocial programming related to sex and socioeconomic status, there are insufficient data on which to base a statement more precise than that prosocial programming can, under some circumstances, increase children's subsequent prosocial behavior.

There is a need for more studies employing typical broadcast television content and naturalistic measures of prosocial behavior to delineate more clearly the program-related, child-related, and environment-related factors that determine the efficacy of the medium in regard to prosocial behavior. However, the evidence is sufficient for us to believe that portrayals in day-to-day broadcasting emphasizing desirable behavior would have a beneficial influence on children.

Learning: The Basic Effect

Learning and Acquisition vs. Performance

The least contestable generalization about the effects of television on young persons is that they learn from the medium. This is the basic effect underlying the more specific ones we have discussed. It is also the basic effect involved in television's conceptually more diffusive but quite likely important effect on varied attitudes and role expectations.

A very wide range of evidence, part of it already evaluated, indicates that a major effect is the acquisition of information, ideas, attitudes, and behavior. To review briefly:

Under various circumstances, pedagogical effects have been demonstrated when television was designed to teach. For example, a variety of topics have been successfully taught in classrooms to a wide range of age groups (Chu and Schramm, 1967); children have learned from *Sesame Street* (Ball and Bogatz, 1970; Bogatz and Ball, 1971), although there is considerable controversy over the range of such effects and the conditions on which they are contingent (Cook et al., 1975); and teenagers have acquired knowledge about the U.S. Constitution from CBS' nationally broadcast National Citizenship Test (Alper and Leidy, 1970).

Young persons report that television is a major source of information for them. The topics are as diverse as drugs (Fejer et al., 1971); politics and government (Chaffee, Ward, and Tipton, 1970; Hawkins, 1974; Hirsch, 1971); Watergate (Hawkins, Pingree, and Roberts, 1975); and the Vietnam war (Alvik, 1968; Hollander, 1971; Tolley, 1973).

Young persons' exposure to televised news and public affairs programs have been shown to be correlated with knowledge of their content. Topics include weather patterns (J. P. Robinson, 1972c) and the Vietnam war (Tolley, 1973). In one instance, dealing with junior- and senior-high-school students' exposure to public affairs programs and knowledge of politics over a six-month period, the data are most justifiably interpreted as demonstrating that the television exposure increased knowledge rather than that high knowledge led to greater exposure (Chaffee, Ward, and Tipton, 1970).

Even when the television program is designed to entertain, facts have been learned—even by very young children. Such learning has been shown to include facts both essential and incidental to the plot (Collins, 1970; Hale, Miller, and Stevenson, 1968; Hawkins, 1973; Katzman, 1972b); sequences in which important events occur (Leifer, et al., 1971); and, the motives and consequences of portrayed behavior (Collins, 1973a, 1973b; Collins, Berndt, and Hess, 1974; Leifer and Roberts, 1972). These findings, discovered during the studying of traits and conditions on which such learning are contingent, are unsurprising; nevertheless, they make it impossible to argue that the young viewers' cognitions are not affected by television.

Data from many sources converge to indicate that television affects young persons' attitudes and expectations. There are studies demonstrating that some teenagers turn to television to learn norms about behavior (Gerson, 1966); that views were affected when there was limited real-life experience with the topic (a finding that is impressive precisely because the data plausibly discriminate between conditions when television will and will not influence [DeFleur and DeFleur, 1967]); that exposure to television is correlated with perceiving the world more in accord with the way it is portrayed in television drama (Gerbner and Gross, 1976); that exposure to a program (*Big Blue Marble*) intended to change attitudes about other peoples results in changed attitudes (Roberts et al., 1974); that viewing motion pictures could alter attitudes on such subjects as capital punishment, race relations, and prison reform (Peterson and Thurstone, 1933); and, that motion pictures portraying black models could improve the self-image of black children (Dimas, 1970).

More than 100 experiments have demonstrated that young children can acquire behavior by observing its portrayal on television. Although few studies have employed complete television programs with their inherent complexities, observational learning from isolated portrayals has been demonstrated in regard to a wide range of behavior, including aggression, sharing, obedience to rules, resistance to temptation, cooperation, asking questions, and the display of affection (for reviews, see Bandura, 1973; Bryan and Schwartz, 1971; Flanders, 1968; Poulos, 1975; Roberts, 1973; Shirley, 1973).

The evidence that children can and do learn from television is impressive. Learning of various kinds has been demonstrated with preschoolers and adolescents, and with truncated scenes and full programs. The task that remains for science is: Further specification of the factors that influence such learning. Further specification of the conditions and contingencies that affect the likelihood that whatever is acquired from television—whether it is fact, idea, attitude, or behavior—will be translated into overt behavior.

There is a great deal that is not clear. Nevertheless, we shall now lay out what can be said at present about these questions. Central to our analysis is the distinction—troublesome but important—between acquisition and performance. it is troublesome because acquisition is unobservable in any direct sense. Kuhn (1973) notes that it is impossible to determine whether a behavior has been acquired unless it is performed. The same holds true for cognitive and affective learning. Acquisition is only measurable in display. The distinction is important because, despite this conceptual ambiguity, it has been demonstrated that changing the circumstances of the performance situation will alter the degree to which there is some display in regard to what has been observed on television (Bandura, 1965a, 1973). As a result, it is clear that acquisition and performance are separate processes and that failure for some display to occur should never be taken as evidence that acquisition has not occurred, for display may occur subsequently when the performance situation has different characteristics.

At the same time, all the variables that affect acquisition will affect performance because the former is a necessary condition for the latter. As a result, separate treatment produces a high degree of redundancy, because many of the same variables affect both indiscriminately.

Our solution:

When referring to the acquisition process, we actually mean "acquisition/performance," or all those variables which influence performance by facilitating acquisition. Such variables thereby provide the necessary conditions for performance, or in some unknown way facilitate both acquisition and performance. And these are the two categories which cannot be empiriclly distinguished because of our conundrum that acquisition can only be measured through performance.

When referring to the performance process, we exclude those variables whose effects on performance are inextricable from their effects on acquisition. We refer only to those variables which affect only the performance of acquired responses.

The Acquisition Process

Acquisition depends on three processes: attention, comprehension, and retention.

In order for a child to acquire a new behavior from a television program he must pay attention to that program and to the relevant information within it, he must comprehend the relevant information, and he must store it for the future. However, in practical terms it is often difficult to obtain independent measures of such interior processes. Frequently a single kind of measure will be employed as an indicator of two or more.* Nevertheless, it is helpful to discuss these processes separately.

Variations in attention, comprehension, and retention may be influenced by a variety of factors. Again, for purposes of clarity, it is convenient to group these factors into three broad categories:

Person-related factors, such as age, sex, personality, level of cognitive development of the young person.

Stimulus-related factors, such as television's content and the way it is presented.

* For example, tests of short-term recall administered after viewing have been used not only as measures of retention, but also of comprehension and attention. Insofar as retention implies attention and comprehension, such measures are valid. But there always exists the possibility that differences obtained using recall measures are due to variations in memory, or even willingness to respond, rather than or in addition to variation in any of the antecedent processes.

Environment-related factors, such as the characteristics of both the specific viewing situation and the young person's living conditions.

Each of the processes can be thought of as a class of dependent or criterion variables. In turn, the categories of factors influencing these processes can be viewed as locating typical classes of independent or predictor variables. The total schema is displayed in figure 5.5.

ATTENTION. We shall discuss two different kinds of attention— that given in general to a stimulus, and the more selective act of focusing on one or more particular components of a given stimulus.*

A number of investigations indicate that there is a good deal of variability in children's attention to the television. Bechtel, Achelpohl, and Akers (1972) used in-home videotape cameras for continuous surveillance of family viewing and found that young persons' viewing behavior included not only periods of concentration on the screen, but also reading, playing with pets, conversations with others, wrestling matches, and so on. Other studies that have used in-home observers to record viewer orientation toward the television during programming report substantially the same results (Ward, Robertson, and Wackman, 1971; Ward and Wackman, 1973).

A few studies examine the relationship between attention and content and presentation. For example, Lesser (1974) and Levin and Anderson (1976) catalogue a variety of stimulus attributes that have been demonstrated in *Sesame Street* research to affect preschoolers' attention. The data indicate that auditory cues such

---

* Some studies—generally those concerned with amount of overall attention— have measured attention in terms of the adjustment of sense organs for optimal stimulation—eye contact with or head orientation toward the television screen. This fairly direct measure assumes that when eyes are oriented toward the screen the child is paying attention. Selective attention, on the other hand, cannot be measured so directly. Rather, various outcomes presumed to depend on selectivity must be employed. Usually inferences about the nature of children's selective attention to television-mediated stimuli are based on short-term recall. This procedure assumes that differences in the types of information recalled immediately following viewing locate the kinds of information selected by the child for attention and cognitive processing. The possibility always exists, however, that differences obtained using recall measures are due to variations in memory or willingness to respond rather than or in addition to variations in attention.

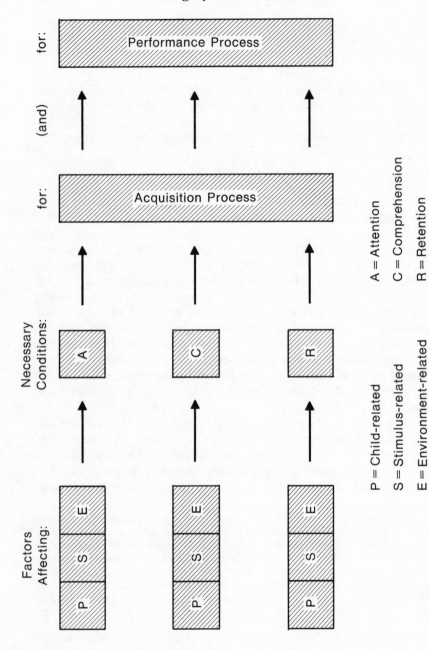

as music and sound effects often serve to draw wandering eyes back to the screen. Similarly, familiar characters or formats often recapture attention. Stimulus factors that sustain preschoolers' attention include such things as humor, diversity of program elements, and anticipation. Finally, attention-directing factors include surprise and incongruity, animation, and action.

Rubinstein, et al. (1974), videotaped the facial expressions of children between six and eight as they viewed two episodes of *Lassie.* Defining attention as "eyes on the television screen" they found that attention increased with amount of vigorous activity portrayed, amount of background music, the presence of animals on the screen, pan camera shots, and camera cuts. Attention decreased when a silent adult female, a woman talking, and a man talking were portrayed. Among preschoolers, however, adult females have been shown to increase attention (Levin and Anderson, 1976). Several studies also indicate that children tend to pay less attention to commercials than to the program material that immediately precedes or follows them (Rubinstein, et al., 1974; Ward, 1972b; Ward and Wackman, 1972a, 1972b; Wartella and Ettema, 1974).

Of course, attention is also a function of a variety of person-related factors. Among the more obvious of these is age. The attention span of the young child is relatively brief but increases with age. Levin and Anderson (1976) write that although television viewing occurs as early as within the first year, the concept of "watching television" occurs at about two-and-a-half years, and after that there are continual increases in duration of attention. Several studies confirm that attention to television increases with age (Rubinstein, et al., 1974; Ward and Wackman, 1972a, 1972b; Wartella and Ettema, 1974). However, at any age there is individual variation. For example, data indicate that the average uninterrupted attention under distracting conditions of preschoolers to a *Sesame Street* segment is about one minute although some preschoolers sit for many minutes as if transfixed.

There is also some evidence that the young viewer's level of cognitive development (largely located by age) may be a determinant of attentional behavior. Piaget's theory of cognitive development (Flavell, 1963; Piaget, 1926) holds that children in the preoperational stage (approximately two to seven years) are generally "perceptually bound." They should therefore be highly sensitive to changes in a message's perceptual attributes. Concrete-operational children (approximately seven to twelve years), on the other hand, have developed greater conceptual skills. They should therefore be sensitive to changes in a message's content as well as in its perceptual attributes.

Consistent with this theory, Wartella and Ettema (1974) found that when content was controlled and only perceptual attributes were allowed to vary, younger children tended to manifest slightly more differentiation in attention. Ward and Wackman (1972a, 1972b), on the other hand, allowed content to vary, whereupon they found that older children showed more differentiation in attention. Rubinstein, et al. (1974), note that the positive relationship between age and attention in their study appeared only for one of two programs—the one that contained a higher level of "talking" and a lower level of action—attributes that would be expected to result in variation dependent on the possession of conceptual skills.

A developmental approach, although one not tied to a theory of different stages of cognitive development, also underlies much of the research into focus of attention. Various investigators have examined the relationship between age and the type of content children focus their attention on. Roberts (1968), for example, found evidence for an age-related shift in the relative amount of attention that children pay to a message's source as opposed to its content. He exposed fourth-, seventh-, and tenth-graders to an audiovisually presented persuasive message and measured immediate recall of attributes of both the message's source and its content. The overall tendency was to focus more on content, but fourth-graders paid relatively more attention to the source, whereas seventh- and tenth-graders focused more on content. Roberts concluded that younger children, less able to deal with the relatively complex relations inherent in the message, turned their attention to the more concrete characteristics of the source. An alternative interpretation is that older children were better able to recognize that the content was more important than its source, hence they were more likely to ignore the source.

There is also evidence that the ability to discriminate between "essential" and "nonessential" information in drama increases with age. However, the data are not without ambiguity. Some studies suggest that the learning of "essential" information (defined as elements necessary to an accurate retelling of the plot) increases with age while the learning of "nonessential" information (room furnishings, characters' dress, names of minor figures, etc.) is curvilinear, increasing then decreasing with age (Collins,

1970; Hale, Miller, and Stevenson, 1968). This suggests that children "learn to learn." For awhile, they absorb all information better as their skills increase, but later they only absorb the more pertinent information as they come to understand what is and is not important. Other studies, however, have found linear increases with age in the learning of both kinds of information (Katzman, 1972b), or a pattern consistent with the "learn to learn" interpretation for one kind of content and inconsistent for another (Hawkins, 1973).

We suspect that several factors are responsible. One is the definition of "essential" and "nonessential" information. The studies define essential information as that necessary for retelling the narrative. Such an assumption may not be tenable for young persons. If we assume that the relative value of any information is an inverse function of the viewer's familiarity with the information and a positive function of its perceived utility, then the importance or "essentialness" of any information can be expected to vary greatly with age (as well as with a variety of other individual and environmental factors). For younger children, a simple lack of experience and knowledge would make most information relatively less familiar, hence more valuable. In addition, the dramatic, age-related changes in needs and interests that characterize childhood would lead to sharp shifts in the kind of information perceived as useful, hence more valuable. At the same time, the degree to which the nonessential is attended to may be a function of the amount of attention that older children need to pay to the essential. Thus, in simpler fare, the learning of the nonessential as well as the essential may show a linear increase with age—as a function of increased cognitive ability. In such a circumstance, attention to the nonessential would operate unimpaired by the need to pay attention to the essential.

In addition, such factors as the child's sex, aspirations, and personality also influence selectivity. Maccoby and Wilson (1957), for example, found that seventh-graders were more likely to pay attention to and recall actions of same-sex characters and of characters who represented their aspired-to social class rather than their current social status. It has been found that black children watch more television shows featuring black characters, and several studies find that the bulk of black children tend to identify with black characters (Clark and Clark, 1950; Greenberg, 1972a; Morland, 1958), although among younger children a great deal of cross-race identification also occurs. Several other studies have also found that attention and responsiveness to symbolic models increase as children perceive those models to be similar to themselves (Rosenkrans, 1967; Tannenbaum and Gaer, 1965).

Attention is also mediated as a function of the sex-appropriateness of the portrayed behavior. For example, Maccoby and Wilson (1957) found that boys focused more on aggressive content and girls more on boy-girl interactions regardless of the sex of the model; Rubinstein et al. (1974) report that boys are more attentive than girls to high action content; and several studies demonstrate that boys pay more attention than girls to scenes of violence (Schramm, Lyle, and Parker, 1961; A. H. Stein and Friedrich, 1972).

Experimental studies of the acquisition of behavior by observing others indicate that children's attention is commanded by such stimulus characteristics as the attractiveness of a symbolic model, the portrayed power of a model, and the portrayed rewards or punishments accruing to a model. These and such other model characteristics as sex, age, social status, and ethnic identification can all be classed as attributes that are correlated with perceptions of different probabilities of receiving reinforcement—the child pays more attention to models with whom identification implies some increased probability of receiving at least vicarious reinforcement (Bandura, 1965a, 1965b, 1969a, 1969b, 1973; Flanders, 1968).

There has been almost no research examining the impact of various environmental conditions on attention. Children's Television Workshop researchers have developed a distraction technique for the pragmatic purpose of testing the ability of various program segments to attract and hold preschoolers' attention (Lesser, 1974), but their concern is more with developing such segments than with the influence of the specific distraction or other viewing conditions. Questions about variations in the location of the television set, the ambience of the viewing situation, and the presence and behavior of others have not been addressed.

COMPREHENSION. In the case of television, comprehension refers to a viewer's understanding and integration of the various parts of a program into a meaningful whole. It implies not only a grasping of the specific actions portrayed, but also of the conditions and contingencies, both explicit and implicit, surrounding whatever actions are portrayed.

From the scientific perspective the concept is a problem, because of the difficulty of establishing external criteria in order to measure what is fundamentally not only an interior but also a relative process. That is, to the extent that a viewer processes any information, some kind of comprehension occurs. To demonstrate that a viewer understands a television program differently from what is defined as "correct" by a producer or a researcher does not show a lack of comprehension, but that comprehension is an active process dependent as much on the receiver as on the message.

Nevertheless, the fundamental goal of most symbolic messages is to elicit in the receiver a mental image similar to the one intended by the sender (Roberts, 1973). Hence most studies of comprehension attempt to compare what is grasped by the reciever either to what was intended by the sender or to what is deemed by some third party to be evident in the message.

This is a justifiable approach. We must warn, however, that it has been demonstrated (Greenberg, 1965) that young children perceive and evaluate programs on different dimensions than do adults who produce them, a population we would expect to be particularly empathic in regard to children. For this reason, as well as what we have already said about individual variation in comprehension, the research cannot be taken as exploring the totality of whatever comprehension occurs.

Not surprisingly, research into the influence of person-related factors on comprehension of television programs by young persons has focused predominantly on age differences: Age locates different levels of experience, and experience influences the mental image against which new information is compared; age locates different levels of cognitive development, and comprehension is a function of the cognitive operations performed on new information; age locates differences in attention, and attention is a necessary condition for comprehension.

Numerous studies have shown that age is positively related to the simple *amount* of information learned from a film or television presentation (Collins, 1970; Halloran, 1969; Hawkins, 1973; Holaday and Stoddard, 1933; Roberts, 1968). Measures of the sheer amount of information recalled from a stimulus, however, are not very good indicators of comprehension in the fullest sense. Rather, comprehension is better assessed by studies that explore the developing child's ability to integrate the information in a television show.

Early research indicated that age was inversely related to recalling events surrounding action or assimilating moral or other ultimate outcomes (Dysinger and Ruckmick, 1933; Himmelweit, Oppenheim, and Vince, 1958). More recently, Leifer et al. (1971) provide even more striking evidence of the failure of very young children to comprehend a dramatic narrative. They showed a children's film to four-, seven-, and ten-year-olds, then asked the children to reconstruct the sequence of events by arranging in the correct order three, five, seven, or nine photographs of central incidents in the story. Only four of the 20 four-year-olds correctly arranged the three photos, and none accomplished the task with seven or nine photos. However, all of the older children arranged the three photos, and 16 of 20 ten-year-olds correctly reproduced the nine-photo sequence. In short, four-year-olds gave little evidence of ability to relate major incidents in a story into a narrative whole, but by the mid-grade-school years the ability was fairly well developed.

Given preschoolers' difficulty with following the sequence of events in a narrative, it is not surprising that they also fare poorly when asked to explain causal relationships, both explicit and implicit, portrayed within programs, and even within episodes. Flapan (1968) reports almost no ability among preschoolers to specify the causal relations among events within a scene but, as with acquisition of information and sequencing ability, a rapid increase in such comprehension with age. Leifer and Roberts (1972) examined age differences in children's understanding of the motivations for and consequences of aggressive acts as portrayed in a sample of commercially broadcast programs, a task which presumably requires the viewer to relate a variety of cues indicating the causes of behaviors. In this study, too, the obtained age differences were dramatic. Kindergarteners showed no understanding; third-graders showed considerable understanding; and twelfth-graders showed almost perfect understanding. Similarly, Leifer et al. (1971) reported little or no understanding of the portrayed feelings and motivations of characters among their preschool subjects, but fairly sound comprehension by the age of ten years.

Piaget's (1926) model of cognitive development, discussed in the preceding section, has been identified as a possible explanation for changes in comprehension of television programs with age. Leifer and Roberts (1972) argue that *consequences* are more frequently portrayed in concrete terms than are motives, and thus should be more readily understood by younger children. Collins (1973b) notes that comprehension of an actor's motives often requires coordination of immediate and distant goals in an extended causal chain. To the extent that younger children are not cognitively ready to handle the implicit, often abstract, relationships underlying motives, and that they tend to "center" on a single immediate event or fact rather than making means–ends causal connections, they should be more likely to grasp actions in terms of immediate, concrete consequences than motives. In addition, there is a good deal of research on Piaget's (1965) model of the development of children's moral judgments to indicate that until about the age of nine or ten, children tend to base their evaluations of actions on the consequences of the act, after which they shift to more intention-based judgments (Collins, Berndt, and Hess, 1974).

Collins, Berndt, and Hess provide support for this model in their demonstration of large changes between the second and fifth grades in children's bases of comprehension of symbolically portrayed aggressive actions. Second graders tended to grasp portrayed aggression in terms of consequences, and none cited motivations of the actors as a basis for evaluating the aggressor. Among fifth-graders, on the other hand, more than 50 percent of the children tested included motives in their explanations of the portrayed aggression, and better than two-thirds based their evaluations of the aggressor on motive. Rule and Duker (1973) also found that eight-year-olds were more likely than twelve-year-olds to base evaluations of an aggressor on consequences.

We also find that age is inversely related to how real television programs and characters are perceived to be (B. S. Greenberg and Reeves, 1976; Halloran, 1969; Lyle and Hoffman, 1972a; Pingree, 1975), and perceived reality is associated with comprehending portrayed events as appropriate or useful in the real world (Bandura, Ross, and Ross, 1963a; Berkowitz and Alioto, 1973; Berkowitz, 1962b; Feshbach, 1972; Schramm, 1968b). Yet, even among a sample of tenth-graders, 25 percent responded that the people on television were just like those in real life (Lyle and Hoffman, 1972a). One study finds that preschool children have trouble understanding a question about the "realness" of television (Lyle and Hoffman, 1972b), suggesting that for young children reality-fantasy may not be a relevant continuum.

Worth and Gross (1974) recently offered a model relevant to this issue. They argue that there is a fundamental difference between the ways in which humans interpret "real" as opposed to "symbolic" events. The former are assessed in terms of knowledge of the world which we know exists (existential meaning). The latter are assessed in terms of meaning based on recognition that the signs are symbolic and that interpretation calls for inferences based on story structure (symbolic meaning). Thus, were one to see a dead body in reality, one might ask "what happened?" whereas the presence of a body on a television screen is likely to elicit the response "What does it mean and how can I tell what happened?" They also posit that the ability to recognize and interpret a symbolic event is developmental, and that young children do not distinguish between real and symbolic situations. Thus, when viewing a television story young children are likely to comprehend actions in terms of the conventional attributes and expectations that constitute their existing social knowledge. This model is consistent with the views of the cognitive developmentalists (Flavell, 1963; Piaget, 1926), who would hypothesize that the skills necessary for symbolic interpretation are not possessed by young children.

Several studies support such a developmental change in the interpretation of mediated narratives (Harlan, 1972; Murphy, 1973). Murphy, for example, showed second-, fifth-, and eighth-grade children a series of photographic slides depicting a doctor working in a hospital, leaving the hospital, walking by and ignoring an accident victim, and continuing home. Second-graders were able to recognize the characters depicted and report the events portrayed. They tended, however, to interpret the narrative in terms of their general social knowledge of the role of doctors, even when such knowledge was contradicted by the information within the slides. Thus, they argued that the doctor did not ignore the accident victim, but probably helped him between slides or saw that he was not hurt, only napping. Highly revealing is the typical reason on which the inference was based: "I think he helped him because that's what doctors are for." In other words, the narrative was comprehended in terms of prior learning about doctors as a class, interpreted as a natural event rather than as any symbolic structure. Older children, on the other hand, talked about their interpretations in terms of "the story," of what *"he* wanted me to think."

No studies have examined the relationship between comprehension of total television programs and child-related factors other than age, although Leifer et al. (1971) do report a failure to find sex differences in children's comprehension of the feelings and motivations of same-sex characters. Several studies do relate other individual characteristics to the perceived reality of television programming. Perceived reality has been found to be positively related to being black (B. S. Greenberg and Dominick, 1969); to being from a family lower in socioeconomic status (B. S. Greenberg and Dominick, 1969; B. S. Greenberg and Gordon, 1972a; Reeves, 1974; Schramm, Lyle, and Parker, 1961), which could account for the finding about blacks; and, in regard to the perceived reality of television violence, to the belief that violent behavior is acceptable (B. S. Greenberg and Gordon, 1972a), and to behaving aggressively (McLeod, Atkin, and Chaffee, 1972b).

Turning to stimulus-related factors, there is a paucity of research concerned with comprehension of complete television programs. There are, however, data from more focused learning experiments. Bandura (1969b), reviewing social learning experiments, writes that learning of specific behaviors is influenced by such conditions as the rate, number, complexity, distribution, and discriminability of modeled stimuli. Thus, for example, we would expect that programming that is repeated, that is presented at a rate and level that a child can handle, and that contains critical features which can easily be discriminated from irrelevant content should all lead to better acquisition. These are all considerations that have been demonstrated to enhance cognitive learning from television that is specifically designed to teach (Ball and Bogatz, 1970; Bogatz and Ball, 1971; Lesser, 1974).

It is reasonable to speculate that the changes in content preferences as children grow older—the progression from cartoons to "children's programs" to more adult fare—is a function of the comprehensibility of content and structure.* Of course, no systematic data support such speculations. Research on content variations that affect children's comprehension of total programs is sadly lacking.

* Cartoons are simple, based on a few clear-cut conventions, and highly episodic and repetitive—all characteristics that would seem to fit the young child's cognitive abilities. Children's adventure and western programs demand more integration of plot materials, but are still highly conventional in form, depending on uncomplicated characterizations and plots and an almost ritualistic sequence of events presented in highly concrete form (e.g., the white hats vs. the black hats). Adult programming, viewing of which tends to be delayed until later childhood or early adolescence, can be characterized as presenting relatively more complex plots and characterizations, conventions providing fewer cues, and demanding the making of inferences rather than containing concrete portrayals.

In sum, there is growing reason to believe that a child's interpretation of the response to television programs depends greatly on his ability to comprehend the total program and the degree to which he perceives the show to represent reality. We know that large differences in comprehension and perceptions of reality are located by age. We know very little, however, about the effect of most other child-related variables, and have just begun to consider how program characteristics and environmental factors might influence comprehension.

RETENTION. Retention is crucial because there may be a long delay between the television viewing experience and opportunity for some relevant overt display to occur (Bandura, 1969a, 1969b, 1971a). If there is no retention, there ceases to be acquisition. Retention is contingent especially upon symbolic encoding, rehearsal, and repetition. Retention of observed stimuli has been demonstrated to be dependent on symbolic encoding by varying the ease of such encoding, with the result that retention varied directly with such ease (Bandura, Grusec, and Menlove, 1966). Symbolic encoding consists of the creation, either in words or images, of a representation of what was observed. This representation can then be stored and recalled to mind (Bandura, 1971a). Encoding has been discussed in the scientific literature primarily in terms of the retention of observed behavior, but it is clear that the retention of attitudes and information also would be dependent on some symbolic system for their storage and recollection.

Retention can be expected to increase with age, because symbolic encoding is directly related to age. Several cognitive theories and some evidence indicate that various stages of cognitive development involve different and increasingly effective representational systems (Bruner, Olver, and Greenfield, 1966; Flavell, 1963; Piaget, 1952). In addition, a number of studies have shown that the spontaneous occurrence as well as the efficiency of encoding are positively related to age (Coates and Hartup, 1969; Flavell, 1963; Flavell, Beach and Chinsky, 1966; Keeney, Cannizzo, and Flavell, 1967; Marsh and Sherman, 1966). That is, younger children will not spontaneously encode unless somehow encouraged to do so.

Retention is also affected by the degree of opportunity and motivation to engage in either explicit or implicit rehearsal of what is observed. Such practice not only serves to stabilize and strengthen what has been acquired, but also serves to provide the viewer with an opportunity to make what has been encoded more accessible. Bandura (1971a) notes that this may be the major benefit of rehearsal, since it appears to be more efficient for a viewer to encode a subjective reconstruction rather than an exact replicate of observed stimuli.

An obvious stimulus factor influencing rehearsal is repetition. The more that information or symbolic behaviors are repeated, the more opportunity the child has to encode them, to rehearse them, or to "streamline" his or her original encoding.

There are a number of characteristics of typical television content that seem particularly fitted to increase children's comprehension. As we saw in chapter 2, analyses of television drama are consistent in their findings that relatively few themes and characterizations tend to dominate. In addition, many of the content characteristics that identify a particular observed portrayal as worthy of attention should also serve to characterize it as worthy of encoding and rehearsal. Thus, studies demonstrating that children more readily recall television or film displays of behaviors that have been portrayed as rewarded (Bandura, 1965b; Bandura, Ross, and Ross, 1963b; Leifer and Roberts, 1972; Rosekrans and Hartup, 1967; Walters and Parke, 1964) are relevant to the retention process as well as to considerations of what mediates performance. Children also tend to recall more of the behaviors of characters with whom they identify, presumably because such identification is associated with anticipation of assuming similar roles or engaging in similar behavior. Hence, children tend to recall more behaviors of same-sex models and sex appropriate behaviors (Maccoby, 1959; Maccoby and Wilson, 1957), and of models who are perceived to be otherwise similar to themselves (Burnstein, Stotland, and Zander, 1961; Rosekrans, 1967).

It also should be noted that there is evidence that scenes which are highly familiar and scenes characterized by conflict and high emotion are particularly likely to be recalled by children (Holaday and Stoddard, 1933; Schramm, Lyle, and Parker, 1961). Indeed, aggressive content in particular appears to engender retention. Bandura and Huston (1961), for example, found that aggressive behavior was recalled by preschoolers regardless of whether the model was rewarded or punished for such behavior.

Finally, there is very little research concerned with the impact of environment-related factors on the retention of content of noninstructional television. Numerous studies of instructional films and television indicate that contexts providing children with the opportunity to rehearse what they have observed, or informing them that they are expected to remember or that they will be tested on what they remember, or providing conditions which make it clear that rewards or punishments will be administered, all result in greater retention (Bandura, 1969b; Chu and Schramm, 1967).

Furthermore, there is some evidence that when parent and child view together, parental comments and directions can increase the child's subsequent recall of what was observed. Ball and Bogatz (1970) found that children whose parents viewed and discussed the content of *Sesame Street* with them learned more than children who viewed without such discussion. Similarly, Atkin and Gantz (1974) report that when parents amplified the content of news programs, the child's recall increased. In cases such as these, it is likely that parental comment not only serves to direct the child's attention to relevant information, but also to motivate and assist the child to encode and rehearse the observed content.

As with attention and comprehension, then, retention has been demonstrated to be a function of the cognitive and symbolic capabilities of the child, the structure and content of the television program, and any environmental factors that serve to cue or motivate encoding or rehearsal.

The Performance Process

Performance refers to the display in real life of acquired responses—whether verbal or behavioral. As we have said, the necessary condition for performance is acquisition and acquisition can only be measured by some sort of performance, so that in practical terms all the variables which affect acquisition also affect performance. In addition, there are many variables which affect performance alone.

Maccoby (1959) illustrates why acquisition and performance must be considered separately. She argues that a child may learn parental behavior by observing his parents, although these behaviors will not be performed until the child becomes a parent. The more general point, to which we and others subscribe (Bandura, 1965b, 1969a, 1969b; 1971a; Bandura and Walters, 1963; Mischel, 1968), is that acquired responses may not occur until the person encounters eliciting conditions—in the Maccoby case, entry into a particular role.

Whether or not a person will display a particular response in a particular situation depends in part upon perceived alternatives available. When there are none, or only a few, the likelihood of display will be affected by the acquisition of new alternatives. Once past early childhood, most humans have acquired a repertoire of responses that may be displayed in a given situation and performance comes more to depend on a number of additional factors.

Bandura (1971a) contends that most human behavior is cognitively mediated and that it is largely controlled by anticipated consequences of prospective actions. For example, children are more likely to aggress against peers than against parents because they expect different consequences for performing the same behavior (Bandura and Walters, 1959).

Such expectations are subjective. The contingencies operating are the perceptions of the person, which are usually only partly governed by objective circumstances. They are also governed by information acquired previously. In other words, perceived contingencies are a function of how the person defines his world—his image of social reality, so to speak (Roberts, 1971).

"Image," here, is not used in any pictorial sense. Rather, it refers to the total of the cognitions relevant to social behavior that the child has acquired—cognitions about what kinds of behaviors are appropriate in various situations, expectations about what kinds of consequences are likely to follow from a given behavior, definitions of the various contingencies that can operate in a situation. In short, it includes all of the components that constitute the social norms and expectations internalized by an individual (Roberts, 1971).

From this perspective, performance is a function of two kinds of factors. The first encompasses the conditions and contingencies operating in the external real-life situation. The second are the individual's cognitions about those conditions and contingencies.

For example, the presence of a policeman will sharply decrease the probability that a teenager will throw a brick through a window. However, a teenager's cognitions about bricks, policemen, and windows will also influence the probability of performance. The teenager who believes that he can outrun the officer, or who expects praise from his peers for such an action, is more likely to break the window than someone who fears or respects the police.

Clearly television content has little or no influence on social behavior to the extent that performance is governed by the first set of conditions. Incentives and conditions in the social environment are not under the control of broadcasters. However, television can influence social behavior to the extent that it influences the norms and expectations that a child brings to the behavioral situation. Most psychologists agree that children's definitions of social reality are largely dependent on socially mediated information, and several have pointed out that the mass media are an important source of such information (Bandura, 1969b; R. Brown, 1965; E. E. Jones and Gerard, 1967; Roberts, 1973).

This line of reasoning underlies Leifer and Roberts' (1972) contention that television's influence on social behavior lies not only in its ability to teach new behavior but also in its contribution to the young person's definition of what constitutes appropriate and inappropriate behavior and what constitutes the situational and behavioral contingencies which should control performance. For example, to the extent that television content influences children to expect that aggressive behavior is frequently rewarded or that submissiveness is the appropriate behavior for a woman, the medium can be expected to influence behavior, although not to a known degree. This is not to imply that television content is more important than other agents of socialization. Indeed, it is generally accepted that television most effectively influences the roles of social behavior either when it reinforces the attitudes, expectations, and definitions promulgated by direct experience and interpersonal communication, or when it defines situations about which other sources have not provided information (B. S. Greenberg, 1974; Klapper, 1960; Roberts, 1971). When its message conflicts with information derived from direct experience or important interpersonal sources, however, its impact may be dramatically, but not totally, reduced. Nevertheless, it is clear that television is a significant agent of socialization and influence on behavior—if only in interaction with other sources of social information, each of which contributes to the child's definition of situations and behaviors appropriate to them.

Performance itself depends, of course, on many of the same stimulus-related, child-related, and environment-related factors that mediate acquisition. We shall quickly review the principal ones.

Content that provides information about the likely consequences of various actions, or about the conditions under which behavior can effectively be carried out, or about what constitutes appropriate behavior in various situations, has been shown to affect the likelihood of children's performance of similar behavior. Several studies indicate that when symbolic behavior is explicitly portrayed as rewarded or punished, subsequent performance of similar behaviors on the part of children respectively increases and decreases (Bandura, 1965a, 1965b; Elliott and Vasta, 1970; Leifer and Roberts, 1972). Similarly, performance is more likely to follow after viewing models who manifest characteristics that imply positive consequences—models who are high in prestige, attractive, powerful (Schramm, 1968b).

Performance of television-mediated behavior has also been shown to increase to the degree that those behaviors are portrayed as justified (Berkowitz and Rawlings, 1963; Collins, Berndt, and Hess, 1974), to the extent that the behaviors are effective even though negatively evaluated (Bandura, Ross, and Ross, 1963b; Zajonc, 1954), and to the extent that they are portrayed by role-appropriate models (Hicks, 1965), or by characters or within situations with which children can easily identify because of perceived similarity. Children's perceptions of the appropriateness of portrayed behaviors also appear to depend on the "reality" of the presentation, the more realistic or true-to-life the content, the more likely viewing is to lead to subsequent performance of observed behavior (Berkowitz, 1962b; Feshbach, 1972). Finally there is some evidence that the frequency and consistency with which certain behaviors are portrayed leads children to perceive those behaviors as appropriate, as reflections of society's norms or definitions of what to expect in the "real" world (Gerbner and Gross, 1976; Leifer and Roberts, 1972).

Characteristics of the child also operate to affect the likelihood of performance of television-acquired behavior. The extent to which television content informs children's definitions of social reality is influenced by the same child-related variables reviewed in connection with the acquisition process. For example, whether a child will associate portrayed behaviors with portrayed consequences, or comprehend particular consequences as positive or negative, or a behavior as useful, or a portrayal as realistic, depends on such child-related characteristics as age and level of cognitive development, sex, or personality. In short, the acquisition of social norms and expectations from television is governed by the same conditions as is the acquisition of any behavior or fact.

There is, however, one additional point about the young person's characteristics and the performance of behavior acquired from television that needs to be noted. Television is only one of many contributors to a definition of social norms and, as noted above, in many instances it may be far from the most important source of such information. Regardless of where young persons acquire social norms and expectations, however, the degree to which they control those young persons' behavior depends on how well they have been internalized. Thus, while for one person inhibition of antisocial behavior may largely depend on some external sanction (such as threat of punishment), for another, performance may be governed by internal controls. An example is the inhibition of aggression because of expectations of self-condemnation.

A number of variables influence the degree to which social norms are internalized, but one of the most important in the present context is age. Socialization is a cumulative process; the more experience a child has with social situations, and the longer he has been exposed to definitions (both explicit and implicit) of the rules of social behavior, the more likely he is to have internalized those rules. It follows that the likelihood that internalized social norms will govern the overt performance of any behavior is inversely related to age.

Considering the relationship between acquisition of television-mediated behavior and age, then, we are faced with a situation where younger children are less likely to learn complex behavioral sequences but more likely to perform the behaviors that they do learn because of lack of internalized norms. Older children, who experience little difficulty acquiring behaviors from television, are also more responsive to internalized social norms—norms which have been defined by many other sources in addition to television. This point becomes particularly critical if one considers the evidence that young children often comprehend and retain specific behaviors and actions portrayed on television, but not the contingencies surrounding them. The preschooler may learn how to hit, and note that hitting frequently occurs; but he may not comprehend the contingencies surrounding such behavior. By virtue of his age, he is also less likely to have internalized controls against hitting, thus is more likely to perform the observed behavior.

There is also evidence that various environment-related variables also affect the likelihood that young persons will perform what they learn from television. An obvious one is the closeness of the match between television's world and the young person's. Berkowitz (1962b) has argued that the more a performance situation is similar to those portrayed on television (such as setting, names of characters, and the like) the greater the likelihood that the child will display the behavior portrayed by television. Berkowitz (1965) reports a series of studies demonstrating that when cues associated with symbolic portrayals of behavior are presented in a performance situation, performance increases. Similarly, a careful reading of the literature on observational learning indicates that subsequent performance of observed behavior increases the more nearly the performance setting matches the symbolic setting (Flanders, 1968; Schramm, 1968b; Shirley, 1973).

Information provided directly to the young person by his environment also influences how he interprets and accepts television-mediated information. When television provides information about social situations and norms which is unavailable to the person from other sources—or from direct experience—that information is likely to guide overt responses if and when the person encounters a situation similar to that portrayed on television. Thus, Peterson and Thurstone (1933) report that the attitudinal impact of movies dealing with various ethnic groups was greater with unsophisticated children—children from homogeneous rural towns as opposed to a large heterogeneous urban center where there was more direct contact with other ethnic groups. Similarly, Siegel (1958) is careful to point out that the impact of a radio program on second-grade children's expectations about the role of taxi drivers was achieved with children who had little or no experience with them. B. S. Greenberg (1972a) also found that children from rural and suburban backgrounds were more likely to state that they utilize television for information about how to behave with black people, while their urban counterparts, who had more direct experience to call on, reported less use of the medium for this purpose. And Gerson (1966) found that when necessary information about dating behavior was not easily found in teenagers' immediate environment, they reported turning to television to get that information, presumably to use as a guide to behavior.

Finally, information and sanctions provided by significant others in the young person's immediate environment also affect both behavior and acceptance of television's messages regarding such behavior. A body of nontelevision research demonstrates that parental behaviors and sanctions, as well as the manner in which these behaviors and sanctions are communicated, significantly shape the expectations and behavior of children (Baumrind, 1972; Maccoby and Jacklin, 1974). More recent, however, are studies indicating that comments made to children by adults while viewing a television program significantly affect the way the child interprets the program and the likelihood that the child will subsequently perform behaviors acquired from the program. As noted earlier, children who viewed *Sesame Street* in the presence of parents who discussed the program with them learned significantly more than did children who viewed alone (Ball and Bogatz, 1970).

McLeod, Atkin and Chaffee (1972a, 1972b) report that parents who interpret television portrayals of violence as inappropriate or unrealistic can reduce the harmful influence of that violence on the children. Hicks (1968) showed that when an adult observed an aggressive film with a child, making either approving or disapproving comments about the violence as it occurred, subsequent imitation by the children was a function of the adult's comments. These findings recall our earlier point that interpersonal sources of communication are frequently the most influential guides to children's behavior. When adults play an active interpretive role, they can significantly moderate television's impact on the behavior of children.

It should also be recalled, however, that evidence reviewed earlier indicates that children are frequently left to their own devices when viewing, and even when they do view in the presence of others, interpretive comments about portrayals are not always made. Bandura (1969b) writes that, "Under conditions of rapid social and technological change, many parental interests, attitudes, and role behaviors that were serviceable at an earlier period may have little functional value for members of the younger generation." For this kind of information, children have little recourse but to turn to society's information-providing institutions, of which television is a major one.

Television as an Agent of Socialization

Our evaluation of the evidence on the role of television in the lives of young people leads us to conclude that it should tentatively be considered a major agent of socialization. We believe that it contends with some force in competition with such other agents as parents, school, community, siblings, peers, and church.

So that what we are saying will not be misunderstood, we shall clarify what we mean by "socialization." Frequently, socialization is conceived in terms of the proscribed and prescribed behaviors that characterize a particular culture. Thus, much of the research focuses on whether television influences children to adhere to or break certain "rules." It is important to keep in mind, however, that the term refers not only to the degree to which children follow the rules and norms of a culture, but also to their learning of the definitions and expectations underlying those rules and norms. That is, the extent to which a child is socialized to adhere to the rules or norms of any category of behavior is a function of how that category is conceptualized by the child, and that conceptualization, that dimension of the child's image of the world, is also a product of socialization (R. Brown, 1965). "Socialization" as used here, then, pertains as much to how the world comes to be defined as to specific behaviors associated with that definition.

The socialization process continues throughout life, and responses to various sources of influence vary depending on the individual's age (Schramm, 1971). This point becomes particularly critical when the focus is on young persons. The period between birth and the end of adolescence is a period of rapid change. In 20 years, a totally dependent infant becomes an independent adult. Needs, interests, experiences, capabilities, all undergo developmental changes, most of which have implications for the relationship between television and the young person (Roberts, 1973). Age locates (a) degree of experience against which to judge new information, (b) qualitatively and quantitatively different cognitive capabilities and strategies by which new information is processed, and (c) differential motoric capabilities for performing a behavior. As a result, although for convenience one must often speak of how television influences "young persons" or "children," it is rapidly becoming apparent that in many instances the question is how it influences and is used by four-year-olds, six-year-olds, ten-year-olds, and perhaps fourteen-year-olds.

We therefore find the lack of developmental research on children's responses to television disturbing. Fewer than 50 of the hundreds of studies reviewed have taken a developmental perspective. We believe this has been an error in scientific strategy.

We would also emphasize that television is only one of a number of influential information sources (socialization agents) available to and used by young persons. We conceive of socialization as dependent upon signals received from outside sources. We would emphasize that television is only one of a number of possibly influential sources. As they always have, parents, siblings, peers, schools, churches, all continue to impinge on how the developing child comes to define and behave in his world. Moreover, each of these agents, including television, affect each other as well as the child, and each is to some extent affected by the child. For example, both young persons and adult members of the audience influence the content of television by their patronage.

The interactions among child, television, and "other" socialization agents is displayed in figure 5.6. Although we have oversimplified the model by collapsing all socialization agents other than television into "other agents," it does emphasize that socialization is a process of many interactions. The young person may be directly influenced by television or by others. Each may be influenced by the young person. Television and other agents also interact.

The core of the diagram locates multiple interactions among the young person, television, and other socialization agents. We suspect that the effect of television on young persons is more likely to be ultimately understood as a result of such multiple interactions than to be direct.

This does not, however, lessen the importance of television in the system. As figure 5.6 shows, *any* socialization agent in the system functions in interaction with other agents. Early analyses of mass-media effects, such as that by Klapper (1960), which at least implicitly discounted the effects of television on the grounds that the medium's influence is usually mediated through a variety of intervening and contingent conditions, miss the point. All social influence, whether emanating from a television program, a parental proscription, or a teacher's lesson, is mediated by conditions and contingencies that derive from other sources of influence. Although it makes research difficult, this is the way the world operates.

To conclude that television contributes to—rather than directly causes—a particular behavior does not imply that the me-

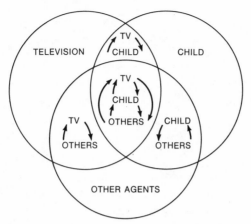

Figure 5.6. Hypothesized relationship between television and other agents of socialization.

SOURCE: Adapted from A. D. Leifer, N. J. Gordon, and S. B. Graves. 1973. *Children and Television: Recommended Directions for Future Efforts.* Center for Research in Children's Television, Harvard University.

dium is not an important agent of socialization. Rather it indicates that television has become a significant contending force among the full array of socialization agents that surround the developing young person.

Chapter

Four Highly Attracted Publics

WE NOW TURN to four other segments of the audience—women, blacks, the poor, and the elderly. These groups are heavy viewers and the object of concern over whether society is fulfilling its responsibilities and obligations to them.

In recent years, there has been increasing attention to the role of the mass media, and in particular television, in their lives. The belief has grown that each has been poorly served by television, and it is clear that in regard to the medium each differs appreciably from the rest of the audience.

Naturally, in looking at what sets these four groups apart we shall also depict the status of the other portions of the audience to which they are compared. What we are actually doing, then, is examining the full range of major social attributes which define distinct relationships with television.

We shall review the evidence in regard to: *portrayals,* with particular attention to stereotyping; *viewing,* with emphasis on the aspects that set the various groups apart; *attitudes and motives,* where the emphasis turns to differences in orientation toward the medium; and finally, *effects.*

Portrayals

When we draw together the many studies of the content of television entertainment and commercials (chapter 2), we can only conclude that over the past two-and-a-half decades portrayals of females and minorities have been stereotypic; women, the poor, minorities, and the elderly have been relatively excluded (table 6.1).

Table 6.1 Television Portrayals by Age, Sex, Ethnicity, and Socioeconomic Status

---

Age

In the eight television seasons between 1967–1968 and 1974–1975, between 1.9 percent and 5.7 percent of all characters in dramas of all kinds during a typical fall week of prime-time and Saturday morning programming were elderly. The average over the eight seasons was 3.9 percent of all dramatic characters (Gerbner et al., 1976).

In Saturday children's cartoon programs, only 4 percent of the human characters were depicted as elderly (Levinson, 1973).

Sex

Of the major characters in noncartoon, prime-time, network dramatic television programs between 1969 and 1972, only 28 percent were women (Tedesco, 1974).

Fifty-one percent of the female characters (1969–1972) were portrayed as married; 32 percent of the males. In addition, 60 percent of the females were unemployed as opposed to 36 percent of the males (Tedesco, 1974).

More than 50 percent of the males on soap operas are represented as professional; approximately one-third of the females are housewives or have lower status positions (Downing, 1974; Katzman, 1972a; Ramsdell, 1973).

In Saturday children's cartoons, males outnumber females 3-to-1. For adult characters the ratio increases to 4-to-1 (Levinson, 1973).

Ethnicity

The percentage of prime-time and daytime ads in which a black appeared more than doubled from 1967 to 1969—4 to 10 percent in prime time and 5 to 12 percent in daytime (Dominick and Greenberg, 1970).

In 1967–1969 blacks were usually shown in commercials with a large number of other people. The median number of people in ads containing blacks for 1967–1969 was 10, 7, and 6 compared to 1.6, 1.7, and 1.9 for those without blacks (Dominick and Greenberg, 1970).

Blacks appear on television less frequently than their distribution in the population (6.3 percent vs. 11 percent). Whites are slightly overrepresented—75 vs. 70 percent, and British characters appear even more frequently than blacks (6.6 vs. 1.4 percent British in the U.S. population) (Seggar and Wheeler, 1973).

The white male has been dominant. He is the typical protagonist of action-adventure—whether western, foreign espionage, science fiction, or urban crime (Gerbner, 1972b; Gerbner and Gross, 1976; Gerbner et al., 1977). He has from the first been far more populous in prime-time drama than in our demography (Smythe, 1954). He is a principal participant in the daytime soap opera (Katzman, 1972a). Professionals and persons without visible means of support have also been overrepresented (DeFleur, 1964; Gerbner, 1972b; Katzman, 1972a; Seggar and Wheeler, 1973; Smythe, 1954). Occupationally, the blue collar viewer typically finds himself staring upward. Most television roles are filled

Table 6.1 Continued

Blacks are overrepresented as professional and technical workers by 18 percent for males and 58 percent for females compared to the actual count for the U.S. population (Seggar and Wheeler, 1973).

More than 60 percent of the Saturday morning children's programs with human characters presented no black or minority characters. There are few black heroes or villains, most are portrayed as good. Over half the villains in these programs have foreign accents (Mendelson and Young, 1972).

In 294 Saturday morning television commercials in 1973, 88 percent of the girls in ads involving just females were shown playing in a bedroom, whereas 63 percent of the boys in ads involving just males showed the boys playing outdoors (Chulay and Francis, 1974).

Of 299 central figures in 199 commercials in 1971, 57 percent were male (increasing to 70 percent at night), 43 percent female; 70 percent of the males were portrayed as authorities, 14 percent of the females. Less than half of the females had their own, independent identity, and only 11 percent were depicted in an occupational setting (McArthur and Resko, 1975).

Socioeconomic Status

All ethnic groups are overrepresented in the professional, technical, and service occupations categories (Seggar and Wheeler, 1973).

"Approximately five in ten characters can be unambiguously identified as gainfully employed. Of these, three are proprietors, managers, and professionals. The fourth comes from the ranks of labor. The fifth serves to enforce the law or preserve the peace on behalf of public or private clients." (Gerbner and Gross, 1976).

There is an underrepresentation of all groups in occupations with little prestige except for service workers where males in all ethnic categories are largely overrepresented by 28 percent for blacks; 36, British; 36, Chicano; 45, European; 20, white) (Seggar and Wheeler, 1973).

In an analysis of occupational portrayals, 30 percent of all males were in professional and technical categories, and 37 of the females. In the actual population, these percentages are 9 and 12 respectively (DeFleur, 1964).

Managers, officials, and proprietors are overrepresented by 24 percent for all males, and 4 percent for all females (DeFleur, 1964).

by persons who are young or middle-aged adults (Gerbner, 1972b; Smythe, 1954). These emphases make the well-situated white male of young to middle years television's typical creature. His secret is simple. He is the ideal object for fantasy for the majority of the audience, whether it is the fantasy of conflict and conquest or of personal trauma and coupling. The effect has been to limit the stage available to others.

The lack of diversification is reinforced by the avoidance of any tarnish to the authority and efficacy of this figure. It is the nonwhite and the foreign born who are more likely to be involved in violence—as perpetrators or victims—and the nonwhite, the foreign born, and women who are more likely to be portrayed as less efficacious by falling victim to violence (Gerbner, 1972b).

When women appear on television, they are typically housewives or serve as sexual magnets. This is true for prime-time drama (Gerbner, 1972b; Smythe, 1954), soap operas (Katzman, 1972a), commercials (McArthur and Resko, 1975), cartoons (Levinson, 1973), and child- and family-oriented programs (Long and Simon, 1974). They are usually dependent on males and are more likely to provide emotional support than to play an instrumental role in achieving a goal. Their submissive status is particularly striking in commercials, where even for household products males typically have the role of professional or expert while women appear as unsophisticated household laborers with irrepressible enthusiasm for the achievement of such domestic pleasures as blazing white shirts.

The elderly and those in low-income occupations hardly appear at all (DeFleur, 1964; Gerbner, 1972b; Seggar and Wheeler, 1973). The distribution of occupations veers strongly from that of the real world toward the affluent, the professional, and the youngish male. The sole exceptions are service activities catering to the needs of social betters. Furthermore, negative characteristics are more frequently attributed to those in lower-status occupations. The bias toward higher-status occupations, however, does result in the overrepresentation, compared to the real world, of blacks and minorities in these positions (DeFleur, 1964; Seggar and Wheeler, 1973).

There are, of course, numerous exceptions in specific programs and series to these statements. Recent seasons have seen numerous programs and commercials with blacks and minorities in some prominence. Several series have featured women. Blacks, because of their success in popular recording, appear frequently on music and variety shows, which these data ignore.

Television too changes with time, although the changes come slowly and often only with the adoption of new policies. For example, in the late 1960s the networks decided to increase the presence of blacks on television, and their appearance in commercials and in dramatic roles increased sharply. They usually appeared in integrated situations, often were associated with law-enforcement, and did not share the degree of villainy attributed to other minorities and the foreign born (Dominick and Greenberg, 1970; Seggar and Wheeler, 1973). No similar policy so far has been enunciated in regard to the portrayal of women, other minorities, and the foreign born, the elderly, or those of low income. We must await the future and new data to see if there are any other noteworthy shifts.

Viewing

Our viewing data (see chapter 3 and table 6.2) are clear:

> Females typically view more than males, and this holds for all ages.
> Viewing is inversely related to social class, for which we take income or education as surrogates.
> Blacks typically view more than whites and have a markedly different relationship with television.
> Elderly persons typically view more than those who are younger.

These facts provide the framework but do not tell the whole story. What they do not make clear is the way television viewing fits differently into the social life of these groups.

Women

Women's closer affiliation with television only becomes clearly visible in adulthood. As we concluded in the last chapter, very young boys and girls probably do not differ in amount of viewing. If there are differences during elementary school, girls would appear to view more than boys. Girls begin their adolescent downturn in viewing earlier. Otherwise, the basic trend is similar to that for the male: increasing viewing during the elementary school years, decreasing viewing through the high school and college years, a sustained valley during the early child-rearing years, and then a gradual increase to the higher viewing—although typically not so high as the childhood peak—of adulthood (Lyle and Hoffman, 1972a; J. P. Robinson, 1972c). As chapter 3 made clear, adult viewing *is* greater among women, most likely because the social roles that are assigned to men more often restrict the time available for television. Indeed, men and women do not differ in viewing when they have the same opportunity (Bower, 1973). It is unlikely that television fits female tastes better, because neither girls nor women have more favorable attitudes toward the medium

Table 6.2 Television Viewing by Age, Sex, Ethnicity, and Socioeconomic Status

Age	Amount of Viewing Median Number of Hours Spent Yesterday Watching Television
Adults 18–64	1.7
Adults 65 and over	2.2
Sex	Average Hours of Viewing Per Week
Males 18–49	21.8
Females 18–49	27.2
Males 50 and over	28.9
Females 50 and over	33.9
Ethnicity	Average Hours of Prime-Time Viewing Per Week
Blacks 18–49	9.8
Whites 18–49	9.1
Blacks 50 and over	8.0
Whites 50 and over	10.2
Income	Average Hours of Viewing Per Week
Under $5000	32.2
$5000–9999	26.0
$10,000–14,999	25.7
$15,000 and above	22.9
Education	Average Hours of Viewing Per Week
One year of college or more	22.8
Less than one year college	27.5

SOURCE: Adapted from Louis Harris 1974. *A Survey on Aging: Experience of Older Americans vs. Public Expectation of Old Age.* New York: Louis Harris and Associates, Inc., p. 209; L. Bogart. 1972b. Negro and white media exposure: New evidence. *Journalism Quarterly,* 49, 15–21; A. C. Nielsen Co. 1976. *Nielsen Television Index.*

(Bower, 1973; Lyle and Hoffman, 1972a). Women, in fact, are less likely than men to name television viewing as a favorite evening activity (Department of Commerce, 1977).

The major point of difference in adult life is the weekday daytime viewing of the housewife (Bogart, 1972b; Meyersohn, 1965). This implies that women's viewing is made particularly discontinuous by being joined with other household and child-rearing tasks undertaken simultaneously. Women are entering the labor force in increasing numbers, which means that their total viewing will decline and the daily pattern of their viewing will change.

Blacks

The relationship of blacks to television is startling because it departs from the general rule for social phenomena. And it is all the more interesting because, while well-documented, it has not been widely remarked upon. Normally, diffrences among ethnic groups in American society, apart from those deriving from the parent culture, are attributable to differences in education and income. This is not the case for blacks and television.

The data indicate clearly that the greater viewing of blacks is not attributable to the greater proportion of households of lower income and education (Bogart, 1972b; Bower, 1973; J. P. Robinson, 1972c). Among whites, social class is inversely related to the viewing of television and to favorable attitudes toward television. The relationship, depending on the specific measure, tends to be sharply attenuated or reversed for blacks. The higher-status black typically views as much or more television, and typically holds about as favorable or more favorable attitudes toward it, then the lower-status black. This affiliation appears to develop early, for black children and adolescents from families of lower socioeconomic status have been found to view more than whites of comparable age and status (B. S. Greenberg and Dervin, 1970).

There is no clear-cut explanation. Blacks adopted television despite their relative exclusion from it until recent years, for the pattern predated the widespread appearance on television of black actors and entertainers. One factor could be television's rise to dominance during the same period that blacks were entering the mainstream of American life, and so they became particularly attuned to the mass media. A related factor could be the dissatisfaction of blacks with the treatment and amount of coverage they receive in magazines and newspapers (Baker and Ball, 1969; B. S. Greenberg and Dervin, 1970; Lyle, 1967; National Advisory Commission on Civil Disorders, 1968), so that the new medium became preferred because it lacked the stigma of older media. In addition, perhaps television seemed to provide the best picture of the larger society into which blacks aspired to enter; and as a result of their relative exclusion from mainstream culture and educational experience over the decades prior to the arrival of television, perhaps blacks did not hold television to be a threat to reading, print media, and books, as many whites did. All of these influences presumably would have their greatest impact on blacks of higher education and income, thus leading to the departure from the pattern that has held so far for whites.

Blacks view about the same amount of television in prime time (Bower, 1973). However, blacks—and particularly black males—view more than whites outside of prime time (Bogart, 1972b). Thus, blacks not only view more, but also do so in a different pattern. Recent data suggest that blacks are becoming increasingly selective in what they view (Department of Commerce, 1977), but whether this signals new disaffection for the medium is moot.

Otherwise, the pattern of viewing for the black public is similar for the population as a whole (Bogart, 1972b; B. S. Greenberg and Dervin, 1970). Females view more than males. Although the data are scant, the lifetime viewing curve appears similar with one important exception. Elderly blacks, unlike elderly whites, tend to view less than those a few years younger.

Lower-Income Persons

Persons of lower income and lesser education also typically watch more television and have more favorable attitudes toward it (Bower, 1973; Bogart, 1972b; B. S. Greenberg and Dervin, 1970). However, there may be some discontinuities to the pattern, for one national sample found no greater viewing among those at the bottom rung educationally than among those a step above. The implication is that some motive inhering in a minimum of sophistication must be present to encourage viewing, after which available time and contrary commitments become factors. Such a perspective fits the positive association that occurred in the same sample between amount of viewing and leisure opportunities among those of lower socioeconomic status, for here again we find television use rising with signs of other interests. The fact that no such association was found for those of higher socioeconomic status presumably reflects the greater limits on unoccupied time as somewhat less favorable attitudes toward the medium (Bower, 1973; Meyersohn, 1965; Samuelson, Carter, and Ruggels, 1963). The pattern that appears to hold is that as we move down the social scale we find an increasingly large role for television until apathy disrupts the trend.

Among those of lower income and education, the pattern of viewing is the same as for the population as a whole. Females and the elderly view more, except for the black elderly. Although there are no specific data available, there is no reason to think the lifetime curve is different.

The Elderly

The elderly clearly view more than those younger (Chaffee and Wilson, 1975; Louis Harris, 1974; Meyersohn, 1965; Schramm, 1968a, 1969). The major exception are blacks over 65, who view less than blacks who are younger. The female elderly, white and black, view more than the male. Data from a recent national survey on the cycle of media consumption with advancing age (figure 6.1) shows an increase in television consumption between the mid-50s and age 70, with a subsequent decline that nevertheless remains higher on the average for those over 80 than for those 55–64, and for that matter higher than for any period of adult life (Louis Harris, 1974). What is most remarkable here is the unambiguous identification of television as the medium of advancing age, for not only does television consume more hours than any other medium (slightly less than half of all media time in these estimates), but it is the sole medium for which consumption rises with advancing age.

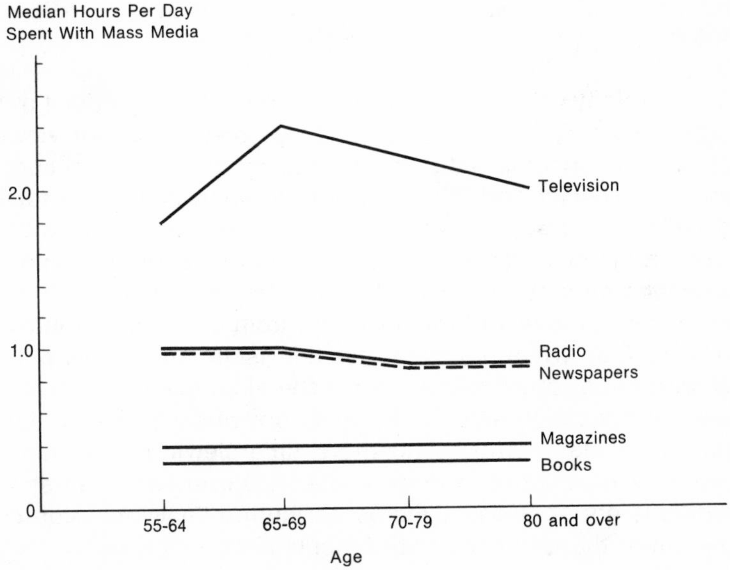

Figure 6.1. Pattern of media consumption with advancing age.

NOTE: For ages 55–64, $N = 486$; 65–69, $N = 1033$; 70–79, $N = 1295$; 80 and over, $N = 469$.

SOURCE: Adapted from *A survey on aging: Experience of older Americans vs. public expectation of old age.* 1974. New York: Louis Harris and Associates, Inc., p. 208.

Table 6.3 Mass Media Consumption by Persons over 65, by Income and Education (Percent Saying "Yes" [N = 2797])

Ever Spend Time:	Income			
	Under $3000	$3000– 6,999	$7000– 14,999	$15,000 and over
Watching television	92	95	96	97
Reading newspapers	76	89	95	97
Listening to the radio	82	84	84	83
Reading magazines	49	68	81	80
Reading books	46	56	67	80

Ever Spend Time:	Education		
	Some High School or Less	High School Grad/Some College	College Grad
Watching television	93	97	97
Reading newspapers	82	95	97
Listening to the radio	81	87	85
Reading magazines	55	85	92
Reading books	46	72	92

SOURCE: Adapted from Louis Harris, 1974. (See table 6.2).

The affinity of the elderly for television is not an artifact of the elderly's typically lower income. Old age means heavier viewing regardless of income, and the inverse relationship between income and viewing and education and viewing that holds for the population as a whole tends to disappear among the elderly. Meyersohn (1965) first reported this departure from the expected socioeconomic pattern on the basis of an analysis of a 1960 national survey. It is reconfirmed by data from a recent national survey (table 6.3), which indicate that television shares this pattern only with radio; other media use by the elderly is quite positively related to education and income. The obvious explanation is the most likely: the elderly spend more time viewing television because they have more time available. However, we shall shortly see, this is not at all the same as attributing heavy telvision consumption to the absence of other activities.

Attitudes and Motives

We are led immediately to speculate about the implications of these patterns of viewing. There are more questions than answers, but there are enough data for arresting if partial portraits.

Women and girls do not hold more favorable attitudes toward television except in regard to television news (Bower, 1973; Lyle and Hoffman, 1972a). The greater viewing by women throughout early, middle, and late adulthood is principally attributable to housewifery while men are at work, and its legacy once men retire, for working men and women do not differ in amount of viewing (Meyersohn, 1965). Here, social role orders the makeup of the television audience by the assignment of women to the home, where the television set offers company and distraction.

One plausible interpretation of the socioeconomic difference is that greater education induces a stronger orientation toward "book culture" which leads to a more negative disposition toward television (Meyersohn, 1965). Spokesmen for blacks, and sometimes those for the poor, may criticize the medium, but the typical viewer is more, not less, favorably disposed toward it.

Among whites, those of lower socioeconomic status clearly hold more favorable attitudes toward television. Blacks just as clearly hold more favorable attitudes than do whites, and this is true even when blacks and whites of equivalent socioeconomic status are compared (Bower, 1973; B. S. Greenberg and Dervin, 1970). One plausible interpretation of the socioeconomic difference is that greater education induces a stronger orientation toward "book culture" which leads to a more negative disposition toward television (Meyersohn, 1965). Spokesmen for blacks, and sometimes those for the poor, may criticize the medium, but the typical viewer is more, not less, favorably disposed toward it.

Blacks in particular are strikingly enamored of television. As table 6-4 makes clear, they differ sharply from whites in believing they have shifted toward viewing more, not less, television and in beleiving that they watch too little television. When blacks were asked, as were whites, to evaluate the performance of television in the 1970 national survey reviewed earlier (chapter 3), many more and often as extreme a difference as four times as many employed the most favorable of the permitted replies to the various queries—there were an extraordinarily greater proportion of "superfans" among them. Furthermore, the inverse relationship between socioeconomic status and favorability toward television that has typified the white public barely holds for blacks while the inverse relationship with viewing is sharply reversed—viewing among blacks increases with education (Bower, 1973).

One marked effect of the relationship between blacks and

Table 6.4 Black Orientation Toward Television by Education

Orientation and Education	Percent of Representative National Sample	
	Blacks	Whites
Declare watching more television than a decade earlier (persons 28 or older)		
Grade school	57	48
High school	48	37
College	60	31
	(N = 133)	(N = 1315)
Believe they watch too little television		
Grade school	27	16
High school	41	21
College	40	14
	(N = 188)	(N = 1658)
Report being "heavy viewers" (35-plus hours per week)		
Grade school	29	40
High school	39	33
College	48	29
	(N = 189)	(N = 1658)

SOURCE: Adapted from R. T. Bower. 1973. *Television and the Public.* New York: Holt, Rinehart, and Winston, p. 49.

television has been increasingly to sever their ties with newspapers. Television, of course, has become over the years clearly the medium aid by the public to be its primary source of news, the most useful and informative, and the least biased or inaccurate (Bower, 1973; Roper, 1975). However, blacks appear to have shifted toward television and away from newspapers at a far faster rate (McCombs, 1968). The shift of blacks toward television as a news source is a major phenomenon of audience behavior of the past decade. Furthermore, the positive orientation of more highly educated blacks toward television and the increasing orientation of blacks toward television as a news source suggest that the trend for blacks has been quite opposite to the apparent decreasing correlation for the population as a whole between level of education and use of television to follow political campaigns (J. P. Robinson, 1971; Robinson and Converse, 1972).

Blacks have different tastes in regard to television entertainment than the white majority (Carey, 1966; Fletcher, 1969; B. S. Greenberg and Dervin, 1970; B. S. Greenberg and Hanneman, 1970; Surlin and Dominick, 1970). As we pointed out earlier (chapter 3), this is partly attributable to the greater proportion of persons of lower socioeconomic status among the black population but also to some degree to ethnic differences. There is more agreement between black and white adults low in socioeconomic status than between blacks of such status and the white majority, but the agreement is very far from perfect (B. S. Greenberg and Dervin, 1970). The national samples we have examined (chapter 3) suggested the conclusion that blacks have a greater preference for action/adventure and less liking for situation comedy and programs featuring families, including action/adventure series featuring family units. We qualified this portrait of black adults with data showing that teenagers from low-income families, but blacks in particular, more frequently preferred programs featuring families—a preference that probably reflects their seeking from the media satisfactions or experiences that are lacking in their own lives. The seeking of such gratifications would be consistent with the finding that young blacks appear to employ the medium more for information about ways to behave, including dating behavior (Gerson, 1966; B. S. Greenberg and Dervin, 1970). As we would expect, there is a greater preference among blacks of all ages for programs featuring black actors and entertainers.

Women differ somewhat from men in their tastes (Bower, 1973; Lyle and Hoffman, 1972a; J. P. Robinson, 1972c; Schramm, Lyle, and Parker, 1961). The divergence becomes noticeable by the first grade. Women tend toward comedy, music, and family programs; men prefer action in drama and sports. Even when actual viewing, not preference, is the measure (which inevitably would involve some inhibition of the display of individual taste) and viewing is confined to evenings and weekends, the differences in regard to comedy and sports appear for adults, although of course the total viewing of men and women during these hours is similar (Bower, 1973). The predominantly housewife audience for soap operas of domestic and interpersonal crisis and game shows trading on human enthusiasm for merchandise certainly implies greater female preference for such fare, for it is hard to believe that the highly competitive television industry would not have developed other kinds of programming if the decades of proprietary research had given any hint that other fare would be preferred.

Women also more frequently plan viewing in advance (Bower, 1973), probably because of the greater time that housewives have to read about coming attractions. Such an interpretation is supported by the fact that planning is inversely related to socioeconomic status, and the greater planning by women occurs only for those high-school or college-educated. Advance planning, therefore, is associated with characteristics that would favor use of other media and greater overall interest in media.

The extent to which television serves different functions for females is obscure. Early radio research discovered that one motive for listening to soap operas was a desire to learn how to solve problems and how to behave in difficult situations (Herzog, 1944, 1954). These findings probably apply to television soap operas. This information motive is consistent with that found for young blacks. It is clearly established that females and males both display greater interest in content that is especially pertinent to them, whether it is recent experience (Boyanowsky, Newtson, and Walster, 1974), identification (Lyle and Hoffman, 1972a; Maccoby and Wilson, 1957), sexual interest (Maccoby, Wilson, and Burton, 1958), or the particular poignance of a portrayal at a certain stage in life (Dysinger and Ruckmick, 1933). The difficulty, of course, is that it is not always clear precisely where pertinence will lie.

National news viewing is greatest for those with the least and the most education (Israel and Robinson, 1972; J. P. Robinson, 1971); this holds for males and females, blacks and whites. This curvilinearity with socioeconomic status probably reflects quite different processes, with lack of experience and interest in other media contributing to greater viewing by those with the least education and greater interest motivating those with the most education. There appears to be strikingly greater credibility among women than among men for television news; in a national survey (Bower, 1973), more than a fourth more adult women chose television as providing "the fairest, most unbiased" news (37 percent of women vs. 29 percent of men), while the proportions naming newspapers were almost identical, thereby eliminating the explanation of general greater trust in the media on the part of women. This naturally leads to speculation over whether any of the factors responsible for this greater orientation toward television than newspapers might be the same as for the similar orientation of blacks. Socioeconomic status also appears to predict choice of entertainment programming, for it is inversely related to the viewing of action-adventure programming (Israel and Robinson, 1972). The poor watch more violence.

The viewing of violence, but not the news viewing, fits the formulation of a proclivity on the part of those with less education and income for mass-media fantasy (Schramm, Lyle, and Parker, 1961), but whether the determining factor is immediate reward, as was originally argued, or salience (fantasy may bring immediate reward, but television violence also may be more salient for those of lower social status), or something else is unclear. The fact of news viewing, and the salience interpretation are consistent with the definitely greater propensity of those of lower socioeconomic status, regardless of age, to believe that they can learn things from television (Bower, 1973; B. S. Greenberg and Dervin, 1970). Thus, television's primary role for the general public as provider of entertainment becomes, for those of lower education and income, modified by the greater degree to which their viewing is motivated by the belief that something can be learned.

The relationship of the elderly to television is distinguished by the singular role it plays in their lives. Television viewing is the predominant leisure-time activity for those over 65 (Louis Harris, 1974; Schramm, 1968a, 1969). Viewing is likely to be planned, with time carefully allotted for favorite programs. (Schalinske, 1968). Tastes also appear to change with aging (R. H. Davis, 1971; Gregg, 1971; Israel and Robinson, 1972; Schalinske, 1968; Schramm, 1969). The elderly clearly have a greater preference for public affairs and news, often declaring it their favorite programming. The entertainment programs most popular with the public as a whole are typically not so popular with the elderly. They are particularly unattracted by action and adventure. Sex-related differences, however, appear to continue with the exception of a common liking for such a perennial older adult favorite as *The Lawrence Welk Show*. Attitudes toward television become more favorable the older the segment of the population queried, and this appears to represent more of a shift attributable to aging than a generational difference (Bower, 1973). A majority of the elderly believe they are fairly portrayed on television, and the portrayal of the elderly is evaluated at least as favorably and possibly more so by the elderly themselves than by those younger (Louis Harris, 1974). Paradoxically, notably fewer among the elderly than among the population as a whole, although still a majority, believe children are "better off" with television (Bower, 1973). This greater skepticism over television's influence on children is shared with those of lower socioeconomic status generally, and because the elderly as a group also have less education, it probably stems from the same source. However, it would be silly to attribute the elderly's involvement with television to the fact that as a group they tend to be of lower socioeconomic status. Other factors are involved, and this is perhaps best demonstrated by the elderly's sharp departure from the norm for those of lower education and income in their greater news viewing.

The obvious explanations for the elderly's use of television are social isolation, growing infirmity, security in routine, and reduced use of other media. These all hold some truth, but one must be cautious because the evidence requires that such hypotheses be carefully qualified. The elderly have been found to prefer programs which invite personal involvement and a relationship to personalities that has been called "parasocial interaction" (Gregg, 1971), but viewing during these later years has not been found to be associated with fewer leisure activities (Meyersohn, 1965) or fewer interpersonal contacts (Cassata, 1967; Graney, 1974), although it has been found to increase with the act of retirement (Cassata, 1967). The implication is that the changed pattern of living associated with advancing age is an influence, but that among the elderly—contrary to much speculation—lesser involvement in activities or interpersonal relationships does not lead to greater viewing of television. The major factors appear to be time available and established media habits. Thus, viewing by elderly men, typically used to working, varies inversely with time spent away from home, while viewing by elderly women, already used to watching more television, is not affected (Meyersohn, 1965). Retirement typically increases the "time on one's hands" that is the predominant rationale offered for viewing (J. P. Robinson, 1972c) and at the same time cuts numerous personal ties, but after this point greater isolation does not appear to be associated with heavier viewing. Infirmity and routine surely play some role, but such factors apply more to the very elderly than those in their first decade after 65. The elderly do not appear to turn away from mass media except for movies (Schramm, 1969), and otherwise their use of media other than television appears to be broadly similar to that of those a decade or more younger (Louis Harris, 1974).

What we know about the elderly and television largely represents the general pattern of media use associated with being older, empirically defined in most cases as "60 and older" or "65 and older." The shifts and changes that may occur as the years and then decades pass after this border are unclear because there are few data that allow us to pursue the media to the end of life in any detail. We reported that a national sample indicates that television use declines somewhat after reaching a peak around age 70 while remaining greater throughout old age than in any previous period (Louis Harris, 1974). The same data indicate considerable continuing use without much change of radio, newspapers, and magazines through the final age category studied, 80 and older. Data from a Wisconsin sample of several hundred adults (Chaffee and Wilson, 1975) suggest that the impression of no change in media other than television may require qualification. Newspaper use climaxed a trend toward increasing use during the later years of life with a peak in the early 70s, after which it declined. Radio and magazine use declined after age 65, with the decline in radio use representing a trend begun in the late 50s. Television news viewing also declined after age 65, but less sharply so than newspaper, radio, and magazine use. This slow but progressive withdrawal from news viewing is consistent with the study of a retirement home with a median age of 80 where documentaries, panel discussions, and other serious treatment of issues on television were not attractive to the elderly, although television remained the principal source of news (Schalinske, 1968). When the media were compared in the Wisconsin sample as sources of information on important problems, television and newspapers were far more frequently said to be relied upon, and these two did not appreciably differ in the frequency of such reliance for the age categories 58–65, 66–73, and 74–89. This pattern of differential media use as a function of purpose is consistent with the finding of Hwang (1974) that among a sample of several hundred elderly persons in Oregon, newspapers and television were about equally named as sources of national news, but newspapers were far more frequently said to be the source for local news. These findings emphasize the importance of motive as a factor in media use; the pattern among the media here alters sharply as the focus narrows the specific functions served.

There is much we do not know, but the scenario that would appear to be most general is one of adaptation to change in which television appears to play a role of some importance. At age 65 there is retirement, and leisure time is markedly increased but the effect is typically greater for males than females because males have more often been employed outside the home; the concomitant is the severing of numerous ties, especially for the formerly employed, and television comes to fill some of this time and to serve as a source of information and stimulation in regard to the outside world that was once provided by interpersonal ties;

with the passage of years, there is some turning away from the contact with external events provided by the media, and this may be associated with physical and mental deterioration that make attention to the media more difficult; but the striking fact is not this progressive diminution of involvement but the continuing high degree of attention to the media and in particular to television.

Effects

Television's influence in other ways on these four segments of the audience is speculative, with certain exceptions. There presumably are behavioral effects, as have been discussed in regard to children and adolescents (chapter 5), and will be examined in the framework of a theoretical model (chapter 8) because these adhere in psychological principles of broad applicability. However, they are modified, as we would expect, by the particular social circumstances that hold for these groups.

Many of the experiments concerned with observational learning, imitation, and instigation to behave in some way, most of which concern television violence and aggression, have included girls and young women as well as boys and young men. Females, like males, acquire new modes of behavior from television; they sometimes imitate, and have their disposition to behave in some way altered, but typically the outcome is modulated by the social norms for the kind of behavior involved (Bandura, 1973; Bandura, Ross, and Ross, 1961; Bandura, Ross, and Ross, 1963a; 1963b; Berkowitz and Rawlings, 1963; Ekman et al., 1972; Eron et al., 1972; Hicks, 1965). Thus, female subjects frequently display less aggression because social sanctions against aggression are greater for females than for males. The governing role of social norms is exemplified by the tendency of females to be less aggressive when provocation is minor but equally as aggressive as males when provocation is strong (Baron, 1977). Presumably, the tendency toward greater effects on males would be reversed for behavior that is normative for females.

The typical pattern is for the influence of a portrayal to vary positively with the normative social power of the portrayed figure, so that male models have more influence even on females, and adults more than peers (Bandura, Ross, and Ross, 1961; Bandura,

Ross, and Ross, 1963a; Nicholas, McCarter, and Heckel, 1971a, 1971b). It appears that race of the portrayed figure also enters; in one experiment blacks demonstrated that they were more influenced by a black model (Nicholas, McCarter, and Heckel, 1971a). The experimental literature pays no attention to socioeconomic status. It is reasonable to hypothesize that effects would be maximal for portrayed figures and for behavior particularly esteemed by those of lower socioeconomic status, but this is speculation. All of the experiments have had children or persons of college age as subjects. The typicality of similar effects on older persons is unknown. Presumably, the instigation of behavior would occur among adults, and such a supposition is supported by the fact that in many of the experiments demonstrating such an effect the subjects have been of college age. Influence on the acquisition of behavior presumably would decline somewhat with age, as the amount of observed behavior on television that is novel decreases. However, the frequency of adults' acting out in real life what they have seen on television—is moot, as the regularity with which airline bomb threats followed broadcasts of Rod Serling's *The Doomsday Flight* (Bandura, 1973) makes dismissal of such an adult phenomenon impossible.

There has been only scant study of influences on norms, values, and knowledge that bear with any particularity on these four publics. The somewhat greater degree to which information of various kinds is a motive for viewing for blacks, those of lower socioeconomic status, and the elderly (Bower, 1973; B. J. Greenberg and Dervin, 1970; Schalinske, 1968) suggest they may be particularly affected. Consistent with this speculation is the finding that the perception of the real world as similar to the way the world is portrayed on television (such as the probability of falling victim to a crime) is correlated with heavier viewing (Gerbner and Gross, 1976; Gerbner et al., 1977). Furthermore, the fact that this tendency is markedly greater among those of lower socioeconomic status, whether or not they are currently light or heavy viewers, encourages the speculation that this socioeconomic difference is the result of viewing. The argument would be that the greater inclination of those of lower socioeconomic status to look upon television as a source of information increases the likelihood that prior viewing would have some influence as well as increasing the impact of current viewing. Such an argument leads us to hypothesize greater influence also on blacks and on the elderly, who hold similar motives for viewing. The finding that the influence of television on children's knowledge about occupations is contingent on lack of real-life experience with persons engaged in them (DeFleur and DeFleur, 1967) suggests that isolation from other sources for *any reason*—geographic, racial, or psychological—may be a key factor. This would lead one to hypothesize greater influence on women as well as on men on topics about which their social roles leave them less informed. The same would be true of blacks, the poor, and the elderly, who in effect are variously isolated from many aspects of social life.

Beyond these various suggestive leads, there is only utter speculation. The most popular is that the way various of these groups are portrayed has an insidious if hard-to-document effect on their self-image and relations with others. C. C. Clark (1969, 1972), for example, has argued that television reinforces the values of a white-dominated society by portraying minorities in subsidiary roles or as enforcers of the rules and laws laid down by that society. Francher (1973) has argued that the emphasis on youth in television advertising—as exemplified by the slogan "It's the Pepsi Generation"—creates anxiety and tension among the elderly, which encourages display of symptoms of intellectual impairment. Gerbner and Gross (1976) depict television as impeding social change and reform through the portrayal in its violent entertainment of those who are more or less powerful in actual society, thereby reinforcing the existing hierarchy. The stereotypic portrayals of female roles in recent years have been particularly attacked on these grounds (Women on Words and Images, 1975). A neo-Marxist view would hold that television serves the economic system by helping to maintain the status quo and by fostering values which make viewers hungry, thirsty, and acquisitive consumers (Hujanen, 1976). From this perspective the game show is a training session. The oldest speculation is that of Lazarsfeld and Merton (1971) that mass media have a "narcoticizing dysfunction" by drawing attention from serious social issues and by substituting absorption in the portrayal of events for effective thought and action. A very plausible argument is that of Bogart (1965), who sees television as having a homogenizing influence by providing common experience across social strata, particularly for blue-collar workers, for whom he believes it provides an introduction to middle-class behavior. An equally plausible view consistent with many of these arguments is that television provides instruction for women, blacks, the poor, and the elderly for their assumption of subordinate roles. Homogenization is not necessarily in conflict with such an outcome. Despite appearances, it need not reflect the diminution of the social hierarchy, but simply an increased and wider acceptance of the norms and values on which the hierarchy depends. These are all viewpoints on whose behalf it is easy to offer logically and rhetorically persuasive arguments but which are so sweeping that it is hard to specify precisely what evidence would lead to their acceptance or rejection.

In sum, we conclude that:

Females, blacks, those of lower socioeconomic status, and the elderly typically are heavier viewers of television.

The dominant figure in television drama is the youthful white male adult, and portrayals of females, blacks, those of lower socioeconomic status, and the elderly tend to be either infrequent, stereotypic, unrepresentative of their status in real life, or dependent.

The four characteristics of sex, ethnicity, social class, and age each identify particular relationships with television that can be defined in terms of use, attitudes toward the medium, motives for viewing, and experience with the medium.

The evidence leads to the speculation that because of psychological and social isolation the four characteristics examined identify publics particularly susceptible to influence by television.

Our focus on these four publics is predicated on the belief that their greater use of television raises questions about their relationships to the medium that should be addressed. We expect women, blacks and other minorities, the poor, and the elderly to receive increasing attention in television studies because of the broader scrutiny being given their treatment by the society. However, our emphasis on group variation should not becloud the fact that the audience is best thought of as individuals who vary with respect to television in accord with sex, ethnicity, socioeconomic status, and age, as well as other variables. The differences that distinguish segments of the audience from one another are always less extreme than those that exist among individuals even within a segment, for the former are based on averages while the latter incorporates the flowering of idiosyncrasy.

Chapter

7

Politics and Purchases

THE GROWTH OF the mass media has been accompanied by concern and at times alarm over their manipulative ability. It is ironic that the mass media can simultaneously engender both devotion and suspicion. Yet each in its turn, from the simplistic assertions of World War I propaganda to the sophisticated productions of contemporary television, has been the object of concern and uneasiness about its manipulative ability.

We shall evaluate television's persuasive prowess by examining two bodies of research that are usually treated separately. One is the scientific literature on television's influence on voting and politics. The other is the scientific literature on television's effectiveness as an advertising medium. We treat them together because in both cases calculated campaigns are conducted through the media with the intent to persuade. We believe that treating together evidence about effects on voting and buying greatly increases understanding about television's capabilities and limits in regard to personal decision-making.

However, we caution against any advance assumption that what holds in regard to politics necessarily holds in regard to day-to-day consumption. It is partly because the differences between the two domains cast the special factors operating within each in sharper, and therefore more discernible, contrast that we have chosen to cover them within the same framework.

There is no doubt that television has drastically altered American politics. We agree with Mendelsohn and Crespi (1970) that television has changed traditional American politics in four ways:

By focusing major attention on the nominating conventions, they are becoming increasingly manipulated and self-conscious in order to hold public attention and make a favorable impression.

⌈   By its command of large audiences, television has replaced
other media and other activities to become one of—often the
⌊major—element around which campaigns are organized.

   Because of its heavy use in campaigns, television has altered
the makeup of campaign staffs, with larger roles going to media experts; and it has altered the distribution of campaign funds, with
more going to the media.

   Television has greatly increased vicarious participation in politics by the individual voter.

   We must emphasize, however, that our focus in regard to
television's political effects is somewhat narrower. We are interested in the influence of television on the political decision-making of the individual voter, although we cannot wholly ignore effects on the larger political framework because they influence
these individual decisions.

   Whenever the evidence permits, we distinguish among the
various possible outcomes, but neither life nor science is always
so neat. Often, we can only speak of attitudes and beliefs that encompass some amalgam of attentional, cognitive, and affective elements. And even when we are dealing with behavior, the attentional, cognitive, and affective components that lie behind the
behavior cannot always be specified. Sometimes, it seems reasonable to accept a behavioral outcome as implying a consistent
set of supporting attitudes and beliefs. It is not wise, however, to
assume such consistency in all instances. As we discuss in other
contexts (chapters 5 and 8), behavior typically is strongly influenced by external factors, such as pressure from others or the
simple lack of an opportunity to display a particular behavior.

   We begin by discussing the intellectual history of the scientific study of television's persuasive influence. This discussion of
the dominant ideas across the years in mass communication research sets the stage for our analysis of the empirical evidence
about the influence of political communications on television,
such as news and public affairs programs, the coverage of conventions and campaign events, and the broadcasting of major
speeches and debates. We then turn to television advertising,
including both political and product advertising.

   Among the topics we shall cover are:

   Significant trends and shifts in the scientific study of the influence of television on voter and consumer decisionmaking.
   The way television influences the priorities and prominence the

public assigns to issues, persons, and symbols—often called the agenda-setting function of television.

The degree to which television affects the public's knowledge about issues, persons, and symbols.

The role of television in shaping attitudes and behavior, and the various uses and gratifications of television viewing.

What advertising research has to say about television and decision-making.

How social and advertising research complement, extend, and qualify each other.

Shifts in Scientific Perspective

Political Research

The benchmark examination of the effects of mass communication on political behavior is the study by Lazarsfeld, Berelson, and Gaudet (1948) of Erie County, Ohio, voters in the 1940 Presidential election. This pretelevision investigation was guided by a concern over mass media's manipulative influence. Describing the Presidential election as "a large-scale experiment in political propaganda and public opinion," the authors attempted to assess the impact of the major mass media—radio and newspapers in that day—on voters' decisions. Subsequent research continued the concern with voting, but expanded the range of effects under scrutiny. Added to the act of voting were formation and change in attitudes about candidates, issues, and political parties. In addition, this broad interest in attitudes led to research on communication situations other than elections. Studies of the direct effects of mass communication on attitudes and opinions were to dominate the research for several decades after Erie County.

This long reign of attitude change as the major dependent variable in communication research is explained by three circumstances. The first is a guiding point of view taken—like many early behavioral theories—almost directly from popular belief, which held that the mass media have strong, direct effects. Schramm and Roberts (1971) call this point of view the "bullet" theory, because members of the mass audience were viewed as easy targets for the persuasive messages fired by the media.

Second is the significant body of empirical evidence that

documented the ability of communications to achieve substantial attitude change. Most prominent was the program of experiments begun in the early 1940s by Hovland and associates (Hovland, Janis, and Kelley, 1953; Hovland, Lumsdaine, and Sheffield, 1949; Rosenberg et al., 1960).

Finally, major new theories of communication and attitude change emerged in the 1950s, which were very attractive to social scientists. The common element was that attitude change and use of communications were conceived of as being used to resolve conflicts or discrepancies among a person's beliefs and perceptions. Such homeostatic theories—for example, Festinger's (1957) theory of cognitive dissonance, Osgood and Tannenbaum's (1955) congruity principle, Heider's (1958) balance model, Newcomb's (1953) symmetry theory of communication acts—guided the testing of dozens of specific hypotheses.

For decades, these factors sustained the preoccupation within communication research with direct effects on individual's attitudes. This preoccupation was well established by the time television appeared in the late 1940s and still largely dominates public thinking about television and other mass media.

However, the scientific examination of the political effects of television by now has largely emerged from this initial preoccupation. As we shall see, these studies have generally failed to corroborate a "bullet" theory of television effects. This failure even has led some to abandon such a theory for its antithesis, a "law of minimal consequences." For others there remained a suspicion that there were demonstrable effects, but that in the 1940s and 1950s scientists had not focused their research on the right questions.

To understand the political role of television it is essential to consider topics other than attitude change. One must consider not only attitudinal effects, but also cognitive and overt behavioral effects, of which voting is only one example. Thus, the history of research on mass media and politics has been marked by the enlargement of the kinds of effects studied, moving from a dominant concern with effects on attitudes and opinions to a broader concern with cognitive and behavioral effects (Becker, McCombs, and McLeod, 1975; Blumler and McLeod, 1974; Kraus and Davis, 1976; McCombs, 1972).

The most obvious of the possible cognitive effects of television is on voters' knowledge of politics. Most of the political arena is out of sight and never directly experienced by the individual citizen. Few ever meet or even see political leaders or monitor their daily official actions. Yet most people have opinions about what these officials should be doing, about their effectiveness and efficiency as leaders, and about their positions on the issues of the day. People obtain the store of knowledge and information that underlies their political beliefs, perceptions, and attitudes largely from the mass media. Television and newspapers create the second-hand political reality that governs much of our political behavior.

The information transmitted by television ranges from basic knowledge of the political system and how it works to sets of facts about immediate and largely transitory news events. Early research on cognitive learning from television tended to emphasize the learning of facts. More recently, social scientists have examined the information acquired from television in a more realistic manner. Rather than framing their questions in a civics-book format, they have asked individuals to indicate areas of great personal interest or concern and then probed the role of the media in providing information relevant to them.

This approach to learning from mass communication underscores another aspect of the possible cognitive effects of television—the role of mass media in determining the salience of topics for an individual or community. Termed the "agenda-setting" function of mass communication, this hypothesized influence of the news media is best summarized by B. Cohen's (1963) remark that while the media may not succeed in telling us what to think, they are "stunningly successful" in telling us what to think *about.* Initial research has documented high correlations between press coverage of political and public issues and the salience of these issues in the public mind (Funkhouser, 1973; McCombs and Shaw, 1972). Such correlations of course are no test of the hypothesis, because the association could as easily reflect the influence of public preoccupations on media content as the reverse; nevertheless, they establish the association necessary to justify further exploration of the proposition. Obviously, no one contends that agenda-setting is an influence process operating at all times and all places on all people. Thus, current research seeks to specify the conditions under which agenda-setting operates (McCombs and Shaw, 1974; McLeod and Becker, 1974; Weaver, McCombs, and Spellman, 1975).

Other current research probing the influence of television on interpersonal agendas marks the transition from concern about television's cognitive effects to a concern with its overt behavioral effects other than voting preferences. There is a growing body of research that indicates a significant impact of television and other mass media on topics of conversation (Atkin, 1973; Chaffee, 1972c; LoSciuto, 1972). Conversely, anticipation of interpersonal communication also influences selection of material from the media with consideration of its high social utility in these subsequent conversations. This may be the major impact of television—as a stimulus for and source of interpersonal conversation. Coupled with television's ability to attract massive audiences, this is a significant social role.

Television also may influence other forms of political behavior and participation. But elaboration of the full nexus of communication and political variables is necessary to trace these outcomes. In short, multivariable theories and models are necessary for complete description and adequate explanation of the political communication process.

Advertising Research

Much like the early research into the effects of political communication, the impetus for early advertising research was to identify behavioral effects. The reason, of course, was a very practical one. The managers of companies that spent huge sums of money for advertising desired proof that company sales benefited from the advertising.

The problem was not one of documenting changes in behavior—company sales do fluctuate and frequently dovetail with fluctuations in advertising campaigns. The major problem faced by advertising research has been to isolate those changes in sales which can be unequivocally attributed to advertising. That has been a herculean task. Advertising is always part of a larger promotional and marketing effort. Factors such as personal selling, availability of the product, retailing activity, public relations, and price also influence buying. Apart from those company activities, sales are influenced by numerous external forces: competitors' actions, economic and social conditions, even weather and climate. It is very difficult to control for these nonadvertising effects in econometric analyses, and laboratory experiments which do control for them suffer from critical problems of external validity.

For these reasons, then, researchers began to examine variables other than behavior for measuring advertising's effectiveness. A benchmark in this effort was Lavidge and Steiner's model (1961) which treated purchase as the final stage in a "hierarchy of effects." As figure 7.1 indicates, advertising moved consumers up the steps of the process, from unawareness to awareness to knowledge, and eventually to purchase. The appropriate task for advertising research was to measure how well advertising moved people from stage to stage. While the model admitted that the steps might not be equidistant or that some consumers might move through more than one step at a time, it still presupposed that the same sequence was followed.

The Lavidge and Steiner model had important implications for advertising research. If it was correct, it would eliminate the

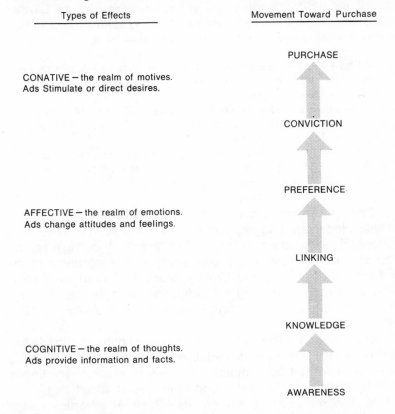

Figure 7.1. "Hierarchy of effects" model of advertising influence.

SOURCE: Adapted from R. J. Lavidge and G. A. Steiner. 1961. A model for predictive measurements of advertising effectiveness. *Journal of Marketing,* published by the American Marketing Association. 25: 59–62.

need to treat sales as a measure of effectiveness. Instead, the research could measure the effect upon the intermediate stages. For example, awareness and recall studies could be used to measure cognitive effects; the semantic differential and other rating scales could be used to measure attitudes.

The model evoked varied reactions. One of the early responses, for example, disputed the notion that each person moved from stage to stage in the purchase process. Instead, asserted Copland (1963), it was more accurate to say that some people who are at the awareness stage will buy the brand, that more of those who are at the knowledge stage will buy it, and that even more of those at the preference stage will buy it.

By the mid-1960s there was enough response to the Lavidge and Steiner model to enable Palda (1966) to review the criticisms and empirical research. His conclusions were pessimistic:

> There was no clear evidence that awareness or knowledge increased the probability of purchase, since each could just as easily follow purchase as precede it.
> Favorable attitudes did seem to increase the probability of purchase, but a change in attitude could and often did occur after purchase—instead of before.
> There was no published evidence that clearly showed that the expression of intent by a consumer to purchase a brand increased the probability of its subsequent purchase.

One of the few empirical tests of the entire Lavidge and Steiner model used aggregate data from 57,000 interviews in 19 national surveys about instant coffee brands. A multiple regression analysis of brand awareness, advertising exposure, attitude, and behavior (as measured by each brand's share of the market) concluded that advertising did influence behavior, but through awareness rather than through attitude change (Aaker and Day, 1974).

Even though numerous studies found evidence contradictory to the Lavidge and Steiner model, nothing has really replaced it. Its most important contribution has been to separate the behavioral from the affective and cognitive effects of advertising.

New interest in research on the effects of advertising—and television advertising in particular—is emerging among social scientists. As several commentators have pointed out in regard to children and television advertising, few social scientists have taken an interest in studying the effects of advertising (Comstock and Lindsey, 1975; Sheikh, Prasad, and Rao, 1974). The only major exception has been those situated within business schools, who have been primarily interested in improving advertising's sales effectiveness. Prominent among the reasons for a lack of scholarly analysis has been skepticism that research would affect advertising practices; concern about inadvertently making a contribution to commerce instead of science; and the belief that advertising does not merit serious study. There are many signs that this situation is changing. The principal factor is increasing concern that television advertising should be regulated in order to protect young viewers from persuasive appeals with harmful impact. This concern is leading to research on whether such regulation is called for, what form it should take, and its effectiveness.

Agenda-Setting by Television

An act such as voting or buying is often the final link in a sequence beginning with simple exposure to and growing awareness of a topic, person, or symbol. While many political messages fail to achieve this final link, there are documented instances of public affairs campaigns that have achieved the full sequence of possible effects (Douglas, Westley, and Chaffee, 1970; Mendelsohn, 1973; Merton, 1946). The sequence is: new or increased attention, cognitive change, affective change, and sometimes altered behavior.

It is ironic that the study of the mass media's political impact began with the final links in the sequence. Although what occurred is understandable, we must add that it was scientifically poor strategy. In recent years, communication research has refocused on earlier links in the sequence which received only secondary attention in the earlier decades of study (Ball-Rokeach, 1974).

One of the major foci of research is attention and awareness. Here is not only the most obvious effect, but possibly one of the most important effects of television and other mass media—an ability to structure our world for us, to direct our attention toward some things and, by default, to direct it away from others. This influence of the mass media has been labeled *agenda-setting*.

Assertions about agenda-setting by the mass media can be found in the literature over past decades (W. C. Clark, 1968;

B. Cohen, 1963; Lippmann, 1922), but the first empirical attempt to validate the notion was made by McCombs and Shaw (1972) in regard to the influence of newspaper and network television coverage on Chapel Hill, North Carolina, voters in the 1968 presidential election. In the few years since the publication of their study, research on agenda-setting by the various mass media has become frequent.

The specific hypothesis McCombs and Shaw posed was that when the media emphasize an event, they influence the audience to see it as important. McCombs and Shaw found very high correlations between the media's emphasis on given issues and their being ranked as important by voters. They argue that agenda-setting by the media is the most plausible interpretation because of the absence of other sources for public affairs information and the tendency for newsmen and their audiences to disagree *a priori* on news values.

Agenda-setting, of course, is not necessarily limited to news. Heavy viewers of television have been found to perceive the crime rate as closer to the incidence of television drama than the lower incidence of real life (Gerbner and Gross, 1976; Gerbner et al., 1977), a perception that probably would heighten the importance of crime in their agenda of public issues. Similarly, children have been found to acquire knowledge about occupations from television drama when real-life examples are absent (DeFleur and DeFleur, 1967), an outcome that given the high proportion of persons concerned with law enforcement in television drama (chapter 2) also implies a heightening in their agenda of crime as a matter of concern.

Each day the gatekeepers of the mass media decide what to cover and what to reject. Furthermore, accounts are not treated equally. Some are detailed and emphasized, others touched on briefly.

Agenda-setting asserts that audiences learn these saliences of the mass media, incorporating a similar set of weights into their personal perceptions of the world. Varying salience of messages is an attribute inevitably imposed by the norms of journalistic practice in all media.

This agenda-setting concept is a hypothesis specifying a strong positive relationship between the emphases of mass communication and the salience of these topics to the individuals in the audience. This concept is stated in causal terms: increased salience of a topic or issue in the mass media influences (causes) the salience of that topic or issue among the public.

Testing the Hypothesis

In the initial empirical exploration of the agenda-setting hypothesis, McCombs and Shaw (1972) found that voters' perceptions of the major issues reflected the *composite* of the mass media coverage, even though the three presidential candiates placed widely divergent emphasis on the individual issues. Voters agreed no more with the agenda that represented news about their preferred candidate than they did with the overall news agenda; they agreed somewhat more if anything, with the media's agenda. The data are displayed in table 7.1. This suggests that voters pay some attention to all the political news in the media regardless of whether it is about, or originated with, a favored candidate. This is contrary to what we would expect if selective exposure and selective perception were fully operative. These concepts, asserting that audiences generally select and recall supportive mes-

Table 7.1 Relationship between Voters' Agenda of Issues and Agenda Transmitted by the News Media in the 1968 Presidential Election

| | Correlation Coefficients For: | | | |
| | Major News Items | | Minor News Items | |
Selected Media	All News	News of Own Party	All News	News of Own Party
CBS				
Voters (H)[a]	.83	.83	.81	.71
Voters (N)	.50	.00	.57	.40
Voters (W)	.78	.80	.86	.76
NBC				
Voters (H)	.57	.76	.64	.73
Voters (N)	.27	.13	.66	.63
Voters (W)	.84	.21	.48	−.33
New York Times				
Voters (H)	.89	.79	.97	.85
Voters (N)	.80	.40	.88	.98
Voters (W)	.89	.25	.78	−.53
Durham Morning Herald				
Voters (H)	.84	.74	.95	.83
Voters (N)	.59	.88	.84	.69
Voters (W)	.82	.76	.79	.00

SOURCE: Adapted from M. E. McCombs and D. L. Shaw, 1972. The agenda-setting function of mass media. *Public Opinion Quarterly*, 36, 176–87.

[a] H = Humphrey voters
N = Nixon voters
W = Wallace voters

sages, frequently have been invoked to "explain" the lack of significant influence by mass communications (Klapper, 1960).

While these initial findings in no way prove that television plays a significant agenda-setting role in politics, they do constitute evidence consistent with such a notion and raise new questions. One of the first was whether the media really set the agenda, or whether they simply reflect an agenda set by their news sources. Funkhouser's (1973) study of the events of the 1960s demonstrates the power of the media to establish an agenda that is not a mere reflection of the events in the real world. He compared trends among three measures—media coverage of events, the degree the public perceived events as a problem, and the actual evolution of the class of events in question. Media coverage was measured by content of three major news magazines—*Time, Newsweek,* and *U.S. News and World Report*—as a proxy for all media, a procedure that gains validity from evidence of high correlations among media in emphasis of coverage (McCombs and Shaw, 1972). While there was a high correlation (.78) between media coverage and what people said the important problems were, there was considerable lag between both these variables and the peaks of the objective indicators for each of the problems studied. For example, coverage of and public concern over the Vietnam war, campus unrest, and urban riots peaked a year or two earlier than did the actual situations themselves.

We also can look at the evidence for a causal linkage between media agendas and personal agendas. Several studies have reported strong associations between the two agendas (Gormley, 1975; McCombs and Shaw, 1972; McCombs, Shaw, and Shaw, 1972; Mullins, 1973), but did not directly measure the direction of influence. Obviously, the notion of agenda-setting asserts that the direction of effect is from media to audience. What empirical support is there for the assertion?

The history of Watergate as a political scandal would appear to exemplify agenda-setting by the media. The *Washington Post* probed into an event and began to outline it as an issue. Slowly, television news, the wire services, and other news media followed suit. Over time, the prominence of Watergate in the news grew and, lagging a bit behind, so did public concern. Television probably further imposed this issue on the public agenda with its extensive live coverage of the Watergate hearings chaired by Senator Sam Ervin (D. K. Davis and Lee, 1974; Kraus and Chaffee,

1974; M. J. Robinson, 1974). Analyzing the behavior of Charlotte, North Carolina, voters interviewed during the 1972 presidential campaign and again in May 1973, at the beginning of the Ervin hearings, Weaver, McCombs, and Spellman (1975) found substantial evidence that high media use led to the increased salience of Watergate as an issue among those with a "high need for orientation," defined as high interest accompanied by uncertainty over allegiance.

Television vs. Newspapers

One of the interesting questions in agenda-setting is the relative efficacy of television and newspapers in influencing personal agendas. The original McCombs and Shaw study found no significant difference between the influence of television and newspapers. But later research reported by McCombs, Shaw, and Shaw (1972) suggest that there is a difference. Their data are displayed in table 7.2. The pattern of a higher correlation between media and personal agenda among those who are frequent users holds for both the newspapers and television. However, the correlation for television is lower, and when the influence of the two media are examined jointly, frequent television use appears to make far

Table 7.2 Correspondence Between Public Affairs Agendas of Citizens and Media Coverage by Frequency of Exposure to Newspapers and Television

Media Orientation	Agreement Between Agenda (Spearman's rho)	
A. Newspaper is principal source		
	Newspaper Exposure	
	Frequent	Infrequent
	+.70	+.38
B. Television is principal source		
	National Television News	
	Frequent	Infrequent
	+.48	+.38
C. Joint Use of Newspapers and Television		
	Newspaper Exposure	
Television Exposure	Frequent	Infrequent
Frequent	+.70	+.38
Infrequent	+.75	+.65

SOURCE: Adapted from M. E. McCombs, D. L. Shaw, and E. Shaw, 1972. The news and public response. Three studies of the agenda-setting powers of the press. Paper presented at the meeting of the Association for Education in Journalism.

less difference than frequent newspaper use. The implication is that the newspaper was more effective than television in setting the agenda.

Analyses of voter agendas and media coverage during the months preceding the 1972 presidential election in Charlotte, confirm but also amplify this impression (McCombs, 1976). Again, newspapers appeared to influence voter agendas throughout the campaign while television did not. By the end of the campaign, television was thoroughly in line in its news coverage with voter agendas, and this appeared to be the result of the medium's conforming to voter interest rather than either influencing it or following the earlier pattern of coverage of the newspaper, although at the very end of the campaign there was some slight evidence of influence on voter agendas by television.

These findings are consistent with those of other investigators. Tipton, Haney, and Baseheart (1975) directly attacked the causal problem of agenda-setting with a design comparing media and voter agendas in early fall with voter agendas in the final weeks of a gubernatorial campaign. The evidence for the direction of effect was quite mixed, but there were consistent strong correlations between the newspaper agendas and personal agendas. However, the correlations both across time and synchronously between television agendas and personal agendas were weak or even negative. This was the case even when the analysis was carried out separately for survey respondents who said they depended mainly on television for their political information. Similar findings of an agenda-setting effect for newspapers, but not television, have been reported by McClure and Patterson (1974) from their study of voters in Syracuse, New York during the 1972 presidential campaign and by Mullins (1973) from his study of young voters on the University of North Carolina campus during the 1972 election.

The importance of cumulative long-term media emphasis in developing the public's political agenda is demonstrated by a lack of agenda-setting when this factor is absent. The Ford-Carter debates during the 1976 presidential campaign were watched by huge television audiences, and in them the candidates stressed certain issues (e.g., the state of the economy) and ignored many others. But two studies by research groups that had previously contributed a good deal of evidence of agenda-setting effects could find no indication of agenda-setting as a consequence of the Ford-Carter debates (Becker, et al., 1977; McLeod, Durall, Ziemke and Bybee, 1977).

The differences between television and newspapers may extend beyond their influence on the public's ranking of issues. In addition to the salience of a topic, issue, or person, there is also the salience of their many attributes. To what extent is our view of a stimulus shaped or influenced by those attributes which the media deem newsworthy? For example, Paletz, Reichert, and McIntyre (1971) have argued that the public's view of the city council as an institution is strongly influenced by newspaper coverage with the result that these local governing groups are perceived to have more expertise and authority than in reality they possess.

Consideration of agenda-setting in terms of the saliences of topics and individuals and their attributes leads to the concept subsuming various related concepts. These include status-conferral, stereotyping, and image-making. Status-conferral denotes the prominence achieved among the public through attention from the media. Stereotyping refers to the heightening of the salience of certain attributes to the exclusion of others, with a resulting deemphasis of real-world variability. Image-making, now a part of political jargon, describes the manipulation of prominence and salience of various attributes of candidates and other public figures.

Two recent studies have documented the agenda-setting influence of the press on the perceived attributes of public issues as well as on the overall set of issues that are salient to voters. D. Cohen (1975) examined the attributes of a local environmental issue in Indiana while Benton and Frazier (1976) studied the salient attributes of a national issue, the economy, among Minneapolis residents.

Using three different measures to probe salient aspects of the local environment issue—development of a large lake area—D. Cohen (1975) found substantial correlations between all three measures of the public agenda and the coverage of the issue in the local newspaper.

Specifically comparing the agenda-setting influence of television and newspapers, Benton and Frazier (1976) conceptualized three levels of agenda-setting. At level 1 is a set of broad issues or topics. This is the focus of most research to date on agenda-setting. They instead focus on two more detailed and differentiated levels of an agenda for a single topic, the economy. These second and third levels constitute various attributes of the larger topic. At level 2 are subissues, including specific problems, causes, and proposed solutions. Examples are "inflation," "unemployment,"

"Arab oil prices," and "tax rebates." At level 3 is specific information about these subissues, such as arguments for or against the proposed solutions or people and groups connected with the proposed solutions.

Stratifying their respondents according to which medium, television or the newspaper, was their most important source of information about the economy, they found for level 2 a high correlation (.81) between the agenda of those for whom newspapers were the primary source and newspaper coverage but only a weak correlation (.27) between television coverage and the agenda of those for whom it was the primary source. At level 3, they again found a substantial correlation between the agenda and coverage among those relying on newspapers (.68) but a marginal correlation (.08) among those relying on television. In both instances, the pattern held even among those expressing greater agreement with the emphasis of the other medium.

In sum, newspapers were found to be more effective in influencing the agenda than television, and their effectiveness increased as the attributes under scrutiny became more detailed and differentiated. These findings certainly do not mean that television never influences the public's agenda, for there is evidence that it does (including the weak correlation in these data at level 2 of the agenda), but they do suggest, as do other data, that the influence of newspapers typically may be stronger—and especially so as the aspects of the agenda become more specific.

There are at least three potential explanations for these preliminary findings and they are not mutually exclusive:

The nature of the media competition in the city studied. Individual television stations and newspapers differ tremendously in the quality of their journalistic product. While the odds would seem to favor television in the match between television network news and local newspapers' coverage of national issues, the preliminary evidence contradicts this. In the match between television and newspaper coverage of local issues, the odds generally—but not always—would favor newspapers.

Audience variables. The audiences for television and newspapers differ on a large number of attributes. Any of these attributes—alone or in combination—might account for the differences in the agenda-setting effects.

The differing nature of the two media. We believe this is the principal explanation. Both McCombs and Shaw (1974) and McClure and Patterson (1974) have commented that some of the characteristics of television news may make it less efficient as a teacher of saliences. With print, each member of the audience can proceed at his own pace, rereading and thinking about the information if he desires. In contrast, television news is a rapid succession of similar items paraded in front of the viewer. Television's more constrained coverage also may be a factor. Television news is equivalent to a newspaper's front page. Once news is "front page," both newspapers and television offer audiences about the same opportunity to learn. But long before many topics make the front page, they begin to appear occasionally in the back pages of newspapers. So by the time both media present a stimulus for learning, newspaper readers already have a number of exposures behind them.

Major Contingent Conditions

No one would contend that agenda-setting operates at all times and all places on all people. If the agenda-setting influence were that universal, American housewives would talk incessantly about the brightness of their laundry.

One psychological concept which begins to explain each individual's focus of attention is "need for orientation" (McCombs, 1967), as suggested by the finding reported earlier that a relationship between media use and acknowledgment of Watergate as an issue was confined to persons for whom such a need was high (Weaver, McCombs, and Spellman, 1975). The underlying postulate is that exposure to the media is in part a function of individual factors making information useful or relevant.

Using data collected from a large sample of Charlotte voters during the 1972 presidential campaign, McCombs and Weaver (1973) found that extensive use of television and the other mass media to follow the campaign increased with the strength of need for orientation.* The greater the need for orientation, the greater use made of mass communication to learn about the campaign, candidates, and issues. Similarly, the higher the need for orientation, the higher the correlation between the voters' agenda of key issues and the television agenda of public issues. Again, the

* Need for orientation was defined in terms of level of interest in politics and level of uncertainty in selecting a candidate to vote for. Those with little interest in politics were defined as having low need for orientation. Among those with high interest, the level of uncertainty was used to identify moderate and high need. Those with high interest and low uncertainty were defined as having moderate need for orientation; those with high interest and high uncertainty were defined as having high need for orientation.

match with the voters was better for newspapers than for television, but there was evidence of agenda-setting by both media.

Another major variable on which the agenda-setting influence of television and newspapers may be contingent to some degree is the frequency politics is discussed with other people. However, the studies to date report contradictory results. McCombs, Shaw, and Shaw (1972) found that the agenda-setting relationship was strongest among Durham, North Carolina, voters with a low level of interpersonal communication. Mullins (1973) found that it was strongest among college students with a high level. We believe that the apparent contradiction, which is associated with differences in sample populations and operational definitions, will be resolved with the collection of additional data and further elaboration of the theory of agenda-setting.

We conclude that:

Television, as well as other mass media, influences the degree of attention the public gives to topics, persons, and symbols, thereby affecting the conduct and outcome of political activity. Television and other mass media also influence the public's perception of reality through selective emphasis on the various attributes of topics and persons in the news.

Television (although the medium sometimes and under some conditions has such effects) is less typically influential than the newspaper, because of the differing characteristics of the two media.

Learning from Television

Television, like other mass media, must compete with many other sources of political information—many of which are well entrenched prior to exposure to the television stimuli of a given campaign. One, interpersonal communication, makes extensive use of feedback; interpersonal messages can be calibrated for every recipient and recalibrated continuously for each recipient. No form of mass communication enjoys that flexibility. Given the powerful competition to mass media from these other sources, it is not surprising that, as we shall see, a change in attitude can only infrequently be unambiguously attributable to television.

A Different Reality

When we regard the acquisition of information and other cognitive changes as the dependent variables, we are in a realm where the competition for television and the other mass media is considerably less. Especially in the political and public affairs arena, mass communication has few competitors. As Lang and Lang (1959, 1968) observe, most of our political world is a second-hand reality conveyed to us by the mass media.

Few persons have any direct contact with the political leaders and issues of the day. How many have ever seen a President of the United States in person, much less held a conversation with him? Even on the lesser level of a congressman or state legislator, few constituents have any personal contact. Knowledge and perceptions of political figures and experience with politics are largely mediated by the mass media.

Television's great contribution to this second-hand reality is its ability to make us spectators for many significant political events. Millions of Americans have now witnessed a President deliver a State of the Union address, followed the weary proceedings of political conventions, and been brought dramatically close to the assassinations of President John Kennedy, Senator Robert Kennedy, and Rev. Martin Luther King. Television has enlarged the scope of our political experience by adding numerous objects for our potential observation. But while television has vastly increased the range of observation, it also has created distortions.

Like the human witness who must rearrange and edit the data passing through his sensory organs and brain, so must television and the other mass media shape the data they transmit (Meyer, 1972d). This is clearly the case for the news reporter who must selectively report to the audience what he or she has directly witnessed. But even the camera as a witness "rearranges" reality (Mandell and Shaw, 1973).

The comparison by Lang and Lang (1968) of television and eyewitness coverage of MacArthur Day in Chicago is the classic documentation of how the media may subtly influence what is perceived. General Douglas MacArthur visited Chicago for a speech after his dismissal in 1951 as commander of American forces in the Korean war by President Harry Truman. Thirty-one observers were stationed at various points from which events were televised: MacArthur's arrival at Midway Airport, his parade through the city and dedication of the Bataan-Corregidor Bridge, and his evening speech at Soldiers Field. Other observers followed the events as portrayed by television.

The impression given by television contrasted sharply with the experience of eyewitnesses. There was also a sharp difference between the attitudes of spectators and the way in which the attitudes were described on television. Those who watched on television experienced seething masses, an exuberant welcome, and a strong focus on the General. On television, the event was described as a celebration, a welcome, and an honoring. Those on the scene seemed to look upon it as a chance to participate in something exciting, and to see a famous man. The eyewitnesses perceived sparse-to-moderate crowds, more curiosity than a desire to welcome the General, and a very limited opportunity to see him.

The Langs speculate that the deviation of the televised account from the experience of those actually present is attributable to the conformity of the television coverage to expectations created beforehand by the media. They concluded that television does not convey reality, but structures it. They attribute this to: television's technological character, in which scenes must be ordered in some sequence and what is shown cast in foreground and background, based on the decisions of television personnel as to what is important; the announcer's structuring of an event, which ties the assorted visual perspectives together; and reciprocal effects, so that events themselves are modified to make them suitable for televising. There is a bias toward combinations of high appeal, since broadcasters want the largest audiences possible.

Acquiring Information

The occasions on which the media deliberately set out to persuade are a tiny portion of the set of messages produced daily. Most television programming, like most of the content of other mass media, is intended to inform and entertain, not persuade. Effects on knowledge and cognition thus would appear to be more pertinent dependent variables than changed attitudes.

Chaffee, Ward, and Tipton (1970) argue that the primary political function of the media is not to persuade, but to stimulate interest in political affairs and provide information about them. Clarke and Kline (1974) have also suggested that "what people learn from communicative activity is a more rewarding topic for media effects research than attitude formation or change." It was this shift in perspective among communication researchers from attitude change to cognitive effects which, among other things, generated the rapidly expanding program of research into the agenda-setting function of the media—research concerned wholly with the cognitive effects of the media.

Voters do acquire vast amounts of information from the mass media. Some illustrative data appear in table 7.3 from a study of the 1948 presidential campaign, before television was a factor. The same voters were queried before and after the campaign, and exposure to mass-media coverage of the campaign was measured. By the end of the campaign, those more exposed had more accurate perceptions of party stands on issues.

Table 7.3 Exposure to the Mass Media and Shifts in Political Knowledge During a Presidential Campaign

	Proportion of Respondents with High Knowledge[a] at End of Campaign Among Those Whose Media Exposure Was:			
Knowledge[a] at Beginning of Campaign	Higher		Lower	
	%	N	%	N
High	57	(173)[b]	43	(110)
High-Middle	58	(97)	21	(79)
Low-Middle	39	(85)	25	(81)
Low	33	(46)	5	(88)

SOURCE: Adapted from B. R. Berelson, P. F. Lazarsfeld, and W. N. McPhee. 1954. *Voting*. Chicago: University of Chicago Press.

[a] Knowledge = At beginning of campaign, measured by accuracy of perception of traditional voting trends within demographic groups, such as Catholics, the poor, etc. At end of campaign, by accuracy of perceptions of party stands on campaign issues. Figures are percentage with three or more accurate perceptions of party stands.

[b] ( ) = Number of respondents.

One plausible explanation is that media exposure was greater for the better informed. Another is that media exposure led to superior knowledge. In fact, both seem to occur. Those better informed prior to the campaign tended to be higher in media exposure during the campaign. However, within each level of precampaign knowledge, those higher in media exposure had greater end-of-compaign knowledge. In short, the strong association between media exposure and knowledge is partly explained by the contribution of the media to knowledge.

Similar findings occur for studies dealing with post-television politics. Trenaman and McQuail (1961) found that voters with the greatest amount of exposure to television in the 1959 British general election were most likely to know where the candidates stood on different issues. However, in the United States, Patterson and McClure (1976) found no difference among Syracuse, New York, voters between those who watched evening network news and those who did not (during the 1972 election) in knowledge of the presidential candidates' stands on issues. The divergence in findings is probably attributable to the extensive political content of British Broadcasting Corporation's election-period programming and the more limited political coverage of network news in the United States. Network news, as we pointed out earlier (chapter 2), probably suffers in informativeness by its emphasis on the visual and the dramatic. On the other hand, Patterson and McClure found that exposure to television advertising for the candidates led to significant learning of their positions on issues—succinct, explicit associations of candidates with positions by television portrayal can increase at least rudimentary political knowledge.

Numerous variables obviously enter into this learning process. Those with greater initial information and interest typically attend more to political content on television, and are thus exposed to a greater quantity of information from which learning may ensue. Those with lesser information and interest are more likely to encounter information new to them. Sometimes exposure means learning of information supportive of predispositions and previously made decisions, but certainly this is not invariably the case. DeVries and Tarrance (1972) present a variety of evidence that use of television for political information is especially vital among independent voters and ticket-splitters.

Certainly a great deal of incidental learning occurs as people watch television. Even those with only peripheral interest in politics inadvertently acquire some political information from television (Converse, 1962). And between elections television documentaries on social issues are powerful teachers of public affairs information for those interested enough to view (Fitzsimmons and Osburn, 1968).

Measuring the Impact of Mass Media

The early research into the relationship between a voter's store of knowledge and use of mass media depends heavily on the introspective replies of survey respondents. This line of inquiry and its findings are summarized in Wade and Schramm's (1969) massive secondary analysis of knowledge items from national surveys conducted during the 1950s and 1960s. For public affairs information during presidential campaigns the proportion of voters naming newspapers as their principal source held constant at about 25 percent between 1952 and 1964. But the proportion of people naming television increased dramatically from 1952 to 1960 and then leveled off. In 1960 and 1964, the proportion naming television had climbed to over 50 percent. This reflects the increasing availability of television as an information medium during that period and, again, its ability to deliver a large audience for political messages.

However, this growth in attention to television does not reflect new interest in political communication attributable to the medium. Television drew off the radio audience for political communication (McCombs and Wilcox, 1968). The data are displayed in figure 7.2. Television's net increase in the proportion of people naming it as their major source of political information is the approximate mirror image of those naming radio. More interesting is the comparison of the increased proportion naming television with the increase in proportion of television households. While the proportion of people naming television as their primary source of information increased 26 percentage points between 1952 and 1964, the proportion of television households increased 53 percentage points, from 37 percent in 1952 to 90 percent in 1964. The primary reason, of course, that television did not keep pace is that acquisition of a television did not mean abandonment of the newspaper as a news source, and sets were appearing in more and more households whose interest in politics was only marginal.

There are two questions to ask about the use of various media for public affairs information: which is the preferred medium or most frequent source of political information? and which medium is used most often? Since most Americans use a variety of public affairs information sources, both topics must be pursued.

For both, television has the larger audience. But the demographic composition of its audience does depend on the question asked. If one is simply asking about use of various mass media to follow politics, then about 70 percent of American adults from all demographic groups make regular use of television for informa-

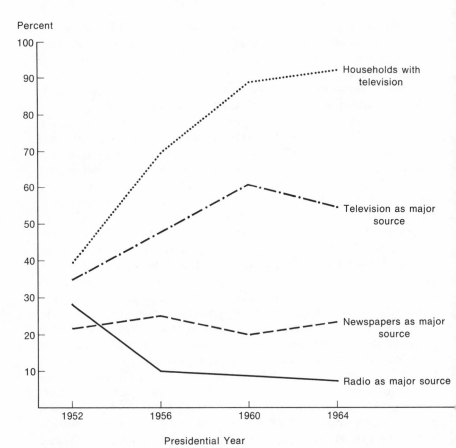

Percent

Figure 7.2. Major sources of information during presidential election campaigns cited by national samples, 1952–1964.

SOURCE: Adapted from M. E. McCombs and W. Wilcox. 1968. Media use in presidential election campaigns. In C. Bush (ed.), *News Research for Better Newspapers,* vol. 3. Washington, D.C.: American Newspaper Publishers Association, pp. 36–39.

tion on campaigns, candidates, and issues. However, when interest centers on the most frequent source of public affairs information, television is most likely to be the source named by people with lower education, females, nonwhites, and farm and blue-collar workers. Newspapers are named with greater frequency and often are found to be the most frequently used source among the highly educated, whites, males, professional, managerial, and white-collar workers, and high-income groups. Regardless of these demographic differences, however, television is the major source of information during political campaigns for the majority of the public.

These findings are based on each respondent's ability to recall and characterize his aggregate use of various mass media as sources of information. Such measures of information acquisition from mass media ostensibly reflect the learning of dozens of discrete items from various media across lengthy and often unspecified periods of time, and are limited in their revelatory power by the dependence on the accuracy and completeness of an individual's knowledge of his sources of information.

There have been many attempts to measure the level of public information directly by eliciting specific factual knowledge, such as the name of the local congressman or the definitions of such terms as "veto" and "filibuster." Correct answers are typically correlated both with amount of exposure to the media and level of education, with the relationship with education strongest.

However, the investigator in such instances is to some degree imposing a formal conception of public affairs knowledge on a probably much more variegated phenomenon. What is required to study the true range and depth of public knowledge is a representative sample of the information held by individuals. Most of the early research fails to meet this standard.

Recent research has thus turned to more respondent-centered approaches. One such technique (Edelstein, 1973) allows the respondent to pose the topic that will be further examined in regard to his state of knowledge and related use of mass media. Another technique is based on message recall (Clarke and Kline, 1974; Miller, Morrison, and Kline, 1974). Replies are elicited about the varied information on a topic recalled from use of a specific media during a specified span of time. Type and number of specific messages "discriminated" or recalled by the individual can be compared for the various mass media across different periods of time.

Using this technique, Clarke and Palmgreen (1974) found that the amount of message discrimination explained substantially more of the variance in knowledge of local issues than did the respondent's level of education. Most previous research—using gross measures of media use—had found education to be the prime predictor of knowledge. For knowledge of national issues, message discriminations and level of education independently explained about equal anounts of variance. Related research by Palmgreen, Kline, and Clarke (1974) in addition found that recall of newspapers was greater than for television for local coverage, but that recall of television was greater than for newspapers for national issues.

In sum, we conclude that:

Television alters political reality by the act of portraying it, and the reality it creates is partially a unique contribution of television because its portrayals differ from those of other mass media.

Television is a major source of information about politics despite its apparent failure to increase public interest in politics.

The recent trend toward trying to measure information acquisition in terms employed by the media consumer suggests that reliance on the mass media for information has been underestimated in the past.

Television and Voting

Politics in America and the Ultimate Mass Medium

Television made its political debut in the United States in the 1952 presidential election. In the presidential contest four years before, only a very few homes had television, but by 1952, the figure was about one out of three. Moreover, these households were those whose occupants were more likely to vote than the average citizen. Like the bulk of regular voters, early television set owners came disproportionately from upper socioeconomic classes. Among the voting population the availability of television was much more widespread than statistics for the general population would suggest. For example, among a panel of midwestern voters studied in 1952, over three-fourths owned sets (Miami University, 1954).

Both the Republican and Democratic national conventions were broadcast in their time-consuming and often monotonous entirety. Millions of American voters obtained their first glimpses of the political party process (Cranston, 1960). The 1952 election also marked the debut of the television political commercial.

Politics was now televised, and the basis was established for widespread and still persistent belief in the efficacy of television for delivering votes to a candidate. This belief has created a new kind of mass communicator, the image-maker. Although the pioneer California image merchants Whitaker and Baxter date from the pretelevision era (Kelley, 1956), image-making became a sought after and talked about activity only with the use of television in political campaigning (Chester, 1969; Hiebert, 1971; Mendelsohn and Crespi, 1970; Nimmo, 1970; B. Rubin, 1967).

There is no question that television reshaped the conduct of national politics in America. Our principal concern here is with its direct influence on the voter.

CRYSTALLIZATION AND REINFORCEMENT. For many Americans, politics does not arouse great fervor. On those rare occasions when it does—such as at the Democratic convention in Chicago in 1968 or on many college campuses during the 1960s—most Americans are appalled. Other historical and continuing indicators of politics' low salience for the average citizen are the low turnout rates for American national elections compared to those in many nations; and the existence of two predominant political parties each encompassing almost the entire spectrum of political beliefs rather than the multiple parties each representing fairly distinct beliefs, which is the pattern in many countries. Men may argue over whether football or baseball is the great American pastime; few persons would contend that it is politics. Indeed, between presidential elections the flicker of political partisanship is barely discernible among a majority of Americans.

Two terms occur frequently in discussions of political communication:

Crystallization—the sharpening and elaboration of cognitive and affective elements relating to a particular topic, person, or symbol in a manner such that future cognitive, affective, and behavioral responses are consistent with the less embellished initial disposition.

Reinforcement—the receipt of information that strengthens the affective response to a particular topic, person, or symbol.

Political campaigns seek to hold the typical adherents of a party while attracting additional support from independents and undecideds. To win, a candidate usually must attract a significant portion of these relatively unaligned voters. The political campaign is a communications package—and television has been a key component since 1952—designed to achieve these goals of party mobilization and attraction of the unaligned (Dawson and Zinser, 1971; Nimmo, 1970).

Many feared that the introduction of television into political campaigns would lead to easy manipulation of the public. This was an extension of the concern over the influence of mass media that long preceded the appearance of television (Smith, 1973). However, neither television nor other mass media before television have been found to result in mass political conversion. The two major studies of political behavior and mass communication prior to television—the 1940 Erie County study (Lazarsfeld, Berelson, and Gaudet, 1948) and the 1948 Elmira, New York, study (Berelson, Lazarsfeld, and McPhee, 1954)—both found minimal shifts from one political camp to another during presidential campaigns. As Joseph Klapper (1960) summed up the pretelevision research: "The tendency of mass communication to reinforce rather than convert has . . . been documented by various . . . studies, and in reference to communications on political and nonpolitical topics."

This pattern continued in 1952 with television very much present in the campaign. Simon and Stern (1955) examined the aggregate impact of television on both voter turnout and party choice in Iowa where, because of a freeze on new television stations then in effect, only one-third of the counties were in range of strong television signals. They compared 30 Iowa counties where 50 percent or more of the families had a television set with the 68 counties where less than half had television. No difference was found in the two sets of counties for either turnout or percentage of the vote going to the Republicans and Democrats. Campbell, Gurin, and Miller (1954) in a national study found only 4 percent of the voters shifting from one side to the other during the campaign; the shifts were self-cancelling with 2 percent shifting each way.

Similar noneffects of exposure to television on voting intentions were found in a study of the 1959 British general election by Trenaman and McQuail (1961). There was no evidence that the viewing of party broadcasts affected either the *vote* or the *attitudes* of voters toward the Labour and the Conservative parties. There was a marked shift toward the Conservative Party during the campaign, but exposure to political content in the mass media was unrelated to that shift. The lack of association was so striking that the authors refer to the presence in voters' minds of a "barrier between sources of communication and movements of attitude in the political field at the General Election."

The findings of Mendelsohn and O'Keefe (1976) on voter behavior during the 1972 presidential campaign do not dispel the impression of a lack of extraordinary shifting in voting decisions as a consequence of exposure to the mass media. However, this painstaking examination of a panel of more than 600 voters in Summit County, Ohio, interviewed at five different points during the campaign successfully elaborates and qualifies the conclusions that would be drawn from earlier studies.

There was no evidence that marked shifts among voters were attributable to either television or newspapers. The impression of media insignificance that cursory examination of the earlier studies might give is nevertheless sharply altered. Television was consistently cited by voters throughout the campaign as the medium most relied upon to follow the campaign; it was the primary source of convention coverage, and remained most relied upon in subsequent weeks. About half of all voters ranked television first throughout the campaign, with about a third citing newspapers, and a minute 5 percent citing interpersonal communication. Exposure to news of the Eagleton resignation as George McGovern's running mate and the Watergate break-in did not appear to affect voting decisions. Nevertheless, various events during the campaign were described by subsets of voters as influential; one of the more significant was the announcement just before election day of a possible Vietnam ceasefire, which was cited by one-sixth of the sample as having some influence. Typically, influence appeared to consist either of reinforcement or crystallization of views already held, although some mind-changing occurred.

The data give little justification for assuming that the media play an insignificant role. Besides the declarations by voters of reliance on the media, the favorability of the image held of the candidate and agreement with the candidate on issues, both factors for which the media are likely to be principal sources, were positively and sizably related to voting decisions.

Crystallization and reinforcement, but not change and conversion, are the effects typically corroborated by scientific evidence. As a result, by the late 1950s many scientists were inclined to accept the law of minimal consequences as the correct statement of the influence of television on politics. This view ignored the possibility that television typically may be more effective as teacher and informant than persuader. For example, British party broadcasts in 1959 resulted in voters with more accurate information about party policies, if not in changed votes (Blumler and McQuail, 1969). The data are displayed in table 7.4. Exposure to party telecasts was associated with initial levels of political knowledge, but exposure also was associated with gains in knowledge during the campaign. The implied precampaign involvement in politics has typically been found to be associated with exposure to political communication during the campaign. However, we also see that such exposure apparently leads to the acquisition of political knowledge.

Table 7.4 Exposure to Political Telecasts and Information Gain in the 1959 British Election

	Number of Party Telecasts Viewed				
	0 (N = 191)	1–3 (N = 142)	4–6 (N = 192)	7–9 (N = 136)	10-plus (N = 87)
Average number of party policies identified correctly before the campaign	1.61	1.79	2.15	2.32	2.16
Average gain in correct identification over the campaign	.28	.37	.71	.66	.49

SOURCE: Adapted from J. G. Blumler and D. McQuail. 1969. *Television in Politics.* Chicago: University of Chicago Press.

It is important not to mistake crystallization and reinforcement for conversion, or the reverse. Substantial correlations between television exposure and ballot decisions are quite common, and could indicate either. For example, in one 1952 study about two-thirds of voters who viewed over half of Stevenson's television appearances during the convention and campaign voted for him, while three-fourths of those who viewed half or more of Eisenhower's appearances voted for him (Miami University, 1954).

The temptation to dismiss such findings as entirely reflecting crystallization and reinforcement is somewhat tempered by the sample's fulsome declaration of influence by television. Sixty-two percent said that television was more influential for them than newspapers, magazines, family and friends, or radio. Given the large proportion of voters that typically reaches a decision by the end of a convention, the correct interpretation, consistent with the findings of Mendelsohn and O'Keefe (1976), is probably not that television markedly altered the outcome of their decisions but that it supplied information evaluated as useful.

THE MEDIUM OF ATTENTION. Television may be the ultimate *mass* medium. It delivers a huge national audience for a single message. Radio undeniably was first to reach a proportionately huge national audience with the same message, but as the replacement of radio by television as the nation's principal source of diversion indicates (chapter 4) radio lacks the audience appeal of the audio-visual medium. Newspapers carry relatively standardized political coverage from the wire services, but the presentation and wording differ from paper to paper.

During television's major political debut at the 1952 conventions, at least three speeches during the Republican and two during the Democratic conventions gained huge national audiences. Overall, the television convention audience was three times larger than either the radio or newspaper audience for the same information.

Given the cyclical rise and fall of the salience of politics for most Americans, the nominating convention is a major factor in restoring that salience and lining up the first major bloc of voters for each candidate. By bringing their pageantry into millions of homes, television has heightened the role of the conventions, and although the repetitiveness from convention to convention and the frequency with which the nominee is predictable before the convention begins may eventually mitigate their impact on public attention, such effects of familiarity to some degree will be offset by the continual addition of inexperienced young voters to the audience, the common interest of the networks and the parties in making coverage interesting, and the invariable suspense about the presidential nominee's running mate. Among American voters, in the typical election some half to two-thirds have made an unalterable decision by the close of the nominating conventions. By the end of the televised convention, the candidate is well on his way. This sendoff is important not only because of the large number of commitments already made, but also because the television audience for politics often declines sharply after the convention and remains small until about ten days before the election.

The fact that most voter decisions take place either during the conventions or during the last ten days of the campaign would appear to suggest some impact for television. These are the two periods in which television delivers its political messages to the largest audiences. During the initial wave of decision-making, television's effect may simply be to stimulate the salience of politics and, as a byproduct, reactivate the voters' partisan predispositions. This is consistent with the high correlations usually found between party identifications and the many voting decisions made in this period. But since the correlation is only slight for the final days of the campaign, it is not so clear how television's influence works in that period.

Part of the conventional wisdom of political advertising is the belief that raising public awareness of a candidate is almost tantamount to winning the election. There are ample political anecdotes about initially obscure and unknown candidates who won election following massive spending on television advertising (Barrett, 1970). Beyond such folk wisdom, there is some scientific evidence that repeated exposure to a stimulus—candidate's name, photograph, slogan, or whatever—results in increased positive affect toward the stimulus. There have been studies by Zajonc and his colleagues that used photographs (Crandall, 1972; Saegert, Swap, and Zajonc, 1973; Zajonc, 1968; Zajonc and Rajecki, 1969) and by Chaffee (1967a, 1967b) that used words in a puzzle, and by Rajecki and Wolfson (1973) that used nonsense syllables in mailed brochures. All found higher ratings for the items appearing most frequently before the subjects.

But there is a caveat in generalizing these experimental findings to the political arena. In an experiment by Rothschild and Ray (1974) dealing specifically with political advertisements, an effect of message repetition on voting intentions was found in only one of the three test campaigns, with the effect limited to less important offices. In another experiment, Becker and Doolittle (1975), using simulated radio political spot ads as a stimulus, found a curvilinear relationship between frequency of exposure and both positive attitudes toward the candidates named and desire for more information about candidates; positive attitudes and the desire for information were greater for those with low or high rather than medium exposure.

Blumler and McQuail (1969) found that the upsurge in Liberal Party support during the 1964 British general election were powerfully assisted by exposure to the party broadcasts during the campaign. Under the British system the parties are allocated a generous portion of television time—13 broadcasts by the three parties during the 17 days of the 1964 campaign—and these programs appear simultaneously on all channels. In 1964, the Liberal Party offered a larger field of candidates than in previous elections and so was entitled to a much larger share of broadcast time. Blumler and McQuail offer a variety of evidence that this greater exposure on television for the Liberal Party is the major explanation for its gains. Particularly, these effects were greatest among those whose motivation for following the political campaign was medium or weak. In other words, for the peripherally involved, exposure *per se* can have persuasive effects.

The balanced coverage given by television in the United States to the Democratic and Republican conventions tends to equate the benefits derived by one or the other of the presidential nominees from public exposure to these party events. Nevertheless, the role of such exposure in stimulating partisanship and reinforcing predispositions means that discordant events or inept behavior associated with the conventions may leave one party in a more favorable position precisely because of the extensive coverage. Many observers believe that Democratic support was seriously weakened by the rioting, made dramatic by television, at the 1968 convention in Chicago. George McGovern was certainly not helped in 1972 when party wrangling delayed his acceptance speech past prime time, thus depriving him of the large audience that had been ready to hear him.

Television can confer status on contenders for the nominations. It can help to create apparent frontrunners. But unless other factors—the efficiency of the candidate's campaign organization or uncontrollable occurrences—all favorably converge, the status conferred by television and the other mass media will not be sufficient to secure the nomination. In 1952, the earlier televised Senate crime hearings had catapulted Estes Kefauver into the race for the Democratic nomination, but he did not secure it. Similarly, in 1972 the media treated Edmund Muskie as the frontrunner for the Democratic Presidential nomination but he fell by the wayside.

Once the nomination is secured, any previous status-conferral is an important asset. In 1952, Eisenhower was well known at the outset of the campaign. Stevenson had to catch up, and never did. Yet initial prominence is no guarantor of victory. Eight years later John Kennedy overtook the better-known Richard Nixon— possibly with the help of their televised debates.

But beyond this first elementary step in the process of winning office—making a candidate's name known to the public—

what specific influences can be attributed to television? The initial impact of television and the other mass media in a political campaign lies in their ability to raise the salience of politics and reactivate and reinforce those partisan predispositions which lie latent in most Americans between elections. The process is illustrated in tables 7.5 and 7.6. We use these data, which are from the 1948 presidential election (in which television was not a factor) because they make their two points so well. Table 7.5 deals with interest in politics; table 7.6 deals with degree of support for a candidate. In both cases, exposure to the mass media during the campaign was associated with greater interest and support at the end of the campaign. We are inclined to attribute this to the influence of the press, because it holds true even when initial interest and support were held constant. Thus, the association cannot be fully explained by those initially high in interest or support seeking out greater exposure during the campaign. For example,

Table 7.5 Mass Media Exposure During a Presidential Campaign and Level of Political Interest

Level of Political Interest at End of Campaign	Level of Political Interest at Beginning of Campaign					
	Great Deal		Quite a Lot		Not Much or None	
Mass Media Exposure:	Higher (N = 192)	Lower (N = 81)	Higher (N = 143)	Lower (N = 133)	Higher (N = 63)	Lower (N = 137)
Great deal	68	42	34	24	10	6
Quite a lot	27	31	53	46	19	20
Not much or none	5	27	13	30	71	74

SOURCE: Adapted from B. R. Berelson, P. F. Lazarsfeld, and W. N. McPhee. 1954. *Voting.* Chicago: University of Chicago Press.

Table 7.6 Mass Media Exposure During a Presidential Campaign and Degree of Support

Degree of Support at End of Campaign	Degree of Support at Beginning of Campaign					
	Very Strong		Fairly Strong		Neutral	
Mass Media Exposure:	Higher (N = 194)	Lower (N = 109)	Higher (N = 166)	Lower (N = 155)	Higher (N = 41)	Lower (N = 94)
Very strong	80	68	36	22	15	5
Fairly strong	13	16	57	54	29	12
Neutral	7	16	7	24	56	83

SOURCE: See Table 7.5.

among those expressing a "great deal" of interest and "very strong" support at the beginning of the campaign, those with greater media exposure were more likely to maintain such dispositions near its end. In both cases, too, higher interest and greater support at the beginning were associated with greater exposure to mass media coverage during the campaign. This illustrates one of the restrictions on the prowess of the mass media—they are more likely to reach those already involved in an endeavor.

Since television commands huge audiences, large numbers of peripherally involved citizens—including the majority among the poor, both black and white—are exposed to its political messages. While the empirical evidence is still limited, we believe that television is the major source of information and influence among these groups. Television is equally available to all the American population regardless of social class. In surveys of three eastern and midwestern cities, B. S. Greenberg and Dervin (1970, 1973) found no difference in access to television among low-income adults and a general population sample of adults, but the low-income adults spent far more time viewing television and reported much greater reliance on television news. Low-income blacks and whites were highly similar across a variety of variables except that blacks relied more on television news while a higher proportion of low-income whites regularly read a newspaper. The implication of this high and relatively uniform degree of exposure to television, a departure from the positive relationship between socioeconomic status and use of print media, is that television probably brings about some degree of public awareness of politics that otherwise would not occur.

The hypothesis of selective exposure, which holds that persons seek out supportive or confirming content and avoid discrepant information, has not been strongly supported for political communication in the mass media (Atkin and Heald, 1976; McCombs, 1972; Mendelsohn and O'Keefe, 1976; M. J. Robinson and Burgess, 1970; Sears and Freedman, 1967; Shaw and Bowers, 1973; Sheinkopf, O'Keefe, and Meeske, 1973; Surlin and Gordon, 1974). Weiss (1969) is probably correct that the balanced journalistic coverage extended by the mass media to the two major parties ensures that most voters are exposed to considerable information that is not particularly supportive of and often is inconsistent with their political views and allegiances. As we point out shortly, selectivity has little chance to operate in the case of televised political commercials because of the brief and unpre-

dictable nature of exposure, and the relative universality of exposure to television further argues that it would be even more immune to the influence of selective exposure than print media.

Easy access to television also increases the likelihood that it
will have an important role as political groups move into the
mainstream. During the 1950s and 1960s the Civil Rights Movement ushered in dramatic increases in political activity among
blacks. Parallel to increases in voter registration, turnout, and
membership in political organizations, McCombs (1968) found
sizable increases among blacks in the use of mass communication, especially the use of television. Using time-series
data constructed from the national presidential year surveys of
the University of Michigan Survey Research Center, table 7.7

Table 7.7 Use of Television and Newspapers To Follow Politics, By Race
(1952–1964)

| | Percent Users by Presidential Year | | | |
| | 1952 | | 1960 | |
Media Use Pattern	Black (N = 171)	White (N = 1728)	Black (N = 172)	White (N = 1782)
High television, high newspaper users	9	23	11	28
Low television, low newspaper users	63	29	56	34
High newspaper, low television users	11	18	17	19
High television, low newspaper users	17	30	11	19

| | 1964 | | Percent Change | |
	Black (N = 159)	White (N = 1411)	Black	White
High television, high newspaper users	19	23	+10	0
Low television, low newspaper users	41	41	−22	+12
High newspaper, low television users	13	18	+2	0
High television, low newspaper users	27	18	+10	−12

SOURCE: Adapted from M. E. McCombs, 1968. Negro use of television and
newspapers for political information, 1952–1964. *Journal of Broadcasting,* 12,
261–66.

shows that the majority of blacks (63 percent) were low media users in 1952. But in 1964 only 41 percent of the blacks remained in the low-media-use group (low use of both television and newspapers to follow politics). Among those who had shifted, 20 percent became high television users and only 12 percent became high newspaper users. We can speculate why newspapers did not share equally in the increase. As awareness of politics develops, television is most likely the medium turned to first because it already is available. Using a television set for political information is a far simpler act than reading a newspaper. As the appetite for political information increases, it is likely that the newspaper is added as a second source of information.

Images and Issues

The mass media influence perceptions of candidates, shaping the images of the contenders in the public mind. Because of its live, pictorial character, and because it emphasizes the personal, the visual, and the emotional, the contribution of television to these images in the public mind is probably greater than that of newspapers, magazines, or radio (Keating, 1972). We have also seen that the mass media influence voters on issues, and particularly their agenda of issues meriting priority where the effect of newspapers generally appears to be greater than that of television.

We know that in most instances, the ballot to be cast in November is consistent with earlier party predispositions. When such party affiliation is a key variable, we sould assume that television contributes elements to the voter's cognitive and affective responses to the candidates which are largely consonant with those held before. However, for some voters the situation is very different.

Among voters reaching a decision during the course of a campaign there is a declining correlation between ballot choice and party identification. For those deciding in the final two weeks of the campaign, the correlation is about zero, partly because these persons have very weak or shifting party ties. This progressive decrease in the consistency of voting decisions and predispositions means that there is opportunity for television and other mass media to influence voters directly.

There is no convincing evidence available on the influence of television or other mass media on such late deciders. When the proportion of undecided and wavering voters in the late stages of the campaign is as large as it was in 1976 (national polls found as many as half the electorate uncertain shortly before election day) the effects of the media may be sizable (Lucas and Adams, 1977).

When late deciders are relatively few—in 1972 perhaps 12 percent of the electorate—the opportunity for the media to affect them is limited because in such cases this small minority tends to be low in political awareness, attention, and interest and less exposed to campaign coverage in newspapers and television (Mendelsohn and O'Keefe, 1976).

There are two conflicting points of view about the origins of voters' images of political personalities. They differ in regard to the degree that candidate images can be described as perceiver-determined or stimulus-determined. The first emphasizes the degree to which the cognitive pictures of candidates held by voters are a function of the attributes of the voter. The second emphasizes the degree to which the mass media shape such pictures.

These conflicting views both reflect interpretations of the various theories of cognitive balance (Festinger, 1957; Heider, 1958; Newcomb, 1953), which posit a drive to achieve consistency among cognitive elements. From the perceiver-determined viewpoint, new stimuli pertinent to images are said to be interpreted in accord with the partisan affiliation and position on issues of the receiver with little or no shift in basic disposition. From the stimulus-determined viewpoint, new stimuli are considered to be capable of establishing a set of cognitions somewhat independent of prior predispositions so that the resulting image may exert pressure for a shift.

The empirical evidence is quite mixed. In the 1960 presidential election McGrath and McGrath (1962) found that Young Democrats and Young Republicans agreed in assigning Kennedy and Nixon to opposite ends of semantic differential scales on 29 of the 50 attributes measured. However, Sigel (1964) challenged their conclusion that perceptions of political figures are stimulus-determined rather than perceiver-determined, arguing that the attributes measured were not highly relevant ones likely to produce psychological stress when nonconsonant with other political cognitions. Sigel presented data, also from the 1960 election, showing that Democrats were more likely than Republicans to assign traits to Kennedy corresponding to their own image of an ideal President. Distinguishing between political and personal components of candidate images, she concluded that the political traits were perceiver-determined, while personal traits, such as person-

ality and appearance, were stimulus-determined and open to influence from television and other sources.

In the 1964 British general election Blumler and McQuail
(1969) compared shifts in party attitudes and candidate images.
Despite the general tendency for candidate ratings to go with
party attitudes, which supports the perceiver-determined viewpoint, there was an important exception. On the cluster of scales
connoting strength of leadership, supporters of the three contending parties shifted their images of the three party leaders in
the same way and to the same extent, which is strong evidence
for the stimulus-determined position. Furthermore, exposure to
television news was significantly associated with these changes
in images of candidate strength.

We are not surprised by these apparent conflicts. The preliminary empirical evidence makes it clear that there are some circumstances when the best prediction of the outcome of exposure
to the mass media will be based on characteristics of the stimuli
and others when it will be based on characteristics of the per-
ceiver. The question for future research is the nature of the circumstances on which effects are contingent.

There are a number of trends in the United States that increase the likelihood that television and other mass media will influence voting in the future through effects on issues and images.
The potency of party identification as a predictor of ballot choice
has been declining over recent elections (Dreyer, 1971; Nie,
Verba, and Petrocik, 1976). One study (Nie, Verba, and Petrocik,
1976) found that between 1960 and 1964, the correlation between
identification with a party and support for the party's candidate
dropped noticeably (from .49 to .39), and in 1972 was negligible
(.14), while the correlation between voter agreement with a candidate on issues and favorable evaluation of a candidate was substantial in 1960 (.47) and increased in 1964 and 1972 (.56).

These trends reflect a decline in party-oriented partisanship
that implies a reduction in the role of television as a reinforcer of
predispositions, because there are fewer precommitted voters for
whom reinforcement would be relevant. A major result has been
the greater influence of issues on the vote, another has probably
been an increase in the potential role of candidate image. The
roles of both image issues were apparently sizable in the Summit
County (Ohio) study of the 1972 election, although image appeared to have somewhat greater influence in this instance (Mendelsohn and O'Keefe, 1976). The Summit County data suggest

that issues and image were decisive in 1972; for McGovern, party was described by supporters as a major factor, while for Nixon, party was said to be minor and issues and image figured more prominently. Given the predominant Democratic registration in the United States, the implication is that in 1972 party allegiance failed to hold those favorably oriented toward the Democratic party from the stronger appeal of the Nixon image and his stand on issues on which voters perceived the two candidates to differ. The weight of particular factors is obviously highly independent on the singular characteristics of each election. Data on the Ford-Carter debates, to be reviewed shortly, do not suggest that image figured overwhelmingly in their impact on voter choice, although it played some role. Other data, however, indicate that the use of television news to verify impressions of candidate image was very important for the unusual number of undecided and wavering voters in this campaign (Lucas and Adams, 1977), although the analyses available to date do not indicate whether this reliance on television for information on images altered in any way the choices that might have been expected on the basis of prior party preferences or socioeconomic and other demographic factors.

We have speculated that certain characteristics of television may make its influence different from that of other mass media. We would not want to give the impression that its prowess is strongly independent of the size of the audience attracted. In the data from that 1952 election when television was first a factor, about the same proportion—between 35 and 40 percent—reported increased positive feelings about Eisenhower after the convention whether they had followed his nomination on television, in the newspapers, or by radio (Miami University, 1954). Patterson and McClure (1976) found no indication that evening network television news contributed to voters' images of the candidates or to their knowledge of the issues. In line with the findings of Graber (1971) and McCombs and Shaw (1972) from the 1968 campaign, they found television's political world dominated by campaign events and speculation over the winners, with little attention to issues. They also found that political commercials on television, which do often present the positions of candidates, if one-sidedly, primarily increased the level of information among television viewers who paid little attention to newspaper coverage of the campaign. These findings, as do many of the others we have reviewed, suggest the quite sensible conclusion that any impact of television is to a large degree a function of the size and breadth of its audience rather than of any particular prowess inhering in a televised message.

The Debates

NIXON-KENNEDY IN 1960. Television made its political debut in 1952. Only eight years later came some of the most dramatic political telecasts of all time—the four television confrontations between Richard M. Nixon and John F. Kennedy. These debates became one of the most studied events in the history of television and politics. One collation shows there were 31 different, independent investigations of their effect on the election (Kraus, 1962).

The debates, carried simultaneously by all three networks, demonstrate the ability of television to assemble a national audience for a political message. The first drew 75 million—the largest audience up to that time in television history. For the next three, the audience fluctuated between 60 and 70 million. By the end of the series, more than 100 million individuals had seen one or more debates (Brown, 1977).

What kind of impact did these debates have on voters? As in previous elections, a sizable proportion of the voting population had already made their decision by the date for the first debate. A Michigan Survey Research Center post-election survey found that 60 percent of voters declared that they had made up their minds by the time of the election. Such a retrospective measure may be quite imprecise, but it leaves little doubt about sizable early decision-making. Any conclusions about who won each debate, about the images of the candidates created, and about attitudes formed or swayed must be qualified to take into account the large numbers of voters likely to build consonant cognitions around their already selected choice. However, more than reinforcement occurred. Carter and Sebald (Carter, 1962; Katz and Feldman, 1962) both found that significant learning took place. There was factual learning about candidates' stands on the issues and there were changes in the salience of the issues. These effects of the debates parallel the television effects found by Trenaman and McQuail (1961) a year earlier in the British general election.

Katz and Feldman (1962), who analyzed the 31 individual studies of the debates, concluded that there was not much evidence of change of attitude or opinion on issues but that the image or public perception of the candidates had been affected.

Democrats reported that their image of Kennedy had improved more often than Republicans reported an improvement in their image of Nixon; Republicans became more favorable to Kennedy than Democrats did to Nixon; and independents moved more toward Kennedy than toward Nixon. In short, cognitions related to image seem both to have crystallized and to have reinforced positive attitudes toward Kennedy more so than for Nixon. This interpretation is buttressed by the additional finding that strength of commitment increased during the debates more among Democrats than among Republicans. Nevertheless, about half of the respondents in the various studies reported no change at all in their images of the two presidential contenders, although of course such self-reports would ignore changes of which the respondents themselves were unaware.

To assess the overall persuasive impact of the debates on the presidential vote of 1960, we shall examine the political context in which the debates occurred. In table 7.8, we see that a trend toward Kennedy-Johnson slowly built up during August and early September (August 17–September 14). Then, in the Gallup Poll taken on the eve of the first debate, the Kennedy trend wavered (September 25). Kennedy-Johnson dropped two percentage points and stood one point behind their Republican opposition.

In the post-debate poll, however, their strength increased by three points while Nixon lost a point (October 12). This appeared

Table 7.8 The Kennedy-Nixon Debates in 1960 and the Trend of Political Support

Gallup Poll Release Date	Percent Saying How They Would Vote, "If the election were held today . . ."[a]		
	Kennedy	Nixon	Undecided
August 17	44	50	6
August 31	47	47	6
September 14	48	47	5
September 25	46	47	7
October 12	49	46	5
October 26	48	48	4
November 4	51	45	4
November 7	49	48	3
Actual vote	50.1	49.9	

SOURCE: Adapted from E. Katz and J. J. Feldman. 1962. The debates in the light of research: A survey of surveys. In S. Kraus (ed.), *The Great Debates*. Bloomington: Indiana University Press, p. 211.

[a] Results include those registered and intending to vote. *N* varied from 1500 to 8000.

to reestablish the Democratic trend. Did the first televised debate—which the evidence indicates the public believed Kennedy won—decide the election?

We may treat the September 25–October 12 Gallup Polls as a before-after measurement of the first debate's effect. When we do so, we find there are two points of view: (1) The first debate had a pro-Kennedy impact; (2) there was already a Democratic trend, which explains any Kennedy gain between the two dates.

Let us examine each.

If we employ only the data for these two dates, we find a significant impact. The Democrats gained support; the Republicans lost support.

But a simple before-after design may be misleading. A time series design utilizing all the data in table 7.8 yields a more comprehensive picture of the 1960 election and the impact of the first television debate on it. With the major exception of the September 25 poll taken just before the first debate, there is a steady trend toward the Democrats. Everything, then, turns on the assumption made for the poll taken on the eve of the debates. If it is assumed that this single deviation from the trend is attributable to sampling error, there remains no evidence in the time series for any impact of the debate. If it is assumed that the debate-eve poll reflects a break in the Democratic trend, there is evidence that the debate enabled the Democrats to recover their momentum.

However, if we question the representativeness of one sample, we must also consider the implications for others. The argument for a pro-Kennedy trend rests on the increase in support for him between August 31 and September 14. If it is assumed that this is attributable to sampling variation, the trend argument becomes untenable.

One solution to possible sampling deviations would be to average the available measures. If the average of all four measures before the first debate, a procedure which maximizes the reliability of the pre-debate estimate by pooling independent samples, and the October 12 post-debate measure are used, the data indicate a pro-Kennedy effect.

We see no way to choose among the alternatives. The data neither confirm the hypothesis of increased votes for the perceived winner, nor the null hypothesis of no such effect. They support the existence of a trend toward Kennedy over the period in which the first debate occurred, and they make it clear that any effect of the debates was small in terms of number of voters influenced. At the same time, the 1960 election makes it clear that an effect small in magnitude in terms of voters may be huge in terms of social influence. In this instance, the election turned on a tenth of a percentage point.

FORD-CARTER IN 1976. A different picture emerges from data on the 1976 debates between Jimmy Carter and Gerald Ford, which were viewed by audiences comparable in size to those for the Nixon-Kennedy debates. We have already observed that the decline in the influence of party identification on voting has limited television's role in reinforcement and increased the likelihood of other effects. The data on the 1976 debates are consistent with an interpretation of increased effects of television.

A survey of a representative panel of about 200 Wisconsin voters (Dennis and Chaffee, 1977) illustrates how the 1976 debates related to their decision-making. The same persons were interviewed before the debates, after the first debate, after all the debates, and finally after the election. This method allows the tracing of changes in vote intentions over time and the relating of those changes to the amount of attention given the debates. Figure 7.3 shows the different patterns of decision-making for three kinds of voters: those who watched the debates regularly, those who didn't watch them, and an intermediate group who watched them occasionally or partially.

The nonviewers can be simply described. Their minds were mostly made up before the debates began, and this was mainly the result of identification with one of the major parties, although their position in the socioeconomic hierarchy had some influence. The images they held of the candidates also had an impact on their final voting decisions.

The occasional viewers changed somewhat more from their pre-debate voting intentions in the actual vote. In the main, they voted on the basis of party affiliation. Most of this effect of party on vote occurred before the debates, but some later reinforcement also appears to have occurred. Apparently this type of voter watched the debates sufficiently to assure himself that his party had nominated a worthy person. Images of the candidates were less important in determining the vote than was the case with the nonviewers. Instead, the images that emerged following the debates were highly predictable from the voting intentions held before them.

A distinctly different picture, and a more complex one,

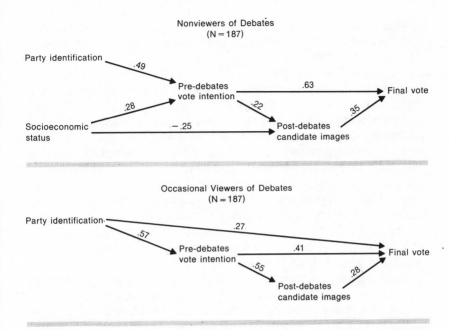

Nonviewers of Debates
(N = 187)

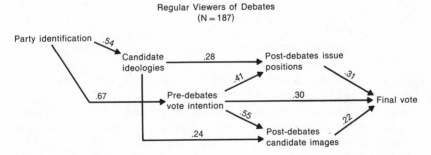

Figure 7.3. Models of 1976 vote decision-making for voters differing in exposure to televised Carter-Ford debates.

NOTE: The coefficients on each arrow indicate the strength of the relationship (standardized regression coefficient). Only those relationships that exceed .20 and that lead to the final vote decision are diagrammed.

SOURCE: J. Dennis and S. H. Chaffee. 1977. Impact of the debates upon partisan, image and issue voting. In S. Kraus (ed.), *The Great Debates: 1976, Ford vs. Carter.* Bloomington: Indiana University Press.

emerges for the group that regularly watched the 1976 debates. For these persons, differences over issues, a quite insignificant factor for the other voters, becomes the strongest predictor of the vote. Images were less important than in the other groups. Party was important in determining preference before the debates, but had no significant impact on the changes that occurred after that time. The general ideological stances of the candidates (liberal or conservative) were also important in the decision-making process. The most interesting finding is that these voters changed the most of any group during the latter stages of the campaign. Ordinarily in studies of political mass communication it is found that the people who are most likely to pay attention to campaign events are also the most partisan, and consequently the least susceptible to influence by what they see in the media. At least in the case of the 1976 debates, this tendency seems to have been reversed (Kraus, 1977).

Data from the same panel survey also indicate that the debates stimulated interpersonal conversation about politics and use of the mass media for additional political information. Such factors, as would be predicted from prior research, were related to viewing of the debates, but viewing in turn appeared to increase further such political involvement.

The weight of the debates in the campaign is suggested by the proportion of the sample in each of the three categories. Of the about 200 respondents, only 20 percent were in the minimal exposure group. Of the remaining 80 percent, half were in the occasional-exposure group and half in the consistent-exposure group. These proportions obviously cannot simply be extrapolated to national voting. Nevertheless, the Wisconsin sample was representative and conformed demographically to the national election samples of Gallup, Daniel Yankelovich, and others, and the prediction of the outcome from the pre-election data was within 2 percent of the actual Wisconsin vote. These factors suggest that the sample can be taken as a rough approximation of national impact. It is quite fair to conclude that nationally there was a very substantial number of voters falling in the third group, showing significant effects of the debates.

On the other hand, there is no evidence in the data on the debates of any agenda-setting in regard to issues (Becker et al., 1977) despite the evidence of various other effects. The implication is that agenda-setting may be confined to continuing exposure to the media rather than brief, relatively singular exposure, however portentous.

The data on the whole give support to the notion that television has the capacity to break through the ordinary barriers of political partisanship and selective exposure. The declining role for candidate image associated with increased attention to the debates suggests that in this context of dramatic confrontation, influence occurred more frequently on issues. This does not diminish in any way the possible influence of image in other contexts, such as an entire campaign. The major implication is that a heavily publicized event televised by all major outlets simultaneously can reach beyond the usual small audience for political news and penetrate the broader electorate. Those Americans who regularly viewed the debates apparently made use of the information gained in their voting decisions. The potential contributions of television to the enlightenment of the democratic process has not been fully explored, but these data suggest that the picture may not be so bleak as critics and detractors of the medium have argued.

Election Day Reporting

An often debated topic is whether in presidential elections the voter turnout or choice in western states is affected by the broadcast of results from eastern states where the pools close earlier or by the accompanying commentary and projections about the likely national winner. Four studies have focused on this issue:

In 1964, 1700 California voters were interviewed the day before the election and after the polls closed. Only 12 percent of the total sample and only 11 percent of those reaching a decision on the final day were exposed to reports and projections, and only 1 percent of the sample changed its vote (Mendelsohn, 1966).

Also in 1964, 2700 voters in California and Washington were interviewed before and after the election. Turnout was almost identical for those exposed and those not exposed to the broadcasts of returns and projections, and only 2.7 of the total sample changed their votes, and there was only minutely more changing among those exposed to the broadcasts (Fuchs, 1966).

Again, in 1964, 364 Californians who voted after the broadcasts began, and 116 Ohio voters, where the polls closed before the broadcasts, were interviewed. Neither turnout nor support for either candidate appeared to differ (Lang and Lang, 1968).

In 1968, 517 Eastern Standard Time voters and 1455 Pacific Standard Time voters were interviewed before and after the election. In the West, only 38 percent had not voted when the broadcasts from the East began, and only 6 percent saw the broadcasts before voting or deciding not to vote. When West and East are compared, 4 percent in the West and 7 percent in the East changed in their decision of whether or not to vote. Seven percent of those exposed to the broadcasts in the West changed their choice, compared to 6 percent in the East (Tuchman and Coffin, 1971).

We conclude that the possibility of political broadcasts prior to the closing of the polls in the West influencing a Presidential election is limited by the small number exposed to such broad-. casts, and that there is no evidence that such broadcasts affect an election. In the four studies, involving two elections and four different samples, neither turnout nor choice were affected. However, we would warn that these findings do not eliminate the possibility that some influence under circumstances different from those of the elections studied might occur. The 1968 election between Humphrey and Nixon was so close that the latter was not declared a winner by political commentators until the following morning, and one would not expect knowledge of early results and projections to have much effect in such an unpredictable situation. On the other hand, the very partisan, strong feelings about Goldwater in 1964 may have prevented defections from voting on either side, despite the early signs of an overwhelming victory by Johnson. What these and most other elections have in common is that the televised prognostications and early trends are consonant with voter expectations, and presumably would have been taken into account in advance in reaching a voting decision. When expectations are disconfirmed, such broadcasts might significantly alter behavior.

These four studies also bear the question of the general influence of forecasts and estimates of the eventual vote, including those of the many national opinion polling organizations. Their implication is that forecasts and estimates do not affect the vote—at least when they are in accord with expectations. This obviously suggests that such advance indicators may play a crucial if less visible role in shaping expectations, for in that capacity they contribute to the framework on which the influence of future forecasts and estimates appears to depend.

Uses and Gratifications

Pursuit of explanations for mass communication behavior has led to renewed interest in the "uses and gratifications" approach to the study of the media (Blumler, 1964; Blumler and Katz, 1974; Katz, 1959; Klapper, 1963; Katz, Blumler, and Gurevitch, 1973). The contrast with the long-dominant effects orientation of mass-communication research (Halloran, 1964; Higbie, 1961; Klapper, 1960; Schramm and Roberts, 1971) is illustrated in figure 7.4. When asking "What are the effects of mass communication?" it is logical for the arrow between Message and Audience to run from left to right. From a uses and gratifications orientation, the arrow should be reversed. Rather than inquiring about what mass communication does to people, we are inquiring into what people do *with* mass communication.

If the law of minimal consequences is correct that television and other mass media have no impact, how do we explain any viewing of political broadcasts? Are lethargy and the seeking of reinforcement the sole factors? Blumler and McQuail (1969) and McLeod and Becker (1974) studied the role in (respectively) the British general election of 1964 and the American presidential election of 1972 of such uses of television as reinforcement, vote guidance, surveillance, and excitement. Their results are largely

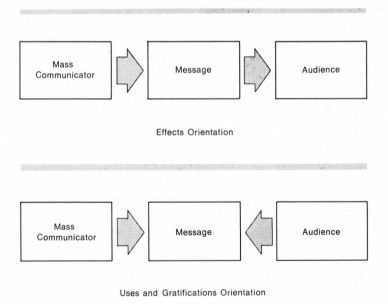

Figure 7.4. Two orientations toward television research compared: The effects orientation vs. the uses and gratifications orientation.

consistent, although there are many points where there is no overlap.

Reinforcement and vote guidance do not appear to fully explain attention to the political content of the mass media. Blumler and McQuail, for example, found that half of their sample could not be said to be primarily so motivated. Motives that were paramount for the other half of the sample were surveillance, or keeping up with the news, and excitement.

Motives appear to operate somewhat independently of exposure; that is, measures of motives and exposure do not relate alike to such variables as campaign interest, activity, and knowledge, or vote change. McLeod and Becker, for example, found motives even more strongly related to such variables than exposure.

A role for excitement-seeking should be expected because its satisfaction is a traditional goal of journalism. Such a factor presumably would be particularly important in the United States, where exposure to political information more often occurs as an adjunct of news viewing or entertainment-seeking than in Great Britain, where the extensive airtime made available to the contending parties means that viewing more frequently occurs as the result of political interest. Coverage at the presidential level may be shaped by journalists' pursuit of the exciting, but the amount is unlikely to be affected. In lesser races, however, the amount of coverage is also likely to be affected. Thus, the excitement of the contest and the televisability of the contenders as perceived by broadcasters was found to determine to a large degree the coverage of the 10 congressional races on the Chicago area in 1972 (K. McGrath, 1975).

There appears to be on the whole a powerful role for motives, although one quite differentiated by their variety. Blumler and McQuail found that among those with high exposure to television, strength of motive for viewing political programs was positively associated with a gain of information during the campaign; this was not true among those with low exposure. They also found that there was no relationship between exposure and gain of information among those who wished guidance about whom to vote for. Here, any gain in information was the function of the motive. On the other hand, McLeod and Becker found that the specific motive of surveillance was associated with some increase in information, but not vote guidance. These findings seem to fit the panel study of Lucas and Adams (1977) of the 1976 presidential election in which television news viewing was related to a voting decision but not knowledge among the unusually large number of undecided and wavering voters. One implication of these findings is that television may serve those seeking guidance primarily through confirming or disconfirming the viewer's image of the candidate rather than by supplying information.

Blumler and McQuail report that the various possible effects were most frequent for those without strong political involvement. They attribute this, probably accurately, to the far greater increase in exposure to political events that an election campaign brings to the less interested. However, McLeod and Becker also report on various motives for avoiding political content—such as a preference for entertainment, a distrust of political, and unassailable partisanship—that would constrain effects on the disinterested. Blumler and McQuail also found that despite exceptions exposure to political content on television was related to a gain in information. Thus, motives cannot be said to be wholly determinant.

These varied findings hopefully will initiate a further exploration of the complex role of uses and gratifications in the political effects of television. They would appear to recast and qualify the conclusion that would be reached from the often-replicated finding that in political campaigns initial level of voter knowledge and subsequent gain in information are positively related to mass-media exposure. However, research has yet to sharply define the precise motives, uses, and gratifications that bring the individual voter to the television set and that mediate the effects of what is viewed there.

In sum, we conclude that:

Television should be judged a unique factor in politics because it represents the fullest technological and sociological expression to date of a mass medium; it can command the largest audience of any medium for the communication of a single message, minimize or eliminate the delay between the occurrence of an event and its coverage, and has the resources of spoken word and moving picture.

Although television has altered the political experience of the individual, the medium functions within a context of numerous influential factors which together restrict its capacity to alter attitudes or behavior.

The capacity of television to wield political influence is further restricted by the American public's typically low level of interest in politics. Nevertheless, television is a major factor in focusing attention on an election and in arousing partisan predispositions, and a major step in this process is the coverage of the conventions, because by their end many voters have made their decisions.

Most voters typically make their decisions early in the campaign, and the correlation between the decisions reached and preexisting dispositions toward the contending parties is so high that the influence of television in terms of numbers of voters affected, apart from crystallizing or reinforcing predispositions, can only be small.

Although most voters reach decisions early in the typical election, there are always some who do not, and the possibility they are influenced by television is enhanced by the much-reduced role of such factors as party allegiance, which are paramount for earlier deciders, although the apparent low level of media use by such atypical voters somewhat restricts any such possibility.

When the proportion of undecided and wavering voters is large and the media use of those yet to reach a decision is that of the typical voter, there is a very large opportunity for television to have some influence.

The trend toward reduced party allegiance reduces the proportion of voters for whom television can reinforce predispositions and increases the likelihood that television can affect voting decisions by shaping images and views on issues, both of which are probably increasing in their importance in voter decision-making.

Television's unique capability to stage a media event that will unfold in the living room, as exemplified by the presidential debates of 1960 and 1976, constitutes the power to penetrate beyond the confines of the usual audience for politics, thereby giving it a potential for unusual and atypical contributions to voter decision-making.

Television is probably a major contributor to the image held by the public of a Presidential or other prominent candidate, but the number of votes which can be said to be influenced by television's contribution independent of other factors typically appears to be relatively small.

Despite the small typical magnitude of television's influence, the social impact can be great because elections are often decided by a narrow margin.

Television's influence on voting decisions occurs in interaction with other variables and is difficult and perhaps impossible to isolate.

There is no evidence that the broadcast in the West of results and projections from the East before the polls have closed has influenced either turnout or voter choice, but because of the unique elements present in every election, these findings do not preclude some influence in the future.

The obtaining of information which might guide political attitudes and behavior is far from the sole motive of individuals for viewing broadcasts with political content, and the political role of television can only be fully understood if the other varied uses and gratifications which political and public affairs content serve for the public are taken into account.

The Lessons of Advertising Research

Television advertising may not invariably have the effects often ascribed to it, but it certainly would appear to be capable of powerful effects. For example:

A two-week, $1 million advertising campaign on the 1972 Summer Olympics telecasts raised the Northwestern Mutual Life Insurance Company from 34th to 3rd place in public recognition of life insurance company names (*TV Guide,* November 9, 1974).

After a two-year advertising confrontation with Goodyear, B. F. Goodrich experienced a 222 percent increase in top-of-mind consumer awareness and moved from last to second place in awareness (*Advertising Age,* 1974b).

A Columbus, Ohio, survey indicated that 20 percent of the viewers said they changed their attitudes about Senator Edward Kennedy after they saw his televised explanation of the Chappaquidick incident in July 1969, and three-fourths of them said their attitudes became more favorable (M. J. Robinson and Burgess, 1970).

In his 1968 Democratic primary campaign against incumbent Senator Gruening in Alaska, Mike Gravel trailed by two to one in the polls on a Friday but on the following Monday, after all three Anchorage television stations had shown a paid Gravel documentary, he had a 55–45 percent margin which he maintained throughout the remainder of the campaign (Napolitan, 1969).

Patterson and McClure (1973) found that over a third of the voters they interviewed changed their intended vote during the campaign, and they conclude that televised political advertising—played a major role in that decision-making.

On the other hand, when Democrat Richard VanderVeen won President Gerald Ford's old Congressional seat in a special election, he did it without using any television advertising—because he could not afford it (*Advertising Age,* 1974a).

The Character of Political Advertising

Political and product advertising share some important similarities. Both attempt to persuade individuals to decide to act. This is something both also have in common with the nonadvertising segments of political campaigns. Both attempt to convince these individuals that what is advocated is consistent with their preexisting attitudes;advertising rarely attempts to change those attitudes. Both also expose the consumer to larger amounts of disjointed and often trivial information.

There are also some important dissimilarities between product and political advertising. These relate primarily to the very different contexts in which the two take place. First, people interested in politics typically have access to more sources of information, opinion, and influence. In addition to the advertising, they also can view news programs and documentaries. In the case of product advertising, access is limited; there aren't many other mass-media sources of information about products, particularly on television. The display of merchandise on game shows is inseparable from advertising. The consumer advocate publications reach only a very small proportion of consumers. The information outside of advertising that is available is often negative—as when products are recalled because of manufacturing defects or dangers.

Second, product advertising is one-sided and seldom presented in the context of confrontation, while political advertising, certainly one-side ad-by-ad, occurs in a context in which confrontation and two-sided messages are common. Television product commercials are deliberately isolated from those of competitors and the practice of citing competitors by name is still infrequent. In politics, there is a great deal of face-to-face confrontation, both explicitly in news conferences and debates, and implicitly in interviews and commentary. In short, product advertising occurs in a context of one-sided communication; political advertising occurs in a context of two-sided communication.

A third dissimilarity relates to the share of the market sought by political candidates as opposed to that sought by product advertisers. A disinfectant spray manufacturer, for example, might be content with 20 percent of the $75 million market. This allows him to be very specific in his appeals to a rather narrowly defined market. By contrast, the political candidate must obtain over 50 percent of the market or he will not be in business after election day! That means he must appeal to a much wider and more heterogeneous segment, and his advertising appeals cannot be too specific or information-laden or he will risk alienating a sizable portion of the market.

A fourth dissimilarity is that the product advertiser is subject to pressures and restrictions by federal, state, and local governments, and must document his claims, while the political advertiser is free to make virtually any claim. The political advertiser has far more latitude in formulating appeals.

Political advertising, of course, also differs from other political communication on television. Intended to persuade, it is more pointed, more succinct, invariably one-sided, and calculated to leave the viewer with a more (or a least no less favorable) disposition toward its subject.

Factors Affecting Learning, Attitudes, and Behavior

There is really no question that advertising does affect learning, attitudes and behavior. There simply is no "does it?" issue; it does. It is equally clear that all advertising under all conditions is not equally effective. We shall focus, then, not on the issue of whether advertising has effects, but on the nature of those effects and the circumstances and conditions on which they are contingent. We shall show that advertising's cognitive and affective effects are dependent upon two major types of contingencies:

Stimulus factor—the type of program in which the advertising appears, the content of the advertising message, and the environment in which it appears;

Receiver factors—the consumer's involvement with the product, attitudes toward advertising, and selective and cognitive processes.

We would be remiss if we did not say that our task is made difficult by the invisibility of much advertising research. Only a small amount of what has been undertaken is available to researchers. Much of the remainder has been kept secret for proprietary reasons or has been discarded because the decision to which the findings were relevant has been made. That factor—in addition to the difficulty of isolating the specific effects of advertising—accounts for the dearth of clear-cut information about advertising's effects.

LEARNING. The efforts to isolate and specify the cognitive effects of advertising have been hampered by lack of agreement about the most appropriate means of studying those effects. Brand awareness is customarily measured by presenting a person with the name of a product category and asking which brands in that category come to mind. The B. F. Goodrich and Northwestern Mutual Life Insurance Company experiences mentioned earlier reflect such "top-of-mind awareness" measures.

However, there is much disagreement about the most common method of measuring learning: aided or unaided recall. These studies are usually conducted the day after the commercial has been telecast; the respondent is asked if he can remember the sponsor of a particular show or if he can remember anything about the commercial.

From the practical point of view of advertising management, an important problem associated with recall is the eventual linkage between recall and whether the product is purchased. In other words, even though advertising researchers separate learning effects from behavioral effects, they must still deal with the question of whether or how learning influences eventual behavior. The evidence from one major study indicates that the relationship is somewhat tenuous. Haskins (1964) reviewed 28 studies which sought to analyze the relationship between recall and behavior. He concluded that even though research had documented that people did learn and could recall information from advertising and other forms of mass communication, the measures of learning (recall and retention) had no pertinent relationship to changes in attitude or behavior.

The use of recall as a measure of learning is further complicated by the fact that the average viewer devotes little attention to the commercial and therefore tends to forget it very quickly. Shulman (1972) analyzed 84 recall studies and compared the recall scores (the percentage of persons who could correctly remember the ad) derived from interviews conducted on the morning after the commercial was telecast to those from interviews on the afternoon of that day. The average recall score was higher for morning interviews, evidence of deterioration of memory over time. One important consequence is that commercials which appear on higher-rated shows will usually have higher recall scores than commercials on lower-rated programs—it takes longer to find persons who watched the lower-rated show and, hence, more of those interviews are conducted in the afternoon.

Whatever the reason—and it would appear that rapid deterioration of memory is probably the major culprit—the most striking thing about the recall of television commercials is the fact that so few people can remember them, even when the measures are taken immediately after the program. In the three hours following the conclusion of the 1975 Super Bowl football game, interviewers reached by phone 642 people in the Miami, Florida, area who said they had watched the game on television. When asked to name the advertising sponsors of the telecast (unaided recall), only 7 percent could correctly name Goodyear, which had shown five commercials during the game. Three sponsors were not remembered by anyone, and others had recall scores below two percent. A startling 25 percent could correctly recall Chrysler's automobile rebate ads, but Chrysler's rebate announcement had been front page news most of the previous week (*Editor and Publisher,* 1975a). Apart from the Chrysler ads, the recall scores were typical. The average recall score for 30-second commercials—which account for nearly 90 percent of all television commercials—was a little over 8 percent in 1973 (*Advertising Age,* 1975).

Another factor which has undoubtedly contributed to the poor recall performance of television commercials has been a condition the advertising industry calls "clutter," the increase in the number of different commercial messages shown during a particular time period. Between 1965 and 1970 there was a 23 percent increase in the number of commercial minutes (total time devoted to commercial messages), but a 61 percent increase in the number of nighttime commercials (J. Walter Thompson, 1970). The increase in the number of commercials was primarily due to the increased use of 30-second instead of 60-second messages. In 1967, 47 percent of the prime-time commercials were 30 seconds long; in 1973, 30-second commercials accounted for 88 percent of the prime-time total. During that same period, the average recall score for prime-time commercials dropped from 9.5 percent to 8.5 percent (*Advertising Age,* 1975).

One manifestation of clutter has been the grouping of several 30-second commercials into one, long commercial break in the program. Any viewer who has watched one of these chains of commercials knows how difficult it is to remember the names of the advertisers. It is not clear from research, however, if position within that chain makes a difference in recall or attention. Steiner (1966) trained college students to observe their family members' behavior while watching television. From those recorded observations, he concluded that attention declined for the subsequent commercials in the chain. Other research has indicated, however, that there is no clear-cut advantage or disadvantage for any position within the chain (*Advertising Age,* 1975).

The evidence of television's effects upon learning must be viewed in light of some important implications of these problems of recall measures:

> The relatively low recall scores from on-air testing (actual commercials seen under normal conditions) provide a benchmark against which to compare recall scores from laboratory experiments.
>
> Recall performance from earlier studies must be viewed in light of increased clutter today.
>
> Low-recall scores from on-air testing reduce the variance in scores, making it more difficult to ascertain the conditions which influence recall.

Keeping in mind the problems of recall, we now turn our attention to the evidence on televised advertising's effects upon learning. We will first look at certain stimulus conditions which mediate those effects: the impact of television as compared to other media, the program environment in which the commercial appears, message content, repetition, and the setting in which the stimulus is received.

Does television make a difference? Is the same commercial message more powerful when seen on the home screen than when read in print, or heard on the radio? Results from laboratory studies suggest the answer is contingent upon the nature of the product being advertised. Buchanan (1964) ascertained his subjects' interest in a product by a mail questionnaire before the experiment. He then brought them to the advertising agency and exposed one group to a television commercial and the other group to a print ad featuring the same product and the same selling points. The next day he telephoned the subjects at their homes to measure recall of the advertising message. For the magazine group, he found that recall increased directly with product interest; no such relationship held for the television group.

McConnell (1970) showed Australian college students some American television commercials, some radio ads developed from the television sound tracks, and some newspaper ads developed from the television ads. He tested for immediate recall and found that effectiveness varied with the product. Television and newspaper were better than radio for a soft drink, television and radio were superior to newspaper for a beer, and the newspaper ad was superior for a men's hair spray.

In another laboratory study (Grass and Wallace, 1974), subjects learned more from the television version than from the print version of the same message. However, this study suffered from more than the usual validity problems because the print ads were seen as slides, even though they were under the control of the subjects.

Unfortunately, we know very little about the relative advertising efficacy of the media under real conditions. From nonadvertising research, however, we have learned that heavy print users are usually aware of more political issues and are generally better informed about issues than are heavy television users (J. P. Robinson, 1972a; Sheinkopf, O'Keefe, and Meeske, 1973).

Does the learning from television advertising depend upon the time of day the commercial is seen? This is an important question for advertisers. Nighttime television has much larger audiences, but the lower costs of daytime commercials permit greater repetition, more exposure, at the same cost. The average recall of a daytime network commercial is about 70 percent of the recall for a prime-time commercial, but the increasing clutter in prime-time may be erasing that advantage. The differences are presumably due to a greater degree of attention paid to nighttime as opposed to daytime programming (J. Walter Thompson, 1970).

Does the program environment make a difference? Will a commercial be more effective if it appears in a drama show, a situation comedy, a musical variety show, or a sports program? Actual strategic decisions show wide variation; some advertisers prefer comedy, some police dramas, and a great many express no preference. The J. Walter Thompson agency (1970) concluded that there was weak evidence for some superiority of drama shows. If true, the reason may be exemplified by the greater attentiveness commanded by movies (table 4.2), which suggests that a compelling story may hold the viewer more firmly before the screen than other entertainment, although it should be said that the same data indicated no marked differences among other types of programming, including drama, except for reduced interest in commercials and news.

This question of program environment is confounded by another important contingency—the popularity of the programs.

The more that viewers like a program, the more likely they are to recall the advertising on it. After reviewing 25 on-air tests of 30-second commercials, Clancy and Kweskin (1971) concluded that attitude toward the program was significantly related to recall while certain other factors—education, age, product usage, and viewing of the entire program—were not. Interviews with Chicago-area housewives revealed an average 24-hour recall score of 23 percent for top-rated (largest audiences) nighttime shows and only 15 percent for low-rated shows (Barclay, Doub, and McMurtrey, 1965). Of course, this is due in part to the fact that it takes longer for the researcher to locate viewers of the lower-rated shows, and the lower recall scores may be due as much to memory loss as to the popularity of the show (Shulman, 1972).

Does the length of the commercial message make a difference? We have already said that almost 90 percent of all prime-time commercials are 30-seconds long. Most research indicates that recall is greater for 60-second commercials, but it is not twice as great. The average recall for a 30-second commercial is about 75 percent of the recall score for a 60-second commercial (Bogart, 1972a; J. Walter Thompson, 1970). Despite the lower recall, most advertisers still prefer the 30-second commercials because their lower cost permits more repetition.

Since almost 75 percent of all United States households had color television sets in 1975, and since virtually all commercials are telecast in color, it is no longer relevant to ask if advertising in color is more effective than black and white. It probably comes as no surprise to learn that studies have shown that viewers have greater and more vivid recall of color advertising than for black and white (Donohue, 1973; Scanlon, 1970; Schaps and Guest, 1968).

We have made several references to advertisers' desire for repetition of their messages. Do people learn more if they are exposed to an advertisement more than once? Research in both the laboratory and the field suggests that repeated exposures are accompanied by an initial increase in learning, but that the rate of learning begins to level off or decline after more exposures. This decline in effectiveness is called "wearout" in advertising jargon. For the individual, it means there is an increase in recall after the second exposure to the message, but the rate of increase becomes less and less with each subsequent exposure. For the aggregate audience, wearout means an increase in recall scores after the second or third exposure, followed by a leveling-off or decline in recall scores after that. The wearout effect has been generally less pronounced in on-air testing than in the laboratory, however, presumably because the aggregate audience is constantly changing; each repeated telecast of the message will reach some persons who are seeing it for the first time as well as some persons who may be seeing it for the fourth or fifth time.

Grass (1968) demonstrated that there is a wearout effect on both attention and learning. He measured attention by using a device that required the subject to keep pushing a foot pedal in order to continue viewing a movie which had commercial messages repeated throughout. The extent to which the subject kept pushing the pedal was taken as an indication of attention. Learning was measured by interviewing the subjects 24 hours after exposure.

Grass's subjects paid more attention to the commercial the second time they saw it than the first time. After that, however, the level of attention declined with repeated exposures. The same wearout effect also occurred for learning, which is not what one would expect. Since there is only so much to learn about a commercial, one might think that learning scores would increase to a plateau and then level off. Grass surmised that viewers begin to forget what they have learned and, since they pay less and less attention to repeated exposures, the learning is not reinforced. Grass and Wallace (1969) found a wearout effect upon learning and attention in field testing as well as in laboratory experiments.

A. Greenberg and Suttoni (1973) reviewed the methodology and the findings of several studies on the wearout effect of television commercials. Among their conclusions: Learning is enhanced by repetition of the message; awareness of new products is enhanced by repetition; interest declines with repetition because people learn all there is to know about the message and lose interest.

As we have seen (chapter 4), television viewing is an often-interrupted, frequently divided focus of attention. The degree of raptness commanded by television apparently is somewhat less for commercials than for programs (Bechtel, Achelpohl, and Akers, 1972; Hsia, 1974; Steiner, 1966). The story of measuring commercial effectiveness as the inverse of toilet flushing during commercial breaks is apocryphal; reduced attention is a fact.

Do competing stimuli or distractions mediate television advertising's cognitive effects? Venkatesan and Haaland (1968) showed subjects a television commercial under varying levels of distraction in the laboratory. A control group saw an unaltered 60-second beer commercial. Those in the visual distraction group heard the same audio soundtrack, but saw unrelated video content. The behavioral distraction group was asked to fill out a questionnaire while watching the untouched commercial. The visual and behavioral distraction group had to fill out the questionnaire while watching the altered commercial. The recall scores (percent recalling the name of the brand) were 95 percent for the control group, 42 for the visual distraction group, 57 for the behavioral distraction group, and 7 percent for the visual and behavioral distraction group. Since there are typically both visual and behavioral distractions present under normal viewing conditions, it is not difficult to see why recall scores are typically as low as they are.

There are many unanswered questions about the stimulus factors which mediate the cognitive effects of television advertising. We know even less about the receiver variables which mediate those effects. However, increased research emphasis is being devoted to receiver variables and information-processing at both the physiological and cognitive levels.

Krugman (1968, 1971) pioneered the study of physiological responses during exposure to advertising. With eye movement cameras, he found that people scanned a print ad to learn the content. When they learned it, they stopped scanning. On repeated exposures to the same ad, the eye movement was less, suggesting that eye movement research could be used to predict how many repetitions were necessary for a person to learn the ad content.

Krugman also analyzed brain-wave activities during exposure to television and magazine advertising. In response to television, the brain waves were slower or more passive, while they were more active and showed more involvement during exposure to magazine advertising. Krugman (1966) also found that for both magazine and television advertising, the number of thoughts relating to something in a reader or viewer's life was greater when attention was primarily directed toward the accompanying editorial content rather than to the advertising itself. He also found that the number of connections was greater when the surrounding content was news rather than light entertainment.

Krugman (1965, 1966, 1968, 1971) regards all of these findings as reflections of involvement. He argues that television is inherently a low-involvement medium because of the relative lack of selectivity of specific content compared to that exercised by a reader, and that as a result, mental processes differ for television and print advertising. Television, he argues, alters the way a product is perceived without affecting evaluative attitudes, that the altered perception may lead to a purchase, and that subsequently attitude will shift to be consistent with the behavior. He believes print advertising is more likely to involve a shift in attitudes, which subsequently leads to a purchase.

Interest in direct responses to advertising has not been limited to eye movement and brain waves, but has also moved into the cognitive realm. Wright (1973) showed advertisements for a hypothetical food product to adult women and asked them to record all their thoughts during the exposure. They also were asked to indicate their attitudes toward the product, the relative importance of the thoughts they had listed, and the origins of each of these thoughts. Wright found that their thoughts could be coded into three categories: counter-argument, source derogation, and support argument. The most common response was counter-argument, or resistance. In other words, the subjects said that as they looked at the ad, they were thinking of arguments against the brand or the selling points of the ad. Some of their responses were source-derogation, in which they discounted the advertising because of the company or because of a general antiadvertising bias. Finally, some of the responses were supportive, or favorable to the brand, the company, and the selling points.

The makeup of these cognitions, Wright concluded, were primarily a function of attributes of the respondent and not the advertising stimulus. Furthermore, he posits that these responses, taken in sum, mediate the effects of advertising, with acceptance dependent upon the net balance among supportive, derogatory, and counter-argumentative cognitions.

Selective processes require attention because of the degree to which phenomena in the past have been attributed either to selectivity of exposure or mental processing as reflected in perception and retention. Voters and consumers certainly have some choice about the messages to which they are exposed. This choice, however, is less for product and political advertising on television than for other television content or much of such advertising in other media. The reason is that the broadcast of particular commercials cannot be divined in advance by the viewer, and they are short enough so that the incentive for channel-switching is minimal. They stand in sharp contrast to lengthy political documentaries, paid-for or ostensibly objective, that permit viewers greater exercise of choice, and for which some selectivity of exposure in accord with partisan disposition has been found to occur (McClure and Patterson, 1974). These circumstances, in conjunction with the lack of evidence for selective exposure as typical of voter response to mass-media political communication, lead us to believe that political commercials may often be quite effective in conveying information to voters. For example, in the Summit County, Ohio, study of the 1972 presidential election (Mendelsohn and O'Keefe, 1976), exposure to commercials was related to greater viewing of television, but there was no relationship between support for a candidate and exposure to his commericals, and apparently because of scheduling differences McGovern commercials were seen more frequently by both Nixon and McGovern supporters. Thus, we are not surprised by the findings of Atkin and Heald (1976) that exposure to such commercials appeared to increase political knowledge, of Patterson and Mc-Clure (1976) that commercials appeared to make a greater contribution to knowledge than exposure to network news, and of Mendelsohn and O'Keefe (1976) that voters who had difficulty in reaching a decision were more likely than others to cite commercials as helpful.

ATTITUDES. The evaluation of television advertising's effects upon attitudes is hampered by the difficulty of separating attitudes toward advertising in general, the particular advertisement, the company, and the product being advertised. This problem, along with that of linking attitudes to behavior, must be kept in mind as we review the evidence.

Does the medium make a difference? How persuasive is television when compared to other media? Surprisingly, the evidence is not only unclear but meager. One study found no difference between television and radio advertisements while a study of nonadvertising messages indicated superiority for radio and print over television.

Baldwin and Surlin (1969) showed three commercials—one for a breakfast cereal, one for chewing gum, and one for a dog food—to one group of subjects and played tapes of the radio versions to another group. The image of all three products improved regardless of the medium. There was difference among the media for the cereal and the gum—but the radio version was superior for the dog food. As the authors caution, however, the artificial laboratory conditions limit the generalizability of the conclusion.

While it was not a test of advertising, Dommermuth's (1974) study sheds some light on the relative persuasiveness of the media. He gave a 20-minute presentation to four different groups: one was given a television program, one a motion picture, a third a radio program, and a fourth a printed message. The subjects rated all the other media "stronger" than television, and radio and print were more persuasive.

How does message content mediate the effects of advertising? Again, the evidence is limited, but at least two factors have been shown to have an effect: the race of the performers in the commercial and the use of refutational arguments in the message.

Primarily as a result of government pressure, advertisers in the late 1960s began to increase the number of black performers in television advertising. This immediately raised some questions. Would there be negative reactions from white viewers? Would the presence of black performers influence the reception of the advertising by the black audience? Studies of black and white adults (Schlinger and Plummer, 1972) and children (Barry and Hansen, 1973) both indicated no negative reactions from whites and that black viewers were more receptive to commercials featuring blacks than they are to all-white commercials.

Another growing trend in advertising strategy is to mention a competitor by name instead of as "Brand X." The Federal Trade Commission has urged this tactic, but many advertisers have been reluctant to do it for fear of generating more favorable attitudes toward, or at least more awareness of, the competition. We do not yet have enough evidence to tell us who benefits the most from this policy, the advertiser, the consumer, or the competitor.

Sawyer (1973) tested simulated refutational commercials in a laboratory experiment. Refutational ads—those which named the competitor or expressed the opposing viewpoint—were more effective in changing attidues than were supportive or one-sided commercials. However, this was more likely with users of the competing brand and after repeated exposures. In other words, the effectiveness of the refutational ads depended upon the consumer's past experience with the brands as well as repetition of the message.

What happens if the commercial is solely negative? In other words, how will attitudes be affected if the viewer sees a commercial which is critical of a product but does not advocate the purchase of another? Lull (1974) tested the effectiveness of such a commercial critical of Bayer aspirin. Attitude change was in the predicted direction (more negative toward Bayer), but it was not significant. Interestingly enough, the greatest change was for subjects who regularly used Bayer; their attitudes moved down the favorable scale, but did not move from favorable to unfavorable.

We mentioned earlier that repetition of the advertising message initially enhances learning, but that after a satiation point is reached the commercial begins to "wear out" or lose effectiveness. The evidence indicates that repetition apparently has a similar effect upon attitudes. Grass (1968) reported that attitudes became more favorable after the second exposure, increased at a decreasing rate until they leveled off, but did not decline as attention and learning did.

Housewives' seven-day television viewing diaries enabled Geiger (1971) to estimate the number of times the women saw commercials for seven different brands of dentifrices and headache remedies. After the seven days, the women were interviewed about their attitudes toward these products and brands. For three brands, increased exposure was accompanied by more favorable attitudes, expressed intentions as to purchase. For the other four brands, intention to purchase either did not change or else declined.

Winter (1973) measured brand attitudes and preferences before and after varying levels of exposure to advertising contained in a comedy shown to women in a laboratory setting. Each exposure had a decreasing effect upon changing attitudes in the direction of the product, more evidence of wearout. The most favorable change occurred among those whose attitudes had the greatest distance to go—those originally unaware and unfavorable. This suggests that conventional television advertising has less impact on persons who have favorable attitudes already, those who are familiar with the brand, or those who have already been exposed to the advertising.

The findings of these experiments suggest that it is plausible to think of distraction, self-confidence, and counter-arguing as interacting in the effectiveness of a persuasive message (Hovland and Janis, 1959; Festinger and Maccoby, 1964; McGuire, 1969), and the few studies of television commercials employing these variables (Barach, 1969; Bither, 1972; Bither and Wright, 1973; Wright, 1973) are consistent with this view. The model that best fits the evidence: Persuasibility is greater among those of lower self-confidence; one plausible explanation is that those with lower self-confidence are less ready to counterargue. Distraction is positively related to persuasive effectiveness of a message because it interferes with the construction of counterarguments. However, distracton may decrease persuasiveness among persons of low self-confidence because its major effect among these persons of scant counterargument is to interfere with receipt of the message. As self-confidence increases, distraction increases persuasive effectiveness; there is interference with counterarguing but some receipt of the message continues. However, as distraction becomes greater, persuasive effectiveness declines; there is interference with receipt of the message as well as with counterarguing. Thus, the effectiveness of a television commercial would remain only partly the function of its contents even when these include elements purposively distractive from the principal message; personality and situational factors will determine whether the communicator's engineering has succeeded.

We said that a person's attitude toward advertising can confound efforts to learn how advertising affects that person's attitude toward a product. What do people think of advertising and how might those attitudes mediate its effects?

We reported earlier (chapter 3) that the 1970 nationwide survey of American adults by Bower (1973) found the public ambivalent over television advertising, with about three-fourths agreeing with the statement that "there are just too many commericals" while about the same proportion agreed that "commercials are a fair price to pay for the entertainment you get." A sizable 30 percent agreed that "I'd rather pay a small amount yearly to have TV without commercials."

Among other results: 65 percent agreed that commercials were too long; 43 percent agreed that commercials were annoying and in bad taste.

On the other hand: 54 percent agreed that some commercials are helpful and informative; 54 percent agreed that some are more entertaining than the program they accompany; 35 percent agreed they frequently welcomed a commercial break—although the reasons for this pleasurable response was not explored.

When asked about products they did not think should be advertised on television, about a third cited cigarettes or other tobacco items, 16 percent cited liquor or beer, and between 4 and 6 percent cited personal undergarments, personal-hygiene items, drugs and medicine, and soaps and detergents. These objections presumably largely reflect the perception of television as a family medium readily accessible to children.

When asked to volunteer objections, the maximum proportion for any single specific complaint was the 15 percent who said that commercials are stupid, unrealistic, or silly. Only 8 percent said commercials were misleading or dishonest, only 2 percent said commercials were too aggressive or hard sell, and only 1 percent said commercials were boring or dull. The low rate of volunteered objections and the fact that slightly less than half (48 percent) agreed with the statement that "I would prefer TV without commercials" suggest that there is not widespread, general antipathy toward television advertising.

How do people feel about the advertising on television as compared to the advertisements they see or hear in other media? The answer depends upon who does—or at least reports—the research.

Newspapers are the "best liked" advertising medium, if one believes *Editor and Publisher* (1975b), the leading newspaper trade publication. It heralded the results of a poll taken by the American Association of Advertising Agencies in which a national probability sample of adults indicated their degree of favorability to newspapers, television, direct mail, magazines, radio, and billboards. Nearly 70 percent of the respondents rated newspaper advertising as "mostly" or "completely favorable," while only 40 percent gave television advertising such marks.

Broadcasting magazine (1976a), on the other hand, reported that the public considers television the "most influential" advertising medium. It reported the results of a national survey commissioned by the Television Bureau of Advertising and conducted by an independent research firm. Television advertising was called the most influential by 82 percent, compared to only 11 percent for newspapers. Television advertising was also rated most authoritative (50 percent compared to 26 percent for newspapers), most up to date (58 percent compared to 23 percent for newspapers), and most exciting (80 percent compared to 3 percent for newspapers and radio and 4 percent for magazines).

There is considerable evidence that negative attitudes toward advertising develop in adolescence, and these attitudes tend to become more negative as the child grows older (McNeal, 1969; Rossiter and Robertson, 1974; Sheikh, Prasad, and Rao, 1974; Ward, 1972a, 1972b).

People do have opinions about advertising in general. How do those attitudes mediate the effects of advertising? Greyser (1973) reported that ads for certain products—soap and detergents, toothpastes and mouthwashes, deodorants and proprietary medicines—experience greater consumer dislike. He also found that people tend to like ads more for products they use than for products they do not use, but we do not know whether use of a product leads to a liking for its commercials or whether liking a commercial leads to use.

BEHAVIOR. There are no publicly available studies which unambiguously relate changes in behavior to exposure to television advertising. Instead, the available studies focus on attentional, cognitive, and affective responses. There are several reasons. One is the difficulty of separating the impact of advertising from other factors. Another is that such research is especially likely to be proprietary and transitory. The third is that the most popular model holds that the direct effects of advertising are alterations in attentional, cognitive, and affective responses, and that these in turn alter the probabilities of a particular decision or act at some possibly much later time when such behavior is opportune and appropriate. Our conclusion that advertising has behavioral as well as other effects derives not from a body of findings but from a frequently observed phenomenon—the fluctuation in the fortunes of politicians and products with alterations in advertising.

In sum, we conclude that:

Political and product advertising, although similar in some respects, differ in many ways because of the different contexts in which each occurs, and political advertising differs in many ways from the political communication surrounding it.

The purposes of advertising research make much of it invisible, so that the quantity and range of findings available for scrutiny is very limited.

There is very little doubt that under some circumstances political and product advertising can have attentional, cognitive, affective, and behavioral effects, although the testing of direct effects is largely limited to the first three.

While observation affirms that advertising does have some effects, advertising research has so far failed to adequately define and isolate them, and has yet to specify the exact relationship among them.

Among the factors upon which the influence of television advertising is contingent are characteristics of the stimulus, including compatibility between what is advertised and the medium employed; repetition, although there are limits to its effectiveness; competing distractions, which inhibit the viewer from engaging in self-protective cognitive processing, such as the rehearsal of counterarguments; and, discretionary attention, which in the case of advertising may be withheld by viewers.

Televised political advertising has unusual capacities to transmit information about issues because of the inclination of television news to stress dramatic events and the images conveyed by candidates and because it reaches some who might avoid television news and public affairs broadcasts.

Political and Advertising Research Compared

We began our analysis with the assumption that we would learn more about the contribution of television to individual decision-making about politics and purchases by treating political and advertising research within the same framework. When done, we concluded that the assumption was valid. However, it is valid for reasons other than that the findings from one domain apply to the other, because both politics and product advertising involve calculated campaigns to persuade the public to make and act on a decision.

We believe television's principal role in decision-making is as a contributor of information. We believe that information almost invariably will have its influence in conjunction with that of many other factors. Thus, television's "direct" effects, when they occur, are typically to alter attentional, cognitive, and affective responses. Sometimes, such alterations increase or decrease the likelihood of the various acts which might have occurred in their absence. In any case, these direct effects of television are part of the varied backdrop of prior experience which inevitably influences the decision-making of an individual.

For two reasons, we do not find the argument compelling, as some do, that when the behavior in question in the real world is the same as would have been predicted prior to exposure to some presumably relevant television there has been no meaningful contribution by television to that behavior. One reason is that when such is the case, we still do not know what would have occurred in the absence of television. The other is that we are hesitant to dismiss such reinforcement as unimportant because the long-term effects of repeated reinforcement, although probably not detectable by the limited tools of social and behavioral science, may not be small.

This formulation applies alike to politics and product advertising.

However, the domains of politics and product advertising differ greatly in several respects. One is the degree to which previous personal involvement plays a role. In politics, previous involvement, usually expressed as party preference or predisposition, is a strong predictor of the eventual decision. There is no comparable orientation in product advertising. Brand loyalty is a fickle flirtation before the allegiance commanded by political predisposition. Another difference is the rhythm of the communicatory experience. Although there are political news and public affairs broadcasts throughout the year, national political campaigns have dramatic beginnings and endings. There is no analogue in televised product advertising. The result is that political decision-making occurs within a forced but always similar calendar, while product decision-making is variable and largely at the command of the decision-maker.

We believe these factors at least partially explain the very different conclusions of research about the effects on purchasing and on voting of television. In the political domain, one assigns television a major role in the providing of information but a highly constrained and comparatively minor one in altering voting decisions. In the product domain, one assigns television a more important role in influencing decisions because other factors are less important.

We have actually been examining three different realms of communication: Product advertising, political advertising, and televised political coverage. In terms of mutual relevance among the findings from these realms, we believe they can most usefully be thought of as arranged in an overlapping fashion, as in figure 7.5. Product advertising and political advertising, although differing in many respects, have much in common. Political advertising and televised political coverage, although also differing in many respects, have much in common. Product advertising and televised political coverage, although sharing some similarities, for the most part are quite different from each other.

In other words, a finding bearing on the effectiveness of product advertising may have some relevance to similar issues concerning the effectiveness of political advertising. A finding bearing on the effectiveness of political advertising may have some relevance to similar issues concerning the influence of general political communication on television. Findings bearing on

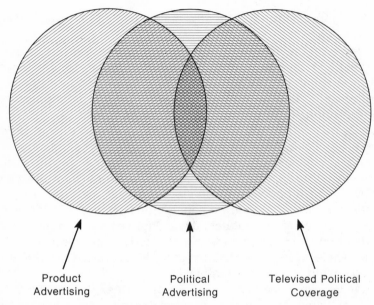

Figure 7.5. Relationship between domains of product advertising, political advertising, and general political communication.

product advertising and general political communication are less likely to have mutual relevance.

The reason for this is the way the three realms of communication are aligned on various dimensions. Some of the similarities and differences are displayed in table 7.9. Political decisions occur within the context of prior involvement, long- and sometimes deeply-held beliefs, a norm that the decision should be based on rational grounds, and a surfeit of information. They also occur within a context in which many other factors can be said to be consistent or inconsistent with any of the possible alternatives, and typically these factors are clearly more consistent with one than another alternative, many messages are two-sided, and sources are often perceived as unbiased. Political advertising differs from political coverage in the ways that it resembles product advertising—in its one-sidedness within messages, perceived bias of the source, typically brief format, and repetitiveness of the message. Political coverage does not entirely escape from one-sidedness because of the frequent, inevitable imbalance within a single presentation and the coverage of conventions that essentially amounts to the display of a party's leaders and policies, although in the long run it is—as content analyses document

Table 7.9 Alignment of Three Realms of Televised Communication on Various Dimensions

	Realm of Communication		
Dimension	Product Advertising	Political Advertising	Televised Political Coverage
Prior involvement	slight	deep	deep
Strength of beliefs	low	high	high
Opportunity for selective exposure	low-to-moderate	low-to-moderate	high
Norm of rationality	low-to-moderate	high	high
Quantity of information	low	high	high
Relevance of other stimuli	low-to-moderate	high	high
One-sidedness	total within presentations	total within presentations	variable within
Perceived bias	high	high	low
Format	brief	brief	mixed, often extended
Message repetition	high	high	moderate

(chapter 2)—roughly balanced in its treatment of the two major parties. Both product and political advertising enjoy some immunity from selective exposure because they occur with less predictability than political coverage, although a politically allergic viewer presumably could escape part of even a brief message by dial-switching. Paid-for political broadcasts other than political commercials, such as documentaries and campaign speeches, are highly similar to political advertising in character, except that the possibility of selective exposure is greatly enhanced.

By such an analysis, we are better able to see when research concerned with one or another of the realms is relevant to another realm. For example, when the circumstances of product advertising are similar to those of either type of political communication, we would expect the outcomes of such communication to be very much the same and research to be mutually relevant. Thus, we would not expect advertising to be particularly effective in altering basic food preferences, which resemble political predispositions except possibly for the norm of rationality as the basis for choice.

We are also better able to understand the special character of varied types of communicatory situations. The fact that persuasive intent is a common factor is important to recognize, but it is very far from the sole attribute of importance. By comparing research when the communicatory situations differ, we begin to understand why outcomes were not the same.

These are our reasons for believing social and advertising research are best treated together. Joint treatment allows us to better recognize relevance and irrelevance and to better recognize the specific factors which characterize communicatory situations.

Chapter

The Psychology of
Behavioral Effects

WE SHALL NOW evaluate the evidence on how television influences behavior. However, we will proceed somewhat differently from previous evaluations of much of this evidence both in our focus and framework.

In many cases, the focus has been on whether or not specific kinds of effects occur. A typical question addressed is, "Does television violence increase children's aggressiveness?" Although we shall provide answers to this kind of question, our focus will be on the psychological processes behind any such effects.* In short, many evaluations have only asked, "Do effects occur?" We also ask, "Why do they occur?"

There are two reasons for our particular emphasis. First, we believe there is sufficient evidence that effects do occur for one to begin by assuming that they do occur. Second, we believe that a great deal of information is lost when the focus is on a specific kind of effect.

* There are three broad classes of process variables which we encompass under the term, "psychological processes." First, there are those that involve television content and the person's immediate perceptions and interpretations of its meaning. Second, there are "black box" processes that hypothetically occur within the individual, and that are common to all forms of behavior. Finally, there are environmental or situational factors that to some degree govern an individual's behavior in the real work in which he lives, independently of what he might want, or has learned how, to do. Although only the second of these three classes includes processes that one might think of as purely psychological, we shall use the term "psychological processes" broadly here to refer to all three types of variables. We do not mean to imply that only psychologists study the effects of television. The literature on which we draw comes from many fields in addition to psychology. In particular, the growing field of communication research, housed mainly in departments of communication, journalism and speech, has made major contributions.

When the *kind* of effect is emphasized, the knowledge gained is limited to the specific kind of effect in question. For example, if we only learn that television violence increases children's aggressiveness, we cannot go beyond the statement of the causal relationship between the two variables. However, if we learn about the processes behind such a causal relationship, we learn far more, because now we may tentatively infer that the same processes may operate to cause additional effects quite different in character. For example, if we conclude that imitation of what is observed on television is a principal factor in such a relationship, we would tentatively hypothesize that other kinds of behavior observed on television also would be imitated.

We also differ from most previous reviews by attempting to integrate the findings from studies conducted within a wide range of theoretical frameworks rather than organizing the findings within one of those frameworks. Our procedure is to first present an explanatory model which fits these findings. Then, we "test" the consistency of this model with the empirical findings by deriving hypotheses from it which each can be individually "tested" by previous findings. At the same time, we identify various hypotheses which cannot be tested by the available data. As a result, our review accomplishes several gains:

> Organizes the highly diverse set of findings from more than 400 studies within a single framework.
> Identifies the kinds of effects which have been demonstrated to occur.
> Presents a model which explains why these effects occur.
> Identifies the strengths of the scientific literature by specifying those hypotheses for which there is support.
> Identifies the weaknesses of the scientific literature by specifying those hypotheses on which the evidence is too inconsistent for tentative inference.
> Identifies the gaps in the scientific literature by specifying those hypotheses and issues on which there are little data so far.

Two important points must be made which are perhaps obvious. The first is that this effort at the integration of a complex and varied scientific literature is exploratory, and conclusions about the correctness of "fit" or merits of the model are tentative. However, it *is* quite clear that at the minimum it is very serviceable in allowing one to cover the studies in an orderly manner, and that it does make clear many areas where new research is called for.

The second is that our presentation reverses the order in which the intellectual activity actually occurred. We begin with the model, and then test it for consistency with the empirical findings. Actually, of course, the model could not be developed without knowledge of the findings and in fact is derived from them. However, the emergence of such a model occurs not in an orderly fashion, but by jumps and starts, and we have decided to focus on the use of the model in interpreting the literature rather than to attempt to tell the story of its development, in which the model would appear in its historically accurate place at the conclusion of the attempt to synthesize the findings.

Among the topics we will cover:

> Background factors which influenced the development of the model, including the nature of previous reviews, certain assumptions and goals, the three different classes of "third variables," and various implications of the model for policy and research.

> The model itself presented in the form of a flow chart illustrating the relationship between the principal concepts believed to play a part in any influence of television on behavior.

> A review of the evidence which resulted in the model's having its particular features, including discussions of how television's influence on a particular act is likely to be influenced by state of *arousal, catharsis, modeling* or *imitation,* nature of the viewer's *response hierarchy, cue properties* of the real-life situation, prior *real-life consequences* for a similar act, *perceived reality* of the television portrayal, and the *opportunity* for performance of the act.

> The implications of the model for the range of behaviors to be studied in the future in regard to television's possible influence.

Background

Previous Reviews

This is far from the first attempt to interpret the empirical evidence on television's effects on behavior. Studies of effects on children began as soon as a sizable number of U.S. homes had television sets (Maccoby, 1951; Riley, Cantwell, and Ruthiger, 1949). By the late 1950s there was a rich literature available for review in connection with the major field studies conducted by Himmelweit, Oppenheim, and Vince (1958) and Schramm, Lyle, and Parker (1961). Both studies tested in rough fashion many hypotheses about television's effects, citing such sources of speculation as Klapper's (1954) concern that television might cause children to grow up too fast by exposing them prematurely to the adult world. Among other hypotheses, they examined two seemingly contradictory ones: that sitting and watching television would make children unduly passive, and that exposure to violence on television would induce them to behave aggressively. Both Himmelweit, Oppenheim, and Vince (1958), and Schramm, Lyle, and Parker (1961) concluded that there did not appear to be grounds for either worry because neither extreme passivity nor extreme aggressiveness was found to be correlated with heavy television viewing.

This "null" inference fit the accepted verdict of that time, which was that the mass media have only limited and minor impact on individual behavior. The conceptual schema which led to such a conclusion was most fully laid out in an influential monograph by Klapper (1960), who stressed that congenial media inputs are selected by audience members ("selective exposure"), that mass media messages are often disseminated through individuals rather than directly ("two-step flow"), and that interpersonal sources outweigh media when the two sources are in conflict ("personal influence"). Direct effects of the media on behavior are said to occur only in the small residuum of instances in which such factors are absent.

In a briefer version of this argument, Klapper (1957) suggests that delinquent behavior and voting exemplify his general principles. The scenario underlying the "limited" or "null" effects view of the mass media is that aggressive youngsters choose to watch violent programs and Democrats prefer to read about Democratic rather than Republican politicians. The main psychological process from that point on, Klapper suggests, is *reinforcement,* or as it is often put, "mere" reinforcement. This would mean that the aggressive youngster becomes more likely to behave aggressively, and the Democrat becomes more firmly committed to his party. Since the "predispositions" were presumably originally learned from the person's social environment, they will continue to be reinforced by life-situation factors as well as by media exposure. Whatever the conditions might be that would break up this seemingly endless spiral of reinforcement of predispositions, the theory holds that they will *not* result from media inputs alone.

This null-effects view contrasts sharply with the conclusions being drawn at the same time by experimental psychologists interested in violence and aggression. They had found violent films an effective means of altering aggressiveness (e.g., Bandura, Ross, and Ross, 1963a, 1963b; Berkowitz, Corwin, and Heironimus, 1963; Feshbach, 1961).

Many social and behavioral scientists nevertheless remained skeptical that effects demonstrated in the laboratory were generalizable to the typical home viewing situation. As they were aware, field studies rarely had lent much support to laboratory findings of media effects (Hovland, 1959).

Behind this juncture lay the evolution of mass communication research. The successful use of mass persuasion by fascist and communist dictatorships in the 1930s alarmed many in the academic community. As one leading social psychologist put it, "It is conceivable that one persuasive person could, through the use of mass media, bend the world's population to his will" (Cartwright, 1949). But when sociologists studied the political power of the media in the 1940 presidential election campaign, they found it to be modest (Lazarsfeld, Berelson, and Gaudet, 1948). Instead, they found in this and a similar study of the 1948 election (Berelson, Lazarsfeld, and McPhee, 1954) considerable evidence of selective exposure and the predominance of personal sources over media in influencing attitudes; their subsequent research focused heavily on such personal influence, with the media taking a decidedly secondary role in any theorizing (Berelson and Steiner, 1964; Katz and Lazarsfeld, 1955). Meanwhile, newly formulated theories in social psychology in the 1950s provided strong support for this shift by predicting that the mind attempts to maintain an equilibrium. Such homeostatic theories—the interpersonal influence models of "balance" (Heider, 1946) and "symmetry" (Newcomb, 1953), and the more purely intrapersonal theories of "congruity" (Osgood and Tannenbaum, 1955) and "cognitive dissonance" (Festinger, 1957)—predicted both selective exposure and personal influence as very general cognitive principles, and one, "cognitive dissonance," explicitly organized the case for the selective exposure hypothesis, and generated an enormous variety of studies (Brehm and Cohen, 1962). Taken as a group, these homeostatic theories were quite congruent with the null-effects conclusions that were being drawn about mass media influences on social attitudes and behavior. This literature constituted most of what was taught as "communication theory" in the training of future specialists in mass communication research in the early 1960s.

There were, of course, social and behavioral scientists at that time who pointed to the laboratory findings of Berkowitz and Bandura, and argued that television could affect behavior. Others concurred with the conclusions of the psychiatrist Wertham (1954) that television was a "school for violence." But wide acceptance of these arguments was deterred by the lack of non-laboratory supporting data and an obvious public reluctance to accept doomsaying about television. One obvious finding in the early studies was that both children and parents welcomed television to their lives. They looked forward to it before they had it, and they spent more time with it than any other activity once it was available (Schramm, Lyle, and Parker, 1961). Had anti-television wisdom issued from academe, it would not have found a very receptive audience; Americans were tuned in to television and would not have heard the message.

The next ten years brought inescapably visible violence. The assassination of President John F. Kennedy was the most dramatic of a series of political murders. Riots broke out in urban racial ghettos, and later in suburbs in the process of racial integration. A series of national administrations gradually involved the United States in the prosecution of a war in Vietnam which eventually fell in public favor. On university campuses, organized opposition to the war evolved into violence itself, and begat officially sanctioned repression in return. Old questions about a national "culture of violence" began to be asked again, and television—as the most prominent expression of cultural values—became the focus of scrutiny. Thoughtful people could no longer comfortably accept the no-effects proposition.

Meanwhile, the accumulated scientific findings of the 1960s were inconsistent with the no-effects theory. Sears and Freedman (1965, 1967), originally young devotees of the selective exposure hypothesis, concluded that the efforts they and others had undertaken to demonstrate it had failed; they announced themselves ready to abandon the hypothesis. Dissonance and other homeostatic theories empirically turned out to predict only a limited range of outcomes. Soon, most social scientists had largely abandoned the homeostatic theories, including the authors of the theories. Another element of the null model, personal influence and the two-step flow, came in for a good deal of conceptual criticism (Arndt, 1968; Bostian, 1970; Lin, 1971; Rosario, 1971; Trol-dahl, 1966). This was encouraged by studies showing a number of important media effects even when interpersonal sources were explicitly controlled (Atkin, 1971; Chaffee, Ward, and Tipton, 1970; Donohue, Tichenor, and Olien, 1972; Douglas, Westley, and Chaffee, 1970; McLeod, Rush, and Friederich, 1968; J. P. Robinson, 1971; Rogers and Shoemaker, 1971; Ward, 1972b). At the same time, laboratory findings were running heavily in support of the inference that exposure to film violence has the immediate, specific effect of increasing aggressiveness (Goranson, 1970). This raised anew the issue of cumulative individual differences—whether extensive exposure to televised violence induces a child to be habitually more aggressive.

Society's concern with violence in general and social psychology's with aggressive effects converged in 1969 when the National Institute of Mental Health (NIMH) sponsored $1 million in new research in connection with the Surgeon General's study of television violence. The political machinations behind this undertaking have been thoroughly described elsewhere (Cater and Strickland, 1975; Liebert, Neale, and Davidson, 1973). What is pertinent here is that the $1 million in research on television violence not only produced many of the studies that we will review later, but it also forced the rather broad community of communication researchers to take a new look at the old hypotheses. When the full range of findings were reviewed, the no-effects model was found to be inadequate (Bogart, 1972c; Chaffee, 1972b; Surgeon General's Scientific Advisory Committee, 1972). Of 20 researchers who contributed to the NIMH project and who later responded to a survey by Paisley (1972), none accepted the hypothesis that "viewing violence has no effect on aggressiveness," nor the view that "viewing television violence decreases aggressiveness." Instead, they concluded either that "viewing television violence increases aggressiveness" or that the relationship between these two variables "depends on a third variable or set of variables."

This evolution in scientific perspective about the influence of the mass media is described in abbreviated form in table 8.1. For ease of communication, four hypothetical "stages" are used to convey the sequence of events. Obviously, reality has been much less nearly organized, the "stages" flow into each other and coexist, although one or another is more clearly dominant at a given time.

Table 8.1 Hypothetical Stages in Evolution of Research on Mass Media Influence

Stage	Prevailing Viewpoint	Empirical Basis
1	Mass media have strong effects	Observation of apparent success of propaganda campaigns Experiments demonstrating immediate attitude change after exposure to messages
2	Mass media largely reinforce existing predispositions, and thus outcomes are likely to be the same in their absence	Evidence of selective perception—persons ignore message contrary to existing predispositions Evidence of personal influence—persons are more influenced by others than the mass media Evidence of negligible influence on voting No relationship observed between exposure to mass media violence and delinquent behavior among the young
3	Mass media have effects independent of other influences which would not occur in the absence of the particular mass media stimuli under scrutiny	Evidence that selective perception is only partially operative Evidence that media influence by setting the context and identifying the persons, events, and issues toward which existing predispositions affect attitudes and behavior Evidence that television violence increases aggressiveness among the young
4	Processes behind effects so far studied may be more general, suggesting new areas for research	New research is finding that under some circumstances television may influence behavior and attitudes other than those related to aggressiveness

Assumptions and Goals

We will give particular emphasis to those third variables—of which there are three very different types. It is not the issue of violence that brings us to this literature.* Our goal is much broader. Tentatively, we assume that the processes governing the one type of outcome hold for other types of outcome.

---

*Many writers approaching this literature have confined themselves to adjudicating the violence-aggression issue, either in favor of the effects hypothesis (e.g., Bogart, 1972a; Goranson, 1969b; Liebert, Neale, and Davidson, 1973; or against it (e.g., Efron, 1972; Kaplan and Singer, 1976; J. L. Singer, 1971); even those who have declined to draw major conclusions have nevertheless seen the major issue as being framed in these terms (e.g., Fuchs and Lyle, 1972).

The Psychology of Behavioral Effects 393

We shall try to accommodate existing findings to the greatest extent possible. In some instances, we shall treat as complementary results treated by others as contradictory. Much of the research has been devoted to antisocial behavior; however, it is clear that it is possible to develop concepts and hypotheses that apply to behavior in general.

We treat television as a functional equivalent to direct personal experience. There are other functional equivalents—among them immediate observation and reports by any means of the experience of others. The term "vicarious" applies alike. We do not thereby suggest that all modes of experience are identical in impact. The influence of experience, whether it is direct or vicarious, is contingent on numerous factors. None of these factors are likely to be wholly independent of the mode of experience.

Television is a particularly important source of vicarious influence. We would attribute this both to the widespread use of television in American life, and to properties of the medium that coincide with factors important for social influence to occur.

Our model of how television influences behavior basically is a description of television's role in learning. Although we do not make any attempt to contribute directly to the various theories of the way behavior changes through learning, we do draw concepts from those theories, such as "stimulus," "reinforcement," and "response hierarchy."

We nevertheless are afraid that the term "learning" may have too narrow a connotation. We would not want to be misunderstood as solely concerned with the acquisition of new behavior, as the term might suggest to some. Nor are we concerned primarily with the acquisition of either facts or values, as others might suppose. Instead, we are concerned with the full range of factors which affect acquisition ("learning" in the narrow sense) and performance, which includes a wide range of attributes of the television stimulus; of the person, including prior experience, and of the real-life nontelevision situation.

We do not consider that it will be sufficient to limit ourselves to two-variable hypotheses of either the stimulus-response or the response-reinforcement variety. The very notion of psychological "processes" behind an effect requires us to deal with at least three variables at a time. There are three classes of three-variable causal relationships, and we outline them before we present our model.

Types of Third-Variable Concepts

The full range of behavioral effects of television has certainly not been demonstrated, nor even explored very extensively. Much two-variable research remains to be done. But it is our view that this research is most likely to lead to enlightened policy if the parts played by additional variables are also examined in the course of testing simple hypotheses about kinds of effects. Assume that there is a general causal connection between television and social behavior. Let us next consider the kinds of roles that might be played by third variables. We shall distinguish three roles the third variable may assume: an antecedent condition, an intervening condition, and a contingent condition.

An *antecedent* condition is an event that must have occurred prior to the person's exposure to television in order for the effect to occur. The relationship with other variables is illustrated in figure 8.1. This antecedent condition is a necessary part of the process that later occurs. For instance, it is often suggested that televised violence "reinforces" previously learned aggressive behavior patterns, thereby making the person more likely to behave aggressively after viewing a violent scene. In this explanation, the necessary antecedent condition is that the person must previously have learned some aggressive behaviors; if he has not, there will be nothing to reinforce, and hence no effect.

An *intervening* condition is a psychological event that occurs between the exposure to television and the subsequent behavior. The relationship with other variables is also illustrated in figure 8.1. The intervening condition can be thought of as a necessary linking mechanism that consists of an immediate response to the television stimulus, and which in turn becomes a stimulus whose consequent response is the behavioral effect in which we are interested. A good example of an intervening condition can be found in the hypothesis of *generalized arousal*. This formulation holds that the direct effect of televised violence is to excite in the person a high degree of motivation to do something—almost anything—of a physical nature. Aggressive behavior is only one of many outlets for this heightened arousal; whether the person lets out a shout, runs around the block, washes the kitchen floor, or perhaps assaults someone, will depend on other factors.

Many of these other factors come under the general definition of *contingent* conditions, which can be thought of as "enabling" or "encouraging" aspects of the social and physical set-

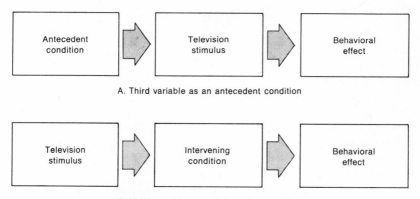

A. Third variable as an antecedent condition

B. Third variable as an intervening condition

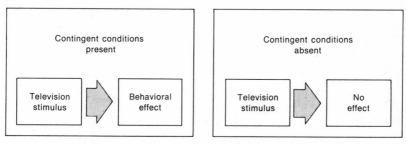

C. Third variable as a contingent condition

Figure 8.1. Three roles of third variables.

ting in which the person finds himself. If appropriate contingent conditions happen to exist, the person's behavior will be affected by the stimulus, but in the absence of such conditions it will not. Again, the relationship with other variables is illustrated in figure 8.1. Situational contingencies are not quite part of the process, but they are necessary for it to operate. The classical example in science is that of a catalyst—a substance in whose presence a specific chemical reaction between two other substances will take place and in whose absence it may not, even though the catalyst itself is not involved in the reaction.

In regard to television's behavioral effects, a moment's thought will suggest many contingent conditions that might govern the occurrence of an effect. An obvious example is the presence of a target. In laboratory studies of violence and aggressive behavior, it is standard procedure to provide the experimental subject with an easy and obvious target—a large doll, or a person to whom shocks can be administered, for instance—so that any direct behavioral effect can be readily observed. Contingencies can also operate to reduce the apparent effect. For example, sanctions may be introduced, such as punishing the child if he behaves aggressively.

A contingent condition is conceptually different from an intervening condition. If a child knows he will be spanked if he hits his baby sister, we have a contingent condition which may partially govern any effects of observing a portrayal of violence on television. When the same portrayal is viewed, but the violent actor is subsequently punished, that portrayal of punishment becomes an intervening condition which may partially govern any effects of the initial portrayal. The contingent condition is external to the process, but influences it; the intervening condition occurs between the stimulus and the effect, or "within" the process.

Implications for Policy and for Science

From a purely psychological point of view, this last distinction would not seem important. It might be perfectly possible to study, and understand, how anticipated punishment operates as a sanction, without worrying about whether the child learns about it from his parents' warning or within the televised stimulus program itself. But from a policy perspective, there is a great deal of difference. The kinds of policies that are devised, and the methods for instituting them, are quite different for parents as opposed to the television industry. To make parents aware of the problem a particular type of television content might pose, and to train them in methods for coping with it in their child-rearing, would require a massive educational program. Only a few such efforts have been successfully carried through (one example is the shift in this century away from corporal punishment and attempts at early weaning). It would be wholly different to attempt to influence television story plot lines, which are quite intricate and in which a single element such as punishment can take on a wide variety of subtle meanings—each of which might be translated by a viewer into a distinct intervening condition, which could lead to a different behavioral effect.

Here we shall not attempt to consider the full range of possible contingencies that might conceivably exist or which experimenters could create in controlled laboratory environments. The conditions that command most of our attention are those suf-ficiently common in the real world for policy to take them into ac-count.

Assessing the importance of a factor in regard to policy requires a rather different kind of methodology from that usually employed to demonstrate the simple existence of such a factor. It is common to describe the difference in terms of experimental "versus" survey methods (e.g., Hovland, 1959), although the two have much in common and within each there is a wide diversity of procedures. But we shall adhere to the convention of using the term "experiment" to refer to studies in which most threats to *internal* validity of an inference are controlled (D. T. Campbell and Stanley, 1966), so that the claimed finding is not subject to many alternative explanations; the terms "survey" and "field study" will be used where a study assesses natural variation across a reason-ably wide variety of persons in their ordinary life-situations, thus encouraging some confidence in the generalizability of findings by meeting various threats to *external* validity of a finding—beyond the particular conditions of the study itself. Before pre-suming to devise policy recommendations based on an inference, one should have evidence of both types; that is, evidence that the hypothesized process indeed operates, and also that it operates often enough to be worth doing something about. As we shall see, such thoroughly studied topics are rare.

Besides considering the relationship between research and public policy, we therefore must also address ourselves to strat-egies for future research, and the role played by process variables in that research. It will be useful to distinguish between research that is designed to *build* theories about the effects of television, and research whose purpose is to *test* hypotheses derived from such theories. As we have indicated, it is clear that whatever be-havioral effects television might have, it does not have them on all viewers at all times. The search for theoretical explanations con-sists first of stating what seem to be plausible antecedent, inter-vening, and contingent conditions for the effect; practically any kind of research—experiments, surveys, case studies, clinical ex-plorations, introspection—might yield such hunches, and the business of organizing them into a coherent theoretical scheme may take place without a great deal of original empirical inves-tigation. A useful theory would consist of a small set of general principles that predict that one will find consistent patterns of relationships across a wide variety of real-world observations. A "theory" about the effect of *one* television program, or applicable only to *one* viewer, would not be of much value; neither would one that is so complicated that we could scarcely comprehend it, nor one that failed to state the conditions under which we should expect it to operate.

A theory is not tested whole; rather, it is used to derive a number of hypotheses that should be true if the total theory is true. Each hypothesis is submitted to empirical test, which means that someone attempts to gather evidence that will indicate whether the specific hypothesis is consistent with real-world observations. These tests may be of either of the types we have discussed above—experimental tests of the validity of the hypothesis, or field studies to assess its generality. Because other, future tests of the same or different hypotheses may not be supportive, hypotheses that survive such tests do not prove the total theory correct, of course, but those which fail to pass empirical tests serve to falsify the larger theory or at least to indicate that its applicability is limited (Popper, 1968).

In experimental tests of hypotheses about process variables, the investigator has enough control over the factor in question either to "create" it for some persons or to withhold it from them, or both. For example, we have discussed the contingent condition hypothesis that parental threat of punishment for aggression might reduce the effect of television violence in producing aggressive behavior. This could be tested experimentally either by introducing that threat for some youngsters, or by guaranteeing them immunity from such a threat. In either case, the children who receive this experimental treatment should be randomly selected by the experimenter.

In a field test of the same hypothesis, such tight control over parents and children by the researcher might not be possible, so that a major element of hypothesis-testing power is sacrificed in order to gain power in generalizing to the typical world in which children watch and react to television. In such a field study, one would look separately at those children whose parents exercise sanctions against aggression, and those who are not under such sanctions. If the latter group exhibited a stronger tendency to be aggressively influenced by television violence, the evidence would be consistent with the hypothesis, but less conclusive than in the case of a controlled experiment on the same point.

The Complete Model

We have chosen to present our model in the form of a flow chart because that is the clearest and most convenient way when many variables can profitably be conceptualized as occurring in sequence. The model has the following features:

> Sequential relationships are specified among the variables that appear most essential to an understanding of the way television influences behavior. These include perceptions of television content (e.g., perceived reality, and perceived consequences of behavior), "black box" intra-individual processes (e.g., generalized arousal, inhibition, reinforcement, and catharsis), and situational contingencies (e.g., opportunity, consequences).
> There is provision for branching to different processes, depending on combinations of the above factors, and on whether the behavioral act in question occurs or not.
> There are cumulative effects over repeated cycles through the hypothesized sequences of events.

The full model will be laid out first, so that the reader can see it whole. It is illustrated in figure 8.2. Despite the apparent complexity, we must emphasize that the model is a gross oversimplification of the complexities of human behavior. After we have presented the overall model, we shall review the evidence regarding its various parts in detail.

The devising of a model of this type forces us to make choices about the relationship among combinations of variables and to formulate an internally consistent and logical overall picture of television's role in influencing behavior. We have also attempted to make the model "externally consistent"—that is, consistent with existing research, which we review here.

Our rendering of the processes is at best hypothetical. One of our intentions is to stimulate such empirical testing in a more organized fashion than has been the case in the past. If subsequent research that tests our propositions demonstrates that they are untenable, then the model will have served its scientific purpose equally as well as it would if subsequent research were to validate it in all respects.

The model represents the itinerary of one person, over time. Its results, summed across many persons, would correspond to aggregate social behavior. The values for the various elements of

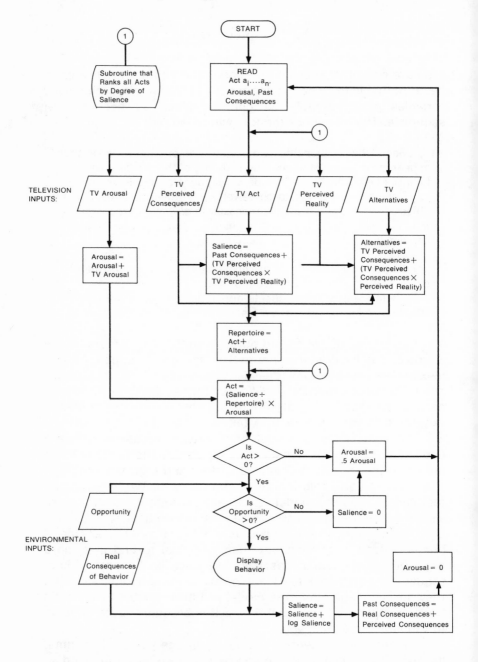

Figure 8.2. Flow chart of model of how television influences behavior.

the model for a given person will depend upon: the probabilities of his experiencing particular television stimuli; the probabilities of his encountering certain environmental contingencies, such as opportunity to act, and rewards or punishments for his acts; his accumulated learning, as a function of these first two sets of factors, over a long series of cycles through the model. This last characteristic of the model is intended to give it an "existential" quality that accords with evidence that a person's prior learning greatly conditions his response to a particular television program in a particular situation.*

Unhappily, when words which have one or more meanings in ordinary English are used to label components of such a model some language problems arise. Sometimes a term will refer to all the stipulations and properties of that stage in the model. At other times, the term will have a more conventional meaning, although obviously it will have that meaning within the context of discussing the model. We regret the departure from English, but our solution when the former is the case is to place the term within brackets—for example, [act], [alternatives], [arousal].

The Principal Components and Their Interrelationship

Our central concept is [act]. This refers to any of the full range of social behavior a person might carry out. It could be an aggressive act, such as hitting or threatening another person, or a "prosocial" act, such as helping or cooperating with another person. Or it might be an erotic, political, or isolated physical act. We can hardly begin to list the possibilities, since they constitute the total set of possible human behaviors. Fortunately for our purposes

---

*We do not include in the model any genetic individual "personality" differences, although there are doubtless such differences between people before they encounter television or social situations in which behavior learned via television might be acted out. For our purposes here, we shall assume that prior personality differences are distributed randomly across different levels of television inputs and situational factors. The latter two categories of influences vary enough from one person to another to account eventually for rather sizable differences among people, without reference to genetic personality factors. In taking this approach, we are following the premise that our long-range goal is the development of *policy*. We are implicitly assuming that policies regarding both television inputs and situational constraints on behavior are within the broad sphere of human control. We will avoid the thorny thicket of contemplating social "policies" regarding the analogous manipulation of genetic personality traits, so, except to the extent that such traits are learned via the processes described in our model, we shall ignore them here.

here, only a few classes of acts have been studied in connection with television, but we should not leave the impression that *only* those that have been studied—or only those that occur on television—are potentially relevant. We should assume at the outset that any form of behavior *might* follow the route we will describe for [act]. If only a few types of acts in fact result from television in daily life, the model should explain why this would be so, in terms of other necessary factors in the process that ordinarily do not occur.

The likelihood of a given person's behaving in conformance with a given [act] is a function of three factors: [salience], the degree to which the particular behavior exists psychologically for the person (Carter, 1965); [repertoire], the summed salience of all possible acts for the person in his present situation (any single act is a fraction of [repertoire]); [arousal], which is the extent to which the person is activated to perform *any* act in his present situation.

Intuitively, we can propose that the probability of the person's performing a particular act is decreased to the extent that he has other possible acts in his repertoire, and increased to the extent that he is aroused to do *something.* These intuitive propositions can be summarized in the equation,

$$[act] = \frac{[salience]}{[repertoire]} \cdot [arousal] \qquad (1)$$

Let us consider the implications of this simple bit of arithmetic. First, if the act is not at all salient for the person, it will not affect his behavior. Second, if he is not at all aroused to act, he will not exhibit the particular act—no matter how salient it is. If there is some degree of arousal, and the act is to some extent salient, it has some probability of occurring. If it is the only act in the person's repertoire, then it is maximally likely, limited only by the degree of arousal. An act that is only a minor item in the person's total repertoire, by contrast, has little chance of occurring in a given instance. Over many trials, given high arousal, however, it would occur occasionally.

This equation is carried throughout our model by the person. It is modified to the extent that events alter the salience of the act, or the total repertoire of acts, or the person's level of situational arousal. Equation 1 is by no means the only theoretical proposition available to us regarding these variables. We have selected it from a number of possible general models of behavior because it will permit us to account for many other factors that are demonstrably related to television and social learning. We invite the reader to accept it tentatively, not as "truth" but as a necessary assumption for understanding the remainder of our model.

We posit that television can affect the salience of an act in two ways: by demonstrating the act, and by attaching negative or positive values to the act.

It seems intuitively obvious that the more often, and the more vividly, a given act is portrayed for a person, the more salient it will become to him. The parameters governing this process are not so well understood as they are generally agreed upon. We presume that this would be a process of learning by observation, which would follow a gradually decelerating or asymptotic learning curve—the first few observations of the act via television (or in real life) should increase its salience markedly, but gradually the impact of a single observation lessens, so that, say, the 100th repetition adds rather little. This would accord with the vast literature on cumulative learning curves (see Keller and Schoenfeld, 1950; Woodworth and Schlosberg, 1963).

The second way is by attaching positive or negative values to the act. For instance, it is common in dramatic plots to indicate that a given act is justified by the circumstances confronting the actor, or that it has positive consequences for the actor or for the community. This is typical, for instance, in westerns and police dramas, where a violent act—such as murder of a criminal—is portrayed as necessary to rid the community of a menace. Attachment of positive values in such ways should increase salience; of negative values, such as demonstrating unhappy consequences, should reduce salience.

We shall review evidence on these particular lines of argument later, after we have outlined our full model. For convenience, meanwhile, we shall use the catch-all term [perceived consequences] to refer to the sum of 'all positive values, minus all negative values, that the person has learned to attach to a given act. This includes such value-connected elements as justification, community needs, and the like, as well as the act's direct consequences for the individual actor.

Later in the model, when the person actually carries out a particular act as a result of the processes we are discussing here, he may experience direct consequences of this behavior. We would expect these [real consequences] to be incorporated into the level of salience he carries with him into subsequent situations, where the act may again become a salient possibility. So later we shall make provision for that eventuality.

Also important, research indicates, is the degree to which the person perceives the televised portrayal as representing reality. The evidence is strong enough on this point for us to consider [perceived reality] to constitute a contingent condition, in whose absence there will be no increase in salience regardless of the degree of exposure to, or consequential values associated with, the act for the person. Therefore we would propose that any increase in the salience of an act attributed to its demonstration on television is a single instance would follow the general formula,

$$[salience] = [past \: consequences] +$$
$$([perceived \: consequences] \cdot [perceived \: reality]) \qquad (2)$$

We have intentionally written this as a multiplicative equation so that if the degree of perceived reality is zero, the increment in salience will also be zero. On the other hand, if the portrayal is perceived by the person as a perfect replica of real-life, then the resultant values associated with its [perceived consequences] will have maximal impact on [salience]. Similarly, if no evaluative consequences are associated with the act, [salience] will not be affected regardless of the extent to which the portrayal is seen as realistic.

Television can also affect both [repertoire] and [arousal]. It affects [repertoire] by changes in the salience of [act], which we have just discussed, and by the additional input of salient alternative behaviors. Without elaborating at this point, we can define this as,

$$[repertoire] = [act] + [alternatives] \qquad (3)$$

leaving [alternatives] for later consideration in connection with situations in which the most salient act does not occur for some reason. As for [arousal], it is conceived to be highly situational, with the level fluctuating markedly. It is intuitively obvious that a person can be aroused by many situational factors in his daily life. There is also good evidence that both the content and form of televised portrayals can be arousing. Decreases in arousal can occur as a result of acting out a given behavior (either the act, or an alternative), and it is possible for television to play some role in such a "cathartic" response as well.

So far, we have considered major factors affecting behavior, and some hypothetical relationships among them, in which television might provide a vicarious experience, depending on its given content elements. Among these elements are display of an act, and of alternative acts; perceived consequences of the act; perceived reality of the portrayal; and the general arousing properties of the televised program. Although the role of viewer characteristics typically would be most pronounced in affecting the perception of consequences and of reality, which are usually the most ambiguous of content factors, in fact all of the content elements are the joint product of attributes of the portrayal and characteristics of the viewer. The meaning of what the viewer receives depends upon how he perceives it. We label the two concepts [perceived consequences] and [perceived reality] simply to emphasize their particular sensitivity in this respect.

Our model must also incorporate factors beyond the context of the viewing experience itself. A person does not carry out behaviors in a social vacuum, however stimulated he might be toward a particular act. At least two kinds of environmental factors have to be taken into account. First, as we have mentioned above, there are the [real consequences] he experiences if he performs the act. The other, and prior, factor is that of [opportunity]. If there is little chance that an appropriate situation for a particular act will present itself to the person, the probability of that act's occurring is small regardless of other factors. Therefore, we should expect social learning—in the sense of acquiring actual behavior patterns—to be most likely when television portrays acts which the person has many opportunities to perform. As an example, we might compare the learning potential from dramatized fisticuffs to that from dramatized rocket warfare in outer space or sexual debauchery in a shiek's harem.

The latter types of portrayals, while we can hardly expect them to result in direct imitative behavior (given the extreme unlikelihood of opportunity) nevertheless interest us for several reasons. One is the possibility of *response generalization*. It is well established in psychology that learning of one behavior also enhances learning of similar behaviors. This would imply, for example, that exposure to rocket warfare might stimulate some kind of warlike behavior in the person—even though he does not have a rocket ship readily available. Secondly, the absence of opportunity for one behavior might reasonably lead to a search for new alternatives, which could lead the person back to television itself in the mode of behavior called *information-seeking*.

A third point is that the space journey and the harem are clearly fantasy portrayals; absence of opportunity might well offer an alternative explanation for the considerable importance that has been attached to perceived reality as a contingent condition in learning from television. It may not be a perception of fantasy (vs. reality) in a television portrayal that short-circuits cognitive learning. Instead, it could be that the lack of opportunity to carry out the fantasy portrayals blocks an effect of such learning at the overt behavioral stage. Here we have chosen to make the cognitive interpretation of the reality-fantasy dimension, because we would like to make a place for *fantasy-play* in our overall model. Although there has been little research on the topic, we consider that there may well be important consequences for learning via television owing to the opportunity provided for children to play in toy rocket ships, or to simulate other activities for which real-life opportunities are not available.

The impact on children's play of motorcycle daredevil Evel Knievel in the mid-1970s was obvious enough to parents of boys throughout the country; and that impact justifies some theoretical concern regarding the role of fantasy-play in learning of behaviors for which real-life opportunities seemingly do not exist. There is evidence that very few children through the age of eight or nine cognitively make the reality-fantasy distinction (Ward and Wackman, 1973); television is taken as simple observation of part of the world, and [opportunity] can be extended to include the chance to carry out the observed behavior in socially approved fantasy-play situations.*

If the value of [act], as defined above in terms of various constituent factors, is greater than zero, we should expect the behavior to occur if, and only if, [opportunity] is present. If not, we would expect the person to seek [alternatives], to the extent that he remains aroused. If so, this behavior might or might not be reinforced, depending on the [real consequences] the person's social environment provides in response. We expect the [salience] of an act that has been emitted to increase as a result of that behavior. Separately, we expect the [perceived consequences] of that act to be altered to a considerable extent

---

*We should expect some differences among children depending on the extent to which they have had toys and other equipment available for this type of experience. In this context, it is worth noting that television programs provide a major source of content themes for the toy industry, as did children's films before television.

by its [real consequences], as experienced by the person. And finally, we assume, on the basis of considerable research on behavioral catharsis, that [arousal] is reduced much more if the act occurs than if it does not. All of these features are built into "return loops" in our model, which bring the person back to the starting point for additional stimulation from television in a new cycle.

An Individual's Itinerary

We can now review our formulation by following a person's itinerary (figure 8.2). From "start," he goes to a point at which all prior learning is summarized in terms of the factors we have identified as potentially important: salience, past consequences, and initial level of arousal. For the very young child entering the model for the first time all of these values except initial arousal can be assumed to be zero. For those persons with some social learning behind them, the saliences of each possible act differ, and are ranked at this point. The most-salient one will be identified for this cycle through the model as [act], and all others will be lumped together for simplicity here as [alternatives]. We would assume that each alternative to [act] is stored separately in the person's memory, and that these alternatives also differ in salience from one another and are subject to fluctuations depending on inputs from television. It is this full [repertoire] of alternative acts, ranked according to their respective saliences, that is referred to as the person's response hierarchy in certain theories of learning.*

In figure 8.4, a number of inputs from television are possible in the next stage. These are posited to influence the person's disposition to perform the act in question. One input is the

---

* Since we think of this hierarchy as representing differential probabilities of the person's emitting the various alternative acts, we can expect some variation from time to time in the behavior that he exhibits; in a Monte Carlo simulation model, behaviors would be sampled from this hierarchy on a *probabilistic* basis, so that over time even rather low-salience acts might occur once in a while. We shall not concern ourselves here with that type of mathematical simulation, however; we shall limit our discussion to the elements that we consider *deterministic* in the sense that they alter the configuration of the response hierarchy from one time to another. This is not to imply that we do not consider probabilistic simulation to be a useful method for analyzing the processes we are considering here; in fact, we consider it a highly promising approach, although more appropriate for a more advanced state of knowledge than is the case here.

[arousal] evoked by the television presentation itself; this we presume is somehow added to the person's initial level of arousal, to determine his overall level of arousal in this situation. A second major input is the degree of [perceived reality]. This will govern the effect on him of a third type of input, the [perceived consequences], as portrayed on television, of the various acts that are displayed. The remaining inputs from television are various acts which again can be separated into a most-salient [act] and less salient [alternatives], which may or may not be identical to the [repertoire] existing prior to exposure to the television portrayal.

The first combining equation following the television inputs is the recalculation of salience as a consequence of new perceived consequences multiplied by the perceived reality associated with their televised portrayal. This, we assume, occurs separately for each alternative act in the person's behavioral repertoire, which is then recalculated accordingly. In theory, this could result in the initially selected act being superseded by one of the alternatives as the most-salient item in the person's repertoire. This would occur if, in a highly realistic portrayal, the most-salient act was demonstrated to have decidedly negative consequences while an alternative act was portrayed as producing more positive consequences. The cognitive process by which the salience of an act is reduced owing to negative consequences is usually called *inhibition.*

The [act] that emerges from this first-stage processing of information from television is, we hypothesize, a strong or weak behavioral disposition depending on the strength of alternative dispositions. The greater the value of [act] relative to [repertoire], the stronger the disposition to behave accordingly. Whether the person will carry out this disposition depends, however, on other factors besides its strength. Specifically, we propose that it depends on [arousal] and on [opportunity] for the behavior in the environmental situation in which he finds himself.

An example of the implications of this early part of the model can be seen in figure 8.3. Here, three hypothetical persons are followed through a set of television experiences. For simplicity, we assume that their initial levels of [arousal] are low, and that they begin with no notion of the [consequences] of either of the two types of behavior in their [repertoires]—aggression and helping. For two of them (Persons A and B) the [saliences] of aggression and helping are initially equal, whereas for the third (Person C) aggression is a somewhat more salient act than is helping.

Initial level of saliences...	aggression = helping	aggression = helping	aggression greater than helping
Initial perceived consequences	zero	zero	zero
Initial arousal	low	low	low
TV Act/Consequence	aggression/negative	aggression/negative	helping/positive
New saliences	aggression less than helping	aggression less than helping	aggression = helping
TV arousal	strong	weak	moderate
TV reality	highly realistic	very unrealistic	somewhat realistic
Resultant act/likelihood...	helping/very likely	helping/unlikely	helping or aggression/ somewhat likely

Figure 8.3. Experiences of three hypothetical persons.

These three persons are then given some rather different television content. Persons A and B both see examples of aggression that has negative [consequences]. Person A, however, sees this portrayed in a highly arousing and realistic context, while Person B see an unrealistic and nonarousing portrayal. The result is that helping becomes a much more likely act for Person A than for Person B. Meanwhile, Person C is seeing a different program, one in which helping has positive consequences; the portrayal is somewhat realistic and the program is moderately arousing. The overall result is that either helping or aggression have become approximately equally likely (which was not the case before), and the probability that any act of either type will occur is greater than in the case of Person B but less than that of Person A.

As we noted earlier, [arousal] is a combination of the person's initial arousal plus the situational arousal evoked by his television experience. This overall [arousal] is multiplied by the strength of the disposition to [act]; if the result is insufficient to evoke the act, the level of arousal is hypothetically reduced somewhat—although not entirely—and the person returns to the early stage of the model and continues to process information from television. If the combination of [act] and [arousal] is sufficient to produce a disposition to carry out the behavior, the person then examines his environment for an [opportunity] to act on this disposition. If no opportunity presents itself, the model specifies that the salience of the act in question is reduced to zero, and the overall level of arousal is reduced to one-half (an arbitrary intermediate value) of what it has been; the person returns to the early stage of processing television information, but with an altered response hierarchy in which the act that had been most salient is no longer a salient element. Repeated presentations of the act could, of course, restore it to a position of salience.

Figure 8.4 illustrates the theoretical impact of [opportunity] on three hypothetical persons we call X, Y and Z. In this example we shall consider three types of social behavior that might be portrayed on television and consequently learned by a viewer: affection toward, cooperation with, and avoidance of other people. The impact of the television portrayal, combined with other factors such as [arousal] and [reality] has been identical on Persons X and Y, in terms of affection; both these persons find this behavior highly salient, as indicated by (+ + +) in figure 8.4. Their secondary behavioral tendencies are different: cooperation in X's case, avoidance in Y's. Person Z is overall less aroused; his tendency toward cooperation is equal to that of Person X, (+ +) in each case; but he has no more salient behavioral tendency at this

	Person X	Person Y	Person Z
First cycle: Repertoire	Affection (+ + +) Cooperation (+ +)	Affection (+ + +) Avoidance (+ +)	Cooperation (+ +) Affection (+)
1st Act tendency	Affection	Affection	Cooperation
Opportunity to Act?	Yes	No	No
Behavior displayed	Affection	None	None
Second cycle: Repertoire	Affection (+ + + +) Cooperation (+)	Avoidance (+ + +) Affection (+ +)	Affection (+ +) Cooperation (+)
2nd Act tendency	Affection	Avoidance	Affection
Opportunity to Act?	Yes	Yes	Yes
Behavior displayed	Affection	Avoidance	Affection
Third cycle: Repertoire	Affection (+ + + + +)	Avoidance (+ + + +) Affection (+)	Affection (+ + +)

Figure 8.4. The impact of opportunity on three hypothetical persons.

beginning stage, so his initial tendency is toward cooperation; he also has some tendency toward affection, but it is quite minimal (+).

Now let us suppose for illustration that each time a person has the [opportunity] to act out his most salient behavioral tendency he will do so; further, let us suppose that this display of behavior increases the salience of it in his [repertoire[by one unit, as represented in figure 8.4 by a (+) sign. Any behavior not displayed because of lack of opportunity we shall assume becomes less salient, and so we shall subtract a (+) sign in such a case.

What happens to our friends X, Y and Z in figure 8.4 as a consequence of lack of opportunity exaggerates the impact we conceive of [opportunity] as having, but it is instructive to consider it even as an overstated case. Person X finds opportunity to display affection, and does so, on the first cycle; this strengthens his tendency toward affection in the second cycle, when once again he finds the opportunity and behaves accordingly; by the beginning of the third cycle, affection is the single and highly salient item remaining in his repertoire. Person Y by contrast finds his tendency toward affection blocked by lack of opportunity in the first cycle; in the second cycle, avoidance has become more salient, and the opportunity for avoidance presents itself; as Y enters the third cycle, his avoidance tendency has been strengthened and affection has nearly vanished from his repertoire. Person Z, finding no opportunity to display cooperation in the first cycle, turns to affection in the second; by the start of the third cycle, his tendency toward affection has become the only item in his repertoire.

Note that even given the simple rules for changing saliences in this hypothetical example a number of important things have happened to the people in figure 8.4. Cooperation, which was originally in the repertoire of both X and Z, never occurs and in a short time has been dropped entirely. Person Y, who initially had a much stronger tendency toward affection than Person Z, loses it almost entirely, and by the third cycle their situations are entirely reversed; because of lack of opportunity, Person Y turns to avoidance behavior.

Real people, with long years of social learning behind them, would of course not respond so dramatically to [opportunity] factors. But even minor effects of this character, aggregated over large numbers of people and many cycles of learning, could eventuate in sizable effects on social life. This simple example should also give the reader an appreciation of our reasons for *not* attempting to be highly quantitative in the development of our simulation model. Our knowledge of the incidence of various behaviors in social interaction, or even on television, is so primitive that one could not begin to attach precise quantitative estimates to any of the processes represented in the general model of figure 8.2. Its value lies in integrating a large number of factors into a coherent—if complicated—whole.

If the person is disposed to carry out the [act], and if he finds an appropriate [opportunity], we propose that he will display the behavior in question. This act then might have either positive or negative [real consequences]. The exercise of the behavior increases its general [salience] by an unknown logarithmic function, which is a mathematical way of representing the decelerating pattern of the typical behavioral learning curve over repeated trials (to attempt to assign an exact value to this function would be premature, given the limited state of knowledge on human behavioral learning). We posit also that the person's [perceived consequences] for the act are modified strongly by its [real consequences] for him, but that his prior store of perceived consequences is also retained in this recalculation; we have arbitrarily weighted real consequences equally with prior perceived consequences in this recalculation. Finally, we propose that the experience of carrying out the act dissipates [arousal] totally, so that it is set back to zero. The person then returns to the beginning of the model with a modified set of values for the elements he has "learned" in connection with the behavior he has displayed. The [salience] of the [act] has been modified by both its exercise (which has increased its salience) and by changes in its [perceived consequences] (positively or negatively depending on the act's real consequences); initial arousal has returned to zero. At this point, the person awaits new stimulation from television, which will begin a new cycle through the model we have outlined above.

Reviewing the Evidence

Of course, our ability to construct our model is no guarantee of its validity. We have designed it to accord with our interpretation of the research literature on the variables we have built into it. We shall now test the model's consistency with the evidence.

Because we focus on our model, we shall not necessarily look at the studies in the same ways that their authors have intended. Instead, we have set for ourselves here an agenda of interdependent hypotheses, which will enable us to examine evidence as it bears upon our propositions. In the sense that this same evidence may also bear upon equally plausible hypotheses we have not incorporated, our interpretation is selective. However, we shall not ignore the existence of evidence that is clearly inconsistent with propositions that we have built into our model.

There are five topics which have been studied in sufficient depth to provide us with data. They are:

Television's contribution to aggressiveness.

Television's influence over constructive, or "prosocial," behavior.

Pornography and erotica, although television *per se* has not been involved.

Television's role in political socialization.

Television's usefulness as a therapeutic tool, particularly in the desensitization of phobic responses.

With the exception of the fifth topic, almost all of the research has involved children or adolescents. Whether this emphasis on youth seriously limits the applicability of the findings to other segments of the population is an empirical question. It can only be answered by testing the hypotheses our model generates with population segments other than the young. In the meantime, we believe that a model which fits the large inventory of findings on these topics should be viewed as generalizable to other topics and different populations in the absence of evidence to the contrary.

Arousal as a Necessary Condition

An important variable in our model is the concept of [arousal]. If the person is not aroused, nothing happens, regardless of television's influence on other factors. On the other hand, arousal by stimuli other than television can be the factor generating an effect on which television may have a profound influence by way of such other factors.

We treat arousal as a necessary (but not sufficient) condition for the overt display of learned behaviors, and we also provide for it to vary over time much more than do other factors in the model.

It can be immediately raised to a level sufficient to activate the person, and then reduced to zero if he does act. It is partially dissipated, even in the absence of overt behavior, by the suspension of action while the person processes information from television.

We have given an important role in the model to this single variable because of recent research which gives empirical support to our main propositions about arousal. To date, however, this research has been disappointingly limited in focusing almost entirely on the question of the stimulation of aggressive behavior. We would hope that our delineation of a general model for all sorts of behavioral learning might stimulate new efforts toward investigation of this variable in connection with nonaggressive social acts that television could "teach."

The typical method employed in the arousal research is the laboratory experiment. Examples are the work of Doob and Konecni, and of Tannenbaum and Zillmann. Before turning to the experimental work, however, we should consider one field survey that lends support to the main thrust of the laboratory studies.

Watt and Krull combined survey data collected by others (McLeod, Atkin, and Chaffee, 1972a) with their own coding of the action quotient of television programs (Krull and Watt, 1973; Watt and Krull, 1974) to assess the extent to which habitual levels of adolescent aggression could be attributed to the arousing characteristics of programs. Their action quotient is based on the frequency with which the action in a program shifts from one locale to another, or the dialogue from one actor to another. This variable, when scored for all evening series programs from careful coding of videotapes, provided greater discrimination among the programs than did various schemes for identifying violence (B. S. Greenberg and Gordon, 1972a; McLeod, Atkin, and Chaffee, 1972a, 1972b). That is, programs appear to vary more on their action quotient than on violence.

When program violence ratings were weighted according to frequency of individual viewing, McLeod, Atkin, and Chaffee (1972b), found positive correlations between the resulting index of exposure to television violence and various measures of aggressive behavior across a variety of samples (see Chaffee, 1972b, for summary). Later, Watt (1973) demonstrated that the violence and action quotient measures *each* explained a significant amount of independent variance in the criterion measure of aggression, when the other independent variable was controlled. Krull (1973) presented some evidence to link program action quotient with physiological arousal, and research is underway to test the strength of this association more completely. Assuming that, as seems likely, high action television programs are capable of arousing a viewer independently of their explicit plot line, the Watt-Krull data make a good presumptive case for testing the role of arousal more specifically under controlled conditions.

These are a very important set of findings. First, they suggest that in some circumstances increased aggression after exposure to television violence outside the laboratory may be attributable in part to factors other than the specific content, and exposure to other kinds of content may also be followed by increased aggression. Second, they demonstrate that other dimensions of television content besides violence are not only measurable (among them such subtleties as the program rhythms reflected in activity level) but also that exposure to such dimensions has measurable effects. The result is to greatly widen the range of processes and effects open to study in the future.

The laboratory studies can be divided generally into a few groups. There have been many demonstrations of the arousing physiological effects of viewing portrayals of aggressive, physically active, erotic, or frustrating fare (K. E. Davis and Braucht, 1971; Doob and Climie, 1972; Doob and Kirschenbaum, 1973; Dysinger and Ruckmick, 1933; Lazarus et al., 1962; Mosher, 1971, 1973; Sternbach, 1962; Tannenbaum, 1971, 1972). Behavioral aggressive effects of arousing portrayals have also been shown frequently (Bandura, 1965a; Bandura, Ross, and Ross, 1963a, 1963b; Doob and Climie, 1972; Mallick and McCandless, 1966; Mann, Sidman, and Starr, 1971, 1973; Mann et al., 1974; Meyer, 1972a, 1972b; Walters and Thomas, 1963; Zillmann, 1969, 1971, 1972; Zillmann, Hoyt, and Day, 1974; Zillmann and Johnson, 1973). There has also been some work by Berkowitz (1974) and his associates on the effect on behavior of "prior arousal" before viewing a violent television episode. In a somewhat different vein, Zillmann (1972) has been concerned with the role of arousal in the "excitation" of aggressive behavior. An earlier treatment was Feshbach's (1961) contention that arousal is a necessary condition for the operation of "catharsis" of aggressive dispositions following exposure to dramatic violence; this hypothesis is somewhat more complicated than the simple arousal formulation of our model, and we shall reserve discussion of catharsis for later.

Our use of the term "arousal" to this point has masked the fact that this concept is looked on by most investigators as a complex combination of cognitive and purely physiological factors. The label that the individual applies to his physiological state is an important factor on which the effects of physiological arousal are partly and possibly wholly contingent. "Cognitive labeling" may be a necessary element if arousal is to have practical consequences.

It is clear that increased aggressive behavior can be brought about by treating experimental subjects in rude and insulting ways (Doob and Wood, 1972; Konecni, 1973, 1975a, 1975b; Konecni and Doob, 1972). However, this is not necessarily the result of physiological arousal alone. As Konecni (1975b) points out, the experimenter's insulting remarks are "social in nature," so that the subjects should be expected cognitively to "label themselves" as angry and accordingly behave more aggressively in a subsequent social situation (Schachter and Singer, 1962).

Such labeling may be necessary to produce any aggressive effect. This interpretation is encouraged by the finding of Zillmann, Katcher, and Milavsky (1972) that when there was a high level of social instigation (or "social arousal"), aggression varied in accord with purely physiological arousal (in this case strenuous exercise). Konecni (1975b) tested the hypothesis in an experiment in which social instigation was manipulated by the experimenter's insults, and nonsocial arousal by the loudness of tones the subject heard prior to each opportunity to aggress by administering shocks to someone. Those subjects who had not been insulted exhibited dramatically less aggression than did the insulted subjects at each of five levels of physiological arousal.

Konecni (1975b, p. 711) takes this as good evidence for the cognitive labeling hypothesis, in that "even the repeated exposure to aversive auditory stimulation did not enhance aggressive behavior, unless the subjects had a good reason for considering themselves angry." He is currently attempting to investigate in greater detail the relationships among arousal, anger, and aggression. The prominence of cognitive labeling in behavior is further emphasized by the tentative evidence that anxiety may lead to the seeking of stimuli that can serve as an explanation for its presence (Boyanowsky, 1977; Boyanowsky, Newtson, and Walster, 1974). Cognitive labeling, which in the case of aggression frequently takes the guise of anger, deserves not only the exploration Konecni proposes for that domain but also examination of its role in other kinds of behavior that may be facilitated by television.

Zillmann has developed a somewhat similar position, a two-factor "excitation-transfer" paradigm (Zillmann, 1969, 1971, 1972). On the basis of Schachter and Singer's (1962) finding that *reports* of arousal were identical in subjects who had received activating agents and those who had received placebos that they had been led to expect would arouse them, Zillmann (1972, p. 927) infers that "excitatory response patterns associated with the various emotional states are non-specific." Accordingly, an adequate formulation of the arousal process requires both a physiological and a cognitive component. As Zillmann (1972, p. 928) puts it, "perception-cognitions guide and thus determine the individual's assessment of the *kind* of emotion he is experiencing, whereas the interoception of his physiological arousal determines the *intensity* of the emotion arrived at cognitively." While this formulation differs only slightly in character from Konecni's, there are much clearer differences between the two schools in the relative emphasis they give to cognitive and physiological factors. Zillmann sees generalized arousal as a sufficient condition for eliciting aggressive behavior, whereas Konecni (1975b) proposes that it is necessary but not sufficient.

Our model does not force a choice between these two viewpoints, but we clearly lean toward the Konecni version in our formula for determining [act] as a multiplicative rather than an additive function of arousal.* We assume that some form of generalized arousal is necessary, and that it must be associated with some cognitive awareness of a specific behavior, in order to produce an overt act. Both the Konecni and the Zillmann formulations, and the data supporting them, are consistent with this general conclusion, which we have incorporated into our model.

The manipulation of commercials and violent films by Wor-

---

*Evidence somewhat against our judgment comes from several experiments. Zillmann (1971) demonstrated that exposure to erotic (nonaggressive) material can elicit aggressive behavior in comparison with a nonerotic, nonaggressive film. Meyer (1972a) replicated this finding, although the erotic film in his study did not produce as much aggressiveness as did a violent film. In a later study, Zillmann, Hoyt, and Day (1974) found that an erotic film produced significantly higher levels of aggressiveness than did two films they labeled "violent" and "aggressive," and the latter two did not differ significantly from a "control" film. While there are enough differences among these studies to render them noncomparable, and while the sampling of both erotic and aggressive-violent materials is far too limited to justify any inferences about the relative arousal-potential of the two types of content, these results as a group support the general conclusion that excitation is to some extent independent of the specific behavior that is being displayed.

chel, Hardy, and Hurley (1976) gives support to arousal as a crucial element, and also illustrates that the source may be some interpolated message or symbol. Subjects viewed in entirety either one of two violent films, *Attica* or *The Wild One,* or the comedy *The Mouse That Roared.* The films were either shown uninterrupted or with four two-minute blocks of commercials every 15 to 20 minutes. Subjects viewing the violent films were interrupted by the greater hostility only when the films were interrupted by the commercials. A plausible explanation is that the interruptions served to frustrate, and thus arouse, the viewers, and this state combined with the presentation of violent models and cues to elicit hostility. The findings also lead to the speculation that arousal induced by films ordinarily dissipates in the course of storytelling, but that such dissipation may be arrested by television's commercial interruptions. This experiment stands apart from those in which subjects are frustrated or angered first, and thus view while arousal is heightened; in this case, the arousal apparently was induced by aspects of the portrayal apart from the violent content itself. The failure of the violent films to inspire greater hostility than the nonviolent comedy warns us that the presence of violence in a portrayal is not sufficient to ensure heightened arousal.

Erotic films have also been used, as one might expect, in the experimental instigation of erotic—rather than aggressive—behavior. K. E. Davis and Braucht (1971) studied effects of exposure to films of heterosexual activity on sexual arousal, physiological arousal, sexual behavior, sexual thoughts, emotional tensions, and attitude questions. They found some short-term effects on the cognitive and affective measures, but no significant differences in measures of overt sexual behavior. Mosher (1971) similarly found no untoward consequences of exposure to explicit sexual films. Tannenbaum (1971) examined emotional arousal as a mediating variable in erotic communication effects, and concluded that a two-factor model involving cognitive and emotional elements of arousal would be needed. This coincides with Konecni's and Zillmann's conclusions.

B. S. Greenberg (1972b) has suggested that young children should be studied, to assess the degree to which they are aroused by various types of content. A study by Osborn and Endsley (1971) measured galvanic skin responses of four- and five-year-olds to televised segments depicting human and cartoon violence and nonviolence. Both physiological (GSR) and cognitive (information recall) reactions were greatest for the human violence program. This positive correlation between the two reactions suggests that the conceptual separation of physiological and cognitive components of arousal may not make so much difference in practice as might be inferred from controlled laboratory studies.

A second element of our model on which evidence is needed is our creation of a loop in which arousal is immediately dissipated to one-half, if the disposition to act is insufficient or if there is no opportunity to act. From this point, the person is cycled back to the stage of processing information from television anew, with reduced arousal. In the case where his disposition to act was suppressed by lack of opportunity, the salience of that act is also set to zero before he reenters the information-processing stage. This latter element of the model can be viewed, over a series of many cycles through the model, as a pattern constituting "act-search" behavior.

As long as arousal remains, the person continues to review potential acts from his repertoire until one occurs to him for which he has some opportunity. This provision in the model would account for the relative ease with which arousal has been demonstrated empirically with regard to aggressive effects (for which opportunity is often present), but the comparative failure to show the comparable result for erotic behavioral effects. Opportunity for the latter is rare; sexual behavior is appropriate—or even possible—only in rather limited social circumstances.

Zillmann (1971) feels that erotic portrayals are potentially more arousing than violent ones. In his excitation-transfer scenario, the erotic film excites a general tendency to act, which is then "transferred" into a behavior for which opportunity is created. In this case, the experimenter provides the subject with a handy opportunity to display a form of aggressive behavior. We may interpolate an intervening stage, at which the act that has been made most salient by the erotic film is some form of sexual behavior. But opportunity for such behavior is blocked by the experimenter, who provides no handy sexual targets and whose presence presumably creates a level of surveillance that discourages auto-erotic behavior. Thus, blocked, the sexual act is dropped from the person's repertoire (its salience set to zero), and alternatives are considered. The alternative for which opportunity exists, aggressive behavior, becomes more likely on subsequent information processing cycles. This account is somewhat different from Zillmann's hypothesis of a "transfer" effect from sexual to aggressive behavior.

Our decision to partially discount the level of arousal immediately during this process of recycling in search of appropriate acts is based on several pieces of evidence indicating that physiological arousal is short-lived when it has been created by filmed and televised portrayals. Doob and Climie (1972) examined the aggressive impact of filmed violence immediately following exposure and, in a second condition, after 20 minutes' delay. The experimental effect of the film clearly deteriorated with delay in measurement. Mann et al. (1974) also conclude that responses elicited by media erotica are fairly transient. Another study (Konecni, 1975a) showed that subjects who were required to wait 13 minutes after being angered gave significantly fewer shocks than those who waited only 7 minutes. Where opportunity for sexual activity exists, of course, we should expect to find behavioral effects—as with any other behavior. Mann, Sidman, and Starr (1971, 1973) report, for instance, that among married couples sexual activity was greater on evenings when erotic films were viewed.

A somewhat complex interaction not accounted for in our model distinguishes between different levels of erotic arousal. Donnerstein, Lipton, and Evans (1974) found that, while highly erotic stimuli combined with anger-arousal produced increased aggression, the effect of mildly erotic stimuli is to reduce subsequent aggression. Another interaction of interest has to do with the role of cognitive variables of the type we have lableled [perceived consequences] that might inhibit aggressive behavior. Zillmann, Mody, and Cantor (1974) induced physiological arousal by having the subjects engage in various levels of physical exercise. They then introduced information about "mitigating circumstances" that would help to explain the behavior of their anger-provoking experimenter. The cognitive labeling apparently introduced by this "mitigation" condition significantly decreased the aggressive effect among those who had exercised moderately, but it made no difference for those who had done so vigorously. The latter were highly aggressive regardless of cognitive input. These latter findings indicate rather clearly that our model is too simple to account for the full range of interactions between physiological arousal and associated cognitive elements that are necessarily connected with it. At the same time, we should stress that the emphasis in research on aggression and

(as almost a sidelight) on sexual behavior has been dispropor-
tionate to the relative potentiality for learning of other kinds of
televised social behaviors. Given a forced choice between adding
one more interaction to the already rich literature regarding these
two types of content and behavior vs. opening up the study of
arousal in relation to different content-behavior areas, we would
argue strongly for the latter.

One way to register that argument is by *not* making our
model as complicated with respect to arousal as it might be. It
should be sufficient to encourage new research directions to set
forth the relatively simple hypotheses that appear in the model.

In sum:

Arousal is proposed as a necessary condition for overt behavior.

It is seen as involving two related components, physiological
excitation and cognitive labeling of that generalized emotion.

It hypothetically combines with behavioral cognitions in a multiplicative fashion, so that it produces a behavioral disposition only
when both of these elements are present.

It is conceived as a highly situational and transitory variable,
subject to abrupt increases as a result of viewing experiences, and
to at least partial dissipation when a behavioral disposition fails to
be translated into an overt act.

Further, arousal is implicitly treated in our model (across many
cycles) as a motivation for a search for appropriate social acts for
which opportunity exists, thus helping to stimulate information-
seeking as well as constituting part of the reaction to information-
processing.

Arousal by television is not required for television to have an influence on behavior. When arousal is sufficiently heightened by
sources other than television to activate the factors encompassed
by our model, all the other television-related influences play their
role.

The Catharsis Controversy

There is one additional point in our model at which arousal un-
dergoes transformation: after the act is question has been displayed in overt behavior, we specify that arousal is set to zero.
While this may seem a radical reduction, it is consistent with our
hypothesis that arousal is subject to dramatic changes from one
situation to the next. It is also consistent with a variety of evidence on "catharsis."

There are actually two catharsis hypotheses: overt behavior results in the reduction of arousal; vicarious behavior results in the reduction of arousal. We incorporate the first in our model; evidence for the second suggests it has highly limited applicability, and we therefore do not include it.

THE OVERT BEHAVIOR HYPOTHESIS. In their landmark psychoanalytic work on frustration and aggression, Dollard et al. (1939) stated that the "expression of any act of aggression is a catharsis that reduces the instigation to all other acts of aggression" (p. 53). This statement embodies a long-accepted folk wisdom; it is not uncommon, for instance, to be advised to "have a good cry and get it out of your system." This idea that an emotional arousal (of many possible types) can be purged through acting it out behaviorally has at least some support in the empirical literature. Mallick and McCandless (1966) proposed a "hydraulic" conception of catharsis, but in a series of three experiments with young children they failed to demonstrate it. On the other hand, Hokanson, Burgess, and Cohen (1963) found that subjects who had been previously aroused exhibited significant decreases in blood pressure only after they had acted out aggression against their frustrator. When substitute targets for their aggression were provided, the blood pressure decreases were greater when these targets resembled the frustrator than when they did not.

Konecni and Doob (1972) analyzed the literature on the catharsis hypothesis, and concluded that there might be an intermediate form of catharsis when the cathartic aggressive act involved the frustrator who had originally aroused the person's aggressive impulse (Doob, 1970; Doob and Wood, 1972). They created an experimental condition in which subjects had an opportunity to aggress against another person before aggressing against their frustrator. Following initial angering of the subjects, this interpolated experience reduced the level of later aggression. Shocks administered in a laboratory situation to the frustrator were considerably stronger among those subjects who were not given the interpolated cathartic opportunity, as compared to the aggression levels against either the frustrator or the interpolated "scapegoat" in the catharsis condition.

Following Bandura's (1973) criticism that subjects in the angered, noncatharsis condition might undergo "self-arousal" while they sat and waited for the test situation, Konecni (1975a) replicated the Konecni and Doob (1972) experiment with an additional condition. To prevent self-arousal among the waiting subjects (who would have time to cognitively label their emotional state as anger, and act accordingly), one group was given math and logic problems to solve; they later exhibited reduced aggression, as did (again) those who in the interim had opportunity to aggress against a scapegoat; both groups were again exceeded in aggression by those who had no opportunity for either behavioral catharsis or diversion. Behavioral catharsis produced the greatest immediate reduction in aggression (7 minutes later), but the diversion condition led to greater delayed reduction (13 minutes later).

Konecni (1975a) concludes that, since aggression is apparently superior to nonaggression in reducing arousal labeled as anger from an aversively high level, "it follows that every instance in which aggression alleviates anger increases the probability that aggression will occur in future cases of anger inducement" (p. 100). This hypothesis, which has certainly not been fully tested, is presented in our model in the form of two functions that follow display of the act. The first is the reduction of immediate arousal to zero following the behavior. The second is the recalculation of [salience]; this variable increases as a result of the exercise of the behavior, but this "reinforcement" effect is modified by the nature of the [real consequences] of the act for the person. Konecni is suggesting that these consequences will be perceived as positive in at least one respect—they will reduce the anger-arousal, which he assumes is an aversive emotional state. For this reason, he concludes that in the long run, "aggression breeds aggression," even where catharsis occurs. Whether such a hypothesis would extend logically—and empirically—to other types of behavior is a thoroughly open question. To date, it has not been researched.

THE VICARIOUS BEHAVIOR HYPOTHESIS. While we have accepted catharsis from Konecni's viewpoint—essentially the original Dollard position—by setting arousal to zero following display of the act, we have not embellished our model with the second, more controversial, complicated hypothesis of vicarious catharsis, which involves a series of contingent relationships that render it a relatively improbable event. We are thus not surprised that it has been observed in only a small minority of studies that have purported to test it. Because it is a complicated hypothesis, but one that has been usurped on behalf of various overly facile interpretations, it has been tested much less often than has been claimed. Because of the debate which has surrounded it, let us review the vicarious catharsis hypothesis in detail, and then examine the relevant evidence.

In the fourth century B.C., Aristotle wrote in his *Poetics:*

> A tragedy is the imitation of an action that is serious and also, as having magnitude, complete in itself; in language with pleasurable accessories, each kind brought in separately in the parts of the work; in a dramatic, not in a narrative form; with the incidents arousing pity and fear, where-with to accomplish its catharsis of such emotions. (Warnock and Anderson, 1959, ch. 7)

The term "catharsis" meant, literally, "purging," and there are several possible interpretations of the nature of the purging process Aristotle had in mind (Else, 1958). Clearly [arousal] would be set to zero, figuratively speaking, under any interpretation; the differences in interpretation have to do with the fate of the elements of [salience] that would survive display of the [act].

Aristotle said nothing, it is clear, about catharsis of aggression. His comment—which is the basis of an elaborate analysis of the structure of an emotionally successful drama—referred specifically to fear and pity. He defined fear as "a pain or disturbance arising from a mental image of impending evil of a destructive or painful sort," a concept that would cover such notions as "anxiety" in modern psychology. For Aristotle, the idea of pity took a much less altruistic form than it might in present-day usage; he defined pity as "a sense of pain at which we take to be an evil of a destructive or painful kind, which befalls one who does not deserve it, which we think we ourselves or some one allied to us might likewise suffer, and when the possibility seems near at hand." Pity, then, seems to be nothing more than a fear that has been evoked by a sense of what today might be called "identification" or "empathy" with an observed victim; emotionally it involves caring about oneself much more thsn it involves caring about the observed victim. (Translations from Cooper, 1932, pp. 107–21.)

We would not concern ourselves with Aristotelian discourse on the emotions, were it not for the fact that they are often cited by proponents of the vicarious catharsis hypothesis as "authority" for the application of this proposition to aggressive behavior. One need not read Aristotle extensively to discover that this is a misappropriation of a venerable concept. Throughout his discussion in the *Poetics* of the ways in which drama affects emotions, Aristotle consistently links the terms fear and pity as if they were a single hyphenated concept—and he does *not* discuss dramatic impact on any other emotions.

This last point is important because in his *Rhetoric* he treats fear and pity as just two of many emotions to which he gives equally extensive consideration. The others include anger, love, hatred, mildness, indignation, and envy, several of which might well be thought of as more closely related to aggressive behavior than are either fear or pity. We should infer, from the textual record, that Aristotle specifically considered all of these emotions, and rejected the hypothesis that any of them except fear and pity could be purged by a process of evoking them through dramatic portrayals.

Of course, one need not appeal to Aristotle in order to set an empirical hypothesis for test today. His "data" were presumably a product of introspection. It could well be that a number of emotional states, including aggressive drive, are subject to vicarious catharsis. If we think of extending the list, some astonishing implications arise. A person in a state of deep emotional depression might be advised to watch a tragedy, rather than a comedy, in order to improve his spirits. Sexual offenders and drug abusers might be force-fed heavy diets of media portrayals of their respective excessive behaviors, for correctional purposes. By the same token, portrayals of socially desirable behaviors might reasonably be kept off the screen, lest they purge their viewers of their inclinations to display such acts. To say the least, we do not advocate such policies, and no provision is made in our general model that would imply that we would expect them to work for the broad variety of social behaviors. Nevertheless, the possibility remains that *under limited conditions* cathartic phenomena can occur. Let us review that evidence in the area of aggression, where it is most persistently pursued.

Feshbach has been the leading exponent of the hypothesis that viewing violent portrayals would inspire aggressive fantasies that would purge the viewer of previously aroused aggressive tendencies without overt aggressive behaviors. He suggests (1955; p. 3):

Fantasy expression of hostility will partially reduce situationally induced aggression. Ideally, this hypothesis might be tested by inducing aggressive drive, measuring the strength of the drive induced and, after an interpolated fantasy activity, measuring the strength of aggressive drive a second time.

Two sequences are subsumed by the hypothesis. In the first phase, arousal is induced but the aroused behavior does not occur. Our model does provide for such a sequence as a result of viewing, although it could also come about from other stimulation. We agree with Feshbach in assuming that arousal can be raised to a high level in one situation, and reduced effectively to zero in the next. The difference comes in the second phase of Feschbach's formulation. We, following Konecni and Doob's evidence, predict catharsis as a result of actual display of the behavior. Feshbach would have no necessary quarrel with this, but his argument would add a second catharsis process, within our loop where information is received, but the act does not occur. The implication of the Feshbach formulation is that vicarious catharsis—in the absence of arousal from a nonmedia source —would require some continuity of viewing, so that prior arousal might occur; this parallels the placement by Aristotle of catharsis at the terminal stage of drama following prior stimulation of the audience.

Feshbach (1955) provided the first evidence for the symbolic catharsis hypothesis. He compared the strength of aggressive drive in three experimental groups. Two groups were insulted, and one was not. Of the insulted groups, one was given an opportunity to express hostility through the construction of thematic apperception test (TAT) stories. This latter group was found to express the least aggressiveness in a subsequent sentence-completion test and on an attitudinal questionnaire. Feshbach later (1956) found that aggressive free play, rather than reducing later aggression in children, increased it among boys and made no difference for girls.

Siegel (1956) was the first to examine this hypothesis with specific attention to the effects "of the aggressive and hostile themes which predominate in many entertainment films, commercial television programs, and comic books." She found no differences between the play behavior of children after watching a film depicting fantasy aggression and after seeing a control film.

Feshbach (1961) pointed out that catharsis could only be expected if the subject had been emotionally aroused *before* experiencing the vicarious aggressive activity. If this condition were not met, he posited that aggression would be facilitated by the fantasy aggression experience. In effect, he was describing what we have outlined as Phases 2 and 1, respectively, above. High emotional arousal (at the end of Phase 1) is a contingent condition required for catharsis to operate. To test this, Feshbach used a 2×2 design in which college students, who had either been insulted or not, watched either an aggressive or a neutral film. From an attitude questionnaire and a word association test he found significantly less aggressive responses for those who had been insulted and then shown the aggressive film. This study, which appears at first glance to satisfy the data requirements of the catharsis model rather well, probably constitutes the high-water mark for that hypothesis in the literature. Most experiments of that time were finding opposite results and subsequent research focused on distinctions regarding cue properties (Berkowitz, 1964) and the type of aggression involved (Feshbach, 1964; Hartmann, 1965), among other factors, in an effort to define the specific conditions that are necessary to develop the cathartic phenomenon. These are considered in detail below.

The search for vicarious catharsis receives little encouragement from two-variable field studies. The catharsis principle would lead one to expect a negative correlation between exposure to television violence and a consistently high level of aggressive social behavior. There are quite a few samples in which, instead, significant positive correlations between these two variables have been reported (Dominick and Greenberg, 1972; Lefkowitz et al., 1972; McIntyre and Teevan, 1972; McLeod, Atkin, and Chaffee, 1972a, 1972b). One field experiment (Feshbach and Singer, 1972) reports the hypothesized negative relationship over an extended time period. Also, the vicarious catharsis hypothesis could draw almost as much support as could the simple learning hypothesis from the fact that a person-by-person matching of aggression with violence viewing scores prepared by McLeod, Atkin, and Chaffee (unpublished) shows a strong "effect" on aggression from low to moderate levels of violence viewing, but no relationship from moderate to high levels of violence viewing. (In our model here, this decelerating function of learning over repeated exposures is accounted for mathematically, by modifying [salience] according to a logarithmic schedule following repeated displays of the behavior.) Methodological critiques of field studies abound, but the main deficiency common to all of them is that they measure cumulative individual differences whereas the catharsis hypothesis is one of immediate specific effects that occur within a very brief timespan. An aroused disposition to act hypothetically increases, then decreases again, during a single sustained exposure to a dramatic presentation, or in two successive phases that are linked closely together in time. If this kind of cathartic phenomenon occurs, it is not likely to be captured by field measurement methods. They are useful for assessing the overall outcome of a person's viewing history, but they do not tap situational shifts in arousal within a single viewing experience.

There are a few experiments that seem to satisfy the empirical requirements laid out by Feshbach (1955), and the weight of evidence seems to be against a vicarious catharsis hypothesis regarding aggressive behavior. One supportive study is Feshbach (1961), which we have already described. We should note again that Feshbach used nonbehavioral criteria, specifically an attitude questionnaire and a word association test. There are a number of studies showing essentially the opposite result; in most of these, the criterion measure is actual display of aggressive behavior, whereas Feshbach's hypothesis and early experiments are consistent in focusing on "projective" measures of prebehavioral aggressive dispositions. Berkowitz and his associates have consistently found increased aggressive behavior in angered subjects following exposure to aggressive models (Berkowitz, 1962a, 1964, 1965; Berkowitz, Corwin, and Hieronimus, 1963; Berkowitz and Rawlings, 1963). Berkowitz interprets this [act] as a consequence of lowering of the person's inhibitions (in our model, [perceived consequences]) against aggression. The behavior outcome is also a function of cue associations that tie the consequent aggressive behavior to the person responsible for angering him. Hokanson, Burgess, and Cohen (1963) found subjects who had been previously aroused exhibited significant decreases in systolic blood pressure only after they had actually behaved aggressively against the person who had frustrated them. There was also a tendency for the decrease in pressure to be greater after aggression against substitute targets that resembled the frustrator than after aggression against those that did not resemble the frustrator.

The predominant view on vicarious catharsis currently seems to be that it occurs as a function of what we have called [perceived consequences] in our model. As Goranson (1970; p. 20) puts it, "it is not the observation of aggressive *attacks* that results in catharsis. Rather, it is the perception of the tragic *results* of aggression that produces catharsis." Even that revised version is not supported by Hartmann's (1969) experiment, in which angered subjects who witnessed filmed reactions of pain during a fight responded more punitively than did those who saw a film focusing on aggressive responses. However, Hartmann (1965) had found that the presence of pain-cues tended to reduce the level of aggression for subjects who had not been previously angered. Thus there seem to be interactions between emotional and cognitive factors which remain to be fully explored.

Looking on the vicarious catharsis hypothesis from a somewhat broader perspective, we would justify our decision not to incorporate it into our model on the following bases: it is proposed for aggressive feelings specifically, not for a wide variety of behavioral dispositions; it is apparently limited to prebehavioral emotional states, not extending to actual behavior; it may be explained by cognitive factors that we shall treat under the rubric of perceived consequences.

By contrast, the behavioral catharsis hypothesis is rather well documented and is accommodated fully in our model. This is not to argue that vicarious catharsis of certain emotions, such as Feshbach's aggressive feelings or Aristotle's fear/pity, never occurs. It is simply to conclude that the hypothesis does not offer much toward our central problem here, which is the specification of a general psychological model for the learning of a variety of social behaviors via television.

Imitation and the Learning of Specific Behavioral Acts

Given that our model isolates the element of the behavioral learning process we call [act] from such related elements as [arousal] and [perceived consequences], one might assume that the process of "learning" a given behavior from a televised portrayal would be quite straightforward. There are, however, a number of different meanings that can be given to the concept of "learning a behavior," and there are several variable elements to be considered. Specifically: differences between direct observation of a behavior, and viewing a televised portrayal of it; differences between concepts of the cognitive acquisition of a "response," and the actual display of that response as an overt behavior; differences between aggression and other socially deleterious behavior, and socially desirable behaviors such as altruism; our concept of the hierarchy of [act] vs. [alternatives] in terms of [salience].

The general question of whether exposure to a given type of behavior can affect display of subsequent similar behavior by the viewer is so conclusively settled as not to be worth our reviewing the research literature in any detail here. Studies that are consistent with that general hypothesis will be examined here for the light they shed on the subordinate issues we have outlined. These findings will, in passing, more than sufficiently document the case for a general principle of imitative social learning.

DIRECT OBSERVATION VS. TELEVISED PORTRAYALS. Even leaving aside the question of perceived reality, to observe an act via television does not present the person with the same set of stimuli as would direct observation. We have intimated that we presume direct observation to be the most powerful form) with vicarious observation via television less than (or at most equal to) the observation of real-life behavior, in terms of learning consequences. Yet, although television eliminates from view some elements of real-life observation, at the same time it provides a concentrated focus) the boundaries of the screen set off the behavior from its surrounding context, which in some cases could be diverting. So there may be conditions under which observation via television constitutes a *stronger* stimulus to imitative learning than does real-life observation. Research on this point would be useful in designing procedures to influence social learning.

Meanwhile there are two bodies of evidence which indicate that the distinction between direct and televised observation need not concern us too much. Bandura, Ross, and Ross (1963a) studied imitative aggression by nursery-school children in four conditions: in one group of children observed a real-life aggressive model; in the second, they saw the same model on film; in the third, they viewed cartoon aggression; in the fourth, they saw no film. The first two groups did not differ in the amount of imitative aggression) or of verbal aggression, subsequently displayed; both these groups exceeded the cartoon and control groups, on both dependent measures. Shifting our focus to prosocial behavior, a series of studies by Bryan and Walbek demonstrate that modeling of filmed portrayals of sharing can be created among grammar school children, just as "behavioral contagion" of directly observed sharing can be effected (Bryan, 1970; Bryan and Walbek, 1970a, 1970b; Walbek, 1969).

Hartley (1964) has criticized experimental demonstrations of modeling partly on the premise that they involve more faithful film depiction of real-life models than is ordinarily the case with broadcast television portrayals. This is correct, but in the long run not especially relevant. Research comparing direct observation explicitly with televised observation, and varying the degree to which the latter ranges between *cinema vérité* and a slickly edited production for broadcast, has not been done. But if such comparative studies were to demonstrate serious attenuation of learning when the broadcast production is too heavily edited, or presented in the context of diversionary content (such as ads), this would simply tell us more about the way television should be presented in order to influence modeling as we wish. The general proposition that such modeling occurs, and that it can be a rather strong effect, does not seem to be in doubt.

FOUR SUBPROCESSES IN MODELING. The leading exponent of the modeling-imitation formulation of social learning theory has been Bandura (1969b, 1971b, 1973). As he has put it, "Social learning theory assumes that modeling influences produce learning principally through their informative functions and that observers acquire mainly symbolic representations of modeled activities rather than specific stimulus-response associations" (Bandura, 1971b; p. 6). He goes on from this global proposition to break down modeling into four subprocesses: attentional processes, retention processes, motoric processes, reinforcement and motivational processes. Flanders (1968; p. 329) sees these as being divided into "two key processes in Bandura's writings . . . acquisition and performance." It is useful in examining the literature to distinguish between the *acquisition* (attention and retention) of a behavior cognitively, and aspects of *performance* (motoric and motivational).

Attentional processes are important because mere exposure to a televised portrayal does not guarantee that the proper cues will be perceived by the viewer. Studies have shown that a variety of factors influence attention, including the observer's model characteristics, incentives, and characteristics (Bandura, 1969b). It may seem obvious that modeling over a sustained period of time requires that the person also retain the symbolic representation he has witnessed. Factors such as rehearsal and identification have been identified as important facilitators of retention. As Bandura notes, retention is often ignored in theories of imitation, and one cannot deny that it has been underresearched.

The distinction between acquisition and performance is a major one, and we have so treated it in our model by interposing a number of contingencies, such as [arousal], [perceived consequences], and [opportunity], between the transmission of an [act] via television and the actual display of the corresponding behavior. Bandura distinguishes between motoric and motivational elements of behavior because they are controlled somewhat differently. Motor behavior is affected by, for example, the rate and level of observational learning and the complexity of the behavior. Motivational processes depend on the presence of positive incentives, which we will deal with in connection with perceived consequences. When a behavior that has been observed fails to be imitated, it cannot necessarily be inferred that it was not learned in the limited sense represented at the [act] stage in our model; if incentives and opportunity later occur, the behavior may be displayed. Liebert (1972) discusses this distinction in terms of acquisition vs. acceptance. We assume that through modeling it is possible to inhibit behaviors, disinhibit them, and to add new behavior to the person's repertoire.

Our emphasis on the distinction between cognitive acquisition and behavioral display finds support in several kinds of evidence. For instance, Hicks (1965) mildly frustrated young children and measured their imitation of adult and child aggressive models. Six months later he remeasured them both on performance of imitative aggression and on recall of the model's actions. The youngsters were able to recall significantly more of the model's behavior than they actually performed.

In a similar vein, Bandura (1965a) came to believe that the perception of adverse consequences for an aggressive response inhibits aggressive behavior. Although the performance of aggressive acts by children did not seem to be increased by observing a model whose aggression was punished, a large number of the children were able to describe in great detail the model's aggressive behaviors, and he comments that:

> Evidently, they had learned the cognitive equivalents of the model's responses but they were not translated into their motoric forms.

These findings highlighted both the importance of distinguishing between learning and performance and the need for a systematic study of whether reinforcement is primarily a learning-related or a performance-related variable. (Bandura, 1965a; p. 590)

In a subsequent experiment, Bandura (1965a) exposed nursery school children to filmed aggression, under experimental conditions of punishment, reward, and no consequences; the expected differences in subsequent aggressive behavior were observed. All of the children were then offered attractive rewards if they could reproduce the behaviors they had seen the models perform; the previous differences among the three experimental conditions disappeared with this new incentive. He concluded that both the inhibition and the disinhibition of a response could be "vicariously transmitted through observation of reinforcing consequences." (Bandura, 1965a; p. 594).

Evidence on the distinction between cognitive and behavioral acquisition of a response is not limited to the domain of aggressive behavior. One prosocial behavior that has been studied in detail is the area of adherence to rules and resistance to temptation. Related studies indicate that a yielding model is likely to have a disinhibitory effect, but there is only marginal evidence suggesting that models can inhibit behavior (Rosenkoetter, 1973; A. H. Stein, 1967). A study by G. M. Stein and Bryan (1972) on rule-adoption by children found that both a model's speech and behavior affected the observer's overt behavior, but the observer's words were influenced only by the corresponding words of the model, not by his overt acts. This finding is at variance with those of Bryan and Walbek (1970a, 1970b) and Walbek (1969), which dealt with altruistic behavior rather than rule-adoption; the latter may be a more compartmentalized cognitive problem for the imitator.

As we have been finding in other areas, the processes involved in modeling are more complex than are the variables representing them in our model. Our observations, and the subsequent research that may be done on these issues, should be considered as amplification of the overall process that the model attempts to organize. Where complicated interactions among subprocesses have been demonstrated, investigators who are intensely interested in one aspect of our overall model may very well find it necessary to develop more elaborate subroutines to more completely describe what they are studying.

PROSOCIAL VS. AGGRESSIVE BEHAVIOR, AND RESPONSE HIERARCHIES. Throughout this analysis, we attempt to extend principles developed in the heavily studied domain of aggression to other kinds of social behavior. However, some research on a variety of behaviors that can be termed "prosocial" also has been reported. These have included helping and sharing behavior in children (Bryan, 1970; Bryan and London, 1970; Bryan and Schwartz, 1971; Bryan and Walbek, 1970a, 1970b; Elliott and Vasta, 1970; Marshall, 1972; Masters, 1972; Midlarsky, 1968; Midlarsky and Bryan, 1967; Poulos, 1977; Poulos and Liebert, 1972; Rosenhan and White, 1967; Staub, 1969; Walbek, 1969); rule adherence and resistance to deviation (Rosenkoetter, 1973; Slaby and Parke, 1971; A. H. Stein, 1967; G. M. Stein and Bryan, 1972; Wolf, 1973; Wolf and Cheyne, 1972); and delay of rewards and gratifications (Bandura and Mischel, 1965; Staub, 1972; Yates, 1974). Other topics such as courage, cooperation, friendliness, persistence at tasks and even question-asking behavior (Zimmerman and Pike, 1972) have received limited attention as well.

We see no particular need to address here the value-laden issue of the relative merits, from the perspective of either society or the individual or his immediate social group, of these different forms of behavior.* Meanwhile we have gone to some effort to argue for the most fundamental assumption in our model, that *all* behaviors are subject to the same processes of learning via television. We shall increasingly draw on research on behavior the investigators (and we) consider socially desirable more often than not to support inferences based on the study of behaviors that we consider socially undesirable in most circumstances. Our labeling of these as "prosocial" and "aggressive," respectively, is not an empirical value judgment, but simply adherence to the language of the literature.†

* Leifer, Gordon, and Graves (1973) have suggested that one area where much work is needed is "research to determine which behaviors are socially valued. We would like to see research and program development presenting these behaviors in ways that will entertain children and encourage them to perform behaviors."

† We recognize that there are circumstances in which aggressive behavior is wholly in order, and settings in which we would feel that the presumed "prosocial" behaviors are dysfunctional for individual, group, or society. The prosocial or antisocial quality of a real-life act depends both on the circumstances and on the subject values of the observers. The two terms are simply convenient code words for the normative judgment about certain classes of behavior in certain situations. We also agree that research on these value judgments is in order, and would be useful as a guide to policy development regarding television as a learning tool.

We are conceiving of the response hierarchy, based on comparative [salience] of [act] and the [alternatives] that constitute the person's [repertoire], as including all of these types of behavior. Inhibition and disinhibition, for instance, are treated in most studies as specific to one form of behavior—aggressive, prosocial, etc. But it is equally acceptable from our viewpoint to treat these as competing behavioral dispositions within the same response hierarchy. To the extent that one class of behaviors becomes more salient, the others become less so. We view this process as probably independent of the relative social merits that might be ascribed to the different acts.

Unfortunately for our purposes, research to date has not been organized in such a way as to demonstrate outcomes in the form of competing response tendencies. Instead, each study selects a dependent variable of interest, such as aggression or helping, and measures the extent to which that single outcome does or does not occur. There are some studies in which operationally the measure of the selected behavior *not* occurring was that the person engaged in an alternative behavior. For instance, Bandura, Ross, and Ross (1961) compared outcomes of their experiment in terms of aggression (hitting, kicking or sitting upon a Bobo doll) vs. nonaggression (playing with tinker toys). Similarly Lovaas (1961) measured aggressive tendencies by the choice of an aggressive toy, from a set that also included a similar nonaggressive toy. But these are essentially forced-choice situations, in which the person must do *something*. They do not allow separate behaviors to compete with one another freely—and they do not permit the outcome of nonbehavior, which would hypothetically result if no single [act] survived the series of contingencies in our model sufficiently to be displayed. We are, then, making a large assumption about the homogeneity of behaviors in our model, without direct supporting evidence. Accordingly, we would wish to see research on social learning via television in which a variety of behaviors (both those positively and those negatively valued by society) are permitted to compete as possible outcomes. This

---

Our main purpose in juxtaposing aggressive and prosocial behaviors in connection with theoretical points that are important in our model is to test the generality of that model, which we propose as extending well beyond both these classes of social behavior. Overall we are reasonably satisfied that we have this type of evidence of generality, where such comparisons have been possible on the basis of research to date.

would require a radical shift in research paradigms within the field.

Some evidence consistent with the thinking represented in our model regarding multiple dependent variables can be found in the studies of Tannenbaum, Zillmann, and others discussed earlier in connection with their hypothesis of generalized arousal (e.g. Zillmann, Hoyt, and Day, 1974). As we noted, it has been demonstrated that exposure to an erotic film induces aggressive behavior. Our model's accounting of this overall outcome would involve two loops through the television-input section of figure 8.4. We may safely assume that the subjects in these experiments (male college students) have had plenty of previous exposure to aggressive models. They are shown erotic films, which we have already inferred will induce general arousal, at least in this age-sex category. We can also infer that such films raise the salience of erotic behaviors in the person's response hierarchy, much as any depiction of any behavior would. Let us assume that the product of this level of [salience] combined with this level of [arousal] is sufficient to create a strong disposition to [act] in an erotic fashion.

But the next choicepoint in the model is [opportunity]. Experimental test situations such as those used by the Zillmann group do not offer the subject much, if any, chance to act out an erotic impulse. The model specifies that in this situation the person returns to information-processing, with the [salience] of the particular [act] seriously reduced (let us say to zero), and [arousal] somewhat reduced (let us say by half). According to Zillmann's argument, [arousal] would still be fairly high, since he proposes that erotic portrayals are more arousing than any other type of media stimuli. This is certainly believable with respect to college males. The person now reenters the input stage, with erotic behavior blocked by lack of opportunity; the remaining [alternatives] in his [repertoire] include, we should confidently assume, some previously learned aggressive behaviors. These may now become the most salient remaining acts, and there remains sufficient [arousal] to evoke them. Further, the experimental situation has been set up very carefully to provide the person with an opportunity to carry out a form of aggressive behavior. Indeed, the person can do little else, and the only question is the degree of aggressive behavior (administering noxious noises) that occurs. Given this opportunity, and the absence of any reason to anticipate inhibiting consequences, we should not be surprised to find that the net "effect" of the erotic film presentation—combined with the rather bizarre experimental situation—is to elicit high levels of aggressive behavior. In effect, then, our assumption that different types of responses reside in a latent hierarchy with some degree of comparative salience is consistent with the Zillmann group's findings.

We have built the concept of [salience] into our model in order to accommodate these findings, but that is not the most compelling reason for our doing so. Our larger purpose, as we have emphasized, is to attempt to design a general model in which the term [act] will function as a symbol referring to all types of social behaviors. The long-range purpose of a formulation of this type is to stimulate new kinds of research. We see experimentation on the broad response hierarchy we have hypothesized here as an important area for innovative study.

Perceived Consequences

As the reader might guess from the frequency with which we have referred to "perceived consequences," we include many disparate contingent variables under this label. Most of the studies in which display of a modeled behavior has been modified by the consequences the person perceives for the act deal with one of four issues:

> The role of anticipated personal reward or punishment for the act. This may be learned either by observing the consequences of the same act for another person, or it may be communicated to the person verbally.
> The influence of justification for the modeled behavior. This may be thought of as a kind of "societal reward" for the act, in that it is justified on the basis of some widely accepted moral principle—usually an element of the story line, as in the case of a portrayal of justified aggression.
> The influence of cue properties of the target of the behavior. This research too has focused most specifically on aggression, although the concepts seem less narrowly applicable to that type of behavior than is the case with justification.
> The role of real consequences of past behavior that was similar to a portrayed act.

ANTICIPATED REWARD AND PUNISHMENT. One of the most widely recognized influences on behavior is reinforcement, or reward and punishment.* There is evidence that the observation of the reward or punishment of an act within a television portrayal also affects the subsequent influence on a viewer of that portrayal.

Bandura, Ross, and Ross (1963b) compared two experimental conditions (plus a control condition), that differed in the consequences the film model received for his aggression. The film showed two children arguing over who would play with a toy. In one condition, the boy who hit and kicked the other eventually won possession of the toy, and was also rewarded with a snack. The announcer identified this boy at the end as the "victor." In the other version, the aggressive child was punished, and the other boy was allowed to keep the toy. (The control film showed the boys in nonaggressive play.)

In a subsequent play situation, those children who had seen the aggressor rewarded exhibited a greater degree of aggressiveness in a subsequent play situation. Those in the aggression-punished condition, although they behaved less aggressively, were able to describe the aggressive model's behavior subsequently, which suggests that the punishment inhibited aggressive behavior but not learning (Bandura, 1965a).

Following this lead, Bandura (1965a) added a third experimental condition, in which the filmed aggressor received neither reward nor punishment. Subsequent aggressive play by the subjects (nursery-school children) was about as high in this condition as in the aggression-rewarded condition. Both were higher than the aggression-punished or control conditions. Again, when the children were later tested for their ability to recall the model's aggressive acts, there were no differences among the experimental groups.

Walters and Parke (1964) also concluded that what happens to a model indicates only the permissibility or nonpermissibility of his actions in a given setting; it does not affect what the observer learns cognitively from the model. Rosekrans and Hartup (1967) varied the consistency of reward; they found that an inconsistently rewarded model was not superior to a control condition or

* Reinforcement can be defined as an environmental contingency that either increases or decreases the probability that a given response will be repeated. Factors that increase the probability are called "positive reinforcers;" those that decrease it, "negative reinforcers." In everyday language, the terms "reward" and "punishment" are substituted for these. Of course, there are some factors which function as reinforcers which cannot be described accurately as either reward or punishment.

a punished model in eliciting imitative aggression, although they replicated Bandura's findings that a consistently rewarded model did produce more imitation than the other three conditions. A number of other studies have also demonstrated a general relationship between reward-punishment contingencies and imitative aggression among children (Bandura and Mischel, 1965; Hicks, 1965; Thelen et al., 1974; Walters, Parke, and Cane, 1965).

In the prosocial area, the possibility of vicarious reinforcement of altruistic behaviors has interested several investigators (Elliott and Vasta, 1970; Harris, 1970; Midlarsky and Bryan, 1967, 1972). Two recent studies of negative reinforcement of altruism demonstrate the complexity of the theoretical issues. Morris, Marshall, and Miller (1973) found in one experiment that first- and second-grade girls were more likely to share things after seeing a peer punished for not sharing, and after seeing a peer receive punishment unrelated to sharing. In a second experiment they found that the "punishment regardless" condition was superior to the "not-sharing/punished" version, for eliciting other prosocial behaviors besides sharing. They concluded that the child who witnessed the punishment that was not tied to any specific behavior may have interpreted her environment as generally dangerous, and consequently relied only on those behaviors that she knew (from prior experience) would not bring punishment. Midlarsky, Bryan, and Brickman (1973) examined the hypothesis that "reinforcing a behavior (altruistic donation) inconsistent with the agent's prior modeling of that behavior will be aversive rather than rewarding, and will produce a decrement in the behavior reinforced." In one experiment, sixth-grade girls were exposed to either a charitable, neutral, or selfish model, who either did or did not express approval for altruism in a game situation. As predicted, the selfish-approval combination produced the least altruistic behavior. This finding was replicated in a later study of third-grade girls, in which race and sex were systematically counterbalanced.

Taken together, these studies lead us to several conclusions about the role of reward or punishment of a portrayal in the eventual influence of that portrayal on a viewer. In sum:

> Reinforcement appears to apply specifically to the performance of a behavior, and not to its cognitive acquisition.*

---

* Although not employed in all theories of learning, reinforcement is treated in most *behavioral* theories as some environmental contingency that either increases or decreases the probability that a given response will be repeated. In some *cogni-*

There seems to be a lack of symmetry between reward and punishment. The anticipation of punishment tends to inhibit display of an act, but anticipation of reward does not appear to increase the act's likelihood beyond the level attained if no consequences, good or bad, were perceived.

There is no exact equation between reward or punishment items in a presentation and the overall perception the viewer draws of the appropriateness of a behavior that is presented. There may be complex interactions between factors in the total presentation that will make it difficult—for most purposes impossible—to design dramatic programs that would follow some sure-fire definable formula for reinforcement.

It appears that reinforcement factors are applicable to a fairly wide range of behaviors—including such different classes of behavior as aggression and altruism.

At the same time, we emphasize that it has not been demonstrated that these various factors are effective except with young children. We suspect that older persons would not be so easily manipulated by attempts at vicarious reinforcement, because of their greater background of experience with different types of behavior.

JUSTIFICATION. For many years, the various codes governing "good taste" and permissible content in the film and television industries have embodied a dualistic approach to the matter of justification of aggression. They have generally proscribed the depiction of crimes of violence and revenge as justifiable. At the same time, they have encouraged the championing of law enforcement efforts—which often are portrayed as extremely aggressive, and which are almost always shown as justified. This distinction between "bad guys" and "good guys" has no parallel in the scientific literature. Instead, the studies consistently demonstrate that justified aggression by a model is more likely to elicit aggressiveness than is unjustified aggression. It should be noted, though, that this finding does not explain what psychological processes operate to produce the phenomenon. We shall consider that question after examining the relevant findings.

---

tive theories, reinforcement is not viewed as necessary for acquisition of *knowledge* of an act. The distinction we make in our conclusion between effects on performance and cognitive acquisition is consistent with this theoretical distinction. In our model, we have taken this theoretical distinction into account by separating the acquisition of [act] (no reinforcement required) from the acquisition of [perceived consequences] (the product of vicarious reinforcement).

Berkowitz and Rawlings (1963) manipulated justification by describing bloody defeat in a boxing film as either "just desserts" or malfortune befalling an innocent. Previously angered subjects for whom the beating was depicted as justly punitive subsequently exhibited higher levels of aggression. Berkowitz, Corwin, and Heironimus (1963) strengthened the design by adding a no-film control group. They concluded that the justified fight film reduced their subjects' restraints against such behavior. Hoyt (1970) added the distinction between justifications of "vengeance" and "self-defense." Vengeance consisted of "the motive of someone previously harmed by another," and self-defense was a "kill-or-be-killed" motive. Since in the experimental-stimulation situation the subjects were angered by another person, Hoyt predicted that justification of the vengeance (which was more closely analogous to the angering experience) would elicit higher levels of aggression than that of self-defense. Finding support for this hypothesis, he pointed out that the "results do suggest that the media code position that violence should be shown in a justified context of aggression may not be appropriate" (Hoyt, 1970; p. 463).

Geen and Stonner (1972) replicated Hoyt's study but with an introduction justifying vengeance; an introduction simply describing a workaday professional fight; and a control, in which no introduction was given to the fight scene. Among angered subjects, the vengeance-justified version produced more aggressive reactions although subjects were not initially angered displayed more aggression after viewing the professional-fight version than after the vengeance version. Experiments by Meyer (1972c) and by Berkowitz and Alioto (1973) also support the general inference that justified aggression tends to have a strong disinhibiting effect on aggressive behavior; these experiments diverge on the issue of whether aggressive models depicted as "real" are more disinhibiting than those presented as fantasy (see below).

Taken together, the studies lead to several conclusions about the role of justification of a portrayed act:

Justification is a story element that does not lend itself easily to any type of behavior other than aggression—at least, no other type of behavior has been studied in connection with justification.

It appears to operate primarily as a disinhibiting factor, countervailing against negative perceived consequences more than it provides a positive stimulus to act aggressively.

It interacts with the motive state of the individual viewer. The more closely the rationale for justifying the model's aggression coincides with the immediate arousal of the viewer, the stronger is the disinhibiting effect.

Industry codes which permit justified aggression by "good guys" do not have scientific support.

CUE PROPERTIES OF THE TARGET. There is considerable evidence that the cues in the situation in which the viewer finds himself after observing a television portrayal partially govern the influence of that portrayal. Berkowitz (1965) pioneered the study of the role of cue properties with three experiments. In the first, the highest levels of expressed hostility against an experimenter who had angered the subjects occurred when he was introduced as a former college boxer, and the subjects were then shown a violent boxing film. A second experiment replicated this finding with some design refinements, including a behavioral measure of aggression (administration of shocks). The third study added a manipulation of justification (see above), which did make some difference; the introduction of the angerer (and later target) as a former boxer, however, elicited more aggressive responses regardless of the justification condition. Berkowitz and Geen (1966) demonstrated the same effect simply by introducing the angerer-target person by the same name as that of the victim in the boxing film (in this case, the film boxer was actor Kirk Douglas, and the target person was introduced as "Kirk"). Geen and Berkowitz (1966) later manipulated the target person, by giving him the same name as either the film victim, or the film victor. The level of subsequent aggression was greatest when the target's name coincided with that of the victim. In another replication (Berkowitz and Geen, 1967), the name of the target person was not introduced until after the film had been seen; the results were similar to those of the previous studies. Geen and Berkowitz (1967) concluded that "aggressive predisposition does not give rise to aggressive actions unless approprate cues are present in the situation."

The importance of target cues is also supported by a finding that young men who were led to believe that an aggressive model was similar to them were more likely to imitate his behavior than were those who were told the model was different from them; this effect held up consistently across reward, punishment, and control conditions of reinforcement (Rosekrans, 1967). Additional research has focused on the target of potential imitative aggression as a cue to the appropriateness of the aggressive act, and on situational cues that have become associated with aggressive behavior in general (Geen and Berkowitz, 1967).

This well-documented line of research buttresses the case for disinhibition as a major psychological process where aggressive behavior is concerned. The unanswered question is the degree to which cues are important in regard to other classes of behavior. The report by Rubinstein et al. (1974) that exposure to a televised portrayal of helping behavior only affected children when very similar opportunities were at hand suggests that situational cues may be important for a wide range of the behavior open to influence by television. In terms of our model, situational cues are one factor upon which [perceived consequences] are dependent. We do not offer it an independent role because we are skeptical about the range of behavior for which it is important and believe that they may be a necessary condition in some circumstances and irrelevant in others. We shall cover other aspects of the influence of the situation in terms of [opportunity].

STORED REAL CONSEQUENCES. Our model makes an important place for environmental reactions to the behavior displayed by the person. We have every reason to assume that human beings learn from their experiences, and that the consequences they perceive for a potential behavior are—after many trials—strongly conditioned by the patterns of reinforcement (including rewards and punishments) for such behavior in the past. This would presumably mean that the laws of instrumental learning apply equally in the areas we have been discussing as in other types of behavior. It is fortunate that we can be confident on this point, since there has been little research to demonstrate it specifically in connection with television. Experimental studies, which dominate the literature, are ordinarily organized around a single trial, rather than following a person longitudinally over many trials. The latter type of research design would be more appropriate to testing this feature of our model. Indeed, most of the experiments we have described have been arranged to insulate the subject from real consequences for his actions.

A few studies have examined the role of adults, as a source of sanctions on children's behavior following media presentations. Hicks (1968) found that adult approval/disapproval significantly influenced imitative aggression. Grusec (1973) examined this with 5- and 10-year-old children, and found that adult disapproval affected aggressive play (in the absence of the adult) only for the older children. In a field survey, Chaffee and McLeod (1972) found that the correlation between exposure to television violence and habitual aggressive behavior was weaker in families where the parents exercised sanctions against aggression by their children; this finding was replicated in eight different samples (see summary in Chaffee and Tims, 1976).

Our premise that real consequences are stored over repeated trials, however, is strongly supported by other bodies of research. One is the extensive literature on human behavior modification (Bandura, 1969a); another is the literature on animal learning (see Skinner, 1971); there is no apparent reason for thinking that the many reinforcement effects that have been demonstrated regarding learned behaviors in general would not apply to those learned via television. In addition, we concluded from our examination of the effects of the reward and punishment of acts portrayed on television that such *vicarious* reinforcement had been demonstrated to have effects. We believe it reasonable to assume that real-life experience would have a stronger impact than analogous vicarious experience.

Perceived Reality of Television

Several field studies provide data on the role played by the degree of reality the viewer perceives in a television portrayal and his psychological reaction to it. Himmelweit, Oppenheim, and Vince (1958) present evidence that children found realistic television violence more uncomfortable than the stylized or stereotypic encounters of the typical western. McLeod, Atkin, and Chaffee (1972a, 1972b) found a correlation between perceptions of reality in television content, and both the exposure to television violence and the display of aggressive behavior. Chaffee and Tims (1976) found that programs viewed by adolescents jointly with their parents were more likely to be perceived as realistic and to be violent than those viewed alone or with other youngsters. B. S. Greenberg, Ericson, and Vlahos (1972) found the same positive relationship between violence viewing and viewing with parents among elementary-school children. Chaney (1970) found an association among young men between perceptions of reality and degree of violence in British programs, and B. S. Greenberg and Reeves (1976) found the opinions of significant others (parents, peers, siblings) influenced the child's evaluations of the reality of television. Gordon (1973) found that children attributed greater reality (and less acceptability) to aggressive action shown in the context of the present-day world, compared to the same acts portrayed as occurring in either earlier or future times. These findings suggest that there is a good deal of variation in the degree to which televised portrayals are seen as realistic, and that this variance is likely to be related to both social and behavioral elements of a person's situation.

We have accorded the variable of perceived reality an important role in our model. Specifically, we have tied it to the domain of [perceived consequences]. The salience of an act for the person is stipulated to be partly a multiplicative function of [perceived consequences] and [perceived reality]. This means that to the degree the presentation is not seen as realistic, the consequences portrayed will have less effect. The corollary is that even a very realistic portrayal will have slight or no effect if scant or no consequences, such as winning, are associated with the act.

Conceptually, by separating the perceptions of reality and consequences from the acquisition of the act itself, we are assuming that the act can be learned without becoming salient as potential behavior. Several experiments suggest that the perceived reality of a portrayal is important for aggressive responses. No comparable body of evidence bears on prosocial behavior. Our model posits that both prosocial and aggressive behavior would be enhanced when a portrayal implies that it bears on reality.

Feshbach (1972) carried out three laboratory studies in which the reality-fantasy nature of the portrayals was manipulated. Although somewhat conflicting, these experiments suggest in general that the highest levels of aggression followed observation of "real" violence. In the most clear-cut of his studies, Feshbach presented the same violent film (a mixture of news and dramatized scenes of a campus confrontation between students and police) with two different introductions; one as news film, in a second as a fictional drama. The level of subsequent aggression (noxious noise) was higher in the reality condition.

Noble (1973) found evidence that exposure to realistic aggressive scenes produces anxiety in young children, and a subsequent decrease in constructive play. Following Himmelweit, Oppenheim, and Vince's (1958) finding that realistic violence was more frightening than stylized violence, he set up an experiment that demonstrated two behavioral effects of realistic film violence: the children were more likely to play destructively, and less likely to play constructively, than if they had seen the less realistic version. Berkowitz and Alioto (1973) got analogous results with college students, in that higher levels of aggressive behavior were found when the subjects were told that the violent film was real than when they were told it was fantasy. Finally, Bandura, Ross, and Ross (1963a) attempted to set up a three-level reality-fantasy continuum, by showing children a real-life aggressive model, the same model on film, and an aggressive cartoon character. Again, the cartoon version was less potent in stimulating aggressive behaviors than were the realistic presentations. The reported difficulty of preschool children in answering questions about the "realness" of television (Chapter 5), however, cautions us that this reality-fantasy dimension may not be so meaningful for very young as for older viewers.

However, it would be unwise to assume that portrayals of violent real events necessarily will have more impact on behavior than a fictional treatment, for the reality assigned to a portrayal derives from the viewer. Fiction holds our attention precisely because it purports to convey some degree of truth; this holds for Tolkien, Hemingway, and Irving Wallace. Our point is emphasized by the finding of Worchel, Hardy, and Hurley (1976) that a documentary of a prison uprising, Attica, did not result in greater hostility on the part of viewers than the famous California motorcycle gang film The Wild One. The authors astutely suggest that explicit labelling may be a crucial factor to overcome the readiness of viewers to become involved in a drama, and thus give themselves over to its reality, fictional or not.

The fact that these studies all point in the same direction is not especially comforting from the viewpoint of our model, since none of them tests our main proposition about perceived reality— that this variable intereacts with perceived consequences in a multiplicative fashion. Instead, all of the research to date has treated perceived reality as an isolated independent variable, which will raise or lower the aggressive tendency. We see no theoretical reason why this should be so, unless the content perceived has some cognitive components that will affect the viewer's conception of the consequences he should expect for the behavior. That is, we expect him to discount portrayed consequences when he believes them to represent fantasy. Our alternatives, given the overall organization of our model, would be to make [perceived reality] a contingency governing either [arousal] or cognitive acquisition of the [act]. In neither case is there research to direct us. Lacking any, we have simply reasoned that arousal seems like too global an emotional state to be greatly controlled by perceptions of reality, and the learning of behavioral acts seems to occur relatively independently of actual display of the behavior—whereas perceived reality clearly has something to do with overt behavior.

The Existence and Likelihood of Opportunity

There yet remains one major variable: the factor of [opportunity] to display the learned behavior. The role of opportunity has not been systematically examined *within* studies, although several experiments make it clear that the display of behavior may depend upon the presence of eliciting conditions (Bandura, 1965b, 1969a, 1969b; Bandura and Walters, 1963; Mischel, 1968), and there is considerable variation *between* studies in the kinds of opportunities offered to subjects. We have remarked, for example, on the Zillmann, Hoyt, and Day (1974) experiment demonstrating that an erotic film can stimulate aggressive behaviors; it should be pointed out that one of the conditions governing this finding is that no opportunity for erotic behavior was provided, whereas an obvious and consequence-free opportunity to behave aggressively was.

According to our model, opportunity is not simply a situational contingency that determines whether or not a behavioral disposition will be carried out. Over many trials, behaviors for which there is more frequent opportunity will be displayed more often, and this experience will in itself reinforce those acts at the expense of others. Some increment in salience is added each time a behavior is displayed, and this tends gradually to make that behavior more salient than others and thus more subject to later learning. We are envisioning, in writing our model this way, a process in which television and environmental events tend to be mutually reinforcing if behaviors that often appear on the screen are similar to those for which opportunity frequently presents itself. Aggression may be such a behavior; there are doubtless others, even though they have not been studied with the same diligence.

Our emphasis on [opportunity], despite the lack of research on the topic, carries several implications:

Programs designed to foster certain patterns of social behavior via television should be planned so that they coincide somehow with situations in which the audience members can display the behavior in question. We should not expect media portrayals to stimulate or disinhibit behaviors for which opportunity is rare, and not contiguous to the viewing situation. This would explain, for example, why exposure to pornography appears to have so little effect on overt sexual behavior (except among couples).

Research should take opportunity factors into account. One implication is studies in which there are multiple behavioral dependent variables, so that one for which opportunity exists could substitute for a more salient one that has been blocked. Another is better simulation of natural settings, closer to real-life opportunities, perhaps by experiments in which opportunity factors are systematically varied instead of being held constant and high as is usually the case. A third is longitudinal research, in the limited sense of studies that extend over a series of trials; almost all of the experimentation we have reviewed has consisted of one-trial learning studies, whereas our model more realistically emphasizes the repetition of learning processes over many trials—some of which inevitably will be blocked by lack of opportunity.

Implications for Future Research

We have presented a model of the psychological processes behind any effect television may have on a viewer's behavior. The model is based on the synthesis of evidence from hundreds of studies. However, on many points there is very little evidence to go on. As a result, the model raises far more questions than it answers. As scientists interested in answers, we are unhappy with this state of affairs. As designers of a model intended to stimulate and direct scientific research, we are pleased.

To summarize the major directions we believe research concerned with the processes behind effects should take:

In regard to [arousal], research should focus on the influence of arousal on behavior other than aggressiveness, on the importance of cognitive labeling of arousal, and on the consequences for the reduction of arousal by lack of opportunity or insufficient disposition to perform an act.

In regard to the catharsis controversy, research should focus on the intriguing hypothesis that "cathartic" reduction of a drive by behavior, such as aggression, should increase the likelihood of similar behavior when a similar drive state occurs (because of the reinforcing effect of drive reduction), and on the proposition that vicarious experience may be "cathartic" for emotions or motives without any analogous effect occurring for behavior.

In regard to the role of imitation and learning, or acquisition of an [act], research should focus on factors that affect retention of acquired acts, and on the influence on an act's display of the response hierarchy and competing response tendencies which make up the psychological context of the acquired act.

In regard to [perceived consequences], research should focus on whether anticipated rewards or punishments, as introduced by a television portrayal, have the same effects for adults as for children, and on the range of behaviors for which environmental cues govern any influence of television.

In regard to [perceived reality], research should focus on the degree to which effects on "prosocial" behavior are dependent on this variable, and on whether it governs the influence of perceived consequences.

In regard to [opportunity], research should focus on the degree to which immediate opportunity is necessary for a television portrayal to affect behavior (and in particular on the effect of the blocking of immediate opportunity, as would occur often in the natural course of events, on the eventual display of an act); on the influence on display of an act of the possibility for some alternative action; and on the simulation of naturalistic research settings (so that displayed acts occur within an environment where opportunity does not differ from the real world).

We would like to add some more general comments. We are disappointed by the limited nature of evidence on each point. The most severe limitation is the enormous emphasis on aggression, at the expense of other types of behavior. Where possible, we have compared the aggression literature with that dealing with prosocial behavior. Usually, the result has been a confluence of inferences. However, it must be recognized that, given the present range of available research, there is some danger of constructing a model that will apply narrowly to aggression plus perhaps the narrow range of prosocial acts that have been studied.

In the laboratory, promising starts have been made in several directions. Bandura (1969a) in particular has stimulated a good deal of work using film as a tool in behavior modification. This includes the systematic "desensitization" of various phobias (Bandura, Blanchard, and Ritter, 1969), the learning of moral judgments (Bandura and McDonald, 1963), and the development of prosocial patterns of behavior (Bandura, Grusec, and Menlove, 1967). Another group has focused on the modification of aggressive behaviors (Bryan and Walbek, 1970a, 1970b; Walbek, 1969; Walters and Willows, 1968), and the acquisition of altruistic behaviors (Bryan and Schwartz, 1971; Bryan and Test, 1967; Bryan and Walbek, 1970a, 1970b; Walbek, 1969). While film rather than television is the usual method in such studies, there is not much reason theoretically to distinguish between the two media; it is pretty well established that film models can be as effective as live behavior models (Bandura, 1973; Bandura and Mischel, 1965; Bandura, Ross, and Ross, 1963a, although live models may be more powerful than film in overcoming very strong inhibitions (Bandura and Menlove, 1968). One impressive study is that of Bandura, Blanchard, and Ritter (1969), in which film models were successful in the desensitization of phobias over snakes; this was manifested both in reduced fear and in increased behavioral approaches to snakes in the test situation. When used in a context of guided participation, media models can clearly be effective in reducing undesirable avoidance behavior patterns (see also Blanchard, 1970).

Another promising direction is the use of television in group psychotherapy. The key element in this process, and one often overlooked by communication scientists who focus exclusively on the "mass broadcast" features of the medium, is that television can be used by a person to observe himself. With the advent of the portable videotape recorder, therapists have been able to show a patient his own behavior, and then help him to modify it. These efforts have included considerable evaluative research (K. G. Bailey and Sowder, 1970). As Danet puts it, "In addition to being provided with the traditional source of feedback within the group itself, there is added a direct confrontation for the patient of his own image. He can place himself in the role of reactor to his own behavior, along with other group members and therapist(s)" (1969:433); see also Danet 1968).

For the psychologically disturbed individual, videotape may help correct errors in self-perception. It may also accelerate behavioral change by removing the opportunity for denial that exists when an individual receives information only from other people (Melnick, 1973). As Berger comments:

Seeing oneself and reflectively re-experiencing meaningful interactions frequently allows a person to acknowledge something about himself which he had not previously been ready to accept from either therapist or other patients who have themselves been more or less ambivalent about making the necessary but perhaps painful confrontation. (1970:23)

However, there is some danger that videotape will have disruptive effects on therapy groups (Danet, 1967; Searle, 1968), and the recent emphasis is on avoiding attention to behavior other than that of immediate therapeutic interest (M. J. Robinson and Jacobs, 1970; Berger, 1970).

Videotape has also been used in family and marital counseling (Alger and Hogan, 1967, 1969; Hogan and Alger, 1966). It is said that a more democratic interaction between client and therapist is created by videotape because both of them have access to the same information. Alger and Hogan (1969:87) point out that videotape recording is "a superb technique for capturing the context of a situation as well as the multiplicity of cueing and other communicational behavior," so that family members see their interactions from a more objective perspective. The critical element is the *realistic* quality of televised presentations. When the person sees himself on the screen, he is aware that what he is viewing really happened and is not the product of someone else's interpretation of the situation.

We are encouraged about the validity of the experimental evidence because variables we have identified as important in understanding commercial broadcast television's effects also seem to be critical in one-on-one therapeutic uses of the medium. These variables include the perception of reality, consequences of behavior, and opportunity to display an act. There seems to be good reason to proceed with experimental attempts to understand the psychological processes implied by television with confidence that the eventual results will be scientifically valuable and socially beneficial.

Chapter

The Future

WE HAVE SET forth what social and behavioral science has to say about the effects of television on human behavior. But what are the implications of our findings for future research?

Our answer will be in three parts. First, we shall examine the role of social and behavioral science in television policy-making. Second, we shall identify topics we believe have priority for scientific scrutiny. Third, we shall offer some solutions to major problems confronting the study of television and human behavior.

The Prospect for Policy-Relevant Research

At first glance, the role for social and behavioral science in television policy-making would seem to be enormous. The issues science addresses are precisely those over which there is public concern—for example, the effects of television violence, the influence of television on children, the portrayal of minorities and women, and the role of television in elections. After a second look, the same observer might conclude that the role is slight, because to date such science has played almost no part in federal regulatory rule-making. Such a view is too pessimistic because it fails to take into account certain distinctions: much of regulatory rule-making is concerned with issues where one cannot expect much use of social and behavioral science because it is not directly and immediately relevant; the number of issues where it is relevant has been increasing; regulatory rule-making is only one part of policy-making, and the potential for social and behavioral science in other policy-making is large.

Regulation and Policy-Making

The two agencies which regulate broadcasting are the Federal Communications Commission (FCC) and the Federal Trade Commission (FTC). The principal agency is the FCC which, among its many responsibilities in regard to electronic communications, is obliged to formulate rules to ensure that the broadcasting industry performs in the public interest. Its sphere includes the assignment of broadcasting channels for various use (such as for educational or commercial broadcasting), the licensing of broadcasters, the determination of the prerogatives of commercial broadcasting vs. such alternatives as pay, cable, and public television, and, to a very limited degree, certain aspects of content. The FTC has a far narrower task. Its regulation of interstate trade includes the obligation to regulate television advertising judged to be part of such trade to protect consumers from deception, misrepresentation, and other chicanery. Its concern with television covers only content of this particular kind.

However, television policy-making (see figure 9.1) is a complex area that includes much more than regulatory rule-making. It consists of two related dimensions: (a) the *target* of action—is the policy for structural or social effects? and (b) the *source* of action—is the policy of a regulatory or of a nonregulatory nature?

STRUCTURAL POLICY-MAKING. Decisions ordering the physical, economic, and operational makeup of the broadcasting industry fall into this category. The FCC and the Congress play the principal roles. Congress, which created the FCC by the Communications Act of 1934, continues to set up the framework within which the agency functions. The new Department of Commerce office on telecommunications policy, replacing a similar entity located directly responsible to the White House, also presumably will help shape the federal regulatory stance. The industry plays a large *ex-officio* role through its support or opposition to proposed steps, and various other groups to a lesser degree affect decision-making. An example are the FCC regulations imposing an obligation on cable operators to carry all local broadcast television signals, both commercial and public, and limiting their prerogative to retransmit distant signals.

SOCIAL-EFFECTS POLICY-MAKING. Decisions in this category are those intended to affect the content of what is broadcast, and evolve from the presumed effects on viewers of the particular kind of content in question. Violence, for example, is typically assumed to have undesirable effects; other examples include public service programming (encouraged), obscentity (discouraged), and advertising (which must meet certain criteria). These and various other classes of content are the target of efforts to alter their character or frequency on television. The industry itself, through its self-regulatory procedures and its decision-making about programming, plays the principal role. However, the FTC and the FCC have a limited regulatory role. Furthermore, Congress and various citizen groups, ranging from consumer advocacy groups to those of religious and moral commitment, have influenced policy by generating pressures to which the industry and the regulatory agencies have responded. An example of social-effects policy-making is the FCC's ruling that cigarette advertising (later banned by Congress) had to be balanced by anti-smoking commercials under the fairness doctrine.

REGULATORY POLICY-MAKING. Decisions in this category involve the stipulation of procedures for the broadcasting industry to follow. The FCC, the FTC, and the Congress are principal parties involved. Various other parties, and in particular the broadcasting industry, influence decisions by their support or opposition. The distinguishing feature is the setting of requirements by government agencies which the broadcasting industry must follow. The great majority involve structural policy-making, but to a very limited degree there is some social-effects policy-making. An example of regulatory policy-making is the FTC ruling that advertisements for toys cannot exaggerate the product's capabilities.

NONREGULATORY POLICY-MAKING. Decisions in this category are intended to influence the programming and advertising that reaches viewers. The industry, through its self-regulatory procedures and programming decisions, plays a major role, as do organized citizens (consumer advocacy, ethnic, and special interest groups) that create pressures to which the industry responds. The various governmental agencies are involved in regulatory policy-making, and in particular the FCC, FTC, and the Congress, also respond to such public pressure and, through threat of action, influence the industry's behavior. The unorganized public's real or anticipated reaction to content is also always a factor in industry behavior. An example of nonregulatory policy-making is the adoption by the broadcasting industry of the "family viewing" code, under which violence and sexually provocative content is restricted during two prime-time hours.

SCIENCE'S ROLE. The role of social and behavioral science in regulatory and structural policy-making has been slight, even though the validity of such policy-making depends on the eventual social outcome, which such science is preeminent at measuring. This makes the situation ironic but understandable. The immediate and primary issues revolve upon the law, economics, and, at the FCC, engineering. This circumstance derives not solely from the claim of such matters, but also from the value to which they presumably should be subordinate and the practical circumstances of policymaking. There is no agreement on what constitutes the public welfare (stipulated by the Communications Act of 1934 as the "public interest, convenience, and necessity"), and no concensus on the criterion—empirical or otherwise—to be invoked in its behalf. There also is a far distance from the locus of a decision to its impact; the halls of regulation and the living room are two worlds. The result is that public welfare has no hypnotic hold on attention.

Even when the regulatory decision involves social-effects policy-making, where social and behavioral science would seem to be directly relevant, its role has been slight. A major reason is the very nature of regulatory deliberations.

Whatever the declared issue, the FCC and the FTC are in fact engaged in arbitrating disputes over access to income. Those whose activities are affected are typically affected economically. This is true whether what is at issue is the right to be in business or the contribution of free air time under the Fairness Doctrine (as it is when the FCC grants a license renewal or requires anti-smoking commercials as a condition for broadcasting cigarette advertising) or the right to broadcast advertising of a certain character (as it is when the FTC sets standards for television advertising).

The result is that the rule-making process is usually an adversary procedure, with the outcome open to judicial appeal. The various parties whose rights to present and future income are at issue must be assured of "due process"—which in this case means action in accord with the various relevant statutes and the procedural rules of the two agencies. It is not surprising, then, that the model followed is that of the judicial process and, as in the civil courts, there is the filing of legal-type briefs by interested parties and the arguing of cases. In each instance, the dispute revolves around the determination of the facts and their evaluation in terms of the obligations of the two agencies, and precedent in previous rule-making and court rulings plays a large part.

The situation is similar at the FCC and FTC, although the mandate of the FTC results in greater attention to impact on the viewing consumer. At both agencies, the root of contention is economic, and rulings may be overturned by court appeal. The makeup of the FCC exemplifies the priorities. Through 1977, half of all commissioners had been lawyers but no economist had served. Lawyers are very visible on the commission staff (from which they often move to highly-paid jobs serving the broadcasting industry); economists regularly occur; sociologists, social psychologists, and other behavioral scientists have been rare enough to be mistaken for the invisible man. The use of data is uncommon; the annual budget in the mid-1970s for research of any type was a modest $400,000, and the commission often relies on statistics compiled by the industry (Cole and Oettinger, 1978).

Social and behavioral science only enters, if at all, through the arguments assembled by the parties in conflict. There is usually no expert evaluation of such "evidence" within the agencies. This would require the absent social and behavioral scientists. Economics is the boldest step toward empirical evidence—as contrasted with legal argumentation—the agencies have taken. "When they want to know something about psychology around here, they ask an economist."

New Issues

The role of social and behavioral science in regulation of television also has been constrained by the federal statute under which the FCC functions and the free-speech guarantee of the First Amendment, both of which limit the degree to which regulation can follow from evidence on the effects of television content. Despite this and the other circumstances we have cited, there is the possibility that it will have a definite role—and in some instances a crucial one—in the future. One reason is the appearance of new issues.

In the mid-1970s, the influence of television advertising on children and adolescents became a topic of debate. New regulatory issues were raised because advertising is widely believed not to enjoy the same protection as news, public affairs, and entertainment.

Although the exact boundaries of FCC and FTC power over broadcast content is a matter of debate, the widely accepted interpretation is:

The FCC is specifically restricted from attempting to regulate program content by its founding statute, the Communications Act of 1934. However, it has in fact done so to a very limited degree in such ways as taking into account in licensing the quantity of public service programming, and by its application of the Fairness Doctrine (which calls for full airing of all sides of a controversial issue), and the equal time requirement (which specifies that political candidates for an office be given access on an equal basis).

The FCC is further constrained by the First Amendment, whose freedom of speech guarantee is judged by most lawyers to extend to all categories of program content within the limits imposed by the Fairness Doctrine and the equal time requirement.

There are no statutory restrictions upon advertising, and in the opinion of most lawyers, the protection of the First Amendment does not extend to it to the same degree as to program content.

Some argue that the FCC could exercise greater influence over programming without coming into conflict with the First Amendment, and others argue that advertising has considerable First Amendment protection.* Some of the answers will evolve from the interplay of rule-making and court rulings. The likelihood is that advertising will become increasingly the subject of regulatory—as well as other policy-making—scrutiny, and that programming will continue to be largely avoided by the FCC.

Television advertising has long been a policy issue. In 1963,

---

* The issue is the degree to which there is an intrusion on the communicatory protection afforded by the First Amendment. Those who assert that the FCC could exercise greater influence over programming would argue that the First Amendment is intended to protect content conceivably relevant to public issues, and that certain television content—such as children's programming and frivolous entertainment (although few would argue that defining "frivolous entertainment" is easy)—is not covered. They would also argue that the FCC in effect already rules on content through the factors it takes into account in licensing broadcasters. They would conclude that rules requiring greater or lesser quantities of certain classes of programming (such as "violent" programs) are consistent with past

the FCC proposed to limit the quantity of advertising permissible, but desisted in the face of industry opposition and a strong House vote for a bill, later abandoned, to prohibit such action (Barnouw, 1975; W. K. Jones, 1967). Presumably, the agency has such authority, although whether it could be applied to limit advertising more severely when there are more children in the audience—as some desire—is less certain. The efforts of the FTC to eliminate deceptive and misleading advertising have been increasing over the years (Emery, 1971). The FCC ruled that cigarette advertising called for anti-smoking public service spots under the Fairness Doctrine, before Congress banned cigarette advertising from television, and this has led to numerous petitions for similar counteradvertising on other topics. The big change in the 1970s was a very sharp focus on possible undesirable effects of television advertising on young viewers.

The new focus is owing to the public interest advocates. In the early 1970s, Action for Children's Television and Robert Choate, who later founded the Council on Children, Media and Merchandising, were challenging the desirability of the advertising that reached children. ACT argued that directing advertising to children, as on Saturday morning children's programming, was unethical because children are emotionally and intellecutally ill-prepared to evaluate persuasive consumer appeals. Choate focused on the nutritional merit of advertised cereals, which he claimed was so questionnable as to pose a health risk. Partial victories were won in the reduction by the broadcasting industry of the quantity of commercials on children's television, and in the upgrading of the nutritional supplements in dry cereals.

These efforts created a new set of issues in regard to the effects of broadcast content to be addressed by social and behavioral science. They include:

> The degree to which children fail to perceive television advertising as a calculated attempt to induce behavior of benefit to the communicator.

---

practices and not in conflict with the First Amendment, as long as broadcasters were left free to function within the guidelines. Those who assert that advertising enjoys considerable First Amendment protection would argue that an advertiser enjoys the right to communicate what he wants to the public as long as he does not violate existing laws, and that advertising is little different from other programming because both are the product of the profit motive. They would also point out that when controversial public issues are deemed to be involved, broadcasters may be required to televise "public interest" commercials, and that advertising is otherwise subject to the same constraints as other content.

The frequency with which television advertising raises or shapes expectations over a product's capabilities beyond what the product can actually deliver.

The various circumstances under which a commercial should be judged to be false or misleading to a young viewer.

The extent to which television advertising pressures children into influencing their parents' buying habits.

The degree to which food preferences and dietary practices, both in the present and, more importantly, in later life, are shaped by television advertising toward foodstuffs doubtful in their contribution to health.

The degree to which the advertising on television of over-the-counter, proprietary drugs encourages young people to abuse them or to turn to illicit drugs.

The degree to which the television advertising of household products that can be dangerous when employed in play (such as certain cleaning substances) encourages children to experiment with them.

The degree to which the exposure of young people to the implied promise in television commercials of social or emotional benefit from purchase engenders materialistic or unrealistic values and attitudes.

The degree to which very early and continuing exposure of children to television advertising leads, with their increasing comprehension of the self-interested nature of commericals, to skepticism about all public communications.

The size of the young audience which can be said to view and understand the sales messages of television commercials.

A crucial question is for what portion of the broadcast day are children's reactions relevant? There are probably always at least a few child viewers. Under what circumstances are they important?

Some would argue that there is no issue unless there is demonstrated harm to the young viewer. We disagree, not because we reject harm as irrelevant, but because we do not accept it as the exclusive criterion. Many of the issues over children's advertising revolve around propriety—the treatment that is deemed appropriate for children. We do not think these issues are less important because of this. Empirical evidence remains important where propriety is the issue because the fact of transgression can only be discerned from the verbiage of dispute with the introduction of an objective criterion. The failure of a child to be able to discriminate between program and advertising content may or may not harm him, but it is perfectly plausible to judge such a circumstance as unacceptable in principle; yet one is powerless to identify when such a condition holds without empirical evidence. We would warn that "harm" is illusory as a more concrete criterion, for its presence or absence inevitably also depends on a subjective definition—although, like other criteria of advertising unacceptability, one that becomes practical only when translated into empirical terms.

• The NAB code's provisions on children and advertising apply only when the advertising is directed at children, the program is intended for children, and children are presumed to be a majority of the audience. As much as 90 percent of children's viewing occurs when these criteria do not apply, and the code—which limits the quantity and otherwise restricts advertising to children—was not operative for more than half of the 40 programs most popular with children in 1975. The broadcasting and advertising industries naturally oppose additional restrictions; various advocacy groups argue that the issue is the number of children reached by a program and not their proportion of the audience or the intent of the broadcaster.

By the mid 1970s, nutrition and the propriety of advertising to children remained important, but the range of issues had widened. The parties involved had come to include not only the advertising and broadcasting industries and a wide range of advocacy groups, and the FTC and FCC, but also the Congress, which began to schedule hearings on children and television advertising (U.S. Congress, 1976a), and the National Science Foundation (NSF) which, under pressure from the Congress and the FTC, has begun funding studies (Adler, 1977) on the topic.

The contention illustrates the central role of economics in television policy-making. Children's programming, most of which is on Saturday mornings, has proven extremely profitable for the broadcasting industry. Despite a decrease in the minutes per hour of advertising endorsed by the NAB code (a step taken voluntarily by the industry in response to the pressure generated by the advocacy groups) the estimated gross revenues for the three networks increased 16 percent between 1974 and 1975 to $78 million.

The decrease was hardly an expunging. It left children's programming with the same upper limit of non-program material as prime time; previously, children's programming had fallen under the more liberal daytime provisions. The result was to leave plenty of advertising for children. There were still probably more minutes of product advertising per hour than in prime time, because of the lesser proportion of non-program material devoted to promotions for other programs. There were certainly more commercials, because of the use of shorter commercials that permitted more to be fitted into a time period (Barcus, 1975). The decreased time may not represent much reduction in the number of commercials reaching children because of the use of shorter commercials (Barcus, 1975). However, the increase in revenues confirms the prediction of an FCC staff's economic forecast that such advertising time could be reduced without adversely affecting income because the demand for such exposure is so great that any effect of a reduction in total time sold would be offset by a higher level of revenue from the remaining time (*Television Digest,* 1976a). One question implied by this development is the degree to which further reductions might be possible without lowering economic returns to the industry.

The more recent position of ACT has been that all advertising should be banned from children's programming on the grounds not only that selling to children is unethical but also that the quality and diversity of programming suffers from the competition to appeal to a mass audience (*Broadcasting,* 1976g). The industry argues that without self-supporting profits there would be no children's programming. ACT would have the FCC require programming for children under its obligation to impose regulations in the public interest. The magnitude of the economic stakes do not suggest any easy success for ACT.

The recent state-of-the-art survey of research on children and television advertising sponsored by NSF (Adler, 1977) observes that policies directed at specific ages are difficult to employ effectively and somewhat impractical—because only about 15 percent of children's viewing occurs during children's programming, and because of the heterogeneity of the audience at any time. We concur that age does not provide a panacea, but not in the implication that age-related policies do not merit consideration.

The broadcasting industry finds some sunshine in wide acceptance of the belief that the nature of audience composition bars the devising of reforms based on age. In fact, precedent gives no succor to such a view. Age is the basis of the current policies followed by the NAB and the networks, and endorsed by the FCC, in which certain strictures are applied only to television directed at children and attracting an audience in which children are in the majority (FCC, 1974).

We would argue quite differently. Rather than concluding from the impossibility of perfect application of an age-specific policy that any such policy is impractical, we would argue for the very careful analysis of audience patterns by age—which might require the collection of new data for a large enough child sample—in order to determine the number of children and hours of programming that might be affected by various possible prohibitions based on the number of children of a certain age in the audience. Then, we believe it would be time to judge the practicality of such a policy on the basis of this empirical evidence of its likely effectiveness.

Both the discord and the emerging role for social and behavioral science were evident at the joint FTC-FCC fact-finding hearings held in Washington in mid-1976, which grew out of a petition to the FCC filed by Massachusetts Attorney General Francis X. Bellotti and signed by 18 other attorneys general asking that televised advertising of over-the-counter drugs be barred before 9 P.M. to protect children (*Broadcasting*, 1976d). The issues were the research evidence on drug advertising's influence on legal and illegal drug consumption, and what action government, broadcasters, educators, or the public should take. Advertising and broadcasting spokesmen asserted there was no evidence of harmful influence. Social and behavioral scientists generally concurred that there was not strong evidence of harmful effect. Several, however, did not believe enough research had been done to give great confidence in such a conclusion. Public interest advocates and others skeptical of the benign influence of drug advertising argued that the issue was partly moral, in that exposure of children to messages arguing for the consumption of drugs is unethical because of the possibility of harmful effect; that the quantity of such advertising made any chance of risk sizable; and, that the findings of a variety of studies would lead one to expect some influence toward an increased disposition to consume drugs.

The disagreement again illustrates the economic nature of television policy-making. In 1973, over-the-counter drug manufacturers spent $265 million on television advertising, about three-fourths of which went for network advertising.* Television is the favorite medium of such companies, with the industry leaders

---

* Includes five internally taken product categories: cough, cold and sinus remedies; digestive aids; headache remedies, sedatives and sleeping products; laxatives; and vitamin preparations and tonics. Does not include the $40.4 million spent by manufacturers of medicated skin products and liniments.

typically spending 75 percent or more of their advertising budgets on it (Council on Children, Media and Merchandising, 1976).

Unlike most FCC and FTC fact-finding efforts, social and behavioral science was prominent. Numerous scientists testified. The Bellotti petition referred to a number of studies. One center of attention was a longitudinal study of 13- to 15-year-old boys over the ensuing 3.5 years sponsored by NBC (Milavsky, Pekowsky, and Stipp, 1975). The principal finding was that exposure to drug advertising was unrelated to later illegal drug use, but was positively although modestly related to over-the-counter drug use; however, the absence of data on whether or not such consumption was gratuitous or inappropriate to symptoms did not permit any inference about whether it constituted "abuse." The FCC-FTC also asked a wide range of social and behavioral scientists for written positions on exposure of young persons to drug advertising and drug abuse.

The FCC rejected the petition on the twin grounds of probable lack of authority to take the action requested and the absence of "empirical evidence to support the claim of a causal connection" between television advertising and drug abuse (*Television Digest,* 1976b). However, one may imagine the pressure that would be created for some action should a study like NBC's appear to demonstrate a connection between exposure to drug advertising and drug abuse. Those concerned over the effects of drug advertising argued that the NBC study should not be considered definitive because it did not answer the question of the very long-term effects of legal drug abuse. Ironically, no one seemed to notice that this set of NBC data could be employed to cast considerable light on such questions by again re-surveying the boys in the original sample, thereby obtaining data on the role of symptomatology in legal drug consumption and on long-range effects of earlier exposure to drug commercials.

The drug issue is just one that is emerging in regard to television advertising. The inconclusiveness of the FCC-FTC hearings is neither surprising nor important. What is important is that they demonstrate the potential role of scientific evidence of social fact as a precursor to regulatory decision-making. The direction of regulatory action cannot be predicted, particularly because it will occur in the context of self-regulatory steps by the advertising and broadcasting industries which may substitute for (and often be in response to threats of) regulation. There is no reason to think that the issues will be confined to the young, because at the root is the viewer's presumed vulnerability and, as the FTC's actions against misrepresentation and deception testify, this is not a state thought to be exclusive to any age group. Children are certain to remain prominent, however; the trend over the past decade at the FTC has been toward increasing aggressiveness on their behalf.

Evaluation

There is also a role for social and behavioral science in evaluating the outcomes of rule-making and of advertising and broadcasting industry practices which in some way might become subject to regulation. This would require some change in the disposition of the FCC and the FTC toward such collection of evidence, but that is not beyond possibility. The children's-advertising issue is a beginning; so, too, is the apparent reaction at the FCC to the scientific evidence on the effects of violent entertainment, expressed in its involvement in the industry's formulation of the "family viewing" code; and there are other very recent instances of attempts to draw on social and behavioral science.

Such evaluation may address itself to the effectiveness of present regulatory requirements, of various alternative regulatory steps, or of industry practices such as in the case of self-regulation, where regulatory action might be weighed.

At any time, the current regulations in effect may be subjected to an empirical test of whether they are achieving their intended effects. At present, the NAB code requires "positive disclosure" of items which must be purchased separately (batteries or accessories necessary to operate toys, for example) and encouragement of "recognized standards of safety," which in some instances implies warnings of possible hazards (NAB Code Authority, 1975). The FTC has made it plain that toy manufacturers risk heavy fines if their commercials misrepresent the operation of their products, such as implying voice control of a mechanical soldier (*Advertising Age,* 1976). It is reasonable to ask whether such restrictions actually help children—or, for that matter, their parents—to better understanding. In the case of warnings, it is reasonable to ask whether there is any risk of increasing the attraction for some portion of the young audience.

An example of the evaluation of existing practice is a recent study of the relationship between presence of a television station in a community and public affairs knowledge (Lucas and Possner, 1975). There was no relationship between news viewing and knowledge of local public affairs in communities without their own television station, but in communities with a station such knowledge was positively associated with news viewing. In the station-less communities, news viewing was associated only with greater knowledge of affairs shared with the neighboring communities with television stations. These data provide support for the FCC concept that local ownership is beneficial, providing special benefits but they also raise the question of what might be done to ensure local news coverage for communities now without stations. It is hard to argue that social and behavioral science could not help to answer such questions.

When a decision is made to consider regulatory action, or to reconsider action already taken, there are usually a number of alternatives. Whatever scientific evidence exists obviously should be reviewed, and sometimes new research may be feasible in order to obtain a sounder basis for a decision. It is in this vein that NSF sponsored an evaluation of the evidence on the effects of common ownership of different media within a market, such as a daily newspaper and a television station, particularly in regard to fairness of news coverage. The study concluded that "most questions about the effects of media ownership concentration on media performance must be answered with the well-known Scotch verdict 'Not proved!'" (Baer et al., 1974). On the surface, this is inconclusive. However, when interpreted in the contest of the evolution of FCC decision-making toward the view that multiple ownership of television and other media in a market is undesirable on its face, because of the risk of one-sided news coverage, for example, it provides considerable guidance by demonstrating that there is no evidence that clear benefits are sacrificed when concentration is discouraged.

The evaluation of industry practices as a prelude to possible regulatory action would also seem to be a possible use of social and behavioral science, particularly in regard to practices considered to be self-regulatory. The "family viewing" code is just one possibility for evaluation. The limits on the authority of the FCC to engage in rule-making on a particular topic obviously pose no problem to such evaluation when it is sponsored by some other entity, such as a private foundation or some federal agency which funds social and behavioral research. It is also likely that possible limits on rule-making do not impose a barrier to the FCC's studying the efficacy of industry procedures. Constitutional or statutory restrictions may bar certain kinds of rule-making, but they would not appear to bar the collection of data in the absence of a specific rule whose legitimacy could be tested in the courts. One reason is that the precise boundaries of FCC and FTC authority are ambiguous until they are tested in court. Another reason is that regulations intended to supplant self-regulatory procedures would have the same intended outcome, but could involve quite different mechanisms, so that the unacceptability of self-regulation as a model for regulatory action is not in and of itself a sufficient argument for eliminating the possibility of regulatory action. The character of an eventual rule would be unknown at the evaluation stage—and it is hard to conceive of a Constitutional or statutory restriction having much force in advance of the action purported to be at variance with it.

The Case of Family Viewing

One way in which social and behavioral science can and will figure in policy-making is by contributing to pressures which lead the industry to adopt self-regulatory measures. "Family viewing" is an example.

In 1974, the pressures on the FCC in regard to violence and sex on television were escalated sharply when the Congress attached a directive to its fiscal appropriation for the agency demanding that the FCC report on the "specific positive actions taken or planned by the Commission to protect children from excessive programming of violence and obscenity" (*Broadcasting,* 1974). The tenor of the demand is conveyed by the fact that the House included a threat of "punitive action"—presumably by parsimony in future appropriations—if the directive were ignored.

Chairman Richard E. Wiley's interpretation of the First Amendment and the Communications Act of 1934 led him to conclude that the agency probably lacked rule-making authority, and that in any case an attempt at rule-making would be unwise because of the precedent of a possible incursion on the First Amendment (Ford Foundation, 1976). The FCC chairman asked the presidents of the three networks to meet with him in Washington. Additional meetings between FCC and industry representatives were held. At some point, Arthur Taylor, then president of CBS, advanced the notion of what came to be called "family viewing"—two hours in the early evening during which sex and violence would be sharply reduced.

The new code was adopted by the three networks in 1975. A

few months later, under network pressure, the National Association of Broadcasters (NAB) at its annual meeting incorporated it into the NAB code. This action brought the non-network independent stations belonging to the association under the code, although full implementation was delayed until September 1977 because of their reliance on reruns, which would not be available in quantity to meet family viewing criteria.*

The code was immediately challenged in federal court in Los Angeles by Hollywood's television writers and producers, with the FCC, the NAB, and the three networks as defendants. The primary formal argument was that the code was the result of governmental duress, constituted "government action" and therefore could not be instituted unless various formal procedures required of the FCC were followed, and amounted to a violation of the First Amendment. *Broadcasting* (1976b) described the issue as the status of "government by raised eyebrow." One motive of the plaintiffs undoubtedly was the admirable disinclination of persons creating in any medium to endure any more interference than avoidable. A second and surely not inconsiderable factor was the threat of lowered profits caused by restricting the time periods in which certain programs could be broadcast when placed in syndication for purchase by individual stations. A third—as the testimony made clear—was that the restrictions made their job more difficult by reducing the range of possible portrayals and treatments and by involving them in continuing contention with the networks over vaguely defined issues.

Four producers, Norman Lear (*All in the Family*), Danny Arnold (*Barney Miller*), Allan Burns (*Rhoda*), and Larry Gelbart (*M*A*S*H**) testified that family viewing had brought numerous disputes and negotiations over content. Lear summarized their displeasure by describing the new situation as an "intolerable climate of pressure and anxiety for creative people" (*Broadcasting*, 1976c).

On November 4, 1976, Federal Judge Warren G. Ferguson ruled in favor of the plaintiffs. The outcome was a shock for those who believed (Geller and Young, 1976) that however questionable

* The compromise reached at the NAB prohibited programming "inappropriate for family viewing" for two hours each evening. The period was to end at 8 P.M. in the Central and Mountain time zones, but at 9 P.M. in the Eastern and Pacific time zones, a discrepancy that has aroused considerable criticism that the policy is less effective for a major portion of the country. Interpretation and application of the code, of course, is left to the networks and the individual broadcasters.

the FCC involvement, the industry had the authority as exemplified in the NAB code of adopting whatever strictures it might deem necessary to deflect congressional and public pressure. The judge's grounds were the application of government duress incompatible with the First Amendment, the inappropriateness of FCC involvement without adherence to formal FCC procedures, and denial to individual broadcasters of prerogatives guaranteed by the First Amendment (United States District Court, November 4, 1976). He concluded that the industry-wide ban deprived broadcasters of their constitutional right to select programming independently. He further ruled that the plaintiffs could sue for any economic damages suffered as a result of the policy. He did not in any way rule against "family viewing" when applied by individual networks or individual broadcasters. What he struck down was the industry-wide adoption of a code as the result of government intervention, an event which he characterized as equivalent to the establishment of official censorship.

The decision raised many more issues than it settled. The network reaction has been to insist that the policy would be maintained by each individually; however, the upward shift in violence that we observed (chapter 3) after the judicial overturn seriously questions the effectiveness of such a stance in the competition for ratings when there is no internetwork agreement. The decision is being appealed and it will probably be several years before the case reaches a judicial end. The belief in the industry is that higher court reversal is unlikely.

The judge's invoking of the First Amendment to preclude industry-wide restrictions on individual broadcasters, even when acceded to by them, has placed the industry's previously sacrosanct shield against governmental and public criticism in jeopardy, and the NAB has ceased to require mandatory subscription to the code by members while simultaneously affirming the need for an industry-wide code (*Broadcasting,* 1976i). One result certainly will be new pressures for federal interference in programming. Congress is expected to be insistent that some means be developed to reduce "sex and violence," and many expect Congress to test fully the protection offered by the First Amendment (*Broadcasting,* 1976h). Public criticism certainly will increase, as exemplified by the campaigns against television violence by the national Parent-Teachers Association and the American Medical Association.

There may also be a quite different kind of pressure emerging from the courts. At this writing, the damage suit brought against NBC over the alleged bottletop rape of a 9-year-old girl by four teenagers, three of them girls, after the portrayal of a similar incident in the made-for-television movie *Born Innocent* will see jury trial. The suit had been dismissed with the court's declaration that the state was "not about to begin using negligence as a vehicle to freeze the creative arts" (Superior Court, San Francisco, 1976). Neither the state appeals nor the U.S. Supreme court concurred that the First Amendment barred the suit. The doctors' new pugnaciousness was evident in this instance in the brief filed in the appeal by the California Medical Society, arguing that the evidence on television violence was strong enough to hold broadcasters "civilly responsible for acts which lead to foreseeable harm" (*Los Angeles Times,* 1977c). Whatever the *Born Innocent* outcome, it could be the first of many such cases. The conviction of Ronald Zamora, 15, in a Florida trial in which the defense for the murder of an elderly woman was "intoxication" by television violence (*Miami Herald,* 1977) does not alter the picture. Broadcaster negligence, and the implications of the First Amendment for such a concept, are issues quite apart from those surrounding the adjudicating of the guilt or innocence of those who commit crimes.

Broadcasting has responded to these varied incursions by attempting to reconstruct its self-regulatory shield. The NAB has sought consensus on the minimizing of violence from the three principal parties—the networks, the stations, and the writers and producers who manufacture television entertainment. It is searching for a means of satisfying critics that self-regulation is effective. The specifics of the NAB code—its stipulations and their phrasing—will be a recurring focus of debate among broadcasters. Yet, there is no evading of the dilemma of laissez faire. As we shall see, the NAB code has been largely symbolic because of the lack of provisions for enforcement, but its symbolic value is reduced without mandatory subscription by member stations (*Broadcasting,* 1977b; *Television Digest,* 1977).

An additional factor is the nascent advertisers' revolt. By the end of 1976, major national advertisers were questioning the advisability of appearing in conjunction with violent programming. Some had suffered embarrassment by being tied to violence (Slaby, Quarfoth, and McConnachie, 1976; *Better Radio and Television,* 1976); J. Walter Thompson, the advertising agency, announced a policy of opposing violence, accompanied by pilot study evidence that a few consumers rejected products if advertised in conjunction with violence. Various advertisers began to declare moralistic opposition to violent entertainment. The American Association of Advertising Agencies urged members to avoid programs with a high level of violence even if the costs of reaching consumers were increased, and the Association of National Advertisers recommended that members intervene in programming decisions to reduce violence (*Broadcasting,* 1977c).

This trend was given impetus by a startling turn in 1976. The advocacy group formed by former FCC Commissioner Nicholas Johnson, the National Citizens Committee for Broadcasting, commissioned a commercial monitoring firm to measure violence. Almost immediately, the monitoring was expanded to include portrayals of alcohol consumption, whose effects on young viewers were the subject of a recent Senate hearing (U.S. Congress, 1976b). The result, at low cost because of the use of a system already operating, are program-by-program tabulations that make possible the identifying of advertisers with violence—or any other content that some party might deem undesirable. The reaction at the networks was dismay and consternation, for here was a guide for the application of pressure on those who in effect pay for broadcasting, and the threat of continuing bickering with anxious advertisers and agencies over the content of the programming where their commercials would be placed. There is considerable irony in these circumstances, because the central mechanism is the product of the industry, which must monitor the advertising that is broadcast to ensure that time purchasers get what they pay for.

Many critics of violent television entertainment have argued for years that the industry would be most susceptible through advertisers. Advertisers, however, are typically conservative in regard to norms and values. Invoking them as a lever to reduce violence is another of those propositions whose implications have never been carefully examined. If they are insensitive or overzealous on violence, or if they extend their censorship to other types of portrayals, the long-term effect may differ considerably from what most of those concerned about violence desire. Nevertheless, as a cynic would expect, the industry appears to be more ready to conform to the desires of its advertising clients (*Broadcasting,* 1977a) than it has been to the complaints of anyone else, including members of Congress.

The future in regard to content is also made problematical by the increasing abandonment of entertainment taboos, as exemplified by the hit of 1975–76, *Mary Hartman, Mary Hartman.* Much of the content—homosexuality, for example—would have been unacceptable a decade ago. This trend should be considered a long-term outcome of television's continuing conflict with motion pictures. A factor in the upward trend of violence over the past decades in both media (Clark and Blankenburg, 1972) is their competition. With television now particularly constrained in regard to violence, we would expect increasing resort to social relations that are startling but defensible as not primarily or blatantly "sexual." This is particularly so because the themes dear to newspaper advice columns and popular psychology seem to thrive in the limited format of the dramatic or comedy series. Thus, we find the industry in the late 1970s fretting with some legitimacy about incursions on its freedom and the prospects for significant, controversial drama while at the same time observers note an increase in themes and portrayals with some apparent degree of sexual tantalization (*Los Angeles Times,* 1977a,b).

It is also reasonable to be skeptical about any reduction of television's contribution to social aggression that may result from a policy such as "family viewing." It may reduce violence, but it is not clear that such reduction is either sufficient in quantity or in the effect on the character of the remaining violence to markedly deter any undesired effects.

The concept does seem to have considerable public support, at least in terms of the expression of public opinion. Nationwide polls both shortly after its inauguration and six months later found about 80 percent of American adults saying they favor "family viewing," although three-fourths or more needed to have it explained to them (Ryan, 1976). This is, of course, no measure of actual public behavior in regard to viewing during the family period. The same polls found that after six months 11 percent of parents said their family viewing habits had changed (although the nature of the change is not described). They found that slightly more than half of adults subscribe to the statement that "there is too much emphasis on sex on television" and almost three-fourths subscribe to the statement that "there is too much violence on television," leading to the conclusion that the public is more concerned about violence than sex—probably because sex is not the subject of vivid portrayals, as is violence. However, experience with "family viewing" resulted in sharp declines in those who believe it will improve television (from 56 to 31 percent) and in parents who find it "very helpful" or "fairly helpful" (from 48 to 39 percent). As has typically been found, the public is inconsistent in its views on restrictions on television: only one-fifth say there should be "stricter controls" but about one-half assert "sex and violence" should be reduced throughout the evening while about one-third say "family viewing" should be continued. In short, the public likes the "family viewing" label, is somewhat disappointed in its execution, supports the idea of reducing "sex and violence," but is not ready to support action that sounds like censorship.

Although the eventual fate of "family viewing" is unknown, it is clear that it represents an innovation in social-effects policy-making. The principal problem in the past in restraining violence has been the competition among the networks for viewers, with none wishing to take any steps which might leave it at a disadvantage. Family viewing introduces a common restraint across networks, thus placing all on an equal basis. It commands attention because such common action is one of the few recourses to achieve alterations in the makeup of programming within the context of a system where content is largely outside the sphere of government influence.

It is also clear that it is an example of policy-making in part traceable to the findings of social and behavioral science. The conclusion of Cater and Strickland (1975) that the Surgeon General's study of television violence, in which the scientific advisory committee concluded that television violence was a probable cause of increased aggressiveness on the part of young viewers (Surgeon General's Scientific Advisory Committee on Television and Social Behavior, 1972), had no effect on industry practice was premature. Although opinion and belief, in Congress and among the public, were certainly critical factors, it is hard to believe that the "family viewing" code would have come into existence had the support of scientific evidence been absent. FCC Chairman Wiley, in fact, has credited the Surgeon General's study with initiating the series of events which culminated in family viewing (see Ford Foundation, 1976). Thus, family viewing illustrates one of the major ways in which social and behavioral science can influence television policy-making—not through its role in the rule-making process, but by affecting the pressures on policy-makers. Sometimes the outcome will be regulatory action, but more often it will be self-regulatory action taken to discourage regulation and placate critics.

Source of Action

	Regulatory	Nonregulatory
Structural	FCC grants and reviews license to broadcast FCC decides on outlets permissible in market FCC sets rules on common newspaper-TV station ownership in same market	Foundations and government give financial support to public television Station license renewals are challenged
Social Effects	Congress prohibits cigarette commercials FCC enforces Fairness Doctrine and equal time requirement FTC sets criteria to police false and misleading advertising	Industry adopts "family viewing" code Networks rule on acceptability of program content Advocacy groups seek reduction in advertising on children's programming

Target of Action

Figure 9.1. Targets and sources of television policy-making.

The Relevance of Research

Policy-making in regard to television involves the whole range of parties whose actions influence the behavior of the advertising and broadcasting industries. The clientele for policy-relevant social and behavioral research is thus very broad.

The principal institutions and their roles are shown in table 9.1. They include the federal regulatory bodies, the television industry in all its diversity, the viewing public, including the noisome advocacy groups, and various interventionist bodies. The regulators make the rules, the industry responds, the public and the interventionist bodies react, and the industry and the regulators respond to the new situation. The process is continual.

There are obviously three different kinds of decisions being made: (1) the decisions which shape the various regulatory stipulations to which the advertising and broadcasting industries must conform, (2) the many decisions on the part of advocacy groups and the public which define the context or the milieu within which these industries function, (3) the decisions made within the advertising and broadcasting industries which constitute their response to regulatory stipulations and to the actions of the various parties outside the regulatory process.

Table 9.1 Principal Actors in Television Policy-Making

Principal Actors	Kind of Decision-making
Federal Regulatory Bodies FCC FTC Congress	Stipulate rules to which industry must conform.
Television Industry Networks Affiliate stations Independent stations Advertising industry Producers/writers	Respond to regulatory stipulations, threats of regulation, and actions of public and interventionist bodies, sometimes by formal self-regulation, often implicitly in daily decision-making.
Viewing Public Advocacy groups General public	Create context of opinion and litigation in which industry and regulatory bodies function.
Interventionist Bodies Educational system Private foundations Government agencies	Respond to industry performance by subsidizing public television or by sponsoring research on television's social role.

Because of the way broadcasting is organized in the United States, policy-making that affects programming often involves the response of the industry to assorted pressures. As we have emphasized, in social-effects policy-making for television the industry is a principal actor. The "family viewing" code has been only the most visible of what in fact is continuing adaptive behavior. As Larsen (1964) points out, the institutions of mass communication typically minimize the risk of interference by policing themselves. Broadcasters fear any extension of regulation, any loss of patronage by advertisers, and any challenges to renewal of station licenses. The concrete expression of these fears is a system of rigorous procedures for self-regulation.

The most publicized is the Television Code of the NAB, which sets forth standards for both programming and advertising. It serves as the prominent symbol of the television industry's self-regulatory activities and largely declares general principles. General standards for advertising are also set by the national Council of Better Business Bureaus and the Association of National Advertisers.

Neither the NAB nor the other codes themselves have any meaningful mechanism for enforcement. For example, the NAB code prohibits the use of hosts or primary cartoon characters in the advertising of products on children's programming. The effective instrument, however, is the broadcast standards department, which interprets and applies such injunctions at each network.

The network criteria for advertising are fairly explicit, although as the new focus on children and advertising illustrates, the particular concerns of such policy are continually open to reexamination and revision, to which social and behavioral science can significantly contribute. It is programming that involves the majority of decision-making. In the mid-1970s, a major concern at the networks was the reduction of violence in television viewed by children. In giving concrete shape to this goal, decisions are made daily by the broadcast standards departments about what can and cannot be portrayed. The treatment of firearms on Saturday morning children's television is an example. In the 1974–75 NBC animated series *Return to the Planet of the Apes* the simian army was allowed to carry guns in pursuit of its human prey but not permitted to fire them at a human target. The strictures imposed at each of the three networks are similar, although there are enough differences so that what has been rejected by one network may be acceptable at another.

The programming that newly appears on the screen each fall is the result of a complex process that begins a year earlier. Decisions follow each other like decks of cards fluttering from a high building until several hundred ideas are reduced to the few series that will be broadcast. The various stages in the process, and the activities involved, are illustrated in figure 9.2.

The "concept" is the motivation and relationship among key characters that defines the nature of the series. Hundreds are typically considered; probably about a hundred receive serious evaluation in terms of what competing networks will do, the personal tastes and intuition of the programming staff, and whatever "theory" is predominant at the time about audience trends— toward action, or comedy, or family adventure, or variety, or whatever. A profile is then constructed for each survivor—about four for every series slot to be filled. The concept is tested for appeal with small samples of potential viewers, and variously modified; audience share and the financial cost of capturing such a share are estimated; a "Bible" or fact book specifying the minutiae of setting, props, and mannerisms to which each episode must adhere is compiled, and a sample script is written. These are the data of final selection. The survivors are intended for fall broadcasting. A tentative fall program schedule is prepared, and for

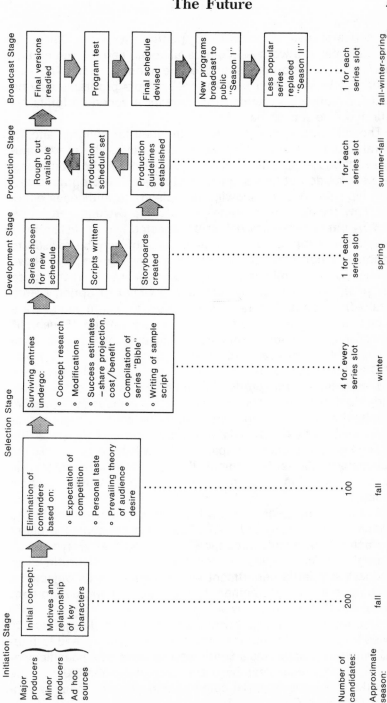

Figure 9.2. Process of series development with activities at each stage.

each series stories are created, and scripts written. "Dailies"—each day's camera work—become available. Then a "rough cut," imperfect in running time, sound, and editing, is ready. The final version follows. With the first episodes, whole programs may be tested for audience reaction. The broadcast schedule for fall is confirmed. The season begins.

The system is similar for series intended for children and for general audiences and for nonseries programs. There are naturally variations in specific instances; television is show business, where events do not flow so much as tumble. The program test—which typically involves showing an episode to audiences either in preview theaters or in homes via a cable system, and is followed by interviews—may detect unexpected like or dislike for a character, and future episodes as yet unshot may be revised to take this reaction into account. Often, a series concept will have its initial—and sometimes only—public appearance in the guise of a "pilot" to test audience appeal the winter or spring before the fall for which it is under consideration. In recent years, there has been a "Season I," and then a quickly assembled "Season II" in which unpopular programs are replaced by new entries from the original set of contenders.

The three parties in the decision-making are the programming department, the production company, and the broadcast standards department. The critical decisions about survivors are made by the programming department. The actual programs are deeply affected by the decisions of producers and writers at the independent production company. Both will have to satisfy the broadcast standards department. It is broadcast standards that sets the rules within which the others attempt to work this show biz magic.

At each of the stages, the evolving episode is reviewed by the broadcast standards department. The basic concept, the script and treatment (available in comic strip form in the "storyboard"), the rough cut, and the final version are all subject to scrutiny. The broadcast standards department will make known its objections or doubts in a written comment to the programming department and the production company.

This intervention only becomes visible when disagreements between the networks and the producers and writers lead to public acrimony. Actually, it is a continuing process. The specificity of the rulings is made clear by these examples submitted by the networks to a congressional committee in proof of industry vigilance (*Television Digest,* 1977):

Although no one is now killed in the conclusion . . . some of the action has been sensationalized to an unacceptable level. For example, when Serpico uses the chaise lounge to bash the heavy's head into the cement wall and then the fight between Serpico and the second heavy is excessive in length and the number of blows exchanged. . . . This episode combines sex and violence in a lascivious way, repeating words in contexts which were objectionable at the script level. . . . Three men attacking and then, raping Carol is clearly beyond what is acceptable. The scene is salacious, too violent and too long. . . . The scene shows us everything—the fights, tearing the dress, a man fumbling with his belt, right to Carol's face as we must assume the sex begins. In an earlier script we allowed a medical question about bleeding after the attack. That never meant nor was it to be construed that we would allow Serpico to see a rivulet of blood running down the inside of her thigh. . . .

Filming of the action which shows "Roger executing Jeff with a judo chop" should avoid being instructional or unduly vicious . . . Please avoid having Karen torture Doris while the latter is in the pool. . . .

The reference to the ice pick having been driven "into the base of the victim's skull" will be changed to something like "and drive it into him". . . . The ice pick should not be seen protruding from his body. . . .

Please eliminate the action of Caesar trying to drive his knee into Braddock's groin. . . .

Critics of broadcasting make much of the fact that the NAB code does not provide wide or strong constraints because many stations are not members and the penalty for persistent violation is no more than removal of the right to display the NAB seal—a mechanism akin to enforcing traffic laws by ripping "I'm a Safe Driver!" stickers from passing violators. From a long-range perspective, however, this weakness is partially overcome by the fact that much of what is known on these stations are syndicated reruns originally produced under the conditions stipulated by the networks. By no act of their own, the programming of the independent and non-NAB stations eventually reflects to a large degree decisions made at the networks.

This system has a major consequence for policy-making. The self-regulatory mechanisms of the broadcast standards departments are a systematic element in the multitude of decisions which lie behind any television program or advertisement. As a result, the mechanism provides a formal means by which pressures from the many parties involved in broadcasting can find expression.

It is important to understand that this expression is likely to be largely negative in direction. The separation of authority that has evolved between those responsible for production and those responsible for enforcing standards leaves no place for positive stipulations on behalf of certain kinds of portrayals. The incentive is to avoid such responsibility because it would greatly increase conflicts over the propriety of content. Producers, writers, and the network executives who express their desires about program content cannot be expected to be influenced by research other than that concerned with popularity, because the goal assigned them by the system is to attract the largest possible audience. The result is that, barring fundamental reorganization of television, social and behavioral science will enter only when its findings have been translated into a prohibition.

In these circumstances, social and behavioral science can influence the industry's policy-making in two ways. One is by compelling industry action. The other is by defining the corrective steps the industry should take.

The attempt to reduce violence is an example of the first. It occurred in response to external pressures fueled if not created by evidence from social and behavioral science. The many analyses of television content which document the stereotypic treatment of sex roles may have similar influence as they provide various women's groups with concrete evidence. The NAB code has already been revised to reduce the quantity of advertising on children's television, and new restrictions on content of such commercials are certainly within the power of the industry if evidence convincing to sufficiently formidable critics were to be offered by science.

The second way in which social and behavioral science can influence self-regulation is through the empirical testing of the validity of the various rulings made by the broadcast standards departments. There are certainly findings in the research to date that bear on the kind of self-regulatory judgments being made. Almost all concern young viewers' reactions to portrayals of violence. For example, it has been found that:

> When a perpetrator is rewarded, or not punished, the likelihood of subsequent aggressiveness by the young viewer increases; when a perpetrator is punished, it decreases (Bandura, 1965a; Bandura, Ross, and Ross, 1963b; Rosekrans and Hartup, 1967).
> When the violence is presented as justified, the likelihood of

subsequent aggressiveness by the young viewer increases. (Berkowitz and Rawlings, 1963; Meyer, 1972c).

When cues are included in the violent portrayal which match cues in real life environment such as similarity of name of victim the likelihood of subsequent aggressiveness by the young viewer increases (Berkowitz and Geen, 1966).

When the perpetrator is depicted as similar to the viewer, the likelihood of subsequent aggressiveness by the young viewer increases. (Rosekrans, 1967).

A portrayal of violent interaction between persons motivated by intent to injure increases the likelihood of subsequent aggressiveness (Berkowitz and Alioto, 1973; Geen and Stonner, 1972).

A portrayal of actual violent interaction between persons is more likely than a fictional portrayal to result in subsequent aggressiveness (Feshbach, 1972).

The presentation of highly exciting material of any kind increases the likelihood of subsequent aggressiveness when that is an appropriate response (Zillmann, 1971; Tannenbaum and Zillmann, 1975).

These and similar aspects of portrayals would escape the broad tabulating of violence in television drama such as that conducted by Gerbner and Gross (chapter 2). However, it is precisely such aspects that are regularly accepted or rejected by the self-regulatory mechanisms of the industry. It is thus unfortunate that there has never been an effort to focus a series of studies on the empirical validity of the rulings made within the industry. There is no reason why such judgments could not be subjected to empirical test. The display of guns not fired at human targets *may* reduce any possible contribution of a cartoon adventure to the aggressive behavior of young viewers, but such a stipulation—which leads to a certain dramatic absurdity—should be grounded in evidence. Production-oriented research designed to answer the questions now settled intuitively would be a large step toward increasing the relevance of social and behavioral science in television policy-making.

There is a third and even more difficult challenge for social and behavioral science in directly enhancing the service rendered the public by television. Television broadcasting is a business engaged in the selling to advertisers of access to audiences, and largely it gains these audiences by the presentation of entertainment. However, it shares with other media a normative and self-acknowledged role to provide news and information, and to some degree to entertain in ways that are socially constructive. It is this norm of social responsibility that justifies the protection of the First Amendment and is the rationale for the regulation of scarce broadcast frequencies by the government.

Research and analysis conducted by the media to guide policy has focused on potential popularity of content. In television, this use of research extends not only to entertainment, but to the selection of on-the-air news personnel and the design of news and public affairs formats as well. This leaves untouched the more important question of the degree to which programming serves various public needs.

Of greatest use would be better evidence on the efficacy of current national television news. Network coverage typically treats news as an episodic event, and emphasizes the event which is amenable to camera coverage. Thus, we have the extraordinary finding that viewing of television news during a presidential election campaign is unrelated to knowledge of candidates and issues while viewing of televised political commercials appears to increase such knowledge (Patterson and McClure, 1976). Yet, many rely largely on television for news and groups which are highly oriented toward television and less likely to supplement television with newspaper and magazine reading include the less educated and blacks (McCombs, 1968; J. P. Robinson, 1971). The occasionally reported lack of a correlation between television news exposure and public affairs knowledge (Patterson and McClure, 1976; J. P. Robinson, 1972c) encourages the speculation that television as a sole news source is inadequate. The networks tacitly acknowledged the possibility by weighing in 1976 the doubling of the time allotted to early evening news, an innovation at least temporarily abandoned because of the opposition of affiliate stations, which find the time more profitable if programmed independently. The substitution of effectiveness for the present research criterion of popular acceptance could provide crucial evidence for constructive reform.

There is also a role for social and behavioral science in the shaping of entertainment by clarifying its psychological impact. It would be naive to argue that research could easily improve programming. Nevertheless, it is clear that television's producers and writers strive for what they perceive to be the most socially meaningful drama and comedy possible within a given format, and increased knowledge of the constructive and destructive roles of entertainment in people's lives conceivably could alter the conceptual framework they inhabit.

Neither of these issues are likely to be directly addressed by the industry because its priorities inevitably lie in audience maximization. This places the challenge before academia, independent research centers, and the private foundations and government agencies which support their activities.

In Conclusion

Our analysis deals with the present system of broadcasting, in which federal regulation plays a large role. This should not be taken to imply that we believe it is the best system possible, although we do believe that it is likely to continue in much the same shape into the future.

There are, of course, many who advocate change. Most reformers argue for a larger role for public television made possible by increased private and governmental subsidy, and it does appear that public television is growing in popularity and may threaten commercial television's revenues by reducing its audience and redirecting advertiser dollars to the underwriting of prestige-winning public programs.* Many argue for reduced regulatory restrictions in regard to the carrying by cable of programming and movies originally broadcast by commercial stations, in order to create a competing system that presumably would offer viewers greater diversity of program choice.

One economist (Owen, 1975) would abandon the present system. He would end FCC regulation on the grounds that in effect it arbitrarily requires public service broadcasting regardless of viewer demand in exchange for the barring of entry of new broadcasters into the market and the protection of the vested economic interests of present license holders. He would abolish public television as it now exists on the grounds that it meets no demonstrated public demand, represents an elitist view of what the public should have, and does so in a very expensive way. More specifically, he would end station licensing, sell present licenses to the highest bidders, limit regulation to the prohibition of newspaper and television ownership in the same market, limit support for public broadcasting to the purchase of commercial air time,

---

* For example, in 1975 four major oil companies—Arco, Exxon, Gulf, and Mobil—spent $35 million on television. Of that sum, 25 percent went to public television—more than the 20 percent to non-network spots and almost half of the 55 percent spent on network advertising (National Broadcasting Company, 1976). Companies can gain more attention than audience share would indicate by heavily promoting their underwriting.

increase the outlets operating in a market to a number that would evolve naturally from the attempt to operate profitably, end all restrictions on pay television, and make cable television time available to all able to pay for it with no control over content by cable system operators. The purpose would be to end government interference in free expression and increase the influence of audience demand—as expressed in its willingness to watch commercial broadcasting or to pay for specialized programming—on the performance of the broadcasting industry. Ostensibly, such a system of open, unrestrained competition would increase the diversity of programming, better satisfy the demands of minority and special interest audiences.

However, the system is likely to continue much as it is for reasons of sociology and politics. A society does not dismantle its major institutions in the absence of public displeasure, and usually that displeasure must reach the level of fury for such transformations to occur. And there is no evidence of great public dissatisfaction with television, and certainly no sign that any dissatisfaction that exists is accompanied by any widespread belief in the desirability of radical reform. Furthermore, the present system has created in the broadcasters who benefit from it a very powerful set of vested interests which will oppose any change. The major source for change will certainly be the various technological developments—cable and pay television, in-home playback, and the provision of special services and information to the home. Their eventual impact of course is unknown, but at present they are being accommodated slowly within the present framework. However, even if the most radical of possible changes were to occur, social-effects policy-making and the need for evidence from social and behavioral science on which to base it would continue. Social effects policy-making derives from public and governmental fear of the media, and from the media's fear of governmental and public wrath; neither are likely to go away.

The pursuit of scientific evidence about the effects of mass communication sometimes seems to trouble people. When television is criticized for what it brings into the home, its defenders often assert that this is a case of "killing the messenger" because the medium, in news and entertainment, only reflects the society. They are quite right that the mass media are often the scapegoat for evils that originate elsewhere. Unfortunately, this view is sometimes accompanied by the belief that "hear no evil, see no evil" is a proper attitude toward evidence of media's effects. The argument is that research is dangerous to free expression because it may end in restrictions on what can be communicated. It is hopefully true that the demonstration of an undesirable effect may alter the decisions that enter into television programming. What the argument overlooks is that there is never a time when decisions are not being made about what is acceptable. Given this fact, we would argue that it is better that such decisions be based on knowledge than made in ignorance. Social and behavioral science did not invent anxiety over the impact of the mass media. It has existed since the first newspapers and popular periodicals. Comic books, pulp fiction, and movies have all been targets of attack. What social and behavioral science can do is provide empirical evidence about the legitimacy of the various claims and counter-claims. Scientific evidence can be liberating as well as confining. It can warn when television may not be acting in society's best interest (as appears to have transpired in the case of violent entertainment), but it can also free television from unjustified attacks when alleged harmful effects appear to be nonexistent (as appears to be the case in regard to the exposure of young viewers to over-the-counter drug advertising and use of illicit drugs).

The potential role of social and behavioral science in television policy-making, which is many-leveled and complex, is large. Its effectiveness depends on the degree to which it credibly addresses the demands for information by the many and varied parties able to influence television—particularly in the exertion of pressure outside regulation, and the degree to which it gives direction to the self-regulatory response of the advertising and broadcasting industries. There is a definite but limited role for social and behavioral science in regulatory action. Its past and potential role in nonregulatory action, particularly in regard to social effects policy-making, is sizable. To equate policy-making with regulation is to ignore the realities of television, and to deprive ourselves of the guidance that social and behavioral science can provide.

Research Priorities

Our agenda for the further scientific examination of television's social impact appears in table 9.2.

Table 9.2 Agenda for Research on Television and Human Behavior

Topic	Issues
I. *Television and socialization*	Television consumes a large portion of the time available to children and adolescents. Public and parental concern about possible negative effects continues, and the possibility of increasing any positive influence merits exploration.
Socially desirable effects	What aspects of portrayals increase the likelihood that viewers will take them as models for their own behavior?
	In what ways are the psychological dynamics involved in prosocial effects similar and dissimilar to those involved in antisocial effects?
	Are there any prosocial effects attributable to violent entertainment?
Role socialization	To what degree does television influence occupational aspirations?
	To what degree does television influence expectations and behavior in regard to persons a viewer encounters such as policemen, doctors, and lawyers?
	To what degree does television influence expectations and behavior in regard to male/female roles?
Political socialization	To what extent does television contribute to the formation of beliefs and values about public affairs?
	To what extent does television affect expectations and intentions about eventual political participation, including voting?
Antisocial behavior	What are the environmental circumstances and psychological processes which enhance the likelihood that television violence will contribute to aggression or antisocial behavior?
	What conditions or circumstances mitigate any contribution of television to aggression or antisocial behavior?
	To what degree is any contribution of television to aggression or antisocial behavior attributable to its capacity to excite or arouse, rather than to specifically violent content?
	To what degree does television violence desensitize viewers in regard to real-life violence, thereby reducing behavioral and attitudinal reactions?
Effects of advertising	To what extent do television food commercials promote dietary and health practices inconsistent with good nutrition?
	To what extent, and by what inadvertent devices, do television product commercials encourage dangerous play, such as with poisonous household cleaners?

Table 9.2 Continued

	To what extent do television drug commercials promote unnecessary consumption of over-the-counter drugs?
	To what extent do television commercials lead to pressures on a parent to purchase items the parent would otherwise ignore?
	To what degree do television commercials mislead young viewers over their self-interested persuasive intent or the nature, quality, and benefits of the product, and what techniques augment or diminish such deception?
Cognitive learning	What is the negative or positive contribution of television viewing to reading and other verbal skills and to nonverbal perceptual capabilities?
	How can the contribution of television viewing to the acquisition of socially valued skills and knowledge be increased?
Television among other agents of socialization	What is the influence of television compared to that of such other agents of socialization as parents, schools, and the community?
	What are the aspects of socialization for which television is an especially important influence?
	What kinds of parental behavior or family conditions increase or decrease the socializing influence of television?
Television viewing patterns	How can the viewing experience be more completely and meaningfully described?
	How does this experience vary by age, sex, and ethnic group?
	What is the import of contextual factors, such as solitary vs. group viewing, the genesis of program choice, and pre- and post-viewing interpersonal communication about television?
II. *Television and politics*	The notion that television or any other mass medium is the single predominant factor in voter decision-making was long ago discredited, but television nevertheless plays an important if more modest role.
News and public affairs coverage	What picture of events reaches the public and what is the degree and character of distortion or bias?
Effects on political beliefs and behavior	How does television interact with other influences in shaping voter decision-making?
	To what degree does television set the public's agenda of issues and persons to which it pays attention?
	What is the role of television in influencing beliefs on major issues of long-term focus, such as Watergate and the Vietnam war?

Table 9.2 Continued

III. *Television and special populations* Minorities Poor Elderly Women	These segments of the audience share two characteristics: each is a high consumer of television and an object of concern in regard to equitable treatment by the society. What are the factors motivating high use? In what ways do tastes and preferences differ? How do these groups perceive themselves as portrayed and how are they portrayed? Are there effects peculiar to these groups? In what ways, if any, are these groups served less well than other segments of the audience?
IV. *Psychological and behavioral effects*	Many new questions about the effects of television have been opened by the research on violent entertainment and children and adolescents.
Arousal hypothesis	To what degree does physiological arousal attributable to the excitatory capacity of portrayals and not the specific kind of content account for behavioral effects?
Dynamics behind effects	Which of the various possible psychological and environmental factors play the predominant role in any behavioral effect?
Prosocial behavior	What are the similarities and dissimilarities with effects on aggressive behavior?
V. *Uses and gratifications of television*	The implication of the public's extensive viewing of television is that various motives and rewards are involved, but their precise role is unclear. What are the varied motives and rewards for viewing television, and how do they vary by kind of content and by characteristics of the viewer? To what degree is any influence on knowledge, attitude or behavior contingent on the viewer's motives or expectations?
VI. *Analysis and monitoring of entertainment content*	One measure of the performance of the industry is what is broadcast. Television can only be evaluated with knowledge of its content. What are the recurring themes and messages related to socially desired behavior? What is the treatment of segments of the population about whose role in society there is some concern, such as the poor, minorities, women, and the elderly?
VII. *Operation and management of television*	Effects proceed from content, and content is the reflection of operation and management. To influence content, the way television operates must be understood.

Table 9.2 Continued

	What are the trends and shifts in violent entertainment as the industry attempts to reduce such content?
News and public affairs decision-making	What are the factors which determine the composition of television news?
Entertainment decision-making	What is the process by which entertainment programming is developed, and what are the loci and nature of decisions that would benefit from social and behavioral science?
	How might public tastes and desires be more accurately and thoroughly measured than by *post hoc* audience ratings?
Alternatives to present system	What is the relationship between the present system of broadcasting and the programming available to viewers, and what differences in programming would be expected with changes in the system?
VIII. *Comparative media systems*	The assets and liabilities of the American system of broadcasting can be better understood in comparison with the systems of other societies. The relationship among the various national systems is little understood.
Media structure and organization	How are the broadcasting systems of other societies differently organized and supported?
Control of media content	How is programming developed and regulated in different systems?
International flow of television content	What are the trends in the distribution and flow of television programming across international boundaries?
IX. *Television and society*	The place of television as an institution among the other institutions of our society merits continuing attention because of the great expenditure of public time for which it is responsible.
	How does television stand in regard to major social institutions, how has it altered the performance of other institutions, and how will it evolve in the future?
	What are the implications of the increased program choice promised by the new technologies of cable, pay-TV, and in-home playback?
	What are the continuing, characteristic, net influences on social life of television as it has evolved in our society?

The major topics are ordered by the degree of interest they command among social and behavioral scientists concerned with television. This ranking, although ultimately subjective, is based on interviews with prominent scientists (for details, see Comstock and Lindsey, 1975). It attempts to represent the degree of attention that can be expected over the next decade if the priorities held at the time of the survey persist.

The actual course of research will certainly differ if financial support does not parallel these interests, or if particularly striking thrusts within any topic draw new interest. This volatility is multiplied within major topics, and for this reason we do not rank-order the subsidiary topics.

The priorities of any individual social or behavioral scientist will reflect his training, interests, and judgment of needs. There is no reason to believe that the consensus of scientists is optimal by any criteria other than for satisfying their intellectual appetite.

There are a number of interests whose prominence is relatively new. This is in part a legacy of the Surgeon General's study. The affirmative conclusion in regard to television's causal role in aggression heightened interest in television's effects and refocused attention.

The new interests include such topics as socially desirable behavior, role socialization, the effects of advertising, the effects on cognitive learning, and the place of television in the matrix of such pretelevision agents as parents. They also include such psychological issues as the dynamics behind any behavioral effects including aggression. Here, the "arousal hypothesis" (the contention that behavioral effects are at least in part attributable to the physiologically measurable excitation induced by a portrayal, and not its specific content) and the factors which might mitigate any contribution to antisocial behavior are newly prominent.

The interests which have endured since television's first days—aggression, politics, content, harm to children—have been transformed in emphasis over the years. New questions are being asked today because of the research of the past.

This has become a period for assessing the state of research on television and human behavior because of the Surgeon General's study, whose 1972 termination is a punctuation mark for the field. The most prominent of recent agendas is that by Katz (1977), prepared for the British Broadcasting Corporation. It has been criticized for too fully accepting the perspectives of broadcasters, for not advocating a critical stance on the part of researchers, for giving inadequate emphasis to the socialization of children as an issue for broadcasting, and for substituting intellectual curiosity for policy-relevance (Filep, 1977; Halloran, 1978). Its breadth, comprehensiveness, and the erudition of its assessment of the tides of scientific scrutiny are undeniably impressive. Our thinking has been enriched by it, as it has by other attempts to impose order on the field (Anderson, Comstock, and Dennis, 1976; Bobrow, 1974; Bogart, 1974; Davison and Yu, 1974; The Ford Foundation, 1976; Hyman, 1974; Katz, Blumler, and Gurevitch, 1973; Leifer, Gordon, and Graves, 1973; Rubinstein, 1973; Social Science Research Council, 1975). Nevertheless, our agenda has its own emphases. This may reflect the imposition of our own vision, an event always somewhat unavoidable in matters of this kind. We hope that it reflects our success in recording the current of scientific events; to borrow from Christopher Isherwood's famous opening to *Goodbye to Berlin* (1954), we have "developed . . . printed, fixed" what we have seen.

Making Science More Articulate

The successful use of research on television and human behavior for practical ends depends partially on the resolution of three problems. They are present wherever social and behavioral science is relevant to policy issues, but they are particularly acute in regard to television because of the character of the medium and the difficulties it poses for scientific study.

Problem I: Increasing confidence in the conclusions drawn from social and behavioral science about television's social influence.

In a single laboratory-type experiment, the role of statistical tests is to ensure that a particular finding is highly unlikely to be the result of sampling anomalies. That role cannot be filled by replication in order to make inferences about events outside the study. Replication does increase confidence that within the limits of the method the finding is real, and it can expand the categories of persons for which a finding can be said to hold; but it does not ensure generalizability to real-life events.

The unhappy fact is that no single method can provide unambiguous evidence of a real-life causal relationship. There is typically a tradeoff between lack of ambiguity for causal inference and the certainty of real-life applicability. There is also typically a tradeoff between flexibility, in terms of ability to study an issue and the diversity of issues that can be studied, and the certainty of real-life applicability. The laboratory-type experiment is strong for causal inference and in flexibility, but direct extrapolation to real-life events is hazardous. The difficulty is that a finding may always in some way be attributable to the artificiality of the circumstances, so that what is "real" within an experiment may not be real in terms of actual events. The more naturalistic circumstances in which data are collected in the field experiment and the survey (whether one-time only or in a panel design) solve the artificiality problem but at the price of flexibility and confidence in drawing causal inferences.

A frequently proposed solution is the substitution of the field experiment for the laboratory-type experiment, because it ostensibly transports the inferential prowess of the latter to naturalistic circumstances. When we examine the field experiments done to date on the effects of television (Feshbach and Singer, 1971; Milgram and Shotland, 1973; Parke et al., 1977; A. H. Stein and Friedrich, 1972; Wells, 1973), we can only conclude that the field experiment, because of the unavoidable need to fit life as it is, courts problems in the case of television which often make interpretation of findings difficult. These problems include the typical need to use intact groups or to depart otherwise from perfect random assignment; the risk, in creating experimental conditions by depriving persons of preferred television fare, of also creating reactive frustration on the part of subjects that itself may be the "cause" of any observed "effect" (Feshbach and Singer, 1971; Wells, 1973); and the possibility of failure to achieve the naturalistic setting on which the credibility of the findings rest (Milgram and Shotland, 1973).

There is also the very special problem of insensitivity when a field experiment is intended to detect the real-life incidence of an effect—a socially important impact may well be overlooked (Milgram and Shotland, 1973). This occurs because the size of the national television audience means that a phenomenon occurring below the threshold of detection by conventional statistical tests would result in a quantity of incidents of sizable magnitude.*

*For example, Milgram and Shotland (1973) expose several hundred persons to an antisocial act in an episode of the television series *Medical Center* and several days later measure the propensity of viewers to perform a similar act when given

These problems are compounded by the frequent high cost of such ventures. We do not argue that field experiments on the effects of television cannot be useful, or that such experiments to date have not produced any valuable data, but only that transporting the rigors of the laboratory-type experiment to real-life settings is easier to advocate than to accomplish and that field experiments are high-risk undertakings.

The survey can provide extremely valuable data, particularly when it is part of a panel design in which the same persons are measured two or more times. The survey is valuable because its data represent phenomena as they occur in real life, including their rareness of frequency and, with a panel design, their trend or oscillation over time. Thus, shifts in television viewing and other behavior can be followed. The weakness is that causal inference is typically not permitted and when a case can be made for it there will be many who will reject the argument. As the often-cited ten-year panel study of the effects of television violence on the aggressiveness of young viewers by Lefkowitz, Eron and colleagues demonstrates (Eron et al., 1972; Eron et al., 1974; Lefkowitz et al., 1972), so many legitimate doubts can be raised about the use of such data by themselves to infer that television is a "probable cause" of some behavior, as these investigators do, that widespread acceptance of such a conclusion is unlikely (Chaffee, 1972b; Howitt, 1972; Huesmann et al., 1973; Kaplan, 1972; Kay, 1972; Lefkowitz, 1972; Pool, 1972; Surgeon General's Scientific Advisory Committee on Television and Social Behavior, 1972). Survey data can often help in narrowing the field of contending causal explanations (Chaffee, 1972a, 1972b), but by itself is unlikely to be persuasive. It is for these reasons of causal ambiguity that the principal investigator of NBC's major panel study of television's effect on children and adolescents (Milavsky and Pe-

---

the opportunity. They find no influence, but the problem is that a rate of effect far lower than would be statistically significant would be socially significant. If one out of a thousand were affected, a national audience of 13 million for a prime-time series would precipitate 13,000 incidents. If the rate of effect for a specific antisocial portrayal were high enough to be detected by an experimental design using a few hundred subjects, one would not need any research to find out, because each night's television would predict the crime wave headlines of the following days. This demonstration of a "null" effect ironically reinforces the arguments of those whose concern is guided by the laboratory-type experiments demonstrating aggressive effects of violent portrayals, which typically involve far fewer subjects because it illustrates how far less frequent in real life such an effect would have to be to be of some social importance.

kowsky, 1973; Milavsky, Pekowsky, and Stipp, 1975) has argued that such panel data should be subjected to analysis by as many alternative statistical models as possible in order to explore the influence on findings of their varying assumptions, and thereby to guard against unjustified conclusions (The Ford Foundation, 1976).

From a scientific perspective, the confusion that sometimes appears to exist is the result of faulty or unsophisticated conceptualization. Different methods typically address somewhat different questions, and conflicts in outcome are often more apparent than real. This division of labor among methods is illustrated in the instance of television violence. The laboratory experiments focus principally on the testing of hypotheses regarding the attributes of the television, situation, and viewer on which any influence of a violent portrayal on subsequent aggressiveness may be contingent, while field experiments principally focus on testing the central hypothesis of a causal relationship between violence viewing and subsequent aggression in as naturalistic and uncontrived a set of circumstances as possible. This emphasis on the inferential specialization of the experiment does not imply disagreement with the view that causal inference ultimately rests on the progressive falsification of possible explanations rather than the positive demonstration of a particular relationship, which necessarily always remains ambiguous because of the infinite number of possible explanations for any event (Popper, 1968). On the other hand, surveys principally focus on the relationships among the various variables of interest as they occur in real life, although thereby they can make crucial contributions to inferences about causal relationships. The variation of results as a function of difference in method is not inconsistency in the sense that the term connotes conflict and disagreement but only the demonstration of disparate facts that must be resolved in the light of the particular strengths and weaknesses of the methods employed.

The problem of the absence of a single genre of method that can produce compelling results in the case of television's effects is exacerbated by the many vested interests within the industry hostile in regard to any conclusion that might bear on industry practice. These interests range from the networks and the NAB to the producers and writers and individual broadcasters. The response of the industry on the violence issue is only the most prominent example. Industry spokesmen repeatedly protested objections to violence, and continued to do so long after laboratory-type experiments began to demonstrate a causal relationship between children's exposure to violent portrayals and subsequent aggressiveness (Baker, 1969; United States Congress, 1955a,b, 1963, 1965). In 1972, Senate hearings began, which reviewed the Surgeon General's study, and the industry began to shift its position (U.S. Congress, 1972, 1974). More recently, producers, writers, and individual stations have opposed the "family viewing" code (*Broadcasting,* 1976b,c,e,f). The nature of television is such that any plausible argument against the credibility of a study is certain to be well and loudly articulated.

The solution is a research strategy that meets as many potential objections as possible. The two possibilities are the use of multiple methods and the continuing elaboration of empirically-tested theory.

Solution One: Use of multiple methods—each with compensating strengths—to study the same issue.

The conclusion of the Surgeon General's advisory committee that the best interpretation of the full array of evidence is that television violence increases the likelihood of aggressiveness on the part of young viewers rested on the consistency of findings of studies employing different methods. To use the committee's language, the conclusion was based on the *convergence* of evidence from laboratory-type experiments and from surveys (Surgeon General's Scientific Advisory Committee, 1972). The former demonstrated a causal relationship within the artificial confines of the experimental setting. The latter demonstrated a positive association in everyday life between the viewing of violence and aggressive behavior that was not attributable to any measured "third" variable, including the one most often proposed as an alternative to television violence as the causal agent in such a correlation—the preference of aggressive persons for more violent entertainment. The conclusion was reached *despite* the doubts about the validity of inferring causation from the Lefkowitz-Eron ten-year panel study completed under the Surgeon General's program, because that study was taken as providing only evidence of a positive association between aggression and viewing of violence, and it did not rest on the evidence from any field experiment.

The obvious lesson is that a combination of methods provides inferential strength beyond that of any single method, and that such strength is particularly crucial for television, which is embedded with so many other factors and where contention and vested interests abound. It would be naive to expect compelling findings from a single study or method. It is more reasonable to search for consistencies across studies and methods.

By multiple methods, of course, we mean some combination of the laboratory-type experiment, the field experiment, and survey methods. Such a combination can be accumulated by adding the missing portions to an existing literature, as occurred in the Surgeon General's case. It is best done by incorporating different methods within the same design or strategy. This has tremendous strengths because the methods can be used to mutually validate various measures, the involvement of the same investigators will increase the likelihood of comparability across the studies, and the particular strengths of a method can be turned to providing evidence beyond the scope of other methods, yet that evidence will gain in value because it emerges from a context in which some findings derived from different methods can be compared. Because of these strengths, a multiple methods strategy is desirable even when a body of evidence based on one of the component methods already exists.

Some of the different functions served by components of a multiple methods design that incorporates a panel study and a set of laboratory-type experiments are presented in table 9.3. Key survey instruments are validated in the laboratory-type experiments, where pencil-and-paper or interview techniques can be combined with behavioral measures, which are difficult to obtain in surveys; the laboratory-type experiment is used to study age groups where survey techniques would be difficult; and the panel provides evidence of real-life relationships not obtainable from the laboratory-type experiment. The implications of the various possible combinations of findings are displayed in table 9.4. One of the benefits of the multiple-methods approach is that, in addition to helping counter criticism that could be raised about evidence from a single method, it more immediately delineates the direction for future research.

Our example combines a panel study with laboratory-type experiments because of the ability of the former to measure the complex dynamics of everyday behavior and the flexibility and inferential power of the latter. In addition, there are methods of statistical analysis which, if certain assumptions are met, make panel data more useful than a one-time only survey for reaching a con-

Table 9.3 Functions Served by Components of Hypothetical Multiple Methods Study

Study Description:
Several age cohorts—for example, an elementary, junior, and senior high school sample—are measured a year apart. Several laboratory-type experiments are conducted with subjects of the same ages. The issue under investigation is television's contribution to behavior and attitudes judged to be important in socialization.

Panel Study:
Measure behavior and attitudes as they occur in real life.

Test existence of real-life association between television and variables of interest.

Measure changes over time.

Narrow range of possible causal explanations for any association between television and variables of interest.

Laboratory-Type Experiments:
Validate pencil-and-paper measures of attitude or a propensity to behave in a certain way by correlation with observed behavior.

Study conditions difficult to measure in real life.

Observe immediate effects on actual behavior.

Study subjects too young for easy use of survey techniques.

Infer causation.

Table 9.4 Implications of Various Outcomes of a Multiple Methods Study

Outcomes		
Panel Study	*Lab-type Experiment*	*Implications*
+	+	Confidence in real-life validity of hypothesis strengthened.
−	+	Focus on aspects of laboratory situation that might be responsible for artifactual or "lab-only" results.
+	−	Focus on aspects of laboratory situation that might inhibit an effect; search for alternative causal explanations.
−	−	Abandon ship! (Look for alternative causal explanations.)

+ = positive finding
− = negative or null finding

clusion about causation (Chaffee, 1972a, 1972b; Heise, 1970; Kenny, 1972, 1973; Pelz and Andrews, 1964; Pelz and Lew, 1970; Rozelle and Campbell, 1969). However, a field experiment can also be profitably combined with other methods. For example, Parke et al. (1977) greatly increased confidence in his findings that violent films increased the aggressiveness of delinquent boys by consistent results not only from three field experiments of several weeks' duration (replication) but also from a laboratory-type experiment (multiple methods).

Solution Two: Continue the elaboration of theory by the empirical testing of hypotheses, with particular attention to meeting objections to theory's relevance to real life.

Theory in social and behavioral science is a coherent explanation of events which leads to the formulation of testable hypotheses. As the hypotheses fail or survive these tests, the theory becomes revised and strengthened. Eventually, a particular finding confirming a hypothesis derives its credibility not only from the data subjecting it to specific test but also from the fact that the theory which produced it is supported by numerous other tests. In this context, "credibility" has two meanings. It means that the confirmation of the hypothesis is more convincing because it is consistent with a larger body of evidence, and also that confidence in its real-life relevance is increased by the fact that the hypothesis is the product of a plausible explanation of events that has received extensive empirical confirmation. Such a hypothesis still might not hold for real-life events, but such a likelihood is reduced by its placement in a context of theory and extensive confirmation—unless one believes that the confirming instances are almost entirely the artifact of method.

The most useful tool for the construction and elaboration of theory is the laboratory-type experiment.

Because of its flexibility, moderate cost, and capacity for causal inference the laboratory-type experiment is the most useful tool for the construction and elaboration of theory. Therefore, we do not believe, as the criticisms of the real-life relevance of the method might be taken to imply, that the laboratory-type experiment cannot contribute important knowledge.

Despite the failure of the laboratory-type experiment to make the Surgeon General's study unnecessary, the status of research on television violence and aggression actually argues strongly on its behalf. It provided the necessary evidence which—when data from surveys demonstrated a positive association in real-life between viewing of violence and aggression—permitted that new data to be interpreted within a causal framework. That framework was greatly strengthened by the fact that the evidence from the laboratory-type experiments sensibly explained a causal relationship in terms of the observational learning theory of Bandura

(1973) and social-psychological formulations of Berkowitz (1962b, 1973).

The elaboration of theory is particularly crucial for the new research on television's contribution to socially desirable behavior. The genesis of such research lies in theory developed largely in connection with television violence and aggression (Bryan, 1971; Bryan and Walbek, 1970b; Rubinstein et al., 1974), which draws much of its appeal from the positive findings of the laboratory-type experiments devoted to that issue and is currently high on the research agenda of social and behavioral scientists interested in television and children (Comstock and Lindsey, 1975). However, it is not at all clear if the paradigm is completely transferable. Aggression involves discrete physical acts, and the prosocial analogue would appear to be some specific, beneficient physical intervention rather than the broader categories of behavior which are sometimes mentioned as possibly able to be affected by television, such as altruism, helping, generosity, and fairness. Antisocial aggression also involves departure from a norm, while prosocial behavior is in accord with a norm, and the observation of another's behavior on television may be less able to increase performance of a sanctioned action whose social approval may have already placed it at its upper limit of an individual's response hierarchy than a negatively sanctioned one whose likelihood of occurrence can be increased simply by reducing the perception of those sanctions. There is also the problem of the evidence that reward or lack of punishment for the perpetrator in a violent portrayal increases the immediate subsequent aggressiveness of a child viewer (Bandura, 1965a; Bandura, Ross, and Ross, 1963b; Rosenkrans and Hartup, 1967). The mechanism would appear to be an alteration in the viewer's expectation of outcome, either in terms of social approval or more concrete payoff, such as greater access to toys. If expected social approval is hard to manipulate because it is already near its ceiling, any effect must depend on payoff, and it is very unclear whether the inconsistency between the act (which is prosocial) and the motive (which is selfish) would be acceptable to many as a means of using television to encourage socially desirable behavior in children. These issues of symmetry between the aggressive and prosocial domains will have to be settled if there is to be extended progress on this new topic.

Establishing relevance to real life is the principal challenge that theory must meet. This occurs indirectly through the consistency of theory with real-world events, even though the uncontrolled character of those events precludes their being used to test the theory. Thus, the demonstration of a positve correlation between viewing of violence and real-life aggression encourages us to accept, at least as a partial explanation, observational learning theory. The theory provides a "why" for the phenomenon that has repeatedly survived empirical tests in laboratory-type experiments. However, relevance is more directly established by specific ties between the experimental evidence and actuality. For example, we readily accept the proposition that nursery school children will imitate aggressive behavior they have seen on television immediately after viewing when conditions are facilitative; there is no chance of being punished and the setting is similar to that of the portrayal—not only because it has been repeatedly demonstrated in the laboratory but because these are circumstances which could match certain, although possibly rare, instances in real life. However, because the ties between the actuality of the experiment and real events are fewer, we are less confident in the prediction that the likelihood of aggressiveness is increased in some later, different situation. It is through such ties that the relevance of the theory itself is established. What is needed, then, are experiments with as many naturalistic qualities as possible. There is nothing inherent in the laboratory-type experiment which prohibits the inclusion of more extensive viewing before and after the portrayal under study, of the possibility of retaliation or punishment for aggression, of aggression against persons rather than things, of settings unlike those of the portrayal, and of ordinary program-length television rather than specially created scenes. Nor is it always unavoidable that a laboratory-type experiment be understood by the subjects as an experiment. An exemplary naturalistic design is that of Steuer, Applefield, and Smith (1971), who manipulated exposure to unabridged violent and nonviolent television programs in a nursery school and found the viewing of the violent programs to be followed by greater interpersonal aggressiveness during normal play.

PROBLEM II: Minimizing the difficulties imposed by the polyglot nature of research on television and behavior.

The topic of television attracts social and behavioral scientists in a wide variety of disciplines. These include social psychology, developmental psychology, marketing and advertising, education, political science, speech, public opinion research, journalism and communications, and sociology. There is only moderate communication across disciplinary boundaries. News of current research flows slowly and the crossing of a disciplinary boundary will often take several years, if it occurs at all. This is not only counterproductive but needless. There is a deep underlying commonality of interests and, in the case of television, research within one discipline typically bears on that in another.

The resulting isolation and compartmentalization of investigators is intensified by the fragmented and unprogrammatic nature of funding. There are numerous government agencies, many private foundations, and in recent years the networks themselves which conduct research on television and behavior. There is no coordination among them. Furthermore, most of the research is funded within programs largely unconcerned with the media. The continuing, focused, sophisticated leadership that can give order and shape to a field has been absent. There have been no means to reduce overlap, avoid redundancy, encourage interdisciplinary cooperation, or ensure that a particular balance or emphasis in activity is achieved.

All of these factors also interfere, of course, with the effective communication of the findings of science to the various parties involved in television policy-making. They can be countered, if not routed, by two steps: undertake research within focused programs, and improve access to information.

Solution One: Undertake research within focused programs.

The Surgeon General's study is the sole instance of a large program of research devoted to the mass media. Whatever its deficiencies, it gives an example of the benefits of a focused effort (table 9.5). They are many.

In the Surgeon General's case, there was a major topic around which the studies were organized—television violence; program management was in the hands of subject specialists who could offer advice and criticism as the research progressed rather than being left to professional administrators; information dissemination and, more importantly, cooperation among investigators was nurtured and encouraged; a review committee immediately initiated the—in this instance, controversy-filled—process of interpreting the findings in the light of prior research; and there was a publication program that leaped several years in putting the results, including both the review committee interpretations and the original new research, before scientists and the public.

Table 9.5 Typical vs. Focused Research Program

Program Component	Typical Program[a]	Focused Program[b]
Operational thrust	Project selection based on peer review for scientific quality, with minimal concern for coherence or fit with other projects. Implied motive is to support scientifically meritorious research.	Project selection based on relevance to a particular topic or issue and contribution to program as a whole, within limits of peer review for scientific quality. Explicit motive is to address a specific issue and cover overlooked areas.
Administrative staff	Professional administrators without extensive knowledge of many of the topics under investigation.	Social and behavioral scientists able to offer advice and counsel during course of projects.
Project solicitation	Formal announcement of availability of support; may be one-time only or describe a recurrent competition.	In addition to formal announcement, administrative staff personally solicits proposals in order to better fulfill program goals.
Project coordination	Projects proceed independently with little or no involvement of administrative staff.	Administrative staff encourages pooling of knowledge and resources among projects.
Dissemination	Report is usually filed with sponsor. Additional dissemination occurs through normal channels—professional meetings, journals, books.	A program-sponsored publication program makes results available shortly after conclusion of the research. Dissemination is far wider than through the discipline-bound channel of professional meetings, and occurs years in advance of normal publication.
Evaluation	Reaction of administrative staff to early draft of report, if one is submitted. Normal evaluation by scientific community when and if dissemination through normal channels occurs.	Specially-assembled review committee evaluates new research in light of prior findings. Committee report hastens process of synthesis of new and old research and entry of new knowledge into scientific and public domains.

[a] Based on a composite of government and private foundation research support.
[b] Based on the Surgeon General's study of television violence at the National Institute of Mental Health, 1969–1972.

There are many other possible configurations for a focused program. There is certainly no reason why several could not function at once, each with its particular emphasis and approach. The essential feature is a sustained effort whose character is dictated by the conditions peculiar to the study of television.

A focused program is obviously *not* a necessary condition for creative scientific research on television and behavior, as numerous studies attest. What it can provide are conditions that increase the likelihood that such research will be pertinent, timely, visible, nonredundant, in line with the intent of the sponsor, and speedily introduced into the mainstream of scientific and public discussion. By so doing, it not only enhances the value of current research, but sets a better foundation for subsequent research.

Solution Two: Improve access to information.

There has been talk for years of the need for some kind of new center devoted to advancing the scientific study of television's influence on society. There is no consensus about the shape it should take. There is agreement that it should be located outside the government (although it could derive support from the government). The disagreement occurs over the functions it would perform, and stems from the fear of some that it might unnecessarily compete with existing activities (The Ford Foundation, 1976).

We would propose an undertaking that would not intrude on present activities or institutional arrangements but for which there is a clear need. Its primary role would be to make needed information more available to social and behavioral scientists. The intent would be to improve the quality of research. A secondary role would be to make information about research more available to potential users in government, broadcasting, and among the public.

This undertaking would have five principal functions:

To collect completed research (books, articles, reports, papers), with particular attention to material—such as investigator's reports to sponsoring agencies and papers delivered at professional meetings—which ordinarily would not reach many scientists.

To summarize completed research in a format designed to meet the needs of users.

To collate information on research in progress.

To disseminate such information to interested parties.

To report regularly on progress and trends, with particular attention to identifying issues and questions that should be addressed.

Such a facility should begin as a test of the feasibility of improving research by increasing the flow of information among scientists by energetic intervention. The analogue would not be that of a library intended to survive indefinitely, but of a demonstration project to be evaluated and possibly terminated after there has been time to assess its ability to achieve its goals. Thus, it would have the added value of possibly providing a model that could be applied to hasten progress in other fields.

The envisaged facility would not follow the passive example of ERIC (Educational Research Information Centers), which disseminates documents upon request. Instead, it would actively seek out its scientific clientele. The principal function would not be passing on the verbatim original, but in disseminating information that would convey the contents sufficiently to make the original unnecessary for many users. Nor would it confine itself to passing on information. One of its major functions would be the analysis of present activity and future needs. And it would not confine itself to completed research, but would also attempt to report on research that is in progress and is therefore largely invisible even to scientists.

Its design and operation would derive from the clientele to be served. A facility that would try to serve many parties equally well probably would serve none optimally, and the steps that would best serve scientists might not best serve other parties. For this reason, such a facility at first should only attempt to meet the specific needs of scientists, with service to others a byproduct. Later, it could try to develop techniques for serving in a more direct way the needs of other parties (such as teachers and parents) or of covering other types of research (such as legal, economic, and structural aspects of television).

There would be no redundancy with any continuing activity. Neither ERIC, the Smithsonian Scientific Information Exchange, the National Institute of Mental Health Clearinghouse, the industry's Television Information Office, nor any other existing agency, either singly or in combination, performs the specified functions.

The potential contribution of such a knowledge facility is high—a judgment based not only on the perceived lack of information flow, but also on the character of the scientific population to be served. It is diverse and compartmentalized, but there are common interests and a wide desire for greater communication. Furthermore, the absolute size of this population is small enough so that the task could be done with a thoroughness and depth not possible for such a mastodonic enterprise as, say, "education."

PROBLEM III: Increasing social and behavioral science's role in television policy-making.

Policy-making and social and behavioral science have at least one attribute in common: a concern for events yet to unfold. Policy of all types is based on expectations about events in the future and the effect on them of present and intervening actions. This is true at the FCC, at the networks, and in the home. Science similarly seeks to predict events on the basis of known past relationships. It would predict, for example, that a young viewer is more likely to behave aggressively if he has just seen a violent television portrayal because such an effect has been repeatedly demonstrated. The same kind of forecast, heightened in salience by public and political pressure, figured in the formulation of "family viewing."

All decisions related to television policy-making—structural, social effects, regulatory, and nonregulatory—derive to some degree from beliefs about the medium's social impact. Social and behavioral science can help all the varied parties involved by clarifying the circumstances likely to favor or disfavor a particular state of affairs. Its role, to their loss, has been constrained by the isolation of policy-makers and social and behavioral scientists from each other. By training, experience, position, and often temperament, they stand apart. Policy-makers lack the knowledge that would make social and behavioral science, despite its frequent ambiguities, helpful to them; social and behavioral scientists lack the knowledge that would help them make research more relevant to practice. This gulf is not one likely to be bridged by an act of God.

One solution: alter the intellectual environment. Another: change the organizational setting in which policy is made.

Solution One: Alter the intellectual environment to provide new guidance to policy-makers and to social and behavioral scientists.

Two things are not clear in regard to television: (1) how social and behavioral scientists should proceed if they are to contribute to policy-making; (2) how policy-makers can make use of social and behavioral science. These questions have not been addressed to any great degree. We need a literature on the process of communications policy-making that clarifies the possible roles of social and behavioral science. The policy-maker would be better able to see its uses, and the scientist better able to deliver useful research.

There are a wide variety of possible topics. They fall into three categories:

Analyses of the future states toward which policy is presumably directed, so that research can be more clearly focused on relevant issues.

Studies of television industry practices, so that research can be addressed realistically to the kinds of decisions actually made.

Reviews of regulatory practices and related governmental activity to identify better the contributions that research might make.

The first amounts to the articulation of goals, and would make it possible to interpret research and to design new studies to identify the factors on which progress toward goals are contingent. This would help the policy-maker and the social scientist focus on the same question. For example, once the goal of greater citizen knowledge of public affairs is stated for the allocation of broadcasting licenses, a criterion is set for the evaluation of evidence on the effects of differences in the way licenses are allocated. Once the goal of minimizing the contribution of television to the aggressive behavior of young children is stated for programming practices, the need for evidence on the aspects of portrayals that increase the likelihood of such behavior becomes clear.

The second is exemplified by two kinds of studies. One is the specification of the precise decisions made in regard to unacceptable program content, so that they can be measured against the available evidence or subjected to new empirical tests. We discussed the need for such a study earlier. The other is the more general examination of daily broadcast operations so that the nature of the business can be better understood. Here, there is an immense body of entertaining and informative personal accounts (for example, Merle Miller and Evan Rhodes's 1964 tale of a programming fiasco, *Only You, Dick Daring!*), some very valuable reportage on certain aspects of operations (such as Les Brown's story of the battle for ratings, *Television: The Business Behind the Box* [1971] and Edward Epstein's portrayal of newscasting, *News from Nowhere: Television and the News* [1973a]), but only a few scholarly analyses of mass media decision-making (Cantor, 1971, 1972; Elliott, 1973). Particularly for social and behavioral scientists, the industry stands unrevealed. Yet, as the possibility of altering broadcast practices by empirically testing the rulings made within the industry on the basis of its codes demonstrates, it is through a knowledge of the way the industry operates that research can be made to bear on practice.

The third would involve the explication of the regulatory process and related governmental activity to clarify the possible uses, abuses, and limitations of social and behavioral research. For example, an evaluation of the ascertainment requirement of the FCC is badly needed. The FCC requires each holder of a commercial or public broadcast license to regularly survey the community by some means to ascertain its needs in regard to broadcaster performance. These studies must meet only a few standards, and there is little comparability across broadcasters; they may often provide little useful information, and they conceivably could be quite unjustified other than as a gesture by the FCC. On the other hand, individual broadcasters may well have developed inventive and useful techniques which could be more widely applied. The Corporation for Public Broadcasting has been sponsoring research to improve ascertainment techniques (NAEB, August 1976), but these studies would have their greatest return when evaluated in the context of the ascertainment requirement for the whole of broadcasting. It is reasonable to suspect that ascertainment could be made both more useful and less burdensome to broadcasters. Another example would be the development of an agenda for research on children and advertising that would aid the decision-making of the FCC and FTC in this contentious area. A third example is the examination by Cater and Strickland (1975) of the particular approach to policy-making exemplified by the Surgeon General's study of television violence. All these kinds of studies are needed because policy-relevant research cannot proceed from an ignorance of policy-making.

Solution Two: Change the organizational setting in which policy is made so that social and behavioral scientists are more directly involved.

The use of social and behavioral science in policy-making depends on the flow of information to policy-makers. At present, that flow is sharply restricted by policy-makers' lack of access to social and behavioral scientists. To varying degrees, this is true for all the parties involved in policy-making—the regulatory agencies, the Congress, the industry, and the various advocacy groups.

The problem is particularly severe at the regulatory agencies and the Congress, whose exposure to social and behavioral science data typically occurs in the heat of a public hearing. From the perspective of the contending parties, it is a matter of "their psychologist (or sociologist)" vs. "our psychologist." The perception is unavoidably much the same for those in the adjudicatory role. The outcome is usually the same as occurs in the courts when each side presents favorable psychiatric testimony: cancellation by conflicting expert opinion. The precise issues, the points of agreement and loci of disagreement, and whatever information might be pertinent tend to be lost.

In the absence of expert interpretation within these bodies, the policy-makers are incapacitated for reasoned judgment by the brevity of exposure. The same situation does not hold outside the behavioral and social realm. The industry and advocacy groups may offer their own economists, but the FCC or whatever government body is involved will typically have its own economists to help interpret the conflicting views.

The solution is the development of stable roles for social and behavioral scientists within these policy-making bodies. This would not only enhance the capability of these bodies to deal with whatever social and behavioral science data might be relevant, but it would also provide a link (where there is now none) that would increase the flow of information from these bodies to social and behavioral scientists. One way to create such roles would be through internships. They would be occupied by scientists, who would carry their new knowledge of the needs and practices of policy-makers back to their colleagues. An alternative is the creation of permanent staff positions for social and behavioral scientists. Another option, although not a substitute for the continuing and intensive attention that staff capability would provide, is the appointment of social and behavioral scientists to major policy-making roles, such as membership on the FCC or FTC. A fourth possibility is the regular instruction of commissioners by short-course or briefing from scientists on relevant evidence outside the contentious framework of the public hearing, which often serves less to inform policy-makers than to display publicly the ostensible concern of the policy-making body and thereby allay criticism. The optimal arrangement would be some combination of such steps to provide continuity and a trusted relationship within a policy-making body and continually increasing sophistication in regard to policy issues by scientists.

Within the industry, there is greater familiarity with social and behavioral science, because its techniques have long been used for business ends. In regard to social effects, however, it typically has followed the pattern that the sociology of organizations would predict by drawing on scientists to defend itself against critics. It has consistently denied the relevance of research, sponsored only by a few studies, and assiduously avoided sponsoring research that might demonstrate negative effects (Baker, 1969). This posture has changed noticeably in recent years. In the 1970s, all three networks sponsored research on social effects, including possibly harmful effects on children. Furthermore, there were a number of innovative efforts, through advisory panels and consulting arrangements, to give program decision-making the benefits, particularly in regard to children's television, of social and behavioral science knowledge. Behind this is the tentative acceptance of the notion that television violence is not without some risk of harm. The desire to avoid public or governmental displeasure has taken a radical new turn, and the industry is pioneering in the use of social and behavioral science in advance of the governmental policy-making bodies.

Advocacy groups pose a special problem. Their very nature implies the selective use of evidence to bolster a position. At the same time, they need a judicious and balanced knowledge of the evidence if they are to select issues and take positions which truly serve the interest of whatever segment of the public they purport to protect. Like the industry, they will certainly draw on social and behavioral science when it appears to fit their preconceptions. The problem is broadening their access to knowledge so that their views are shaped by fact rather than prejudice. One cannot expect them to invest heavily in the search for such information when the same resources could be devoted to their combative activities. For these reasons, we argue that there is an unmet need for providing these groups with the services of social and behavioral scientists outside their normal operating budgets. The most feasible means would be a set of internships financed by some private foundation or public agency; an alternative would be a specialized consulting service, similarly supported, to serve these groups.

The common thread through all these suggestions is to remove partisanship from the use of knowledge. It is naive to expect that those involved in policy-making will make good and unbiased use of social and behavioral science if reliable, trusted sources of information are not available. Our first solution was to enrich the available intellectual capital; our solution here is to adopt new mechanisms for the application of that capital to policy-making.

Social and behavioral science can tell us much about the role of television in society, thereby helping us to make the most of this compelling medium. It often cannot give an unequivocal answer. It cannot answer questions where values are decisive. What it can do is test our best judgment against the sole corrective to impassioned opinion—evidence that could falsify that judgment. It is a corrective and a liberator. Its strength is that it is not designed to flatter us. In this it is like the law. Both consist of rules of procedure and evidence by which facts are evaluated in reaching a conclusion. Neither ensure that truth is reached, only that the possibility of error is minimized. Neither flatter by ensuring the validation of a point of view. The admonition of logic and dispassionate assessment which adhere in each are not always in line with our impulses. Social and behavioral science is also like the law in its fragility before abuse. If we ask questions beyond its capacity, bend it to fit the case at hand, varying evidentiary standards in accord with our preconceptions, we shall lose the help it can provide, leaving us only the guidance of the opinions from which we originally sought protection.

References

Aaker, D. A., and G. S. Day. 1974. A dynamic model of relationships among advertising, consumer awareness, attitudes, and behavior. *Journal of Applied Psychology,* 59, 281–86.

Adler, R. (ed.). 1977. Research on the effects of television advertising on children. Washington, D.C.: Government Printing Office, 1977.

Advertising Age. 1974a. Democrat won in Michigan with TV-less campaign. February 25, p. 4.

Advertising Age. 1974b. Goodrich, not Goodyear, works at telling it straight. October 7, p. 63.

Advertising Age. 1975. How (and how not) to solve TV clutter. April 21, pp. 57–58.

Advertising Age. 1976. Toy makers put on notice as FTC tests new strategy. February 16, p. 2.

Albert, R. S. 1957. The role of the mass media and the effect of aggressive film content upon children's aggressive responses and identification choices. *Genetic Psychology Monographs,* 55, 221–85.

Alger, I., and P. Hogan. 1967. The use of videotape recordings in conjoint marital therapy. *American Journal of Psychiatry,* 123(11), 1425–30.

—— 1969. Enduring effects of videotape playback experience on family and marital relationships. *American Journal of Orthopsychiatry,* 39, 86–94.

Allen, C. L. 1965. Photographing the TV audience. *Journal of Advertising Research,* 5, 2–8.

Alper, W. S., and T. R. Leidy. 1970. The impact of information transmission through television. *Public Opinion Quarterly,* 33, 556–62.

Altheide, D. L. 1976. *Creating Reality: How TV News Distorts Events.* Beverly Hills, Calif.: Sage.

Alvik, T. 1968. The development of views on conflict, war and peace among school children: A Norwegian case study. *Journal of Peace Research,* 2, 171–95.

Anderson, K., G. Comstock, and N. Dennis. 1976. Research on television and the young. *Journal of Communication,* 26(2), 98–107.

511

Andison, F. S. 1977. TV violence and viewer aggression: A cumulation of study results, 1956–1976. *Public Opinion Quarterly* 41(3), 314–31.

Aristotle. *See*, Cooper, 1932; Else, 1958; Warnoch and Anderson, 1950.

Arndt, J. 1968. A test of the two-step flow in diffusion of a new product. *Journalism Quarterly*, 45, 457–65.

Atkin, C. K. 1971. How imbalanced campaign coverage affects audience exposure patterns. *Journalism Quarterly*, 48, 235–44.

—— 1973. Instrumental utilities and information seeking. In P. Clarke (ed.), *New Models for Mass Communication Research. Sage Annual Reviews of Communication Research*, vol. 2., pp. 205–42. Beverly Hills, Calif.: Sage.

—— 1975. The effects of television advertising on children. Second year experimental evidence. Final report to the Office of Child Development. Department of Communication, Michigan State University.

Atkin, C. K., and W. Gantz. 1974. How children use television news programming: Patterns of exposure and effects. Paper presented at the meeting of the International Communications Association. New Orleans, April.

Atkin, C., and Heald, G. 1976. Effects of political advertising. *Public Opinion Quarterly*, 40, 216–28.

Baer, W. S., H. Geller, J. A. Grundfest, and K. B. Possner. 1974. *Concentration of Mass Media Ownership: Assessing the State of Current Knowledge*. Santa Monica: The Rand Corporation, R-1584-NSF.

Bailey, G. A., and L. W. Lichty. 1972. Rough justice on a Saigon street: A gatekeeper study of NBC's Tet execution film. *Journalism Quarterly*, 49, 221–29; 238.

Bailey, K. D. 1975. Political learning and development: Continuity and change in childhood political orientations, 1973–1975. Unpublished manuscript, University of Maryland.

Bailey, K. G., and W. T. Sowder, 1970. Audiotape and videotape self-confrontation in psychotherapy. *Psychological Bulletin*, 74, 127–37.

Bailyn, L. 1959. Mass media and children: A study of exposure habits and cognitive effects. *Psychological Monographs*, 73, (1, Whole No. 471).

Baker, R. K. 1969. The views, standards, and practices of the television industry. In R. K. Baker and S. J. Ball (eds.), *Violence and the media. A staff report to the National Commission on the Causes and Prevention of Violence*. Washington, D.C.: Government Printing Office, pp. 593–614.

Baker, R. K., and S. J. Ball. (eds.). 1969. *Violence and the media. A staff report to the National Commission on the Causes and Prevention of Violence*. Washington, D.C.: Government Printing Office.

Baldwin, T. F., and C. Lewis. 1972. Violence in television: The industry looks at itself. In G. A. Comstock and E. A. Rubinstein (eds.), *Television and Social Behavior. Vol. 1, Media Content and Control*. Washington, D.C.: Government Printing Office, pp. 290–373.

Baldwin, T. F., and S. H. Surlin, 1969. The contribution of the visual element in television commercials. *Journalism Quarterly,* 46. 607–10.

Ball-Rokeach, S. J. 1974. The information perspective. Paper presented at the meeting of the American Sociological Association, Montreal, August.

Ball, S. J., and G. A. Bogatz, 1970. *The First year of Sesame Street: An Evaluation.* Princeton: Educational Testing Service.

Bandura, A. 1965a. Influence of models' reinforcement contingencies on the acquisition of imitative responses. *Journal of Personality and Social Psychology,* 1, 589–95.

—— 1965b. Vicarious processes: A case of no-trial learning. In L. Berkowitz (ed.), *Advances in Experimental Social Psychology.* New York: Academic Press, vol. 2, pp. 1–55.

Bandura, A. 1969a. *Principles of behavior modification.* New York: Holt, Rinehart and Winston.

—— 1969b. Social-learning theory of identificatory processes. In D. A. Goslin (ed.), *Handbook of Socialization Theory and Research.* Chicago: Rand McNally, pp. 213–62.

—— 1971a. Analysis of modeling processes. In A. Bandura (ed.), *Psychological Modeling: Conflicting Theories.* Chicago: Aldine-Atherton, 1971a. pp. 1–62.

—— 1971b. *Social Learning Theory.* New York: General Learning Press.

—— 1973. *Aggression: A Social Learning Analysis.* Englewood Cliffs, N.J.: Prentice-Hall.

Bandura, A., E. B. Blanchard, and B. Ritter. 1969. Relative efficacy of desensitization and modeling approaches for inducing behavioral, affective, and attitudinal changes. *Journal of Personality and Social Psychology,* 13, 173–99.

Bandura, A., J. A. Grusec, and F. L. Menlove. 1966. Observational learning as a function of symbolization and incentive set. *Child Development,* 37, 499–506.

—— 1967. Vicarious extinction of avoidance behavior. *Journal of Personality and Social Psychology,* 5, 16–23.

Bandura, A., and A. C. Huston. 1961. Identification as a process of incidental learning. *Journal of Abnormal and Social Psychology.* 63, 311–18.

Bandura, A., and F. J. McDonald. 1963. The influence of social reinforcement and the behavior of models in shaping children's moral judgments. *Journal of Abnormal and Social Psychology,* 67, 274–81.

Bandura, A., and F. Menlove. 1968. Factors determining vicarious extinction of avoidance behavior through symbolic modeling. *Journal of Personality and Social Psychology,* 8, 99–108.

Bandura, A., and W. Mischel. 1965. Modification of self-imposed delay of reward through exposure to live and symbolic models. *Journal of Personality and Social Psychology,* 2, 698–705.

References

ι, A., D. Ross, and S. A. Ross. 1961. Transmission of aggression through imitation of aggressive models. *Journal of Abnormal and Social Psychology,* 63, 575–82.
—— 1963a. Imitation of film-mediated aggressive models. *Journal of Abnormal and Social Psychology,* 66, 3–11.
—— 1963b. Vicarious reinforcement and imitative learning. *Journal of Abnormal and Social Psychology,* 67, 601–7.
Bandura, A., and R. H. Walters. 1959. *Adolescent Aggression.* New York: Ronald.
—— 1963. *Social Learning and Personality Development.* New York: Holt, Rinehart and Winston.
Barach, J. A. 1969. Advertising effectiveness and risk in the consumer decision process. *Journal of Marketing Research.* 6, 314–20.
Barclay, W. D., R. M. Doub, and L. T. McMurtrey. 1965. Recall of TV commercials by time and program slot. *Journal of Advertising Research,* 5(2), 41–47.
Barcus, F. E. 1975. *Weekend commercial children's television—1975.* Newtonville, Mass.: Action for Children's Television.
Bardwick, J. M., and S. I. Schumann. 1967. Portrait of American men and women in TV commercials. *Psychology.* 4(4), 18–23.
Barnouw, E. 1975. *Tube of Plenty: The Evolution of American Television.* New York: Oxford University Press.
Baron, R. A. 1977. *Human Aggression.* New York: Plenum Press.
Barrett, M. (ed.). 1970. *The Alfred I. duPont-Columbia University survey of broadcast journalism, 1969–1970. Year of challenge, year of crisis.* New York: Grosset and Dunlap.
Barry, T. E., and R. W. Hansen. 1973. How race affects children's TV commercials. *Journal of Advertising Research,* 13, 63–67.
Baumrind, D. 1972. Socialization and instrumental competence in young children. In W. W. Hartup (ed.), *The Young Child: Reviews of Research.* Washington, D.C.: National Association for the Education of Young Children, vol. 2, pp. 202–24.
Bechtel, R. B., C. Achelpohl, and R. Akers. 1972. Correlates between observed behavior and questionnaire responses on television viewing. In E. A. Rubinstein, G. A. Comstock, and J. P. Murray (eds.), *Television and Social Behavior.* Vol. 4, *Television in Day-to-Day Life: Patterns of Use.* Washington, D.C.: Government Printing Office, pp. 274–344.
Becker, L. B., and Doolittle, J. C. 1975. Repetitious political advertising and evaluations of and information seeking about candidates. *Journalism Quarterly,* 52, 611–17.
Becker, L. B., M. E. McCombs, and J. M. McLeod. 1975. The development of political cognitions. In S. H. Chaffee (ed.). *Political Communication: Issues and Strategies for Research.* Vol. 4 of Sage Annual Reviews of Communication Research. Beverly Hills, Calif.: Sage, 1975.
Becker, L., D. Weaver, D. Graber, and M. McCombs. 1977. Influence of

the debates on public agendas. Unpublished manuscript, Syracuse University.

Belson, W. A. 1959. Effects of television on the interests and initiative of adult viewers in Greater London. *British Journal of Psychology*, 50, 145–58.

—— 1977. Television violence and the adolescent boy. Paper presented at the British Association for the Advancement of Science, Aston University at Birmingham, England, September 6.

Benton, M., and P. J. Frazier. 1976. The agenda-setting function of the mass media at three levels of information-holding. *Communication Research*, 3, 261–74.

Berelson, B. 1948. Communications and public opinion. In W. Schramm (ed.), *Communications in Modern Society*. Urbana: University of Illinois Press, pp. 167–85.

Berelson, B. R. 1959. The state of communication research. *Public Opinion Quarterly*, 23, 1–15.

Berelson, B. R., P. F. Lazarsfeld, and W. N. McPhee. 1954. *Voting*. Chicago: University of Chicago Press.

Berelson, B. R., and G. Steiner. 1964. *Human Behavior: An Inventory of Scientific Findings*. New York: Harcourt, Brace and World.

Berger, M. M. 1970. Confrontation through videotape. In Berger (ed.), *Videotape Techniques in Psychiatric Training and Treatment*. New York: Brunner/Mazel, pp. 18–35.

Berkowitz, L. 1962a. *Aggression: A Social Psychological Analysis*. New York: McGraw-Hill.

—— 1962b. Violence in the mass media. In *ibid.*, pp. 229–55.

—— 1964. Aggressive cues in aggressive behavior and hostility catharsis. *Psychological Review*, 71, 104–22.

—— 1965. Some aspects of observed aggression. *Journal of Personality and Social Psychology*, 1965, 2, 359–69.

—— 1973. Words and symbols as stimuli to aggressive respones. In J. F. Knutsen (ed.), *Control of Aggression: Implication from Basic Research*. Chicago: Aldine-Atherton.

—— 1974. Some determinants of impulsive aggression: Role of mediated associations with reinforcements for aggression. *Psychological Review*, 81, 165–76.

Berkowitz, L., and J. T. Alioto, 1973. The meaning of an observed event as a determinant of its aggressive consequences. *Journal of Personality and Social Psychology*, 28, 206–17.

Berkowitz, L., and R. G. Geen. 1966. Film violence and the cue properties of available targets. *Journal of Personality and Social Psychology*, 3, 525–30.

—— 1967. Stimulus qualities of the target of aggression: A further study. *Journal of Personality and Social Psychology*, 5, 364–68.

Berkowitz, L., R. Corwin, and M. Heironimus. 1963. Film violence and subsequent aggressive tendencies. *Public Opinion Quarterly*, 27, 217–29.

Berkowitz, L., R. D. Parke, J. Leyens, and S. G. West. 1974. Reactions of juvenile delinquents to "justified" and "less justified" movie violence. *Journal of Research in Crime and Delinquency*, 11, 16–24.

Berkowitz, L., and E. Rawlings. 1963. Effects of film violence on inhibitions against subsequent aggression. *Journal of Abnormal and Social Psychology*, 66, 405–12.

Better Radio and Television. 1976. Horror shows lose support. 16(3).

Bither, S. W. 1972. Effects of distraction and commitment on the persuasiveness of television advertising. *Journal of Marketing Research*, 9(2), 1–5.

Bither, S. W., and P. L. Wright. 1973. The self-confidence-advertising response relationship: A function of situational distraction. *Journal of Marketing Research*, 10, 146–52.

Blanchard, E. B. 1970. The relative contributions of modeling, informational influence, and physical contact in the extinction of phobic behavior. *Journal of Abnormal Psychology*, 76, 55–61.

Blatt, J., L. Spencer, and S. Ward. 1972. A cognitive developmental study of children's reactions to television advertising. In E. A. Rubinstein, G. A. Comstock, and J. P. Murray (eds.), *Television and Social Behavior.* Vol. 4, *Television in Day-to-Day Life: Patterns of Use.* Washington, D.C.: Government Printing Office, pp. 452–67.

Blumler, J. G. 1964. British television—the outlines of a research strategy. *British Journal of Sociology*, 15, 223–33.

Blumler, J. G. and E. Katz (eds.). 1974. The Uses of Mass Communications: Current Perspectives on Gratifications Research. Sage Annual Reviews of Communication Research, vol. 3. Beverly Hills, Calif.: Sage.

Blumler, J. G. and J. M. McLeod, 1974. Communication and voter turnout in Britain. In T. Leggatt (ed.), *Sociological theory and survey research.* London: Sage Publications, pp. 265–312.

Blumler, J. G., and D. McQuail, 1969. *Television in Politics: Its uses and influences.* Chicago: University of Chicago Press.

Bobrow, D. B. 1974. Communication and the political system. In W. P. Davison and F. T. C. Yu (eds.), *Mass Communication Research: Major Issues and Future Directions.* New York: Praeger.

Bogart, L. 1965. The mass media and the blue-collar worker. In A. Shostak and W. Gomberg (eds.), *Blue-Collar World: Studies of the American Worker.* Englewood Cliffs, N.J.: Prentice-Hall, pp. 416–28.

—— 1972a. *The Age of Television* (3rd ed.). New York: Frederick Ungar.

—— 1972b. Negro and white media exposure: New evidence. *Journalism Quarterly*, 49, 15–21.

—— 1972c. Warning, the Surgeon General has determined that TV violence is moderately dangerous to your child's mental health. *Public Opinion Quarterly*, 36, 491–521.

—— 1974. The management of mass media. In W. P. Davison and F. T. C. Yu (eds.), *Mass Communication Research: Major Issues and Future Directions.* New York: Praeger.

Bogatz, G. A., and S. J. Ball. 1971. *The second year of Sesame Street: A continuing evaluation.* 2 vols. Princeton: Educational Testing Service.

Bostian, L. R. 1970. The two-step flow theory: Cross-cultural implications. *Journalism Quarterly,* 47, 109–17.

Bottorff, A. 1970. Television, respect, and the older adolescent. Master's thesis, University of Wisconsin.

Bower, R. T. 1973. *Television and the public.* New York: Holt, Rinehart and Winston.

Boyanowsky, E. I. 1977. Film preferences under conditions of threat: Wetting the Appetite for violence, information, or excitement? *Communication Research,* 4, 133–44.

Boyanowsky, E. O., D. Newtson, and E. Walster. 1974. Film preferences following a murder. *Communication Research,* 1, 32–43.

Brehm, J., and A. Cohen. 1962. *Explorations in cognitive dissonance,* New York: Wiley.

Broadcasting. 1974. Wiley feels heat from TV's screen. October 21, p. 41.

—— 1976a. The people's choice: TV is voted best advertising medium. January 12, p. 29.

—— 1976b. Family time heads for trial where objectors say it hurts. April 5, p. 39.

—— 1976c. Producers talk of frustrations of family hours. May 3, p. 26.

—— 1976d. Little support for Bellotti petition emerges at FTC-FCC panels. May 24, p. 26.

—— 1976e. Stations wash their hands of family viewing at Denver hearing. July 12, p. 23.

—— 1976f. Family-viewing suit is coming down to wire. July 19, p. 25.

—— 1976g. ACT berates FCC for lack of positive stand. September 20, 1976, pp. 63–64.

—— 1976h. Rough road forecast as result of family-viewing court decision. November 22, 1976, pp. 29–30.

—— 1976i. NAB to confront TV networks on sex, violence. December 20, p. 22.

—— 1977a. Networks think it's for real as advertisers scramble for antiviolence bandwagon. February 14, pp. 29–30.

—— 1977b. NAB talking up its efforts to talk down TV violence. March 21, pp. 29–34.

—— 1977c. ANA to members: Don't just take what the networks are handing out. October 31.

Brodbeck, A. J. 1955. The mass media as a socializing agency. Paper presented to the American Psychological Association Symposium on Children and the Mass Media, San Francisco.

Brown, J. R., J. K. Cramond, and R. J. Wilde. 1974. Displacement effects of television and the child's functional orientation to media. In J. G.

Blumler and E. Katz (eds.), *The Uses of Mass Communications: Current Perspectives on Gratifications Research.* Beverly Hills, Ca.: Sage. pp. 93–112.

Brown, L. 1971. *Television: The Business behind the Box.* New York: Harcourt Brace Jovanovich.

—— 1977. *The New York Times Encyclopedia of Television.* New York: Times Books.

Brown, R. 1965. *Social Psychology.* New York: Free Press.

Bruner, J. S., R. R. Olver, and P. M. Greenfield. 1966. *Studies in Cognitive Growth.* New York: Wiley.

Bryan, J. H. 1970. Children's reactions to helpers: Their money isn't where their mouths are. In J. Macaulay and L. Berkowitz (eds.), *Altruism and helping behavior.* New York: Academic Press, pp. 61–76.

Bryan, J. H. 1971. Model affect and children's imitative altruism. *Child Development,* 42, 2061–65.

Bryan, J. H., and P. London, 1970. Altruistic behavior by children. *Psychological Bulletin,* 73, 200–211.

Bryan, J. H., J. Redfield, and S. Mader. 1971. Words and deeds about altruism and subsequent reinforcement power of the model. *Child Development,* 42, 1501–8.

Bryan, J. H., and T. Schwartz. 1971. Effects of film material upon children's behavior. *Psychological Bulletin,* 75, 50–59.

Bryan, J. H., and M. Test. 1967. Models and helping: Naturalistic studies in aiding behavior. *Journal of Personality and Social Psychology,* 6, 400–7.

Bryan, J. H., and N. Walbek. 1970a. Preaching and practicing generosity: Children's actions and reactions. *Child Development,* 41, 329–53.

—— 1970b. The impact of words and deeds concerning altruism upon children. *Child Development,* 41, 747–57.

Buchanan, D. I. 1964. How interest in the product affects recall: Print ads vs. commercials. *Journal of Advertising Research,* 4(1), 9–14.

Burnstein, E., E. Stotland, and A. Zander. 1961. Similarity to a model and self-evaluation. *Journal of Abnormal and Social Psychology,* 62, 257–64.

Cameron, P., and C. Janky. 1971. The effects of TV violence upon children: A naturalistic experiment. *Proceedings of the 79th annual convention of the American Psychological Association.* Washington, D.C.: American Psychological Association, pp. 233–34.

Campbell, A., G. Gurin, and W. E. Miller. 1954. *The Voter Decides.* Evanston, Ill.: Row, Peterson.

Campbell, D. T., and J. C. Stanley. 1966. *Experimental and Quasi-Experimental Designs for Research.* Chicago: Rand-McNally.

Cantor, M. G. 1971. *The Hollywood TV Producer.* New York: Basic Books.

—— 1972. The role of the producer in choosing children's television content. In G. A. Comstock and E. A. Rubinstein (eds.), *Television and Social Behavior.* Vol 1, *Media content and control.* Washington, D.C.:

Government Printing Office, pp. 259–289.

Carey, J. W. 1966. Variations in Negro/white television preferences. *Journal of Broadcasting*, 10, 199–212.

Carter, R. F. 1962. Some effects of the debates. In S. Kraus (ed.), *The Great Debates*. Bloomington: Indiana University Press, pp. 253–70.

—— 1965. Communication and affective relations. *Journalism Quarterly*, 42, 203–12.

Carter, R. F., and B. S. Greenberg. 1965. Newspapers or television: Which do you believe? *Journalism Quarterly*, 42, 29–34.

Cartwright, D. 1949. Some principles of mass persuasion, selected findings of research on the sale of U.S. war bonds. *Human Relations*, 2, 253–67.

Cassata, M. B. 1967. A study of the mass communications behavior and the social disengagement behavior of 177 members of the Age Center of New England. Doctoral dissertation, Indiana University.

Cater, D., and S. Strickland. 1975. *TV Violence and the Child: The Evolution and Fate of the Surgeon General's Report*. New York: Russell Sage Foundation.

Chaffee, S. 1967a. Salience and pertinence as sources of value change. *Journal of Communication*, 17, 25–38.

—— 1967b. Salience and homeostasis in communication process. *Journalism Quarterly*, 44, 439–44.

—— 1972a. Longitudinal designs for communication research: Cross-lagged correlation. Paper presented at the meeting of the Association for Education in Journalism, Carbondale, Illinois, August.

—— 1972b. Television and adolescent aggressiveness. In G. A. Comstock and E. A. Rubinstein (eds.), *Television and Social Behavior*. Vol. 3, *Television and Adolescent Aggressiveness*. Washington, D.C.: Government Printing Office, pp. 1–34.

—— 1972c. The interpersonal context of mass communication. In F. G. Kline and P. J. Tichenor (eds.), *Current Perspectives in Mass Communication Research*. Vol. 1 of *Sage Annual Reviews of Communication Research*. Beverly Hills, Ca.: Sage, pp. 95–120.

—— 1976. Comparing television to other agencies of socialization. Unpublished manuscript, Mass Communications Research Center, University of Wisconsin.

Chaffee, S. H., and J. M. McLeod. 1972. Adolescent television use in the family context. In G. A. Comstock and E. A. Rubinstein (eds.), *Television and Social Behavior*. Vol. 3, *Television and Adolescent Aggressiveness*. Washington, D.C.: Government Printing Office, pp. 149–72.

Chaffee, S. H., J. M. McLeod, and C. K. Atkin. 1970. Parent-child similarities in television use. Paper presented at the meeting of the Association for Education in Journalism, Washington, D.C.

—— 1971. Parental influences on adolescent media use. *American Behavioral Scientist*, 14, 323–40.

Chaffee, S. H., J. McLeod, and D. B. Wackman. 1966. Family communication and political socialization. Paper presented at the meeting of the Association for Education in Journalism, Iowa City, Iowa, August.

———. 1973. Family communication patterns and adolescent political participation. In J. Dennis (ed.), *Socialization to Politics: A Reader.* New York: Willey, pp. 349–64.

Chaffee, S. H., and A. R. Tims. 1976. Interpersonal factors in adolescent television use. *Journal of Social Issues.* 32(4), 98–115.

Chaffee, S. H., L. S. Ward, and L. P. Tipton. 1970. Mass communication and political socialization. *Journalism Quarterly,* 1970. 47, 647–59; 666.

Chaffee, S. H., and D. Wilson. 1975. Adult life cycle changes in mass media use. Paper presented at the meeting of the Association for Education in Journalism, Ottawa, Ontario, August.

Chaney, D. C. 1970. Involvement, realism and the perception of aggression in television programmes. *Human Relations,* 23, 373–381.

Chester, E. W. 1969. *Radio, Television and American Politics.* New York: Sheed and Ward.

Childers, P. R., and J. Ross. 1973. The relationship between viewing television and student achievement. *Journal of Educational Research.* 66, 317–319.

Choate, R. B. 1973. The selling of the child. Statement before the Consumer Subcommittee of the Committee on Commerce. United States Senate. New York City, February 12.

———. 1975. Statement before the Subcommittee on Communications of the Committee on Interstate and Foreign Commerce. United States House of Representatives. Washington, D.C., July 14.

Chu, G. C., and W. Schramm. 1967. *Learning from Television.* Stanford, Ca.: Institute for Communication Research, Stanford University.

Chulay, C., and S. Francis. 1974. The image of the female child on Saturday morning television commercials. Paper presented at the meeting of the International Communication Association, New Orleans, April.

Clancy-Hepburn, K., A. A. Hickey, and G. Nevill. 1974. Children's behavior responses to TV food advertising. *Journal of Nutritional Education,* 6, 38–41.

Clancy, K. J., and D. M. Kweskin. 1971. TV commercial recall correlates. *Journal of Advertising Research,* 11(2), 18–20.

Clark, C. C. 1969. Television and social controls: Some observations on the portrayal of ethnic minorities. *Television Quarterly,* 8, 18–22.

Clark, C. C. 1972. Race, identification, and television violence. In G. A. Comstock, E. A. Rubinstein, and J. P. Murray (eds.), *Television and social behavior.* Vol. 5, *Television's effects: Further explorations.* Washington, D.C.: Government Printing Office, pp. 120–184.

Clark, D. G., and W. B. Blankenburg. 1972. Trends in violent content in selected mass media. In G. A. Comstock and E. A. Rubinstein (eds.), *Television and social behavior.* Vol. 1. *Media content and control.* Washington, D.C.: Government Printing Office, pp. 188–243.

Clark, K., and M. P. Clark. 1950. Emotional factors in racial identification and preferences in Negro children. *Journal of Negro Education,* 19, 169–78.

Clark, W. C. 1968. The impact of mass communication in America. *Annals of the American Academy of Political and Social Science,* 378, 68–74.

Clarke, P. 1963. An experiment to increase the audience for educational television. Doctoral dissertation, University of Minnesota.

Clarke, P., and F. G. Kline. 1974. Media effects reconsidered: Some new strategies for communication research. *Communication Research,* 1, 224–40.

Clarke, P., and P. Palmgreen, 1974. Media use, political knowledge and participation in public affairs. Paper presented at the meeting of the International Sociological Association.

Clarke, P., and L. Ruggels. 1970. Preferences among news media coverage of public affairs. *Journalism Quarterly,* 47, 464–71.

Cline, V. B., R. G. Croft, and S. Courrier. 1972. Desensitization of children to television violence. *Journal of Personality and Social Psychology,* 27, 360–65.

Clotfelter, J., and B. G. Peters, 1974. Mass media and the military: Selected ratings of fairness. *Journalism Quarterly,* 51, 332–34.

Coates, B., and W. W. Hartup. 1969. Age and verbalization in observational learning. *Developmental Psychology,* 1, 556–62.

Coates, B., H. E. Pusser, and I. Goodman. 1976. The influence of "Sesame Street" and "Mister Rogers' Neighborhood" on children's social behavior in the preschool. *Child Development,* 47, 138–44.

Coffin, T. E. Television's impact on society. 1955. *American Psychologist,* 10, 630–41.

Coffin, T. E., and S. Tuchman. 1972a. A question of validity: Some comments on "Apples, oranges, and the kitchen sink." *Journal of Broadcasting,* 17, 31–33.

—— 1972b. Rating television programs for violence: A comparison of five surveys. *Journal of Broadcasting,* 17, 3–20.

Cohen, B. 1963. *The Press and Foreign Policy.* Princeton: Princeton University Press.

Cohen, D. 1975. A report on a non-election agenda-setting study. Paper presented at the meeting of the Association for Education in Journalism.

Coldevin, G. O. 1971. The effects of mass media upon the development of transnational orientations. Doctoral dissertation, University of Washington.

Cole, B. and M. Oettinger. 1978. *Reluctant Regulators.* Reading, Mass.: Addison, Wesley.

Collins, W. A. 1970. Learning of media content: A developmental study. *Child Development.* 41, 1133–42.

Collins, W. A. 1973a. Developmental aspects of understanding and evaluating television content. Paper presented at the meeting of the Society for Research in Child Development, Philadelphia, March.

——— 1973b. Effects of temporal separation between motivation, aggression, and consequences: A developmental study. *Developmental Psychology,* 8, 215–21.

——— 1974. Aspects of television content and children's social behavior. Final report, July, University of Minnesota, Grant No. OCD-CB-477, Office of Child Development, Department of Health, Education, and Welfare.

Collins, W. A., T. J. Berndt, and V. L. Hess. 1974. Observational learning of motives and consequences for television aggression: A developmental study. *Child Development,* 45, 799–802.

Collins, W. A., and S. A. Zimmermann. 1975. Convergent and divergent social cues: Effects of televised aggression on children. *Communication Research,* 2, 331–46.

Columbia Broadcasting System, Office of Social Research. 1974. *A Study of Messages Received by Children Who viewed an Episode of Fat Albert and the Cosby Kids.* New York: Columbia Broadcasting System, Inc.

——— 1976. Network prime-time violence tabulations for 1975–76 season. Unpublished manuscript, April.

Comstock, G. A. 1972. New research on media content and control. In G. A. Comstock and E. A. Rubinstein (eds.), *Television and Social Behavior.* Vol. 1, *Media Content and Control.* Washington, D.C.: Government Printing Office, pp. 1–27.

Comstock, G. A., and Lindsey, G. 1975. *Television and Human Behavior: The Research Horizon, Future and Present.* Santa Monica, Calif.: The Rand Corporation. R-1748-CF.

Connell, R. W. 1971. *The Child's Construction of Politics.* Melbourne: University of Melbourne Press.

Converse, P. E. 1962. Information flow and the stability of partisan attitudes. *Public Opinion Quarterly,* 26, 578–99.

Cook, T. D., H. Appleton, R. F. Conner, A. Shaffer, G. Tamkin, and S. J. Weber, 1975. *"Sesame Street" Revisited.* New York: Russell Sage Foundation.

Cooper, L. *Rhetoric of Aristotle.* 1932. New York: Appleton-Century.

Copland, B. D. 1963. An evaluation of conceptual frameworks for measuring advertising results. In *Proceedings of the 9th Annual Conference, Advertising Research Foundation,* pp. 72–77.

Council on Children, Media and Merchandising. 1976. *May 1976 joint FTC/FCC hearings on over-the-counter drug advertising, television and children—a fact sheet.* Washington, D.C.: The Council.

Courtney, A. E., and T. W. Whipple. 1974. Women in TV commercials. *Journal of Communication,* 24, 110–18.

Crandall, R. 1972. A field extension of the frequency-affect findings. *Psychological Reports,* 31, 371–74.

Cranston, P. 1960 Political convention broadcasts: Their history and influence. *Journalism Quarterly,* 37, 186–94.

Cunningham and Walsh. 1958. *Videotown. 1948–1957.* New York: Cunningham and Walsh Publishers.

Cutler, N. E., and A. S. Tedesco. 1974. Differentiation in television message systems: A comparison of network television news and drama. Paper presented at the meeting of the International Communication Association, New Orleans, April.

Danet, B. N. 1967. Self-confrontation by videotape in group psychotherapy. Doctoral dissertation, University of Minnesota.

—— 1968. Self-confrontation in psychotherapy reviewed. *American Journal of Psychotherapy,* 22(2), 245–57.

—— 1969. Videotape playback as a therapeutic device in group psychotherapy. *International Journal of Group Psychotherapy,* 19, 433–40.

Davis, D. K. 1974. Self and social orientations and television use. Paper presented at the meeting of the International Communication Association, New Orleans, April.

Davis, D. K., and J. Lee. 1974. An approach to the analysis of panel data: The Watergate hearings and political socialization. Paper presented at the meeting of the Association for Education in Journalism, San Diego, California, August.

Davis, K. E., and G. N. Braucht. 1971. Reactions to viewing films of erotically realistic heterosexual behavior. In *Technical Report of the Commission on Obscenity and Pornography.* Vol. 8, *Erotica and Social Behavior.* Washington, D.C.: Government Printing Office, pp. 68–96.

Davis, R. H. 1971. Television and the older adult. *Journal of Broadcasting,* 15, 153–159.

Davison, W. P. and F. T. C. Yu (eds.) 1974. *Mass Communication Research: Major Issues and Future Directions.* New York: Praeger.

Dawson, P. A., and J. E. Zinser. 1971. Broadcast expenditures and electoral outcomes in the 1970 congressional elections. *Public Opinion Quarterly,* 35, 398–402.

Dawson, R. E., and K. Prewitt. 1969. *Political Socialization.* Boston: Little, Brown, and Co.

Department of Commerce. 1977. *Social Indicators 1976.* Washington, D.C.: Government Printing Office.

DeFleur. M. L. 1964. Occupational roles as portrayed on television. *Public Opinion Quarterly,* 28, 57–74.

DeFleur, M. L., and L. B. DeFleur. 1967. The relative contribution of television as a learning source for children's occupational knowledge. *American Sociological Review,* 32, 777–89.

Dennis, J., and S. Chaffee. 1977. Impact of the debates upon partisan, image and issue voting. In S. Kraus (ed.), *The great debates: 1976, Ford vs. Carter.* Bloomington: Indiana University Press.

DeRath, G. 1963. The effects of verbal instructions on imitative aggression. Doctoral dissertation, Michigan State University.

DeVries, W., and L. Tarrance, Jr. 1972. *The Ticket-Splitter: A New Force in American Politics.* Grand Rapids, Mich.: Eerdmans Publishing.

524 References

Diener, E., and DeFour, D. In Press. Does television violence enhance program popularity? *Journal of Personality and Social Psychology.*

Dimas, C. 1970. The effect of motion pictures portraying black models on the self-concept of black elementary school children. Doctoral dissertation, Syracuse University.

Doll, H. D., and B. E. Bradley. 1973. A study of the objectivity of television news reporting of the 1972 presidential campaign. Paper presented at the meeting of the Speech Communication Association, New York, November.

Dollard, J., L. Doob, N. Miller, O. Mower, and R. Sears. 1939. *Frustration and Aggression.* New Haven: Yale University Press.

Dominick, J. R. 1973. Crime and law enforcement on prime-time television. *Public Opinion Quarterly,* 37, 241–250.

—— 1977. Geographical bias in national TV news. *Journal of Communication,* 27, 94–99.

Dominick, J. R., and B. S. Greenberg. 1970. Three seasons of blacks on television. *Journal of Advertising Research,* 10(2), 21–27.

Dominick, J. R., and B. S. Greenberg. 1972. Attitudes toward violence: The interaction of television, exposure, family attitudes, and social class. In G. A. Comstock and E. A. Rubinstein (eds.), *Television and Social Behavior.* Vol. 3, *Television and Adolescent Aggressiveness.* Washington, D.C.: Government Printing Office, pp. 314–335.

Dominick, J. R., and G. E. Rauch. 1972. The image of women in network TV commercials. *Journal of Broadcasting,* 16, 259–65.

Dommermuth, W. P. 1974. How does the medium affect the message? *Journalism Quarterly,* 51, 441–47.

Donnerstein, E., S. Lipton, and R. Evans. 1974. Erotic stimuli and aggression: Facilitation or inhibition. Unpublished manuscript, Southern Illinois University.

Donohue, G. A., P. J. Tichenor, and C. N. Olien. 1972. Gatekeeping: Mass media systems and information control. In F. G. Kline and P. J. Tichenor (eds.), *Current Perspectives in Mass Communication Research.* Beverly Hills, Ca.: Sage. pp. 41–69.

Donohue, T. R. 1973. Viewer perceptions of color and black-and-white paid political advertising. *Journalism Quarterly,* 50, 660–65.

Doob, A. N. 1970. Catharsis and aggression: The effect of hurting one's enemy. *Journal of Experimental Research in Personality,* 4, 291–96.

Doob, A. N., and R. J. Climie. 1972. The delay of reinforcement and the effects of film violence. *Journal of Experimental Social Psychology,* 3, 136–42.

Doob, A. N., and H. M. Kirshenbaum. 1973. The effects on arousal of frustration and aggressive films. *Journal of Experimental Social Psychology,* 9, 57–64.

Doob, A. N., and L. Wood. 1972. Catharsis and aggression: Effects of annoyance and retaliation on aggressive behavior. *Journal of Personality and Social Psychology,* 22, 156–62.

Douglas, D. F., B. H. Westley, and S. H. Chaffee. 1970. An information campaign that changed community attitudes. *Journalism Quarterly,* 47, 479–87.

Downing, M. 1974. Heroine of the daytime serial. *Journal of Communication.* 24,(2), 130–37.

Drabman, R. S., and M. H. Thomas. 1974a. Does media violence increase children's toleration of real-life aggression? *Developmental Psychology,* 10, 418–21.

—— 1974b. Exposure to filmed violence and children's tolerance of real life aggression. Paper presented at the meeting of the American Psychological Association, New Orleans.

Dreyer, E. C. 1971. Media use and electoral choices: Some political consequences of information exposure. *Public Opinion Quarterly,* 35, 544–53.

Dubanoski, R. A., and D. A. Parton. 1971. Imitative aggression in children as a function of observing a human model. *Developmental Psychology,* 4, 489.

Dysinger, W. S., and C. A. Ruckmick. 1933. *The Emotional Responses of Children to the Motion Picture Situation.* New York: Macmillan.

Edelstein, A. S. 1973. An alternative approach to the study of source effects in mass communication. *Studies of Broadcasting,* 9, 6–29.

Editor and Publisher. 1975a. Millions watched the Super Bowl and the Godfather . . . but few of them remembered the TV commercials. February 22, p. 12.

—— 1975b. Newspapers are public's favorite ad medium. March 29, p. 12.

Efron, E. 1971. *The News Twisters.* Los Angeles: Nash Publishing.

—— 1972. A nonsolution to a nonproved problem produced by a noninvestigation of a nonresolved controversy over a nondefined threat to nonidentifiable people. *TV Guide,* 20(48), 30–36.

Ekman, P., R. M. Liebert, W. V. Friesen, R. Harrison, C. Zlatchin, E. J. Malmstrom, and R. A. Baron. 1972. Facial expressions of emotion while watching televised violence as predictors of subsequent aggression. In G. A. Comstock, E. A. Rubinstein, and J. P. Murray (eds.), *Television and Social Behavior.* Vol. 5, *Television's Effects: Further Explorations.* Washington, D.C.: Government Printing Office, pp. 22–58.

Eleey, M. F., G. Gerbner, and N. Tedesco. 1972a. Apples, oranges, and the kitchen sink: An analysis and guide to the comparison of "violence ratings." *Journal of Broadcasting,* 17, 21–31.

—— 1972b. Validity indeed! *Journal of Broadcasting,* 17, 34–35.

Elliott, P. 1973. *The Making of a Television Series: A Case Study in the Sociology of Culture.* New York: Hastings House.

Elliott, R., and R. Vasta. 1970. The modeling of sharing: Effects associated with vicarious reinforcement, symbolization, age and generalization. *Journal of Experimental Child Psychology,* 10, 8–15.

Ellis, G. T., and F. Sekyra. 1972. The effect of aggressive cartoons on the behavior of first grade children. *Journal of Psychology,* 81, 37–43.

Else, G. F. 1958. *Aristotle's Poetics: The Argument.* Cambridge, Mass.: Harvard University Press.

Emery, F. E. 1959a. Psychological effects of the Western film: A study in television viewing. I. The theoretical study: Working hypotheses on the psychology of television. *Human Relations,* 12, 195–213.

—— 1959b. *Ibid.* II. The experimental study. *Human Relations,* 12, 215–32.

Emery, W. B. 1971. *Broadcasting and Government: Responsibilities and Regulations.* East Lansing: Michigan State University Press.

Epstein, E. J. 1973a. *News from Nowhere: Television and the News.* New York: Random House.

—— 1973b. The values of newsmen. *Television Quarterly,* 10, 9–33.

Eron, L. D. 1963. Relationship of T.V. viewing habits and aggressive behavior in children. *Journal of Abnormal and Social Psychology.* 67, 193–96.

Eron, L. D., L. R. Huesmann, M. M. Lefkowitz, and L. O. Walder. 1972. Does television violence cause aggression? *American Psychologist,* 27, 253–63.

Eron, L. D., M. M. Lefkowitz, L. O. Walder, and L. R. Huesmann. 1974. Relation of learning in childhood to psychopathology and aggression in young adulthood. In A. Davis (ed.), *Child Personality and Psychopathology: Current Topics.* Vol. 1. New York: Wiley.

Fechter, J. V., Jr. 1971. Modeling and environmental generalization by mentally retarded subjects of televised aggressive or friendly behavior. *American Journal of Mental Deficiency,* 76, 266–67.

Federal Communications Commission. 1974. *Children's television report and policy statement.* Washington, D.C.: Government Printing Office, June. 1989

Fejer, D., R. G. Smart, P. G. Whitehead, and L. LaForest. 1971. Sources of information about drugs among high school students. *Public Opinion Quarterly,* 35, 235–41.

Feshbach, S. 1955. The drive-reducing function of fantasy behavior. *Journal of Abnormal and Social Psychology,* 50, 3–11.

—— 1956. The catharsis hypothesis and some consequences of interaction with aggressive and neutral play objects. *Journal of Personality,* 24, 449–62.

—— 1961. The stimulating versus cathartic effects of a vicarious aggressive activity. *Journal of Abnormal and Social Psychology,* 63, 381–85.

—— 1964. The function of aggression and the regulation of aggressive drive. *Psychological Review,* 71, 257–72.

—— 1969. The catharsis effect: Research and another view. In R. K. Baker and S. J. Ball (eds.), *Violence and the Media. A Staff Report to the National Commission on the Causes and Prevention of Violence.* Washington, D.C.: Government Printing Office, p. 461–72.

—— 1972. Reality and fantasy in filmed violence. In J. P. Murray, E. A. Rubinstein, and G. A. Comstock (eds.), *Television and Social Behavior.* Vol. 2, *Television and Social Learning.* Washington, D.C.: Government Printing Office, pp. 318–45.

Feshbach, S. and R. D. Singer. 1971. *Television and Aggression: An Experimental Field Study.* San Francisco: Jossey-Bass.
—— 1972. Television and aggression: A reply to Liebert, Sobol, and Davidson. In G. A. Comstock, E. A. Rubinstein, and J. P. Murray (eds.), *Television and Social Behavior,* Vol. 5, *Television's Effects: Further Explorations.* Washington, D.C.: Government Printing Office, pp. 359–66.
Festinger, L. 1957. *A Theory of Cognitive Dissonance.* Evanston, Ill.: Row, Peterson.
Festinger, L., and N. Maccoby. 1964. On resistance to persuasive communications. *Journal of Abnormal and Social Psychology,* 68, 359–66.
Filep, R. (ed.) 1977. *Social Research and Broadcasting: Proceedings of a Symposium.* Los Angeles: Annenberg School of Communications, University of Southern California.
Fitzsimmons, S. J., and H. G. Osburn. 1968. The impact of social issues and public affairs television documentaries. *Public Opinion Quarterly,* 32, 379–97.
Flanders, J. P. 1968. A review of research on imitative behavior. *Psychological Bulletin,* 69, 316–37.
Flapan, D. 1968. *Children's Understanding of Social Interaction.* New York: Teachers College Press.
Flavell, J. H. 1963. *The Developmental Psychology of Jean Piaget.* Princeton: Van Nostrand.
Flavell, J. H., D. R. Beach, and J. M. Chinsky. 1966. Spontaneous verbal rehearsal in a memory task as a function of age. *Child Development,* 37, 283–99.
Fletcher, A. D. 1969. Negro and white children's television program preferences. *Journal of Broadcasting,* 13, 359–366.
The Ford Foundation. 1976. *Television and children: Priorities for research.* Report of a conference at Reston, Virginia, November 5–7, 1975. New York: The Ford Foundation.
Foundation for Child Development. 1977. National survey of children. Summary of preliminary results. Unpublished manuscript, Foundation for Child Development, New York.
Francher, J. S. 1973. "It's the Pepsi generation. . . ." Accelerated aging and the television commercial. *International Journal of Aging and Human Development,* 4, 245–55.
Frank, R. S. 1973. *Message dimensions of televison news.* Lexington, Mass.: Lexington Books.
Frideres, J. S. 1973. Advertising, buying patterns and children. *Journal of Advertising Reserach,* 13, 34–36.
Friedman, H. L., and R. I. Johnson. 1972. Mass media use and aggression: A pilot study. In G. A. Comstock and E. A. Rubinstein (eds.), *Television and Social Behavior,* Vol. 3, *Television and Adolescent Aggressiveness.* Washington, D.C.: Government Printing Office, pp. 336–60.
Friedrich, L. K., and A. H. Stein. 1973. Aggressive and prosocial television programs and the natural behavior of preschool children. *Monographs of the Society for Research in Child Development,* 38(4).

—— 1975. Prosocial television and young children: The effects of verbal labeling and role playing on learning and behavior. *Child Development,* 46, 27–38.

Fryear, J. L., and M. H. Thelen. 1969. Effect of sex of model and sex of observer on the imitation of affectionate behavior. *Developmental Psychology,* 1, 298.

Fuchs, D. A. 1966. Election-day radio-television and Western voting. *Public Opinion Quarterly,* 30, 226–36.

Fuchs, D. A., and J. Lyle. 1972. Mass media portrayal—sex and violence. In F. G. Kline and P. J. Tichenor (eds.), *Current Perspectives in Mass Communication Research.* Beverly Hills, Ca.: Sage, pp. 235–64.

Funkhouser, G. R. 1973. Trends in media coverage of the issues of the '60s. *Journalism Quarterly,* 50, 533–38.

Galst, J. P., and M. A. White. 1976. The unhealthy persuader: The reinforcing value of television and children's purchase-influencing attempts at the supermarket. *Child Development,* 47, 1089–96.

Geen, R. G., and L. Berkowitz. 1966. Name-mediated aggressive cue properties. *Journal of Personality,* 34, 456–65.

—— 1967. Some conditions facilitating the occurrence of aggression after the observation of violence. *Journal of Personality,* 35, 666–676.

Geen, R. G., and D. Stonner. 1972. Context effects in observed violence. *Journal of Personality and Social Psychology,* 25, 145–150.

Geiger, J. A. 1971. Seven brands in seven days. *Journal of Advertising Research,* 11, 15–22.

Geller, H., and G. Young. 1976. *The family viewing hour: An FCC tumble from the tightrope?* Palo Alto, Calif.: Aspen Institute Occasional Paper.

Gentile, F., and S. M. Miller. 1961. Television and social class. *Sociology and Social Research,* 45, 259–64.

Gerbner, G. 1972a. Comments on "Measuring violence on television: The Gerbner index," by Bruce M. Owen (Staff Research Paper, Office of Telecommunications Policy). Unpublished manuscript, Annenberg School of Communications, University of Pennsylvania.

—— 1972b. Violence in television drama: Trends and symbolic functions. In G. A. Comstock and E. A. Rubinstein (eds.), *Television and Social Behavior.* Vol. 1, *Media Content and Control.* Washington, D.C.: Government Printing Office, pp. 28–187.

Gerbner, G., and L. Gross. 1976. Living with television: The violence profile. *Journal of Communication,* 26(2), 173–99.

Gerbner, G., L. Gross, M. F. Eleey, S. Jeffries-Fox, M. Jackson-Beeck, and N. Signorielli. 1976. *Violence Profile no. 7: Trends in Network Television Drama and Viewer Conceptions of Social Reality: 1967–1975.* Philadelphia: Annenberg School of Communications, University of Pennsylvania.

Gerbner, G., L. Gross, M. F. Eleey, M. Jackson-Beeck, S. Jeffries-Fox, and N. Signorielli. 1977. *Violence profile no. 8: Trends in network television drama and viewer conceptions of social reality, 1967–1976.* Philadelphia: Annenberg School of Communications, University of Pennsylvania.

Gerson, W. M. 1966. Mass media socialization behavior: Negro-white differences. *Social Forces*, 45, 40–50.

Goldberg, M. E., and G. J. Gorn. 1974. Children's reactions to television advertising: An experimental approach. *Consumer Research*, 1, 69–75.

—— 1977. Material vs. social preferences, parent-child relations, and the child's emotional responses. Three dimensions of response to children's TV advertising. Paper presented at the Telecommunications Policy Research Conference, Airlie House, Virginia, March.

Goranson, R. E. 1969a. The catharsis effect: Two opposing views. In R. K. Baker and S. J. Ball (eds.), *Violence and the Media. A Staff Report to the National Commission on the Causes and Prevention of Violence.* Washington, D.C.: Government Printing Office, pp. 453–59.

—— 1969b. A review of recent literature on psychological effects of media portrayals of violence. In *ibid.*, pp. 395–413.

—— 1970. Media violence and aggressive behavior: A review of experimental research. In L. Berkowitz (ed.), *Advances in Experimental Social Psychology*, vol. 5. New York: Academic Press, pp. 1–31.

Gordon, T. F. 1973. *The Effects of Time Context on Children's Perceptions of Aggressive Television Content.* Philadelphia: Temple University, School of Communications and Theater.

Gormley, W. 1975. Newspaper agendas and political elites. *Journalism Quarterly*, 52, 304–8.

Gorn, G. J., M. E. Goldberg, and R. N. Kanungo. 1976. The role of educational television in changing the intergroup attitudes of children. *Child Development*, 47, 277–80.

Graber, D. 1971. The press as opinion resource during the 1968 presidential campaign. *Public Opinion Quarterly*, 35, 168–82.

Graney, M. J. 1974. Media use as a substitute activity in old age. *Journal of Gerontology*, 29, 322–24.

Grass, R. C. 1968. Satiation effects of advertising. In *Proceedings of the 14th Annual Conference, Advertising Research Foundation*, pp. 20–28.

Grass, R. C., and W. H. Wallace, 1969. Satiation effects of TV commercials. *Journal of Advertising Research*, 1969, 9(3), 3–8.

—— 1974. Advertising communication: Print vs. TV. *Journal of Advertising Research* 14(5), 19–23.

Greenberg, A., and C. Suttoni. 1973. Television commercial wearout. *Journal of Advertising Research*, 13, 47–54.

Greenberg, B. S. 1965. Television for children: Dimensions of communicator and audience perceptions. *AV Communication Review*, 13, 385–96.

Greenberg, B. S. 1972a. Children's reactions to TV blacks. *Journalism Quarterly*, 49, 5–14.

—— 1972b. Televised violence: Further explorations. In G. A. Comstock, E. A. Rubinstein, and J. P. Murray (eds.), *Television and Social Behav-*

ior. Vol. 5, *Television's Effects: Further Explorations.* Washington, D.C.: Government Printing Office, pp. 1–21.

—— 1974. Gratifications of television viewing and their correlates for British children. In J. Blumler and E. Katz (eds.), *The Uses of Mass Communications: Current Perspectives on Gratifications Research. Sage Annual Reviews of Communication Research,* vol. 3. Beverly Hills, Ca.: Sage, 71–92.

Greenberg, B. S., and B. Dervin. 1970. *Use of the Mass Media by the Urban Poor.* New York: Praeger.

—— 1973. Mass communication among the urban poor. In C. D. Mortensen and K. K. Sereno (eds.), *Advances in Communication Research.* New York: Harper and Row, pp. 388–397.

Greenberg, B. S., and J. R. Dominick. 1969. Racial and social class differences in teen-agers' use of television. *Journal of Broadcasting,* 13, 331–44.

Greenberg, B. S., P. M. Ericson, and M. Vlahos. 1972. Children's television behavior as perceived by mother and child. In E. A. Rubinstein, G. A. Comstock, and J. P. Murray (eds.), *Television and Social Behavior.* Vol. 4, *Television in Day-to-Day Life: Patterns of Use.* Washington, D.C.: Government Printing Office, pp. 395–409.

Greenberg, B. S., and T. F. Gordon. 1972a. Children's perceptions of television violence: A replication. In G. A. Comstock, E. A. Rubinstein, and J. P. Murray (eds.), *Television and Social Behavior.* Vol. 5, *Television's Effects: Further Explorations.* Washington, D.C.: Government Printing Office, pp. 211–30.

—— 1972b. Perceptions of violence in television programs: Critics and the public. In *ibid.* Vol. 1, *Media Content and Control.* Washington, D.C.: Government Printing Office, pp. 244–58.

Greenberg, B. S., and Hanneman, G. J. 1970. Racial attitudes and the impact of TV blacks. *Educational Broadcasting Review* 4(2), 27–34.

Greenberg, B. S., and B. Reeves. 1976. Children and the perceived reality of television. *Journal of Social Issues,* 32(4), 86–97.

Greenberg, E., and H. J. Barnett. 1971. TV program diversity—New evidence and old theories. *American Economic Review,* 61, 89–100.

Gregg, P. W. 1971. Television viewing as parasocial interaction for persons aged 60 years or older. Master's thesis, University of Oregon.

Greyser, S. A. 1973. Irritation in advertising. *Journal of Advertising Research,* 13(1), 3–10.

Grusec, J. E. 1973. Effects of co-observer evaluations on imitation: A developmental study. *Developmental Psychology,* 8, 141.

Haavelsrud, M. 1971. Development of concepts related to peace and war: An international perspective. Paper presented at the meeting of the American Psychological Association. Washington, D.C.

Hale, G. A., L. K. Miller, and H. W. Stevenson. 1968. Incidental learning of film content: A development study. *Child Development,* 39, 69–77.

Halloran, J. D. 1964. *The effects of mass communication with special ref-*

erence to television. Leicester: Leicester University Press (Television Research Committee Working Paper No. 1).

—— 1969. A report on several evaluations of children's reactions to a prize-winning film for young children (ages five to eight years) from the Second Prix Jeunesse Competition, Munich 1966. In *Second Progress Report and Recommendations.* Leicester, England. Television Research Committee, Leicester University Press, pp. 77–94.

—— 1978. Social Research on Broadcasting: Further Development—or Turning the Clock Back? *Journal of Communication,* 28(2), 120–32.

Hanratty, M. A., R. M. Liebert, L. W. Morris, and L. E. Fernandez. 1969. Imitation of film-mediated aggression against live and inanimate victims. *Proceedings of the 77th annual convention of the American Psychological Association.* Washington, D.C.: American Psychological Association, pp. 457–58.

Hanratty, M. A., E. O'Neal, and J. L. Sulzer. 1972. The effects of frustration upon the imitation of aggression. *Journal of Personality and Social Psychology,* 21, 30–34.

Harlan, T. A. 1972. Viewing behavior and interpretive strategies of a photographic narrative as a function of variation in story title and subject age. Master's thesis, Annenberg School of Communications, University of Pennsylvania.

Louis Harris and Associates, Inc. 1974. *A survey on aging: Experience of older Americans vs. public expectation of old age.* Conducted for the National Council on the Aging, Inc. New York: Louis Harris and Associates, Inc.

Harris, M. 1970. Reciprocity and generosity: Some determinants of sharing behavior. *Child Development,* 41, 313–28.

Hartley, R. L. 1964. *The impact of viewing "aggression": Studies and Problems of Extrapolation.* New York: Columbia Broadcasting System, Office of Social Research.

Hartmann, D. P. 1965. The influence of symbolically modeled instrumental aggression and pain cues on the disinhibition of aggressive behavior. Doctoral dissertation, Stanford University.

—— 1969. Influence of symbolically modeled instrumental aggression and pain cues on aggressive behavior. *Journal of Personality and Social Psychology,* 11, 280–88.

Haskins, J. 1964. Factual recall as a measure of advertising effectiveness. *Journal of Advertising Research,* 4(1), 2–8.

Hawkins, R. P. 1973. Learning of peripheral content in films: A developmental study. *Child Development,* 44, 214–17.

—— 1974. Children's acquisition of current events information in the context of family, peers, media use and pre-existing attitudes. Doctoral dissertation, Stanford University.

Hawkins, R. P., S. Pingree, and D. F. Roberts. 1975. Watergate and political socialization: The inescapable event. *American Politics Quarterly,* 3, 406–22.

—— 1967. Anxiety and preference for television fantasy. *Journalism Quarterly* 44, 461–69.

Hazard, W. R. 1967. Anxiety and preference for television fantasy. *Journalism Quarterly,* 44, 461–469.

Head, S. W. 1954. Content analysis of television drama programs. *Quarterly of Film, Radio and Television,* 9, 175–94.

Heffner, R. D., and E. H. Kramer. 1972. Network television's environmental content. Unpublished manuscript, Rutgers University.

Heider, F. 1946. Attitudes and cognitive organization. *Journal of Psychology,* 21, 107–12.

Heider, F. 1958. *The Psychology of Interpersonal Relations.* New York: John Wiley and Sons.

Heise, D. R. 1970. Causal inference from panel data. In E. F. Borgatta (ed.), *Sociological Methodology 1970.* San Francisco: Jossey-Bass, pp. 3–27.

Herzog, H. 1944. What do we really know about daytime serial listeners? In P. F. Lazarsfeld and F. N. Stanton (eds.), *Radio Research 1942–1943.* New York: Duell, Sloan, and Pearce, pp. 3–33.

—— 1954. Motivations and gratifications of daily serial listeners. In W. Schramm (ed.), *The Process and Effects of Mass Communication.* Urbana, Ill.: University of Illinois Press, pp. 50–55.

Hess, R. D., and H. Goldman. 1962. Parents' views of the effects of television on their children. *Child Development,* 33, 411–26.

Hess, R. D., and J. V. Torney. 1967. *The Development of Political Attitudes in Children.* Chicago: Aldine.

Hetherington, E. M., and G. Frankie. 1967. Effects of parental dominance, warmth, and conflict on imitation in children. *Journal of Personality and Social Psychology,* 6, 119–25.

Hickey, N. 1972. What America thinks of TV's political coverage. *TV Guide,* April 8, 6–11.

Hicks, D. J. 1965. Imitation and retention of film-mediated aggressive peer and adult models. *Journal of Personality and Social Psychology,* 2, 97–100.

—— 1968. Effects of co-observer's sanctions and adult presence on imitative aggression. *Child Development,* 38, 303–9.

Hiebert, R. E. (ed.). 1971. *Political Image Merchants: Strategy in New Politics.* Washington, D.C.: Acropolis.

Higbie, C. E. 1961. 1960 election studies show broad approach, new methods. *Journalism Quarterly,* 38, 164–70.

Hill, J. H., R. M. Liebert, and D. E. W. Mott. 1968. Vicarious extinction of avoidance behavior through films: An initial test. *Psychological Reports,* 22, 192.

Himmelweit, H. T., A. N. Oppenheim, and P. Vince. 1958. *Television and the Child.* London: Oxford University Press.

Himmelweit, H. T., and B. Swift. 1976. Continuities and discontinuities in media usage and taste: A longitudinal study. *Journal of Social Issues,* 32(4), 133–56.

Hirsch, H. 1971. *Poverty and Politicization.* New York: Free Press.

Hofstetter, C. R. 1976. *Bias in the News.* Columbus: Ohio State University Press.

Hogan, P., and I. Alger. 1966. Use of videotape recording in family therapy. Paper presented at the meeting of the American Ortho-Psychiatric Association.

Hokanson, J. E., M. Burgess, and M. F. Cohen. 1963. Effects of displaced aggression on systolic blood pressure. *Journal of Abnormal and Social Psychology,* 67, 214–18.

Holaday, P. W., and G. D. Stoddard. 1933. *Getting Ideas from the Movies.* New York: Macmillan.

Hollander, N. 1971. Adolescents and the war: The sources of socialization. *Journalism Quarterly,* 58, 472–79.

Holsti, O. R. 1969. *Content Analysis for the Social Sciences and Humanities.* Reading, Mass.: Addison-Wesley.

Hovland, C. I. 1959. Reconciling conflicting results derived from experimental and survey studies of attitude change. *American Psychologist.* 14, 8–17.

Hovland, C. I., and I. L. Janis (eds.). 1959. *Personality and Persuasibility.* New Haven: Yale University Press.

Hovland, C. I., I. L. Janis, and H. H. Kelley. 1953. *Communication and persuasion.* New Haven: Yale University Press.

Hovland, C. I., A. A. Lumsdaine, and F. D. Sheffield. 1949. *Experiments in mass communication.* Princeton: Princeton University Press.

Howard, J. A., J. M. Hulbert, and D. R. Lehmann. 1973. An exploratory analysis of the effect of television advertising on children. *Proceedings of the American Marketing Association.* Washington, D.C.: The Association.

Howitt, D. 1972. Television and aggression: A counterargument. *American Psychologist.* 27, 969–70.

Hoyt, J. L. 1970. Effect of media violence "justification" on aggression. *Journal of Broadcasting,* 14, 455–64.

Hsia, H. J. 1974. Audience recall as tolerance toward television commercial breaks. *Journalism Quarterly.* 51, 96–101.

Huesmann, L. R., L. D. Eron, M. M. Lefkowitz, and L. O. Walder. 1973. Television violence and aggression: The causal effect remains. *American Psychologist,* 28, 617–20.

Hujanen, T. 1976. *Immigrant broadcasting and migration control in Western Europe.* Tampere, Finland: Institute of Journalism and Mass Communication, University of Tampere.

Hwang, J. C. 1974. Aging and information seeking. *Communication* (Journal of the Communication Association of the Pacific), July.

534   References

Hyman, H. H. 1959. *Political Socialization.* New York: Macmillan-Free Press.
Hyman, H. H. 1974. Mass communication and socialization. In W. P. Davison and F. T. C. Yu (eds.), *Mass communication research: Major Issues and Future Directions.* New York: Praeger.
Isherwood, C. 1954. Goodbye to Berlin. In C. Isherwood, *The Berlin Stories.* New York: New Directions.
Israel, H., and J. P. Robinson. 1972. Demographic characteristics of viewers of television violence and news programs. In E. A. Rubinstein, G. A. Comstock, and J. P. Murray (eds.), *Television and Social Behavior.* Vol. 4, *Television in Day-to-Day life: Patterns of Use.* Washington, D.C.: Government Printing Office, pp. 87–128.
Jacobs, T. 1971. Advertising and children: Investigation by Nader's Raiders. In E. Sarson (ed.), *Action for Children's Television: The First National Symposium on the Effect on Children of Television Programming and Advertising.* New York: Avon.
Jacobson, H. K. 1969. Mass media believability: A study of receiver judgments. *Journalism Quarterly, 46,* 20–28.
Jennings, M. K., and R. G. Niemi. 1973. The transmission of political values from parent to child. In J. Dennis (ed.), *Socialization to Politics: A Reader.* New York: Wiley.
Johnson, R. L., H. L. Friedman, and H. S. Gross. 1972. Four masculine styles in television programming: A study of the viewing preferences of adolescent males. In G. A. Comstock and E. A. Rubinstein (eds.), *Television and Social Behavior.* Vol. 3, *Television and Adolescent Aggressiveness.* Washington, D.C.: Government Printing Office, pp. 361–71.
Johnstone, J. W. C. 1974. Social integration and mass media use among adolescents: A case study. In J. G. Blumler and E. Katz (eds.), *The Uses of Mass Communications: Current Perspectives on Gratifications Research.* Beverly Hills, Ca.: Sage, pp. 35–47.
Jones, E. E., and H. B. Gerard. 1967. *Foundations of Social Psychology.* New York: Wiley.
Jones, W. K. 1967. *Cases and Materials on Regulated Industries.* Brooklyn: The Foundation Press.
Kaplan, R. M. 1972. On television as a cause of aggression. *American Psychologist, 27,* 968–69.
Kaplan, R. M., and R. D. Singer. 1976. Television violence and viewer aggression: A reexamination of the evidence. *Journal of Social Issues, 32(4),* 35–70.
Katz, E. 1959. Mass communication research and the study of popular culture: An editorial note on a possible future for this journal. *Studies in Public Communication, 2,* 1–6.
—— 1977. *Social Research on Broadcasting: Proposals for Further Development.* London: British Broadcasting System.
Katz, E., J. G. Blumler, and M. Gurevitch, 1973. Uses and gratifications research. *Public Opinion Quarterly, 37,* 509–23.

Katz, E., and J. J. Feldman. 1962. The debates in the light of research: A survey of surveys. In S. Kraus (ed.), *The Great Debates.* Bloomington: Indiana University Press, p. 211.

Katz, E., and M. Gurevitch. 1976. *The Secularization of Leisure: Culture and Communication in Israel.* Cambridge, Mass.: Harvard University Press.

Katz, E., M. Gurevitch, and H. Haas. 1973. On the use of mass media for important things. *American Sociological Review,* 38, 164–81.

Katz, E., and P. Lazarsfeld. 1955. *Personal Influence.* New York: Free Press.

Katzman, N. I. 1972a. Television soap operas: What's been going on anyway? *Public Opinion Quarterly,* 36, 200–12.

—— 1972b. Violence and color television: What children of different ages learn. In G. A. Comstock, E. A. Rubinstein, and J. P. Murray (eds.), *Television and Social Behavior.* Vol. 5, *Television's Effects: Further Explorations.* Washington, D.C.: Government Printing Office, pp. 253–308.

—— 1973. *One Week of Public Television: April 1972.* Washington, D.C.: Corporation for Public Broadcasting.

—— 1974. *Community Survey, Sacramento, California.* Washington, D.C.: Corporation for Public Broadcasting.

Katzman, N. I. *Public television program content: 1975.* Washington, D.C.: Corporation for Public Broadcasting.

Katzman, N. I., and K. Farr, 1975. *CPB Report—Focus on Research.* Nos. 2, 3, 4, and 6. Washington, D.C.: Corporation for Public Broadcasting.

Katzman, N. I., and S. Lasselle. 1974. *Community Survey, San Jose, California.* Washington, D.C.: Corporation for Public Broadcasting.

Kay, H. 1972. Weaknesses in the television-causes-aggression analysis by Eron et al. *American Psychologist,* 27, 970–73.

Keating, J. P. 1972. Persuasive impact, attitudes, and image: The effect of communication media and audience size on attitudes toward a source and toward his advocated position. Doctoral dissertation, Ohio State University.

Keeney, T. J., S. R. Cannizzo, and J. H. Flavell. 1967. Spontaneous and induced verbal rehearsal in a recall task. *Child Development,* 38, 953–66.

Keller, F. S., and W. N. Schoenfeld. 1950. *Principles of Psychology.* New York: Appleton-Century-Crofts.

Kelley, S. 1956. *Professional Public Relations and Political Power.* Baltimore: Johns Hopkins University Press.

Kenny, D. A. 1972. Threats to the internal validity of cross-lagged panel inference, as related to "Television violence and child aggression: A follow-up study." In G. A. Comstock and E. A. Rubinstein (eds.), *Television and Social Behavior.* Vol. 3, *Television and Adolescent Aggressiveness.* Washington, D.C.: Government Printing Office, pp. 136–40.

Kenny, D. A. 1973. Cross-lagged and synchronous common factors in panel data. In A. Goldberger and O. D. Duncan (eds.), *Structural Equation Models.* New York: Seminar Press.

536   References

Klapper, J. T. 1954. The comparative effects of the various media. In W. Schramm (ed.), *The Process and Effects of Mass Communication.* Urbana, Ill.: University of Illinois Press, pp. 91–105.
—— 1957. What we know about the effects of mass communication: The brink of hope. *Public Opinion Quarterly, 21, 453–74.*
—— 1960. *The Effects of Mass Communication.* New York: Free Press.
—— 1963. Mass communication research: An old road resurveyed. *Public Opinion Quarterly, 27, 515–27.*
Kniveton, B. H. 1973. Social class and imitation of aggressive adult and peer models. *Journal of Social Psychology, 89, 311–12.*
Konecni, V. J. 1973. Experimental studies in human aggression: The cathartic effect. Doctoral dissertation, University of Toronto.
—— 1975a. Annoyance, type and duration of postannoyance activity, and aggression: The "cathartic effect." *Journal of Experimental Psychology: General,* 104(1), 76–102.
—— 1975b. The mediation of aggressive behavior: Arousal level versus anger and cognitive labeling. *Journal of Personality and Social Psychology, 32, 706–12.*
Konecni, V. J., and A. N. Doob. 1972. Catharsis through displacement of aggression. *Journal of Personality and Social Psychology, 23, 379–87.*
Kraus, S. (ed.). 1962. *The Great Debates. Bloomington: Indiana University Press.*
Kraus, S. (ed.). 1977. *The Great Debates: 1976, Ford vs. Carter.* Bloomington: Indiana University Press.
Kraus, S., and S. H. Chaffee (eds.). 1974. The Ervin Committee hearings and communication research. *Communication Research, 1,* special issue.
Kraus, S., and D. Davis. 1976. *The Effect of Mass Communication on Political Behavior.* University Park: Pennsylvania State University Press.
Krugman, H. E. 1965. The impact of television advertising: Learning without involvement. *Public Opinion Quarterly, 29, 349–56.*
—— 1966. The measurement of advertising involvement. *Public Opinion Quarterly, 30, 583–96.*
—— 1968. Processes underlying exposure to advertising. *American Psychology, 23, 245–53.*
—— 1971. Brain wave measures of media involvement. *Journal of Advertising Research, 11,* 3–9.
Krull, R. 1973. Program entropy and structure as factors in television viewership. Doctoral dissertation, University of Wisconsin.
Krull, R., and J. H. Watt, Jr. 1973. Television viewing and aggression: An examination of three models. Paper presented at the meeting of the International Communication Association, Montreal, April.
Kuhn, D. Z. 1973. Imitation theory and research from a cognitive perspective. *Human Development, 16,* 157–80.
Lambert, W. E., and O. Klineberg. 1967. *Children's Views of Foreign People.* New York: Appleton-Century Crofts.

Lang, K., and G. E. Lang. 1953. The unique perspective of television and its effects: A pilot study. *American Sociological Review,* 18, 3–12.
—— 1959. The mass media and voting. In E. Burdick and A. J. Brodbeck (eds.), *American Voting Behavior.* Glencoe, Ill.: Free Press, pp. 217–35.
—— 1968. *Politics and Television.* Chicago: Quadrangle Books, 1968.
Langton, K. P. 1967. Peer group and school and the political socialization process. *American Political Science Review,* 61, 751–58.
Langton, K. P., and M. K. Jennings. 1968. Political socialization and the high school civics curriculum. *American Political Science Review,* 62, 852–57.
—— 1969. Acquisition of political values in the schools. *American Political Science Review,* 63, 51–65.
Larsen, O. N. 1964. Social effects of mass communication. In R. E. L. Faris (ed.), *Handbook of Modern Sociology.* New York: Rand McNally, pp. 348–81.
Larsen, O. N., L. N. Gray, and J. G. Fortis. 1963. Goals and goal-achievement in television content: Models for anomie? *Sociological Inquiry,* 33, 180–96.
Lavidge, R. J., and G. A. Steiner. 1961. A model for predictive measurements of advertising effectiveness. *Journal of Marketing,* 25, 59–62.
Lazarsfeld, P. F., B. Berelson, and H. Gaudet. 1948. *The People's Choice.* New York: Columbia University Press.
Lazarsfeld, P. F., and R. K. Merton. 1971. Mass communication, popular taste, and organized social action. In W. Schramm and D. F. Roberts (eds.), *The Process and Effects of Mass Communication.* (rev. ed.) Urbana, Ill.: University of Illinois Press, pp. 554–78.
Lazarus, R. S., J. C. Speisman, A. M. Mordkoff, and L. A. Davison. 1962. A laboratory study of psychological stress produced by a motion picture film. *Psychological Monographs.* 76 (34, Whole No. 553).
Lefkowitz, M. M. 1972. Letter to Honorable John O. Pastore, and letter to Dr. Ithiel de Sola Pool. In U.S. Congress, Senate Committee on Commerce. Hearings before the Subcommittee on Communications. *Surgeon General's Report by the Scientific Advisory Committee on Television and Social Behavior.* 92nd Congress, 2nd Session. March 21–24, 1972. Washington, D.C. Government Printing Office, pp. 90–91; 93–94.
Lefkowitz, M. M., L. D. Eron, L. O. Walder, and L. R. Huesmann. 1972. Television violence and child aggression: A followup study. In G. A. Comstock and E. A. Rubinstein (eds.), *Television and Social Behavior.* Vol. 3, *Television and Adolescent Aggressiveness.* Washington, D.C.: Government Printing Office, pp. 35–135.
—— 1977. *Growing Up To Be Violent.* Elmsford, N.Y.: Pergamon Press.
Leifer, A. D., W. A. Collins, B. M. Gross, P. H. Taylor, L. Andres, and E. R. Blackmer. 1971. Developmental aspects of variables relevant to observational learning. *Child Development,* 42, 1509–16.
Leifer, A. D., N. J. Gordon, and S. B. Graves. 1973. Children and televi-

sion: Recommended directions for future efforts. Center for Research in Children's Television, Harvard University, May Final Report to the Office of Child Development, Department of Health, Education and Welfare.

Leifer, A. D., and D. F. Roberts. 1972. Children's responses to television violence. In J. P. Murray, E. A. Rubinstein, and G. A. Comstock (eds.), *Television and social behavior.* Vol. 2, *Television and Social Learning.* Washington, D.C.: Government Printing Office, pp. 43–180.

Lemert, J. B. 1974. Content duplication by the networks in competing evening newscasts. *Journalism Quarterly,* 51, 238–44.

Lesser, G. S. 1974. *Children and Television: Lessons from Sesame Street.* New York: Random House.

Levin, S. R., and D. R. Anderson. 1976. The development of attention. *Journal of Communication,* 26, 126–35.

Levinson, R. M. 1973. From Olive Oyl to Sweet Polly Purebread: Sex role stereotypes and televised cartoons. *Journal of Popular Culture,* 9, 561–72.

Leyens, J. P., R. D. Parke, L. Camino, and L. Berkowitz. 1975. Effects of movie violence on aggression in a field setting as a function of group dominance and cohesion. *Journal of Personality and Social Psychology,* 32, 346–60.

Liebert, D. E., J. N. Sprafkin, R. M. Liebert, and E. A. Rubinstein. 1977. Effects of television commercial disclaimers on the product expectations of children. *Journal of Communication,* 27, 118–24.

Liebert, R. M. 1972. Television and social learning. Some relationships between viewing violence and behaving aggressively. In J. P. Murray, E. A. Rubinstein, and G. A. Comstock (eds.), *Television and Social Behavior.* Vol. 2, *Television and Social Learning.* Washington, D.C.: Government Printing Office, pp. 1–42.

Liebert, R. M., and R. A. Baron. 1972a. Short-term effects of televised aggression on children's aggressive behavior. In J. P. Murray, E. A. Rubinstein, and G. A. Comstock (eds.), *Television and Social Behavior.* Vol. 2, *Television and Social Learning.* Washington, D.C.: Government Printing Office, pp. 181–201.

—— 1972b. Some immediate effects of televised violence on children's behavior. *Developmental Psychology,* 6, 469–75.

Liebert, R. M., L. E. Fernandez, and L. Gill. 1969. The effects of a friendless model on imitation and prosocial behavior. *Psychonomic Science,* 16, 81–82.

Liebert, R. M., J. M. Neale, and E. S. Davidson. 1973. *The Early Window: Effects of Television on Children and Youth.* Elmsford, N.Y.: Pergamon Press.

Liebert, R. M., and R. W. Poulos. 1974. Television as a moral teacher. In T. Lickona (ed.), *Man and Morality: Theory, Research, and Social Issues.* New York: Holt, Rinehart and Winston.

Liebert, R. M., M. D. Sobol, and E. S. Davidson. 1972. Catharsis of aggression among institutionalized boys: Fact or artifact. In G. A. Comstock, E. A. Rubinstein, and J. P. Murray (eds.), *Television and Social Behavior*. Vol. 5. *Television's Effects: Further Explorations*. Washington, D.C.: Government Printing Office, pp. 351–59.

Lin, N. 1971. Information flow, influence flow and the decision-making process. *Journalism Quarterly, 48*, 33–40.

Lippmann, W. 1922. *Public Opinion*. New York: Macmillan.

Long, B. H., and E. H. Henderson. 1973. Children's use of time: Some personal and social correlates. *Elementary School Journal, 73*(4), 193–99.

Long, M. L., and R. J. Simon. 1974. The roles and statuses of women on children and family TV programs. *Journalism Quarterly, 51*, 107–10.

Los Angeles Times. 1977a. Commentary: Porno chic on increase. April 11.

—— 1977b. Old bedfellows: Sex, violence. April 22.

—— 1977c. TV violence: Doctors join fight. May 22.

LoSciuto, L. A. 1972. A national inventory of television viewing behavior. In E. A. Rubinstein. G. A. Comstock, and J. P. Murray (eds.), *Television and Social Behavior*. Vol. 4, *Television in Day-to-Day Life: Patterns of Use*. Washington, D.C.: Government Printing Office, pp. 33–86.

Lovaas, O. I. 1961. Effect of exposure to symbolic aggression on aggressive behavior. *Child Development, 32*, 37–44.

Lowry, D. T. 1971a. Agnew and the network TV news: A before/after content analysis. *Journalism Quarterly, 48*, 205–10.

—— 1971b. Gresham's law and network TV news selection. *Journal of Broadcasting, 15*, 397–408.

—— 1974. Multiple measures of network TV news bias in campaign '72. Paper presented at the meeting of the International Communication Association, New Orleans, April.

Lucas, W. A., and W. C. Adams, 1977. The undecided voter and political communication in the 1976 presidential election. Paper presented at the meeting of the Southwestern Political Science Association, Dallas, April.

Lucas, W. A., and K. B. Possner. 1975. *Television News and Local Awareness: A Retrospective Look*. Santa Monica: The Rand Corporation, R-1858-MF.

Lull, J. T. 1974. Counter advertising: Persuasibility of the anti-Bayer TV spot. *Journal of Broadcasting, 18*, 353–60.

Lyle, J. 1967. *The News in Megalopolis*. San Francisco: Chandler.

—— 1972. Television in daily life: Patterns of use. In E. A. Rubinstein, G. A. Comstock, and J. P. Murray (eds.), *Television and Social Behavior*. Vol. 4. *Television in Day-to-Day Life: Patterns of Use*. Washington, D.C.: Government Printing Office, pp. 1–32.

—— 1975. *The People Look at Public Television 1974*. Washington, D.C.: Corporation for Public Broadcasting.

Lyle, J., and H. R. Hoffman. 1972a. Children's use of television and other media. In E. A. Rubinstein, G. A. Comstock, and J. P. Murray (eds.), *Television and Social Behavior*. Vol. 4, *Television in Day-to-Day Life: Patterns of Use*. Washington, D.C.: Government Printing Office, pp. 129–256.

Lyle, J., and H. R. Hoffman. 1972b. Explorations in patterns of television viewing by preschool-age children. In E. A. Rubinstein, G. A. Comstock, and J. P. Murray (eds.), *Television and Social Behavior*. Vol. 4. *Television in Day-to-Day Life: Patterns of use*. Washington, D.C.: Government Printing Office, pp. 257–73. ,

Lyle, J., and R. A. Stone. 1971. One hour of TV news equals about 10 columns of a newspaper page. *ANPA News Research Bulletin No. 16*, November 24, pp. 103–115.

McArthur, L. Z., and B. G. Resko. 1975. The portrayal of men and women in American television commercials. *Journal of Social Psychology, 97*, 209–20.

McClure, R. D., and T. E. Patterson. 1974. A comparison of the agenda-setting influence of television and newspapers. Paper presented at the Syracuse University Conference on Agenda-Setting, Syracuse, New York.

Maccoby, E. E. 1951. Television: Its impact on school children. *Public Opinion Quarterly, 15*, 421–44.

—— 1954. Why do children watch television? *Ibid., 18*, 239–44.

—— 1959. Role-taking in childhood and its consequences for social learning. *Child Development, 30*, 239–252.

—— 1964. Effects of the mass media. In M. Hoffman and L. W. Hoffman (eds.), *Review of Child Development Research*. Vol. 1. New York: Russell Sage Foundation, pp. 323–48.

Maccoby, E., and C. N. Jacklin. 1974. *The Psychology of Sex Differences*. Stanford, Calif.: Stanford University Press.

Maccoby, E. E., and W. C. Wilson. 1957. Identification and observational learning from films. *Journal of Abnormal and Social Psychology, 55*, 76–87.

Maccoby, E. E., W. C. Wilson, and R. V. Burton. 1958. Differential movie-viewing behavior of male and female viewers. *Journal of Personality, 26*, 259–67.

McCombs, M. E. 1967. Editorial endorsements: A study of influence. *Journalism Quarterly, 44*, 545–48.

McCombs, M. E. 1968. Negro use of television and newspapers for political information, 1952–1964. *Journal of Broadcasting, 12*, 261–66.

—— 1972a. Mass communication in political campaigns: Information, gratification, and persuasion. In F. G. Kline and P. J. Tichenor (eds.), *Current Perspectives in Mass Communication Research*. Beverly Hills, Ca.: Sage, pp. 169–94.

—— 1972b. Mass media in the marketplace. *Journalism Monographs, No.*

24. Lexington, Kentucky: Association for Education in Journalism, August.

—— 1976. Press and public agendas of community issues. Paper presented at the meeting of the American Association for Public Opinion Research, Asheville, North Carolina, May.

McCombs, M. E., and D. L. Shaw. 1972. The agenda-setting function of mass media. *Public Opinion Quarterly,* 36, 176–87.

—— 1974. A progress report on agenda-setting research. Paper presented at the meeting of the Association for Education in Journalism, San Diego, August.

McCombs, M. E., D. Shaw, and E. Shaw. 1972. The news and public response. Three studies of the agenda-setting power of the press. Paper presented at the meeting of the Association for Education in Journalism.

McCombs, M. E., and D. Weaver. 1973. Voters' need for orientation and use of mass communication. Paper presented at the meeting of the International Communication Association.

McCombs, M. E., and W. Wilcox. 1968. Media use in presidential election campaigns. In C. Bush (ed.), *News Research for Better Newspapers,* vol. 3. Washington, D.C.: American Newspaper Publishers Association, pp. 36–39.

McConnell, J. D. 1970. Do media vary in effectiveness? *Journal of Advertising Research,* 10(5), 19–22.

McGrath, J. E., and M. F. McGrath. 1962. Effects of partisanship on perceptions of political figures. *Public Opinion Quarterly,* 26, 236–48.

McGrath, K. 1975. Social science in the newsroom. An agenda-setting approach to covering the 1974 elections. Paper presented at the meeting of the Association for Education in Journalism.

McGuire, W. J. 1969. The nature of attitudes and attitude change. In G. Lindzey and E. Aronson (eds.), *The Handbook of Social Psychology.* Vol. 3, *The Individual in a Social Context.* 2nd ed. Reading, Mass.: Addison-Wesley, pp. 136–314.

McIntyre, J. J., and J. J. Teevan, Jr. 1972. Television violence and deviant behavior. In G. A. Comstock and E. A. Rubinstein (eds.), *Television and Social Behavior.* Vol. 3, *Television and Adolescent Aggressiveness.* Washington, D.C.: Government Printing Office, pp. 383–435.

McLeod, J. M., C. K. Atkin, and S. H. Chaffee, 1972a. Adolescents, parents, and television use: Adolescent self-report measures from Maryland and Wisconsin samples. In G. A. Comstock and E. A. Rubinstein (eds.), *Television and Social Behavior.* Vol. 3, *Television and Adolescent Aggressiveness.* Washington, D.C.: Government Printing Office, pp. 173–238.

—— 1972b. Adolescents, parents and television use: Self-report and other-report measures from the Wisconsin sample. In *ibid.,* pp. 239–313.

McLeod, J. M., and L. B. Becker. 1974. Testing the validity of gratification measures through political effects analysis. In J. G. Blumler and E. Katz (eds.), *The Uses of Mass Communications: Current Perspectives on Gratifications Research.* Beverly Hills, Calif.: Sage Publications, pp. 137–64.

McLeod, J. M., S. H. Chaffee, and H. S. Eswara. 1966. Family communication patterns and communication research. Paper presented at the meeting of the Association for Education in Journalism, Iowa City, Iowa, August.

McLeod, J., S. Chaffee, and D. Wackman. 1967. Family communication: An updated report. Paper presented at the meetings of the Association for Education in Journalism, Boulder, Colorado, August.

McLeod, J., J. Durall, D. Ziemke, and C. Bybee. 1977. Expanding the concept of debate effects (tentative title). In S. Kraus (ed.), *The great debates: 1976, Ford vs. Carter.* Bloomington: Indiana University Press.

McLeod, J. M., R. R. Rush, and K. H. Friederich. 1968. The mass media and political knowledge in Quito, Ecuador. *Public Opinion Quarterly,* 32, 575–87.

McLeod, J. M., S. Ward, and K. Tancill. 1965. Alienation and the uses of the mass media. *Public Opinion Quarterly,* 29, 583–94.

McNeal, J. U. 1969. An exploratory study of the consumer behavior of children. In J. U. McNeal (ed.), *Dimensions of consumer behavior.* New York: Appleton-Century-Crofts, pp. 255–75.

McNeil, J. C. 1975. Feminism, femininity, and the television series: A content analysis. *Journal of Broadcasting* 19(3), 259–69.

Mallick, S. K., and B. R. McCandless. 1966. A study of catharsis of aggression. *Journal of Personality and Social Psychology,* 4, 591–96.

Mandell, L. M., and D. L. Shaw. 1973. Judging people in the news—unconsciously: Effect of camera angle and bodily activity. *Journal of Broadcasting,* 17, 353–62.

Mann, J., L. Berkowitz, J. Sidman, S. Starr, and S. West. 1974. Satiation of the transient stimulating effects of erotic films. *Journal of Personality and Social Psychology,* 30, 729–35.

Mann, J., J. Sidman, and S. Starr. 1971. Effects of erotic films on the sexual behavior of married couples. In *Technical Report of the Commission on Obscenity and Pornography.* Vol. 8. Washington, D.C.: Government Printing Office, pp. 170–254.

—— 1973. Evaluating social consequences of erotic films: An experimental approach. *Journal of Social Issues,* 29, 113–32.

Marsh, G., and M. Sherman. 1966. Verbal mediation of transposition as a function of age level. *Journal of Experimental Child Psychology,* 4, 90–98.

Marshall, H. M. 1972. The effect of vicarious punishment on sharing behavior in children. Doctoral dissertation, Dartmouth College.

Masters, J. C. 1972. Effects of social comparison upon the imitation of neutral and altruistic behaviors by young children. *Child Development,* 43, 131–42.

Meadow, R. G. 1973. Cross-media comparison of coverage of the 1972 presidential campaign. *Journalism Quarterly,* 50, 482–88.

Melnick, J. 1973. A comparison of replication techniques in the modification of minimal dating behavior. *Journal of Abnormal Psychology,* 81, 51–59.

Mendelsohn, H. A. 1966. Election-day broadcasts and terminal voting decisions. *Public Opinion Quarterly,* 30, 212–25.

—— 1973. Some reasons why information campaigns can succeed. *Ibid.,* 37, 50–61.

Mendelsohn, H. A., and I. Crespi. 1970. *Polls, Television, and the New Politics.* San Francisco: Chandler.

Mendelsohn, H. A., and G. J. O'Keefe. 1976. *The People Choose a President: Influences on Voter Decision Making.* New York: Praeger.

Mendelson, G., and M. Young. 1972. *Network Children's Programming: A Content Analysis of Black and Minority Treatment on Children's Television.* Newtonville, Ma.: Action for Children's Television.

Menzies, E. S. 1971. Preferences in television content among violent prisoners. Master's thesis, Florida State University.

Merton, R. K. 1946. *Mass Persuasion.* New York: Harper and Row.

Meyer, T. P. 1972a. The effects of sexually arousing and violent films on aggressive behavior. *Journal of Sex Research,* 8, 324–31.

—— 1972b. The effects of verbally violent film content on aggressive behavior. *AV Communication Review,* 20(2), 160–69.

—— 1972c. Effects of viewing justified and unjustified real film violence on aggressive behavior. *Journal of Personality and Social Psychology,* 23, 21–29.

—— 1972d. News reporter bias: A case study in selective perception. *Journal of Broadcasting,* 16, 195–203.

Meyersohn, R. B. 1965. Leisure and television: A study in compatibility. Doctoral dissertation, Columbia University.

—— 1968. Television and the rest of leisure time. *Public Opinion Quarterly,* 32, 102–12.

Meyerson, L. J. 1966. The effects of filmed aggression on the aggressive responses of high and low aggressive subjects. Doctoral dissertation, University of Iowa.

Miami Herald. 1977. Mom: Zamora spoon-fed in front of TV. Oct. 4, 1977.

Miami University, Department of Marketing. 1954. *The Influence of Television on the Election of 1952.* Oxford, Ohio: Oxford Research Associates, Inc.

Midlarsky, E., and J. H. Bryan. 1967. Training charity in children. *Journal of Personality and Social Psychology,* 5, 408–15.

—— 1972. Affect expressions and children's imitative altruism. *Journal of Experimental Research in Personality,* 6, 195–203.

Midlarsky, E., J. H. Bryan, and P. Brickman. 1973. Aversive approval: Interactive effects of modeling and reinforcement on altruistic behavior. *Child Development,* 44, 321–28.
—— 1973b. Aversive approval: In *Palmer Quarterly,* 14, 229–60.
Milavsky, J. R. 1977a. Private communication.
—— 1977b. Invited address. American Psychological Association, San Francisco, August 29.
Milavsky, J. R., and B. Pekowsky. 1973. Exposure to TV "violence" and aggressive behavior in boys, examined as process: A status report of a longitudinal study. Unpublished manuscript, Department of Social Research, National Broadcasting Company.
Milavsky, J. R., B. Pekowsky, and H. Stipp. 1975. TV drug advertising and proprietary and illicit drug use among teenage boys. *Public Opinion Quarterly,* 39, 457–81.
Milgram, S., and R. L. Shotland. 1973. *Television and Antisocial Behavior: Field Experiments.* New York: Academic Press.
Miller, M., and E. Rhodes. 1964. *Only You, Dick Daring!* New York: Sloane.
Miller, P. V., A. J. Morrison, and F. G. Kline. 1974. Approaches to characterizing information environments. Paper presented at the meeting of the International Communication Association.
Mischel, W. 1968. *Personality and assessment.* New York: Wiley.
Morland, J. K. 1958. Racial recognition by nursery school children in Lynchburg, Virgina. *Social Forces,* 37, 399–410.
Morris, W. N., H. M. Marshall, and R. S. Miller. 1973. The effect of vicarious punishment on prosocial behavior in children. *Journal of Experimental Child Psychology,* 15, 222–36.
Mosher, D. L. 1971. Psychological reactions to pornographic films. In *Technical Report of the Commission on Obscenity and Pornography,* vol. 8. Washington, D.C.: Government Printing Office, pp. 255–312.
—— 1973. Sex differences, sex experience, sex guilt, and explicitly sexual films. *Journal of Social Issues,* 29, 95–112.
Mullins, E. 1973. Agenda setting on the campus: The mass media and learning of issue importance in the 1972 election. Paper presented to the Association in Journalism, Fort Collins, Colorado, August.
Murphy, J. P. 1973. Attributional and inferential strategies in the interpretation of visual communications: A developmental study. Doctoral dissertation, University of Pennsylvania.
Murray, J. P. 1972. Television in inner-city homes: Viewing behavior of young boys. In E. A. Rubinstein, G. A. Comstock, and J. P. Murray (eds.), *Television and Social Behavior.* Vol. 4, *Television in Day-to-Day Life: Patterns of Use.* Washington, D.C.: Government Printing Office, pp. 345–394.
Murray, R. L., R. R. Cole, and F. Fedler. 1970. Teenagers and TV violence: How they rate and view it. *Journalism Quarterly,* 47, 247–55.

Mussen, P., and E. Rutherford. 1961. Effects of aggressive cartoons on children's aggressive play. *Journal of Abnormal and Social Psychology,* 62, 461–64.

NAEB Letter on Research. 1976. Washington, D.C.: National Association of Educational Broadcasters, August.

Napolitan, J. 1969. *The Election Game and How to Win It.* Garden City: Doubleday and Co.

National Advisory Commission on Civil Disorders. 1968. *Report.* New York: Bantam Books.

National Association of Broadcasters Code Authority. Toy Advertising Guidelines, 1975. 3rd ed., January 1.

National Broadcasting Company, Social Research Department. 1976. *Public Television.* New York: National Broadcasting Company.

Neale, J. M. 1972. Comment on "Television violence and child aggression: A follow-up study." In G. A. Comstock and E. A. Rubinstein (eds.), *Television and Social Behavior.* Vol. 3, *Television and Adolescent Aggressiveness.* Washington, D.C.: Government Printing Office, pp. 141–48.

Newcomb, T. M. 1953. An approach to the study of communicative acts. *Psychological Review,* 60, 393–404.

Nicholas, K. B., R. E. McCarter, and R. V. Heckel. 1971a. The effects of race and sex on the imitation of television models. *Journal of Social Psychology,* 85, 315–16.

—— 1971b. Imitation of adult and peer television models by white and Negro children. *Ibid.,* 317–18.

Nie, N. H., S. Verba, and J. R. Petrocik. 1976. *The Changing American Voter.* Cambridge: Harvard University Press.

Nimmo, D. 1970. *The Political Persuaders.* Englewood Cliffs, N.J.: Prentice-Hall.

Niven, H. 1960. Who in the family selects the TV program? *Journalism Quarterly,* 37, 110–11.

Noble, G. 1973. Effects of different forms of filmed aggression on children's constructive and destructive play. *Journal of Personality and Social Psychology,* 26, 54–59.

O'Conner, R. D. 1969. Modification of social withdrawal through symbolic modeling. *Journal of Applied Behavior Analysis,* 2, 15–22.

O'Connor, J. J. 1977. How ABC got to the top. *New York Times,* October 19.

Osborn, D. K., and R. C. Endsley. 1971. Emotional reactions of young children to TV violence. *Child Development,* 42, 321–31.

Osgood, D. E., and P. H. Tannenbaum. 1955. The principle of congruity in the prediction of attitude change. *Psychological Review,* 62, 42–55.

Owen, B. M. 1972. *Measuring violence on television: The Gerbner index.* Staff Research Paper, Office of Telecommunications Policy. Springfield, Va.: National Technical Information Service.

Owen, B. M. 1975. *Economics and Freedom of Expression: Media Structure and the First Amendment.* Cambridge, Mass.: Ballinger.

Owen, B. M., J. H. Beebe, and W. G. Manning, Jr. 1974. *Television Economics.* Lexington, Mass.: Lexington Books.

Paisley, M. B. 1972. Television and social behavior: Violence done to policy research. Paper presented at the meeting of the Pacific Chapter of the American Association of Public Opinion Researchers.

Palda, K. S. 1966. The hypothesis of a hierarchy of effects: A partial evaluation. *Journal of Marketing Research,* 3, 13–24.

Paletz, D. L., and M. Elson. 1976. Television coverage of presidential conventions: Now you see it, now you don't. *Political Science Quarterly,* 9, 109–31.

Paletz, D. L., P. Reichert, and B. McIntyre. 1971. How the media support local governmental authority. *Public Opinion Quarterly,* 35, 80–92.

Palmgreen, P., F. G. Kline, and P. Clarke. 1974. Message discrimination and information holding about political affairs: A comparison of local and national issues. Paper presented at the meeting of the International Communication Association, New Orleans, April.

Parke, R. D., L. Berkowitz, J. P. Leyens, S. G. West, and R. J. Sebastian. 1977. Some effects of violent and nonviolent movies on the behavior of juvenile delinquents. In L. Berkowitz (ed.), *Advances in Experimental Social Psychology.* Vol. 10. New York: Academic Press, Inc., pp. 135–172.

Parker, E. B. 1960. The functions of television for children. Doctoral dissertation, Stanford University.

—— 1963. The effects of television on library circulation. *Public Opinion Quarterly,* 27, 578–89.

Patterson, T. E., and R. D. McClure. 1973. Political advertising: Voter reaction. Paper presented at the meeting of the American Association for Public Opinion Research, Asheville, North Carolina, May.

—— 1976. *The Unseeing Eye.* New York: G. P. Putnam.

Pearlin, L. I. 1959. Social and personal stress and escape television viewing. *Public Opinion Quarterly.* 23, 255–59.

Pelz, D. C., and F. M. Andrews. 1964. Detecting causal priorities in panel study data. *American Sociological Review,* 29, 836–48.

Pelz, D. C., and R. A. Lew. 1970. Heise's causal model applied. In E. F. Borgatta (ed.), *Sociological Methodology 1970.* San Francisco: Jossey-Bass, pp. 28–37.

Peterson, R. C., and L. L. Thurstone. 1933. *Motion Pictures and the Social Attitudes of Children.* New York: Macmillan.

Piaget, J. 1926. *The Language and Thought of the Child.* New York: Harcourt Brace.

—— 1952. *The Origins of Intelligence in Children.* New York: International Universities Press.

—— 1965. *The moral judgment of the child.* New York: Free Press.

Pingree, S. 1975. A developmental study of the attitudinal effects of nonsexist television commercials under varied conditions of perceived reality. Doctoral dissertation, Stanford University.

Pool, I. de Sola. 1972. Correspondence to Dr. Monroe M. Lefkowitz. In U. S. Congress, Senate Committee on Commerce. Hearings before the Subcommittee on Communications. *Surgeon General's Report by the Scientific Advisory Committee on Television and Social Behavior.* 92nd Congress, 2nd Session. March 21–24, 1972. Washington, D.C.: Government Printing Office, pp. 91–92.

Popper, K. 1968. *The Logic of Scientific Discovery.* (3rd ed., rev.) New York: Harper and Row.

Poulos, R. W. 1975. Television's prosocial effects: A positive look at the medium. Unpublished paper, State University of New York, Stony Brook.

Poulos, R. W., and E. S. Davidson. 1971. Effects of a short modeling film on fearful children's attitudes toward the dental situation. Unpublished manuscript, State University of New York, Stony Brook.

Poulos, R. W., and R. M. Liebert. 1972. Influence of modeling, exhortive verbalization, and surveillance on children's sharing. *Developmental Psychology,* 6, 402–8.

Pride, R. A., and B. Richards. 1974. Denigration of authority? Television news coverage of the student movement. *Journal of Politics,* 36, 637–60.

Pride, R. A., and D. H. Clarke. 1973. Race relations in television news: A content analysis of the networks. *Journalism Quarterly,* 50, 319–28.

Pride, R. A., and G. L. Wamsley. 1972. Symbol analysis of network coverage of Laos incursion. *Journalism Quarterly,* 49, 635–40.

Pynchon, T. 1974. *Gravity's Rainbow.* New York: Bantam.

Rajecki, D. W., and C. Wolfson. 1973. The ratings of materials found in the mailbox: Effects of frequency of receipt. *Public Opinion Quarterly,* 37, 110–14.

Ramsdell, M. L. 1973. The trauma of TV's troubled soap families. *Family Coordinator,* 22(3), 299–304.

Rees, M. B. 1967. Achievement motivation and content preferences. *Journalism Quarterly,* 44, 688–92.

Reeves, B. B. 1974. Predicting perceived reality among elementary school children. Master's thesis, Department of Communication, Michigan State University.

Riley, J. W., Jr., F. V. Cantwell, and K. Ruthiger. 1949. Some observations on the social effects of TV. *Public Opinion Quarterly,* 13, 223–24.

Riley, M. W., and J. W. Riley. 1951. A sociological approach to communication research. *Public Opinion Quarterly,* 15, 444–60.

Roberts, D. F. 1968. A developmental study of opinion change: Source orientation vs. content orientation at three age levels. Doctoral dissertation, Stanford University.

—— 1971. The nature of human communication effects. In W. Schramm and D. F. Roberts (eds.), *The Process and Effects of Mass Com-*

munication. (rev. ed.) Urbana: University of Illinois Press, pp. 347–87.
—— 1973. Communication and children: A developmental approach. In I. de Sola Pool and W. Schramm (eds.), *Handbook of Communication.* Chicago: Rand McNally, pp. 174–215.

Roberts, D. F., R. P. Hawkins, and S. P. Pingree. 1975. Do the mass media play a role in political socialization? *The Australian and New Zealand Journal of Sociology,* 11, 37–43.

Roberts, D. F., C. Herold, M. Hornby, S. King, D. Sterne, S. Whiteley, and L. T. Silverman. 1974. Earth's a Big Blue Marble: A report of the impact of a children's television series on children's opinions. Unpublished manuscript, Institute for Communication Research. Stanford University.

Robertson, T. S., and J. R. Rossiter. 1977. Children's responsiveness to commercials. *Journal of Communication,* 27, 101–6.

Robinson, J. P. 1969. Television and leisure time: Yesterday, today, and (maybe) tomorrow. *Public Opinion Quarterly,* 33, 210–23.
—— 1971. The audience for national TV news programs. *Public Opinion Quarterly,* 35, 403–5.
—— 1972a. Mass communication and information diffusion. In F. G. Kline and P. J. Tichenor (eds.), *Sage Annual Reviews of Communication Research.* Vol. 1, *Current Perspectives in Mass Communication Research.* Beverly Hills, Calif.: Sage, pp. 71–93.
—— 1972b. Television's impact on everyday life: Some cross-national evidence. In E. A. Rubinstein, G. A. Comstock, and J. P. Murray (eds.), *Television and social behavior.* Vol. 4, *Television in day-to-day life: Patterns of use.* Washington, D.C.: Government Printing Office, pp. 410–31.
—— 1972c. Toward defining the functions of television. In *ibid.,* pp. 568–603.

Robinson, J. P., and J. G. Bachman. 1972. Television viewing habits and aggression. In G. A. Comstock and E. A. Rubinstein (eds.), *Television and Social Behavior.* Vol. 3, *Television and Adolescent Aggressiveness.* Washington, D.C.: Government Printing Office, 1972, pp. 372–82.

Robinson, J. P., and P. E. Converse. 1972. The impact of television on mass media usages: A cross-national comparison. In A. Szalai (ed.), *The Use of Time: Daily Activities of Urban and Suburban Populations in Twelve Countries.* The Hague: Mouton and Co., pp. 197–212.

Robinson, M. J. 1974. The impact of the televised Watergate hearings. *Journal of Communication,* 24(2), 17–30.

Robinson, M. J. and P. M. Burgess. 1970. The Edward M. Kennedy speech: The impact of a prime time television appeal. *Television Quarterly,* 9(1), 29–39.

Robinson, M. J., and A. Jacobs. 1970. Focused video-tape feedback and behavior change in group psychotherapy. *Psychotherapy: Theory, Research and Practice,* 3, 169–72.

Rogers, E. M., and F. F. Shoemaker. 1976. *Communication of Innovations: A Cross-Cultural Approach.* 2nd ed. New York: Free Press.

The Roper Organization, Inc. 1973. *What people think of television and other mass media: 1959–1972.* New York: Television Information Office.
—— 1975. *Trends in public attitudes toward television and other mass media, 1959–1974.* New York: Television Information Office.
Rosario, F. Z. 1971. The leader in family planning and the two-step flow model. *Journalism Quarterly,* 48, 288–97.
Rosehan, D. L., and G. M. White. 1967. Observation and rehearsal as determinants of prosocial behavior. *Journal of Personality and Social Psychology,* 5, 424–31.
Rosekrans, M. A. 1967. Imitation in children as a function of perceived similarities to a social model of vicarious reinforcement. *Journal of Personality and Social Psychology,* 7, 307–15.
Rosekrans, M. A., and W. W. Hartup. 1967. Imitative influences of consistent and inconsistent response consequences to a model on aggressive behavior in children. *Journal of Personality and Social Psychology,* 7, 429–34.
Rosenberg, M. J., C. I. Hovland, W. J. McGuire, R. P. Abelson, and J. W. Brehm (eds.). 1960. *Attitude Organization and Change.* New Haven: Yale University Press.
Rosenkoetter, L. I. 1973. Resistance to temptation: Inhibitory and disinhibitory effects of models. *Developmental Psychology,* 8, 80–84.
Rossiter, J. R., and T. S. Robertson. 1974. Children's TV commercials: Testing the defenses. *Journal of Communication,* 24(4), 137–44.
Rothschild, M. L., and M. L. Ray. 1974. Involvement and political advertising effect: An exploratory experiment. *Communication Research,* 1, 264–85.
Rozelle, R. M., and D. T. Campbell. 1969. More plausible rival hypotheses in the cross-lagged panel correlation technique. *Psychological Bulletin,* 71, 74–79.
Rubin, B. 1967. *Political television.* Belmont, Calif.: Wadsworth.
Rubin, P. A. 1974. *A quantitative comparison of the relative performance of VHF and UHF broadcast systems.* Washington, D.C.: Corporation for Public Broadcasting.
Rubinstein, E. A. 1973. Television and the young viewer. Unpublished manuscript, State University at Stony Brook, Department of Psychiatry.
Rubinstein, E. A., R. M. Liebert, J. M. Neale, and R. W. Poulos. 1974. *Assessing Television's Influence on Children's Prosocial Behavior.* Stony Brook, N.Y.: Brookdale International Institute. (Occasional paper 74-11.)
Rule, B., and P. Duker. 1973. The effects of intention and consequences on children's evaluations of aggressive acts. *Journal of Personality and Social Psychology,* 27, 184–90.
Russo, F. D. 1971. A study of bias in TV coverage of the Vietnam War: 1969 and 1970. *Public Opinion Quarterly,* 35, 539–43.
Ryan, M. 1976. Family viewing time: Has it passed the test? *TV Guide,* June 5, pp. 5–10.
Saegert, S., W. Swap, and R. B. Zajonc. 1973. Exposure, context, and in-

terpersonal attraction. *Journal of Personality and Social Psychology,* 25, 234–42.

Samuelson, M., R. F. Carter, and L. Ruggels. 1963. Education, available time and use of mass media. *Journalism Quarterly,* 40, 491–96.

Sargent, L. W., and G. H. Stempel. 1968. Poverty, alienation and mass media use. *Journalism Quarterly,* 45, 324–26.

Savitsky, J. C., R. W. Rogers, C. E. Izard, and R. M. Liebert. 1971. Role of frustration and anger in the imitation of filmed aggression against a human victim. *Psychological Reports,* 29, 807–10.

Sawyer, A. G. 1973. The effects of repetition of refutational and supportive advertising appeals. *Journal of Marketing Research,* 10, 23–33.

Scanlon, T. J. 1970. Viewer perceptions on color, black and white TV: An experiment. *Journalism Quarterly,* 47, 366–68.

Schachter, S., and J. E. Singer. 1962. Cognitive, social, and physiological determinants of emotional state. *Psychological Review,* 69, 379–99.

Schalinske, T. F. 1968. The role of television in the life of the aged person. Doctoral dissertation, Ohio State University.

Schaps, E., and L. Guest. 1968. Some pros and cons of color TV. *Journal of Advertising Research,* 8(2), 28–39.

Schlinger, M. J., and J. T. Plummer. 1972. Advertising in black and white. *Journal of Marketing Research,* 9, 149–53.

Schramm, W. 1968a. Leisure roles. In M. W. Riley and A. Forner (eds.), *Aging and Society.* Vol. 1, *An Inventory of Research Findings.* New York: Russell Sage Foundation, pp. 511–35.

—— 1968b. *Motion Pictures and Real-Life Violence: What the research says.* A working paper for the Motion Picture Association of America. Stanford, Calif.: Institute for Communication research, Stanford University.

—— 1969. Aging and mass communication. In M. W. Riley, J. W. Riley, Jr., and M. E. Johnson (eds.). *Aging and Society.* Vol. 2, *Aging and the Professions.* New York: Russell Sage Foundation, 1969, pp. 352–76.

—— 1971. The mass media in the North American life cycle. *Publics et techniques de la diffusion collective.* Brussels: Editions de l'Institute de Sociologie, University Libre de Bruxelles, 1971.

Schramm, W., J. Lyle, and E. B. Parker. 1961. *Television in the Lives of Our Children.* Stanford, Calif.: Stanford University Press.

Schramm, W., and D. F. Roberts (eds.). 1971. *The process and effects of mass communication.* Rev. ed. Urbana: University of Illinois Press.

Searle, P. R. 1968. The effect of videotape feedback on the behavior of counseling groups. Doctoral dissertation, Brigham Young University.

Sears, D. O., and J. L. Freedman. 1965. The effects of expected familiarity with arguments upon opinion change and selective exposure. *Journal of Personality and Social Psychology,* 2, 420–26.

—— 1967. Selective exposure to information: A critical review. *Public Opinion Quarterly,* 31, 194–213.

Seggar, J. F., and P. Wheeler. 1973. World of work on TV: Ethnic and sex representation in TV drama. *Journal of Broadcasting,* 17, 201–14.

Shaw, D., and T. Bowers. 1973. Learning from commercials: The influence of TV ads on voter political agenda. Paper presented to the Association for Education in Journalism, Fort Collins, Colorado, August.

Sheikh, A. A., V. K. Prasad, and T. R. Rao. 1974. Children's TV commercials: A review of research. *Journal of Communication,* 24(4), 126–36.

Sheinkopf, K. G., M. T. O'Keefe, and M. Meeske. 1973. Issues vs. images in the 1972 presidential campaign strategies. Paper presented at the meeting of the Association for Education in Journalism, Ft. Collins, Colo., August.

Shirley, K. W. 1973. Television and children: A modeling analysis review essay. Doctoral dissertation, University of Kansas.

Shulman, A. 1972. On-air recall by time of day. *Journal of Advertising Research,* 12(1), 21–23.

Siegel, A. E. 1956. Film-mediated fantasy aggression and strength of aggressive drive. *Child Development,* 27, 365–78.

Siegel, A. E. 1958. The influence of violence in the mass media upon children's role expectations. *Child Development,* 29, 35–56.

Sigel, R. S. 1964. Effect of partisanship on the perception of political candidates. *Public Opinion Quarterly,* 28, 488–96.

Silverman, L. T. 1977. Effects of *Sesame Street* programming on the cooperative behavior of preschoolers. Doctoral dissertation, Stanford University.

Simon, H. A., and F. Stern. 1955. The effect of television upon voting behavior in Iowa in the 1952 presidential election. *American Political Science Review,* 49, 470–77.

Singer, B. D. 1970. Violence, protest and war in television news: The U.S. and Canada compared. *Public Opinion Quarterly,* 34, 611–16.

Singer, J. L. (ed.). 1971. *The Control of Aggression and Violence: Cognitive and Physiological Factors.* New York: Academic Press.

Skinner, B. F. 1971. *Beyond Freedom and Dignity.* New York: Knopf.

Slaby, R. G., and R. D. Parke. 1971. Effect on resistance to deviation of observing a model's affective reaction to response consequences. *Developmental Psychology,* 5, 40–47.

Slaby, R. G., G. R. Quarfoth, and G. A. McConnachie. 1976. Television violence and its sponsors. *Journal of Communication,* 26(1), 88–96.

Smith, A. 1973. *The Shadow in the Cave: A Study of the Relationship between the Broadcaster, His Audience and the State.* London: George Allen and Unwin Ltd.

Smythe, D. W. 1954. Reality as presented by television. *Public Opinion Quarterly,* 18, 143–56.

Social Science Research Council. 1975. A profile of televised violence. Report submitted by the Committee on Television and Social Behavior of the Social Science Research Council. Unpublished manuscript, New York, July.

Staub, E. 1969. Effects of variation in permissibility of movement on children helping another child in distress. *Proceedings of the American Psychological Association,* 77, 385–86.

—— 1972. Effects of persuasion and modeling on delay of gratification. *Developmental Psychology,* 6, 166–77.

Stein, A. H. 1967. Imitation of resistance to temptation. *Child Development,* 38, 157–69.

Stein, A. H., and L. K. Friedrich. 1972. Television content and young children's behavior. In J. P. Murray, E. A. Rubinstein, and G. A. Comstock (eds.), *Television and Social Behavior.* Vol. 2, *Television and Social Learning.* Washington, D.C.: Government Printing Office, pp. 202–317.

Stein, A. H., L. K. Friedrich, F. Deutsch, and C. Nydegger. 1973. The effects of aggressive and prosocial television programs on the social interaction of preschool children. Paper presented at the meeting of the Midwestern Psychological Association, Chicago, May.

Stein, G. M., and J. H. Bryan. 1972. The effect of a television model upon rule adoption behavior of children. *Child Development,* 43, 268–73.

Steiner, G. A. 1963. *The People Look at Television.* New York: Knopf.

Steiner, G. A. 1966. The people look at commercials: A study of audience behavior. *Journal of Business,* 39, 272–304.

Sternbach, R. A. 1962. Assessing differential autonomic patterns in emotions. *Journal of Psychosomatic Research,* 6(2), 87–91.

Steuer, F. B., J. M. Applefield, and R. Smith. 1971. Televised agression and the interpersonal aggression of preschool children. *Journal of Experimental Child Psychology,* 11, 442–47.

Stevenson, R. L., R. A. Eisinger, B. M. Feinberg, and A. B. Kotok. 1973. Untwisting *The News Twisters:* A replication of Efron's study. *Journalism Quarterly,* 50, 211–19.

Stipp, H. 1975. Validity in social research: Measuring children's television exposure. Doctoral dissertation, Columbia University.

Stoessel, R. E. 1972. The effects of televised aggressive cartoons on children's behavior. Doctoral dissertation, St. John's University.

Superior Court of the State of California, San Francisco. 1976. Memorandum of Intended Decision, *Olivia Niemi* v. *National Broadcasting Company, Inc.* and *Chronicle Broadcasting Co.,* No. 681-053, September 17.

Surgeon General's Scientific Advisory Committee on Television and Social Behavior. 1972. *Television and Growing up: The Impact of Televised Violence.* Report to the Surgeon General, United States Public Health Service. Washington, D.C.: Government Printing Office.

Surlin, S. H., and J. R. Dominick. 1970. Television's function as a "third parent" for black and white teen-agers. *Journal of Broadcasting,* 15, 55–64.

Surlin, S. H., and T. F. Gordon. 1974. Selective exposure and retention of political advertising: A regional comparison. Paper presented at the meeting of the International Communication Association, New Orleans, April.

Szalai, A. (ed.). 1972. *The Use of Time: Daily Activities of Urban and*

Suburban Populations in Twelve Countries. The Hague: Mouton and Co.

Tannenbaum, P. H. 1976. Emotional arousal as a mediator of erotic communication effects. In *Technical Report of the Commission on Obscenity and Pornography.* Vol. 8, Washington, D.C.: Government Printing Office, pp. 326–56.

—— 1972. Studies in film- and television-mediated arousal and aggression: A progress report. In G. A. Comstock, E. A. Rubinstein, and J. P. Murray (eds.), *Television and Social Behavior.* Vol. 5, *Television's Effects: Further Explorations.* Washington, D.C.: Government Printing Office, pp. 309–50.

Tannenbaum, P. H., and E. P. Gaer. 1965. Mood change as a function of stress of protagonist and degree of identification in a film viewing situation. *Journal of Personality and Social Psychology,* 2, 612–16.

Tannenbaum, P. H., and D. Zillmann. 1975. Emotional arousal in the facilitation of aggression through communication. In L. Berkowitz (ed.), *Advances in Experimental Social Psychology.* Vol. 8. New York: Academic Press, pp. 149–92.

Tasch, M. O. 1970. Modeling of pro-social behavior by pre-school subjects of high and low self-esteem. Doctoral dissertation, Syracuse University.

Tedesco, N. S. 1974. Patterns of prime time. *Journal of Communication,* 24, 119–24.

Television Digest. 1976a. Network children's revenues up. November 22, pp. 2–3.

Television Digest. 1976b. Wiley's Christmas list. December 13, pp. 1–2.

—— 1977. Violence—Here and abroad. May 2, pp. 1–3.

Thelen, M. H. 1971. The effect of subject race, model race, and vicarious praise on vicarious learning. *Child Development,* 42, 972–77.

Thelen, M. H., D. McGuire, D. W. Simmonds, and T. J. Akamatsu. 1974. Effect of model-reward on the observer's recall of the modeled behavior. *Journal of Personality and Social Psychology,* 29, 140–44.

Thelen, M. H., and W. Soltz. 1969. The effect of vicarious reinforcement on imitation in two social-racial groups. *Child Development,* 40, 879–87.

Thomas, M. H., and R. S. Drabman. 1974. Some new faces of the one-eyed monster. Paper presented at the meeting of the Society for Research in Child Development, Denver.

J. Walter Thompson. 1970. Review of research on television's communication effectiveness. Unpublished manuscript, J. Walter Thompson, New York, November.

Tipton, L., R. D. Haney, and J. R. Baseheart. 1975. Media agenda-setting in city and state campaigns. *Journalism Quarterly,* 52, 15–22.

Tolley, H., Jr. 1973. *Children and War: Political Socialization to International Conflict.* New York: Teachers College Press. Columbia University.

Topping, M. C. 1965. The cultural orientation of certain "Western" characters on television: A content analysis. *Journal of Broadcasting, 9,* 291–304.

Torney, J. V. 1972. The influence of current affairs broadcasting upon pupil attitudes toward politics. In *Television and World Affairs Teaching in Schools.* London: Atlantic Educational Publications, 1972. pp. 12–18.

Torney, J. V., and D. N. Morris. 1972. *Global Dimensions of U.S. Education: The Elementary School.* New York: Center for War/Peace Studies, 1972.

Trenaman, J., and D. McQuail. 1961. *Television and the Political Image. A Study of the Impact of Television on the 1959 General Election.* London: Methuen.

Troldahl, V. C. 1966. A field test of a modified "two-step flow of communication" model. *Public Opinion Quarterly, 30,* 609–23.

Tuchman, S., and T. E. Coffin. 1971. The influence of election night television broadcasts in a close election. *Public Opinion Quarterly, 35,* 315–26.

TV Guide. 1974. Do commercials really sell you? November 9, p. 4.

United States Commission on Civil Rights. 1977. *Window Dressing on the Set: Women and Minorities in Television.* Washington, D.C.: Government Printing Office.

United States Congress. 1955a. Senate Committee on the Judiciary. Hearings before the Subcommittee to Investigate Juvenile Delinquency. *Juvenile Delinquency (television programs).* 83rd Congress, 2nd session. June 5–Oct. 20, 1954. Washington, D.C.: Government Printing Office.

—— 1955b. *Ibid.,* 84th Congress, 1st session. April 6–7, 1955. Washington, D.C.: Government Printing Office.

—— 1963. Senate Committee on the Judiciary. Hearings before the Subcommittee to Investigate Juvenile Delinquency. *Juvenile delinquency.* Part 10. *Effects on Young People of Violence and Crime Portrayed on Television.* 87th Congress, 1st and 2nd sessions. June 8, 1961–May 14, 1962. Washington, D.C.: Government Printing Office.

—— 1965. *Ibid.,* Part 16. *Effects on young people of violence and crime portrayed on television.* 88th Congress, 2nd session. July 30, 1964. Washington, D.C.: Government Printing Office, 1965.

—— 1972. Senate Committee on Commerce. Hearings before the Subcommittee on Communications. *Surgeon General's Report by the Scientific Advisory Committee on Television and Social Behavior.* 92nd Congress, 2nd session. March 21–24, 1972. Washington, D.C.: Government Printing Office.

—— 1974. *Ibid., Violence on Television.* 93rd Congress, 2nd session. April 3–5, 1974. Washington, D.C.: Government Printing Office.

—— 1976a. House Committee on Interstate and Foreign Commerce. Hearings before the Subcommitteee on Communications. *Broadcast Advertising and Children.* 94th Congress, 1st session. July 14–17, 1975. Washington, D.C.: Government Printing Office.

—— 1976b. Senate Committee on Labor and Public Welfare Hearings before the Subcommittee on Alcoholism and Narcotics. *Media Images of Alcohol: The Effects of Advertising and other Media on Alcohol Abuse, 1976.* 94th Congress, 2nd session. March 8 and 11, 1976. Washington, D.C.: Government Printing Office.

United States District Court, Central District of California. 1976. *Writers Guild of America, West, Inc.* v. *Federal Communications Commission* (No. CV 75-3641-F) and *Tandem Productions, Inc.* v. *Columbia Broadcasting System, Inc.* (No. CV 75-3710-F), November 4.

Venkatesan, M., and G. A. Haaland. 1968. Divided attention and television commercials: An experimental study. *Journal of Marketing Research,* 5, 203–5.

Wackman, D. B., G. Reale, and S. Ward. 1972. Racial differences in responses to advertising among adolescents. In E. A. Rubinstein, G. A. Comstock, and J. P. Murray (eds.), *Television and Social Behavior. Vol. 4, Television in Day-to-Day Life: Patterns of Use.* Washington, D.C.: Government Printing Office, pp. 543–53.

Wackman, D. B., E. Wartella, and S. Ward. 1977. Learning to be consumers: The role of the family. *Journal of Communication,* 27, 138–51.

Wade, S. E. 1971. Adolescents, creativity, and media: An exploratory study. *American Behavioral Scientist,* 14, 341–51.

Wade, S. E., and W. Schramm. 1969. The mass media as sources of public affairs, science and health knowledge. *Public Opinion Quarterly,* 33, 197–209.

Walbek, N. H. 1969. Charitable cognitions and actions: A study of the concurrent elicitation of children's altruistic thoughts and deeds. Master's thesis, Northwestern University.

Walters, R. H., M. Leat, and L. Mezei. 1963. Inhibition and disinhibition of responses through empathetic learning. *Canadian Journal of Psychology,* 17, 235–43.

Walters, R. H., and R. D. Parke. 1964. Influence of response consequences to a social model on resistance to deviation. *Journal of Experimental Child Psychology,* 1, 269–80.

Walters, R. H., R. D. Parke, and V. A. Cane. 1965. Timing of punishment and the observation of consequences to others as determinants of response inhibition. *Journal of Experimental Child Psychology,* 2, 10–30.

Walters, R. H., and E. L. Thomas. 1963. Enhancement of punitiveness by visual and audiovisual displays. *Canadian Journal of Psychology.* 17, 244–55.

Walters, R. H., and D. C. Willows, 1968. Imitative behavior of disturbed and nondisturbed children following exposure to aggressive and non-aggressive models. *Child Development,* 39, 79–89.

Wand, B. 1968. Television viewing and family choice differences. *Public Opinion Quarterly,* 32, 84–94.

Ward, S. 1972a. Children's reactions to commercials. *Journal of Advertising Research,* 12(2), 37–45.

—— 1972b. Effects of television advertising on children and adolescents.

In E. A. Rubinstein, G. A. Comstock, and J. P. Murray (eds.), *Television and Social Behavior.* Vol. 4, *Television in Day-to-Day Life: Patterns of Use.* Washington, D.C.: Government Printing Office, pp. 432–451.

Ward, S., D. Levinson, and D. B. Wackman. 1972. Children's attention to television advertising. In *ibid.,* pp. 491–515.

Ward, S., G. Reale, and D. Levinson. 1972. Children's perceptions, explanations, and judgments of television advertising: A further exploration. *ibid.,* pp. 468–90.

Ward, S., and T. S. Robertson. 1972. Adolescent attitudes toward television advertising: Preliminary findings. In *ibid.,* pp. 526–43.

Ward, S., T. S., Robertson and D. B. Wackman. 1971. Children's attention to television advertising. Proceedings of the Association for Consumer Research Conference, College Park, Maryland.

Ward, S., and D. B. Wackman. 1972a. Television advertising and intrafamily influence: Children's purchase influence attempts and parental yielding. In E. A. Rubinstein, G. A. Comstock, and J. P. Murray (Eds.), *Television and Social behavior.* Vol. 4, *Television in Day-to-Day Life: Patterns of Use.* Washington, D.C.: Government Printing Office, pp. 516–25.

—— 1972b. Family and media influences on adolescent consumer learning. In *ibid.,* pp. 554–67.

—— 1973. Children's information processing of television advertising. In P. Clarke (ed.), *New Models for Mass Communication Research. Sage Annual Reviews of Communication Research.* Vol. 2 Beverly Hills, Calif.: Sage, 1973. Pp. 119–146.

Ward, S., D. Wackman, and E. Wartella. 1977. *How Children Learn to Buy: The Development of Consumer Information-Processing Skills.* Beverly Hills, Calif.: Sage, 1977.

Warner, M. 1971. Organizational context and control of policy in the television newsroom: A participant observation study. *British Journal of Sociology,* 22, 283–94.

Warnock, R., and G. K. Anderson, 1950. *The World in Literature.* Chicago: Scott, Foresman.

Wartella, E., and J. S. Ettema. 1974. A cognitive developmental study of children's attention to television commercials. *Communication Research,* 1, 69–88.

Watt, J. H., Jr. 1973. Television viewing and aggression: An examination of the catharsis, facilitation, and arousal models. Doctoral dissertation, University of Wisconsin.

Watt, J. H., Jr., and R. Krull. 1974. An information theory measure for television programming. *Communication Research,* 1, 44–68.

Weaver, D. H., M. E. McCombs, and C. Spellman. 1975. Watergate and the media: A case study of agenda-setting. *American Politics Quarterly,* 3, 458–72.

Weisbrod, C. S., and J. H. Bryan. 1972. Filmed treatment as an effective fear reduction technique. Master's thesis, Northwestern University.

Weiss, W. 1969. Effects of the mass media of communication. In G. Lindzey and E. Aronson (eds.), *The Handbook of Social Psychology.* Vol. 5, *Applied Social Psychology.* 2nd ed Reading, Mass.: Addison-Wesley, pp. 77–195.

Wells, W. D. 1973. Television and aggression: Replication of an experimental field study. Unpublished manuscript, Graduate School of Business, University of Chicago.

Wertham, F. 1954. *Seduction of the Innocent.* New York: Rinehart.

Winick, C., L. G. Williamson, S. F. Chuzmir, and M. P. Winick. 1973. *Children's television Commercials: A Content Analysis.* New York: Praeger.

Winter, F. W. 1973. A laboratory experiment of individual attitude response to advertising exposure. *Journal of Marketing Research,* 10, 130–40.

Wolf, T. M. 1972. A developmental investigation of televised modeled verbalizations on resistance to deviation. *Developmental Psychology,* 6, 537.

—— 1973. Effects of televised modeled verbalizations and behavior on resistance to deviation. *Developmental Psychology,* 8, 51–56.

Wolf, T. M., and J. A. Cheyne. 1972. Persistence of effects of live behavioral, televised behavioral, and live verbal models on resistance to deviation. *Child Development,* 43, 1429–36.

Women on Words and Images. 1975. *Channeling Children: Sex Stereotyping in Prime-Time TV.* Princeton, N.J.: Women on Words and Images.

Woodworth, R. S., and H. Schlosberg. 1963. *Experimental Psychology.* New York: Holt.

Worchel, S., T. W. Hardy, and R. Hurley. 1976. The effects of commercial interruption of violent and nonviolent films on viewers' subsequent aggression. *Journal of Experimental Psychology,* 2, 220–32.

Worth, S., and L. Gross. 1974. Symbolic strategies. *Journal of Communication,* 24, 27–39.

Wright, P. L. 1973. The cognitive processes mediating acceptance of advertising. *Journal of Marketing Research,* 10, 53–62.

Yates, G. C. R. 1974. Influence of televised modeling and verbalization on children's delay of gratification. *Journal of Experimental Child Psychology,* 18, 333–39.

Zajonc, R. B. 1954. Some effects of the "space" serials. *Public Opinion Quarterly,* 18, 367–74.

—— 1968. Attitudinal effects of mere exposure. *Journal of Personality and Social Psychology Monograph Supplement,* 9, 1–27.

Zajonc, R. B., and D. W. Rajecki. 1969. Exposure and Affect: A Field Experiment. *Psychonomic Science,* 17, 216–17.

Zillmann, D. 1969. Emotional arousal as a factor in communication-mediated aggressive behavior. Doctoral dissertation, University of Pennsylvania.

—— 1971. Excitation transfer in communication-mediated aggressive behavior. *Journal of Experimental Social Psychology, 7,* 419–34.

—— 1972. The role of excitation in aggressive behavior. In *Proceedings of the Seventeenth International Congress of Applied Psychology, 1971.* Brussels: Editest.

Zillmann, D., J. L. Hoyt, and K. D. Day. 1974. Strength and duration of the effect of aggressive, violent, and erotic communications on subsequent aggressive behavior. *Communication Research, 1,* 286–306.

Zillmann, D., and R. C. Johnson. 1973. Motivated aggressiveness perpetuated by exposure to aggressive films and recuced by exposure to nonaggressive films. *Journal of Research in Personality, 7,* 261–76.

Zillmann, D., A. H. Katcher, and B. Milavsky. 1972. Excitation transfer from physical exercise to subsequent aggressive behavior. *Journal of Experimental Social Psychology, 8,* 247–59.

Zillmann, D., B. Mody, and J. R. Cantor. 1974. Empathetic perception of emotional displays in films as a function of hedonic and excitatory state prior to exposure. *Journal of Research in Personality, 8,* 335–49.

Zimmerman, B. J., and E. O. Pike. 1972. Effects of modeling and reinforcement on the acquisition and generalization of question-asking behavior. *Child Development, 43,* 892–907.

Name Index

Subject Index

Selected List of Rand Books

Baer, Walter S. 1974. *Cable Television: A Handbook for Decision-making.* New York: Crane, Russak & Company, Inc.

Baer, Walter S., et al. 1974 *Cable Television: Franchising Considerations.* New York: Crane, Russak & Company, Inc.

Bagdikian, Ben H. 1971. *The Information Machines: Their Impact on Men and the Media.* New York: Harper and Row.

Bretz, Rudy. 1971. *A Taxonomy of Communication Media.* Englewood Cliffs, New Jersey: Educational Technology Publications.

Bretz, Rudy. 1976. *A Handbook for Producing Educational and Public-Access Programs for Cable Television.* Englewood Cliffs, New Jersey: Educational Technology Publications, Inc.

Carpenter-Huffman, P., R. C. Kletter, and R. K. Yin. 1975. *Cable Television: Developing Community Services.* New York: Crane, Russak and Company, Inc.

Park, Rolla Edward. 1973. *The Role of Analysis in Regulatory Decision-Making.* Lexington, Mass.: D. C. Heath and Company.

Rivkin, Steven R. 1974. *Cable Television: A Guide to Federal Regulations.* New York: Crane, Russak and Company, Inc.